RELIGION AND SOCIETY IN
T'ANG AND SUNG CHINA

RELIGION AND SOCIETY IN T'ANG AND SUNG CHINA

Edited by
Patricia Buckley Ebrey
and
Peter N. Gregory

University of Hawaii Press
Honolulu

97 96 95 94 93   5 4 3 2 1

*This volume was made possible by a
grant from the National Endowment
for the Humanities, an independent
federal agency.*

Library of Congress Cataloging-in-Publication Data
Religion and society in T'ang and Sung China / edited by Patricia
   Buckley Ebrey and Peter N. Gregory.
      p.   cm.
   Papers originally presented at a conference held in Hacienda
   Heights, Calif., 1989.
      Includes bibliographical references and index.
      ISBN 0–8248–1530–0
      1. China—Religious life and customs—Congresses.   2. China-
   -History—T'ang dynasty, 618–907—Congresses.   3. China—History-
   -Sung dynasty, 960–1279—Congresses.   I. Ebrey, Patricia Buckley,
   1947–   . II. Gregory, Peter N., 1945–   .
   BL1802.R45   1993
   200'.951'09021—dc20   93–20371
                                                                    CIP

Designed by Paula Newcomb

Contents

Acknowledgments

With support from the National Endowment for the Humanities, during fall of 1988 the editors of this volume organized a weekly symposium at the University of Illinois at Urbana-Champaign to investigate some of the interactions between religion and society during the T'ang and Sung dynasties. Our larger goal was to work toward a more holistic and integrated understanding of Chinese culture. Diversity and variation we knew existed, but we wanted to learn more about how diverse ideas and practices coexisted and worked together to create, maintain, and reproduce the larger whole. Participants were asked to look especially for evidence of interconnections: links between social and religious changes, between political or economic developments and religious ideas or practices, between folk religion and institutional religion, between Confucian philosophy and changes in the social and religious landscape, between the ways religious and secular groups were organized. They were also asked to think about how power of various sorts shaped these interconnections. In October 1989 we reassembled many of the symposium participants for a conference at Hsi-lai Temple in Hacienda Heights, California. All of the chapters in this volume were first presented at that conference.

In preparing the work presented in this volume, the authors and editors have incurred many debts. The support of the National Endowment for the Humanities and the Office of International Programs and Studies of the University of Illinois made it possible for us to invite many highly knowledgeable scholars to participate in the symposium or conference in addition to those represented in this volume. These include Timothy Barrett, Carl Bielefeldt, Raoul Birnbaum, Peter Bol, Beverly Bossler, Kaiwing Chow, Edward Davis, Ruth Dunnell, Bernard Faure, Robert Gimello, Robert Hymes, Lionel Jensen, Miriam Levering, Wai-yi Li, Victor Mair, John McRae, Daniel Overmyer, William Powell, Gregory Schopen, Gary Seaman, Lynn Struve, and Richard von Glahn. Each of the chapters that makes up this volume owes much to the insights, analyses, and critiques these scholars contributed to our intense and wide-ranging discussions of religion and society in the T'ang and the Sung. The two reviewers for the University of Hawaii Press made a number of helpful suggestions that have improved the volume as a whole. We also are grateful to the hospitable staff of Hsi-lai Temple, which proved to be an excellent location for a conference of this sort. Finally we must thank the University of Illinois students who assisted us in running the symposium or putting together the volume, most notably Mary McGowan, Alan Baumler, and Ch'iu-yüeh Lai.

Introduction

The T'ang (618–907) and Sung (960–1279) dynasties were times of great change, both social and religious. The economy grew spectacularly, the population doubled, migration brought more and more people to the fertile south, and printing led to a great increase in the availability of books and a comparable increase in the level of literacy. Buddhism became a fully sinicized religion that penetrated deeply into ordinary life. New cults and sects appeared and flourished. Ch'an became the dominant force within institutional Buddhism; Celestial Heart and Thunder Rites teachings gained prominence within Taoism; local gods such as Wen-ch'ang came to be worshiped all over the country; and office-holding gods, such as the gods of city walls, became a common feature of the popular pantheon. Even Neo-Confucianism, often thought of simply as an intellectual movement, was in many ways a new sect, in which followers were asked to alter fundamentally their patterns of daily life and even to worship at shrines to Confucian heroes.

Religion in its broadest sense had, of course, always played a major part in the lives of the Chinese people. From ancient times, gods, ghosts, and ancestors were familiar figures in people's worlds. From medieval times on so were those who had the greatest knowledge and expertise in these matters: Buddhist monks, Taoist priests, local mediums, and sorcerers. Religious rituals, symbols, and ideas conveyed basic understandings about the nature of the cosmos and humanity's place in it. Ideas ranging from the interdependence of the living and the dead to karma and reincarnation were diffused through culture and society, influencing behavior not generally characterized as religious.

Sociologists and anthropologists have developed many hypotheses about links between religion, culture, and society. These range from Durkheimian views of religion as a collective representation of the group, to Weberian ones of religion as a rationalization of culturally imputed meanings, to Marxist ones of religion and ideology as superstructure, to functionalist ones that stress expressive or integrative roles played by ideas and religious rites. Scholars of modern China have made use of these theories in sophisticated studies of religion in its social context, including the role of local cults in defining community boundaries, the social uses of divination, the connections between inheritance and ancestor worship, and the ways the state can exert hegemony in religious matters. These studies pose many of the questions that underlie the chapters in this volume: How were changes in religious practices related to changes in the larger society? What were the effects of elite efforts to control, label, or channel religious activities? What were the agents or processes by which ideas or practices spread? What roles did religious experts play in the lives of laypersons? What sorts of religious communities existed?

Sources, not surprisingly, limit the questions we can pursue. For the authors of chapters in this volume, the three greatest deficiencies of surviving sources turned out to be the relative scarcity of evidence concerning the illiterate, the compartmentalization of much of the written record, and the uneven coverage over time. The scarcity of sources for the illiterate is too common a problem to require elaboration. Compartmentalization means that traditions—Buddhism, Taoism, and Confucianism—are made to appear more autonomous than they were in fact. Thus the conventions of literary genres downplay many of the phenomena we wish to study. A dynastic history biography of a high official who was a devout Buddhist might record his official career in detail but make no reference to his Buddhist practices. Even a privately compiled epitaph might make no more than passing reference to this more private side of his life. If his collected works do not survive and references to him in the writings of his contemporaries are scarce, we might never know of his Buddhist interests. Buddhist and Taoist literature shows similar tendencies.

Because printing led to books being produced in hundreds of copies, it is not surprising that many more titles survive from the Sung than from the T'ang. Uneven coverage goes beyond this, however. State activities are better documented for the early than the late T'ang, but private writings survive in greater abundance for the late T'ang. Sources of all kinds are relatively scarce for the early tenth century between the two dynasties. Documentation of the affairs of the central government are much better for the Northern Sung than for the Southern Sung, but not until the Southern Sung do sources for local society survive in any abundance. Quantitative estimates are especially difficult. We can often say that a phenomenon occurred in a certain period, but we are on shakier ground when we imply it had gained in popularity. Were local mediums more common in the late Sung than in the early T'ang? Or do the types of sources likely to mention them survive in greater quantities for later periods? Analyzing regional spread can be just as frustrating.

In part because of these historiographical difficulties, this volume is focused disproportionately on the Sung—only one of the chapters (Hansen's) deals substantially with the T'ang, although other chapters discuss the T'ang in passing (Kleeman's) or use it as a point of reference (Teiser's and Foulk's). We have nonetheless decided to preserve "T'ang" in the title for two reasons. The first is to reflect the origins of the project and its concern with questions of social and religious change. The second, more significant reason is that it is impossible to make any assessment of what was new in the Sung without reference to the T'ang. In our introductory overview (Chapter 1), we have thus tried to restore some temporal balance by sketching the major changes in religion and society during the seventh through thirteenth centuries in order to provide a broader historical context in which to view the specific changes discussed in the chapters that follow.

One of the major changes in religious practice during the T'ang-Sung period—the transformation of local gods into gods worshiped all over the country—is the topic of Terry Kleeman's contribution. By tracing the history of the cult of Wen-ch'ang, the God of Literature, he is able to show how a fearsome local serpent god became anthropomorphized, first as a wonder-worker capable of repelling foreign invaders and later as a patron of the literati taking the civil service examinations. Particularly significant is Kleeman's use of the Taoist scriptures "revealed" to a medium through spirit writing in 1168. Kleeman thus does not look at this cult only from the perspective of officials or literati observers; he is also able to incorporate the perspective of the cult's most ardent adherents. Taoist temples and priests were active in spreading Wen-ch'ang's revelations and officiating at his temples. At the same time, priestly intercessors were not necessary to gain access to Wen-ch'ang, a feature of the cult Kleeman relates to a general increase in access to the sacred realm in Sung times.

During T'ang and Sung times, not only did specific deities come to be worshiped in many places, but office-holding gods became more and more prominent in the Chinese pantheon. Valerie Hansen, in her chapter here, examines the history of one of the best known of the offices that gods could hold—that of god of the city wall. She deals with the interconnections between religious traditions, in this case between Indian Buddhism and the Chinese folk pantheon. Her evidence suggests that the model of the office-holding god came from the spread of the cult to the Indian god Vaiśravaṇa via the small Central Asian kingdom of Khotan. Vaiśravaṇa came commonly to hold the post of guardian of monasteries and, like the later city wall gods, could be referred to by either his name or his post. As in the case of the Wen-ch'ang cult, Taoist priests played a role in the history of the gods of walls, but Hansen stresses how the Taoist clergy, through relabeling the gods, tried to subordinate them to the higher gods in Taoist pantheons. At least as important in the history of the cult, in her view, was the desire of the devotees of local gods to see them honored by the government with the title of god of city walls.

Bureaucratic imagery and the cultural and religious creativity of laypersons are also major themes in Stephen Teiser's study of the emergence of what came to be the dominant Chinese view of postmortem judgment. This was the idea that the dead must proceed through ten subterranean tribunals where the Kings of Purgatory review their sins and merits and rule on their fate in their next life. Already by the tenth century, manuscripts preserved in Tun-huang illustrated this conception of purgatory, synthesizing elements of Buddhist and non-Buddhist origin. Drawing connections between ritual experts and the spread of ideas, Teiser relates the spread of the idea of purgatory to the use of illustrated scrolls by the ritual specialists called on to perform ceremonies for the welfare of the dead. Technological changes such as the use of stencils in mass-producing paintings of the ten kings, he contends, further advanced the standardization of popular conceptions.

The authors of the first three chapters all make great efforts to see the local, popular, unofficial side of Chinese religion, to see what developed without elite leadership, or even despite opposition by authorities. The rest of the chapters give more attention to such authorities as the Buddhist and Taoist establishments, the state, and the Confucian literati elite and the ways these authorities influenced and were influenced by the wider religious world.

The great monasteries of the Sung, the public monasteries patronized by the court and administered by the state bureaucracy, are the subject of Griffith Foulk's chapter. He challenges the widely held picture that the prosperity of the Ch'an monastic institution in the Sung dynasty marked the beginning of a long process of decline within Chinese Buddhism, arguing that such a picture is ultimately an outgrowth of Sung Ch'an mythology in its attempt to construct a "golden age" in the late T'ang and Five Dynasties periods. After sorting through the evidence for the historical origins of distinctly Ch'an monasteries in the T'ang, Foulk turns to the organization and daily practices of monasteries in the Sung. He describes the sorts of ceremonies held in the various halls, including the daily and monthly offerings made before images of former abbots in the patriarchs hall, annual ceremonies celebrating the Buddha's birth, enlightenment, and entry into nirvāṇa in the Buddha hall, the recitation ceremonies in the sangha hall, and the debates and sermons held in the dharma hall. The abbot, selected by the local prefect from among those with appropriate qualifications in the Ch'an lineage, had authority over all affairs in the monastery, including contact with potential donors and other outsiders. Below him were monastic officers, acolytes being groomed for official posts, the main body of ordained monks, novices, and the lay postulants. The notion that Ch'an monasteries were distinctly different from other Buddhist monasteries, Foulk argues, is largely a product of the Ch'an attempt to create a history for itself that would justify the special privileges it acquired in the Sung.

One of the major functions Buddhist institutions came to play in

Chinese society related to the conduct of funeral rituals. Patricia Ebrey looks at three aspects of contemporary funeral practices that disturbed Confucian scholars such as Ssu-ma Kuang, Cheng I, and Chang Tsai: avoiding the *sha* spirits, Buddhist services for the dead, and selection of grave sites according to the principles of geomancy. To these scholars, such practices were superstitious nonsense, based on faulty understandings of death and the connections between the living and the dead. Ebrey then looks at the actions of the state with regard to these practices. Even though the state was largely staffed by men with training in the Confucian classics, she found that, when laws, regulations, publication programs, and the example of the throne are all considered, one organ of the state often gave tacit support to the practices that another organ outlawed. The influence of the state then, she argues, probably lay more in providing a model of how to cope with contradictions than in suppressing deviancy or promoting a single, coherent system of funeral ritual.

Many religious activities provoked more consistent state response than did noncanonical funeral practices. As Judith Boltz shows, local officials were expected to keep an eye on the shrines in their counties or prefectures. The spirit realm deserved official protection when it aided in maintaining order but had to be subjugated when it did not. Gods that demanded human sacrifice or made other extortionate demands had to be suppressed, their shrines shut down, their keepers dismissed or charged with fraud. Because of such policies, the recurrent struggles between the governed and the governors often were acted out as struggles between officials and local gods. Drawing especially on Hung Mai's rich collection of stories about life in south China in the twelfth century, Boltz shows the many forms such struggles could take. Sometimes local officials would call on experts in Taoist exorcistic rites to aid them, and in a few cases officials themselves mastered such rites in their efforts to gain control over spirits, sorcerers, devotees, and any other local forces resisting their jurisdiction. Boltz concludes with an intriguing speculation on the secret weapon within the arsenal of the Thunder Rites that ultimately enabled local officials to prevail. Her chapter is thus particularly rich in describing the more fearsome side of Chinese religion.

Judith Berling shows us the more romantic side of Taoist ritual experts. She examines the career of Pai Yü-ch'an, an expert in Thunder Rites, who was also a poet, the author of works on physiological alchemy, and the chronicler of a major cult. Pai Yü-ch'an interacted with secular men of letters, who saw him as an iconoclastic free spirit. Much of his contact with lay believers and mildly curious Confucian scholars took place at sacred places, especially the mountain temples that dotted the Chinese landscape and provided sites for the visits of pilgrims and tourists alike. Pai traveled extensively and often commemorated his visits in poems. His willingness to cross social, intellectual, and sectarian boundaries, Berling suggests, was typical of the fluid religious ethos of the Sung.

Pai Yü-ch'an spent much of his time at a hermitage on Mount Wu-i, famous also as the site of an academy founded by the great Neo-Confucian philosopher Chu Hsi (1130–1200). The ritual activities of Neo-Confucian academies and the ways they resembled Buddhist and Taoist monasteries and hermitages are the subject of Linda Walton's chapter. Academies invariably had shrines at which past heroes or worthies were venerated with offerings of food, drink, and incense, in much the same way ancestors were venerated in homes, local gods or bodhisattvas at temples, or Ch'an patriarchs at Ch'an monasteries. Like comparable rituals performed elsewhere, these rituals of veneration enhanced the sense of community and common purpose among scholars at an academy. Walton also explores the rivalry between academies and Buddhist and Taoist establishments, all of which were often located on the same mountains. Sometimes local officials aided academies by confiscating temple lands and giving them to temples; sometimes officials sided instead with the monasteries.

The research presented in this volume uncovers many little-studied features of the T'ang and Sung religious world: gods that communicate through spirit writing; Ch'an monks as absorbed in devotional exercises as in meditation; scholars who use veneration of maligned officials as subtle forms of political protest; local residents who try to enhance their power by asserting the power of their gods or getting them titles; officials who seek the most up-to-date techniques to master occult forces. Yet the authors and editors are all too well aware that we are far from a holistic view of Chinese religion in this period. In part because of the limitation of sources, and in part because there are not enough scholars able to master and interpret the sources that do survive, a great many questions have not yet even been posed. We hope that the research presented here will stimulate investigation into important topics largely untouched in this volume, such as the ways patrons influenced the formulation of ideas and practices; the forms of exchange that linked lay communities to clergy; the effects of major innovations in doctrines on common practices or beliefs; the importance of art-historical materials for assessing popular piety; the influence of Tantric Buddhism on Taoist ritual; the social context for the rise of female deities in the Sung; the importance of lineage *(tsung)* as an organizing principle common to Buddhism, Taoism, and Confucianism; or the extent to which the elite participated in a common cultural discourse that cut across the ideological divisions that separated different religious traditions. The historical changes that took place during the Tang-Sung transition also call for research into the the role played by the social, political, and institutional developments that occurred during Five Dynasties period.

Abbreviations

CTS	*Chiu T'ang shu* (Peking: Chung-hua shu-chü, 1975)
HJAS	*Harvard Journal of Asiatic Studies*
HKSC	*Hsü kao-seng chuan,* by Tao-hsüan, *T* no. 2060
HTC	*Hsü tsang ching,* reprint of *Dainippon zokuzōkyō* (Taipei: Shin-wen-feng, n.d.)
HTS	*Hsin T'ang shu* (Peking: Chung-hua shu-chü, 1975)
HY	*Tao-tsang tzu-mu yin-te,* Harvard-Yenching Sinological Index Series, no. 25 (Peking, 1935, rpt. 1966)
ICC	*I-chien chih,* by Hung Mai (Peking: Chung-hua shu-chü, 1981)
JAOS	*Journal of the American Oriental Society*
JAS	*Journal of Asian Studies*
P	Pelliot collection of Tun-huang manuscripts in the Bibliothèque national, Paris
S	Stein collection of Tun-huang manuscripts in the British Museum, London
SHY	*Sung hui yao chi-pen* (Taipei: Shih-chieh shu-chü, 1964)
SKCS	*Ssu-k'u ch'üan-shu.* Taipei: Commercial Press, 1983.
SKSC	*Sung kao-seng chuan,* by Tsan-ning, *T* no. 2061
SJSY	*Sung-jen chuan-chi tz'u-liao so-yin,* by Ch'ang Pi-te and Wang Te-i (Peking: Chung-hua shu-chü, 1988)
SPPY	*Ssu-pu pei-yao,* revised edition (Taipei: Chung Hwa Book Co., 1965–1966)
SPTK	*Ssu-pu ts'ung-k'an* (Shanghai: Commercial Press, 1919–1936)
SS	*Sung shih* (Peking: Chung-hua shu-chü, 1974)
SYTFC	*Sung-Yüan ti-fang chih ts'ung-shu.* Taipei: Ta-hua shu-chü, 1980.
T	*Taishō shinshū daizōkyō,* edited by Takakusu Junjirō and Watanabe Kaigyoku (Tokyo: Taishō issaikyō kankōkai, 1924–1932)
TSCC	*Ts'ung-shu chi-cheng.* Shanghai: Commercial Press, 1935–1937.
TPKC	*T'ai-p'ing kuang-chi* (Peking: Jen-min wen-hsüeh ch'u-pan-she, 1959)

RELIGION AND SOCIETY IN T'ANG AND SUNG CHINA

CHAPTER I

THE RELIGIOUS AND HISTORICAL

LANDSCAPE

Peter N. Gregory and Patricia Buckley Ebrey

Two of the best-known emperors in Chinese history are Hsüan-tsung (r. 713–755) of the mid-T'ang and Hui-tsung (r. 1101–1125) of the mid-Sung. Each presided over a brilliant court only to end his reign in tragedy, forced to abdicate after his capital was seized by former allies. A comparison of their reigns brings to the fore some changes in China during the T'ang and Sung periods.

In 710 Hsüan-tsung had placed his father on the throne and ousted the consort family that had dominated the court during the reign of his uncle. Two years later Hsüan-tsung took the throne himself and set about curbing the power of imperial relatives and Buddhist monasteries, both of which had gained strength during the long period of Empress Wu's domination and the reigns of her two sons. To deal with declines in tax revenue caused by absconding peasants, Hsüan-tsung ordered a new census of his fifty million subjects for use in the "equal-field" system by which land was allotted and taxes collected. Although the population had been steadily shifting toward the south, over half his subjects still lived in the north. Indeed, T'ang forces—often led by non-Chinese generals—exerted control over large regions beyond China proper along the trade routes through Central Asia; these armies generally proved more than a match for the Turks, Tibetans, Uighurs, and Khitans along China's northern and western borders.

Hsüan-tsung's capital, Ch'ang-an, a planned city laid out on a square grid, was home to perhaps a million people and certainly the largest city in the world at that time. It was a cosmopolitan city, attracting traders and pilgrims from much of Asia. Goods from distant regions —horses, jewels, musical instruments, textiles, even religions—were sources of endless fascination to the T'ang elite residing in Ch'ang-an and the secondary capital, Lo-yang. To feed the population of the capital, hundreds of thousands of bushels of tax grain had to be brought in, grain from the south making part of the journey along the Grand Canal. Although over 300,000 strings of cash were minted each year, it was not nearly enough for the demand, leading to counterfeiting that could not be suppressed even by the imposition of the death penalty.

Three of China's greatest poets, Wang Wei (701–761), Li Po (701–762), and Tu Fu (712–770), lived during Hsüan-tsung's reign, and poetic talent was greatly admired among the elite. In most years of this reign, between twenty and thirty-two men were selected, based on their knowledge of the classics and their poetic skills, as "presented scholars" (chin-shih) in the palace examinations. Men who had gained office in this way, moreover, provided some of the court's most prominent officials. Yet family pedigree was still as great an asset as literary skill. In 713 a two-hundred-chapter genealogical catalogue of the great families of the realm was presented to the emperor, providing him with up-to-date assessments of the relative ranking, in terms of family background, of the elite of his society. After the year 720, aristocrats dominated the political scene at court, and after 736 Hsüan-tsung allowed Li Lin-fu (d. 752), an aristocrat proud of his family background, to run the government for him as chief minister.

Hsüan-tsung may have started his reign with efforts to curb the political and economic power of the great monasteries, but he was not anti-Buddhist. In 739 there were said to be over three thousand monasteries and two thousand nunneries in the land. Hsüan-tsung was especially receptive to teachers of the newly introduced Esoteric teachings, such as the Indian masters Śubhakarasiṃha and Vajrabodhi and the Central Asian Amoghavajra. In 726 he called on Vajrabodhi to perform tantric rites to avert drought, and in 742 he held the incense burner while Amoghavajra recited mystical incantations to aid the victory of T'ang forces. Hsüan-tsung was especially attracted to Taoism, and state sponsorship of Taoism was carried out on an unprecedented scale during his reign. Nor did he neglect state Confucianism. In 725 he led an imperial cortege to the holy mountain of T'ai Shan to perform the most awesome of state rites, the feng and shan sacrifices, performed only twice before during the dynasty.

The father of thirty sons and twenty-nine daughters, Hsüan-tsung is remembered in popular culture above all for his infatuation during his late years with Yang Kuei-fei (d. 756), a consort who shared his interest in music and dance. When the general she had favored, An Lu-shan (d. 757), rebelled in 755, Hsüan-tsung had to flee the capital. His mutinous troops forced him to have Yang Kuei-fei killed; already over seventy and depressed by the turn of events, he willingly abdicated to his son.

Almost four centuries later, in 1100, Hui-tsung came to the throne at the age of nineteen. Politics in his time did not focus on consort families or splits between aristocrats and men without such pedigrees as it had in the T'ang. Rather the bureaucracy and the educated class were divided between the institutional reformers, eager to continue and expand the programs first begun by Wang An-shih (1021–1086), and the conservatives, who bitterly opposed them. Both sides drew many of their arguments from recent trends in Confucian thinking. Hui-tsung sided with the reformers and in 1101 appointed Ts'ai Ching (1046–1126) as his chief councillor, a post Ts'ai held for much of Hui-tsung's reign. Leaders of the antireform party were forbidden even to enter the capital. Their writings were also banned; officials and candidates for office were no longer to cite leading intellectuals of the prior generation such as Ssu-ma Kuang (1019–1086), Ch'eng I (1033–1107), and Su Shih (1036–1101).

During the nearly four centuries that separated these two emperors, China's external context had undergone vast changes. In the early eighth century Buddhism had been the universal religion of all of Asia. By the early twelfth century Buddhism had declined in India, and Islam had gained hold in previously Buddhist regions of Central Asia. The Khitans had built a strong state that united the traditional nomadic lands with agricultural areas settled largely by Han Chinese. The Sung state, as a consequence, could not control territories nearly as large as those the T'ang had controlled under Hsüan-tsung and had to live with the uncertainty of a powerful neighbor to its north.

Within its constricted borders, the Sung state under Hui-tsung nevertheless had about twice as many people as Hsüan-tsung's China (about one hundred million), over half of whom now lived in the agriculturally productive south. The government no longer attempted to interfere with the distribution of land, which could be freely bought and sold. Ten to twenty times as much cash circulated in this society than ever had during the T'ang. Indeed, in 1107 there were over twenty-six million strings worth of paper money outstanding, not to mention copper cash and silver bullion. The capital, K'ai-feng, conveniently located near the north end of the Grand Canal and not far from major deposits of coal and iron, was about as populous as Ch'ang-an had been at its height but was more of a commercial city, dominated as much by markets of all sorts as by palaces and government offices. Having learned how to tax commerce, the government derived much of its revenue from commercial taxes.

The great prosperity of China at the turn of the twelfth century had probably given the reformers the confidence that the scope of government activity could be greatly expanded. Welfare projects of many sorts were established, such as hospitals for the indigent and public graveyards. A national school system was instituted, with those passing at successive levels able to enter the national university and eventually take the *chin-shih* examination. In the year 1112, over seven hundred men succeeded in the final examination, the most successful of about two hundred thousand students in the county or prefectural schools. A few years later the students in the national university, numbering in the thousands, were demonstrating to make their voice heard in political debates.

Hui-tsung was a great patron of Taoism. In 1114 he called for the collection of all Taoist texts for the purpose of compiling a complete Taoist canon, the first to be printed in Chinese history. This canon probably included Hui-tsung's commentary on the *Lao Tzu* and some of his liturgical texts. In 1116 the Taoist Lin Ling-su (1076–1120) was presented at court and was soon directing ritual pageants and giving lectures on the newly revealed scriptures of his Shen-hsiao sect. He identified Hui-tsung as the son of the Jade Emperor and the sovereign of the Divine Empyrean. Hui-tsung's faith in Lin and other Taoist masters led to efforts to curb or transform Buddhism. In order to have Shen-hsiao temples throughout the country, many Buddhist monasteries were forcibly converted to Taoist temples, and their monks urged to become Taoist priests. In 1120 Buddhist monasteries were prohibited from increasing their lands and no new ordination certificates were to be issued for five years.

Hui-tsung's greatest talent may have been as a painter and calligrapher. Not only did he use the resources of the throne to build up the imperial painting collection (his catalogue lists over six thousand paintings), but he also personally developed new styles in calligraphy and bird and flower painting. His painting style, in particular, proved influential as he personally instructed the painters employed at the court to paint his way. In popular culture Hui-tsung's absorption in aesthetic and religious matters are blamed for his loss of the throne, indeed, the dynasty's loss of north China. His government had allied with the Jurchen to oppose the Khitan; the Jurchen then turned on them and in 1126 attacked K'ai-feng. Hui-tsung and his heir apparent were captured and taken to the far northeast; he died in captivity in 1135 at the age of fifty-four *sui*.

The comparison of these two reigns leaves out much that happened during late T'ang and early Sung, especially the century and more in which military men held center stage and new political institutions were created. Yet it highlights the magnitude of the transformations. The population had doubled. Commerce and urbanization had grown spectacularly. Printing had been invented, and the price of books dropped to perhaps one-tenth what it had been. The Confucian classics and the Buddhist and Taoist canons had all been published in their entirety. The size of the educated class had grown manyfold and become more oriented toward civil service examinations. New "sects" of Confucianism, Taoism, and Buddhism had altered the relations among these teachings and their social and political roles.

The magnitude of these changes should not so dazzle us that we fail to notice the continuities. The international context may have changed, but a native dynasty still ruled. Scholars trained in the classics still were recruited to serve as officials. Buddhist monasteries still were a worry to emperors. Individuals—like these two emperors—were often attracted to ideas or practices of divergent Confucian, Taoist, and Buddhist origin.

The majority of the population were peasants whose day-to-day lives were marked more by sameness than by change. It is as important to understand these forces limiting changes as to understand the ones nudging them on.

Naitō Kōnan, writing in the teens and twenties, was the first to argue for a major historical divide between T'ang and Sung and to label the period from Sung on as "modern." He put particular emphasis on the decline in the aristocracy, the rise of the examination-based elite, the growth of cities, and the development of forms of popular culture. Scholars coming after him often emphasized economic developments as the most fundamental changes triggering or stimulating other transformations. Few would today question that major economic and demographic changes occurred, but we now also recognize that regional economic developments were not synchronized and there was no simple linear development, with some areas on the forefront and others taking longer to catch up.[1] Studies that focus on particular regions have greatly enhanced our understanding of the social and political effects of economic development and the means by which the state attempted to impose order on society in varied circumstances.[2]

The decline of the aristocracy and the rise of an examination-based elite was not a simple or sudden event. One of the most crucial steps occurred in the Sui period (581–618), when recruitment to office was reformed and members of eminent families could no longer gain low-level bureaucratic posts in their home prefectures or commanderies merely on the appointment of local administrators. Thereafter, to serve in office, aristocrats had to meet standards set by the central government. They did this quite successfully through the T'ang, in part because of the flexibility of the recruitment system and the large number of posts available; still their independence had been fundamentally undermined.[3] In the Northern Sung the rise of an examination-based elite was fostered not only by the civil service recruitment system but also by state support for the expansion of education, especially through endowing local schools with land.[4] Yet even in the Northern Sung, many features of the T'ang aristocratic families were successfully imitated by the families of the men who gained leading posts early in the dynasty. Until about 1100 the most successful of such families lived in the capitals, married with each other regardless of regional origin, and placed most of their sons in the higher offices of the bureaucracy generation after generation.[5]

The social significance of the expansion of the examination system has been debated by scholars. Some see the examination system more as a tool for perpetuating status than a means of attaining it. In one prefecture, within a few decades of the dynasty's founding, most of those who passed the *chin-shih* examination came from families that had been members of the local elite for a generation or longer.[6] Despite the six- or sevenfold increase in the numbers of men gaining *chin-shih,* the sons of officials had better chances than most of getting these degrees, and hereditary privilege *(yin)* still accounted for a high and rising proportion of all officials recruited.[7] Still, it is impossible to deny the social and political significance of those who did rise from relative obscurity to national prominence.[8]

Urbanization, denser networks of settlements, greater interregional commerce, and a great increase in the size of the educated class must all have affected how religious ideas and practices were spread. Not only did these avenues apparently foster the spread of local cults (a topic discussed in several of the chapters to follow), but they also led to new forms of interaction between elite and uneducated commoners. For every man who attempted the civil service examinations, there must have been quite a few who spent enough time in school to learn to read or write but who did not continue long enough to master the classics. It thus became more likely that every county, if not yet every market town, had schools and learned men. Ordinary peasants would be more likely to have contact with them—as tenants, kinsmen, neighbors, and so on. Local elites contributed generously to the construction of Buddhist and Taoist temples, in part as a way to show their community-mindedness. Because of their official responsibilities, local officials had to oversee these cults and might also perform ceremonies at them or even pay for their construction. Religious activities thus were an arena in which the educated and the illiterate routinely came into contact, contact that may have had consequences quite outside the sphere of religion.

SOME FUNDAMENTAL RELIGIOUS ORIENTATIONS

Despite the enormous changes that occurred in Chinese religion over the millennia, many of its central themes can be traced back to the earliest historical times. Before looking at the changes in the religious practices and beliefs that occurred during the T'ang and Sung dynasties, it might therefore be prudent to consider some of the broad continuities in which such change took place. By any reckoning one of the cardinal religious practices running throughout the entire span of Chinese history is ancestor worship. The centrality of ancestors is related to a cluster of practices and concerns within Chinese religion and society. It is predicated on the belief that there is a continuity between the living and the dead; the living and the dead can affect one another because they share the same substance *(ch'i),* uniting them within a single, corporate kinship body. Indeed, this kinship structure is so important for the Chinese understanding of what it means to be human that it is taken as a model for human relationships in general. The reverence and awe associated with ancestors reflects the sacred character of the family as a locus of value. It is also connected with the paramount emphasis placed on filial piety. Confucians emphasized that proper respect for one's parents was the root of moral development. One of the principal demands of filial piety, moreover, was to produce sons who would continue the patriline so that the performance of the ancestral rites would not fall into abeyance.

The ancestors were also at the center of the religious practice of the earliest historical dynasty, the Shang (1766–1122 B.C.). The Shang religious/political order, as David Keightley has suggested, can be pictured as two triangles, one on top of the other.[9] The upper or "heavenly" triangle was populated by the deified ancestors of the imperial family. At its apex was Shang-ti, the Lord on High, who had the power to affect the overall weal of the dynasty. He could, for example, grant fruitful harvest and lend divine assistance in battle; he had dominion over rain, thunder, wind, drought, the fate of the capital, the king's person, and epidemics. Beneath Ti the royal ancestors were arranged hierarchically according to generation. The greater power of the more senior generations was exercised in progressively less personal ways; whereas recently deceased ancestors (who were still remembered as personalities) might plague the living, the dead of more distant generations lost their human individuality and operated according to their rank to affect the state as a whole. Ancestors could intercede with Ti.

At the apex of the lower or "earthly" triangle was the king. The concentration of political power in his person was justified by his ability to communicate with the ancestors through divination and to influence them through sacrifices. The connection between the two realms was reciprocal; while the king depended on the ancestors, the ancestors also depended on the king's grain offerings, animal and human sacrifices, and wine libations for their sustenance. The relationship between the king's political power and his control over the channels of communication with the spiritual realm, a theme relevant to later periods as well, is evidenced in several chapters in this volume.[10]

Just as king and ancestors were mutually dependent in Shang theology, later Chinese gods and their devotees likewise depended on one another. Devotees depended on gods to grant their requests, and gods depended on devotees to make the sacrifices necessary for their sustenance. Indeed, there was a clear reciprocity at work in the transactions that characterized much of Chinese religious practice.[11] Thus, during a severe drought in 823, could Po Chü-i (772–846) chide the Black Dragon of the North: "We are asking you for a favor, but you depend on us for your divinity. Creatures are not divine on their own account, it is their worshippers that make them so. If within three days there is a real downpour, we shall give your holy powers credit for it." He warns another deity that if he "just sits calmly watching while the crops go dry, it will not only be a disaster for the people, it will also be a disgrace for you."[12] If, on the one hand, a deity proved not to be efficacious *(ling)*, people would no longer sacrifice to him, his shrine would be neglected and his name forgotten, and a new deity would eventually be found who responded to their prayers. On the other hand, the more efficacious a god proved to be, the more people would sacrifice to him, and the more people sacrificed to him, the greater his efficacy would seem.

As the power of the imperial institution expanded in later centuries, so too did its dominion over the spiritual world, and the popular pantheon eventually became subsumed within the imperial bureaucracy—a process that gathered irreversible momentum in the Sung, when Chinese religion assumed the basic form it was to have throughout the rest of the imperial period. The state thus came to exercise its power to promote and demote gods. As a representative of the state, a Confucian official embodied a power that eventually proved more awesome than that of the local deities that fell under his jurisdiction, although, as Judith Boltz's chapter shows, this process often involved a battle won at great cost. In late imperial times a local magistrate might even have the image of a recalcitrant deity dragged out of its temple and publicly whipped for its failure to fulfill the responsibility encumbent on its office.[13]

The most suggestive point Keightley makes in his study of Shang modes of religious conception is that religious and political power were conceived in the same terms, as part of a single continuum.[14] He thus argues that the "this-worldly" and "rationalistic" values often associated with Chinese political culture were reflected in the habits of thought and action sanctified in Shang religious life. What is particularly striking about Shang theology is that the logic in which it was conceived can be characterized in terms that we usually reserve for the secular world: Shang ancestor worship was hierarchical, contractual, routinized, impersonal, and rational—in short, it was "bureaucratic" in Weber's sense of the term.[15] Authority was vested in an ancestor on the basis of his generational rank within the kinship hierarchy and had nothing to do with his moral qualities as a person. In Weberian terms, it was based on the charisma of office rather than the charisma of person—a point broadly applicable to the general notion of religious authority within China (as true for an emperor as for a Ch'an master) and related to the obsession with maintaining proper ritual forms.[16] The state was always suspicious of the disruptive potential of personal charisma, whether in the form of a local medium or a messianic prophet, and did its best either to suppress it or to rechannel its energies into more established modes of religious expression.

Just as the terms in which the Shang royal house conceived their ancestral spirits apply to what we in the West would regard as more appropriate for secular matters, so too was the secular world endowed with religious value. The lack of a clear distinction between secular and sacred has enormous significance for appreciating the religious dimension of Confucianism, which many in the West have wrongly seen as a strictly secular body of moral and political reflection. For Confucianism the realm of human activity is itself the locus of the sacred; religious meaning is found by locating oneself within a human community rather than by gaining access to a separate "sacred" realm[17]—hence the enormous importance of ritual, which sacralizes human interaction.[18]

While ancestor worship and kinship organization can be characterized as "bureaucratic," bureaucracy itself became a metaphor for conceiving the structure of religious power and the organization of the supernatural realms. Already by the Han (206 B.C.–A.D. 220) the netherworld was thought of as a "subterranean spirit administration" governed by bureaucratic strictures.[19] The pantheon of Taoist transcendents *(hsien)* and perfected *(chen-jen)* that took form in the centuries after the fall of the Han was modeled after the Han bureaucracy.[20] In the Sung the Taoist pantheon became merged with the popular pantheon into one vast bureaucracy whose reaches encompassed both terrestrial and celestial postings, as Terry Kleeman observes in the conclusion to his chapter. And it was the Sung transformation of the pantheon that defined the basic contours of Chinese religion for the remainder of the imperial period. Thus the bureaucratic character of Chinese religion, upon which so many modern observers have commented, can be traced back to some of the earliest modes of Chinese religious thought and behavior.[21]

As gods became bureaucratized, they also took on characteristics of scholar-officials—in a word, they became Confucianized. In the process originally local zoomorphic gods and nature spirits often were reidentified as the deified spirits of deceased heroes and officials (see the chapters in this volume by Hansen and Kleeman). There was a less edifying side to this practice as well, reflecting the realities people faced in dealing with the power of officialdom. Like officials, gods needed to be bribed to respond favorably. The ten kings who presided in judgment over the fate of the dead in their purgatorial tribunals reflected the darker side of this development, in which the Chinese experience of the arbitrary character and harsh reality with which bureaucratic justice was often meted out altered the purely mechanistic and impersonal operation of karmic recompense (see Teiser's chapter).

Kingly rule and sacred power were also linked through the doctrine of the mandate of heaven *(t'ien-ming)*, an idea propagated by the founders of the Chou dynasty (1122–256 B.C.). As a historical myth of dynastic cycles, the mandate of heaven held that the emperor retained his mandate to rule so long as his virtue *(te,* moral charisma) was bright. If he neglected his sacred duties and acted tyrannically, heaven would display its disfavor by sending down ominous portents and natural disasters. If the emperor failed to heed such warnings, heaven would withdraw its mandate. Then disorder would increase, the political and social order would fall into chaos, and heaven would eventually select the most virtuous as the one upon whom to bestow a new mandate to rule. The blending of political and religious power was here qualified by the important proviso that the retention of the mandate was contingent upon the emperor's moral rectitude. The empire was accordingly held as a sacred trust. Heaven was seen as a cosmic moral force that intervened providentially in human history; moral values were built into the way the universe worked and were expressed in human history. Consequently, history could be read as a mirror of heaven's will. The emperor mediated between heaven and the realm of human beings, and his virtue ensured the proper harmony of the two sides. The mandate of heaven also established the sacred character of the emperor as the "Son of Heaven" and thus reflected the Chinese notion of universal kingship—the emperor's political and religious authority extended to "all under heaven."

Although the mandate of heaven is usually identified with Confucianism, Anna Seidel has shown that Taoism developed by appropriating the symbolism and meaning of the various portents and regalia that had became associated with the bestowal of the mandate in the Han.[22] Taoist ordination rites, for example, were referred to using terms that signified the bestowal of the mandate. The same terms were used for Taoist rites of imperial investiture during the Six Dynasties.[23] Moreover, the various talismans, charts, registers, writs, and tallies that were transmitted during these ceremonies were "elaborations upon the Han theme of imperial treasure objects, the presence of which guaranteed the imperial mandate."[24]

A third cluster of ideas that shaped the development of Chinese religion centers on what Joseph Needham has characterized as the organismic view of the universe, which was articulated systematically in the cosmological theory formulated during the Han.[25] The universe was accordingly seen as a self-generating, self-sustaining, and self-regulating organism, in which each part was organically related to every other part through an elaborate network of correspondences. This vision included the well-known ideas of yin and yang, the five elemental phases, and *ch'i*. Yin and yang refer to the primal polarity of feminine and masculine forces (earth and heaven, dark and light, cold and hot, and passive and active, for example) that emerged when the primordial chaos split; the universe of diversified phenomena was generated through their intercourse and continues to operate according to the rhythms of their dynamic interaction. The five elemental phases (water, fire, wood, metal, and earth) are at once fundamental forces and qualities. As fundamental forces, they are in ever-flowing cyclical motion.[26] They were thus linked with theories of historical cycles and dynastic succession, and speculation about the order of their succession was an increasingly important obsession in Han apocryphal and prophetic texts concerned with politically vital questions of dynastic renewal and succession. As fundamental qualities (fluidity, solidity, heat, and so forth), they represent basic categories in terms of which all phenomena can be classified. They thus correspond to various other sets of categories (e.g., seasons, cardinal points, tastes, smells, colors, musical notes, calendrical signs, numbers, planets, dynasties, historical periods, bodily organs, sense organs, feelings) in such a way that a disturbance in any one category will resonate with the corresponding element in every other category (just as when a note is played on a musical instrument the same note will resonate on a similarly tuned instrument). In this way elements within human beings constantly resonate with outside forces in a complex interaction of microcosmic and macrocosmic forces. *Ch'i* is a term without English equivalent that overlaps categories we tend to think of as distinct—such as energy and matter, or mental and physical.[27] Etymologically it traces back to a graph meaning "breath," "air," and "vapor." As the basic psychophysical stuff of which the universe is composed, it is the resonating or conducting medium through which the five elemental phases affect one another.

Although these cosmological ideas do not figure heavily in the chapters to follow, they became part of the general Chinese world view and were related to a broad range of popular beliefs and practices that cannot be subsumed under the label of any tradition. They were the foundation on which Chinese medicine developed and the basis of geomantic practice just as they were reflected in the lofty reaches of Hua-yen Buddhist metaphysics of interpenetration and Neo-Confucian cosmology. They occupied an especially important place in Taoist theory and practice. They also express some basic orientations that are noteworthy because they are fundamentally different from those of Western religions. The organismic view of the universe involves the interfusion of microcosm and macrocosm; human beings are thus an integral part of the natural order. Since the universe, moreover, is engendered through a process of natural gestation, there is no need for a transcendent god who stands outside of his creation. Rather, the generative force and ordering principle is wholly immanent within the workings of the universe, both as a totality as well as in each of its parts.

A METAPHOR FOR CHINESE RELIGION

Although there is much that we do not know about Chinese religion during the T'ang and the Sung, it is nevertheless clear not only that the modes of Chinese religious practice and belief then were varied and complexly interrelated, but also that they were undergoing major changes. For simplicity's sake, we can discuss medieval Chinese religion in terms of four unequal traditions. The three institutionalized religions of Buddhism, Taoism, and Confucianism stood at some remove from the more diffuse popular tradition. Unlike the popular tradition, Buddhism, Taoism, and Confucianism were all based on a set of canonical texts. They were all also to varying degrees hierarchically organized, with their own professional "clergy" at the top.[28] In contrast to the popular tradition, which was rooted in local religious practice, the claims of the three "great" traditions were universal (or at least national) and their justification transcended any localized set of practices or beliefs.

Although these four traditions can be discussed separately, it is important to bear in mind that they were in constant interaction. Taoism, for example, cannot be fully understood outside the context of Buddhism and Confucianism, on the one hand, and the popular tradition, on the other. A good way to conceptualize this situation is to adapt a metaphor introduced by Eric Zürcher, according to which Buddhism, Taoism, and Confucianism can be pictured as three pyramid-shaped peaks sharing a common mountain base.[29] As the peaks arise out of the same mass of undifferentiated "popular" practice and belief, they begin to take form as discernible traditions. This metaphor should not be construed to mean that the high traditions developed out of the popular tradition—the vertical interaction was complex and went both up and down.[30] The higher the peaks rise, the more clearly they are differentiated from the other peaks and the more their ranks narrow into a professional, literate elite. Conversely, as one descends the peaks, the more they merge into the area of popular religious practice that cannot clearly be labeled Buddhist, Taoist, or Confucian.

Of the three great traditions, Buddhism was the most institutionalized, and it is therefore easier to demarcate its lines of stratification. It can thus serve as a general model to illustrate how this metaphor applies. In the most general terms, Buddhism was composed of three broad strata. The uppermost comprised a celibate clergy of monks and nuns who had been fully ordained according to the Vinaya regulations. These were religious professionals who had "left the family" (ch'u-chia; pravrajita) in order to seek salvation as defined by Buddhist soteriology. Although in actuality many, if not most, monks and nuns did not hope to realize the ultimate goal of Buddhahood in their lifetimes, their vocation, at least, was assured to direct them on the path to it. They were also a legally privileged group, being exempt from taxes, corvée labor, and military service. Below them were the lay men and women who had taken the triple refuge in the Buddha, dharma, and sangha, followed the five precepts (not to kill, steal, lie, engage in illicit sexual activity, and imbibe

intoxicants), supported the monastic community with alms, and may perhaps have also practiced vegetarianism (either during specified periods or throughout the year). A pious layperson during the T'ang or the Sung might also belong to a Buddhist society dedicated to the periodic group recitation of a particularly efficacious scripture, have taken a collective vow to be born in a Buddhist paradise, or have contributed funds to have a holy image consecrated. In any case, the defining characteristic of this group is that it comprised people who, to varying degrees, had made a conscious commitment to Buddhist goals, although the goals in their case were more likely to be proximate ones—such as the accumulation of the spiritual merit that would bring worldly benefit in this life and those to follow as well as ensure progress on the Buddhist path in future lives—rather than the ultimate goal of Buddhahood.[31] The lower portions of this group imperceptibly shade into the lowest tier, which comprised others who did not identify themselves as Buddhists but on occasion might take part in popular Buddhist festivals or might address prayers to various Buddhas or bodhisattvas much as they would to non-Buddhist deities. A merchant thus might commission a statue upon the successful completion of a dangerous caravan journey in fulfillment of a vow made to a bodhisattva, or a woman might beseech Kuan-yin (Avalokiteśvara) to grant her the birth of a son. This group did not subscribe to Buddhist soteriological goals but turned to Buddhism for more immediate, "worldly" benefits having to do with health, prosperity, fertility, and good luck.

Of course there were enormous differences within these three broad groups, depending on a variety of factors such as status, education, gender, aptitude, and motivation. Although objective factors of social position and gender were always important determinants, the more subjective ones having to do with piety and ambition were especially significant in determining position within a Buddhist context and could to some extent overcome the limitations that such objective factors imposed in a more secular context. Buddhism thus created its own partially independent status system. Clearly one of its appeals (stronger in the T'ang when the avenues of social mobility were more restricted than in the Sung) was that it offered the possibility of a prestigious and influential career to the talented and ambitious whose family background would have barred them from more conventional channels of success within the imperial bureaucracy. Although Buddhism did not provide an equal opportunity for women to achieve positions of prominence, it did offer them a haven within which they could escape the frequently oppressive demands of marriage and family life. The legally privileged status of the monastic ranks also attracted many who sought to escape taxation and military service. Moreover, the secure if often meager livelihood of the monastery offered a haven for the hungry and destitute, and the institution thus also provided a broad social service by absorbing many who could not succeed or otherwise find a place in the secular world.

Within the ecclesiastical ranks alone, there was a finely graded hierarchy, with the highest echelon occupied by an elite core, who were likely to be specialists in a particular scripture, doctrinal tradition, or ritual practice; they were the eminences who were most likely to be appointed to the abbacy of a prominent monastery or recognized by the court for their accomplishments. On this most elite level, in terms of our metaphor there is, in fact, not a single peak at the top, but several peaks, each representing a different sectarian tradition (such as T'ien-t'ai or Ch'an), and it was mainly at this rarefied altitude that the differences between the different "schools" of Buddhism had real significance. Below the general population of monks and nuns, there were the postulants (hang-che), laypersons who lived in the monastery awaiting the opportunity to receive ordination. There was also, blurring the boundary between religious and laic, a population of "irregular" monks that the government sought to control with only partial success—persons who would not have been recognized as monks by the religious establishment and secular authorities but who were treated as such by the people (the kind of persons Teiser speculates were instrumental in spreading the mythology of the ten kings during the Sung).

There were also vast differences among the laity, among whom were members of every social class—a fact that is especially important to note in the case of the lowest levels of our model. Popular practices, such as the Yü-lan-p'en, or ghost festival, held on the fifteenth day of the seventh lunar month, were engaged in by Buddhists and non-Buddhists alike, from the most elite member of the clergy to the ordinary illiterate villager. Although all social levels took part in such popular practices, they meant very different things to different groups. Thus for a learned monk like Tsung-mi (780–841), who wrote a scholastic commentary on the scripture on which the festival was based, Mu-lien's rescue of his mother expressed the "greater" filiality of Buddhist monastic life; for common villagers it probably served more as a cathartic exorcising of their fear of ghosts.[32]

Although we know far less about the structure of Taoist religious organization, it too can be broken down into a similarly tiered tripartite division, in which the same kind of determinant factors were presumably operative. The line separating the religious professional from the pious layperson, however, cannot be so clearly drawn for Taoism as in the case of Buddhism. Kristofer Schipper has argued that in the T'ang there was "an overall system that had integrated all major Taoist traditions."[33] Taoist ranks were accordingly graded in terms of a hierarchical series of ordinations corresponding to the three major divisions (*tung,* "caverns") in the Taoist canon, which, in turn, reflected a ranking of the three major Taoist traditions. The lowest stages of ordination allowed progressive access to the scriptures and liturgy of the Celestial Masters (or Cheng-i) tradition. The scriptures and liturgy of the Ling-pao (Numinous Treasure) tradition were successively transmitted in the next series of stages. The final stages involved initiation into the Shang-ch'ing, or Supreme Clarity, tradition containing the Mao Shan revelations. During these ordinations, the appropriate scriptures and their corresponding registers (*lu*) would be transmitted along with a matching set of disciplinary rules (*chieh*). The registers contained the names of the spirit soldiers that a particular ordination empowered one to control. Certain ritual functions could only be conducted by priests with a certain ordination rank, although it is not clear what specific liturgical functions various ordinations empowered one to perform. The lowest ranks probably corresponded to Buddhist laypersons. Only with the transmission of the Rules of the Beginning of Perfection (*ch'u-chen chieh*) did one "leave the family" (*ch'u-chia*), a Buddhist term seeming here to connote not so much a separation from lay society as a more specialized level of professionalization. From the Tun-huang manuscripts Schipper surveys, it seems that many Taoist priests in the T'ang married and lived in the community rather than residing in abbeys or leading itinerant lives as peripatetic adepts. The situation is more complicated in the Sung, when new Taoist movements arose and boundary lines in general tended to become more porous, as suggested by several of the chapters in this volume. Thus figures like Pai Yü-ch'an (1194–1229) (the subject of Judith Berling's chapter) or Wang Che (1112–1170) (the founder of the Ch'üan-chen, or Complete Perfection, tradition of Taoism) could to a large extent operate outside the bounds of ordinary Taoist establishments. Moreover, the Ch'üan-chen tradition gradually began to evolve a Taoist monastic order in the late Sung or Yüan. At the bottom of this tripartite division would be people who did not identify themselves as Taoists but might supplicate a deity in a Taoist temple or participate in the communal celebration of a *chiao* (offering or fête) led by a Taoist priest. Thus candidates on their way to the capital to take the imperial examinations might solicit the divine assistance of Lord Wen-ch'ang in obtaining the *chin-shih* degree.

In the case of Confucianism, there were no institutions truly analogous to monasteries. Nor were there formal rituals of ordination comparable to the Buddhist "leaving the world" or Taoist investiture signifying transition from a secular to a more hallowed status. Rather, two hierarchies stood in some degree of competition with each other: one of political office and the other of scholarship. In both T'ang and Sung times, the state made knowledge of the Confucian classics a criterion for selecting its officials, so its officials can be seen as a sort of Confucian elite. These officials, moreover, had clerical roles in organizing and orchestrating the state cults associated with the emperor's worship of heaven and earth. But officials were not in any exclusive sense clerics. They also served as military advisors, financial officers, editors, historians, judges, and teachers, their responsiblity being to help the emperor rule the country in whatever way he needed them.

Those who did not rise in government might still gain widespread esteem for their scholarship and wisdom. During the course of the Sung, as competition for office grew more intense, it became particularly common for intellectual leaders to assert the independence of scholarship from political office. As discussed in Linda Walton's chapter here, by the Southern Sung Confucian scholars were developing an institutional base for themselves through academies.

An intermediate layer in the Confucian peak can perhaps be recognized among those who had studied the Confucian classics but had not made a profession of office holding, teaching, or writing. Great numbers of men who studied for the examinations but never passed them had to support themselves in other ways. They could still maintain a literary way of life, adhering as closely as they could to the manners and values of officials and prominent teachers. The bottom layer, like that of the Buddhist and Taoist hierarchies, is not easily defined. Can one speak of Confucian lay followers? Would it include all those who accepted the importance of the Confucian virtues, such as filial piety, the separation of the sexes, and loyalty to superiors? Would it include all those who practiced the rituals promoted by Confucian scholars, such as ancestral rites and mourning austerities? If so, it would include virtually all ethnic Chinese. If, however, it were to include only those who refused to practice rituals that Confucian scholars opposed, such as Buddhist funerals, then it would comprise a much smaller segment of the population.

We must not forget that our model is a metaphor and try to push it too far. Like any metaphor, it is certainly too simple to circumscribe the richness of the Chinese religious situation during the T'ang and the Sung. Some might even object that its hierarchical nature gives undue emphasis to the "elite" traditions within the overall landscape of Chinese religion. There were always teachings and practices that cut across the neat divisions suggested by our metaphor. In the case of Buddhism, for example, the bodhisattva precepts were open to both the religious and the laic and were often administered collectively in huge ceremonial gatherings that could include a thousand or more persons. Members of all groups made pilgrimages to sacred mountains, such as Mount Wu-t'ai, in the hope of experiencing the numinous presence of the deity manifested there. Some of the ideas related to Buddhist theories of the inexorable decline of the religion undercut the belief in the value of the monastic life and held that the desperation of the final age *(mo-fa)* called for more radical solutions.[34] The Teaching of the Three Stages (San-chieh chiao), for instance, pushed the doctrine of the universality of the Buddha-nature in all beings to the point of obliterating all distinctions, not only between clerics and laity, but even between Buddhist and non-Buddhist. Like the bodhisattva Never-Disparaging (Ch'ang-pu-ch'ing; Sadāparibhūta) in the *Lotus Sūtra,* followers of this teaching were enjoined to revere everything as inherently Buddha, even heterodox gods and demonic spirits.[35] Messianic hopes centered on the imminent coming of the future Buddha, Maitreya, and the consequent salvation of the elect, also undercut established religious boundaries.[36] Perhaps the most important set of beliefs and practices that cut across the various social strata within Buddhism were those associated with the Pure Land, which rendered rebirth in the Western Paradise of Amitābha open to any who would but call on that Buddha's name with a sincere heart.

All the same, our metaphor is still useful for suggesting how the similarities and differences among the different traditions can be conceptualized both laterally and vertically. The social composition of the peaks and the mountain base reflects the structures through which religious change operated, yielding a model that is more textured and flexible than a simple bipartite split between "high" and "low" or "elite" and "popular" culture.[37] As Chinese society itself changed and became more complex during the Sung, so too did the social composition within the various strata. Overall the different sections of peaks and mountain would have been made of roughly parallel segments of the population for all three traditions, with the qualification that the highest Buddhist and Taoist ranks would have been somewhat more open than for Confucianism, although how much so probably varied considerably with general social change. With the increased channels of mobility and generally more complex society in Sung, the openness of Buddhism and Taoism was probably less important then than during the T'ang.

One further point that our metaphor brings out well is that, in the very process of becoming more self-consciously differentiated as distinct religions, the various traditions also tended to assume similar shapes. The tendency of the different peaks to mirror one another reflects the fact that influence also flowed laterally from tradition to tradition. The highest tier in all three traditions tended to be drawn from the same social strata; all were literate and had access to the high tradition in general. Although the members of this group might disagree with one another on sectarian lines, in many cases they could probably communicate better with one another than with their uneducated fellow religionists. The rivalry between the members of different traditions for patronage and prestige and their consequent self-conscious attempt to differentiate their teachings from one another were probably important reasons why, even though the content of the various traditions was different (and could be clearly identified as Buddhist, Taoist, or Confucian), the structures that they assumed were often similar. For instance, ancestral halls in Sung Ch'an monasteries (as described in the chapter by Foulk) and Neo-Confucian academies (as described in the chapter by Walton) were arranged in similar ways, and the rituals performed within them followed the same basic structure (only the identity of the ancestors enshrined was different). Even though they may not have differed so much in terms of what they actually did, the different traditions often put forward conflicting interpretations of the meaning of such rituals. Again, by the Sung period, Buddhism, Taoism, and Confucianism (and the various subtraditions within them) tended increasingly to conceive of themselves as lineages *(tsung),* and religious authority was passed down through lineage structure. The importance of lineal transmission also gave added weight to the ritual connection of master and disciple.

BUDDHISM

Buddhism always stood apart from the other Chinese religions because of its foreign origin, a handicap that it never entirely overcame. Our earliest evidence of its presence in China goes back to the first century A.D., but it did not begin to make inroads into Chinese culture until after the collapse of Han in 220. It was only during the ensuing centuries of political disunion—when the official Confucianist ideology on which the Han imperium had been based was discredited and "barbarian" regimes controlled the north—that Buddhism began to become assimilated into Chinese life. The process was a long and uneven one and proceeded along different lines in the north and the south. It was further complicated by the fact that during these three and a half centuries Indian Buddhism itself was in the process of continual development and profound change—these were the years of prodigious literary and theological creativity when the so-called Greater Vehicle (Mahāyāna) emerged as an expansive missionary movement reaching out across Central Asia and on into China. With the political unification achieved by the Sui in 589 and continued by the T'ang, Buddhism became thoroughly integrated into almost all levels of Chinese life—so much so that China during the T'ang could be characterized as a Buddhist country.

Buddhism represented China's first encounter with another higher civilization,[38] and the history of Buddhism in China surely represents one of the most fascinating and well-documented cases of cultural interaction in world history. In the process, Buddhism profoundly transformed Chinese culture at the same time that it was also profoundly transformed by Chinese culture. Indian Buddhism reflected a radically different world view and religious orientation that challenged some of the fundamental Chinese values and called into question some of the basic Chinese assumptions about the place and role of human beings in the world—factors that played a major role in the way Chinese responded to and adapted Buddhism. Buddhism had originated in India as part of a wide-scale religious and social movement that sought salvation in radical world renunciation. The world of family and social responsibility that was at the center of Chinese religious life was seen as part of the world of bondage from which the individual must escape. The soteriological split between the world of bondage and that of liberation—between saṃsāra and nirvāṇa in Buddhist terminology—was mirrored in the social division of monastic and lay practitioners.

Such a starkly dualistic division of the world into secular and sacred realms was undercut by developments within Mahāyāna Buddhism, which was beginning to take form in India when Buddhism was being introduced to China. Mahāyāna developed a sophisticated body of doctrine that deconstructed the duality of saṃsāra and nirvāṇa, holding that such a bifurcated view was itself a reflection of the epistemological error that was the fundamental cause binding beings to the wheel of suffering. Liberation was thus to be attained not so much by escaping from the world of bondage as by seeing through the underlying duality in terms of which such a world was conceptually constructed. Hence liberation could only be achieved within the world of suffering, just as an unsullied lotus flower can only blossom when rooted in the muddy bottom of a pond. From the fifth century on, Chinese Buddhist theologians capitalized on those aspects of Mahāyāna doctrine that found religious meaning in the world to develop their own uniquely sinicized versions of the religion—a point never fully recognized by Neo-Confucian critics and their modern students.

Such developments on the theological plane were related to and justified a host of new salvific possibilities on a practical level, ones that opened up the ultimate goal of Buddhahood to all. As the "Great Vehicle" ferrying all beings across the waters of birth and death to the other shore of liberation, Mahāyāna Buddhism offered a vast pantheon of celestial Buddhas and bodhisattvas who could not only rescue devotees from danger but also bring insight and visions. Hopes focused on rebirth in various Pure Lands, made possible through the grace of their celestial Buddhas, gave Buddhists of all levels of sophistication assurance of salvation.

Despite such theological and practical developments, the earlier dualism was still reflected in the social organization of the religion, centered as it was on the monastic institution, and the real or putative "world-denying" character of monastic life never ceased to provide ready fodder for Confucian-minded critics. The extraterritorial claims of the order challenged the emperor's claim of universal sovereignty, and a large body of nonproductive religious continually aroused the suspicion of officials.

Modern scholars are generally agreed that it was during the T'ang that Chinese Buddhism reached its mature form with the emergence of the fully sinicized traditions of T'ien-t'ai, Hua-yen, Pure Land, and Ch'an. The ideas developed by these traditions—especially that all beings are endowed with an enlightened nature, thereby insuring the universality of Buddhahood, and the affirmation of the phenomenal world as the proper field of salvific action—became the unquestioned axioms on which all subsequent Chinese Buddhist teaching and practice were based.

It was not only on the doctrinal front that the developments within T'ang Buddhism laid the foundation on which the subsequent tradition was built. Institutionally as well the T'ang represented a watershed period. The basic forms of ritual and meditation practice, the structure of liturgy, ordination procedures, the daily regime of monastic life, the administrative framework of the monastic organization, and the basic contours of church-state relations were all developed in the early T'ang. Along with the development of uniquely Chinese traditions in the T'ang, the Chinese landscape also became transformed by the presence of bodhisattvas and Buddhist holy sites so that for East Asia the sacred geography of China came to displace India as the center of the Buddhist world. The government patronized mountains sacred to Buddhists, and a network of national pilgrimage sites was established during the T'ang. The manifestation of Mañjuśrī bodhisattva of Mount Wu-t'ai became so renowned as to attract pilgrims from India.

Even though there are good grounds for emphasizing the formative character of the T'ang in the evolution of authentically Chinese forms of Buddhist practice and belief, the oft-accompanying corollary that the Sung marked the beginning of a long and inexorable decline does not follow. Research on the emergence of Ch'an, one of the major developments within Buddhism during the T'ang-Sung period, illustrates this point. Ch'an has been the focus of much of the best work by the present generation of scholars of Chinese Buddhism. As the most thoroughly "sinicized" form of Chinese Buddhism, it is often held up as the paradigm for understanding the complex process by which Buddhism became assimilated into Chinese forms of religious expression. Since Ch'an also emerged as the predominant form of institutional Buddhism in the Sung, its development provides a means of refracting some of the problems and issues important for understanding the changes that took place in Buddhism from T'ang to Sung.

Although the traditional picture of Ch'an as a "mind-to-mind transmission" can be traced back to the late seventh or early eighth century, the theory on which this view was based did not assume final form as a set formula until the Sung. This theory, linking Chinese Ch'an masters to the historical Buddha through an unbroken patriarchal succession, came to be encapsulated in the well-known formula retrospectively attributed to Bodhidharma—the legendary figure believed to have brought Ch'an to China in the first part of the sixth century—namely, that Ch'an is "a special transmission that is independent of the doctrinal teachings and that does not rely on the written word but, by directly pointing to the human mind, enables humans to see their nature and realize their Buddhahood."[39] Sung Ch'an historians looked back to the T'ang as a golden age and celebrated the sayings and doings of the great masters of the late-eighth and ninth centuries as embodying its true spirit. Inherent in this picture is the assumption that by the Sung period Ch'an had somehow fallen from its once exemplary state. Variations of this basic picture continue to inform modern Japanese scholarship, which sees the institutionalized and "syncretic" character of Ch'an practice in the Sung as a "corruption" of the "pure" spirit it displayed in the T'ang. Because of the enormous role that Japanese scholarship has played in shaping the study of Chinese Buddhism, Western scholars are only now becoming aware of and beginning to free themselves from the assumptions behind this picture.

As Griffith Foulk shows in his chapter, such a historical vision is a myth that tells us more about the ideals and self-conception of Ch'an in the Sung than it does about the actual history of Ch'an in the T'ang. Modern scholars have accordingly begun to turn away from Sung sources, a task made possible by the discovery of a number of Ch'an records and treatises among the vast trove of documents recovered from the cave temples at Tun-huang. Taking advantage of the window opened up by these texts, they have been busy rewriting the history of Ch'an in T'ang times.[40] It is now clear that T'ang-dynasty Ch'an did not represent a unified and clearly articulated movement. Rather, the Ch'an of that period was characterized by its wide diversity. The Ch'an records and treatises from Tun-huang as well as the more comprehensive account of Tsung-mi reveal that there was no distinctively "Ch'an" teaching or practice. Instead there were a variety of often contending traditions emphasizing different Buddhist teachings and practices or different approaches to the same practice. The ideas that Ch'an adapted were part of the common fare of sinicized Mahāyāna doctrine that had already been developed by the more scholastic T'ang traditions and articulated in various apocryphal texts.[41] What was perhaps unique, as John McRae has suggested, is a new rhetorical style based on a heightened sensitivity to the danger inherent in all dualistic formulations.[42]

If the existence of Ch'an as a distinct institution in the T'ang has been rendered problematic, there is no doubt that the Ch'an institution represented the dominant form of organized Buddhism in the Sung. Some three-quarters of the Buddhist monasteries that received an imperial name plaque in the Sung were designated as Ch'an establishments.[43] Although Sung Ch'an historians looked back to the T'ang as their golden age, this vision is really a testament to the vitality and creativity of Sung —and not T'ang—Ch'an. By any reliable historical measure, it was only in the Sung that Ch'an came into its own, and it is to the Sung that we must look to discover its "golden age."

The increasing awareness of the importance of the Sung in shaping our understanding of the past helps to free us from the hold that the Sung vision of Ch'an has had in mediating our picture of Ch'an in the T'ang. One of the most important results of such a historical deconstruction is that the field has now been opened for scholars to begin to look at Ch'an outside of the artificial parameters imposed by its sectarian ideology. Researchers need now turn to the continuities of Ch'an with the Chinese Buddhist tradition as a whole as well as with indigenous non-Buddhist forms of religious practice and belief. The direction of Bernard Faure's recent work suggests the fruitfulness of such an approach.[44] By examining various "cultic" aspects of Ch'an, Faure has suggested how Ch'an was connected with more "folk" and "popular" forms of Chinese and Buddhist religiosity. In a similar manner, although not specifically concerned with Ch'an as such, Raoul Birnbaum's work on deity cults, sacred mountains, and vision quests has shown the value of investigating Chinese Buddhist practices from a perspective that cuts across sectarian lines.[45] Such approaches offer the refreshing prospect of breaking the field of Chinese Buddhism out of its relative insulation by enabling us to understand it within the broad context of Chinese religion.

If the Tun-huang documents have been indispensable for reconstructing Ch'an history, they have been equally important for other exciting developments in our understanding of how Buddhism was linked with more "popular" forms of Chinese religion. In this regard one of the most significant discoveries from Tun-huang were the so-called transformation texts *(pien-wen)* dating back to the first half of the eighth century. In a fascinating, erudite, and truly monumental work of cross-cultural scholarship, Victor Mair has used these texts to show how the Indian practice of picture recitation was carried to China in the T'ang. Not only are these texts valuable in providing a glimpse of popular Buddhist religiosity, but Mair has gone on to show how the episodic form of picture storytelling shaped the narrative structure of Chinese fiction and drama.[46]

One of the most important transformation texts concerns the journey of Mahāmaudgalyāyana (Mu-lien) to the netherworld to save his mother. This Buddhist legend was the central myth on which the popular ghost festival *(yü-lan-p'en)* was founded. In his pioneering study, Stephen Teiser has shown how this festival not only was based on canonical and popular Buddhist sources but also resonated with a larger symbolic field characteristic of medieval Chinese popular religion as a whole. The more popular elaboration of the Mu-lien myth in the transformation texts emphasized the centrality of filial devotion, and the ghost festival enabled Buddhists to incorporate the strong Chinese sentiments of filial piety within the structure of a popular festival.[47]

A number of the texts that have come to light in the Tun-huang materials had been lost owing to their effective suppression as apocrypha by the state in full collusion with the Buddhist establishment,[48] and the proscription of such texts provides insight into the process of the formation of the canon. Kyoko Tokuno has shown how the various catalogues of Buddhist scriptures compiled between 374 and 730 had a largely proscriptive function. Many texts excluded from the canon as apocryphal were seen as subverting the authority of the state and the Buddhist establishment.[49] Of course numerous texts admitted into the canon were also apocryphal, in the sense that they masked their Chinese authorship by purporting to be translations of originally Indian works. Such canonical and noncanonical apocryphal works provide an invaluable window into popular religion, and scholars are only now beginning to mine their riches. Their study gives us fresh insight into popular amalgamations of Buddhist and Taoist ideas during the fifth and sixth centuries, and the messianic visions revealed in some of these texts clearly reflect the eschatological concerns of Taoism.[50] Other apocryphal texts admitted into the canon, as Robert Buswell's exemplary study of the *Vajrasamādhi Sūtra* has shown,[51] can be used to clarify the character of the sinicized doctrines that became the basis of Chinese Buddhist belief and practice.

TAOISM

The precise contours of the Taoist tradition, "China's indigenous high religion," are more difficult to delineate.[52] As a religious movement, Taoism began with the Way of the Celestial Masters (T'ien-shih tao) in the second century A.D., and Michel Strickmann has argued forcefully that the term "Taoist" be restricted to those who trace their spiritual warrant back to Chang Tao-ling, the original celestial master. Indeed, the Mao Shan revelations of the fourth century, the great ritual innovations of the Sung, and contemporary Taoist masters in Taiwan all claim the dispensation received by Chang from Lord Lao the Most High (T'ai-shang Lao-chün, the deified Lao Tzu) in A.D. 142 as the ultimate source of their authority.[53]

The Way of the Celestial Masters was in many ways different from the quietistic philosophy found in the *Lao Tzu* and the *Chuang Tzu,* the two great classics of the third century B.C. that many still regard as the inspiration behind Taoism. Anna Seidel traces the roots of Taoism to the "ecstatic cults of folk religion" and suggests that the influence of the *Lao Tzu* and the *Chuang Tzu* on the later religion was to some extent comparable to that of Greek philosophy on Christianity.[54] She has also shown how Taoist symbolism drew much from the prophetic and apocryphal texts *(ch'an-wei)* written during the Han dynasty.[55] The first of these, presented to court at the end of the first century B.C. was titled *T'ai-p'ing ching* (Scripture of great peace), a name that was to play a significant role throughout subsequent Taoist history. These texts were written at a time when there was grave anxiety that the Han was in danger of losing its heavenly mandate to rule, and they accordingly display an obsession with portents signaling heaven's will and reflect the belief that heaven conferred various treasure-objects *(pao)* as a token of its mandate.[56] In the Later Han (A.D. 25–220) the texts eventually proclaim themselves such treasure-objects. Since they were concerned with the religious legitimation of political authority, they were potentially subversive, and the mere possession of such a text could be seen as a claim to the throne. Just as prophetic texts played a major role in the reassertion of Han rule after the Wang Mang interregnum (A.D. 9–23), so, as the Later Han reached a crisis of authority, could they be used against it, and they were accordingly proscribed. The *fang-shih* who authored these texts were forced to go underground.

Following R. A. Stein, Seidel has argued that the first Taoist groups in Szechwan—the Way of the Great Peace and the Way of the Celestial Masters—saw themselves as recreating on a spiritual level the lost cosmic unity of the Han order and that the early Taoist priesthood was organized on the model of the Han bureaucracy.[57] Such appropriation of imperial symbolism underlines the fact that Taoism did not arise as a challenge to state authority. The Celestial Masters' submission to the secular authority of Ts'ao Ts'ao in 215 set the pattern for the religion's relations with the state for succeeding periods. Thereafter, Taoist priests served as part of the apparatus of dynastic legitimation, and the ruling dynasties, in turn, usually granted Taoism official recognition. Although Taoism may have drawn heavily from popular religious practices, it always defined itself, as Stein has shown, in contrast to popular practices,[58] and it thereby aligned itself with the state in the suppression or reform of popular cults. Taoist priests, after all, saw themselves as members of the same celestial hierarchy in which the emperor had his rightful place and so had little reason to subvert the established order.

Taoist deities were also seen as having a different nature than deities of the popular religion: they were celestial rather than terrestrial. They therefore did not accept the blood sacrifices typically offered to chthonic forces at local shrines, for they were pure stellar essences and not spirits of the dead. Neither did they exercise their power through intimidation as did the demonic forces of "excessive cults" *(yin-ssu);* nor were they in the business of granting the kind of material boons for which popular deities were most often supplicated. These stellar deities also had their counterparts within the human body, and their macro-microcosmic resonance made it possible for the Taoist adept to absorb their essences into the appropriate bodily organ in the course of meditation. Taoist gods, moreover, were a part of the celestial bureaucracy, whose ranks the Taoist adept would join, according to level of initiation, at death.

The association of Taoist texts with imperial treasure-objects also helps to explain the sacred character of many Taoist texts, which were often valued less for their philosophic content than for their talismanic power. Indeed, the transmission of sacred texts was central to Taoist rites of initiation, and the rightful possession of such texts gave one religious authority in this world and guaranteed one's sanctified status in the next. The accompanying registers of the names of the various spirit forces that different textual transmissions put at one's command were connected with the notion of the sovereign's power over spirits and the forces of nature. The centrality of texts and their proper transmission also underscore the fact that Taoism, in contradistinction to the popular traditions, was always a literate tradition. The main channel of communication with spiritual powers in Taoist ritual, as Schipper has emphasized, typically took place through the burning of written memorials in classical Chinese.[59]

The formative period of Taoism occurred during the fourth and fifth centuries with the Mao Shan and Ling-pao revelations. The first of these grew out of a series of visions granted to Yang Hsi (330–ca. 386) by a host of perfected from the Heaven of Supreme Clarity *(shang-ch'ing)* during the years 364 to 370. The resultant scriptures, biographies of the perfected, and other writings were later codified and annotated by T'ao Hung-ching (456–536). These texts built on the earlier Celestial Masters movement as well as on a rich body of alchemical lore and longevity practices associated with Ko Hung (283–343) and the *Pao-p'u tzu* (Master who embraces simplicity); they concerned themselves with methods of visionary meditation and meditative alchemy aimed at ensuring one's place among the ranks of the perfected in the hereafter.[60] The Ling-pao scriptures were composed during the late 390s by Ko Ch'ao-fu (fl. 400) and subsequently codified by Lu Hsiu-ching (406–477). These texts offered access to even more exalted celestial realms than their Mao Shan predecessors. They also appropriated Mahāyāna Buddhist ideas then in currency. Whereas the Mao Shan scriptures were focused on the quest for individual immortality, the Ling-pao scriptures addressed the universal salvation of humankind, and a concern with individual meditation was replaced with an institutionalized clergy, moral codes, collective liturgies, and state rituals. The Ling-pao texts defined the basic liturgical structure still used in Taoist ritual today.[61]

The Taoist canon began to take shape sometime around the end of the fourth or the beginning of the fifth century. Lu Hsiu-ching's 471 catalogue grouped Taoist texts into three "caverns" *(tung),* and this tripartite division became the fundamental organizational principle of all subsequent versions of the canon. The first and highest of these divisions was reserved for the Supreme Clarity or Mao Shan scriptures, the second for the Ling-pao scriptures, and the third and lowest for the *Scripture of the Three Sovereigns (San-huang ching).* Four supplements were added in the sixth century to accommodate the *Tao-te ching,* the *T'ai-p'ing ching,* various alchemical texts, and Celestial Masters material.[62]

Although far too little is known about Taoism in the T'ang, it seems that this was largely a period in which the achievements of the Six Dynasties movements were consolidated.[63] Even though no new scriptural revelations or movements occurred during the seventh through ninth centuries, Taoism enjoyed a privileged and semiofficial status under the T'ang court. The T'ang imperial house claimed descent from Lao Tzu, and the patronage of the religion was used as a means of bolstering dynastic prestige. Early T'ang emperors linked Taoism with the state cult and imperial family, and by the end of the seventh century a network of state-sponsored monasteries had been established throughout the empire. During Kao-tsung's reign (649–673) the practice of having imperial princesses receive Taoist ordination was begun,[64] and the *Tao-te ching* was made a compulsory text for the civil service examinations. Taoism received its greatest imperial sponsorship during the reign of Hsüan-tsung (r. 713–756), who, among other measures, had an imperial commentary to the *Tao-te ching* issued under his name, raised the importance of the *Tao-te ching* and other Taoist texts within the examination system by instituting a separate Taoist exam, promoted a nationwide system of schools for the study of Taoism, established the worship of Lao Tzu as an imperial ancestor, and brought the cult of the five sacred mountains under Taoist control.[65] Hsüan-tsung also tried to assemble all extant Taoist texts and compile them into a canon, copies of which were then distributed to Taoist temples throughout the land. Although subsquent T'ang emperors failed to maintain Hsüan-tsung's level of patronage, they continued to draw on the ideological resources of Taoism to maintain the strength of their line.

The second great period of Taoist creativity occurred in the Sung, when there was a proliferation of new ritual texts, the formation of new sects, and the widescale incorporation of popular deities within the Taoist pantheon. Taoism once again became the official religion in the early eleventh century, but it was not until the twelfth century during the reign of Hui-tsung that a veritable renaissance took place. This efflorescence was inaugurated by a new dispensation, which proclaimed the emperor's cosmic origin as the sovereign of the Divine Empyrean (Shen-hsiao). The Divine Empyrean was central and supreme among the nine empyreans, and the other Taoist orders, whose spiritual authority derived from the other celestial palaces, were thus all subordinate to Shen-hsiao. A much augmented sixty-one-chapter version of the *Scripture of Salvation (Tu-jen ching),* a Ling-pao text originally in one chapter, was central to this revelation, and the recitation of this text was supposed to ensure the security and prosperity of the state. This text was also placed at the head of the first complete printing of the Taoist canon carried out under Hui-tsung's sponsorship, and its placement there entailed a major reorganization of the canon that has been replicated in all subsequent editions.[66]

The Shen-hsiao movement rose to preeminence at a time when the dynasty, under imminent threat by non-Chinese forces to the north, sought every means possible to safeguard its security. Hui-tsung also offered special homage to Hsü Sun as a national guardian. Renowned as a queller of demonic creatures, a healer, and a paragon of filial piety, Hsü Sun was a hazy third- or fourth-century figure around whom a thriving cult had developed by the late T'ang. A series of new revelations occurred between 1129 and 1131, shortly after the Sung was forced to relocate in the south, that formed the basis for the emergence of the Loyal and Filial Way of the Pure and Perspicacious (Ching-ming chung-hsiao tao) as an important Taoist movement in the Southern Sung.[67]

The canon printed toward the end of Hui-tsung's reign also contained the new Celestial Heart ritual texts.[68] These were part of a growing body of therapeutic ritual and talismanic lore that burgeoned during the Sung and culminated in the Clarified Tenuity (Ch'ing-wei) revelations, which synthesized earlier Taoist practices together with the new Thunder Rites and Tantric ritual.[69] These Sung period therapeutic rites went beyond earlier Taoist ritual meditation. Rather than merely visualizing Taoist deities within the sanctuary of their bodies, adepts were now able to embody the deity that the rites empowered them to control. As Boltz's chapter documents, these powerful demonifugic rites proved their worth to many magistrates seeking to assert their political control over often-resistant local forces in the south.

Several new Taoist movements also developed under the Chin dynasty (1115–1234) in the north. The only one of these to last, however, was Ch'üan-chen (Complete Perfection), established by Wang Che in the twelfth century. This ascetic movement, drawing on Confucian moral teachings and Ch'an meditation practice, evolved into a full-fledged monastic Taoist tradition.

POPULAR RELIGION

Popular religion is difficult to circumscribe. Not only is the definition of the word "popular" a thorny problem,[70] the problem of sources is also most acute in the case of popular religion. The popular traditions were largely oral and therefore did not leave a record of practices and beliefs. Many of the accounts that we are forced to rely on thus represent the point of view of the literate elite, which more often than not was critical of popular religion. The compartmentalization of the written record also makes it more difficult to get a holistic picture of popular practices and tends to reinforce the belief that there was a larger gap between popular and elite practices than there probably ever was. Many popular practices were popular precisely because they were engaged in by members of all strata of society; hence "popular" should not be understood as being necessarily opposed to elite.[71] The popular tradition also tended to be diffuse, and to lack an organized priesthood. Its local and unsystematic character meant that there was always a wide range of variation and inconsistency, making historical generalization a treacherous business.

We should be careful not to hypostatize popular religious practice and belief as constituting an autonomous religious tradition that was wholly separate from the three institutionalized traditions of Buddhism, Taoism, and Confucianism—although it includes much that falls outside the parameters of these traditions. Even though these traditions often defined themselves in contrast to popular practices, there was much in Buddhism, Taoism, and Confucianism (as our earlier model suggests) that was truly popular and never fully under the control of the religious establishment, such as cult centers, pilgrimages, miracles, portents, exorcism, and so on.

Popular religion centered on the family and community and was linked to immediate concerns of health, long life, good fortune, success, and happiness. As such, it expressed beliefs and values that pervaded Chinese society as a whole, and many of its features have already been mentioned in passing. It included worship of ancestors, household gods, and local deities; participation in annual communal festivals; sacrifice to gods embodying natural forces and phenomena; divination; belief in ghosts; observance of taboos based on ideas of pollution; exorcism; and spirit mediumship. Many of its practices had roots in the prehistoric past, yet it was never static. The Six Dynasties period was characterized by a general opposition to local cults by the combined forces of Confucian officialdom, Taoism, and Buddhism. Starting in the T'ang, however, the suppression of local deities began to give way to strategies of appropriation, and by the end of the Sung, the popular pantheon had come to assume the basic shape that it was to retain down until modern times. In the process, the nonhuman and often fearsome identity of local deities became overlaid by a more civilized guise, often that of a martial hero, former official, or Taoist saint.

The process by which deities became integrated into the established pantheon during the Sung is reflected in the number of titles that were granted to gods by the government. Hansen has noted that there was "a sudden increase in the number of titles granted in the 1070s and a sharp spate of activity in the early 1100s under the emperor Hui-tsung, followed by continuous grants through the twelfth century."[72] Government recognition of gods, like patronage of Buddhism and Taoism, harnessed the spiritual resources of the land for the protection of the dynasty. Recasting gods as supernatural officials in the same bureaucracy to which actual officials belonged bolstered the authority of those officials. The rationalization of gods into a bureaucratic structure coincided with the extension of imperial power on the local level, and local resistance to government encroachment was frequently played out on a supernatural plane (see Boltz's chapter). Gods represented different communities and groups, and their promotion provided a way in which different communities and groups could call attention to their importance.

Although gods' powers surpassed those of mortals, they exercised them much as humans did, sometimes with benevolence and sometimes with vengeance. As the gods became anthropomorphized, their needs were increasingly understood in human terms. Not only did they need offerings of meat, wine, or grain for their sustenance, but they also craved human recognition in the form of images, temples, and titles. The state of a god's image or temple was a reflection of that god's power; if it was poorly kept up, the god's ability to perform miracles would be diminished. If a new image was painted or carved or if a temple was refurbished, however, the god would reward devotees with new miracles. Gods communicated their needs to humans through spirit possession, dreams, and visions, and humans divined gods' needs through various forms of oracles (such as spirit writing, moonblocks, and divination sticks). Official recognition meant that the god's name would be listed in the register of sacrifices, local officials would perform rituals at the god's temple biannually in the spring and autumn, and the government would contribute to the maintenance of that temple.

The principle of reciprocity that bound gods and their devotees together meant that the popular pantheon was always responsive to social change. Scholars have accordingly shown how changes in the popular pantheon reflect broader changes affecting Chinese society at large. David Johnson, for example, has argued that the origin and spread of city gods (*ch'eng-huang shen,* "gods of walls and moats") was related to the emergence of a new commercial or mercantile elite made possible by the growth of cities as commercial centers, a process that began in the late T'ang and gained momentum throughout the Sung.[73] In her contribution to this volume, Valerie Hansen puts forth a different hypothesis on the origin of the city god, suggesting a Buddhist prototype in the monastic guardian Vaiśravaṇa.

As gods shed their zoomorphic skins and became incorporated into a state-sanctioned bureaucratic structure as exemplars, there was a side of the popular tradition (often associated with shamanist practices and demonic power) that was forced to go underground or subsist at the margins of established religion. The numinous always had the power to erupt in unpredicable ways and disrupt the established order. New technologies of exorcism and magic were invented to deal with them, such as Celestial Heart (T'ien-hsin) and Thunder Rites, discussed in Boltz's chapter in this volume.

CONFUCIANISM

Buddhism, Taoism, and popular religion developed in the context of deeply rooted religious orientations concerning ancestors and rulers that were generally associated with the Confucian tradition. The relationship between these traditions and Confucianism was complex, and the direction of influence is often difficult to determine. There were also many parallel developments that cannot be understood in terms of strict unilinear influence. On a practical level, moreover, these traditions had to deal with a state staffed by officials trained in the Confucian classics. The precariousness of their relationship to the Confucian state imposed constraints on the direction and scope of their development and necessitated various degrees of compromise in order to secure patronage and avert suppression.

The vitality of these religions and their hold on people's imaginations helped stimulate the major reorientation of Confucian learning that occurred during the T'ang and the Sung dynasties. This revival is generally credited to a series of great writers and teachers who agreed on some basic premises but differed in many particulars. All Neo-Confucians from Han Yü (768–824) in the late T'ang to Chu Hsi (1130–1200) in the Southern Sung were committed to achieving in their own day long-recognized Confucian virtues and goals, such as a stable social and political order in which children were filial, subordinates loyal, and rulers wise. Many of them tried to define an orthodox core to Confucianism, uncontaminated by heterodoxies of any sort. A much smaller number of Confucian leaders, most notably Chang Tsai (1020–1077), the Ch'eng brothers, and Chu Hsi, developed theoretical explanations of the workings of the cosmos and of human nature that could be seen as alternatives to Buddhist and Taoist cosmologies.

The early Neo-Confucians themselves stressed their break with the past. From the time of Mencius until their own day, they claimed, the true teachings had not been transmitted, owing largely to the pernicious influence of Buddhism and Taoism. Intellectual historians of the twentieth century have largely accepted this claim, if taking a more detached view. It has long been common to think of Confucianism as moribund from late Han times on, as those inclined toward philosophical speculation or the search for spiritual values were attracted to Taoism and especially Buddhism. This decline in Confucianism coincided with the decline in the authority of the imperial state and even of Chinese civilization as the Han dynasty imperium broke up and non-Chinese tribes gained control of the north China plain. The reestablishment of a strong state under the T'ang led to a revival of state Confucianism and renewed interest in Confucian values of service to the state and emperor on the part of many educated men. When confronted with grave political crises in the late eighth and ninth centuries, a few men like Han Yü, Liu Tsung-yüan (773–819), and Li Ao (ca. 772–836) called for finding answers in ancient Confucian texts and the social and political values they taught, or, in their terms, reviving the "way of the sages."

Where modern scholars have departed most fully from Neo-Confucianism's own version of its history is in assessing the role of Buddhism. Confucians in the late T'ang and Northern Sung who looked anew to ancient Confucian texts were often explicitly hostile to Buddhism—wishing to free China of its influence—yet the questions they phrased and the concepts they used demonstrate to modern scholars that they were men of a post-Buddhist China. They could no longer think about humankind and the cosmos in the way Han Confucians had, and they felt compelled to pose questions about the ontological basis of their teachings that had never been asked before. Particularly important here was the emergence of Ch'an in mid-T'ang. As compared to other forms of Buddhism, the ideas about mind and nature in the more sinicized Ch'an could be absorbed more easily by scholars working in a Confucian framework.[74]

Research of the last decade has added greatly to our understanding of the interconnections between changes in the state, the political environment, Buddhism, and Neo-Confucianism. Confucianism in the early T'ang has been shown to have been more vital and creative than many had supposed, but undeniably state-centered. Confucian scholars worked out the ritual programs of the early T'ang emperors and stressed the links between their activities and the needs of the state.[75] Well into the T'ang period Confucian scholars industriously engaged in building state schools and writing histories, belles-lettres, and commentaries to the classics.[76] Both Howard Wechsler and David McMullen show state support for Confucian activities coexisting effectively with state patronage of Buddhism and Taoism and private commitment to either religion on the part of many Confucian officials. Neither the state nor the scholarly community felt compelled to sustain exclusive positions or to demarcate the limits of what was admissible. This pluralistic attitude also colored attitudes toward differences of interpretation within Confucianism; "when emperors might be actively committed simultaneously to such very different belief systems as Buddhism and Taoism, the fact that there were divergencies within the Confucian exegetical tradition cannot have seemed of itself important."[77]

The rebellion of An Lu-shan in the mid-eighth century brought on a political crisis and intellectual ferment. The state agencies that had provided the focus for scholarly activities deteriorated, forcing the scholarly community to reappraise its political and cultural roles. Peter Bol, focusing on the learning of the *shih-ta-fu* (literati-officials), relates the break between early and late T'ang to changes in the social character of the elite. In the aristocratic society of the early T'ang, when men from families of great prestige could count on getting official posts, he argues, men of learning saw their task as preserving and perpetuating cultural forms —especially literary ones but also other forms such as rituals and customary usages. In this environment the received traditions, passed down through the generations, were to be treasured as they mediated between individuals and the ancient classical sources of authority. From late T'ang on, however, scholars started to discard these traditions and turn directly to the classics to find "the way of the sages," a tendency that can also be seen in approaches to literary writing, a pursuit at least as typical of T'ang *shih-ta-fu* as the study of the classics.[78]

Han Yü has long been seen as a key precursor of eleventh century Neo-Confucianism. For Han Yü work as a writer and as a Confucian were not two compartmentalized activities but one role unified by his vision of the Confucian scholar. He did not see the "ancient literature" style he so brilliantly developed as simply a literary style but rather thought of it as the way to convey the truths of the Confucian tradition that had been fully realized in the ancient sages. Han Yü is known for his virulent attack on Buddhism and his call for appropriating its monasteries, burning its books, and laicizing its monks and nuns, but as Charles Hartman shows, he was by no means uninfluenced by Buddhist ideas, especially the Ch'an ones so pervasive in his social milieu.[79]

Many of the early Sung leaders of the Neo-Confucian movement were politically engaged men, and the significance of the historical context to an understanding of their ideas has long been recognized. Men like Fan Chung-yen (989–1052), Ou-yang Hsiu (1007–1072), Ssu-ma Kuang (1019–1086), and Wang An-shih (1021–1086) saw themselves as confronting great social and political crises; it was to deal with concerns of state that they formulated their Confucian programs.[80] These scholar-statesmen also supported the work of teachers committed to reviving Confucianism; Fan Chung-yen, for instance, recommended Hu Yüan (993–1059), Li Kou (1009–1059), and Sun Fu (992–1057) to government teaching posts. Compared to the scholar-statesmen, these teachers often took a narrower view of Confucianism and echoed Han Yü's anti-Buddhist rhetoric; Sun Fu, for example, wrote that allowing a teaching of the barbarians to bring disorder to "the teachings of our sages" was a great humiliation to Confucian scholars.

The steady increase in the size of the educated class added substance to the middle reaches of the Confucian peak and contributed to the intellectual ferment of the eleventh century. Leading teachers could attract hundreds of students, most of whom intended to attempt the civil service examinations. Yet their students did not learn only what would be tested by the state examiners. They discussed with their teachers more abstract subjects such as the nature of sages and the way to restore government by sages. The growth in the importance of the examination system as a means of access to office forced scholars to reconsider the relations between the state, the educated elite, and society more generally. Because such a high proportion of the educated class participated in the civil service examinations, the state had unprecedented opportunities to shape the intellectual activities and orientations of the elite. Out of fear that students would devote their efforts disproportionately to subjects tested in the examinations, scholars engaged in bitter controversies over what the examinations should test. In other words, what scholars should study was both an intellectual and a political question. Whether the state should establish more schools, whether poetry should be tested on the examinations, whether character could be evaluated objectively in any written test were questions of state that divided the scholarly community. Revisions in recruitment procedures were initiated by Fan Chung-yen and Han Ch'i (1008–1075) in 1043 and by Wang An-shih in 1071. These reforms included not merely changes in the sorts of questions on the exams but also expansion of the state-run school system. The growth in the educated class can perhaps also help explain why, by the Southern Sung, Ch'eng I's emphasis on self-cultivation was proving more attractive than the emphasis on reforming the world of his more activist contemporaries. Ch'eng I's views give extraordinary autonomy to the individual to discover truth within himself, and this personal cultivation is seen as more fundamental than service to the ruler. By acting morally, educated men were benefiting society; governmental service, while desirable, was not essential to self-worth. Although Ch'eng I came from a well-established official family, his ideas had appeal to the growing *shih-ta-fu* class whose members had local standing but less and less chance of ever becoming officials.[81]

Chu Hsi was the most important of those who developed Ch'eng I's ideas in the Southern Sung. His personal contribution to the development of Neo-Confucianism is now widely recognized.[82] Despite the recent outpouring of scholarship on Chu Hsi, it has also come to be widely appreciated that only retrospectively does the Ch'eng-Chu school take a central place in intellectual history. Bol argues that the mainstream of literati learning in the Northern Sung was men like Wang An-shih and Su Shih.[83] Ira E. Kasoff has shown that Chang Tsai was an independent thinker, not a follower of the Ch'engs.[84] Hoyt Tillman has demonstrated the lively interaction among the twelfth-century intellectual community.[85]

The cultural context in which Neo-Confucianism developed included all the religious richness discussed earlier in this chapter. Although it is possible to present the history of Neo-Confucianism as following a dynamic internal to the Confucian scholarly discourse, much is gained when the context is broadened. Donald Munro, for instance, frequently brings Buddhist ideas in to explicate Chu Hsi's ideas, whether he was absorbing a Buddhist distinction or rejecting a Buddhist premise. In his study of Tsung-mi, Peter Gregory has shown how Chu Hsi's theory of human nature was based on a conceptual model articulated by T'ang Buddhists.[86] Neo-Confucianism was also formulated in a world in which Taoism and folk religion were important components of everyday life. Confucian scholars' criticisms of popular cults are among our better sources for these cults.[87] Geomancy, cremation, and other popular practices related to handling death, mourning, and ancestral sacrifices were part of the context for Neo-Confucian efforts to redefine distinctly Confucian family rituals.[88]

Few scholars today look on Neo-Confucianism as a strictly secular phenomenon. Neo-Confucians were very much interested in questions of ultimate meaning, of the ontological basis of humanity and the cosmos.[89] Moreover, the attempts of leading teachers to ground their daily lives in structures that would recreate for them the basic verities and aid their spiritual quests often led to the creation or elaboration of rituals not unlike those of their supposed rivals. Academies, for instance, devoted considerable energies to staging rites to former sages. At home many Neo-Confucian teachers treated ancestral rites with the piety much of the population reserved for gods.

To return to the mountain metaphor, the revival and reorientation of Confucianism from the T'ang to the Sung dynasties can be conceived as a restructuring of the Confucian peak. In the early T'ang the top reaches of the Confucian peak, like the Buddhist and Taoist ones, consisted of men who were highly educated in literary traditions and also held ranks within an institutional hierarchy. During the course of the T'ang-Sung period, however, teachers and writers operating largely outside the orbit of the state came to be recognized as key leaders of the Confucian movement. The middle reaches of the Confucian peak swelled in Sung times with the expansion of education and the growing popularity of studying for the examinations. As the proportion of the population educated in the Confucian classics and knowledgeable about current scholarly concerns grew, one can suppose that ordinary, uneducated people were more likely to have contact with Confucian scholars and hear directly or indirectly of Confucian principles from local teachers, lineage leaders, or community leaders. This is not to suggest that the Confucian program to win back the common people from "superstition," Buddhism, and Taoism may have been successful; however, the Confucian presence in local communities was sufficiently strengthened to keep the other religions from making further inroads on popular belief and practice and to ensure that Confucian traditions would retain a hold.

The social and religious landscape sketched in this chapter, it should be reiterated, was constantly evolving. Each of the four traditions was differently constituted in the twelfth century than it had been in the eighth. All adapted to and were stimulated by the same social, economic, and political changes: population growth, urbanization, commercialization, printing, altered relations with Central Asia, settlement of the South, and so on. Equally important, Buddhism, Taoism, Confucianism, and popular religion adapted to and were stimulated by changes in one another. Even though we have discussed each tradition separately, we must stress that none was wholly autonomous; throughout this period, changes in one had complex effects on all of the others. The revival of state Confucianism in the early T'ang occurred in the context of imperial patronage of Buddhism and Taoism. The intellectual sophistication of Buddhist doctrine in T'ang times attracted the interest of educated men who did not identify themselves as Buddhist. The social, political, and economic success of Buddhist monastic establishments stimulated imitations—not merely Taoist monasteries and Confucian academies but also charitable granaries and lineage estates. Buddhist cults to Vaiśravaṇa, Mañjuśrī, and Kuan-yin so closely paralleled the development of cults outside the Buddhist tradition—such as the god of walls and moats and Wen-ch'ang discussed in this volume—that chains of influence are extremely difficult to sort out. The reorientation of Confucian learning from late T'ang times on had effects on the ways officials discharged their responsibility to supervise local religious establishments. These examples of interconnection and influence should suffice to remind us of the dynamic and interrelated nature of change in religion and society over these centuries.

NOTES

1. Robert M. Hartwell, "Demographic, Political, and Social Transformations of China, 750–1550," *HJAS* 42 (1982): 365–442; Joseph P. McDermott, "Charting Blank Spaces and Disputed Regions: The Problems of Sung Land Tenure," *JAS* 44 (1984): 13–41.

2. Yoshinobu Shiba, "Urbanization and the Development of Markets in the

Lower Yangtze Valley," in John Winthrop Haeger, ed., *Crisis and Prosperity in Sung China* (Tucson: University of Arizona Press, 1975); Winston Wan Lo, *Szechwan in Sung China: A Case Study in the Political Integration of the Chinese Empire* (Taipei: University of Chinese Culture Press, 1982); Robert P. Hymes, *Statesmen and Gentlemen: The Elite of Fu-chou, Chiang-hsi, in Northern and Southern Sung* (Cambridge: Cambridge University Press, 1986); Richard van Glahn, *The Country of Streams and Grottoes: Expansion, Settlement, and the Civilizing of the Sichuan Frontier in Song Times* (Cambridge: Harvard University Press, 1987).

3. David G. Johnson, *The Medieval Chinese Oligarchy* (Boulder: Westview Press, 1977), esp. pp. 131–141; Patricia Buckley Ebrey, *The Aristocratic Families of Early Imperial China: A Case Study of the Po-ling Ts'ui Family* (Cambridge: Cambridge University Press, 1978), esp. pp. 93–112.

4. See Thomas H. C. Lee, *Government Education and Examinations in Sung China* (Hong Kong: The Chinese University Press, 1985).

5. Hartwell, "Transformations," pp. 405–425.

6. See Hartwell, "Transformations," p. 419, and Hymes, *Statesmen and Gentlemen*, pp. 29–61.

7. John W. Chaffee, *The Thorny Gates of Learning in Sung China: A Social History of Examinations* (Cambridge: Cambridge University Press, 1985). See also Winston W. Lo, *An Introduction to the Civil Service of Sung China* (Honolulu: University of Hawaii Press, 1987), pp. 79–114.

8. Richard L. Davis, *Court and Family in Sung China, 960–1279: Bureaucratic Success and Kinship Fortunes for the Shihs of Ming-chou* (Durham: Duke University Press, 1986), esp. pp. 167–187; Lee, *Government Education and Examinations*.

9. "The Religious Commitment: Shang Theology and the Genesis of Chinese Political Culture," *History of Religions* 17.3–4 (1978): 211–225; Keightley's ideas are further developed in "Shang Divination: The Magico-Religious Legacy," in Henry J. Rosemont, Jr., ed., *Explorations in Early Chinese Cosmology, Journal of the American Academy of Religion Thematic Studies* 50.2 (Chico, CA: Scholars Press, 1984), pp. 11–34; and "Legitimation in Shang China" (paper delivered at the Conference on Legitimation of Chinese Imperial Regimes, Asilomar, CA, June 1975).

10. See Kwang-chih Chang's "Ancient China and Its Anthropological Significance," in *Symbols* (Spring/Fall 1984), in which he argues that the development of ancient Chinese civilization was associated with a "differentiated access to means of communication—instead of the means of production" (p. 2). See also Chang's *Art, Myth, and Ritual* (Cambridge: Harvard University Press, 1983).

11. It did not apply, however, in the case of Buddhist deities or female deities; see P. Steven Sangren, "Female Gender in Chinese Religious Symbols: Kuan Yin, Ma Tsu, and the 'Eternal Mother,' " *Signs* 9.1 (1983): 4–25.

12. Arthur Waley, *The Life and Times of Po Chü-i (772–846 A.D.)* (London: Allen & Unwin, 1949), p. 148.

13. See Alvin P. Cohen's "Coercing the Rain Deities in Ancient China," in *History of Religions* 17.3–4 (1978): 244–265.

14. Here Keightley's remarks should give pause to those who would see the spiritual world as a "projection" of the political world: "religious belief and prac-

tice had a social reality of their own, and . . . religion and society interacted synergetically . . . producing results which neither could have achieved without the other" ("The Religious Commitment," p. 222).

15. "Bureaucratic," according to Keightley, refers to "the actions and values characteristic of bureaucrats," whom he goes on to define as "men or women, usually specialists, whose actions are validated by their titles and jurisdictions, systematically related to one another in relatively impersonal and routinized ways by a hierarchic system of defined regulations and duties, appointed and promoted on the basis of stipulated, written criteria, such as merit and seniority" ("The Religious Commitment," p. 214, n. 12).

16. While the Confucian stress on the primacy of moral character attempted to curb the despotic potential of an exclusive emphasis on charisma of office, the importance of the charisma of office was reaffirmed in an equal emphasis on ritual propriety. The classical debate between Mencius and Kao-tzu in *Mencius* VI.A.5–6 about whether *i* (duty, righteousness) is internal or external centers on identifying the location of charisma.

17. Jonathan Z. Smith's notion of "locative" (in contradistinction to "utopian") religion is especially apt in the Chinese case; see his "The Influence of Symbols on Social Change: A Place on Which to Stand," *Worship* 44 (1970): 457–474.

18. See Herbert Fingarette's provocative discussion in *Confucius—the Secular as Sacred* (New York: Harper and Row, 1972).

19. Anna Seidel, "Traces of Han Religion in Funeral Texts Found in Tombs," in Akitsuki Kan'ei, ed., *Dōkyō to shūkyō bunka* (Tokyo: Hirakawa shuppansha, 1987), p. 27; see pp. 46–47 for a brief summary of the main features of this netherworldly bureaucracy.

20. See R. A. Stein, "Remarques sur les mouvements du taoïsme politicoreligieux au IIe siècle ap. J.C.," *T'oung Pao* 50.1–3 (1963): 1–78; and Anna Seidel, "Imperial Treasures and Taoist Sacraments: Taoist Roots in the Apocrypha," in Michel Strickmann, ed., *Tantric and Taoist Studies in Honour of R. A. Stein*, vol. 2: *Mélanges chinois et bouddhiques* 21 (1983): 291–371.

21. See, for example, Arthur P. Wolf's classic article "Gods, Ghosts, and Ancestors," in idem, ed., *Religion and Ritual in Chinese Society* (Stanford: Stanford University Press, 1974), pp. 131–182.

22. See her "Imperial Treasures and Taoist Sacraments."

23. Ibid., pp. 308–309.

24. Ibid., p. 292.

25. See "The Fundamental Ideas of Chinese Science," chapter 13 in Needham, *Science and Civilization of China*, vol. 2: *History of Scientific Thought* (Cambridge: Cambridge University Press, 1956). This correspondential cosmology is further explored by Manfred Porkert in *The Theoretical Foundations of Chinese Medicine: Systems of Correspondence* (Cambridge: MIT Press, 1978). See also John Major, "Myth, Cosmology, and the Origins of Chinese Science," *Journal of Chinese Philosophy* 5 (1978): 1–20.

26. The five phases are arranged in terms of two major cyclical patterns: in the first they successively generate one another, wood producing fire (by being burned as fuel), fire producing earth (by producing ashes), earth producing metal (by producing metallic ore), metal producing water (through condensation), and

water producing wood (by nourishing plants); in the second they successively overcome one another, wood conquering earth (wooden tools can dig up the earth), metal conquering wood (metal tools can carve wood), fire conquering metal (by melting it), water conquering fire (by extinguishing it), and earth conquering water (by damming it).

27. A. C. Graham well indicates the range of meaning encompassed by the term in his *Two Chinese Philosophers: Ch'eng Ming-tao and Ch'eng Yi-ch'uan* (London: Lund Humphries, 1958): "*Ch'i*, a common and elusive word in ordinary Chinese speech as well as in philosophy, covers a number of concepts for which we have different names in English or none at all. . . . *Ch'i* is quite concrete; it really is, among other things, the breath in our throats. It is the source of life, dispersing into the air at death; we breathe it in and out, and feel it rising and ebbing when we are angry, failing in a limb which grows numb; we smell it in odors, feel it as heat or cold, sense it as the air or atmosphere of a person or a place, as the vitality of a poem, or as the breath of spring which quickens and the breath of autumn which withers; we even see it condensing as vapor or mist. . . . Matter is merely *ch'i* in a very dense and inert state" (p. 31).

28. Or, in the case of Confucianism, what functioned analogously as a clergy; see Jean Lévi's "Les fonctionnaires et le divan: luttes de pouvoirs entre divinités et administrateurs dans les contes des Six Dynasties et des T'ang," *Cahiers d'Extrême-Asie* 2 (1986), and "Les fonctions religieuses de la bureaucratie céleste," *L'homme* 101 (1987).

29. At the very end of Zürcher's "Buddhist Influence on Early Taoism," *T'oung Pao* 65.1–3 (1980): 146.

30. See Robert Redfield's classic study *Peasant Society and Culture: An Anthropological Approach to Civilization* (Chicago: University of Chicago Press, 1956).

31. The distinction between ultimate and proximate soteriological goals has been insightfully developed by Carl Bielefeldt in "No-Mind and Sudden Awakening: Thoughts on the Soteriology of a Kamakura Zen Text," in Robert E. Buswell, Jr., and Robert M. Gimello, eds., *Paths to Liberation: The Mārga and Its Transformations in Buddhist Thought* (Honolulu: University of Hawaii Press, 1992), pp. 476–478.

32. For a vivid account of the cathartic effect of the story of Mu-lien's rescue of his mother, as dramatized in operas often presented during the ghost festival in later imperial times, see David Johnson, "Actions Speak Louder Than Words: The Cultural Significance of Chinese Ritual Opera," in idem, ed., *Ritual Opera, Operatic Ritual: "Mu-lien Rescues His Mother" in Chinese Popular Culture* (Berkeley: Publications of the Chinese Popular Culture Project, 1989), pp. 1–43.

33. Schipper, "Taoist Ordination Ranks in the Tunhuang Manuscripts," in Gert Naudorf, Karl-Heinz Pohl, and Hans-Hermann Schmidt, eds., *Religion und Philosophie in Ostasien (Festscrift für Hans Steininger)* (Königshausen: Neumann, 1985), p. 131.

34. The literature on Buddhist theories of decline is prodigious; the most recent and best study, by Jan Nattier, is *Once Upon a Future Time: Studies in a Buddhist Prophecy of Decline* (Berkeley: Asian Humanities Press, 1991).

35. The study of this movement was pioneered by Yabuki Keiki; for more recent appraisals see Jamie Hubbard, "Salvation in the Final Period of the

Dharma: The Inexhaustible Storehouse of the San-Chiao-Chiao" (Ph.D. dissertation, University of Wisconsin, 1986); as well as Mark Lewis, "The Suppression of the Three Stages Sect: Apocrypha as a Political Issue," and Antonino Forte, "The Relativity of the Concept of Orthodoxy in Chinese Buddhism: Chih-sheng's Indictment of Shih-li and the Proscription of the Dharma Mirror Sutra," both in Robert E. Buswell, Jr., ed., *Chinese Buddhist Apocrypha* (Honolulu: University of Hawaii Press, 1990). This movement was so effectively suppressed by the state with the full collusion of the Buddhist establishment that, were it not for the chance survival of some of its literature at Tun-huang, we would know virtually nothing at all about its teaching or have any hint of its considerable popularity in the T'ang—a salutary reminder to historians of the often fortuitous character of the sources on which they must perforce rely to reconstruct their picture of the past.

36. See Eric Zürcher, " 'Prince Moonlight': Messianism and Eschatology in Early Medieval Chinese Buddhism," *T'oung Pao* 68.1–3 (1982): 1–75, and Michel Strickmann, "The *Consecration Sūtra*: A Buddhist Book of Spells," in Buswell, ed., *Chinese Buddhist Apocrypha,* pp. 75–118.

37. See also the ninefold grid developed by David Johnson in his introduction to the volume he edited with Andrew J. Nathan and Evelyn Rawski, *Popular Culture in Late Imperial China* (Berkeley: University of California Press, 1985).

38. And up until the time of the encounter with Western imperialist powers the only one of significance.

39. The complete, four-phrase formula first appears in the *Tsu-t'ing shih-yüan,* compiled by Mu-an Shan-ch'ing in 1108; see *HTC* 113.66c.

40. For some of the more recent of these see John R. McRae, *The Northern School and the Formation of Early Ch'an Buddhism* (Honolulu: University of Hawaii Press, 1986); Bernard Faure, *La volonté d'orthodoxie dans le bouddhisme chinois* (Paris: Centre national de la recherche scientifique, 1988); and Peter N. Gregory, ed., *Sudden and Gradual Approaches to Enlightenment in Chinese Thought* (Honolulu: University of Hawaii Press, 1987).

41. See Peter N. Gregory, *Tsung-mi and the Sinification of Buddhism* (Princeton: Princeton University Press, 1991); Robert E. Buswell, Jr., *The Formation of Ch'an Ideology in China and Korea* (Princeton: Princeton University Press, 1989).

42. See "Shen-hui and the Teaching of Sudden Enlightenment in Early Ch'an Buddhism," in Gregory, ed., *Sudden and Gradual.*

43. See Foulk's chapter in this volume.

44. See *The Rhetoric of Immediacy: A Cultural Critique of Chan/Zen Buddhism* (Princeton: Princeton University Press, 1991).

45. See, for example, *Studies on the Mysteries of Mañjuśrī* (Society for the Study of Chinese Religions, 1983); "Thoughts on T'ang Buddhist Mountain Traditions and Their Context," *Tang Studies,* no. 2 (1984); and "The Manifestation of a Monastery," *JAOS* 106 (1986). See also Robert M. Gimello, "Chang Shan-ying on Wu-t'ai Shan," in Susan Naquin and Chün-fang Yü, eds., *Pilgrims and Sacred Sites in China* (Berkeley: University of California Press, 1992), pp. 89–149.

46. See Mair, *Tun-huang Popular Narratives* (Cambridge: Cambridge University Press, 1983); *T'ang Transformation Texts* (Cambridge: Harvard Univer-

sity Press, 1989); and *Painting and Performance: Chinese Picture Recitation and Its Indian Genesis* (Honolulu: University of Hawaii Press, 1989).

47. See Teiser, *The Ghost Festival in Medieval China* (Princeton: Princeton University Press, 1988).

48. Volume 85 of the Taishō tripiṭaka reproduces fifty-six such texts (nos. 2865–2920) from the Stein (British Museum), Pelliot (Bibliothèque national), and Japanese collections of Tun-huang manuscripts.

49. See Kyoko Tokuno, "Evaluation of Indigenous Scriptures in Chinese Buddhist Bibliographic Catalogues," in Buswell, ed., *Chinese Buddhist Apocrypha*.

50. See Strickmann, *Consecration Sūtra*; and Zürcher, " 'Prince Moonlight.' "

51. *The Formation of Ch'an Ideology in China and Korea.*

52. For an authoritative survey of Taoism and Taoist studies, see Anna Seidel, "Chronicle of Taoist Studies in the West, 1950–1990, *Cahiers d'Extrême-Asie* 5 (1989–1990): 223–347, which contains a lengthy bibliography. Good short accounts of Taoism can be found in Farzeen Baldrain's overview article and John Lagerwey's "The Taoist Religious Community," in *The Encyclopedia of Religion* (New York: Macmillan, 1987), 14.288–317. We would like to thank Stephen Bokenkamp for his helpful comments on this section on Taoism.

53. Strickmann has argued this point on numerous occasions; see, for example, his "On the Alchemy of T'ao Hung-ching," in Holmes Welch and Anna Seidel, eds., *Facets of Taoism: Essays in Chinese Religion* (New Haven: Yale University Press, 1979), pp. 165–166; and his review article "History, Anthropology, and Chinese Religion," *HJAS* 40.1 (1980): 207–211.

54. These themes are developed most fully in Seidel, *Taoismus: Die inoffizielle Hochreligion Chinas* (Tokyo: Deutsche Gesellschaft für die Natur- und Völkerkunde Ostasiens, 1990).

55. See her "Imperial Treasures and Taoist Sacraments."

56. See also Max Kaltenmark, "Ling-pao: note sur un terme du taoïsme religieux," *Annuaire du Collège de France* 67 (1968): 411–415.

57. See Seidel, "Imperial Treasures and Taoist Sacraments"; and Stein, "Les mouvements du taoïsme politico-religieux."

58. R. A. Stein, "Religious Taoism and Popular Religion from the Second to Seventh Centuries," in Welch and Seidel, eds., *Facets of Taoism*, pp. 53–81.

59. See Kristofer M. Schipper, "The Written Memorial in Taoist Ceremonies," in Wolf, ed., *Religion and Ritual in Chinese Society*, pp. 310–324; see also his "Vernacular and Classical Ritual in Taoism," *JAS* 45.1 (1985): 21–58.

60. See Michel Strickmann, "The Mao Shan Revelations: Taoism and the Aristocracy," *T'oung Pao* 63 (1977): 1–64; idem, *Le taoïsme du Mao Chan: chronique d'une révélation,* Mémoires de l'Institut des hautes études chinoises 17 (Paris: Presses universitaires de France, 1981); idem, "On the Alchemy of T'ao Hung-ching," in Welch and Seidel, eds., *Facets of Taoism*, pp. 123–192; and Isabelle Robinet, *La révélation du Shangqing dans l'histoire du taoïsme* (Paris: Publications de l'École française d'Extrême-Orient, 1984), vols. 1 and 2.

61. See Stephen R. Bokenkamp, "Sources of the Ling-pao Scriptures," in Strickmann, ed., *Tantric and Taoist Studies* 2.434–486; see also Catherine Bell, "Ritualization of Texts and Textualization of Ritual in the Codification of Taoist Liturgy," *History of Religions* 27.4 (1988): 365–392. For a study of Taoist ritual,

see John Lagerwey, *Taoist Ritual in Chinese Society and History* (New York: Macmillan, 1987).

62. See Judith Magee Boltz's article "Taoist Literature," in *The Encyclopedia of Religion* 14.317–329; the articles on Taoist Literature by Stephen Bokenkamp and Judith Magee Boltz in William H. Nienhauser, Jr., ed., *The Indiana Companion to Traditional Chinese Literature* (Bloomington: Indiana University Press, 1986), pp. 138–174; as well as Judith M. Boltz's *A Survey of Taoist Literature: Tenth to Seventeenth Centuries* (Berkeley: Institute for East Asian Studies, 1987). See also Ninji Ōfuchi, "The Formation of the Taoist Canon," in Welch and Seidel, eds., *Facets of Taoism,* pp. 253–267.

63. The most thorough account of Taoism in the T'ang is Timothy Barrett's "Taoism under the T'ang," in Denis Twitchett, ed., *The Cambridge History of China,* vol. 4: *Sui and T'ang China,* part 2 (Cambridge: Cambridge University Press, forthcoming); see also Franciscus Verellen, *Du Guangting (850–933), Taoïste de cour à la fin de la Chine médiéval* (Paris: Collège de France, 1989).

64. For an account of the ordination of the Chin-hsien and Yü-chen princesses in 711, see Charles D. Benn, *The Cavern-Mystery Transmission: A Taoist Ordination Rite of A.D. 711* (Honolulu: University of Hawaii Press, 1991).

65. See Charles Benn, "Religious Aspects of Emperor Hsüan-tsung's Taoist Ideology," in David W. Chappell, ed., *Buddhist and Taoist Practice in Medieval Chinese Society,* Buddhist and Taoist Studies 2 (Honolulu: University of Hawaii Press, 1987), pp. 127–145.

66. See Michel Strickmann, "The Longest Taoist Scripture," *History of Religions* 17.3–4 (1978): 331–351; see also Boltz, *Survey,* pp. 26–30.

67. See K. M. Schipper, "Taoist Ritual and Local Cults of the T'ang Dynasty," in Michel Strickmann, ed., *Tantric and Taoist Studies in Honour of R. A. Stein,* vol. 3: *Mélanges chinois et bouddhiques* 22 (1985): 812–834; and Boltz, *Survey,* pp. 70–78.

68. See Boltz, *Survey,* pp. 33–38.

69. Ibid., pp. 38–41.

70. See Catherine Bell, "Religion and Chinese Culture: Toward an Assessment of 'Popular Religion,' " *History of Religions* 29.1 (1989): 35–57.

71. Chang Shang-ying (1043–1122) provides an excellent example of this point. Even though he belonged to the higher echelons of the social and political elite and was thoroughly versed in the literate traditions of Confucianism, Buddhism, and Taoism, he wrote a brief work describing his pilgrimage to Mount Wu-t'ai that brims with the kind of miraculous events that are the very stuff of popular piety; see Gimello, "Chang Shang-ying on Wu-t'ai Shan." See Valerie Hansen's useful discussion of the differences between "popular religion" and "textual religions" in her *Changing Gods in Medieval China, 1127–1276* (Princeton: Princeton University Press, 1990), p. 13. In his overview of "Chinese Religion" in *The Encyclopedia of Religion,* Daniel Overmyer has defined popular religion as "the religion of the whole population except those who specifically opted out of it, such as orthodox Taoist priests, Buddhist monks, Confucian scholars, and state officials in their public roles" (3.281).

72. Hansen, *Changing Gods,* p. 80.

73. See his classic article "The City-God Cults of T'ang and Sung China," *HJAS* 45.2 (1985): 363–457.

74. An example of an influential work that stresses Buddhism's role as stim-

ulus is Fung Yu-lan, *A History of Chinese Philosophy,* vol. 2, trans. Derk Bodde (Princeton: Princeton University Press, 1953), esp. pp. 407–424.

75. See Howard J. Wechsler, *Offerings of Jade and Silk: Ritual and Symbol in the Legitimation of the T'ang Dynasty* (New Haven: Yale University Press, 1985).

76. See David McMullen, *State and Scholars in T'ang China* (Cambridge: Cambridge University Press, 1988).

77. Ibid., p. 259.

78. Peter K. Bol, *"This Culture of Ours": Intellectual Transitions in T'ang and Sung China* (Stanford: Stanford University Press, 1992).

79. Charles Hartman, *Han Yü and the T'ang Search for Unity* (Princeton: Princeton University Press, 1986). For other important thinkers of this period, see Timothy H. Barrett, *Li Ao: Buddhist, Taoist, or Neo-Confucian?* (Oxford: Oxford University Press, 1992); and Jo-shui Chen, *Liu Tsung-yüan and Intellectual Change in T'ang China, 773–819* (Cambridge: Cambridge University Press, 1993).

80. See especially the following by James T. C. Liu; "An Early Sung Reformer: Fan Chung-yen," in John K. Fairbank, ed., *Chinese Thought and Institutions* (Chicago: University of Chicago Press, 1957), pp. 105–131; *Reform in Sung China: Wang An-shih (1021–1086) and His New Policies* (Cambridge: Harvard University Press, 1959); and *Ou-yang Hsiu: An Eleventh-Century Neo-Confucianist* (Stanford: Stanford University Press, 1967).

81. See Bol, *"This Culture of Ours."*

82. An international conference on Chu Hsi held in 1982 has led to a volume drawing together some thirty studies ranging widely over specific ideas in Chu Hsi's oeuvre and his place in Chinese philosophy; see Wing-tsit Chan, ed., *Chu Hsi and Neo-Confucianism* (Honolulu: University of Hawaii Press, 1986). See also Daniel K. Gardner, *Chu Hsi and the Ta-hsüeh* (Cambridge: Harvard University Press, 1986); and idem, *Learning to Be a Sage: Selections from the Conversations of Master Chu, Arranged Topically* (Berkeley: University of California Press, 1990). Donald Munro has creatively analyzed Chu's conceptual categories through a study of his imagery; Munro's method brings to the fore key tensions in Chu's thinking, such as the tension between the need for self-discovery of moral truths and the need for obedience to established, external rules of conduct; see Munro, *Images of Human Nature: A Sung Portrait* (Princeton: Princeton University Press, 1988). Chu's roles as an educator and as an intellectual leader of the educated class have been explored in various chapters in Wm. Theodore de Bary and John W. Chaffee, eds., *Neo-Confucian Education: The Formative Stage* (Berkeley: University of California Press, 1989), especially the chapters by de Bary, Bol, Kellerher, and Chu.

83. See Bol, *"This Culture of Ours."*

84. See Ira E. Kasoff, *The Thought of Chang Tsai (1020–1077)* (Cambridge: Cambridge University Press, 1984).

85. See his *Utilitarian Confucianism: Ch'en Liang's Challenge to Chu Hsi* (Cambridge: Harvard University Press, 1982), and his more recent *Confucian Discourse and Chu Hsi's Ascendancy* (Honolulu: University of Hawaii Press, 1992). See also Winston Wan Lo, *The Life and Thought of Yeh Shih* (Hong Kong: Chinese University of Hong Kong Press, 1974).

86. In his *Tsung-mi and the Sinification of Buddhism*. See also Yü Ying-shih, "Intellectual Breakthroughs in the T'ang-Sung Transition" (paper presented at the panel on "Trends and Turning Points in Chinese History," Association of Asian Studies Annual Meeting, 1986); and Robert M. Gimello, "Prolegomenon to a Study of Wen-tzu Ch'an: Learning, Letters, and Liberation in Northern Sung China" (paper presented at the conference on "Religion and Society in China, 750–1300," held at Hsi Lai Temple, Hacienda Heights, 1989). Gimello documents the social intercourse between Ch'an monks and literati in the Sung and also discusses parallels between major cleavages in each tradition over attitudes toward the accumulated written tradition.

87. See Hansen, *Changing Gods in Medieval China*.

88. See Patricia Buckley Ebrey, *Confucianism and Family Rituals in Imperial China: A Social History of Writing about Rites* (Princeton: Princeton University Press, 1991).

89. See the various chapters in Chan, ed., *Chu Hsi and Neo-Confucianism,* and also Tu Wei-ming, *Confucian Thought: Selfhood as Creative Transformation* (Albany: SUNY Press, 1985).

GLOSSARY

Akitsuki Kan'ei　秋月觀暎
An Lu-shan　安祿山
Ch'an　禪
ch'an-wei　讖緯
Chang Tao-ling　張道陵
Chang Tsai　張載
Ch'ang-pu-ch'ing　常不輕
Cheng-i　正一
ch'eng-huang shen　城隍神
Ch'eng I　程頤
chen-jen　真人
ch'i　氣
chiao　醮
chieh　戒
chin-shih　進士
Ching-ming chung-hsiao tao　淨明　忠孝道
Ch'ing-wei　清微
Chu Hsi　朱熹
ch'u-chen chieh　初真戒
ch'u-chia　出家
Ch'üan-chen　全真
Chuang Tzu　莊子
Fan Chung-yen　范仲淹
fang-shih　方士
feng　封

Han Ch'i　韓琦
hang-che　行者
hsien　仙
Hsü Sun　許遜
Hsüan-tsung　玄宗
Hua-yen　華嚴
Hui-tsung　徽宗
i　義
Kao-tsung　高宗
Ko Ch'ao-fu　葛巢甫
Ko Hung　葛洪
Kuan-yin　觀音
Lao Tzu　老子
Li Ao　李翱
Li Kou　李覯
Li Lin-fu　李林甫
Li Po　李白
Lin Ling-su　林靈素
ling　靈
Ling-pao　靈寶
Liu Tsung-yüan　柳宗元
lu　籙
Lu Hsiu-ching　陵修靜
Mao Shan　茅山
mo-fa　末法
Mount Wu-t'ai　五台山

Mu-lien　目蓮
Naitō Konan　內藤湖南
Ou-yang Hsiu　歐陽修
Pai Yü-ch'an　白玉蟾
pao　寶
Pao-p'u tzu　抱朴子
pien-wen　變文
Po Chü-i　白居易
San-chieh chiao　三階教
San-huang ching　三皇經
shan　禪
Shang-ch'ing　上清
Shang-ti　上帝
Shen-hsiao　神霄
shih-ta-fu　士大夫
Ssu-ma Kuang　司馬光
Su Shih　蘇軾
Sun Fu　孫復
T'ai-p'ing ching　太平經
T'ai Shan　泰山
T'ai-shang Lao-chün　太上老君
Tao te ching　道德經
T'ao Hung-ching　陶弘景

te　德
T'ien-hsin　天心
t'ien-ming　天命
T'ien-shih tao　天師道
T'ien-t'ai　天台
Ts'ai Ching　蔡京
Ts'ao Ts'ao　曹操
tsung　宗
Tsung-mi　宗密
Tu Fu　杜甫
Tu-jen ching　度人經
tung　洞
Wang An-shih　王安石
Wang Che　王嚞
Wang Mang　王莽
Wang Wei　王維
Wen-ch'ang　文昌
Yabuki Keiki　矢吹慶輝
Yang Hsi　楊羲
Yang Kuei-fei　楊貴妃
yin　蔭
yin-ssu　淫祠
Yü-lan-p'en　盂蘭盆

CHAPTER 2

THE EXPANSION OF THE WEN-CH'ANG

CULT

Terry F. Kleeman

The religious world of late imperial China was dominated by several national deity cults. Although various claims were made upon these deities by representatives of the state cult and China's two institutionalized religions, Taoism and Buddhism, they were de facto autonomous gods, worshiped by laypersons or local religious professionals hired by the laity in temples owned and operated by a community. The reasons for the rise and spread of these cults remains one of the most important and least studied topics in Chinese religious history. One of these cults was that to Wen-ch'ang, the "God of Literature." The Sung dynasty was the crucial point in the cult's history when the cult was redefined and first broke out of its regional boundaries to become a nationwide phenomenon. By Ming and Ch'ing times Wen-ch'ang was well established as patron deity of the civil service examinations as well as a divine judge who promulgated voluminous morality tracts *(shan-shu)* detailing proper and improper conduct. But an alternate name for the god, the Divine Lord of Tzu-t'ung (Tzu-t'ung ti-chün), points to his origin as a local nature deity of a small town in northern Szechwan.

We are fortunate that sources permit us to trace the cult of Tzu-t'ung from a very early stage in its development down into the present. The earliest reference to the cult, in a fourth-century local history of the Szechwan area, is followed by a legend of uncertain date (probably late Six Dynasties or early T'ang) associating him with a late fourth-century chieftain, and then by references to the same legend by several T'ang literati. Imperial patronage of the cult began during the T'ang. Five Dynasties sources preserve two legends about the god, one contemporary, the other assimilating an ancient tale from another part of Szechwan into the cult. In the Sung there is suddenly a plethora of information, including records of imperial enfeoffments, tales of the god's efficacy in predicting examination results, inscriptions commemorating sites sacred to the god or dedicating temples to him, and elegies from passing poets. The most valuable source is a group of scriptures revealed during the latter half of the twelfth century and attributed to the deity himself.

These scriptures were revealed to a spirit-writing medium named Liu An-sheng in a temple near Ch'eng-tu beginning in 1168. They include a new recension of the *Scripture of the Great Grotto (Ta-tung hsien-ching),*[1] the central scripture of the fourth-century Mao Shan revelations; a *Precious Register (Kao-shang ta-tung Wen-ch'ang ssu-lu tzu-yang pao-lu),*[2] containing the esoteric names and images of deities necessary to activate the *Scripture;* a short account of the god's origin and apotheosis called the *Secret Biography of Ch'ing-ho (Ch'ing-ho nei-chuan),*[3] and a divine title *(hao)* of the god.[4] The masterwork of this revelation was a lengthy prosimetric autohagiography of the god called the *Book of Transformations (Hua-shu).*[5] This work wove strands of disparate legends and traditions that had come to be associated with the cult together with original material to form a continuous narrative that traces the god from his primordial origins through a series of human incarnations and divine careers, culminating in his ascension to heaven on a white donkey and his assumption of celestial office as administrator of the Ministry of Emoluments and keeper of the Cinnamon Record.

In tracing the history of Chinese deity cults, previous studies have largely focused on two types of sources: inscriptions commemorating the erection or renovation of a temple and government documents, especially those recording the conferral of an official title.[6] These are, to be sure, invaluable sources, and it is on the basis of such sources that most of the history of the cult to Wen-ch'ang must be written. But such sources have definite limitations. They are written by literati—most often officials, former officials, or members of their social milieu. More significant, they were written in an official or quasi-official capacity, and expressions of religious sentiment or sensational accounts of supernatural occurrences were frowned upon. Because both types of documents have as their intended audience this same scholar-official elite, and ultimately some abstraction like "posterity," they are primarily concerned with demonstrating that the deity in question is a proper god, worthy of worship by classical standards of orthodoxy. It is inevitable in such documents that certain aspects of a given cult be emphasized and others excluded. Further, the records themselves are incomplete. Local gazetteers from the Sung and Yüan survive only from the southeast, and the gazetteers themselves are not comprehensive in listing cults of a region at the time of composition. Records of governmental enfeoffments are similarly fragmentary.[7] Both types of sources provide only a partial and biased view of the cult.

The *Book of Transformations* and other documents from the twelfth-century revelations are less limited. The "author" was literate and, judging from the quality of the composition and references to ritual procedures, well versed in classical learning, most likely an aspiring or failed examination candidate.[8] But he was also steeped in Taoist lore. He may have been an ordained priest, since he was familiar with a major scripture like the *Scripture of the Great Grotto* and refers to himself as an "Attending Transcendent of the Phoenix Bureau" (the phoenix being the bird that transmits messages from the heavens). Moreover, as a spirit medium, he must have come into contact with a wide range of cult adherents and was no doubt familiar with the entire gamut of supernatural powers with which the god was credited. His familiarity with a variety of cult activity is evident in the *Book of Transformations*.

The *Book of Transformations* conveys its didactic messages in two ways: through the example of the god's conduct during human incarnations and through the rewards and punishments he deals out as a god. His avatars personify the scholar-official ideal and include several lifetimes of devoted and principled service to the state. Other virtues manifested in these lifetimes include filial piety, charity toward one's fellow clan members and friends, concern for widows and orphans, military defense of the state, the promotion of Han Chinese culture, and caring for the sick. It is this exemplary aspect of the work that most clearly reveals its elite origins.

The actions of Wen-ch'ang as a god in the *Book of Transformations* reveal the powers claimed for him and the specializations for which adherents sought him out.[9] Most basic of these was his power over the elements, and he is shown controlling rain, wind, fire, and flood; lightning/thunder is his special attribute, and he casts "thunder shuttles" down from on high to destroy evildoers. These natural powers and his authority to summon "divine troops" *(shen-ping)* are invoked for the protection of China and the Szechwan region in particular. In addition, he can fly, manifest himself at any time or place in any form he chooses, and summon forth and question both the living (during sleep) and the dead. Most important, he sits at the apex of the divine intelligence service, receiving reports from every tutelary deity and city or mountain god. A good example of his functions on the local level is found in the sixtieth chapter of the *Book of Transformations*. A devout family of believers in the city of Ch'eng-tu is set upon by bandits and a particularly pious young daughter is about to be raped when she calls on the god:

"You hungry villains invade our home. The Divine Lord Chang does not know about you yet!" When she had finished speaking, the Director of Fates of her house, Ts'ui Hsüan, and the ancestral spirits of the Chih family reported the emergency to me. I then sent a deputy, Fu Hsing, at the head of a hundred supernatural troops to subdue them. All of the bound people, from Ch'üan-li on down, were released, and all of the villains were captured. The next day these events were reported to the village headman, who memorialized them to the commandery. All were executed.[10]

The god's employment of these powers reveals the type of events his adherents expected him to control. He had a commitment to justice, demonstrated in his punishment of wicked officials—both temporal and divine—in his intervention in wrongly adjudicated criminal cases, and in his enforcement of accurate weights and measures. His curative function, especially with regard to demonically inspired illness, is evident in his subjugation of the plague demons.[11] He is also a provider of progeny, both instructing mortals on the type of conduct that entitles them to offspring and incarnating himself as the son of particularly worthy individuals. Finally, his supervision of the examinations is stated explicitly in the apotheosis at the end of the work: "Because of my unstinting devotion to the classics through many incarnations as a scholar, the Thearch commanded me to take charge of the Cinnamon Record in the Heavenly Bureau. All local and national examinations, rankings, colors of clothing, salaries, and enfeoffments were memorialized to me, and even promotions and demotions within the civil and military bureaucracies were under my supervision."[12] Already in the twelfth century Wen-ch'ang had become a complex figure appealing to multiple constituencies.

THE DEVELOPMENT OF THE CULT WITHIN SZECHWAN

The earliest records of the god and his cult derive from the fourth-century *Hua-yang-kuo chih*.[13] At that time the god was a fearsome serpent called simply "The Viper" (E-tzu), who struck down his foes with awful bolts of lightning. He was worshiped with annual offerings of "thunder shuttles," wondrous slivers of celestial stone that the god would cast to earth to cause lightning.[14] The people would gather these slivers at sites where lightning had struck, but they were careful to supply the Viper with only ten each year, lest the destruction he wreak through them be too great.

Already in the fourth century one corpus of legend, that of the Five Stalwarts, had become associated with this serpent deity.[15] The Five Stalwarts (Wu-ting) were five mighty siblings who are said to have performed wondrous feats of strength in the service of King K'ai-ming of Shu (fourth century B.C.). King K'ai-ming lost the state of Shu to Ch'in, and history consequently portrays him as somewhat dissolute. It is said that the King of Ch'in tried to subvert Shu through a gift of five beauties and that K'ai-ming dispatched the Five Stalwarts to welcome the *femmes fatales* at the border. At this point the Viper appeared, and the Stalwarts gave chase. When the gigantic serpent slithered into a mountain cave, the five strongmen seized his tail and, heaving upon it, brought down the entire mountain on both themselves and the maidens.

The god portrayed by Ch'ang Ch'ü, author of the *Hua-yang-kuo chih,* is typical of the object of worship of a local nature cult. This zoomorphic deity controls the primordial forces of nature and is worshiped at a sacred spot, in this case a cave high atop Sevenfold Mountain (Ch'i-ch'ü shan, just north of Tzu-t'ung). Such primeval figures were often recast as more acceptable deities in conventional sources, but there is as yet no evidence of conscious manipulation of the god's image in order to make it conform to the norms of Confucian society, no attempt to anthropomorphize or impute a sense of morality.

This primitive simplicity was not destined to survive long. A legend arose about an encounter between an anthropomorphized Chang E-tzu and the fourth-century Ch'iang chieftain Yao Ch'ang. The main outlines of this story as recorded in a tenth-century geographical work are as follows: Chang E-tzu encounters Yao Ch'ang in Ch'ang-an. Chang invites Yao to visit him should Yao ever make it to northern Szechwan. Years later, while in Szechwan, Yao receives a supernatural summons to Chang's abode, which turns out to be a temple.[16] Li Shang-yin (813?–858), in referring to this legend a century earlier, had mentioned a magical scepter, giving control over the divine legions, that Chang bestowed upon Yao.[17]

Although the first reliable references to the legend date from the mid-T'ang, it seems likely that it took form during Yao's lifetime or not long after Yao's death in 393.[18] This appearance of a god in human form is perhaps not as sudden a development as it seems. It may be that there were those espousing a human identity for the god when Ch'ang Ch'ü was writing some decades before but that this view was not yet dominant or that Ch'ang was relying on dated reports.

In any case, Chang E-tzu is quite different from the Viper. The Viper represented the crude, primordial power of nature, and he exercised this power directly and willfully. He could be propitiated directly by anyone through material offerings. Chang E-tzu is a much more complex figure. He commands the supernatural forces of Heaven. His actions are directed by a prescient knowledge of men and their fate, a knowledge that permits the god to choose Yao Ch'ang as the recipient of his bounty without any entreaty or offering on Yao's part. Nor is any claim ever made in any version of the legend concerning Yao's virtuous conduct or his support of legitimate Chin rule. Chang E-tzu is drawn to Yao, it would seem, by a personal affinity rather than by moral or political considerations.

The next image of Chang E-tzu comes from some four centuries later. Chang E-tzu is said to have met and given succor to the refugee Li

Lung-chi, the famous emperor Hsüan-tsung of the T'ang (r. 712–756). No contemporary accounts of this encounter survive. A century later Emperor Hsi-tsung (r. 874–888), also fleeing from the capital and perhaps influenced by the tale of Hsüan-tsung's meeting, visited the god's temple and requested aid. Hsi-tsung offered up his own sword to the god, hoping to receive the power over the legions of the netherworld that had once been bestowed upon Yao Ch'ang, and was promised aid.[19]

The god in these T'ang tales possesses the same powers and attributes as in the Yao Ch'ang story. But the tales show the beginnings of a transformation from willful independence to principled cooperation with the directing powers of the universe. Rather than supporting a local, non-Chinese warrior because of a personal affinity, the god now supports the legitimate ruler of China against rebels, although he must still be entreated to action. Thus national concerns begin to take precedence over local ones, the public weal over personal favoritism.[20] Eventually the identity of Chang E-tzu became too confining for this deity, and he came to be referred to by a more general term, but two tales of Chang E-tzu from the tenth century reveal the survival of an earlier phase of the cult's development.

The first is a tale of considerable antiquity, first recorded in the *Hou Han shu*.[21] It tells of a tiny magical snake found by an old woman of Lin-ch'iung (western Szechwan) and raised in her home. When the predations of the grown snake on local livestock become too great, the county magistrate directs the woman to surrender the creature. She fails to do so, the magistrate orders her death, and the snake, transformed into a dragon, inundates the entire town in revenge, creating Lake Ch'iung. The tenth-century version of this tale differs only slightly from the original (the old woman has become an old couple), except in identifying the snake as Chang E-tzu.[22]

The second tale is contemporary with the tenth-century one. It identifies Yüan-ying, son and designated successor to Wang Chien, king of Former Shu (847–918), as a were-snake, possessed of numerous serpentine traits such as black, snakelike eyes, exposed teeth, nocturnalism, and a "vicious, evil, vile, and lewd" character.[23] At the end of this account readers are informed that Yüan-ying was the sprite *(ching)* of Chang E-tzu, referred to as "the snake in the temple."

Both these tales are remarkable in that they testify to the survival into the tenth century of the snake cult in Tzu-t'ung. Although the last written reference to the snake had been some six centuries earlier, the cult had apparently survived among the populace, though perhaps only at the level of oral transmission. It was, moreover, dynamically alive, actively incorporating serpent cults from other parts of Szechwan. The Yüan-ying tale is perhaps not from the hand of an adherent of the cult, but it testifies to the identification of the cult in the popular imagination with a serpent deity.[24] Both legends depict a god who is amoral and motivated solely by personal ties. The Yüan-ying story, perhaps reflecting its noncultic origins, soon was forgotten, but the tale of the Ch'iung Lake dragon became a central element of cult lore and two centuries later was incorporated into the *Book of Transformations,* albeit in a sanitized and moralized version.[25]

The first accounts of the god from the Sung reveal a further development beyond the image of the mature Chang E-tzu of the late T'ang. In the year 1000 the god intervenes in a local rebellion in Ch'eng-tu and is rewarded with an official title at the rank of "king."[26] The god now acts spontaneously on behalf of public order and legitimate rule. He no longer need be supplicated with offerings in order to respond to threats to the public interest. Interestingly, nowhere in accounts of the rebellion or the god's subsequent canonization is the god referred to as Chang E-tzu; rather, he is consistently called simply "the god of Tzu-t'ung."

The god did not attract national attention again until the twelfth century. A series of titles and epithets were bestowed upon him and his divine family from 1105 through 1172.[27] In 1154 the god's title was fixed as the Loyally Aiding and Broadly Rescuing King of Manifest Heroism and Ardent Martial Valor (Ying-hsien wu-lieh chung-yu kuang-chi wang). The title reflects a deity conceived of solely as a martial spirit.

PERSONAE AND ROLES OF THE GOD

The taxonomy of personae and roles presented below is based on both historical sources and revealed scriptures. The revelations mark the full maturity of the god's complex identity, and no significant additional personae or roles have been credited to the god in the subsequent six centuries.

THE VIPER. The Viper was the primordial zoomorphic nature deity par excellence. As argued above, the cult to the Viper was still alive in the tenth century, though perhaps primarily among people whose religious views were seldom reflected in formal historical, geographic, or philosophical sources. At the time of the composition of the *Book of Transformations,* this persona was incorporated into the more complex deity of that time: the encounter with the Five Stalwarts is treated as an example of the god's concern for the protection of Szechwan; the inundation of the town of Ch'iung-tu is portrayed as an overzealous and misguided attempt to claim vengeance for the old woman, who as the mother of the god in a previous life had suffered horribly and died at the hands of the family of Empress Dowager Lü, the Lüs now having been reborn as inhabitants of the town.[28] That these tales were sanitized rather than excluded from cult documents testifies to the appeal of these accounts of the god's power.

CHANG E-TZU. Chang E-tzu was the mysterious wonder-worker created when the Viper was anthropomorphized. He is a romantic figure, and poets sang of his encounter with Yao Ch'ang as late as the eleventh century.[29] The most human of the god's personae, the Chang E-tzu persona was also the most popular with later rationalizing critics, who sought the origin of every local deity cult in homage to some real-life hero. Even today most accounts of the cult or the temple complex in Tzu-t'ung trace the cult back to this phantom, often identifying him with a Chang Yü who fought a battle in northern Szechwan during the fourth century.[30]

THE GOD OF TZU-T'UNG. During the Sung the term commonly applied to the god was simply the "god of Tzu-t'ung." In most accounts this god has one of two functions: he is a martial protector of the populace and the legitimate ruling dynasty against social disorder and foreign invasion, and he is an oracle responding to inquiries concerning the examinations. It is as protector of the Szechwan region that the god of Tzu-t'ung became the patron deity of that region.

TRANSCENDENT CHANG. A local god of Ch'eng-tu also called Chang Chung(-tzu), Transcendent Chang is the patron of childbirth. The legendary material surrounding Chang Chung and his opposition to the Five Stalwarts was incorporated into the *Book of Transformations,* and the god of the *Book of Transformations* clearly functions at times as a fertility god, but no mention is made in that work of Transcendent Chang per se. I have, in fact, found no explicit identification of Transcendent Chang with the god of Tzu-t'ung before the Ch'ing dynasty. Moreover, Transcendent Chang has his own distinct iconography, and most sources treat him as an independent deity. This overlap of the two identities points to a partially assimilated cult. It would seem that the early lore of Transcendent Chang was stripped from his cult and appropriated by the Tzu-t'ung cult. It is possible, however, that the Chang Chung material was originally independent and that it was the Transcendent Chang cult that unsuccessfully tried to assimilate this body of lore to itself before a stronger claim was made by the Tzu-t'ung cult.

THE DIVINE LORD OF TZU-T'UNG. The Divine Lord of Tzu-t'ung was the apotheosized Taoist deity created by the revelations of the later twelfth century. The god provides a model, through the course of his own incarnations and divine postings as recorded in the *Book of Transformations,* for proper service to the state, effective means of self-cultivation, and appropriate conduct as a local, terrestrial deity. The Divine Lord of Tzu-t'ung is eventually rewarded for his millennia of virtuous conduct and diligent devotion to his duties by his appointment to head the Wen-ch'ang Palace, wherein the fate of officials and would-be officials is decided. The Divine Lord was also credited with powers of healing and exorcism. The oracular function of the god of Tzu-t'ung has been expanded; the Divine Lord reveals himself through the planchette and in dreams in order to convert all of humanity and save them from the disasters of the impending kalpa.

WEN-CH'ANG. The ancient astral deity Wen-ch'ang first appears in the *Elegies of Ch'u* and had a secure place within the official state calendar of sacrifices since the Han.[31] Actually a constellation rather than a star, it also named a group of deities, subsuming within itself such important stellar luminaries as the Director of Fates (Ssu-ming) and the Director of Emoluments (Ssu-lu). When the Divine Lord of Tzu-t'ung came to be credited with many of the responsibilities and powers of the Director of Emoluments, it became feasible to claim for the god the position of head of the Wen-ch'ang palace, this being the six stars of the constellation conceived of as the seat of administration of a single, appointed divine bureaucrat. His earthly temples came to be called Wen-ch'ang Palaces as well, and soon the god was known simply as Wen-ch'ang.[32] The identification of the god with this asterism was of immense importance in gaining the support of orthodox "Confucian" scholars.[33] The classical antecedents and the place of the star within the early canon of sacrifices sanctioned the worship of this stellar deity throughout the empire, whereas strictly speaking a local hero like the god of Tzu-t'ung should receive cult offerings only in his native place. The actual functions of the deity do not differ significantly from those of the Divine Lord of Tzu-t'ung, except in that it was under the name of Wen-ch'ang that the god became best known as a judge of popular morality.

To the above names by which the god was known and addressed might be added the enfeoffment titles bestowed by the government beginning in the T'ang, but these titles are really ranks, locating the god within the hierarchy of the imperial canon of sacrifices, and such titles are regularly glossed with one of the names listed above. There was a complex interplay between these personae and the roles or functions the god was thought to perform. Below I delineate seven roles that the god has been known to fulfill:

NATURE DEITY. The primitive, amoral deity known as the Viper had a special relationship with the town of Tzu-t'ung founded upon a long-standing relationship of mutual benefit. The locals regularly supplied the god with offerings and he, in return, protected them and looked after their interests. There is little place in such a cult for abstract categories of right and wrong. The bonds established were extremely enduring, and it is likely that long after the cult to the god of Tzu-t'ung had grown beyond its local associations, some segment of the local populace in Tzu-t'ung continued to worship the god as a nature deity.

朱衣

魁星

文昌

Figure 2.1. Ch'ing dynasty painting of Wen-ch'ang with Chu-i and K'uei-hsing.
(From Henry Doré, *Researches into Chinese Superstitions*, part 2, vol. 6, fig. 8)

WONDER-WORKER. The wonder-worker is Chang E-tzu, prescient possessor of the magic scepter giving control over the legions of the other world. Both sagacious and mystifying, he is typical of the shaman-recluse found in so many stories of transcendents. This role would seem to be largely a literati construct with little cultic reality. Cult lore from the tenth century continued to depict Chang E-tzu as a snake.

MARTIAL PROTECTOR. The role of martial protector is related to the wonder-worker Chang E-tzu's control over supernatural troops. It is also, I believe, a result of the location of the primary cult site, just before reaching the mountains that mark the border with Shensi on the road from Ch'eng-tu to Ch'ang-an. Being on the border of this region, the god must have been expected to play his part in repelling foreign invaders, and in the *Book of Transformations* he does, fending off or trying to fend off first Fu Chien, then the Khitans, and finally the Mongols. The god is also the protector of each believer's person. His legions of infernal troops protect the faithful, sleeping and waking, from demonic and necromantic attacks.

PATRON OF THE EXAMINATIONS. The role of patron of examinations was not unique to the god of Tzu-t'ung. In fact, it was fairly common for gods of the Sung to become involved in the examination business, trading predictions and promises of aid for support. The god of She-hung, who was worshiped in some of the same temples as the god of Tzu-t'ung, shared this specialty.[34] Still, this specialization seems to have held special importance for the Tzu-t'ung cult, and it is regularly pointed out as the distinguishing feature of the cult from the thirteenth century down to the present.[35]

JUDGE OF MORALITY. The role of judge of morality is to a degree inherent in that of patron of the examinations. Success on the exams and in one's subsequent career is determined by personal conduct, and the god who keeps a record of moral transgressions and good deeds might influence one's fate. He does this through his stewardship of the Cinnamon Record, the celestial register of merit and demerit, and his oversight of an otherwordly censorate that constantly observed and recorded the behavior of all individuals within China, regardless of age, sex, or status.

EVANGELIST. Perhaps the god's most startling role is that of evangelist. Not content merely to adjudicate from on high, even after his apotheosis the god continues to descend into this world to set an example of proper conduct and personally to lead the people to the right path.[36] He manifests in physical form and through dreams, but his favorite vehicle is the planchette. Through spirit writing he distributes ethical teaching, gives personal advice, and transmits talismans of power. It is in this role that the god promulgates the many morality books attributed to him.

PROVIDER OF PROGENY. The role of provider of progeny may have its roots in the serpent god, a symbol of fertility in many cultures. It is also firmly rooted in the god's role as an incarnating exemplar of proper conduct and as a cosmic judge. It is through moral excellence that one wins the right to progeny and specifically to the type of successful progeny who could pass the examinations and better the family's circumstances. In rare cases the god could be inspired personally to incarnate as the son of a particularly virtuous individual, thus assuring for the family an illustrious future.[37] We have noted above the complex relationship between the god in this role and Transcendent Chang.

Early accounts of Chinese religion characterized each deity using a persona or role like those delineated above, and in this regard they were no doubt influenced by native informants. Thus, de Groot, Doré, and Hodous all portray the god I discuss as the "God of Literature" as a patron of the scholar-official elite and of little concern to anyone outside this restricted group.[38] Several recent scholars have tried to show that there is a process of historical development within such characterizations. Harrell and Baity, on the basis of fieldwork on Taiwan, demonstrated how minor cults to the disturbed souls of those who had died a violent death could evolve into full-fledged deity cults.[39] Cohen pointed out that a similar process was discernible in the development of the cult to a historical figure such as Shih Hu (294–349).[40] More recently, James Watson has shown that individuals within a very limited geographic context can maintain "diametrically opposed representations" of the same god.[41] Assuming that Chinese deity cults spread because of government patronage and that pluralist interpretations of the god existed because of government tolerance, he argues that "the state imposed a structure but not the content . . . promoted symbols and not beliefs."[42] Prasenjit Duara has presented a somewhat more sophisticated interpretation, in which he discusses the "superscription" of new identities or functions onto existing gods by the state, using the Ch'ing promotion of the cult to Kuan-ti as his example.[43] He points out that it was precisely because of the various understandings of Kuan-ti among divergent social groups, which he characterizes as a "semantic chain," that the cult provided an effective tool with which the Ch'ing state promoted its legitimacy.[44]

The Tzu-t'ung cult confirms the existence of both historical development and synchronic diversity. In historical terms, there is a definite progression from nature deity to hero, and eventually to celestial arbiter. Other elements of the god's image, like his roles as provider of progeny and patron of the examinations, are less easily integrated into a neat developmental model. It is evident that one conceptualization of the god is not abandoned as the next is adopted. The sources do not show a definitive role for the state in defining the god's image. The T'ang canonizations of Chang E-tzu merely confirm an identity established in the Yao Ch'ang legend. The Sung enfeoffments as a protector have their roots in the miraculous aid offered by the god in suppressing a local rebellion. The Taoist identity of the god, including his sole authority for the supernatural supervision of the examinations, was first claimed for the god in the revelations to Liu An-sheng but was not recognized by the government until 1316. In each case, new developments in the god's image occurred spontaneously within the local cult and were only recognized by the government after the fact. Within the god's diverse following there were those whose image of the god accorded closely with that required by the interests of the state. It is for this reason that some developments in the god's image were confirmed by the state almost immediately, whereas others had to wait over a century. But in no case were innovations in the god's image initiated by the state.

EXPANSION OF THE CULT BEYOND SZECHWAN

The Tzu-t'ung cult expanded into southeast China from its original center in Szechwan. It seems to have done so in several stages. By the late twelfth century, belief in the god had spread throughout Szechwan and was particularly well established in the traditional capital of the region, Ch'eng-tu. When the revealed scriptures of Liu An-sheng appeared, they seem to have enjoyed immediate popularity, and they were soon transmitted to the national capital of Lin-an (modern Hangchow). By 1177 the *Secret Biography of Ch'ing-ho* was well enough known in the capital to be inscribed in stone by a man from Kuei-chi.[45] It is not certain that the god possessed at this time an independent temple in the capital, but there must have been at least a subsidiary shrine to him, probably within the Taoist abbey on Mount Wu, where his temple was eventually established.

The early transmission of the cult to the capital is best explained by recourse to Skinner's theory of regional cores.[46] A cult prominent in the Szechwanese regional center of Ch'eng-tu should, according to this model, spread most readily to other regional cores and especially to the national center.[47] In more concrete terms it is possible to imagine the cult at this point being spread by officials and merchants (whose sons may aspire to official posts) as well as itinerant religious professionals. The examination god of the Szechwan region must have been the object of worship of a considerable number of Szechwanese examination candidates who had been attending palace examinations at the capital since the beginning of the Southern Sung. By the end of the thirteenth century, there is explicit confirmation that the god was worshiped by aspirants to officialdom from all over the empire.[48] The *Secret Biography* portrays the god specifically as a representative of the officials, stating, "For seventy-three incarnations I have been a scholar-official *(shih-ta-fu),* and never have I mistreated the people or abused my clerks."[49] But, though we may theorize that the god's identity as patron of scholars was dominant at this point in Hangchow, his image was not one-dimensional. The *Secret Biography* tells of the apotheosis of a historical Chang Ya(-tzu), and the iconography of the stele reveals that the snake identity was not wholly absent.[50]

Although the cult was popular among a certain segment of the capital population by 1177, widespread acceptance seems to have required a longer time. The cult first spread gradually among the populace of southern Szechwan and from there moved down the Yangtze. A later chapter of the *Book of Transformations* (composed in 1194) refers to a flurry of cult activity in southern Szechwan during the 1190s.[51] This excitement, which was prompted by a series of planchette revelations and the distribution of magical talismans in the god's name, stretched along the Yangtze well into Hupei.[52] The god commented, "Now around Fu and K'uei (modern Fu-ling and Feng-chieh) my numinous responses shine forth brightly and my perfected, primordial power is thereby confirmed."[53]

Trade between Szechwan and the southeast had boomed since the fall of the Northern Sung, much of this trade transported by men of Szechwan. For this reason large numbers of Szechwanese had come to occupy the shores of the Yangtze River all along its course to the sea. Lu Yu (1125–1210) tells of whole villages in central Hupei occupied solely by natives of Szechwan and their local affines.[54] The cult must have spread very quickly among these émigré communities. In fact there is record of a temple established to the god in Ch'u-chou (modern Ch'u-hsien, Anhwei) in 1210, a good twenty-five years before the first clear record of independent temples in Nanking and Hangchow.[55]

What was the nature of the cult transmitted through southern Szechwan and down the Yangtze at this time? The revelations that gave impetus to cult expansion at the end of the twelfth and the beginning of the thirteenth centuries portrayed a complex deity of diverse specializations and interests. People turned to him in times of trouble for aid in dealing with human problems like personal security, infertility, ill health, demonic possession, legal entanglements, family separation, and so forth. It would seem that the examination god persona was not dominant at this time and place. Instead his abilities to cure illness and deliver blessings seem to have been most in demand.

Because of the dearth of Sung sources on Szechwan, the official attitude toward this phase of the cult and its sudden expansion can only be inferred. It may have existed in a sort of twilight of tolerance, eyed suspiciously by local magistrates who could not fault its pro-Sung, proauthority teachings but did not trust the meetings and the excitement. The cult shared with some of the groups responsible for disruptive religious uprisings during the Sung the practice of vegetarianism, and this teaching seems to have become more entrenched as time went on.[56] In any case, I have found no record of official patronage of the cult at this time, and most of the revelations we know of seem to have taken place in small towns where no officials were stationed.

Beginning with the first Mongol incursions into Szechwan in the 1230s, the southeast saw a new wave of interest in the god, stimulated by the immigration of large numbers of Szechwanese literati into the region. In 1235 and 1236 new temples were erected in Nanking and Hangchow, and in the ensuing decades more seemed to sprout up all over the southeast.[57]

The Taoist church played a special role in this expansion.[58] The identity claimed in the revelations of 1168 to 1181 was above all a Taoist identity, and cult practices seem to have centered on a Taoist scripture. The first recorded worship of the god outside Szechwan took place in the form of a Taoist offering *(chiao)*. When the wave of officially sponsored temple building in the southeast began in the 1230s, often the altar from a side hall in the local Taoist abbey was being moved into a new, independent building.[59] The temple in Ningpo was established by a Taoist priest, and the first temple in Hangchow was established within a Taoist abbey.[60]

I have presented what information can be assembled on the course of expansion of the cult and tried to give some idea of the diversity of the group worshiping the god. It remains to explain why this expansion occurred. Previous studies have largely confined themselves to how the cult to a given god is transferred from one place to another. The explanations have largely been of the kind given above: migrants, merchants, mendicant religious professionals, or government officials introduced the gods of their native regions to areas they traversed or in which they were stationed. Such studies telling how a god became known in a foreign region resemble closely studies of how technological advances were transmitted from culture to culture. The precise avenue of transmission in both cases is usually lost to history. Unlike technology, where direct material benefits result from adoption, the reasons for a given cult becoming established in a new region and attracting continuing support generation after generation are unclear.[61] Unless an expatriate community could support its own temples—and I have noted that by 1177 the cult to the god of Tzu-t'ung had already ceased to be a strictly Szechwanese and Szechwanese-expatriate phenomenon—some aspect of the cult must have caused local people to shift their support and limited resources from a local cult to that of the new arrival.

In the case of the cult to the god of Tzu-t'ung, I believe it was the power of ongoing revelation that drove the cult's expansion. This god had spoken as no other god before him, telling in the first person of his lives of hardship and denial, his failures and his achievements, but above all of the ultimate success of his personal program of self-cultivation and his apotheosis as one of the most exalted of the celestial divinities. He now continued to speak with evangelistic fervor, seeking to convert *(hua)* the masses through his own personal transformations *(hua)*. In an inscription of 1207 from Tzu-t'ung, he pledged to appear in every small town in Szechwan and told the faithful to await his next manifestation. More and more mediums found that he spoke to them as well. Spirit writing, which is too often thought of in the Sung as a sort of parlor game with some poor scullery maid sent into trance to summon up the literary greats of the past, became for the Tzu-t'ung cult an evangelical broadcasting network, through which a high god was able to communicate directly with his flock.[62] He did not merely answer their questions but preached to them the advantages of a virtuous life and wrote for them his potent personal talismans to heal their bodies and repel demonic or sepulchral assaults on their souls. Thus in his spirit writing as well the god fulfilled the varied roles of oracle, healer, protector, and evangelist.

The cult did not lose its diverse following as it gained acceptance among the literati. An inscription from the sixteenth century still testifies to the richness of the god's personae and the variety of his flock: "Nowadays there are three types of people who pray and sacrifice to Lord Wench'ang. There are those who worship him revering his martial exploits. . . . There are those who worship him because he has his hand wrapped about the handle of civil government *(wen-ping)*. . . . There are those who worship him because they say that the god aids the Southern Dipper in implanting new life *(chu-sheng)*."[63]

We are fortunate in the case of the cult to the god of Tzu-t'ung in that we have documents like the inscription quoted above and a source like the *Book of Transformations*. For all too many cults we have only official records, and we are in constant danger of mistaking the unmentioned for the nonexistent. One way we can try to make up for some of the gaps in our record is by being sensitive to the different specializations attributed to a given god and the names by which he is addressed. A single god can mean different things to people of different class, occupation, age, sex, and interests.

CONCLUSION

What broader generalizations can be made on the basis of the development of the cult to the god of Tzu-t'ung about the development of Chinese religion? It would seem, as is contended by several of the authors in this volume, that the Sung marked a watershed in Chinese religious history, a transition from the classical system of Han through T'ang to the world view that survives even today in Chinese communities around the world. Specifically, there emerged in the Sung national deity cults that quickly came to form the focus of religious devotion for the great majority of the Chinese people, both elite and commoner.

This transition was not simply the diffusion of local cults beyond the confines of their original community, though such diffusion did indeed occur. Cults that dominate an entire region had existed long before. The cult to the Eight Gods of the state of Ch'i recorded in the "Treatise on the Feng and Shan Sacrifices" of the *Shih chi,* with its focus on Ch'ih-yu, is an example of an archaic cult that extended over an area the size of a modern province. The Tzu-t'ung cult was from our earliest records linked through a corpus of myths to the regional center of Ch'eng-tu. The tenth century legends discussed above show the god manifesting both in Ch'eng-tu and in a city considerably to its west. The enfeoffment of 1001 was for services the god performed in Ch'eng-tu. We can assume that by the tenth century, if not earlier, the cult had penetrated through a large portion of northern Szechwan.

Nor was the change in the religious world simply the result of official recognition and sponsorship of local cults. There are records of official recognition of cults as early as the Six Dynasties, and many modern cults received their first honors during the T'ang. The first two titles of the god of Tzu-t'ung were awarded in the eighth and ninth centuries. It may well be that there was an increase in the number of titles awarded during the Sung, but the very partial nature of T'ang records of enfeoffments (neither of the titles awarded to the god of Tzu-t'ung are recorded in the *T'ang hui-yao*) makes it difficult to assess this change.

I would like to propose as a working hypothesis that at least some of the changes that occurred during the Sung can be understood as an increasing integration of and improved access to the Chinese sacred realm. I believe that these changes are evident in the relations between popular religion and both Buddhism and Taoism, but in the following discussion I will focus on the Taoist material, with which I am most familiar.

Integration of the Sacred Realm

The traditional religious world of the Han through T'ang dynasties had been bifurcated into two continuums. The first was a ritual continuum of sacrificial religion that encompassed both the state cult and the local nature and hero cults of what is commonly termed popular religion. The second was a realm of institutionalized religion that emerged in the second century and consisted of China's two "higher" religions, Taoism and Buddhism. The first continuum was defined by the practice of bloody sacrifice, and within the continuum questions of orthodoxy and heterodoxy centered on whether a given individual or community had the right to offer sacrifice to a certain deity. The institutionalized religions were defined in contrast to this first continuum by their rejection of bloody sacrifice.[64] In this realm debates on heterodoxy tended to focus on which of the two traditions was correct.

By Sung times the boundaries between these two continuums had begun to break down. Taoism had long rejected the traditional bureaucracy of otherworldly officials—consisting of gods of the dead, nature spirits, and local deities—in favor of the exalted, purified realms of the Perfected and a celestial bureaucracy culminating in the Three Pures. Now in the Sung the two bureaucracies were reinterpreted as being different levels of one continuous supernatural administration. It was considered proper that one would pass through a succession of terrestrial postings before attaining to the ranks of the Perfected. Thus before his final apotheosis and assumption of an astral office, the Divine Lord of Tzu-t'ung is assigned to a series of terrestrial offices in which he performs services for the mortals under his supervision and receives in recompense from them bloody sacrifice. His appointment to these offices as well as his final apotheosis are mandated by the Great Thearch of Jade Augustness (Yü-huang ta-ti), a reflex of the supreme Taoist deity, the Primordial Heavenly Worthy (Yüan-shih t'ien-tsun).[65]

In a parallel development, during the Sung Taoism claimed a role of caretaker in relation to the popular pantheon, a role it maintains to this day.[66] Shrines and altars to popular deities were often established in subsidiary positions within Taoist abbeys and temples. Scriptures devoted to the new class of national deities were included in the Taoist canon. Today in Taiwan Taoist priests officiate at traditional *chiao* festivals in honor of local deities *(wang-yeh),* many of whom were originally demons and were certainly not the recipients of Taoist worship.[67] I cannot be sure when such celebrations began, but I suspect that their roots are to be found in the Sung integration of the sacred realms of popular and institutionalized religion.

A full understanding of why this integration occurred must await further study, but some factors seem evident at this point. Residents of a certain community or region had a vested interest in promoting the fortunes of their guardian deity. Valerie Hansen has shown that one strategy they employed was to pursue official recognition.[68] Another was to seek a place for their god within the established pantheons of Taoism and Buddhism. Both courses of action increased the prestige of the deity and provided justification for worshiping the deity beyond the confines of the home community. The Tzu-t'ung cult was successful in both these pursuits. But the representatives of institutionalized religion must also have had something to gain from the recognition of local deities. Most likely they expected to gain donations from patrons of the cult, both at the time of the establishment of a shrine and on a continuing basis thereafter. Moreover, the introduction of the image of a god with a current reputation for efficacy *(ling)* could only enhance the prestige of their institution.

Improved Access to the Sacred Realm

I use the phrase "improved access to the sacred realm" to mean that men and women without the status of religious professionals came to have direct relationships with exalted levels of the sacred realm.[69] This theme is prominent in Judith Boltz's contribution to this volume, in which she demonstrates how local officials took spiritual affairs into their own hands, performing exorcisms and other rituals. Judith Berling points out that a prominent figure in Sung Taoism, Pai Yü-ch'an, had received no formal ordination. Stephen Teiser's chapter shows that the belief in the ten kings permitted laypersons to circumvent the traditional offerings to the sangha, securing the well-being of their ancestors through direct offerings to these ten monarchs of the netherworld. The same tendency is evident in the Tzu-t'ung cult. The *Precious Register* contains rituals that have as one of their primary goals success in the examinations and the attainment of government office. These rituals are designed to be performed not, as is common in Taoist ritual collections, by an ordained Taoist priest on behalf of the aspirant but by the aspirant himself.[70] The faithful also had direct communication with the Divine Lord of Tzu-t'ung through spirit writing, as discussed above. Another development was the revelation of a set of oracle slips *(ch'ien)*, through which anyone who visited a Tzu-t'ung temple could consult the god.[71] Many of these features are common to other national deity cults that arose at this time, the most prominent example being Kuan-ti, who also communicated through spirit writing and oracle slips.

I can propose only very general reasons for this increased access. The changes evident in Sung society, including increased interregional trade and travel, the monetization of the economy, increased immigration, urbanization, and the development of communications, all must have expanded the horizons of the individual and encouraged people to look beyond the confines of their traditional world, the village community. The extent to which the examination system resulted in true social mobility has been the subject of some debate,[72] but whatever the historical reality, there was definitely a myth of the examinations abroad during the Sung that made the world seem more open and full of possibilities to those men who aspired to something better than their status at birth. The increasing integration of the realms of institutionalized and popular religion must also have made the high gods of Taoism and Buddhism seem less distant and forbidding. All these factors combined to encourage the men of Sung to approach the gods directly, without benefit of priestly intercessor.

The multivalent character of Chinese deities both facilitated integration and increased access. A body of worshipers used to thinking of a god in a variety of ways was able to accept another aspect to the deity's identity much more easily than a group that adhered to a single, rigidly defined image of a god. In the case of the Divine Lord of Tzu-t'ung, transformation was an attribute of the god since at least the tenth century, and his apotheosis as a stellar Taoist deity was interpreted as simply the final and most spectacular of a long series of spiritual metamorphoses.[73] An institutionalized religion seeking to win the support of the followers of a given god, however, could count on the deity's more popular personae to draw in worshipers who could not understand and felt no need for the aid of an austere Taoist deity in his celestial palace. A congregation deriving from a variety of social, educational, and devotional backgrounds could be drawn to a single temple and their contributions used to support worship of an esoteric pantheon comprehensible to only a limited number of religious professionals and erudite laypersons.

The more direct relationship with high gods, which I have characterized as improved access, was promoted at least in part by similar considerations. If the exalted deity with which one sought to communicate had a popular identity as well, this made that deity more approachable, less distant. Traditional Taoist divinities were frigid and inhuman in their crystalline purity, often little more than the personification of cosmic forces, and could be invoked only through esoteric ritual performed by duly ordained priests. A god like the Divine Lord of Tzu-t'ung had experienced many human incarnations, had loved, married, raised children, and had even in a fit of filial vengeance murdered, suffered, repented, and been forgiven. He could be expected to understand the problems of a human supplicant and be moved by his plight. Moreover, even after his apotheosis, the Divine Lord continued to manifest in this world, and, much like Lü Tung-pin, could turn out to be the man standing next to you in the marketplace.[74] As a reward for special virtue, he might actually be born into your house as your son, thus assuring the family's fortunes. Yet this was the same god who sat in judgment on high, observing the conduct of all individuals and determining how they should be rewarded or punished, whether they would succeed or fail in life, and whether they would be granted posterity or become an "orphan soul" (ku-hun) after death.

So there was revolutionary change within age-old continuity. The same gods of antiquity were worshiped in new settings, with new, more exalted identities not replacing but supplementing the old. Buddhism and Taoism also maintained their traditional pantheons but assimilated new figures from the popular realm that both broadened and diluted their appeal, because though more people worshiped Buddhist or Taoist deities, they also increasingly took matters into their own hands, bypassing the priesthood to interact directly with the divine. This was the Sung religious revolution upon which the religious world of late imperial China was constructed.

NOTES

1. Two texts of this scripture in the Taoist canon clearly derive from this revelation, the *T'ai-shang wu-chi tsung-chen Wen-ch'ang ta-tung hsien-ching* (HY 5) and the *Yü-ch'ing wu-chi tsung-chen Wen-ch'ang ta-tung hsien-ching chu* (HY 103).

2. HY 1204.

3. Comprising the first section of the eponymous HY 169.

4. Recorded in HY 169.2b–3a.

5. This work constitutes the first seventy-three "transformations" *(hua)* of the later *Book of Transformations,* contained in the first three chapters of the *Tzu-t'ung ti-chün hua-shu* (HY170) and in many other transmitted editions.

6. Recent studies using the *I-chien chih*—such as those by Judith Boltz, in both her "Taoist Rites of Exorcism" (Ph.D. dissertation, University of California, Berkeley, 1985) and her contribution to the present volume, and Valerie Hansen, in her *Changing Gods in Medieval China, 1127–1276* (Princeton: Princeton Universtiy Press, 1990)—are notable, and welcome, exceptions.

7. The thirteenth-century enfeoffments of Wen-ch'ang recorded in the *Ch'ing-ho nei-chuan* (HY 169), for example, are not to be found in the *Collected Documents of the Sung (Sung hui-yao kao).*

8. *The Book of Transformations* is replete with classical references. To cite only a few, chapters 24 and 25, attributing poems of the *Shih ching* to the god in an earlier incarnation, are based on the historical explanations of these poems offered by the commentator Mao Heng, and the Lungstone *(fei-shih),* on which he makes a plea for justice in chapter 22, is recorded only in the *Chou li.*

9. At the 1989 Hsi-lai Temple conference, Robert Hymes argued that references to divine powers in a document like this represent only claims and that we cannot be sure that there was any cultic reality behind these claims. I believe Hymes' fears to be largely unfounded. The cult to Wen-ch'ang by the twelfth century was not a small, malleable movement but rather an established cult with at least nine hundred years of history in the Szechwan region. Any document written to gain the adherence of such a large group of people must have relied heavily on established cult lore and stuck fairly closely to the accepted image of the god. Once such a scripture was accepted as authentic, it is unlikely any innovations contained therein (and it seems to me that they must have been on the literati-oriented side of the cult) would have been rejected by the faithful. If they had been, the scripture itself would be unlikely to survive transmission through the centuries. In any case, in the case of the Wen-ch'ang cult each of the powers or specializations mentioned below can be shown to be a viable element of the cult at a later date.

10. Terry F. Kleeman, "Wenchang and the Viper" (Ph.D. dissertation, University of California, Berkeley, 1988), p. 401.

11. This incident actually occurs during an incarnation, but after he has awoken to his true divine identity.

12. Kleeman, "Wenchang and the Viper," pp. 451–452.

13. Ch'ang Ch'ü, *Hua-yang-kuo chih,* Kuo-hsüeh chi-pen ts'ung-shu edition (Shanghai: Commercial Press, 1958), 3.22; Liu Lin, ed., *Hua-yang-kuo chih chiao-chu* (Ch'eng-tu: Pa-Shu shu-she, 1984), 3.145.

14. On various stones related to the production of thunder and lightning, see Feng Yen, *Feng Shih wen-chien chi chiao-cheng* (Harvard-Yenching Index Series, Supplement No. 7, Peking, 1933), pp. 21–24; and Kleeman, "Wenchang and the Viper," pp. 10–12.

15. This legend, alluded to in the sources cited in note 1, is related in full in *Hua-yang-kuo chih* 3.29; *Hua-yang-kuo chih chiao-chu* 3.190.

16. Yüeh Shih, *T'ai-p'ing huan-yü chi* (Taipei: Wen-hai ch'u-pan-she, 1963), 84.7a.

17. P'eng Ting-ch'iu, ed., *Ch'üan T'ang-shih* (Peking: Chung-hua shu-chü, 1960), 539.6171.

18. Yao Ch'ang did not leave the sort of historical legacy that might stimulate mythmakers living long after his death. Since Yao was ultimately unsuccessful, there was little advantage to be gained for the Tzu-t'ung cult by allying their god with such a figure after his fate became clear. Similarly, any cult to Yao Ch'ang established at the place of his death in Shensi province would gain little by claiming an alliance with a local deity of remote Szechwan. I suspect the legend was created by Yao at a time when he was contemplating a campaign against Szechwan. In such a situation, the god that had foiled a plot from Ch'in once would be a very useful figure to claim as a supporter. A version of the tale found in some versions of the *Shih-liu kuo ch'un-ch'iu* is of doubtful authenticity but, if authentic, would confirm this dating. See T'ang Ch'iu, ed., *Shih-liu kuo ch'un-ch'iu chi-pu,* Basic Sinological Series edition (Peking: Commercial Press, 1958), 50.379. It is difficult to envision a plausible scenario for the creation of this tale at a date much later than the fifth century. In any case, a somewhat later date would not disturb the sequence of development presented here.

19. Hsi-tsung's encounter with the god was noted by those in his retinue and commemorated in a poem by Wang To (?–884). Both the poem and the circumstances of its composition are set forth in Chi Yu-kung, *T'ang-shih chi-shih* (Shanghai: Chung-hua shu-chü, 1965), 65.983.

20. This change may well have been instigated by the emperor or members of his retinue, but their efforts were successful in reshaping the cult—or at least one segment of it.

21. Fan Yeh, *Hou Han shu* (Peking: Chung-hua shu-chü, 1971), 86.2852. Concerning this legend, see Max Kaltenmark, "La légende de la ville immergée en Chine," *Cahiers d'Extrême-Asie* 1 (1985): 1–10.

22. Wang Jen-yü, *Chien-wen chi,* quoted in *TPKC* 312.2466–2467.

23. Sun Kuang-hsien (d. 968), *Pei-meng so-yen,* quoted in *TPKC* 458.3749.

24. I think it unlikely that this tale was designed to disparage the deity by recalling a serpentine identity of the god that had been eliminated from contemporary cult belief. The recorder of this tale, Sun Kuang-hsien (d. 968), begins

with two identifications of the god, first as the snake in the Five Stalwart legend discussed above, then as the snake raised by Mister Chang in the Ch'iung Lake legend. He then notes that his contemporaries refer to the god as Chang E-tzu, maintaining the character for "viper" that is so often emended in official sources, and affirms that the god is extremely numinous or magically powerful *(ling)*. Sun continues to relate the tale of Yüan-ying's serpentine nature, his death in rebellion, and the subsequent possession of the temple invoker by E-tzu. Sun concludes, "Through this the people of Shu came to realize that Yüan-ying was the sprite or essence *(ching)* of the snake in the temple." Thus both explanations of the origins of the cult offered by Sun assume that the god is a violent snake deity responsible for numerous deaths, and he twice affirms that people of his day conceived of the god as a snake. Although Yüan-ying is described as "evil," Chang E-tzu is referred to as a "god" *(shen)* and described as *ling,* a term that usually refers to the god's ability to answer prayer and punish insult. There is no methodological justification for assuming that an account that portrays a god as less than completely moral in his actions is from an opponent of the cult. Jean DeBernardi has shown that even such well-established bastions of orthodoxy as Kuan-ti and T'ai-shang Lao-chün can be used to "invert social norms . . . and to elevate the hedonistic values of the underworld as a social ideal" ("The God of War and the Vagabond Buddha," *Modern China* 13.3 [1987]: 311), and many scholars have noted the origins of deity cults in cults to the violent dead.

25. *The Book of Transformations* (chapters 64 and 65) justifies the god's actions by identifying the murdered with the oft-reviled Empress Lü of Han and her family and by claiming an obligation of blood revenge for the god because of the treatment of his mother by the empress in a previous life. Even so, the god is cashiered from his divine office and imprisoned for years as punishment (chapter 66).

26. *SHY Li* 20.55a–b.

27. *SHY Li* 20.56a, lists titles or epithets conferred upon the god of Tzu-t'ung or his family in 1105, 1119, 1132, 1147, 1154, 1159, 1169, and 1172.

28. This apparently became an important element of cult lore. When a temple was erected to three gods of Szechwan in Nanking in 1261, the local gazetteer mentioned as characteristics of the god his supervision of civil affairs and his blotting out the stain of his mother's unjust death *(Ching-ting Chien-k'ang chih* [*SYTFC* edition, 1262], 44.37a).

29. See Sung Ch'i, *Ching-wen chi (SKCS),* 8.8b–9a.

30. See Wang Tai-sheng, "Chang Hsien-chung yü Tzu-t'ung miao," *Ssu-ch'uan wen-wu* 4 (1985), p. 51. On Chang Yü's historical exploits, see Michael C. Rogers, *The Chronicle of Fu Chien: A Case of Exemplar History* (Berkeley: University of California Press, 1968), p. 137.

31. David Hawkes, *The Songs of the South: An Anthology of Ancient Chinese Poems by Qu Yuan and Other Poets* (Middlesex: Penguin Books, 1985), p. 197. For records of official sacrifices to Wen-ch'ang, see *Shih chi* 27.1293, *Han shu* 6.1275, and *Chin shu* 11.291.

32. The first explicit reference to the god by this title seems to be in the Yüan canonization of 1316, recorded in *Ch'ing-ho nei-chuan* (HY 169), 6a–b. The rescript accompanying this canonization also refers to the temple on Sevenfold Mountain as the "Palace of Wen-ch'ang."

33. When Chou Hung-mo submitted a memorial in 1488 attacking, among others, the Tzu-t'ung cult, it was precisely this identification of the god with the asterism Wen-ch'ang at which he directed his arguments. See *Ming shih* 50.1308, *Li-pu chih-kao (SKCS)*, 84.23a. Chao I (1727–1814) also focuses on this point, saying, "As for the stars of Wen-ch'ang, they have no connection with Tzu-t'ung." See *Kai-yü ts'ung-k'ao* (Shanghai: Commercial Press, 1957), 35.765. Similarly, when Yao Ying (1785–1852) wrote supporting the cult, he titled his essay "A human spirit can be taken to stand for the Wen-ch'ang asterism" and addressed directly the arguments of what he termed "students of the classics" *(ching-sheng)*. See *K'ang-yu chi-hsing* (Pi-chi hsiao-shuo ta-kuan edition, *hsü-pien*, vol. 44), 6.9a–b.

34. See the entry on the Traveling Temple to the Three Kings of Shu in Fu-chou in *Fu-chou-fu chih,* quoted in *Yung-le ta-tien* (Taipei: Chung-wen ch'u-pan-she, 1981), 10950.4550A, fol. 8a.

35. See Wu Tzu-mu, *Meng-liang lu* (Pi-chi hsiao-shuo ta-kuan edition, vol. 6), 14.6a; T'ien Ju-ch'eng, *Hsi-hu yu-lan chih* (Taipei: Shih-chieh shu-chü, 1963), 12.164; Lewis Hodous, *Folkways in China* (London: A. Probsthain, 1929), 1.267. Chaffee discusses the cult to the god of Tzu-t'ung along with other examination cults, citing several stories about the god. See John W. Chaffee, *The Thorny Gates of Learning in Sung China: A Social History of the Examinations* (Cambridge: Cambridge University Press, 1985), pp. 179–180.

36. This is particularly clearly stated in the "Inscription to the Grotto of the Flying Auroras" *("Fei-hsia tung chi")* of 1207, in Chang Yü-chia, ed., *E-mei-shan chih pu* (Taipei: Ming-wen shu-chü, 1980 photo reprint of 1713 edition), 9.1a–2a. There he speaks of stopping in every small town to promote moral transformation.

37. As, for example, in the case of a man who was rewarded in this way for not wasting rice. See Lu Ts'an (1494–1551), *Keng-ssu pien (TSCC edition)*, 3.66–67.

38. J. J. M. de Groot, *Les fêtes annuellement célébrées à Emoui* (Amoy): *Étude concernant la religion populaire des Chinois,* trans. by C. G. Chavannes (Paris: Leroux, 1886), pp. 162–165; Henry Doré, *Researches into Chinese Superstitions,* trans. by M. Kennelly, S.J. (Shanghai: T'usewei Printing Press, 1920), part 2, vol. 6, pp. 39–58; Hodous, *Folkways in China,* pp. 75–77.

39. C. Stevan Harrell, "When a Ghost Becomes a God, " in Arthur P. Wolf, ed., *Religion and Ritual in Chinese Society* (Stanford: Stanford University Press, 1974), pp. 193–206; Philip C. Baity, *Religion in a Chinese Town,* Asian Folklore and Social Life Monographs 64 (Taipei: Orient Cultural Service, 1975).

40. Alvin P. Cohen, "Coercing the Rain Deities in Ancient China," *History of Religions* 17.3–4 (1978): 244–263.

41. James L. Watson, "Standardizing the Gods: The Promotion of T'ien Hou ('Empress of Heaven') along the South China Coast, 960–1960," in David Johnson et al., eds., *Popular Culture in Late Imperial China* (Berkeley: University of California Press, 1985), p. 322.

42. Ibid., p. 323.

43. Prasenjit Duara, "Superscribing Symbols: the Myth of Guandi, God of War," *JAS* 47.4 (1988): 778–795.

44. Ibid., p. 791.

45. Juan Yüan, *Liang-Che chin-shih chih* 9.55b–57a, reprinted in Shih-k'o shih-liao hsin-pien (Taipei: Hsin-wen-feng), 14.10417–10418.

46. For a succinct explanation and defense of Skinner's theory, see Daniel Little and Joseph W. Esherick, "Testing the Testers: A Reply to Barbara Sands and Ramon Myers's Critique of G. William Skinner's Regional Systems Approach to China," *JAS* 48.1 (1989): 90–99.

47. Little and Esherick note that "to the extent there is interregional trade, it will occur between high-level central places within different macroregions" and paraphrase Skinner's larger hypothesis by saying that "noneconomic phenomena (such as the spread of heterodox movements and rebellions, the structure of the imperial bureaucracy, and the cultural horizon of the peasant) are better understood when placed within the spatial framework of macroregions" ("Testing the Testers," p. 91).

48. Wu Tzu-mu, commenting on the temple to the god in Lin-an, notes, "Scholars from all four quarters who attend the examinations in search of fame all pray to him." See Wu Tzu-mu, *Meng-liang lu* (Pi-chi hsiao-shuo ta-kuan edition, vol. 6), 14.6a.

49. HY 169.1a.

50. In his comments on this stele, Juan Yüan notes that within the nimbus surrounding the god's head are two figures riding on snakes (*Liang-Che chin-shih chih* 9:55b–57a).

51. Planchette altars were established near the modern cities of Ta-tsu, An-yüeh, Ya-an, and P'eng-hsi. A preface to the *Scripture of the Great Grotto* was revealed near P'eng-hsi and a celestial title near An-yüeh. In addition a *chiao*-type festival was held for the god near Fu-ling and talismans called "Vermillion Petitions to Bless the Populace" were produced. See chapter 94 of the *Wen-ti hua-shu* (Tao-tsang chi-yao edition). Cf. *Tzu-t'ung ti-chün hua-shu* 4.27a–b (where the reign name must be emended from Shao-hsing to Shao-hsi) and 4.29a–b.

52. Chapter 94 tells of a temple established to the god's father in modern Huang-mei, Hupei. See Kleeman, "Wenchang and the Viper," pp. 77–78.

53. *Wen-ti hua-shu* 90.87a.

54. Chun-shu Chang and Joan Smythe, *South China in the Twelfth Century* (Hong Kong: Chinese University Press, 1981), p. 141.

55. *Ming i-t'ung chih (SKCS),* 18.6b.

56. On the rebellion of Fang La and others said to "observe vegetarianism and serve demons," see Chikusa Masaaki, *Chūgoku bukkyō shakaishi kenkyū* (Kyoto: Dōhōsha, 1982), pp. 199–259. The last three chapters of the *Tao-tsang* edition of the *Book of Transformations,* written around 1267, lay special stress on vegetarianism and the necessity to avoid the killing of all sentient beings.

57. This expansion has been chronicled by Morita Kenji, "Bushō teikun no seiritsu: chihōshin kara kakyo no kami e," in Umehara Kaoru, ed., *Chūgoku kinsei no toshi to bunka* (Kyoto: Kyoto University Institute for Humanistic Studies, 1984), pp. 389–418. See also Hansen, *Changing Gods,* pp. 143–145.

58. I follow Sivin and Strickmann in understanding by the term "Taoist" members of self-conscious social groups practicing communal rituals and sharing a core body of doctrine and practice associated with Chang Tao-ling. See Nathan Sivin, "On the Word 'Taoist' as a Source for Perplexity, with Special Reference to the Relations of Science and Religion in Traditional China," *History of Religions*

17 (1978): 303–330, and Michel Strickmann, "On the Alchemy of T'ao Hung-ching," in Holmes Welch and Anna Seidel, eds., *Facets of Taoism: Essays in Chinese Religion* (New Haven: Yale University Press, 1979), pp. 164ff.

59. Such was the case with the Traveling Temple of the Perfected Lord of Tzu-t'ung in Yen-chou. See *Ching-ting Yen-chou hsü-chih* (Sung-Yüan ti-fang chih ts'ung-shu edition), 4.4a.

60. *Yen-yu Ssu-ming chih* (*SYTFC* edition), 18.30b; *Hsien-ch'un Lin-an chih* (*SYTFC* edition), 73.17a.

61. Kristofer Schipper outlines the financial difficulties involved in creating and maintaining a local temple in "Comment on crée un lieu-saint local: À propos de danses et légendes de la Chine ancienne," *Études chinoises* 4.2 (1986): 41–61.

62. I do not mean that each medium's production was in some sense controlled by the main temple at Tzu-t'ung but rather that each new pronouncement would circulate among the cult centers and lead to a general coordination of message.

63. Kuo K'uei, "Wen-ch'ang-tz'u chi," in *Kuo Tzu-chang chi* (1571 edition), 1.9a–b.

64. On the distinction between Taoism and popular religion, see Rolf A. Stein, "Religious Taoism and Popular Religion from the Second to Seventh Centuries," in Welch and Seidel, eds., *Facets of Taoism*. The Buddhist teaching of *ahiṃsā* naturally precluded the sacrifice of living creatures. The traditional sacrificial offerings in these two religions are literary documents in Taoism and flowers and incense in Buddhism. Note that the two continuums are defined in terms of practice rather than practitioners. There were no doubt always individuals who participated in both, just as there were whole communities who rejected one or the other.

65. The Great Thearch of Jade Augustness occupies a position parallel to that of the Primordial Heavenly Worthy as the supreme deity at a different level of the Taoist pantheon. Kubo reports that, among Taoists in modern Taiwan and Southeast Asia, the two are considered the same god; see Kubo Noritada, *Dōkyō no kamigami* (Tokyo: Hirakawa shuppansha, 1986), p. 129.

66. K. M. Schipper notes that local deities (whom he refers to as "popular saints") began to appear in Taoist liturgical sources in the middle of the T'ang and cites the example of Hsü Sun, who entered the Taoist pantheon in the Southern Sung. See his "Taoist Ritual and Local Cults of the T'ang Dynasty," in Michel Strickmann, ed., *Tantric and Taoist Studies in Honour of R. A. Stein,* vol. 3: *Mélanges chinois et bouddhiques* 22 (1985), p. 831, n. 44.

67. On *wang-yeh* cults, see Paul Katz, "Demons or Deities?—The *Wange* of Taiwan," *Asian Folklore Studies* 46 (1987): 197–215; and Liu Chih-wan, *Chung-kuo min-chien hsin-yang lun-wen chi* (Taipei: Lien-ching ch'u-pan shih-yeh kung-ssu, 1983).

68. Hansen, *Changing Gods,* pp. 79–104.

69. An earlier version of this chapter characterized this change as "democratization," but this term proved to have too many irrelevant connotations for other participants in the conference. I reluctantly reject Timothy Barret's suggestion of "Americanization" as being too culture-specific in its interpretation, leaving me with the rather clumsy locution used here. Note that the term "democratization" is used by Western scholars of church history to refer to a very similar process of

laicization in regard to mystical experience in the late Middle Ages; see Steven Ozment, *The Age of Reform, 1250–1550* (New Haven: Yale University Press, 1980), p. 115.

70. Nathan Sivin notes that such direct performance of ritual was already common in the alchemical tradition of self-cultivation during the Six Dynasties (personal communication, September, 1990). Thus this development may reflect the extension of an alchemical practice into the devotional side of Taoism.

71. See *Hsüan-chen ling-ying pao-ch'ien* (HY 1289). This text is not explicitly dated, but references in the preface to the *Secret Biography of Ch'ing-ho* and conditions in the temple on Sevenfold Mountain point to a twelfth- or thirteenth-century date.

72. The various positions are deftly summarized in Chaffee, *The Thorny Gates of Learning,* pp. 9–13.

73. The theme of a god undergoing transformations was present at least as early as the Han, when the *Scripture of the Transformations of Lao-tzu (Lao-tzu pien-hua ching)* was written. This work differs from the *Book of Transformations* in that Lao-tzu passes through a series of earthly incarnations but does not lose his supernatural identity and does not undergo a process of development; see Anna Seidel, *La divinisation de Lao Tseu dans le Taoïsme des Han* (Paris: École française d'Extrême-Orient, 1969).

74. Legends of Lü Tung-pin, who attained a special level of devotion among followers of the Complete Perfection (Ch'üan-chen) school of Taoism, center on his manifesting himself at unexpected places in disguise and dropping enigmatic hints as to his true identity; see Farzeen Baldrian-Hussein, "Lü Tung-pin in Northern Sung Literature," *Cahiers d'Extrême-Asie* 2 (1986): 133–169.

GLOSSARY

Chang 張
Chang Chung(-tzu) 張仲 (子)
Chang E-tzu 張蚩 (惡) 子
Chang Hsien 張仙
Chang Ya(-tzu) 張亞 (子)
Chang Yü 張喻
Chang Yü-chia 張玉甲
Ch'ang Ch'ü 常璩
Chao I 趙翼
Chi Yu-kung 計有功
Ch'i-ch'ü shan 七曲山
Ch'iang 羌
chiao 醮
Chien-wen chi 見聞集
ch'ien 籤
Ch'ih-yu 蚩尤
Chin shu 晉書
ching 精

ching-sheng 經生
Ching-ting Chien-k'ang chih 景定建康志
Ching-ting Yen-chou hsü-chih 景定嚴州續志
Ching-wen chi 景文集
Ch'ing-ho nei-chuan 清河內傳
Ch'iung-ch'ih 邛池
Ch'iung-tu 邛都
Chou Hung-mo 周洪謨
Chou li 周禮
chu-sheng 注生
Ch'u-chou 滁州
Ch'u-hsiang Wen-ch'ang Hua-shu 出象文昌化書
Ch'üan T'ang-shih 全唐詩
E-mei shan chih pu 峨眉山志補
E-tzu 蚩子

Fan Yeh　范曄

Fang La　方臘

"Fei-hsia tung chi"　飛霞洞記

fei-shih　肺石

Feng-shih wen-chien chi chiao-cheng
　封氏閩見集校正

Feng Yen　封演

Fu　涪

Fu Chien　苻堅

Han shu　漢書

hao　號

Hou Han shu　後漢書

Hsi-hu yu-lan chih　西湖遊覽志

Hsi-tsung　僖宗

Hsien-ch'un Lin-an chih　咸淳臨安志

Hsü Sun　許遜

Hsü Sung　徐松

Hsüan-chen ling-ying pao-ch'ien
　玄真靈應寶籤

Hsüan-tsung　玄宗

hua　化

Hua-shu　化書

Hua-yang-kuo chih　華陽國志

Juan Yüan　阮元

K'ai-ming (king of Shu)　蜀開明王

Kai-yü ts'ung-k'ao　陔餘叢考

K'ang-yu chi-hsing　康輶紀行

*Kao-shang ta-tung Wen-ch'ang ssu-lu
　tzu-yang pao-lu*　高上大洞文昌司錄
　紫陽寶籙

Keng-ssu pien　庚巳編

ku-hun　孤魂

Kuan-ti　關帝

K'uei　夔

Kuo Tzu-chang　郭子章

"Li"　禮

Li Fang　李昉

Li Lung-chi　李隆基

Li-pu chih-kao　禮部志稿

Li Shang-yin　李商隱

Liang-Che chin-shih chih　兩浙金石志

Lin-ch'iung　臨邛

ling　靈

Liu An-sheng　劉安勝

Lu Ts'an　陸粲

Lu Yu　陸游

Lü Tung-pin　呂洞賓

Mao Heng　毛亨

Meng-liang lu　夢粱錄

Ming i-t'ung chih　明一統志

Ming shih　明史

Pai Yü-ch'an　白玉蟾

Pao-lu　寶籙

Pei-meng so-yen　北夢瑣言

P'eng Ting-ch'iu　彭定求

San-chiao ho-liu sou-shen ta-ch'üan
　三教合流搜神大全

shan-shu　善書

Shao-hsi　紹熙

Shao-hsing　紹興

She-hung　射洪

shen　神

shen-ping　神兵

Shih chi　史記

Shih ching　詩經

Shih Hu　石虎

Shih-liu kuo ch'un-ch'iu　十六國春秋

shih-ta-fu　士大夫

Ssu-lu　司祿

Ssu-ming　司命

Sun Kuang-hsien　孫光憲

Sung Ch'i　宋祁

Sung hui-yao kao　宋會要稿

Ta-tung hsien-ching　大洞仙經

T'ai-p'ing huan-yü chi　太平寰宇記

T'ai-p'ing kuang-chi　太平廣記

T'ai-shang Lao-chün　太上老君

*T'ai-shang wu-chi tsung-chen
　Wen-ch'ang ta-tung hsien-ching*
　太上無極總真文昌大洞仙經

T'ang Ch'iu　湯球

T'ang hui-yao　唐會要

T'ang-shih chi-shih　唐詩紀事

T'ien Ju-ch'eng　田汝成

Tzu-t'ung　梓潼

Tzu-t'ung ti-chün　梓潼帝君

Tzu-t'ung ti-chün hua-shu　梓潼帝君
　化書

Wang Chien　王建

Wang Jen-yü　王仁裕

Wang To　王鐸

wang-yeh　王爺

Wen-ch'ang　文昌

Wen-ch'ang ta-tung hsien-ching　文昌
　大洞仙經

Wen-ch'ang tz'u-chi　文昌祠記

wen-ping　文柄
Wen-ti hua-shu　文帝化書
wu-ting　五丁
Wu Tzu-mu　吳自牧
Yao Ch'ang　姚萇
Yao Ying　姚瑩
Yen-yu ssu-ming chih　延祐四明志
Ying-hsien wu-lieh chung-yu kuang-
　chi wang　英顯武烈忠佑廣濟王

Yung-le ta-tien　永樂大典
Yü-ch'ing wu-chi tsung-chen
　Wen-ch'ang ta-tung hsien-ching chu
　玉清無極總真文昌大洞仙經註
Yü-huang ta-ti　玉皇大帝
Yüan-shih t'ien-tsun　元始天尊
Yüan-ying　元膺
Yüeh Shih　樂史

CHAPTER 3

GODS ON WALLS: A CASE OF INDIAN
INFLUENCE ON CHINESE LAY RELIGION?

Valerie Hansen

The parallels between earthly administrators and bureaucratic gods have struck most observers of nineteenth- and twentieth-century Chinese religion.[1] Like government officials, Chinese gods have been thought to hold office for a specified term, to respond to orders from above, and to behave with the caprice of officials everywhere. At the top of the two hierarchies are the human emperor and his divine counterpart, the Jade Emperor; at the bottom, the district magistrates and their divine equivalents, the wall-and-moat gods *(ch'eng-huang shen)*, often called city gods.[2] Office-holding gods appear quintessentially Chinese. Who besides the Chinese would imagine a heaven peopled by godly bureaucrats?

The ancient Chinese conceived of a bureaucratically organized pantheon, but the assumption of positions as monastic guardians or as wall-and-moat gods by local deities was a relatively late phenomenon. Local gods who held office did not exist in classical times, and they certainly postdated the introduction of Buddhism in the early centuries A.D. The rise of local gods who held office reflected the influence of Indian Buddhism in general and, I will argue, the cult to one Indian god, Vaiśravaṇa, in particular. The evidence is admittedly far from conclusive, but to me it is sufficiently persuasive to set down here.

Like many other religious changes, the introduction of this type of deity took place during the T'ang and became standardized with the massive increase in title granting by the Sung government. Both Vaiśravaṇa and the wall-and-moat gods were associated with walls. The texts cited in this chapter do not always specify where exactly the temples of these gods were located, however. Sometimes, the sources say, the temples were next to gates, sometimes in watchtowers above gates *(ch'eng-lou)*, or sometimes on the northwest corner of the walls.[3] The temples could have been built on fortifications that did not provide entry into the city; they could as well have been in lean-to structures propped against the city walls.[4] Wherever their exact location, they were always on or by walls. A visitor to a building with a shrine to either Vaiśravaṇa or the local wall-

and-moat god might not know the identity of the god, but the visitor would know the task of the deity was to protect the edifice or city. Local residents were more likely to know the names and even the preapotheosis biographies of the deity. The gods to be discussed in this chapter performed their task of guarding a city, monastery, or building, even when their devotees did not know their names.[5]

In the period before the T'ang, Buddhist and Taoist practitioners and their Confucian counterparts, government officials, regularly attacked indigenous deities and tried to replace them with new gods.[6] In the next phase stories were told of itinerant monks who converted local gods to Buddhism: previously carnivorous deities acknowledged the superiority of Buddhist teachings and eschewed meat offerings. Then, sometime during the seventh and eighth centuries, Chinese began to put images of the Indian god Vaiśravaṇa (in Chinese, P'i-sha-men) on the walls or by the gate of any edifice they wanted him to protect.

In the fourth phase Vaiśravaṇa seems to have become the prototype first for monastic guardians (ch'ieh-lan shen) and then for wall-and-moat gods. Buddhists began to appoint local deities to positions watching over their monasteries: the stories about Kuan Yü's appointment at Yü-ch'üan monastery pin this development down to the ninth and tenth centuries. Soon Taoists and Confucian administrators constructed their own pantheons. The association of Vaiśravaṇa with walls suggests that the rise of wall-and-moat gods in the late T'ang and Sung also followed Vaiśravaṇa's lead.[7] In the Sung the Taoist clergy began to relabel the gods. Relabeling the gods meant that the Taoist clergy could claim to rule over the gods. By assigning the gods to their positions as gods of walls and moats, the clergy made these office-holding gods subordinate to the higher gods in Taoist pantheons. So the clergy could claim, but their claims alone did not mean that the laity accepted the rankings implied by the new labels.

SUPPRESSING THE GODS

Conflict marked the pre-T'ang legacy of relations between China's three organized religions and local gods. Starting even before the unification of the empire in 221 B.C. and continuing in later periods, Confucian officials challenged indigenous gods to contests of power, tore down their temples, and encouraged the worship of former administrators in their stead. Similarly, in the early fourth century, members of the Celestial Masters sect sought to distinguish impure local gods from pure, and thus more powerful, Taoist ones. And Buddhists alerted local deities to the dangers of a meat-eating diet and occasionally even administered lay vows to them. The Confucian, Buddhist, and Taoist justifications for and means of taming local gods differed, but their ultimate goal was the same: they wanted to transform local practices into something less bloodthirsty than what had existed before.

In the predynastic period, representatives of the central government sought to control the different hazards of the wilderness, usually by expelling the wild tigers who preyed on local people or by channeling the waters that periodically flooded. At the same time they moved against local gods of whose cults they did not approve. Before Li Ping could complete his irrigation works in Szechwan, for example, he had to fight a local river god in hand-to-hand combat.[8] The conflicts with indigenous gods that some officials provoked when they dug new irrigation systems suggest that Jean Lévi is right to equate the quelling of natural and divine forces.[9] As the uncontrolled rivers must be channeled before an area is safe to live in, so too must the local people and their gods be conquered. These conquerors could in turn become gods; the local people eventually built a temple to Li Ping.[10]

Like Confucian officials, the Taoists distinguished sharply between permissible and forbidden local cults. Rolf A. Stein makes a strong case that whatever the Taoists advocated they defined as pure; whatever their rivals did for the support of the local people was impure.[11] The Taoists did not hesitate to tear down temples to impure gods or to build temples to pure ones. According to Ko Hung, writing in the fourth century, Ko Hsüan, the mythical founder of the Ling-pao branch of Taoism, defoliated a tree, killed birds, and burned down the temple of an insolent deity.[12] A later biography of Hsü Sun, who lived sometime in the third or fourth century, reports that Hsü erected a temple to a female deity who had appeared to him, but he had no compunctions about using wind and lightning to tear down another temple. Once he had uprooted the trees around the shrine, he told the local inhabitants; "I have already exorcised this demonic shrine. You have no need to worship there."[13] The same account relates that the people of Ching-yang (Szechwan) so revered their prefect that they built a shrine to Hsü after he resigned and left their district.[14]

Like their Taoist and Confucian counterparts, Buddhists also attacked local cults. One tale, set at the end of the fourth century, concerns a Buddhist monk who visited a temple in Nan-k'ang (Kiangsi). The image burst into tears on seeing him; it turned out that the monk was an old friend of his. The image addressed the monk saying; "My crimes are great. Can you absolve me?" The monk recited sūtras and persuaded the god to show his true form. The god then manifested himself as a snake. When he listened to the sūtras, blood came out of his eyes. After seven days the snake expired, and his cult died out too—no doubt to the delight of the monk, who would have been pleased at the superior strength of Buddhism.[15] Bernard Faure has argued that several similar tales about monk-snake encounters show the superior power of Buddhist teaching, which offered a higher understanding of reality, over unruly local gods.[16]

When officials in later periods advocated a strategy of suppression, they often cited the example of Ti Jen-chieh (630–700), the most famous deity-buster of the T'ang. His biography in the official history claims that, repelled by local religious practices, he tore down 1700 temples in the Chiang-nan region, leaving only temples to genuine ancient heroes, the Great Yü, Wu T'ai-po, Chi Cha, and Wu Tzu-hsü.[17] In 688, Ti indignantly asked a local god: "How can you continue to receive unmerited temple offerings and indiscriminately waste livestock? I am empowered to govern this area, and, implementing an urgent request, I order your temple burnt, the platforms leveled, the grass screens eliminated, and the feather canopies reduced to smoke. You should leave quickly and cause no trouble to the people. When this order arrives, treat it as law."[18] Here Ti voices the Confucian distaste for excessive meat offerings—a point on which the Confucians agreed with both Buddhists and Taoists, though on different grounds. Some analysts have suggested that Ti's ousting of Hsiang Yü's spirit, who was said to have caused the deaths of several magistrates in Hu-chou (Chekiang), showed that government officials were ultimately able to control local religious practices.[19] Supporting this view is the list of temples from the first extant Hu-chou gazetteer.[20] Ti would no doubt have been heartened to see that the temples still standing in 1202 that claimed a T'ang founding date were to heroes, early settlers, generals, and virtuous officials—just the kinds of gods whose worship he advocated.[21]

As Ti's campaign shows, the one-time suppression of local cults was easy to effect. A righteous official or indignant monk could simply summon a group of laborers to dismantle one temple, or 1700 temples, and be done with it. But to sustain the suppression—to prevent the rebuilding of temples or to ban prayer within people's houses—demanded a level of control that neither clergy nor administrators of the premodern period commanded. Four centuries after Ti had ousted Hsiang Yü's spirit from the yamen, the cult to him was still active.[22] Cults even less to Ti's liking also survived his suppression. A collection of tales from the end of the eighth century tells of a mountain temple to a Hu-chou woman named Li:

> She had mastered techniques of the Way and could walk on water. Her husband grew angry and killed her. Seven hundred years have passed from her death until today, but her appearance is just as if she were alive. She majestically lies on her side. People come from far and near to pray to her. If they are sincere, then they can reach the temple. If they are not, the wind will turn their boats back and they will not reach the temple. These days, her

image is bathed and manicured once a month. Every day her body is adorned. Her appearance is soft and pliant, just like someone sleeping. It seems that she attained the Way.[23]

No doubt the handling of the mummy would have repelled Ti Jen-chieh. The cult survived his suppression, however, perhaps because it was popular with local people or perhaps because it lay in the mountains. Thus, coexisting with the officially approved cults of the T'ang was another stratum of gods, whose cults rose and fell in spite of official and clerical opposition but whose existence remains largely unrecorded because of it.

CONVERTING THE GODS

Increasingly throughout the late T'ang and the Sung, local clergy of whatever stripe began to recast local gods in terms more acceptable to themselves. This shift was neither conscious nor unilateral; attacks on local cults continued as well. At first, individual monks, working on their own initiative, came up with new unsystematized labels for local gods. Much less schooled than the highly learned monks resident in the capital, these monks lived in local communities where indigenous gods were worshiped and, accordingly, had much more incentive to win the support of their devotees.

Epigraphical evidence allows a glimpse of how one such monk proceeded. Sometime during the T'ang dynasty, a monk heard that a local god in Shao-hsing (Chekiang) accepted human sacrifices. The monk went to the god's temple and began to meditate. The god took many shapes, but the monk did not respond. "Then the god realized his errors and manifested his real body with three attendants. They bowed and converted to Buddhism. They accepted the way of the five precepts [not to kill, steal, commit adultery, lie, or drink] and the three refuges [in the Buddha, dharma, and sangha]. When receiving offerings, they would not consume meat or blood."[24] In this contest between the local god and the Buddhist clergy, the monk's strength derived from meditation was greater than the god's own power and made it possible for him to best the god. As in other Buddhist accounts, the monk who had this vision credited the god and his attendants with a suddenly acquired awareness of their sins. We may wonder, though, whether the god's devotees also knew of his decision to accept only herbivorous offerings.

This tale suggests what in fact became the standard Buddhist approach to dealing with local gods. Often a monk had a dream or vision in which the deity accepted the supremacy of the Buddha. As a result, the god no longer posed a threat. As in the Shao-hsing text, such monks did not concern themselves with what local devotees thought. The devotees, in turn, may well have continued to view the deity just as they had before —and probably continued to make meat offerings.

One development spanning the Six Dynasties and the T'ang was the introduction of new cults to righteous officials and to Buddhist and Taoist figures. Officials and clergy contended that they had eliminated unclean local cults, and that lay people worshiped only beneficent, vegetarian gods. Once Buddhist proselytizers had eliminated local gods (or at least torn down their temples), they often offered purer alternatives for worship by introducing deities like Kuan-yin (Avalokiteśvara), the bodhisattva of compassion, and circulating miracle tales about them.[25] Unlike other popular gods, Kuan-yin was not identified with or worshiped in just one place. As a bodhisattva Kuan-yin could appear anywhere. Dedicatory colophons from Tun-huang manuscripts indicate that the worship of Kuan-yin, Ti-tsang (Kṣitigarbha), and the god of Mount T'ai had become common by the ninth and tenth centuries.[26]

THE CULT TO VAIŚRAVAṆA

The centuries that witnessed the rise of the Kuan-yin cult also saw the assumption of office by local gods. The best way to trace this change through the scant sources is first to examine the history of the cult to Vaiśravaṇa, an originally Indian god introduced to China from Khotan, where he served as a guardian deity for the Khotanese royal family and kingdom. Indeed, it seems that Vaiśravaṇa forms a missing link between the early indigenous Chinese gods and the later office-holding ones. Like the deified humans of earlier periods, such as Li Ping and Hsü Sun, he retained his own identity and was always referred to by a transliteration of his Sanskrit name, P'i-sha-men. Unlike local gods, his temples came to be located all over China (and Japan as well). If one installed a statue of Vaiśravaṇa in the northern watchtower of a city or in the main gate of a monastery, then he watched over the designated city or monastery. The history of his cult suggests that the idea of a office-holding deity, specifically a monastic guardian, may have originated in India and entered China via Central Asia.[27]

Because it is impossible to map precisely the history of any cult that entered China before the twelfth century when the first extant gazetteers were written, the initial stages of the history of Vaiśravaṇa's cult in China can only be partially reconstructed. Vaiśravaṇa was the patronymic of the Indian god of wealth, Kubera, and the god was called by either name.[28] Vaiśravaṇa was one of four Buddhist Heavenly Kings from India who presided over the directions (ssu-t'ien-wang; catur mahārāja); he watched over the north of Mount Sumeru. He is often pictured carrying a halberd, money bag, or mongoose; sometimes an attendant carries one of these items for him.[29] The first surviving depiction of him as one of four guardians appears on a railing in Bhārhut, India, and dates to the second century B.C.[30]

From India the cult moved to Central Asia, specifically to Khotan,[31] where the god was called Vaiśravana, Vaiśramana, and, more popularly, Vrrīśamaṃ.[32] Given Khotan's position to the north of India, it made eminent sense that the guardian of the north should watch over it. Chinese and Tibetan texts tell of the Buddha delegating to Vaiśravana the task of protecting the Central Asian kingdom of Khotan.[33] A third-to-fourth-century Khotanese monastery at Rawak, excavated by Sir Aurel Stein, contained a pair of statues who stood by the sides of one gate. Between each statue's legs were the head and buxom chest of a small woman.[34]

This depiction of Vaiśravana is a visual reference to the legendary founding of Khotan; the kings of Khotan all claimed descent from Vaiśravana. As Hsüan-tsang recounts in his *Record of a Journey to the West (Ta T'ang hsi-yü chi)* (completed in 646), the founder of the kingdom had no son.

> Fearing lest his house should become extinct, he repaired to the temple of Vaiśravana and prayed to him to grant his desire. Forthwith the head of the image opened at the top, and there came forth a young child. Taking it, he returned to his palace. The whole country addressed congratulations to him, but as the child would not drink milk, he feared he would not live. He then returned to the temple and again asked [the god] for means to nourish him. The earth in front of the divinity then suddenly opened and offered an appearance like a breast. The divine child drank from it eagerly.[35]

Why show a buxom woman at Rawak and not a breast emerging from the ground? Alexander Soper offers this ingenious explanation: "The outer gate guardians at Rawak in the Khotan vicinity, who were found standing each with the well-developed bust of a diminutive woman rising from the pedestal between his feet, represent an artist's re-interpretation of this story. A shape like a breast, rising alone out of the earth, would have been a startling sight and one not easy to comprehend; how much better to convey the same idea by showing a traditional mother-figure, like an earth goddess."[36]

The story of the breast enjoyed wide circulation in eighth-century China. Under the entry for Khotan (Yü-t'ien) in his dictionary, Hui-lin (750–820) summarized Hsüan-tsang's version and then added his own comment: "Today this realm actually is one of four cities in the An-hsi (Kucha) region. Within its walls there is a seven-storied wooden temple to Vaiśravana. The deity resides in the upper story of the tower and is very efficacious."[37] Although Hui-lin indicates that Vaiśravaṇa's image was in a tower on the Khotanese city walls, other depictions from eighth-century Khotan show him flush with the wall, next to a gate. A sculpture from the late-eighth-century shrine at another Khotanese site, Dandān-Uiliq, shows Vaiśravaṇa standing on top of a demon by a doorway.[38] His head is missing, but he carries his characteristic money bag in his right hand. On the lower left is a fresco of a woman with a small boy at her side who appears to want milk, another variation, perhaps, on the earth-breast miracle. In eighth-century Khotan, Vaiśravaṇa was depicted sometimes as a relief figure embedded in a wall by gates, sometimes in watch-towers on city walls.

Vaiśravaṇa—P'i-sha-men, as he was called in Chinese—continued to be associated with walls and gates in China. By the tenth and eleventh centuries, legends circulated in China that suggested the worship of the god had been introduced to China from Khotan and explained why P'i-sha-men's statue always appeared on wall towers, often in the northwest corner of city walls. The ninth-century *Ritual Regulations of P'i-sha-men (P'i-sha-men i-kuei)*,[39] the late tenth-century *Biographies of Eminent Monks Compiled in the Sung (Sung kao-seng chuan)*[40] and *Synoptic History of the Sangha Compiled in the Great Sung (Ta Sung seng-shih lüeh)*,[41] the early twelfth-century *Collectanea of the Patriarchal Hall (Tsu-t'ing shih-yüan)*,[42] and the thirteenth-century *General History of the Buddhas and Patriarchs (Fo-tsu t'ung-chi)*[43] all contain different versions of the same legend concerning P'i-sha-men's introduction into China by the famous Tantric monk Amoghavajra (Pu-k'ung; var. Ta-kuang-chih) (705–774). Here, in full, is the ninth-century version, entitled "The Heavenly King of the North, the Great P'i-sha-men":

In 742, the five nations of the 'Abāssid Caliphate[44] and Samarkand surrounded the city of An-hsi [Kucha]. On the eleventh day of the second month came a request for troops to save them. The emperor told the Ch'an teacher I-hsing: "Reverend sir, An-hsi has been surrounded by the 'Abāssid Caliphate and Samarkand.[45] . . . There is a request for troops. An-hsi is twelve thousand *li* [four thousand miles] from the capital [now Sian]. The troops will travel eight months before they get to An-hsi. Thus I have no way to help them."

I-hsing said, "Why doesn't your majesty ask the troops of the the Heavenly King of the North, P'i-sha-men, to send help."

The emperor said, "How can I obtain help?"

I-hsing said, "Call the barbarian[46] monk Amoghavajra and you can obtain help."

An edict was issued summoning Amoghavajra to the court. The emperor called the monk for no other reason than that the city of An-hsi had been surrounded by enemy troops of the five nations. . . .

Amoghavajra said, "Your majesty should carry an incense burner to the place where I will conduct the ritual. And your majesty should pray to the Heavenly King of the North to send divine troops to save them."

The emperor quickly entered the ritual area and prayed. Before [Amoghavajra] had recited the secret words twice seven times, the emperor suddenly saw two to three hundred divine beings wearing armor and standing in front of the ritual area. The emperor asked the monk, "Who are these people?"

Amoghavajra said, "This is Tu-chien, the second son of P'i-sha-men, the Heavenly King of the North. He will lead the heavenly soldiers to save An-hsi and accordingly has come to take his leave."

The emperor provided food offerings and sent them off.

Then, in the fourth month of that year, a memorial came from An-hsi, which said that at midday on the eleventh day of the second month [the same day the emperor and Amoghavajra had prayed] thirty *li* [ten miles] to the northeast of the city dark clouds and fog had appeared. In the fog were beings whose bodies were one *chang* [ten feet] tall. About three to five hundred beings all wore gold armor. After dusk came the sound of drums and loud cries. The sound reverberated three hundred *li* [one hundred miles]. The trembling of the earth and the shaking of the hills stopped after three days. The frightened troops of the five nations all retreated. The soldiers appeared inside the barracks. Moreover, golden rats chewed the strings of their bows and crossbows and destroyed their other weapons so that none could be used.

There were some old men unable to flee. The troops I was in charge of wanted to hurt them. From the sky came a voice that said, "Let them go. Killing is not allowed." After a moment we looked back and saw a great bright light above the northern gate tower of the city. P'i-sha-men, the Heavenly King, had manifested himself above the tower. He looked liked the portraits of the Heavenly King.[47]

This is a dramatically compelling story. In a time when it would have taken troops eight months to get to An-hsi and it took two months for a memorial to arrive, only P'i-sha-men's troops could arrive quickly enough to save the surrounded city. The drama is heightened by the two months' lapse between the emperor's vision of P'i-sha-men and the confirmation of his appearance in An-hsi. Once again, a monk plays the decisive role in introducing the worship of a new god; Amoghavajra's identification of the figure who appears as P'i-sha-men's son is crucial to the story. His rats infiltrate the ramparts around the enemy camp, and he himself chooses to appear above the northern(!) gate tower of the city.

In fact, the tale is too exciting to be true. Matsumoto Bunzaburō provides five reasons why the events of this tale could not have happened in 742. The most damning among them are that Amoghavajra was not in China between 741 and 746 and that I-hsing (b. 683) died in 727.[48] Other legends linking the introduction of the cult to P'i-sha-men with Khotan also circulated in the Sung. One eleventh-century catalogue of paintings reports that an emissary to Khotan, sent to the T'ang emperor Hsüan-tsung to copy a portrait of Vaiśravaṇa, painted it in 725 for the temple in K'ai-feng.[49]

Do these Sung legends contain any elements of truth? Although the episode of P'i-sha-men's manifestation above the gate tower could not have taken place in 742, his cult did exist in China at the time. The god figures prominently in *The Golden Light Sūtra (Suvarnaprabhāsa-sūtra)*, which Dharmarakṣa first translated into Chinese at the beginning of the fifth century. P'i-sha-men was worshiped in his own right by around 600. Two of the guardian kings at fifth-century Yün-kang cave 8 who grasp lances in one hand and possibly purses in the other might be P'i-sha-men. The remains of what may have been stone breasts lie at their feet.[50] The first certain depiction of P'i-sha-men in China dates to the early T'ang (or slightly before) and is at Lung-hsing monastery, Chiung-hsia, Szechwan, suggesting that the cult came first to northwest China from Central Asia. As at Rawak, a small female figure stands between P'i-sha-men's legs.[51] And the first textual evidence outside the Buddhist canon is from the official histories: the nickname of Chien-ch'eng, a son of the founder of the T'ang, emperor Kao-tsu (r. 618–626), was P'i-sha-men.[52] The official histories do not explain why he had this nickname, but it is possible that the T'ang emperors looked to P'i-sha-men to protect their ruling house in the same way he was thought to protect the Khotanese.[53] Whatever the reason, Chien-ch'eng's nickname testifies to the importance of the deity P'i-sha-men in the early seventh century.

The linking of Amoghavajra and the cult to P'i-sha-men in the legend is significant. Amoghavajra did translate the *Heavenly King P'i-sha-men Sūtra (P'i-sha-men t'ien-wang ching)*, a shortened version of *The Golden Light Sūtra*.[54] Amoghavajra played a real role in the religious exchanges between Khotan and China, actively propagating the worship of Mañjuśrī and Samantabadhra. Raoul Birnbaum calls Amoghavajra "one of the most extraordinary figures in the history of Chinese Buddhism: charismatic speaker and passionate teacher, tireless translator and effective writer, ritual master and magician, advisor and preceptor to three emperors, builder of major temples, transmitter and consolidator of tantric teachings in China."[55] Linguistic evidence testifies that the cult came into China from Khotan. The T'ang pronunciation of P'i-sha-men, Bhi-sha-man, represented the Chinese transcription of the Khotanese popular form, Vrrīśamaṃ.[56]

The cult continued to spread in the succeeding century. A time of frequent contact with Khotan, the eighth century—with its fighting, epidemics, and chaos—prompted a sense that the end of a cosmic era was imminent, and both the *Candragarbha-sūtra (Yüeh-tsang ching)* and the *Sūryagarbha-sūtra (Jih-tsang ching)* argued that Khotan was the one place where the law would be protected.[57] As Khotan acquired a reputation as a center for Buddhist studies, many Chinese flocked there. On their return journeys, they brought back texts prophesying the end of the kalpa, such as Fa-ch'eng's (ca. 780–860) 851 translation of *Śākyamuni Buddha's Record of the Total Destruction of the Counterfeit Dharma Era (Shih-chia-mou-ni ju-lai hsiang-fa mieh-chin chih-chi)*, in which P'i-sha-men leads a group of monks to a safe haven.[58]

Epigraphical evidence from the ninth century reveals that, as P'i-sha-men entered China, his iconography changed. In India he carried a lance, money bag, or mongoose. In China he holds a spear or trident in his right hand and a stūpa in his left. An 839 inscription from a temple to P'i-sha-men in Flourishing T'ang (Hsing-t'ang) monastery begins by saying; "He who is P'i-sha-men, the Heavenly King, is the emissary of the Buddha. He grasps a crooked spear *(wu-kou)* in his right hand, and his left hand holds up a stūpa."[59] A fragmentary 882 text from Kung-hsien, Honan, quotes a sūtra as saying; "The north has a god called P'i-sha-men. He obtained salvation in Khotan. His body is that of a king. The god's achievements [gap in text]. . . . [His left hand] grasps a gold spear; the right holds a stūpa." The text continues; "[The devotees] reverently erected his image to the left of the three gates. Above he protects the dharma *(fo-fa)* and brings peace to the empire *(kuo-t'u)*."[60] As in Khotan, P'i-sha-men's function was not only to serve as guardian of the dharma but more generally to serve as guardian of the empire as well. Similarly, *The Golden Light Sūtra* had promised his protection for those who patronized Buddhist teaching.

Many depictions of P'i-sha-men found at Tun-huang confirm the standardization of his iconography by the tenth century. A few woodblock prints from Tun-huang suggest that P'i-sha-men was worshiped both as one of the four guardian kings and as a deity in his own right. Four unbound paintings of the guardian kings were found at Tun-huang along with four pages from the *Heart Sūtra* and a simple cover. A dedicatory colophon is dated 890. The guardian kings of the east, south, and west carry weapons in both hands, but P'i-sha-men, the guardian of the north, has a trident-shaped staff in one hand and a stūpa in the other.[61] So, even when depicted with the other three kings, he stands out as specifically charged with protecting the dharma. A 947 text accompanying a woodblock print of P'i-sha-men from Tun-huang claims: "The northern ruler governs all the bad ghosts and deities of the empire. If one can expel his own faults and pray sincerely, then one may happily receive full protection and good fortune."[62] Having so described his purpose, the military governor, Ts'ao Yüan-chung, ordered the carving and printing of the text and accompanying illustration.[63] Reproduced in fig. 3.1, this print contains many of the standard iconographic features associated with Vaiśravaṇa. He is depicted standing on the hands of the earth goddess; his left hand holds a stūpa while his right hand holds a halberd. The

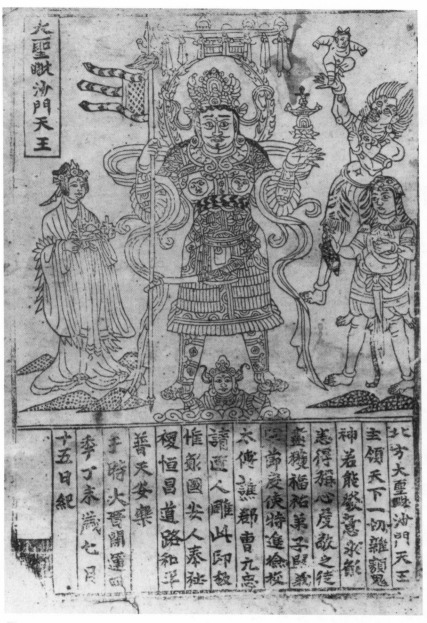

Figure 3.1. P'i-sha'men with attendants. Tun-huang cave 17, Five Dynasties, dated 947. (Stein Collection, British Museum)

lower figure to his left holds a mongoose (linking him with Kubera), and the upper figure to his left holds an infant (recalling the legendary founding of Khotan). His daughter, Śrī Devī, stands to his right.

The legend of 742 bears another look, not because it was true, but because the commentaries to it reveal so much about the history of the cult in the Sung. Tsan-ning (919–1002) added to his version in his *Sung Biographies of Eminent Monks Compiled in the Sung:* "As a result the emperor ordered an image of this heavenly king to be placed in the watchtowers *(ch'eng-lou)* of the cities throughout the various circuits."[64] In another work, *Synoptic History of the Sangha,* Tsan-ning repeated the story under the heading "Heavenly King of Watchtowers" *(Ch'eng-tu t'ien-wang):*

> The emperor accordingly ordered the military governors of the different circuits to each put up and make offerings to an image of the Guardian King and his retinue on the northwest corner of the city walls. He also ordered Buddhist monasteries to place an image in their outer buildings.
>
> Even today, on the first day of each month, the prefectures all present incense, offerings of food, songs, and dancing. They call it making the Heavenly King happy.[65]

At the beginning of the eleventh century Mu-an Shan-ch'ing wrote: "Today the images are placed on the walls around the prefectural government offices or in monasteries or barracks because of this [miracle]."[66] And Chih-p'an added in the mid-thirteenth century: "Today [images of] P'i-sha-men are installed in buildings, in watchtowers, and on barracks because of this [miracle]."[67]

The story of Amoghavajra and Vaiśravaṇa, like so many other legends, is a just-so tale told to explain a real phenomena: the appearance of Vaiśravaṇa's images in cities, barracks, and monasteries all over China. Southern Sung (1127–1276) gazetteers bear out these commentators' descriptions: those from Yen-chou (Chin-te county, Chekiang), Hang-chow (Chekiang), T'ai-chou (Chekiang), and Fu-chou (Fukien) all list temples to the god in government offices and monasteries. Those in Yen-chou and T'ai-chou were built on the northwestern city walls.[68] The discussion above of P'i-sha-men's purported appearance to the emperor in 742 should make us leery of Sung accounts of events taking place in the T'ang and Five Dynasties, but I list them separately because they testify to the geographical spread of the cult to Szechwan, Shansi, and Hopei by Sung times (see table 3.1). So, by the end of the Sung, P'i-sha-men, who had begun his career as a foreign guardian king of the north, had come to serve as a guardian figure all over China.

What was P'i-sha-men doing on the walls or in the gate towers of cities and monasteries? Exactly what an increasing number of wall-and-

Table 3.1 P'i-sha-men's Miracles According to Sung Sources

YEAR	PLACE	EVENT	SOURCE
627–649	Ch'ang-an, Shansi	P'i-sha-men's son, Na-t'uo, appears	*SKSC, T* 50.791a
761	Ta-t'ung, Shansi	rebels hide in P'i-sha-men's temple	Ssu-ma Kuang, *Tzu-chih t'ung-chien* (Peking: Ku-chi ch'u-pan-she, 1956), 222.7109
795	P'ing-shan, Hopei	P'i-sha-men appears	*SKSC, T* 50.874a
860–873	Ch'eng-tu, Szechwan	P'i-sha-men appears and frightens away rebel troops	*SKSC, T* 50.882a
870	Shuo county, Shansi	P'i-sha-men appears to descendant of T'ang ruling house	*Chiu Wu-tai shih* (Peking: Chung-hua shu-chü, 1975), 25.332–333
934	T'ai-yüan, Shansi	P'i-sha-men appears on wall	*Chiu Wu-tai shih* 75.988
935	Ta-ming, Hopei	armor named for P'i-sha-men	*Chiu Wu-tai shih* 47.643

moat gods and monastic guardians began to do: protecting these places. There are striking similarities among these different gods. People called P'i-sha-men both by his name or by his position, guardian king. The cult to P'i-sha-men grew before the assumption of office by local gods in the ninth and tenth centuries, when woodblock printing came into widespread use. Accordingly, sources are much richer for the end of the T'ang than for the beginning, and thus any chronology must be tentative and any assertion of causation provisional. Nevertheless, the evidence that we do have suggests that the widespread popularity of the Indian god Vaiśravaṇa encouraged the spread of monastic guardians and then wall-and-moat gods.

KUAN YÜ: FROM POPULAR GOD TO MONASTIC GUARDIAN

Kuan Yü provides a good example of a god who began as a local god and became a monastic guardian only in the ninth century, after many local gods had taken up office.[69] A hero of the Three Kingdoms period, Kuan Yü died in 219 and was awarded a posthumous title in 260. He does not appear in the the earliest accounts of the founding of Yü-ch'üan monastery by the famous monk Chih-i (538–597), the founder of the T'ien-t'ai school of Buddhism. Chih-i's disciple and biographer Kuan-ting (561–632) says of the site of the monastery that it was formerly desolate and mountainous. The gods, wild beasts, and snakes were ferocious, but Chih-i decided to found a monastery there. A drought occurred that summer, and the local people thought the gods were angry. Chih-i went to the source of the stream and pronounced a spell. Rain followed.[70]

What a nice demonstration of the Buddhists' superior strength! Reminiscent of earlier tales about the suppression of indigenous cults, this anecdote highlights the civilizing qualities of Buddhism. Once the monastery had been established, neither animals nor gods posed a threat to the inhabitants. Kuan Yü does not appear in either an early seventh-century inscription nor in one dated 722, which features the Ch'an teacher Shen-hsiu (606–706) rather than Chih-i.[71]

Given the strength of the Chinese oral tradition, it is always dangerous to assume that the written record provides the only version of a legend, but these early texts indicate that, in the period before local gods took office, Chih-i was perfectly capable of founding the monastery without Kuan Yü's assistance. Kuan Yü makes his debut in a text dated 820, which says that a temple to him is located to the northwest of the monastery. It tells of his appearance to Chih-i, his offer to donate land for the construction of the monastery, and his request that Chih-i leave the site. The same night there was a terrible storm. In the morning a pile of high-quality, neatly stacked lumber appeared, presumably to be used in building the monastery. The minister of works to the military governor of Ching-nan, Yin P'ei-chün, claimed in a text to commemorate a renovation of the temple that Kuan Yü determined "whether the district flourishes or declines, whether the annual harvest is plentiful or barren." As a final proof of Kuan Yü's power, Yin reported that a white snake appeared on the building day and that the monks of the monastery all thought it miraculous.[72] This enthusiastic language, so characteristic of inscriptions to popular deities, suggests why Kuan Yü came to be linked to Chih-i's sixth-century founding of the monastery only in the ninth century. He had in the meantime become simply too powerful a local deity for the Buddhists to ignore or to try to suppress.

An inscription from a Soochow monastery tells of another god who, like Kuan Yü, appeared in a vision to donate land to a monastery; the title of this text specifically refers to the deity Ku Yeh-wang as a *ch'ieh-lan shen,* or monastic guardian. In 944, on the night that a monastery was completed, the spirit of a Six Dynasties official, Ku Yeh-wang, accompanied by two attendants, showed himself to a dreaming carpenter and said: "This is my former residence. It has already fallen into ruins. Today you built a monastery on top of my house. I am very pleased

about this Buddhist monastery. Please put up my image, and I will protect this monastery." The next day the carpenter told two monks what he
had dreamt, but they remained skeptical. That night he dreamt again of
Ku Yeh-wang, who said: "How can you not believe me? You need only to
look where the foundation of the former monastery borders on the
water. There is an old stele that will serve as proof." The next day the
monks found the stone, were convinced, and put up images of Ku and his
attendants.[73] In a 1046 version of the same events, the carpenter has
dropped out, and the deity appears to the two monks directly,[74] suggesting that the *ch'ieh-lan* deities began with the support of local people and
the monks gradually overcame their own resistance to them. A quid pro
quo is at work in both versions. Because the monastery does not displace
the temple, the god's original devotees are pleased. And because the local
deity agrees to serve the Buddha as protector, the Buddhists can (and do)
claim a superior position.

Accounts about Kuan Yü did not include a similar dialogue between
god and monk until the eleventh century, when Chang Shang-ying
(1043–1122), a famous lay practitioner of Ch'an Buddhism, wrote a
highly embellished version of Kuan Yü's investiture as guardian deity.[75]
Kuan Yü assumed various shapes and appeared to Chih-i: "Tigers and
leopards howled and paused. Snakes and pythons coiled up and stared.
Ghosts and sprites cackled and screamed. With bloody lips and sharp
teeth, hair in disarray, spirit soldiers were fierce and angry. Of ghostly
aspect and hideous substance, one by one, they rapidly assumed a thousand different shapes."[76] The unintimidated monk angrily asked them to
identify themselves. Kuan Yü gave a brief account of his life and then
said: "I preside over this mountain. I am fond of only what has been
killed, and I eat only raw meat." Then he admitted to the monk that his
strength had been spent in the contest, offered to donate his hill to him,
and, with his son, promised to protect the dharma forever.[77]

Thus it was only in the Sung that Kuan Yü acquired the full biographical accoutrements of monastic guardian and that the conception of
the monastic guardian's role had taken shape—so that Kuan Yü in Hupei
and Ku Yeh-wang in Kiangsu could bear the same label of *ch'ieh-lan
shen.* The Buddhist guardian deities resembled the wall-and-moat gods
in that both were conceived of as slots to be filled by local gods, who
sometimes were called by name and sometimes by label.

WALL-AND-MOAT GODS: THE EFFECTS OF
GOVERNMENT RECOGNITION

The earliest sources, from the sixth and seventh centuries, refer to wall-
and-moat gods only as a type of god similar to a mountain or stream

deity.[78] They are simply nameless gods who watch over city walls. Later on, in the ninth and tenth centuries, after many local gods took office, devotees began to think of individual deities as holding the position of wall-and-moat god. They called them either by position (wall-and-moat god of a given place) or by name.

One of the earliest texts to mention the wall-and-moat gods is the official history of the Northern Ch'i dynasty, which describes a battle in 555 for Ying-ch'eng (now Wu-ch'ang, Hupei), where enemy troops blockaded the city: "Everyone had given up hope. The prefect agonized alone, and the people were frightened. Mu-jung Yen led with loyalty and righteousness. Moreover he was pleased to soothe them. Within the city walls, there was one temple, commonly called the wall-and-moat god. Prayer took place there on both official and private occasions. Thus, following the desires of both officers and soldiers, [Mu-jung] led everyone to pray there. They hoped to obtain divine protection."[79] And so they did: a wind came up, and the troops dispersed, although Mu-jung and his troops were finally defeated. Even though the wall-and-moat god was an indigenous deity, he was thought to perform the same type of miracles Vaiśravaṇa was credited with centuries later. And, like Vaiśravaṇa, his temples were associated with walls. Notice that, because the term *ch'eng-huang* had not yet come into wide use, this author has to explain who the wall-and-moat god is.

The wall-and-moat god in this tale appears to be a god who presided over the city walls just as other gods presided over mountains and rivers. Even before China was unified in 221 B.C., devotees had made offerings to the walls around cities.[80] The ritual codes of the T'ang suggest the practice continued. Following the 726 controversy in the T'ang court about the advisability of reordering the classical text of *The Book of Rites (Li-chi)*, Chang Yüeh (667–730) was appointed to draft a new code with the help of four scholars. In 732, two years after Chang's death, *The Ritual Code of the Kai-yüan (713–741) Period in the Great T'ang (Ta T'ang Kai-yüan li)* was issued.[81] Included among its provisions were rituals to be conducted on the local level in the case of too much rain: prayers were to be offered to the gates of the city walls *(ch'eng-men)* in both prefectures and counties.[82] *The Compendium of Administrative Law of the Six Divisions of the T'ang Bureaucracy (Ta T'ang liu-tien;* issued in 738) also specifies: "If there is too much rain, [officials of] the capital should honor the several gates. [The ceremony to] each gate should be separated by three days. Each day honor one. If the rain does not stop, then pray to the hills and streams, marchmounts, seas, and rivers. If, after three days, the rain has still not stopped, then pray to the altar of grain *(she-chi)* and the ancestral temples."[83] The inclusion of the city-gate gods in this list suggests that they were just like the gods of the hills and rivers. The term "wall-and-moat" *(ch'eng-huang)* appears in neither of these compilations, but Chang Yüeh, the compiler of the K'ai-yüan Code, does use the term in a prayer dated 717 to the wall-and-moat god of Ching-chou (Hupei): "The [gods of] hills and swamps circulate life force *(ch'i)* to derive their efficacy. The wall-and-moat [gods] use accumulated yin as power *(te)*."[84] Chang explains why the god was thought to be able to bring an end to rain: because the power of wall-and-moat gods is based on yin forces and excessive rain is also caused by yin, they can make the rain stop. The wall-and-moat god of Ching-chou is analogous to the god of any hill or swamp; as mountain or swamp deities guard specific mountains and swamps, wall-and-moat gods preside over a city's walls. Chang does not refer to the wall-and-moat god as a position held by a given deity.

Even in the late eighth or early ninth century, an anonymous author of a Taoist text still felt the need to explain the origins of the wall-and-moat god. The text purports to be Li Ch'un-feng's (602–670) commentary on a revelation given to the Taoist patriarch Chang Tao-ling at the end of the second century.[85] The author appends the following gloss on the term "wall-and-moat" *(ch'eng-huang)*:

> The text above formerly just said earth shrines *(she-miao)*. There was no wall-and-moat god.
>
> The wall-and-moat deity originated from the tomb of King Jui of Wu in the middle of the Wu kingdom [the region just north of the Yangtze]. Subsequently in the time of the Chin [265–419], the wall around the capital of Wu that the prefect Liu Wen-ching was building reached the tomb. That night the walls all collapsed, and the earth was completely removed by shadow spirit troops. On the next day the wall could not be seen, and the earth could not be obtained. The situation continued like this for seven or eight more times.
>
> The prefect then ordered his men at night to catch the offenders. During the night, one prince came out from the earth and was followed by several tens of thousands of soldiers. Still, the man whom the masses had grabbed cursed them saying: "I am King Jui of Wu. My tomb is two *chang* [twenty feet] underneath the earth. How can your lordship cruelly build over my tomb? Every night I have people make the walls collapse and have the earth removed. There is no other evil being.
>
> "If your lordship could move the wall and make it curve one hundred paces away from my tomb, I would protect the wall and the lives of the people and animals, and bring peace for generations."
>
> The prefect accordingly left the tomb intact, moved the wall, and built a temple. Thus originated the wall-and-moat divine officers.[86]

In this account the wall-and-moat god is not just a nameless god who watches over the city walls. He has gained an identity. He is King Jui of Wu, the *ch'eng-huang* god of this city. Like the legend of Vaiśravaṇa's

742 appearance, this is a just-so story that seeks to explain a real phenomenon: the appearance of wall-and-moat gods all over China by the eighth and ninth centuries. Lack of supporting documentation makes it difficult to accept the author's claim that King Jui of Wu was the first wall-and-moat god.

Sometime between the eighth and tenth centuries, the wall-and-moat god began to be thought of as a position different gods could hold in the underworld bureaucracy. In a commentary to instructions on how to petition to expel evil gods and ghosts, the anonymous author of the King Jui of Wu tale equates the relationship of wall-and-moat gods with earth shrines *(she-miao)* to that of prefectures with counties: "Just as first prefectures and then counties follow each other in eliminating evil-doers, so too do the wall-and-moat and earth-shrine [gods] send these documents to each other in order to apprehend demons."[87]

Itinerant Taoists, like the unschooled Buddhists who told of gods converting to Buddhism, probably encouraged the worship of wall-and-moat gods as they were propagating their own version of hell.[88] The parallel divine and bureaucratic hierarchies of later Taoism were not fully worked out in the eighth century, but some Taoists seem to have glimpsed the potential usefulness of city gods in their struggle to mark themselves off from local cults. A given local god could be designated a god of walls and moats and so be subsumed into a Taoist pantheon without alienating any original devotees. Never shy about (though always loath to admit) borrowing from their Buddhist colleagues, these Taoists may have seen the city gods as a counterpart to monastic guardians.

Other T'ang sources indicate that the bureaucratic conception of the wall-and-moat god was not limited to Taoists. One late-eighth-century tale suggests the links between hell and the rise of the cult to the god of walls and moats. A finance official from Hsüan-chou (Hsüan-ch'eng, Anhwei) is prematurely summoned to the underworld, where the presiding officer decides to send him back. The officer turns out to be a god of walls and moats, who had himself served as the prefect of Hsüan-chou before his death.[89] A ninth-century account of a visit to hell, contained in a Buddhist anthology, recounts that the wall-and-moat god who presided over hell granted the narrator five more years of life.[90] Finally, one tale from the late ninth or early tenth century shows just how close the heavenly and earthly bureaucracies had become. As a Szechwanese merchant was praying at the White Horse (Pai-ma) temple after his return from a trip, he heard the god say: " 'You and I have known each other for many years now. I am about to leave this area. Accordingly I say goodbye to you.' The surprised guest asked, 'Where are you going?' He replied, 'I have been appointed to be a wall-and-moat god of Hunan. The emperor has promoted me because of the slight virtue I showed to the people of San-hsia.' "[91] The bureaucratic analogy is complete. The god is not just an individual who happens to be the wall-and-moat god of San-hsia. He actually has a term in office. As in the earthly bureaucracy, the wall-and-moat god serves at the pleasure of the emperor. And, as in the earthly bureaucracy, he is promoted on the basis of virtuous service.

If the wall-and-moat god served in a heavenly bureaucracy modeled on the earthly bureaucracy, what, then, did the earthly bureaucrats make of the wall-and-moat gods? Every indication is that before 900 T'ang bureaucrats paid little heed to them.

Li Yang-ping begins a 759 inscription from Chin-yün (Chekiang) by observing: "The wall-and-moat god is not in the register of sacrifices *(ssu-tien)*. His temples are located all over Wu-Yüeh [the Lower Yangtze valley]."[92] Li's observations mesh with what little is known about the circumscribed nature of the T'ang register of sacrifices. The register was a list of all local gods at whose temples officials were authorized to make offerings, usually in the fall and spring. By the Sung, being listed in the register also implied eligibility to receive government funds for temple repairs;[93] it is not clear whether or not it meant this during the T'ang.

The evidence about granting titles to deities during the T'ang is sparse. The administrative code of the T'ang lists titles given to mountains and rivers, starting with the promotion of the god of the Lo River to marquis *(hou)* in 688.[94] In 746 the marchmounts were given titles.[95] In 747, the emperor explained: "Since the five marchmounts have already been enfeoffed as kings, the four rivers should be promoted to the rank of lord *(kung)*."[96] The T'ang emperors saw themselves as innovators. The 748 edict promoting the Northern Peak (Heng Mountain in Shansi) claims: "The former emperors did not make kings of the five peaks nor lords of the four rivers."[97] For the most part, the T'ang rulers seem to have limited themselves to giving nature gods titles, but other gods received titles as well, as Terry Kleeman shows in this volume.

The wall-and-moat gods may not have received titles, but they were worshiped all over the empire. Surviving prayers of T'ang officials indicate a wide geographic scope for the cult to the wall-and-moat god, encompassing temples in Chekiang, Hupei, and Kwangsi.[98] At the end of the T'ang, Li Shang-yin's prayers show that the wall-and-moat gods continued to be associated with protecting cities. He wrote: "I reverently make offerings to the god of walls and moats who dredges moats and upholds the walls—the means to secure our borders."[99]

In the years before 900 the cult to the wall-and-moat gods seems to have survived without active government support. The situation began to change, possibly in the late T'ang, with a title grant in 898 to a wall-and-moat god in Hua-chou (Shensi),[100] and certainly in the Five Dynasties period.[101] In 908 the Latter Liang awarded the title of marquis to the wall-and-moat god of Yüeh-chou (Shao-hsing), who happened to be the former magistrate.[102] In 934 the Latter T'ang promoted the wall-and-moat gods of Hangchow, Hu-chou, and Yüeh-chou.[103] And, in 950, the wall-and-moat god of Meng-chou (Kwangsi) was rewarded for protecting his city from an attack by enemy troops.[104] The awarding of titles fostered the continued growth of the cult in the early Sung. Ou-yang Hsiu included Li Yang-ping's 759 comment about the register of sacrifices in his epigraphical catalogue and appended a note: "But now [in the mid-eleventh century], [temples to the wall-and-moat god] are not just in the Wu-Yüeh region. They are all over the empire, but there are few in counties [as opposed to prefectures]."[105] The title granting of the Five Dynasties probably encouraged the cult, but through the first hundred years of Sung rule (960–1060), the designation of local gods as wall-and-moat gods remained on a largely ad hoc basis.

One tightly compressed inscription from the early eleventh century tells of a mother-son pair of gods with multiple identities, only one being that of wall-and-moat god. The mother became a vegetarian, Buddha-fearing dragon, her son, a god of walls and moats. The text begins by describing a mountain on which an official lived during the Three Kingdoms period. Following his death, his wife met and slept with an unidentified old man; their son was transformed into a dragon. In 589, the dragon-mother met a monk, asked to receive the precepts, and said she wanted to hear the dharma. So far the narrative follows the standard pattern for converting local gods. A monastery, containing a dragon hall, was founded on the site. In 619 the name of the prefecture was changed to T'ai-chou, and the ancient residence of the official was made into the new yamen. Everyone agreed that the dragon-mother's son was the wall-and-moat god.[106]

The mention of the wall-and-moat god comes out of nowhere. The author's awkward attempt to make sense of the two gods' changing roles highlights the fluid nature of divinity in the T'ang and the Sung. The career paths of the dragon god and his mother embody all the changes in the pantheon taking place before the eleventh century: the conversion of local gods to Buddhism as well as their assumption of positions as city gods.

The strong links between the monastery and the mother-son pair suggest that the resident Buddhists may have had something to do with the son's appointment as god of walls and moats. It was yet another way to enhance the god's following among the people of T'ai-chou. Not just the guardian of a monastery, the dragon son (like Vaiśravaṇa) guarded other structures as well. By protecting the yamen, he became the god of walls and moats for the entire prefecture (and was thereby eligible for government funds). Might the idea of the god of walls and moats as a position to be held by a given deity—the dragon in this case—have been a transmutation of Vaiśravaṇa and the monastic guardians?

Why would the T'ai-chou Buddhists label the dragon son a wall-and-moat god? Designation as a *ch'eng-huang* and placement in the government register of sacrifices offered real benefits. The dragon son was awarded his first title during the Wu-Yüeh reign, received a plaque (the first stage of official recognition) in the Cheng-ho (1111–1117) reign, and was promoted in 1129, 1138, 1168, 1196, 1198, 1200, and 1204.[107] A group of supporters must have been continuously petitioning local officials on his behalf. Other gods were being honored at the same time. Kuan Yü, the monastic guardian at Yü-ch'üan monastery, received his first title in 1069.[108]

Starting in the late eleventh and early twelfth centuries, the government sharply increased its investment in local pantheons, as a comparison of the administrative law codes of the T'ang, Five Dynasties, and Sung shows. These codes, incomplete as they are, suggest the scope of government activity in the pre-Sung period; neither compilation lists more than twenty titles for the duration of the T'ang or Five Dynasties period.[109]

The incomplete lists of titles granted to deities in the Sung administrative law code total over two hundred pages, and they show that the number of titles granted in one year shot up in 1075 to thirty-seven and remained at a high level from then on.[110] Local people petitioned for titles, and the government sent inspectors from neighboring prefectures to check the god's claim to have performed miracles. Once they had confirmed the veracity of the miracles, they recommended the god's promotion. Independent evidence confirms the expansion of the government's role: the turn-around time between the appearance of a new god and the government's award of a title shrank to a decade or two by the twelfth century. The Sung central government, pressed on its northern borders by Jurchen and then Mongol invaders and financially strapped as well, found the awarding of titles a good way to maintain a presence in local society. The express desire of the central government was to harness the gods' power.

The increase in title-granting activity in the late eleventh and early twelfth centuries was so sudden that one astute observer, Chao Yü-shih (1175–1231), wrote about the resulting variations in titles given to wall-and-moat gods: "Local wall-and-moat gods differ and are not of one type. Now these temples verge on being everywhere in the empire. Some have received name plaques from the central government, and some, noble ranks. Of those who have not yet received official titles, some have assumed the name of the god from neighboring prefectures, and some have taken a legendary appellation. Those in the prefectures differ, and those in the counties are not the same."[111] Chao hints at the ingenuity of the devotees of untitled gods: we may infer that the people whose gods did not have official titles would create a claim for their local god in the hope that he would eventually receive government recognition. There follows a long list of wall-and-moat gods with their inconsistent titles. Some had four-character titles, some two. Some were marquises, some kings. In the period between 1075 and the 1130s, officials at the Court of Imperial Sacrifices (T'ai-ch'ang ssu) who were in charge of issuing titles could hardly keep up with all the requests flooding their office. It was impossible for them to award the same kinds of titles to wall-and-moat gods, especially since their long and uneven development meant there were many different types: "P'eng-chou (Szechwan) not only has a *ch'eng-huang* temple, it also has a temple to the outer wall of the city *(lo-ch'eng)*. Fen-i county of Yüan-chou (Kiangsi) not only has a *ch'eng-huang* temple, it also has a temple to the moat around the county government offices *(hsien-huang)*. These are without precedent."[112] No wonder the Sung bureaucrats awarded these different wall-and-moat gods different titles!

Like bureaucrats everywhere, the Sung officials in the title-granting branch of the government thought in specific categories. Two later compilations suggest that the category of wall-and-moat god took shape at the time of the expansion of the title-granting system at the end of the eleventh century. The Sung administrative code gives twenty-one different examples of temple plaques given to wall-and-moat gods in the period from 1102 to 1170. This list is incomplete, but the grouping together of the wall-and-moat gods testifies to the existence of a bureaucratic category. It is followed by lists of earth gods *(t'u-ti)*, dragon temples, hill gods, and water gods.[113] The official history of the Sung confirms the existence of these categories, saying that "marchmount and river gods, wall-and-moat gods, immortals and Buddhas, mountain gods, dragon gods, stream and river gods, as well as [the gods of] other small temples in counties and prefectures" who could respond with miracles to prayer all received titles.[114]

The twelfth century was a time of great government activity and correspondingly high awareness on the part of devotees. Only a few years after the increase in government grants, devotees dreamt of gods who asked them for government titles.[115] In making their petitions to the government, a given god's followers indicated a thorough, even competitive, knowledge of the titles neighboring gods had. In 1270, when the people of South Bank (Nan-hsün) township in Hu-chou, Chekiang, petitioned the government to include two local gods in the register of sacrifices, they said: "For example, the local god of New Market (Hsin-shih) township, in Te-ch'ing county, is also administered by this prefecture. The local god of that township has already been granted a temple plaque. Only South Bank has not yet carried out the procedures to get the earth god into the register of sacrifices. It really is a gap in the register of sacrifices."[116]

Because a god who fit into a preexisting category had a much better chance of being given a title, devotees realized that labeling a local god a wall-and-moat god might help to get him (or her) a title.

THE WALL-AND-MOAT GODS AND
TAOIST PANTHEONS

The devotees of popular gods were not alone in their desire to play the government title-granting system. The government's system was so influential that Taoist Celestial Heart (T'ien-hsin) masters decided to use it to differentiate between legitimate and illicit gods rather than confining themselves to strictly Taoist standards. Permissible or legitimate gods (cheng-shen) were those in the government's register of sacrifices, impermissible gods, those outside it.[117] The author of the first T'ien-hsin ritual compendium (preface dated 1116), Yüan Miao-tsung (fl. 1086–1116), had been an itinerant Taoist.[118] Like the earlier Buddhist monks who found it easier to convert local deities than to tear down their temples, Yüan proposed a simple approach: wholesale adoption of the government's register of sacrifices.

Other T'ien-hsin compilations accepted Yüan's standard.[119] A spirit code that applies penal law to the gods says: "Any spirit whom the nation does not record in the register of sacrifices, who wildly brings spiritual retribution or deceives the people and makes unauthorized good or ill fortune, shall be exiled to a distance of three thousand li [one thousand miles]."[120] Here, of course, is the classic Taoist stance: the practitioner, who ranks above popular deities, is therefore entitled to issue orders to them and to punish them. One text in the late Yüan compilation Tao-fa hui-yüan (A corpus of Taoist ritual) is addressed to the "legitimate (cheng) deities who hold official appointment and are entitled to receive bloody offerings from a district."[121] By the Sung, Taoists, having reconciled themselves to the fact that most popular gods ate meat, incorporated these gods into their pantheons, although far below Taoist immortals and purer deities.

A biography written in 1274 of Marshal Wen Ch'iung (b. 702) expresses one Taoist attitude toward popular deities perfectly. In 961 a drought occurred in Wen-chou (Chekiang), Marshal Wen's hometown. People prayed to the God of the Eastern Peak, but a cloud appeared with Marshal Wen's name written on it. Then it rained, and the local people wanted to build a temple to him. Marshal Wen possessed a commoner and said: "I do not value temple offerings and official titles. If you want to reward my merit, please don't petition the [earthly] court." He feared that the emperor would grant him a title. This is the final twist in the Taoists' attempt to coexist with the government register of sacrifices. Marshal's Wen's refusal to become a popular god—to enjoy food offerings, receive a government title, or have a temple—came to the attention of his superiors, and he enjoyed a successful career in the Taoist bureaucracy.[122] In fact, his promotion within the Taoist hierarchy hinged on his very refusal to accept the trappings of popular worship.

Given the craze for government titles and recognition sweeping early-twelfth-century China, it made no sense for Taoists to try to impose their own standard of orthodoxy. They lacked the financial and human resources to carry out canonization procedures on the scale that the government did, and there was no guarantee that anyone would value their rankings anyway. Hung Mai's *Record of the Listener (I-chien chih),* which allows glimpses of popular understanding that sources in the Taoist canon rarely do, tells of one god who valued his government title more highly than a Taoist title. In 1130, Erh-lang, who had a temple in Lang-chou county, Szechwan, appeared in a dream to an official and said: "I formerly received the rank of king. I descended to deal with worldly things; accordingly, my post was to govern everything, good and bad fortune, winning and losing. In 1110 the emperor [Hui-tsung] changed my title to immortal. Although the name was pure and reverent, my power was dissipated. No one has come to ask me about the myriad affairs of humans."[123] Once the god's original title was restored to him, his powers returned as well. The populace did not necessarily share the Taoist view that the higher up in the Taoist order, the better.

The wall-and-moat god happened to hold a position in Taoist pantheons and to be a lay deity as well. Taoist sources from the Sung testify to the existence of complex pantheons with the God of the Eastern Peak (or the Jade Emperor) at the top, then the wall-and-moat god, and then the earth gods. The T'ien-hsin practitioners even used the correct bureaucratic verbs to petition *(tsou)* the divine emperor, make requests to *(shen)* the God of the Eastern Peak, and inform *(tieh)* the city gods.[124]

This Taoist pantheon was thought to work with a fine precision. The practitioner had only to identify the official who presided over the particular problem he confronted and petition him with the appropriate forms, and the god would respond.[125] It was a nice scheme, but the people of the Sung did not necessarily accept it. In 1195, Hung Mai states, a malaria victim secretly spent the night at a temple to the wall-and-moat god in the hope that his illness would be cured. He dreamt that he saw the wall-and-moat god addressing seven or eight yellow-robed subordinates: "I have received the emperor's edict to spread plague in this area. You are each the earth god of one district. How dare you delay?" Only one earth god protested, saying the people in his district were virtuous and should not be punished. The wall-and-moat god responded: "This is a celestial command. You are a lowly functionary. You must carry out this order." He then granted the earth god's request that he fill his quota only with young children. When the plague broke out, people of all ages were struck in other districts, but only the children in that particular district fell sick. On their recovery, the local people collected money to build a temple to the earth god.[126]

Because Hung Mai identified the narrator, Chou Weng, only as a

Soochow resident, he must not have been a Taoist practitioner. He clearly viewed the earth gods as subordinate to the god of walls and moats, and the latter in turn as subordinate to the emperor. On first reading, this tale confirms the acceptance of Taoist rankings of the gods in the popular mind. Certainly the god of walls and moats seems to outrank earth gods and to be able to issue orders to them. But, on reflection, it turns out that actual performance of the god is more important than purported rank. In the Soochow plague it was a lowly earth god who protected his devotees from the officious wall-and-moat god and the bloodthirsty emperor. After the plague abated, everyone raised money to build a temple to thank the earth god—not the god of walls and moats and not the emperor—for his kindness. The narrator did not care where a given god ranked in Taoist pantheons. His main concern, like that of laypersons throughout the T'ang and the Sung, was performance. The god who could respond to prayer, who could prevent (or at least minimize) the plague, was the god who deserved to be rewarded. And if that god happened to rank lower than another in Taoist pantheons, so be it.

CONCLUSION

It is common knowledge that the introduction of Buddhism marked a new era in Chinese history. The influence of Indian culture was felt not just in religion but in Chinese painting, sculpture, music, and literature—in all of the high arts. Less commonly acknowledged are the effects of Indian and Central Asian culture on Chinese mass culture.

In the pre-Buddhist period, laypersons worshiped a variety of gods, of whom nature deities and former humans were the most important. Throughout the T'ang, the Five Dynasties, and the Sung, members of the Buddhist, Taoist, and Confucian establishments struggled to come to terms with these indigenous gods. Early on they tore down temples to unclean gods and tried to replace them with gods more to their liking. Later, monks had visions in which these gods renounced a meat diet and accepted Buddhist precepts. Laypersons began to worship bodhisattvas like Kuan-yin and Mañjuśrī.

Buddhist monks also introduced the cult of the guardian of the north, Vaiśravaṇa, an originally Indian deity who was very popular in Khotan. In China, this same god, P'i-sha-men, often held a stūpa in his right hand, indicating his role as the guardian of the dharma, and his shrines were located next to the gates of monasteries. He also protected cities, and his temples were often built in the watchtowers on the northwest corner of city walls.

In the pre-Buddhist period, the Chinese had prayed to unnamed deities of city gates. Following the introduction of the cult to P'i-sha-men, and the proliferation of monastic guardians, wall-and-moat gods gained in popularity. Low-level monks, Taoist practitioners, and Confucian officials—possibly following the lead of P'i-sha-men—also assigned local gods positions in different hierarchies. Some gods like Kuan Yü assumed posts as monastic guardians, some like the dragon son of T'ai-chou, as wall-and-moat gods. Like P'i-sha-men, the wall-and-moat gods were associated with city walls. Like P'i-sha-men, they guarded cities. And also like P'i-sha-men, they had specific identities, often related to their preapotheosis lives. By the early tenth century, the wall-and-moat god had become the bureaucratic god with which we are so familiar today. He served a given term as wall-and-moat god and was promoted within the divine hierarchy on the basis of his performance.

Because the massive expansion of title granting in the eleventh century presented devotees with an opportunity to further honor their gods, many seized the chance to present local gods as wall-and-moat gods. Relabeling local gods proved to be a far more successful strategy than suppressing them; offering them tangible benefits was even more successful. As a result, local gods assumed office in pantheons all over China by the end of the thirteenth century and retained them in the centuries to follow.

NOTES

1. I would like to thank all the participants in the Hsi-lai Temple conference for their comments. I am especially grateful to Judith Boltz for her rigorous critique when we met in Los Angeles, Victor Mair for providing a wealth of references that made it possible to push back the date of Vaiśravaṇa's cult in China, and Peter Gregory and Pat Ebrey for their thorough editing. Professor Zhang Guangda provided me with many references during the spring of 1989, and his wife, Xu Tingyun, graciously allowed me to use his library during July and August that same year. Cynthia Brokaw, Daniel Getz, James B. Stepanek, Kojima Tsuyoshi, Nathan Sivin, Barend ter Haar, and Judith Zeitlin all read and criticized earlier drafts of this chapter. The Committee on Scholarly Communication with the People's Republic of China and the U. S. Information Agency funded my stay in China.

2. For the clearest description, see Arthur P. Wolf, "Gods, Ghosts, and Ancestors," in idem, ed., *Religion and Ritual in Chinese Society* (Stanford: Stanford University Press, 1974), pp. 131–182. Not all gods fit into the bureaucratic scheme. Wolf notes two categories of gods: officials *(shih),* such as wall and moat gods, and sages *(fu),* such as Ma-tsu (p. 140). Other scholars further specify that neither goddesses, such as Ma-tsu, nor Buddhist deities, such as Kuan-yin, are considered to be divine officials; see, for example, P. Steven Sangren, "Female Gender in Chinese Religious Symbols: Kuan Yin, Ma Tsu, and the 'Eternal Mother,' " *Signs* 9.1 (1983): 4–25, and Robert P. Weller, *Unities and Diversities in Chinese Religion* (Seattle: University of Washington Press, 1987).

3. Wu Hung, personal communication, April 30, 1990.

4. Nancy Steinhardt, personal communication, April 29, 1990.

5. Office-holding gods were by no means the only gods worshiped in medieval China. The first extant lists of divinities from Southern Sung (1127–1276) gazetteers show that most of the gods worshiped did not hold office of any type. They were local deities who had temples in just one place. Some were the spirits of a given mountain, stream, tree, or house. Others were formerly human. During their lifetimes they had established some tie, however tenuous, to the place where they were subsequently worshiped. Having been born in a village, died there, served as an official there, or even just visited there once, they answered (or were thought to) the prayers of local people for rain, good health, safety, and progeny. These gods had just one identity. If human, they were called by the name they had had before their deaths and subsequent apotheoses; if nature gods, they were called the god of a particular mountain or stream.

6. Classifying government officials as members of the clergy poses some problems. See Jean Lévi's "Les fonctionnaires et le divin: luttes de pouvoirs entre divinités et administrateurs dans les contes des Six Dynasties et des Tang," *Cahiers d'Extrême-Asie* 2 (1986): 102; and "Les fonctions religieuses de la bureaucratie céleste," *L'homme* 101 (1987): 35–57. Lévi makes a compelling argument that local administrators formed a Confucian clergy. Here I modify his usage slightly according to my own definitions of lay and clergy: "Because, in sharp contrast to the eclectic laity, the clergy viewed different religious traditions as mutually exclusive technologies for tapping into the powers of the universe, they chose to limit themselves to ritual techniques associated with just one doctrinal tradition. A layman could consult any god or practitioner to his liking, but the clergyman could not" (Valerie Hansen, *Changing Gods in Medieval China, 1127–1276* [Princeton: Princeton University Press, 1990], p. 41). When acting in an official capacity, such as conducting ceremonies or tearing down banned temples, bureaucrats did behave as a kind of clergy. But, as Judith Boltz shows in her chapter in this volume, when they consulted other religious specialists in attempts to cure illness or solve other problems, then they acted like laypersons.

7. Teng Ssu-yü suggested that Vaiśravaṇa and the *ch'eng-huang* gods might be linked in his "Ch'eng-huang k'ao," *Shih-hsüeh nien-pao* 2.2 (1935): 269–270.

8. Li Fang (925–996), ed., *T'ai-p'ing yü-lan* (Peking: Chung-hua shu-chü, 1960), 882.5a–5b.

9. Lévi, "Les fonctions religieuses de la bureaucratie céleste," pp. 45–46.

10. *TPKC* 313.2477, citing *Lu-i chi* (tenth century).

11. "Religious Taoism and Popular Religion from the Second to the Seventh Centuries," in Holmes Welch and Anna Seidel, eds., *Facets of Taoism: Essays in Chinese Religion* (New Haven: Yale University Press, 1979), pp. 53–81.

12. Ko Hung, *Shen-hsien chuan* (Kuang Han Wei ts'ung-shu edition) 7.8b–9a; Lévi, "Les fonctionnaires et le divin," p. 102.

13. Pai Yü-ch'an, *Ching-yang Hsü chen-chün chuan* 33.4b–5a, in his *Hsiu-chen shih-shu* (HY 263); Lévi, "Les fonctionnaires et le divin," p. 102; K. M. Schipper's "Taoist Ritual and Local Cults of the T'ang Dynasty," a study of the hagiographies of Hsü, dates this text to the early thirteenth century, in Michel

Strickmann, ed., *Tantric and Taoist Studies in Honour of R. A. Stein,* vol. 3: *Mélanges chinois et bouddhiques* 22 (1985): 825.

14. Pai Yü-ch'an, *Ching-yang Hsü chen-chün chuan* 33.5a in his *Hsiu-chen shih-shu* (HY 263).

15. *TPKC* 295.2346, citing *Yu-ming lu* (fifth century).

16. Bernard Faure, "Space and Place in Chinese Religious Traditions," *History of Religions* 26.4 (1987): 337–356.

17. *CTS* 89.2887.

18. *TPKC* 315.2495–2496, citing *Wu-hsing chang-ku chi* (as only this one anecdote is taken from this book, the source cannot be dated), translated into French in Lévi, "Les fonctionnaires et le divin," p. 89. See also Levi's "Les fonctions religieuses de la bureaucratie céleste," p. 53.

19. Miyakawa Hisayuki, "Kō U shin no kenkyū," in *Rikuchōshi kenkyū: shūkyōhen* (Kyoto: Heirakuji shoten, 1964), pp. 391–414; David Johnson, "The City-God Cults of T'ang and Sung China," *HJAS* 45.2 (1985): 428–431; *TPKC* 295.2349, citing *I-yüan* (fifth century)

20. *Chia-t'ai Wu-hsing chih* (Sung-Yüan ti-fang chih ts'ung-shu edition), 13.9a–20b.

21. It is only possible to compile a partial list of temples in any given area after the appearance of the first gazetteers. For a list of deities from Hu-chou that I have reconstructed from different sources, please see Appendix 3 of my *Changing Gods,* pp. 179–195.

22. *Chia-t'ai Wu-hsing chih* (Sung-Yüan ti-fang chih ts'ung-shu edition), 13.12a–13a, 13.14a.

23. *TPKC* 293.2333, citing *Chi-wen* (last quarter of the eighth century).

24. This inscription was recarved in 1233 on the basis of a rubbing circulating in the area, which purportedly dated to the T'ang (*Yüeh-chung chin-shih chih* [Shih-k'o shih-liao hsin-pien edition], 5.20b).

25. Makita Tairyō, *Rikuchō koitsu Kansein okenki no kenkyū* (Kyoto: Heirakuji shoten, 1970).

26. Kanaoka Shōkō, "Tonkō bunken ni mirareru shoshin shobosatsu shinkō no ichi yōsō," in *Yoshioka hakase kanreki kinen dōkyō kenkyū ronshū—dōkyō no shisō to bunka* (Tokyo: Kokushokan gyōkai, 1977), pp. 429–456.

27. See the entry under "Bishamon" in Paul Demiéville, ed., *Hōbōgirin,* 1st fascicle: A–Bombai (Tokyo: Maison Franco-Japonaise, 1929); Matsumoto Bunzaburō's "Tobatsu Bishamon kō," in his *Bukkyōshi zakkō* (Osaka: Sōbunsha, 1944; originally 1939), pp. 273–313; Miyazaki Ichisada's study of this god, "Bishamonten shinkō no tozen ni tsuite," in his *Ajiashi kenkyū,* vol. 2 (Kyoto: Tōyōshi-kenkyū-kai, 1959; originally 1941), pp. 304–335; Phyllis Granoff, "Tobatsu Bishamon: Three Japanese Statues in the United States and an Outline of the Rise of this Cult in East Asia," *East and West* 20 (1970): 144–167; and Yoritomo Motohiro, *Chūgoku mikkyō no kenkyū* (Tokyo: Daitō shuppansha, 1979), pp. 147–181.

28. See Alice Getty, *Gods of Northern Buddhism: Their History, Iconography and Progressive Evolution Through the Northern Buddhist Countries* (New York: Dover, 1988; originally 1928), p. 156, for a discussion of the god's names in different languages.

29. Ibid., 156–162.

30. Alexander Coburn Soper, *Literary Evidence for Early Buddhist Art in China* (Ascona: Artibus Asiae Publishers, 1959), p. 232.

31. Hsüan-tsang mentions that he was also worshiped in Balkh, on the Oxus River. See *Ta T'ang hsi-yü chi* 1, in *T* 51.872c10–13; Samuel Beal, *Si-yu-ki, Buddhist Records of the Western World: Translated from the Chinese of Hiuen Tsiang (A.D. 629)* (London: Trübner & Co., 1884), vol. 1, pp. 43–45.

32. Harold W. Bailey, *The Culture of the Sakas in Ancient Iranian Khotan* (Delmar, NY: Caravan Books, 1982), p. 8.

33. *Ta-fang-teng-ta-chi-ching* 55, in *T* 13.368a17–18; F. W. Thomas (ed. and trans.), *Tibetan Literary Texts and Documents Concerning Chinese Turkestan, Part I: Literary Texts* (London: Royal Asiatic Society, 1935), p. 90.

34. M. Aurel Stein, *Ancient Khotan: Detailed Report of Archaeological Explorations in Chinese Turkestan* (Oxford at the Clarendon Press, 1907), pp. 494–495, fig. 67, plates 14c, 14d.

35. *Ta T'ang hsi-yü chi* 12, in *T* 51.943b16–20. Translation by Beal, *Buddhist Records of the Western World,* vol. 2, p. 311, slightly modified. Tibetan sources vary slightly. The late-seventh-century *Prophecy of Gośṛṅga* tells of a breast arising from the earth to feed the founding king of Khotan, who was the son of Aśoka. *The Annals of the Li Country* (from the ninth or tenth centuries) report that, when Aśoka visited Khotan with a concubine, she had a vision of Vaiśravaṇa and then became pregnant. Because fortune-tellers predicted the son would succeed Aśoka before he died, both Aśoka and his consort abandoned the child. "In the sequel a breast arose from the earth, and, sucking thereat, he did not die: later he received the name Earth-breast." F. W. Thomas, *Tibetan Literary Texts and Documents Concerning Chinese Turkestan* (London: Royal Asiatic Society, 1935), pp. 17, 99.

36. Soper, *Literary Evidence,* p. 240.

37. *I-ch'ieh ching yin-i* 11, in *T* 54.375c16. Discussed in Yoritomo, *Mikkyō,* p. 155. Hui-lin compiled the book in 788, and its final version dates to 806–807 (John R. McRae, *The Northern School and the Formation of Early Ch'an Buddhism* [Honolulu: University of Hawaii Press, 1986], p. 325, n. 159).

38. Stein, *Ancient Khotan,* pp. 252–253, figs. 30 and 31, plate 2. Chinese-language documents from this site date to 781–790 (p. 267).

39. *P'i-sha-men i-kuei, T* no. 1249, is falsely attributed to Pu-k'ung. The text is not mentioned by his biographers nor does it appear in eighth-century catalogues of his work. Yoritomo Motohiro notes that Annen lists this book as having been brought back to Japan by the pilgrim Shūei after his trip to China in 862–865 (*Sho ajari Shingon mikkyō burui sōroku* 2, in *T* 55.1127b14). Yoritomo dates the text to the ninth century (*Mikkyō,* p. 152).

40. Tsan-ning, *SKSC* 1, in *T* 50.714a1–11. Chou Yi-liang provides a full translation of this version on pp. 305–306 of his "Tantrism in China," *HJAS* 8 (1944–1945): 241–332.

41. Tsan-ning, *Ta Sung seng-shih lüeh* 2, in *T* 54.254a22–254b16.

42. Mu-an Shan-ch'ing, *Tsu-t'ing shih-yüan* (postface dated 1108), 6, in *HTC* 113.78a9–78b5.

43. Chih-p'an (1220–1275), *Fo-tsu t'ung-chi* 40, in *T* 49.375b4–13.

44. Emending *ta-shih* (big stone) to *ta-shih* (big eat), the strongest of the

western countries and so the 'Abāssid Caliphate. Michael T. Dalby, "Court Politics in Late T'ang Times," in Denis Twitchett, ed., *The Cambridge History of China*, vol. 3: *Sui and T'ang China, 589–906, Part 1* (New York: Cambridge University Press, 1979), p. 609.

45. A six-character gap follows. Presumably it gave the names of the other three countries surrounding An-hsi.

46. Pu-k'ung, born in Central Asia, was the child of an Indian father and a Sogdian mother (Stanley Weinstein, *Buddhism under the T'ang* [New York: Cambridge University Press, 1987], p. 56).

47. *P'i-sha-men i-kuei*, in *T* 21.228b6–228c1. Thanks to Marston Anderson for his help with the translation. Herodotus tells a similar story about Hephaestus, who sent mice to help an Egyptian priest in a battle with an Arabian army: "But when their [the Egyptians'] enemies came, there spread out against them [the Arabs], at nightfall, field mice, which gnawed their quivers through, and through, too, the bows themselves and the handles of their shields, so that on the next day they fled, defenseless, and many of them fell" (Herodotus, *The History*, trans. by David Greene [Chicago: University of Chicago Press, 1987], p. 193).

48. Matsumoto, *Bukkyōshi zakkō*, pp. 287–290. Chou Yi-liang summarizes the reasons in "Tantrism in China" p. 305, n. 103. Weinstein also rejects the veracity of the tale on the grounds that the early biographies of Amoghavajra do not mention the event (*Buddhism under the T'ang*, p. 170, n. 41).

49. Kuo Jo-hsü (fl. 1074), *T'u-hua chien-wen chih* (Peking: Jen-min mei-shu ch'u-pan-she, 1963), edited by Huang Miao-tzu, 5.121. Translated in Alexander Coburn Soper, *Kuo Jo-hsü's Experiences in Painting (T'u-hua chien-wen chih): An Eleventh Century History of Chinese Painting Together with the Chinese Text in Facsimile* (Washington, D.C.: American Council of Learned Societies, 1951), p. 79. See also Chou, "Tantrism in China," p. 305, n. 103.

50. Granoff, "Tobatsu Bishamon," p. 155, fig. 11; Soper, *Literary Evidence*, p. 234, n. 39.

51. Granoff, "Tobatsu Bishamon," p. 155, fig. 12.

52. *HTS* 79.3540.

53. Alternatively, his father may have feared being overthrown by him (as the fortune-tellers had prophesied the breast-milk drinking child would overthrow his father before he died). Ironically, it was Chien-ch'eng's brother, Shih-min, who forced Kao-tsu to abdicate in his favor, after killing Chien-ch'eng and another brother at Hsüan-wu gate. See Howard J. Wechsler, "The Founding of the T'ang Dynasty: Kao-tsu (r. 618–26)," in Twitchett, ed., *The Cambridge History of China* 3.182–187.

54. Granoff, "Tobatsu Bishamon," p. 152. Pu-k'ung's disciple Yüan-chao listed his works in his biography, *Tai-tsung ch'ao tseng ssu-k'ung ta-pien-cheng Kuang-chih san-tsang ho-shang piao chih chi*, in *T* 52.839c4. Of the many works with the word P'i-sha-men in the title that are attributed to him (*Pei-fang P'i-sha-men t'ien-wang sui-chün hu-fa i-kuei*, *T* no. 1247; *Pei-fang P'i-sha-men t'ien-wang sui-chün hu-fa chen-yen*, *T* no. 1248; *P'i-sha-men i-kuei*, *T* no. 1249; and *Pei-fang P'i-sha-men Tuo-wen-pao-tsang t'ien-wang-shen miao-t'o-lo-ni pieh-hsing i-kuei*, *T* no. 1250), only the *P'i-sha-men t'ien-wang ching* is listed in this catalogue.

55. In his *Studies on the Mysteries of Mañjuśrī: A Group of East Asian Man-*

dalas and Their Traditional Symbolism, Society for the Study of Chinese Religions Monograph 2 (1983), p. 25.

56. Harold W. Bailey, The Culture of the Sakas in Ancient Iranian Khotan (Delmar, NY: Caravan Books, 1982), p. 6. I am grateful to Victor Mair for the suggestion to check the Khotanese pronunciation and for this reference, and to Hugh Stimson and Stanley Insler for establishing the T'ang pronunciation and its Khotanese origins.

57. Joanna Williams, "The Iconography of Khotanese Painting," East and West n.s. 23.1–2 (1973): 114; Chang Kuang-ta (Zhang Guangda) and Jung Hsin-chiang, "Tun-huang 'jui-hsiang chi,' jui-hsiang t'u chi ch'i fan-ying te Yü-t'ien," in Ho Tuan-t'ien, ed., Tun-huang T'u-lu-fan yen-chiu lun-wen-chi, vol. 3 (Peking: Pei-ching ta-hsüeh ch'u-pan-she, 1986), pp. 123–125. The Candra-garbha-sūtra and the Sūryagarbha-sūtra were translated into Chinese in 566 and recast in Khotanese in the eighth century (Jan Nattier, "The Candragarbha-Sūtra in Central and East Asia: Studies in a Buddhist Prophecy of Decline" [Ph.D. dissertation, Harvard University, 1988], pp. 57–59). Śākyamuni charges Vaiśravaṇa with protecting his scriptures, relics, and images in the beginning of this sūtra (ibid., pp. 197, 239). Nattier summarizes the contents of three later Khotanese adaptations (now preserved only in Tibetan) of the decline and ultimate disappearance of the dharma. Vaiśravaṇa and another goddess, Śri-Mahādevi, guide a group of monks and nuns from Khotan to Tibet in all three (pp. 77–97).

58. Shih-chia-mou-ni-ju-lai hsiang-fa mieh-chin chih-chi, in T 51.996c 1–15; Wu Chi-yü (trans. Fukui Fumimasa and Higuchi Masaru), "Daihan koku daitoku—Sanzō hōshi—hōsei den kō" in Makita Tairyō and Fukui Fumimasa, eds., Kōza Tonkō: Tonkō to Chūgoku bukkyō (Tokyo: Daitō shuppansha, 1984), pp. 383–414. Hsiang-fa was the second of the three periods of decline of the dharma: cheng-fa (the age of the genuine teachings), hsiang-fa (the age of the counterfeit teachings, in which understanding of spiritual matters became blurred), and mo-fa (the dissolution of the teachings). See Raoul Birnbaum, "Sound and Music in the Experience of T'ang Buddhist Visionaries: A Preliminary Consideration," forthcoming in Yip Ming Mei, ed., Selected Essays in Chinese Buddhist Music (Hong Kong).

59. P'eng Shu-hsia, ed., Wen-yüan ying-hua (Taipei: Hua-lien ch'u-pan-she, 1965), 819.6a–b.

60. Pa-ch'iung shih chin-shih pu-cheng (Shih-k'o shih-liao hsin-pien edition), 77.21b–23a.

61. Chienfotung xviii: 002 (Stein's transcription and numbering of the Thousand Buddha Caves [Ch'ien-fo-tung] at Tun-huang as found in his Serindia and still used by the Delhi Museum). Photo-reproduction given in plate 90, vol. 4, and textual description page 1016, vol. 2, of Sir Aurel Stein's Serindia: Detailed Report of Explorations in Central Asia and Westernmost China (Oxford at the Clarendon Press, 1921). Now in the Delhi Museum. For more depictions of Vaiśravaṇa, see color plate 65 and black-and-white plates 109, 110, 111, in Roderick Whitfield's Art of Central Asia: The Stein Collection in the British Museum, vol. 1: (New York: Kodansha International, 1982). By the Ming, if not earlier, musical instruments had replaced the kings' weapons. Most of the China International Travel Service–sponsored guardian kings one sees in China today carry lutes, not weapons. I am very grateful to Chhaya Haesner, keeper of the

Central Asian art collection in the Delhi Museum, for discussing the iconography of the different Tun-huang prints with me.

62. Chienfotung xxxvi: 002. Photo-reproduction given in plate 100, vol. 4, and textual description page 969, vol. 2, of Stein's *Serindia*. Now in the Delhi Museum. Due to gaps in the text and mistaken characters, this translation is tentative.

63. This woodblock is now in the Stein collection in the British Museum (registration no. 1919.1–1.0245). Max Loehr discusses this and three other prints cut at the same time in his *Chinese Landscape Woodcuts from an Imperial Commentary to the Tenth-Century Printed Edition of the Buddhist Canon* (Cambridge: Belknap Press of Harvard University, 1969), pp. 7–8. See also Arthur Waley, *A Catalogue of Paintings Recovered from Tun-huang by Sir Aurel Stein* (London: British Museum, 1931), no. 245; Roderick Whitfield, *The Art of Central Asia: The Stein Collection in the British Museum* (Tokyo: Kodansha International, 1982–1985), vol. 2, fig. 153; and Roderick Whitfield and Anne Farrer, *Caves of the Thousand Buddhas* (New York: George Braziller, 1990), p. 104, fig. 85, and p. 106.

64. Tsan-ning, *SKSC* 1, in *T* 50.714a10; Chou, "Tantrism in China," p. 306.

65. *Ta Sung seng-shih lüeh* 2, in *T* 54.254b9–13.

66. Shan-ch'ing, *Tsu-t'ing shih-yüan* 6, in *HTC* 113.78b4–5.

67. *Fo-tsu t'ung-chi* 40, in *T* 49.375b13.

68. *Ching-ting Yen-chou hsü chih* 4.5b (Sung-Yüan ti-fang chih ts'ung-shu edition); *Hsien-ch'un Lin-an chih* 73.4b (Sung-Yüan ti-fang chih ts'ung-shu edition); *San-shan chih* 33–38 (Sung-Yüan ti-fang chih ts'ung-shu edition); *Chia-ting ch'ih-ch'eng chih* (Sung-Yüan ti-fang chih ts'ung-shu edition), 31.4a. Miyazaki has drawn on these chapters to compile a list of seventeen temples and the dates they received name plaques from the central government ("Bishamonten," p. 322).

69. For more about Kuan Yü's cult, please consult Inoue Ishii, "Kan U shibyō no yūrai narabi ni hensen," *Shirin* 26 (1941): 41–51, 242–283; Masami Harada, "Kan U shinkō no ni san no yōso," *Tōhō shūkyō* 8–9 (1955): 29–40; Gunter Diesinger, *Vom General zum Gott: Kuan Yü (gest. 220 n. Chr.) und seine "posthume Karriere"* (Frankfurt: Haag & Herchen, 1984); Prasenjit Duara, "Superscribing Symbols: The Myth of Guandi, Chinese God of War," *JAS* 47.4 (1988): 778–795. Because of the dubious reliability of anecdotes told in later periods about the T'ang and the Sung, I have restricted my discussion to those tales about Kuan Yü that were recorded between 750 and 1300.

70. Kuan-ting, *Sui T'ien-t'ai Chih-che ta-shih pieh-chuan*, in *T* 50.195a26–b3. The account in Tao-hsüan's *HKSC* (*T* 50.566c7–10) is clearly based on Kuan-ting's account. See also Inoue, "Kan U shibyō," p. 47. I am indebted to Peter Gregory for suggesting and providing me with copies of these references.

71. *Kuo-ch'ing pai-lu*, in *T* 46.819b9–820c11; Inoue, "Kan U shibyō," p. 47; Tung Kao et al., eds., *Ch'üan T'ang-wen* (Peking: Chung-hua shu-chü, 1983), 231.1a–4b.

72. *Ch'üan T'ang-wen* 684.14b; Inoue, "Kan U shibyō," p. 47.

73. *Chiang-su chin-shih chih* (Shih-k'o shih-liao ts'ung-shu edition), 7.43a–44b.

74. Ibid., 8.50b–52a.

75. Faure recounts a similar story about Kuan Yü and Shen-hsiu from the eighteenth-century compendium *Shen-hsien t'ung-chien* 14, part 4, p. 2a ("Space and Place," p. 351).

76. *Shan-yu shih-k'o ts'ung-pien* (Shih-k'o shih-liao ts'ung-shu edition), 21.7a–8b; Inoue, "Kan U shibyō," p. 49.

77. *Shan-yu shih-k'o ts'ung-pien* (Shih-k'o shih-liao ts'ung-shu edition), 21.7a–8b; Inoue, "Kan U shibyō," p. 49.

78. The secondary literature concerning the wall-and-moat gods is extensive. My debt to David Johnson's path-breaking study of the *ch'eng-huang* god ("The City-God Cults of T'ang and Sung China") should be obvious in the pages that follow. I have found two other more recent articles very helpful as well: Hayata Mitsuhiro, "Jōkōshin shinkō no hensen ni tsuite," *Tōyō no shisō to shūkyō* 5 (1988): 39–56; and Kojima Tsuyoshi, "Jōkōbyō seido no kakuritsu," *Shisō* 6 (1990).

79. Li Pai-yao (565–648) and Li Te-lin (530–590), *Pei-ch'i shu* (Peking: Chung-hua shu-chü, 1972), 20.281.

80. The term *ssu-yong* refers to the city walls. *Ch'un-ch'iu tso-chuan cheng-i* 30.1941a (ninth year, Hsiang reign) and 48.2086a (eighteenth year, Chao reign), in Juan Yüan, ed., *Shih-san ching chu-shu* (Peking: Chung-hua shu-chü, 1980).

81. David McMullen, "Bureaucrats and Cosmology: The Ritual Code of T'ang China," in David Carradine and Simon Price, eds., *Rituals of Royalty: Power and Ceremonial in Traditional Societies* (New York: Cambridge University Press, 1987), pp. 181–236.

82. Hsiao Sung (664–749) et al., *Ta T'ang Kai-yüan li*, Ikeda On, ed., photolithographic reprint of 1886 edition (Tokyo: Tōkyō kenkyūkai, 1972), 70.6b–7a, 73.6b–7a.

83. Chang Chiu-ling, *Ta T'ang liu-tien* (*SKCS* edition), 4.23a.

84. *Ch'üan T'ang-wen* 233.9a–b.

85. I am grateful to Timothy Barrett for his help with this text and for allowing me to read his manuscripts, "Towards a Date for the *Chin-so liu-chu yin*" and "Buddhism, Taoism, and the Rise of the City Gods." On the basis of internal evidence about a Tibetan attack, he tentatively assigns the text to the reign of T'ai-tsung (762–779) but adds the following caveat: "For the time being, however, assigning it more vaguely to the 'late eighth or early ninth centuries' is about as far as it is possible to go" ("Towards a Date for the *Chin-so liu-chu yin*," p. 4). Judith M. Boltz thinks the text may date to the Sung (*A Survey of Taoist Literature: Tenth to Seventeenth Centuries* [Berkeley: Institute of East Asian Studies, 1987], p. 262, n. 42).

86. *Chin-so liu-chu yin* (HY 1009), 25.7a–b.

87. Slightly altering David Johnson's translation of this passage from *Chin-so liu-chu yin* (HY 1009), 25.13a–b ("City-God Cults," p. 436). See also 25.7a–b for an instance in which the author adds the *ch'eng-huang* god to the commentary following the *she-chi* shrines in the main text.

88. David Johnson argues that a mercantile class was behind the spread of the cult to the city god. Although my understanding of the mechanism for the dispersion of the cult differs from his, I am indebted to him for much of the data I cite here. I disagree with him primarily in his reading of the term *"ch'i-lao"*

("elders"): "They were commoners, but must have enjoyed considerable prestige; and they were wealthy, or could raise money from the community thanks to their standing. I submit, therefore, that they were representatives of the mercantile or commercial elite of Chin-yün [the site of the city god temple in question]" (pp. 419–420). The term *ch'i-lao* constantly occurs in temple inscriptions as a way to characterize devotees who do not hold office. It is better strictly glossed as elders; it is still used in Hong Kong for all those villagers over sixty years old. In itself, it carries no commercial connotations. I have found Barend ter Haar's comments most suggestive: "This notion has been elaborated on most recently by David Johnson in his study of the city god. He assumes that merchants were responsible for the spread of the cult, and not officials or ordinary people. As he himself states, this assumption is extremely hard to prove. He bases his argument on the striking distribution of the city god cult along trade routes. Such a pattern can be demonstrated for many cults, but, in our opinion, is not, in itself, sufficient to prove that merchants were the main group responsible for the spread of the city god cult. Many other traveling groups, such as monks and priests, doctors and quacks, seasonal and permanent migrants, also moved along these trade routes" ("The Genesis and Spread of Temple Cults in Fukien," in E. B. Vermeer, ed., *Development and Decline of Fukien Province in the 17th and 18th Centuries* [New York: E. J. Brill, 1990], p. 354). This is an admittedly difficult question, given the almost total lack of direct evidence. It seems to me, however, just as likely that the itinerant clergy were involved with the propagation of the cult.

89. *TPKC* 303.2399–2400, citing the lost work *Chi-wen*. Johnson dates this tale to the third quarter of the eighth century and translates part of it ("City-God Cults," p. 393, n. 113, 436).

90. *TPKC* 124. 873–874, citing *Pao-ying lu* (ninth century), translated in Johnson, "City-God Cults," p. 446.

91. *TPKC* 312.2469, citing *Nan-ch'u hsin-wen* (late ninth or early tenth century), translated in Johnson, "City-God Cults," p. 437.

92. *Chin-shih ts'ui-pien* (Shih-k'o shih-liao ts'ung-shu edition), 91.21a–b. Li's comments about the geographical distribution of the temple match those in the hell tale cited above: "The custom of Wu is to fear ghosts. Every prefecture and county definitely has a wall-and-moat god" (*TPKC* 303.2399).

93. *SHY, Li* 20.1a, 4a–b (Taipei: Hsin-wen-feng ch'u-pan-she, 1962); Hansen, *Changing Gods,* p. 84.

94. Wang P'u, *T'ang hui-yao* (Peking: Chung-hua shu-chü, 1955), 47.833.

95. *CTS* 9.219.

96. *CTS* 9.221.

97. *Chin-shih ts'ui-pien* 88.4a.

98. *Ch'üan T'ang-wen* 568.22a, 23a (Han Yü); 293:12a–b (Chang Chiu-ling); 781:2a–6a (Li Shang-yin).

99. *Ch'üan T'ang-wen* 781.4b–5a.

100. *Chin-shih ts'ui-pien* 156.8b–11b. As the editor notes, this inscription contains enough errors to cast doubt on its authenticity.

101. Wang P'u, *Wu-tai hui-yao* (Shanghai: Commercial Press, 1937), 11.192.

102. *Liang-che chin-shih chih* (Shih-k'o shih-liao ts'ung-shu edition), 4.1a–3a; *Yüeh-chung chin-shih chih* (Shih-k'o shih-liao ts'ung-shu), 1.65a–66b.

103. Wang Ch'in-jo, *Ts'e-fu yüan-kuei* (Peking: Chung-hua shu-chü, 1960, 1982), 34.12b–13a.

104. *Ts'e-fu yüan-kuei* 34.15b.

105. *Chi-ku-lu pa-wei* (Shih-k'o shih-liao hsin-pien edition), 7.2b–3a.

106. *T'ai-chou chin-shih-lu* (Shih-k'o shih-liao hsin-pien edition), 2.14a–16b. David Johnson provides analysis and translation of selected passages of this text in "City-God Cults," pp. 379–388.

107. *Chia-ting ch'ih-ch'eng chih* 31.1b; *Ch'ih-ch'eng-chi* 11.6a (*SKCS* edition).

108. *Hu-pei sheng t'ung-chih* 18, as cited in Inoue, "Kan U shibyō," part 2, p. 52.

109. *T'ang hui-yao* 47.833–835; *Wu-tai hui-yao* 11.192–193.

110. Figure 1, "Titles Granted to Popular Deities Year by Year," in Hansen, *Changing Gods,* p. 80. My remarks in this section summarize chapter 4, "The Granting of Titles," and the citations to original sources are all there.

111. Chao Yü-shih, *Pin-t'ui lu* (Shanghai: Ku-chi ch'u-pan-she, 1983), 8.103–105.

112. Ibid.

113. *SHY, Li* 20.17b–19a (wall-and-moat gods), 19a–20b (earth gods), 65a–82b (dragon gods), 84a–110b (mountain gods), 111a–131a (water gods).

114. *SS* 105.2562.

115. *ICC, Ting* 10:622, *Ping* 1:371; Hansen, *Changing Gods,* pp. 93–94.

116. *Wu-hsing chin-shih-chi* (Shih-k'o shih-liao hsin-pien edition), 12.22a; Hansen, *Changing Gods,* p. 124.

117. *T'ai-shang chu-kuo chiu-min tsung-chen pi-yao* (Secret essentials on assembling the perfected of the most high for the relief of the state and the deliverance of the people) (HY 1217), 1.6a.

118. Boltz, *A Survey of Taoist Literature,* p. 33.

119. Robert Hymes (in an unpublished paper, "Way and Byway: Taoist Saints' Cults and Exorcist Masters in Sung and Yüan China") disagrees with Boltz about the dating of the *Shang-ch'ing T'ien-hsin cheng-fa* (Correct rites of the Celestial Heart of Shang-ch'ing; HY 566) and *Shang-ch'ing ku-sui ling-wen kuei-lü* (Ordinances governing the specters, a numinous text from the marrow of Shang-ch'ing; HY 461). Hymes thinks both are late Northern Sung texts, Boltz, both late Southern Sung. In either case, both see the T'ien-hsin school as forming a consistent tradition in the twelfth and thirteenth centuries.

120. *Shang-ch'ing ku-sui ling-wen kuei-lü* (HY 461), 1. 9a; *T'ai-shang chu-kuo chiu-min tsung-chen pi-yao* (HY 1217), 6.9a; translated in Hymes, "Way and Byway," p. 22.

121. *Tao-fa hui-yüan* (HY 1210), 251.16b.

122. *Ti-ch'i shang-chiang Wen t'ai-pao chuan* (The biography of Grand Guardian Wen, commander-in-chief of the earth spirits; HY 779), 1.3b. John Lagerwey paraphrases this text in *Taoist Ritual and Society* (New York: Macmillan, 1987), p. 243. See also Boltz, *Survey of Taoist Literature,* pp. 97–99.

123. *ICC, Ping* 17:508–509.

124. *ICC, Ping* 8:430; *Shang-ch'ing t'ien-hsin cheng-fa* (HY 566), 4.8a.

125. See Robert Hymes' discussion of what happened when incompletely trained Taoists tried to carry out these rituals in "Way and Byway."

126. *ICC, Chih-ching* 6:927–928.

GLOSSARY

An-hsi 安西
chang 丈
Chang Chiu-ling 張九齡
Chang Shang-ying 張商英
Chang Tao-ling 張道陵
Chang Yüeh 張說
Chao Yü-shih 趙與時
cheng-fa 正法
cheng-shen 正神
ch'eng-huang (shen) 城隍（神）
ch'eng-lou 城樓
ch'eng-men 城門
Ch'eng-tu t'ien-wang 城闍天王
Chi Cha 季札
Chi-ku-lu pa-wei 集古錄跋尾
Chi-wen 紀聞
ch'i 氣
Chia-t'ai Wu-hsing chih 嘉泰吳興志
Chia-ting Ch'ih-ch'eng chih 嘉定赤
　城志
Chiang-su chin-shih chih 江蘇金石志
ch'ieh-lan shen 伽藍神
Chien-ch'eng 建成
Chih-i 智顗
Chih-p'an 志磐
Ch'ih-ch'eng-chi 赤城集
Chin 晉
Chin-shih ts'ui-pien 金石萃編
Chin-so liu-chu yin 金鎖流珠引
Chin-yün 縉雲
Ch'in-ting ch'üan T'ang-wen 欽定全
　唐文
Ching-ting Yen-chou hsü chih 景定
　嚴州續志
Ching-yang Hsü chen-chün chuan
　旌陽許真君傳
Chiu Wu-tai shih 舊五代史
Chou Weng 周翁
Ch'un-ch'iu tso-chuan cheng-i 春秋
　左傳正義
Erh-lang 二郎
Fa-ch'eng 法成
fo-fa 佛法
Fo-tsu t'ung-chi 佛祖統紀
Han Yü 韓愈
hou 侯
hsiang-fa 像法

Hsiang Yü 項羽
Hsiao Sung 蕭嵩
hsien-huang 縣隍
Hsin-shih 新市
Hsing-T'ang 興唐
Hsiu-chen shih-shu 修真十書
Hsü Sun 許遜
Hsüan-tsang 玄奘
Hsüan-tsung 玄宗
hu-fa shen 護法神
Hu-pei sheng t'ung chih 湖北省通志
Hui-lin 慧林
I-ching 義淨
I-ch'ieh ching yin-i 一切經音義
I-chien chih 夷堅志
I-hsing 一行
I-yüan 異苑
Jih-tsang ching 日藏經
Juan Yüan 阮元
Jui 芮
jui-hsiang 瑞像
jung 榮
Kao-tsu 高祖
Ko Hsüan 葛玄
Ko Hung 葛洪
Ku Yeh-wang 顧野王
Kuan-ting 灌頂
Kuan-yin 觀音
Kuan Yü 關羽
kung 公
Kuo-ch'ing pai-lu 國清百錄
Kuo Jo-hsü 郭若虛
kuo-t'u 國土
li 里
Li Ch'un-feng 李淳風
Li Fang 李昉
Li Pai-yao 李百藥
Li Ping 李冰
Li Shang-yin 李商隱
Li Te-lin 李德林
Li Yang-ping 李陽冰
Liang-Che chin-shih chih 兩浙金石志
Ling-pao 靈寶
Liu Wen-ching 劉文景
lo-ch'eng 羅城
Lu-i chi 錄異記
Ma-tsu 媽祖

mo-fa　末法

Mu-an Shan-ch'ing　睦庵善卿

Mu-jung Yen　慕容儼

Nan-ch'u hsin-wen　南楚新聞

Nan-hsün　南潯

Ou-yang Hsiu　歐陽修

Pa-ch'iung shih chin-shih pu-cheng　八瓊室金石補正

Pai-ma　白馬

Pai Yü-ch'an　白玉蟾

Pao-ying lu　報應錄

Pei-ch'i shu　北齊書

Pei-fang P'i-sha-men t'ien-wang sui-chün hu-fa chen-yen　北方毘沙門天王隨軍護法真言

Pei-fang P'i-sha-men t'ien-wang sui-chün hu-fa i-kuei　北方毘沙門天王隨軍護法儀軌

Pei-fang P'i-sha-men To-wen-pao-tsang t'ien-wang-shen miao-t'o-lo-ni pieh-hsing i-kuei　北方毘沙門多聞寶藏天王神妙陀羅尼別行儀軌

P'eng Shu-hsia　彭叔夏

P'i-sha-men　毘沙門

P'i-sha-men i-kuei　毘沙門儀軌

P'i-sha-men t'ien-wang ching　毘沙門天王經

Pin-t'ui lu　賓退錄

Pu-k'ung　不空

San-shan chih　三山志

Shan-yu shih-k'o ts'ung-pien　山右石刻叢編

Shang-ch'ing ku-sui ling-wen kuei-lü　上清骨髓靈文鬼律

Shang-ch'ing T'ien-hsin cheng-fa　上清天心正法

she-chi　社稷

she-miao　社廟

shen (god, deity)　神

shen (make requests to)　申

Shen-hsien chuan　神仙傳

Shen-hsien t'ung-chien　神仙通鑑

Shen-hsiu　神秀

Shih-chia-mou-ni ju-lai hsiang-fa mieh-chin chih chi　釋迦牟尼如來像法滅盡之記

Shih-min　世民

Shih-san ching chu-shu　十三經注疏

ssu-tien　祀典

ssu-t'ien-wang　四天王

ssu-yung　四墉, 四廍

Sui T'ien-t'ai chih-che ta-shih pieh-chuan　隋天台智者大師別傳

Sung kao-seng chuan　宋高僧傳

Ta-fang-teng-ta-chi-ching　大方等大集經

Ta-kuang-chih　大廣智

Ta Sung seng-shih lüeh　大宋僧史略

Ta T'ang hsi-yü chi　大唐西域記

Ta T'ang k'ai-yüan li　大唐開元禮

Ta T'ang liu-tien　大唐六典

Tai-tsung ch'ao tseng ssu-k'ung ta-pien-cheng Kuang-chih San-tsang ho-shang piao chih chi　代宗朝贈司空大辯正廣智三藏和上表制集

T'ai　泰

T'ai-ch'ang ssu　太常司

T'ai-chou chin-shih-lu　台州金石錄

T'ai-p'ing yü-lan　太平御覽

T'ai-shang chu-kuo chiu-min tsung-chen pi-yao　太上助國救民總真秘要

T'ang hui-yao　唐會要

Tao-fa hui-yüan　道法會元

Tao-hsüan　道宣

te　德

Ti-ch'i shang-chiang Wen T'ai-pao chuan　地祇上將溫太保傳

Ti Jen-chieh　狄仁傑

Ti-tsang　地藏

tieh　牒

T'ien-hsin　天心

T'ien-t'ai　天台

Tsan-ning　贊寧

Ts'ao Yüan-chung　曹元忠

Ts'e-fu yüan-kuei　冊府元龜

tsou　奏

Tsu-t'ing shih-yüan　祖庭事苑

Tu-chien　獨健

T'u-hua chien-wen chih　圖畫見聞誌

t'u-ti　土地

Tung Kao　董誥

Tzu-chih t'ung-chien　資治通鑑

Wang Ch'in-jo　王欽若

Wang P'u　王溥

Wen Ch'iung　溫瓊

Wen-yüan ying-hua　文苑英華
Wu　吳
Wu-hsing chang-ku chi　吳興掌故集
Wu-hsing chin-shih chi　吳興金石記
wu-kou　吳鉤
Wu-tai hui-yao　五代會要
Wu T'ai-po　吳太伯
Wu Tzu-hsü　伍子胥
Wu-Yüeh　吳越
yin　陰
Yin P'ei-chün　尹裴均

Ying-ch'eng　郢城
Yu-ming lu　幽明錄
Yü　禹
Yü-ch'üan　玉泉
Yü-t'ien　于闐
Yüan-chao　圓照
Yüan Miao-tsung　元妙宗
Yüeh-chung chin-shih chih　越中金石
　志
Yüeh-tsang ching　月藏經

CHAPTER 4

THE GROWTH OF PURGATORY

Stephen F. Teiser

Sometime around the tenth century China witnessed the ascendancy of a concept of the afterlife that for the next thousand years constituted the definitive model for imagining and alleviating the fate of the dead. Whatever one's station in life and however virtuous or vile one's moral bearing, one could be certain that a journey through the realm of purgatory awaited one after death. In this vision of the afterlife the spirit of the deceased is led through a series of ten tribunals, each under the direction of a king who functions as an even more powerful version of the magistrates staffing the bureaucracy of the Chinese empire. In each hall the king and his assistants review their records, which note in minute detail almost every action the subject performed while alive. When the registers are incomplete, verbal warning and physical torture are used to encourage the dead person to confess all accumulated sins. After leaving the tenth and final court, the person is released from the grips of the ten kings to be reborn in a state determined by the moral balance of his or her past actions. If meritorious acts predominate, then the person will ascend to the pleasurable states of existence. If, like most people, the person has committed more sins than good deeds, he or she will be reborn as an animal, hungry ghost, or hell being.

A particular class of mortuary rites provided one of the only hopes of gaining relief from the almost universal fate of postmortem punishment. Rather than being a closed loop in which one's future state of rebirth was determined entirely by the moral quality of one's past life, the traditional Chinese system was always and everywhere open to the possibility of ritual manipulation. At any point along the way—during one's lifetime but especially after one's death—the act of offering spirit money to any of the ten kings would reduce one's suffering in purgatory and help to secure a happier state of rebirth.

The Chinese notion carries with it a whole series of associations, some very much like and some very much unlike the concept of purgatory as it developed in late medieval Europe. Many of the basic components of the European conception are absent in China, foremost among them a belief in the immortality of the soul and a final judgment. Since medieval China lacked these essential ingredients of Christian eschatology, it might seem imprudent even to use the term "purgatory" in reference to China. Yet, without ignoring the divergences, there is enough of an overlap between the European and Chinese conceptions to warrant the use of a single, general term. Le Goff formulated a preliminary characterization of the European concept: "Briefly, it was an intermediary other world in which some of the dead were subjected to a trial that could be shortened by the prayers, by the spiritual aid, of the living."[1] The time of purgatory was defined as the period between death and rebirth, while the space of purgatory was imagined to be underneath the earth. Like the European concept, the Chinese understanding of the fate of the dead was premised on the development of highly sophisticated systems of penal law and moral retribution capable of operating in all possible worlds. It also assumed an intimate connection between the living and the dead, without which all mortuary ritual would have been fruitless.

The development of this notion of purgatory marks an important transition in the history of Chinese civilization. In the history of Chinese religion the system of the ten kings represents a mature synthesis of Indian and Chinese deities in one coherent administration. Similar syntheses had been attempted in the Six Dynasties and the early T'ang dynasty, but few had survived in actual practice, and those that did never achieved as broad a circulation as the ten kings. Offerings to the ten kings also constituted a significant shift within the history of Chinese mortuary practice. Prior to the reign of the ten kings, the Buddhist and Taoist priesthoods were important mediators—and beneficiaries—in securing a better lot for one's ancestors. Some families were able to assist their deceased ancestors without the intervention of specialists, but still the role of Buddhist and Taoist priests during the medieval period was greater, if only for lack of alternatives, than it was in later times. When the ten kings came to dominate the dark regions, descendants began to call on religious specialists bearing less formal ties to Buddhist and Taoist institutions, and some families sent offerings directly to the ten kings without the participation of either of China's organized churches.

The rule of the ten kings, however, was not achieved by a simple process of religious conversion or by mere philosophical assent. The ten kings came to dominate Chinese thought and action concerning the afterlife at the same time that China passed from its "middle ages" to what some social historians call its "early modern" period. The ten magistrates of the netherworld were one of the most important developments in Chinese civilization below ground, while changes in China's economy, social structure, and kinship organization were occurring aboveground.

MEDIEVAL VIEWS OF PURGATORY

The Six Dynasties and the early T'ang dynasty saw numerous attempts to explain what happens at death, to describe the judgment of the spirit and the process of rebirth, and to offer methods for mitigating the effects of karmic retribution. The modern conception of purgatory evolved slowly out of the imaginings and the social formations of medieval China. When the new conception appeared in the tenth century, it tended to supplement rather than to replace the earlier forms.

Although evidence is scanty and much remains unknown, it is clear that the fate of the dead was a concern of virtually all social classes and all forms of Chinese religion during the first several centuries A.D. Archeological reports on graves of this period demonstrate a surprising multiplicity of views—many of them maintained outside the purview of organized religion—concerning the fate of the dead. Already in Han times Mount T'ai (T'ai shan) was viewed as an abode of the dead, and the pantheon of gods residing at Mount T'ai was viewed in bureaucratic terms. The memorials and grave goods buried with a corpse gave a dual message to the members of that bureaucracy. On the one hand, descendants expressed the hope that the gods would show leniency in judging the cases of their ancestors, while on the other hand, living family members implored the gods to keep the dead in their rightful place so that the world of the living could be securely insulated from the pollution and the demonic mishaps associated with death.[2] A well-founded fear of government surveillance—exercised by the messengers, scribes, and gods of heaven's bureaus and earth's offices—seems to have been an essential component of organized Taoism dating from its very inception. One of the basic themes of the *Classic of Great Peace (T'ai-p'ing ching)* is that Heaven periodically surveys the actions of humans, records them on special tablets, and adjusts lifespans accordingly. Later Taoism elaborated on this core idea, describing rank after rank of functionaries who could be found in the heavens, below the earth, and within the body.[3]

Other descriptions of the fate of the dead appear in a variety of Buddhist sources, both those translated into Chinese from Indic originals and those produced on Chinese soil to meet the more particular demands of the times. Several sects of early Indian Buddhism (the Sarvāstivādin, later Mahīśāsaka, Vātsīputrīya, Sammatīya, and Pūrvaśila) argued in favor of the idea of an "intermediate existence" (Skt. *antarābhava,* Ch. *chung-yu*), a period that begins at death and lasts until one is reborn in another form. These sects generally argued that there could be neither spatial nor temporal discontinuity between the moment of death and the moment of rebirth; these two forms of life had to be connected by an intermediate stage.[4] One who existed in this liminal condition was endowed with a correspondingly liminal body. Like other bodies it needed nourishment, but, perhaps because it was viewed under the form of a hungry ghost, it could subsist only by "eating smells" (derived from the Sanskrit term *gandharva*, Ch. *shih-hsiang*).[5] Seven days after death, such a being could, under the right circumstances, achieve rebirth. Scholastic sources describe the Oedipal urge that motivates rebirth. The being who exists in the intermediate stage, if male, would be aroused by the sight of his future mother or, if female, would be attracted to her future father. If the prospective parents happened to be having intercourse on the seventh day after the liminoid's death, then it would be implanted immediately into its new mother's womb. If the seven-day rhythm was not fortuitous, then the purgatorial being had to pass another period of seven days—repeated up to seven times for a total of forty-nine days—before achieving rebirth.[6] The forty-nine day period of purgatorial existence inspired a form of mortuary ritual characteristic of Mahāyāna Buddhism throughout East Asia. In medieval China there are numerous references to memorial offerings held every seven days in Buddhist, Taoist, and secular literature.[7] One of the most complete versions of the ritual is to be found in the *Consecration Scripture (Kuan-ting ching),* an apocryphal scripture that Michel Strickmann has convincingly dated to the middle of the fifth century.[8] The mortuary rituals described in this source are dominated by a numerology based on the seven-day periods. When a family member dies, descendants are urged to invite Buddhist monks to uphold a special regimen of fasting for seven days and seven nights and to recite the *Consecration Scripture* forty-nine times. Descendants themselves are instructed to light seven-tiered lamps that contain seven lights per tier, to hang up spirit banners forty-nine feet long, and to save the lives of forty-nine creatures.[9]

Some concepts of the afterlife inspired by Buddhist ideas dispensed with the septenary symbolism of purgatory in favor of other methods of organization. An early-sixth-century encyclopedia mentions systems of sixty-four hells, thirty hells, eighteen hells, as well as the more orthodox belief in eight hells, each containing sixteen smaller compartments of punishment.[10] Although one was reborn in these hells for only one lifetime, they were not exactly purgatorial. Rather than intermediate stages through which each person had to pass before achieving rebirth, they were seen instead as one of six possible destinations (or "courses"; Skt. *gati*, Ch. *tao* or *ch'ü*) in which one could be reborn.

A few generalizations will have to suffice to distinguish these medieval forms of purgatory from the later system of the ten kings. First, and perhaps most important, in most instances of mortuary ritual described in the early texts, the family of the deceased hired the services of a religious priesthood, either Buddhist or Taoist, to assist in the ritual. Even when the sangha was not called in to help, the participation of the monkhood and the extra merit that monks could assure were ideals to which most families aspired. As Gernet has clearly shown, the medieval circuit of exchange between descendants and ancestors depended on the involvement of the Buddhist church (and, to a lesser extent, the Taoist church) as mediator. Rather than sending goods directly to the ancestors to assist them in the afterlife, offerings were made directly to the Buddhist sangha, an action that multiplied many times the blessings that then accrued to the ancestors.[11] Such a system of ostentation was uniquely well suited to the social economy of medieval Chinese religion; it was formed in a world dominated by an established, land-holding gentry class and by an equally prosperous Buddhist church that counted among its property not only land but also the families who farmed the land, not simply Buddhas and bodhisattvas but also the gold, silver, and bronze used to cast their images. Nor should it be forgotten that during the T'ang dynasty the so-called societies, the basic purpose of which was to defray the high cost and to cope with the unpredictable advent of funeral services, drew their membership not on the basis of kinship or residence but rather on the basis of formal lay affiliation with Buddhist temples.[12] As the institutions characteristic of medieval society gave way to new forms of social and economic organization in the late T'ang and early Sung dynasties, the cycle of exchange that helped to define the old institutions changed too.

The waning of the middle ages did not bring a sudden end to the patronage of monks and monasteries on the part of grieving families. Recent studies have shown clearly that those with money continued to pay monks to perform funeral services during the Sung dynasty and that monasteries retained a central position in the local society and economy of the late Ming and early Ch'ing dynasties.[13] What characterized the world of death in postmedieval times was not the disappearance of the old ideal, but rather the proliferation of other kinds of specialists, bearing less exclusive ties to Buddhist and Taoist institutions, who could be called on for help. In dealing with death in the modern period, families had greater choices, just as the Buddhist and Taoist priesthoods faced keener competition from other kinds of ritual specialists.

Finally, purgatory in medieval times was also imagined through metaphors that, like much of medieval Chinese thought, were linked to an exclusively or at least identifiably Buddhist view of existence. Many of the deities of the otherworld retained their Sanskrit names, and their biographies showed that they had lived previously in India. They remained demonstrably Buddhist and more clearly "foreign." The concept of purgatory after the medieval period had not lost all traces of Buddhist influence. As the next section of this chapter will demonstrate, the later notion of judgment after death was indebted quite heavily to the Buddhist notion of karma. But the later concept, unlike the medieval view of purgatory, was couched in language drawn from Chinese bureaucratic practice. In medieval times very few local metaphors were used to portray the purgatorial realms. The modern concept of purgatory supplanted the medieval one precisely because it sought greater accommodation with the demands of Chinese kinship and the realities of Chinese government.

THE NEW CONCEPT OF PURGATORY

Historiographic prudence has led most scholars to put forward the conservative, but ultimately untenable, hypothesis that the concept of a purgatorial realm administered by the ten kings made its first appearance in Chinese history in the year 926, which is the earliest certain dating of

Figure 4.1. Frontispiece illustration to a tenth-century copy of *The Scripture of the Ten Kings* (P 2870). Śākyamuni sits in the center, his disciples Śāriputra and Maudgalyāyana to the right and left (Śākyamuni's left and right). The monk Taoming kneels to the right of the altar, the Boys of Good and Evil to the left. Kings one through five are seated to the right from bottom to top; King Yama wears a cap with dangling pearls. Kings six through ten are seated to the left from top to bottom. (Photograph courtesy of the Bibliothèque Nationale, reproduced with permission)

one of the manuscript copies of *The Scripture of the Ten Kings (Shih-wang ching)*.[14] The mythology and rituals contained in this text are fully formed, and it remains highly doubtful that such a complex system would appear out of nowhere to be put down on paper for the first time in northwestern China in the early tenth century. In fact I have found two possible references to the purgatory of the ten kings in numerous earlier sources. The earliest is a brief notation in a Buddhist catalogue compiled in 664, which attributes *An Essay on the True Karma of the Ten Kings (Shih-wang cheng-yeh lun)* to a monk named Fa-yün, who lived around 660.[15]

Whichever date represents the first appearance of the ten kings in surviving sources, it is in the tenth-century copies of *The Scripture of the Ten Kings* that the modern conception of purgatory achieves its most convincing form. The formal title of the text is *The Scripture Spoken by the Buddha to the Four Orders on the Prophecy of King Yama Concerning the Feasts Practiced as Preparation Before Death and During the Seven Weeks of Intermediate Existence, for Rebirth in the Pure Land (Fo-shuo yen-lo wang shou-chi ssu-chung ni-hsiu sheng-ch'i-chai wang-sheng ching-t'u ching)*, which is why it is usually called simply *The Scripture of the Ten Kings*. The scripture opens in typical sūtra style, describing the audience of gods who have come to hear one of the last sermons of the historical Buddha, Śākyamuni. The audience includes not only the standard Indian Buddhist list of gods and bodhisattvas, but also figures indigenous to the Chinese underworld, like the Magistrate of Mount T'ai (T'ai-shan fu-chün), the Officer of Fate (Ssu-ming) and the Officer of Records (Ssu-lu), as well as numerous scribes and jailers. When all have arrived, the Buddha begins his sermon.

In the major portion of the scripture, the Buddha preaches the advantages of making offerings to the ten kings. Although individuals are allowed to make offerings on their own behalf while still alive, thereby piling up a store of money in preparation for the time after death when they will need it most, the Buddha's instructions are directed primarily to living family members, who are supposed to send offerings on behalf of the deceased. The Buddha explicitly instructs the functionaries of the underground offices to show special leniency to all souls whose families have sent offerings on their behalf: "The Law is broad and forgiving. You can be lenient with all sinners. When sons and daughters who are compassionate and filial cultivate merit and perform sacrifices to raise the dead, repaying the kindness shown in giving birth to them and supporting them, or when during the seven weeks they cultivate feasts and commission statues to repay their parents' kindness, then you should allow them to attain rebirth in the heavens." Later, a hymn warns the audience of the dangers that await the ancestors and promises the living that their suffrages will avert all torment for the dead:

At one hundred days dead people are subjected to more annoyances;
Their bodies are cangued and shackled and they are wounded by whips.
If sons and daughters exert themselves in cultivating merit,
Then [the dead] will be spared from dropping into the underground prisons,
    those places of
eternal suffering.[16]

The first seven sacrifices are to be conducted during the first forty-nine days after death, with the offerings destined for the first seven kings: the Far-Reaching King of Ch'in (Ch'in-kuang wang) during the first week, the King of the First River (Ch'u-chiang wang) during the second week, the Imperial King of Sung (Sung-ti wang) during the third week, the King of the Five Offices (Wu-kuan wang) during the fourth week, King Yama (Yen-lo wang) during the fifth week, the King of Transformations (Pien-ch'eng wang) during the sixth week, and the King of Mount T'ai (T'ai-shan wang) during the seventh week. These rituals should be followed by three more: the eighth, one hundred days after death, with offerings sent to the Impartial King (P'ing-teng wang); the ninth, one year after death, to the King of the Capital (Tu-shih wang); and the tenth three years after death, to the King of the Cycle of the Five Paths (Wu-tao chuan-lun wang) (see appendix 4.1).

When the dead person first arrives in purgatory, envoys riding black horses are dispatched to his or her old home to verify whether the person's descendants are performing the rituals. The scripture promises that if the family does send offerings, then as the deceased reaches each court he or she will be pardoned from the usual tortures and sent on to the next court. The text reserves the greatest reward for the end of the journey: no matter how terrible one's deeds during life, the deceased will be dispatched through the portals of life in the tenth court to attain rebirth in the heavens.

The plight of those hapless individuals whose families fail in their obligations to the ten kings is described to stirring effect in other portions of the scripture. Some versions of the text are accompanied by pictures interspersed in the narrative. These crudely drawn scenes portray a sinner with a wooden cangue encircling his neck, his hands bound, and his feet sometimes in shackles. In this position he is led from one torture to the next. In some chambers he is nailed down to a wooden bed with metal spikes; in others more specialized forms of mutilation are applied. Should a sinner claim to be unjustly punished, he or she is led before the karma mirror, usually shown in the fifth court, which unerringly reflects a person's deeds in past lives (see fig. 4.2). As if these trials were not enough, the scripture makes it painfully clear that, after surviving the tortures of these ten chambers, the sinner who lacks posthumous support from his or her family will be assigned a path of rebirth lower than his or her most recent life as an animal, hungry ghost, or hell being.

Figure 4.2. The fifth court of purgatory, as shown in a tenth-century copy of *The Scripture of the Ten Kings*. King Yama is seated behind the desk. At bottom right an inmate (wearing a cangue) is forced in front of the mirror, which reflects his previous deeds. Two other sinners wait their turn at bottom left. In the background at the top sits Ti-tsang Bodhisattva, accompanied by a golden lion and the monk Tao-ming. (Photograph of a modern Japanese collotype [in the author's collection], reproduction of the original in the collection of Satō Han'ai, now held in the Kubōsō Kinen Bijutsukan outside of Kyoto)

The philosophy of *The Scripture of the Ten Kings* represents a synthesis of Indian and Chinese concepts that later ages were to find completely convincing. The structure of the ten posthumous rituals combines the Buddhist notion of a forty-nine day period of purgatory punctuated by seven offerings with the traditional Chinese pattern of memorial services held one hundred days, one year, and three years (in the twenty-fifth or twenty-seventh month) after death. The bureaucrats themselves constitute a similar mixture. The first, third, sixth, and ninth kings have no attested precedents, but the form of their names sounds Chinese, so most modern studies presume that they are of Chinese origin. The seventh king is unmistakably Chinese, his cult at Mount T'ai being well established before the entry of Buddhism. The second king oversees the passage of souls over the Buddhist River Styx, the fifth king is portrayed in the *Vedas* as lord of the underworld and was absorbed at an early date into Indian Buddhist cosmology, and the tenth king controls the Buddhist cycle of rebirth; these three kings are regarded as Indian imports. The pedigrees of the fourth king and the eighth king are disputed. The title of the fourth, the King of the Five Offices, appears in the idealized Han dynasty accounts of the Chou government, but it may also be of Buddhist provenance, since heavenly messengers from the "Five Offices" were part of the Buddhist pantheon. And the name of the eighth king has been traced both to early Buddhism, where it is simply an epithet for King Yama (fifth in our series), and to the Manichean traditions known in medieval China. The totals: out of ten kings, one is undeniably Chinese, four are probably Chinese, three are purely Indian, one is claimed by both sides, and one could be either Indian or Persian.

However mixed the system may have been in terms of origins, it is clear that all members of the bureaucracy cooperated in administering a single invariant law. The written part of the text says that all of the gods report to Śākyamuni Buddha, and some of the frontispiece illustrations show the ten kings and their assistants arrayed in two neat rows under Śākyamuni's gaze. I would suggest that rather than interpreting the law of karma and the principle of bureaucracy as two essentially antithetical concepts, we should instead allow for the possibility, demonstrated in both the words and the pictures of *The Scripture of the Ten Kings*, that the Indian and Chinese notions were successfully synthesized.

The textual history of *The Scripture of the Ten Kings* provides an unusually instructive example of the way religious texts weathered the shift from medieval to modern Chinese civilization.[17] The longer recension consists of a handwritten scroll containing a narrative written in prose, hymns *(tsan)* composed in poetry, opening prayers to Amitābha Buddha, and pictures (usually numbering fourteen) illustrating the progress of the spirit through the underworld. Based on our knowledge of its use in later periods, it seems reasonable to assume that this kind of text was originally produced more as an object for ritual use than as a merely literary creation or a simple depiction of a particular scene.[18] In all likelihood it was not simply copied and then immediately shelved away in a temple library. Rather, it is my guess that it was carried by local priests to memorial services, where, once unrolled, the family of the deceased sang its hymns and told its story as a way of bringing relief to the spirit of the ancestor pictured in its illustrations. Since both text and pictures were done by hand—probably by two different hands—and in light of the high cost of producing handwritten copies, it is likely that the surviving copies of this version drew a rather expensive fee for rental.

A second type of manuscript copy is shorter. It contains merely a narrative and lacks both pictures and hymns. Written on both scrolls and in the format of a large, bound booklet, this recension was probably chanted by monks.

A third kind of manuscript copy, of which only one survives, represents a further stage in the development of the Chinese "book." It is a tiny bound booklet, measuring 5.3 by 4.9 centimeters. It contains the hymns and ritual instructions of the longer recension but no illustrations. I suspect that this copy of the text was owned by a ritual specialist for his own private use, as were many texts bound in the same fashion.[19] An officiant could use such a text for private study and take it along to funeral services as an *aide-mémoire,* especially when illustrated copies were rare or when the mourning family could not afford them.

The text of *The Scripture of the Ten Kings* also exists in a form that came into its heyday in Sung times, a bound folio printed from wooden blocks. These printed editions for the most part retain the ritual formulae and hymns contained in the earliest manuscripts, but they lack pictures. Like most forms of the printed book, they were in all likelihood accessible to a broader range of people than the audience for the same text in medieval times.

The range of functions of the actual texts of *The Scripture of the Ten Kings* thus serves as a neat summary of the growth of the idea of purgatory, which began on the outskirts of the Buddhist church in medieval times and, once detached from the control of religious specialists and the wealth of great families, spread quickly throughout all classes of society.

Evidence for the hegemony of the ten kings over the realm of purgatory becomes quite widespread, both sociologically and geographically, beginning in the tenth century. What follows is a selective survey of the manifestation of the ten kings in art, literature, and funerary practice in the tenth century and after.

The sight of the ten kings arrayed in two neat rows, originally part of the frontispiece to the tenth-century copies of *The Scripture of the Ten Kings,* was also a scene worthy of depiction in its own right. Numerous paintings survive from the tenth century that show the ten kings seated before Ti-tsang (Kṣitigarbha) Bodhisattva.[20] Some of the ten kings are mentioned in a short prose piece written by the T'ang statesman Ssu-k'ung T'u (837–908) on the occasion of a local celebration in Shansi.[21] An epigraphical collection preserves notice of statues of the ten kings that were commissioned by a man named Tu Liang in late 910 or early 911 in Szechwan.[22] An encyclopedia compiled in the mid-tenth century by the monk I-ch'u, who lived most of his life in eastern China, quotes several lines from *The Scripture of the Ten Kings.*[23] A painting now held in the Musée Guimet and dated to the year 983 depicts the ten kings seated in circular fashion around Ti-tsang Bodhisattva (see fig. 4.3).[24] Yet other evidence points to the existence of paintings of the ten kings in Honan during the late tenth century.[25]

Notices on contemporary customs written in the twelfth and thirteenth centuries testify to the popularity of the ten kings in mortuary ritual. A Buddhist layman of the twelfth century describes the harrowing experiences that await one after death: "On the road ahead you see no

Figure 4.3. Painting on silk dated 983 from Tun-huang depicting Ti-tsang Bod-hisattva as lord of the six paths. Ti-tsang Bodhisattva is seated in the center. At top the six paths float to the left and right. Immediately below Ti-tsang are Tao-ming and the lion, and below them are seated four magistrates. The ten kings are arranged in clockwise rotation starting at top right. The bottom panel contains, from left to right, Yin-lu Bodhisattva, a dedication dated T'ai-p'ing hsing-kuo 8/XI/14 (20 December 983), and portraits of the donor and her servants. (Muséee Guimet [MG 17662]. Photograph copyright Réunion des Musées Nationaux)

light, and looking around you see no companions. Crossing to the other shore of the Nai-ho you see them, all of them in desperate pain. Everyone going through the portal at the Ghost Gate trembles with fear. In the other world only seven days have passed, but in the dark world you are forced to have an audience with the ten kings. The officers of the bureau who hold the case books lack all human feeling, and the prison guards carrying pitchforks never smile."[26]

Hung Mai (1123–1202) reports secondhand on the experience of one Yü I-lang, who took ill in the year 1192 and was dragged into the wilds by two ghost guards. When they came to throngs of people wading across the river of hell, they alone were able to cross by bridge. On the other side they were welcomed by other ghost messengers and countless birds and beasts. Up ahead were more than a thousand monks. The story continues: "When they came to a building, the messengers led him inside. At the top of the chamber, he saw ten men seated separately. They were wearing the clothes of a king. When Yü asked where he was, he was told, 'These are the ten kings of the subterrestrial administration.' " The kings and their assistants questioned Yü about his previous actions and decided to add two years to his life in recognition of the many times he had saved the lives of animals. Yü was then returned to the light of day to live out his extended lifespan, and when he returned home, he found that the judgment of the kings had been written in several lines of vermilion characters across his palm.[27]

Probably the most impressive display of the ten kings is found in a colossal rock carving of an underworld scene at Ta pao-ting shan near Ta-tsu (midway between Chungking and Ch'eng-tu) in the province of Szechwan.[28] The scene is one among thirty-one huge tableaux constituting a kind of folk Buddhist "theme park" that was constructed between 1177 and 1249. Some highlights of a tour of the pilgrimage center would have included scenes of the six realms of existence, representations of Vairocana (P'i-lu-she-na) Buddha, statues of the Thousand-Armed Avalokiteśvara (Kuan-yin), portrayals of Śākyamuni's entry into nirvāṇa, scenes from Śākyamuni's birth and childhood, illustrations of the kindness shown by parents to children stressing the importance of filial devotion, representations of the Pure Land presided over by Amitābha Buddha (A-mi-t'o fo), statues of a local Tantric monk whose secular name was Liu Pen-tsun, and a local version of the ten ox-herding pictures of the Ch'an school. Given the large number of indigenous Chinese scriptures ("apocrypha") inscribed there together with the placement of the scenes at the viewer's eye level, most scholars argue that the clientele for such a religious center was probably illiterate or semiliterate common folks with an interest in but certainly no formal ties to Buddhism. The planning and supervision of the carving of Ta pao-ting shan is attributed to a man named Chao Chih-feng, born in 1149 near Ta-tsu.

The organization of Ta pao-ting shan suggests that pilgrims toured the scenes in a set pattern, with the scenes of hell constituting the twentieth exhibition. The carving is divided into three horizontal panels. In the top panel Ti-tsang Bodhisattva stands at the center. Above he is flanked by a grouping of ten anonymous Buddhas, while below he is flanked by the ten kings of purgatory. Each king is identified by his standard name, and beside each king are inscribed moralistic passages describing the fate of the dead. Most of these passages reproduce verbatim the text of *The Scripture of the Ten Kings,* including the merit one can accumulate "if one commissions the copying of this scripture and the drawing of images."[29] The middle panel consists of ten scenes of punishment in the various hells, and the lower panel presents seven examples of retribution for specific sins.

Thirteenth-century sources provide some idea of the variation in mortuary practices involving the ten kings. A Buddhist history completed in 1237 reports on two different techniques for sending offerings to the ten kings: "Some people revere the method of bestowing blessings on the dead, whereas others hold assemblies in preparation for their own demise."[30] An anonymous work dating from the middle of the century also mentions the premortem practice and suggests that a class of "common monks" (*yung-seng*—undistinguished? unordained? illiterate? unvirtuous? entrepreneurial?) encouraged people in Hangchow to "send treasury money" (*chi-k'u*) to the ten kings before death. Such money was credited to the personal account in the underworld on which each person drew in order to achieve birth and which, at death, had to be reimbursed in order to pass successfully through purgatory.[31] The terminology here ("common" or "run-of-the-mill" monks) has sociological significance, because it suggests that, whether the author was a Buddhist monk or a non-Buddhist member of the literati, he may have believed that the "monks" in question entered the order by irregular means, corrupted the order with unorthodox practices, or sought financial support outside the legally certified channels of Buddhist monasticism.

It is likely that by the end of the thirteenth century the dispatch of offerings to the ten kings on behalf of a deceased family member was an activity that occurred primarily outside the Buddhist and Taoist churches. The custom was so well established that ecclesiastical authorities could not help but take notice. This surmise would explain why the Buddhist monk Chih-p'an (ca. 1260) described the practice and attempted to offer an origin myth that would legitimize it but ended by admitting that he could only find precedents in scriptural and historical texts for the names of six of the ten kings—and most of those precedents came from non-Buddhist sources.[32] Also by this time Buddhist authorities had come to accept the attribution of *The Scripture of the Ten Kings* to a monk named Tsang-ch'uan of Ta-sheng-tz'u ssu in Ch'eng-tu—about whom absolutely nothing is known—but they still refused to allow *The Scripture of the Ten Kings* into the Buddhist canon.

Offerings to the ten kings likewise remained marginal to the Taoist church in the twelfth and thirteenth centuries. In fact, the Taoists attempted to build on the popularity of the ten kings by renaming them in distinctively Taoist terms. Thus there is a work contained in the Taoist canon entitled *The Scripture Spoken by the Exalted Heavenly Venerable Who Saves From Suffering Concerning the Cancellation of Faults and the Extinction of Sins.*[33] In this text the Taoist divinity known as the Exalted Heavenly Venerable Who Saves From Suffering preaches the advantages of making posthumous offerings to an exclusively Taoist set of ten purgatorial gods. The Taoist gods are called by the title "true lord" *(chen-chün)* rather than "king," but in all other respects the rituals addressed to them are identical to the nondenominational services involving the ten kings. Their names, together with those of another set of ten Taoist divinities called "celestial venerables" *(t'ien-tsun),* are listed in appendix 4.2. One liturgy even admits that its audience is probably more familiar with the ten kings of purgatory than with the Taoist true lords. After listing the ten true lords, *The Ceremonial Rules of the Ten Kings of the Underworld Offices Who Bring Salvation (Ti-fu shih-wang pa-tu i)* then points out that each of the ten is commonly called by his name in the standard system. The language typically goes: "Burn incense and make offerings to the Dark Offices. The first court is that of the True Lord of Great Plainness and Mysterious Breadth, whom people in our time call the Great Far-Reaching King of Ch'in."[34] This locution, together with what we know of the relations between Taoism and other forms of Chinese religion around this time, suggests that the Taoist church attempted to weld its own theology onto the widespread worship of the ten kings by redefining the standard system in more exclusive terms.

By the fourteenth century pictures of the ten kings were a familiar sight throughout China and were gaining popularity in Korea and Japan.[35] Their fame in China was due in part to the use of stencils in mass-producing a new iconographic form. Several hundred paintings that in this century are housed in collections in Japan, Europe, and the United States were originally produced in just a few ateliers in Ning-po associated with the Chin and Lu families in the late twelfth and early thirteenth centuries. These paintings consist of ten scrolls, each scroll depicting one of the ten kings. The iconographic details have achieved a high degree of standardization, and the paintings lack any narrative form.[36]

The persistence of purgatory in the Ming and Ch'ing dynasties and in modern times is a fascinating phenomenon that goes far beyond the limits of this chapter. Here it will suffice to mention only a few of the most noticeable manifestations. The domain of the ten kings is fleshed out in considerable detail along with lists of the specific forms of punishment attaching to specific forms of sin in a genre known as the "Jade Calendar" *(Yü-li)*, named after the yearly account books in which the gods of the otherworld record each person's good and evil actions. Most copies of this inexpensive tract contain illustrations. Some copies purport to date from the eleventh century, but the early seventeenth century is a more likely period of authorship.[37] The courts of the ten kings are the subject of numerous "precious scrolls" *(pao-chüan)* in later times.[38] In contemporary times the ten kings continue to exert their authority over the dead. A book entitled *Journey Through Hell (Ti-yü yu-chi)* was dictated over a two-year period in the 1970s in T'ai-chung, Taiwan, by a spirit medium as he made his way through the ten courts.[39] Scrolls of the ten kings are an especially common sight at contemporary Taiwanese funerals. The ones with which I am familiar are owned by ritual specialists, who hang them around the funeral shed constructed outside the home. The scrolls serve to instruct the living and to assist them in securing safe passage for the dead.

THE BROADER CONTEXT

Several important historical questions remain to be answered. Although there were precedents in earlier centuries, there is nevertheless an undeniable explosion of interest in the ten kings beginning in the early tenth century, when they apparently first achieved systematic representation in *The Scripture of the Ten Kings.* By the time that the dust settles in the fourteenth century, the reign of the ten kings in every corner of the Chinese empire is beyond the suspicion of even the most rebellious or the most agnostic of dissenters. Anyone acquainted with Chinese history will note immediately the synchronicity of this epochal shift of authority in the underworld with the social, economic, and political realignments that historians have commonly identified as the transition from "medieval" to "early modern" China. In the pages that follow I explore the connections between these two transitions—one in the world of the dead and the other in the realm of the living—by focusing on three topics: the deinstitutionalization of mortuary ritual, the relationship between religion and society, and the commercialization of purgatory.

It is of vital importance to state in the clearest possible terms that the myths and rituals involving the ten kings of purgatory in the tenth through fourteenth centuries were not located exclusively within the organized religions of Buddhism and Taoism. Rather, they were an expression of the most long-lasting and "diffused" form of religious activity in China, the cult dedicated to the ancestors.[40] Often the locus of services held for the ancestors in purgatory was the home, not the Buddhist or Taoist temple. As will be shown below, the material proceeds from the offerings made during these services were not restricted to Buddhist or Taoist churches. Hence, although the sources for this period are regrettably silent on the question of who, if anyone, officiated at these rituals, in all likelihood when religious specialists were hired by families to assist in memorial services, they had at best only a tenuous and unofficial tie with Buddhist and Taoist churches. I would, then, caution against dubbing the mythology of the ten kings as "Buddhist." The religion of the ten kings had its historical roots in several different forms of Chinese religion: in an indigenous concern for the fate of the ancestors, in an originally local cult dedicated to the spirit of Mount T'ai, in an essentially Buddhist cosmology that depended on the idea of karma and a pantheon of Indian deities, and in a system of divine surveillance elaborated most fully in the Taoist religion. The ten kings operated within the broad context of a general mix of Chinese religious ideas, in which Buddhist concepts were an important ingredient but not necessarily the determining factor. Even to call the religion of the kings "lay Buddhist" would be to assume, contrary to all evidence, that its members had purposefully and ceremonially taken refuge in Buddhism or had consistently distinguished themselves as Buddhists. Similarly, to refer to the notion of purgatory as "syncretic" is to attribute a lack of coherence—an unreasoned assemblage of parts that ought not be put together—to a system that provided a consistently successful way of dealing with death for over one thousand years. And to label such a religious phenomenon "popular" is not so much wrong as it is imprecise, for the term obscures many of the crucial sociological facts we know about who participated in the religion of the ten kings, and when and where the rituals were held.

The noninstitutional character of the ten kings of purgatory becomes even clearer in view of rituals directed toward several analogous sets of deities that were claimed by both Buddhism and Taoism. Beginning in medieval times and continuing well beyond the fourteenth century, both the Buddhist and Taoist churches urged their lay members to gather ten times per month for special services called *chai* (connoting both "fast" and "feast"), during which members of the celestial bureaucracy descended to judge people's behavior and to make reports to their superiors. According to the Buddhist system, if one correctly performs the requisite ritual, then after one's death one's sins will be remitted for a specific number of kalpas and one will avoid suffering in a specific hell. The tenth-century texts that prescribe such rituals take the following form: "On the first day of the month the Boys of Good and Evil descend. If one invokes Dipaṃkara Tathāgata Buddha and upholds the feast, then one's sins will be wiped away for forty kalpas and one will not fall into the Hell of Knives and Swords."[41] The days of the month, the names of the descending functionaries, and the names of the Buddhist deities to invoke are listed in appendix 4.3.

Similarly, texts collected in the Taoist canon prescribe feasts on the same ten days of the month, but here a group, and sometimes two groups, of exclusively Taoist deities descend to pass judgment. A sixth-century text, for instance, explains that on the first day of the month, the god of the Big Dipper sits in judgment over the Northwest and that he sends down his assistants, "The Envoys Who Carry Letters," to inspect the behavior of devotees.[42] The days of the month, directions, names of the gods, and names of their assistants are listed in appendix 4.4.

The Buddhist and Taoist feast days provide a helpful contrast to the system of purgatory and its rituals. The Buddhist and Taoist systems were organized and propagated by their respective churches, whereas the purgatorial system grew up largely outside of institutional religion. The Buddhist and Taoist feast days were followed mostly by people who identified themselves self-consciously as either lay devotees or monks, whereas those who made offerings to the ten kings of purgatory constituted the majority of Chinese people in the tenth through fourteenth centuries, that is, peasants having little or no exclusive ties to either Buddhism or Taoism. And the institutional feasts were held regularly, whereas offerings to the ten kings depended for their timing on the unpredictable shadow of death.

In addressing the relationship between religious and social change, it is tempting to isolate the two systems "religion" and "society" and to proceed as if they formed clearly bounded domains possessing universal validity. Once so stated, the shortcomings of such a dichotomy become obvious, as do the twin prejudices that usually follow from the assumption of an unvarying separation of the social and the religious. Against certain interpreters of Weber, who tend to portray religious ideology as the only motivating factor in social change, we need to acknowledge the social and economic factors that changed the kind of relationship that the living had with the dead. Similarly, against some exaggerations of materialism, it must be recognized that a certain space had to be cleared theoretically—that a great deal of philosophical work had to be done—before a new kind of economic activity became possible.[43] This chapter is not the place to develop a broader theoretical framework for construing the relationship between the new society of the Sung dynasty and its new concept of the afterlife, but several concrete suggestions may help in avoiding a reductive or monocausal understanding.

The bureaucrats of purgatory assumed power around the same time that a new society and a relatively new form of government administration began to take shape during the Sung dynasty. A more precise picture of this process must necessarily await further research by social historians. In the meantime it is important to follow the suggestion of Emily Martin Ahern that the authority exercised by these two kinds of bureaucrats not be assumed a priori to be different in nature. Rather, in early modern times it was possible to imagine only one kind of governmental power, held by both officials on earth and officials underground.[44] The two levels of government exercised the same kind of power, not a "secular" power on one level and a "religious" power on the other.

New ways of dealing with the dead also found their analogues in changes in the kinship system at the end of the T'ang and the beginning of the Sung dynasties. Although the medieval ideal of conspicuous expenditure and the donation of land never disappeared entirely, it was certainly surpassed in popularity by the less costly method of sending token money to the ancestors. Although final salvation of the dead was not thereby assured, help for the dead and solace for the living could at least be achieved by far greater numbers of people and at a lower price. Just how this development is related to the expanded role of the descent group in other realms of ritual activity remains an important but as yet unanswered question.[45]

From a comparative perspective, it becomes clearer that what emerges in the tenth century and gains dominance soon after is not simply a new form of mortuary ritual or a new structure of society but rather a new morality, commercial in tone and optimistic in outlook. In both Europe and Japan in the twelfth and thirteenth centuries, as in China just a few hundred years earlier, the development of a new morality entailed a number of other changes. As scholars of medieval Japan have pointed out, the new morality strengthened ties between the living and the dead; it provided hope for all of imperfect virtue; it answered religious concerns about death while validating the secular structures of everyday life; through it religious specialists found a more central place in society; and it was based not so much on fear as on the optimistic attitude that the dead could be saved.[46]

The conjunction of gods, death, and commerce caught the eye of one of the earliest European travelers to China. Reading through Marco Polo's (1254–1324) travelogue, one is struck by the recurrence of certain phrases. What Marco Polo says here of Cacanfu (Ho-chien fu, in Chih-li) he repeats constantly of other locales: "Cacanfu is a noble city. The people are Idolaters and burn their dead; they have paper-money, and live by trade and handicrafts."[47]

As is well known, paper money was used widely for commerce in the twelfth and thirteenth centuries, attendant upon the great revolutions in commerce, urbanization, and printing that the recent generation of Japanese historians has documented so fully. Evidence offered in a beautiful work by Hou Ching-lang demonstrates that by the twelfth century not only had paper money become the standard item offered to the bureaucrats of purgatory, but a new system of religious economy was also in operation. Each person was born into this world by borrowing money from the bank of the otherworld. Each person stayed alive only so long as the term of repayment had not ended. At death, each person was required to repay in full the loan contracted at birth. One could send installment payments during one's lifetime in order to lessen the amount due on the final payment, but most people needed to send the greatest amount at the time of death. In theory the ten kings of purgatory were the chief executive officers of this banking organization, although Buddhism and Taoism added their own ranks of administrators, accountants, clerks, and messengers to the system. Hou describes the system and its relationship to contemporaneous developments in economy:

> In summary, the whole theme of obtaining life, including the notion of debt, repayment, and the organization of the Treasury, rests on the same base as the theme of Fundamental Destiny which is implied in the texts studied and of which it appears to be the origin. According to this ancient conception, each individual is in correspondence with the organization of the otherworld, just as he has a place in the organization of the empire. He exists, so to speak, on two levels: if his destiny deteriorates in the otherworld, he must restore it on earth, the structures of the otherworld reflecting the political structures of the empire, the registers of the otherworld comprising an actual census of the terrestrial population in imitation of the registers of the Empire, well conducted beginning in the third century B.C. This organization of the otherworld, this connection with everyone, we find again in the conception of the purchase of life, along with debt and repayment, but transposed on an economic plane at a time, we should note, when the organization of banking was tied to commercial development facilitated by loans, which naturally set the idea of debt in a positive light.[48]

As Hou notes elsewhere, paper money had been used in funerals as early as the seventh century, well before the social and economic developments that made it the preeminent token of exchange during the Sung dynasty.[49] This means that an economy based on paper money in China developed first in the realm of the afterlife. The system of religious economy in the twelfth century was already in place during the T'ang dynasty, when, it must be assumed, the authority of an otherworldly government guaranteed the value of spirit money. The "underground" economy required only the development of commercial institutions aboveground to achieve its full articulation.

By the thirteenth century the decisive shifts in the religion of purgatory and, conjointly, in the economy of religion had already occurred. In the medieval religious economy, the ideal funeral service involved hiring monks to chant scriptures, commissioning a statue made of precious metal, or paying to have a scripture copied by scribes. The goal was sending merit to the deceased, but as a rule the means entailed the expenditure of large sums of money. In the thirteenth century the same end could be achieved by almost all classes, since even poor people could afford a little spirit money, which was inexpensive in this world but dear in the next. Salvation was not only cheaper, it was made more uniform, since everyone alive had, by definition, borrowed money that they or their descendants had to repay.

The widespread use of paper money was yet another factor in the deinstitutionalization of mortuary practice after medieval times. In the medieval economy, the family of the deceased had given land or material goods to Buddhist and Taoist churches. In later times the churches lost their position within the Chinese economy, owing in part to changes in the legal and customary systems of land tenure and to new commercial structures that became new centers of economic power. In addition to the great temples there developed new beneficiaries of the economy of death. First, to purchase imitation money, one had to pay real money to people who printed and sold spirit money, who were probably connected to the newly emerging groups of artisans and merchants. There were undoubtedly other persons who found employment in the funerary economy by renting copies of their paintings of purgatory and by assisting in funerals. However, they had few affinities with Buddhist and Taoist priests and probably resembled more the newly emerging class of ritual and performance specialists, those people who could draw on a rich stock of liturgy and opera to entertain the living and to bring relief to the deceased at funerals. Second, once spirit money was purchased, it had to be transmitted—transformed by fire—to the functionaries of purgatory. The transformed currency went not to the treasuries of Buddhist or Taoist temples, those great repositories of medieval wealth, but rather to the bureaucrats of the otherworld, the representatives of a new social and economic order.

The ultimate benefit, of course, was still dedicated to the salvation of the ancestors. But as time went on that merit could be secured through institutions that developed only at the end of the medieval period. To insure the good fortune of the ancestors, paper money first had to be purchased from specialists who printed it, and then it had to be transmitted downward to the ten kings of purgatory.

Appendix 4.1

THE TEN KINGS OF PURGATORY

ORDINAL NUMBER OF KING	TIME AFTER DEATH	NAME OF KING
1	7 days	Far-Reaching King of Ch'in Ch'in-kuang wang
2	14 days	King of the First River Ch'u-chiang wang
3	21 days	Imperial King of Sung Sung-ti wang
4	28 days	King of the Five Offices Wu-kuan wang
5	35 days	King Yama Yen-lo wang
6	42 days	King of Transformations Pien-ch'eng wang
7	49 days	King of Mount T'ai T'ai-shan wang
8	100 days	Impartial King P'ing-teng wang
9	one year	King of the Capital Tu-shih wang
10	three years	King of the Cycle of the Five Paths Wu-tao chuan-lun wang

Appendix 4.2

THE TAOIST GODS

ORDINAL NUMBER	TRUE LORD	CELESTIAL VENERABLE
1	True Lord of Great Plainness and Mysterious Breadth T'ai-su miao-kuang chen-chün	Celestial Venerable, the Jade Jewel, Augustly Exalted Yü-pao huang-shang t'ien-tsun
2	True Lord of Dark Virtue and Calm Rest Yin-te ting-hsiu chen-chün	Celestial Venerable of Dark Truth and Ten Thousand Blessings Hsüan-chen wan-fu t'ien-tsun
3	True Lord of Penetrating Brightness and Universal Quiescence Tung-ming p'u-ching chen-chün	Celestial Venerable of the Extreme Ultimate of Great Mystery T'ai-miao chih-chi t'ien-tsun
4	True Lord of the Five Spirits of Dark Virtue Hsüan-te wu-ling chen-chün	Celestial Venerable of the Darkly Exalted Jade Dawn Hsüan-shang yü-ch'en t'ien-tsun
5	True Lord of the Most Excellent Shining Spirit Tsui-sheng hui-ling chen-chün	Celestial Venerable, the Exalted Sage Who Crosses to Immortality Tu-hsien shang-sheng t'ien-tsun
6	True Lord of Jeweled Reverence and Brightness Complete Pao-su chao-ch'eng chen-chün	Celestial Venerable Who Loves Birth and Measures Life Spans Hao-sheng tu-ming t'ien-tsun
7	True Lord of Dark Virtue and Mysterious Birth Hsüan-te miao-sheng chen-chün	Celestial Venerable, the Great Spirit, Vacuous and August Ta-ling hsü-huang t'ien-tsun
8	True Lord of Unsurpassed Right Salvation Wu-shang cheng-tu chen-chün	Celestial Venerable of Immeasurably Great Splendor Wu-liang ta-hua t'ien-tsun
9	True Lord of Flying Demons and Extensive Rewards Fei-mo yen-ch'ing chen-chün	Celestial Venerable of Jade Vacuity, Bright and August Yü-hsü ming-huang t'ien-tsun
10	True Lord of the Awesome Spirit of the Five Transformations Wu-hua wei-ling chen-chün	Celestial Venerable of the Truly August Penetrating Spirit Chen-huang tung-shen t'ien-tsun

Source: Ti-fu shih-wang pa-tu i (HY 215), pp. 4a–12a.

Appendix 4.3

DEITIES OF THE TEN FEASTS IN BUDDHISM

ORDINAL NUMBER OF FEAST	DAY OF MONTH	DESCENDING FUNCTIONARY	BUDDHIST DEITY INVOKED
1	1	Boys of Good and Evil Shan-o t'ung-tzu	Dipaṃkara Tathāgata Buddha Ting-kuang ju-lai fo
2	8	Prince T'ai-tzu	Bhaiṣajyaguru vaiḍūryaprabha Buddha Yao-shih liu-li-kuang fo
3	14	Inspector of Life Spans and Officer of Records Ch'a-ming ssu-lu	Thousand Buddhas of a Worthy Kalpa Hsien-chieh ch'ien-fo
4	15	Great General of the Five Paths Wu-tao ta-chiang-chün	Amitābha Buddha A-mi-t'o fo
5	18	King Yama Yen-lo wang	Avalokiteśvara Bodhisattva Kuan-shih-yin p'u-sa
6	23	Great General of Heaven T'ien ta-chiang-chün	Vairocana Buddha Lu-she-na fo
7	24	Magistrate of Mount T'ai T'ai-shan fu-chün	Kṣitigarbha Bodhisattva Ti-tsang p'u-sa
8	28	Śakra, Emperor of Heaven T'ien-ti shih	Amitābha Buddha A-mi-t'o fo
9	29	Four Kings of Heaven Ssu t'ien-wang	Bhaiṣajyarāja and Bhaiṣajya-samudgata Bodhisattvas Yao-wang yao-shang p'u-sa
10	30	Great Brahmā, King of Heaven Ta-fan t'ien-wang	Śākyamuni Buddha Shih-chia-mou-ni fo

Source: Ta-sheng ssu-chai jih, no. 1164, *T* no. 2849.

Appendix 4.4

DEITIES OF THE TEN FEASTS IN TAOISM

ORDINAL NUMBER OF FEAST	DAY OF MONTH	DIRECTION	CHIEF GOD	ASSISTANT
1	1	NW	Big Dipper Pei-tou	Messenger Who Transmits Letters Ch'uan-hsin shih-che
2	8	N	Ghost of the Big Dipper Who Oversees Death Pei-tou ssu-sha kuei	Messenger of the Red Chariot Ch'ih-ch'e shih-che
3	14	NE	Messenger of the Great One T'ai-i shih-che	Messenger of the Administrator of Offices Tien-ssu shih-che
4	15	E	Emperor of Heaven T'ien-ti	Three Offices of Heaven, Earth, and Water, the Messenger of the Inspector T'ien-ti-shui san-kuan, Chien-ssu shih-che
5	18	SE	One of Heaven T'ien-i	Messenger of the Board of Robbery Tsei-ts'ao shih-che
6	23	S	Eight Spirit Messengers of the Great One T'ai-i pa-shen shih-che	Attendant of Talismans and Memorials Fu-chang shih-tsung
7	24	SW	North Star Pei-ch'en	Three Generals Who Protect Residences Shou-chai san-chiang-chün
8	28	W	Lower Great One Hsia-t'ai-i	Messenger of the Prince of Heaven T'ien-kung shih-che
9	29	Nadir	Middle Great One Chung t'ai-i	General of the Various Offices Chu-kuan chiang-chün
10	30	Zenith	Upper Great One Shang t'ai-i	Messenger of the Emperor of Heaven T'ien-ti shih-che

Source: T'ai-shang tung-hsüan ling-pao yeh-pao yin-yüan ching (HY 336), *T* 4. 10a–10b.

NOTES

1. Jacques Le Goff, *The Birth of Purgatory,* trans. Arthur Goldhammer (Chicago: University of Chicago Press, 1984), p. 4.

2. On Mount T'ai, see Édouard Chavannes, *Le T'ai chan: Essai de monographie d'un culte chinois,* Annales du Musée Guimet, vol. 21 (Paris: Ernest Leroux, 1910). For a convenient compendium of grave "contracts," see Ikeda On, "Chūgoku rekidai boken ryakkō," *Tōyō bunka kenkyūjo kiyō* 86 (1981): 193–278. For an important analysis of Han dynasty mortuary ritual and the bureaucracy of the otherworld, see Anna Seidel, "Traces of Han Religion in Funeral Texts Found in Tombs," in Akizuki Kan'ei, ed., *Dōkyō to shūkyō bunka* (Tokyo: Hirakawa shuppansha, 1987), pp. 21–57. See also Ying-shih Yü, " 'O Soul, Come Back!' A Study in the Changing Conceptions of the Soul and Afterlife in Pre-Buddhist China," *HJAS* 47.2 (1987): 363–395.

3. See Michel Soymié, "Notes d'iconographie chinoise: Les acolytes de Ti-tsang," part 1, *Arts asiatiques* 14 (1966): 45–78.

4. See *A-p'i-ta-mo ta p'i-p'o-sha lun (Mahāvibhāṣā),* 69, trans. Hsüan-tsang (602–664), *T* 27.356c–358a; and André Bareau, *Les sectes bouddhiques du Petit Véhicule* (Saigon: École française d'Extrême-Orient, 1955), p. 283.

5. See Nakamura Hajime, *Bukkyōgo daijiten* (Tokyo: Tōkyō shoseki kabushiki kaisha, 1975), 1.144a.

6. *A-p'i-ta-mo chü-she lun (Abhidharmakośa),* 9, Vasubandhu, trans. Hsüan-tsang (602–664), *T* 29.46a–47a.

7. For a convenient listing of the Buddhist sources, see Mochizuki Shinkō, *Bukkyō daijiten,* third edition (Kyoto: Sekai seiten kankō kyōkai, 1954–1971), 2.1809a–1810a. For the secular references, see, for example, Wei Shou (506–572), ed., *Wei shu* (Peking: Chung-hua shu-chü, 1974), 83B.1834–1835; and Li Yen-shou (ca. 629), ed., *Pei shih* (Peking: Chung-hua shu-chü, 1974), 80.2688. For Taoist sources, see *T'ai-shang tung-hsüan ling-pao yeh-pao yin-yüan ching* (HY 336), 8.5b–7a; and *T'ai-shang tz'u-pei tao-ch'ang hsiao-tsai chiu-yu ch'an* (HY 543), 10.7b.

8. See his "The *Consecration Sūtra:* A Buddhist Book of Spells," in Robert E. Buswell, Jr., ed., *Chinese Buddhist Apocrypha* (Honolulu: University of Hawaii Press, 1990), pp. 75–118.

9. *Kuan-ting ching* 12, *T* 21.535b.

10. *Ching-lü i-hsiang* 49, 50, Pao-ch'ang (ca. 516), *T* 53.258b–268c. For a survey of the Buddhist concepts of hell available to fifth-century Chinese thinkers, see Étienne Lamotte, trans., *Le traité de la grand vertu de sagesse de Nāgārjuna (Mahāprajñāpāramitāśāstra)* (Louvain-la-Neuve: Institut orientaliste, 1949), 2.955–957, n. 2.

11. See Jacques Gernet, *Les Aspects économiques du bouddhisme dans la société chinoise du Ve au Xe siècle* (Saigon: École française d'Extrême-Orient, 1956), pp. 191–224; and Stephen F. Teiser, *The Ghost Festival in Medieval China* (Princeton: Princeton University Press, 1988), pp. 196–213.

12. See Chikusa Masaaki, *Chūgoku bukkyō shakaishi kenkyū,* Tōyō shi kenkyū sōkan, no. 34 (Kyoto: Dōhōsha, 1982), pp. 477–557; Naba Toshisada, "Bukkyō-shinkō ni motozukite soshiki serararetaru chūbantō godai ji no shayū ni tsuite," *Shirin* 24.3, 24.4 (1939); and idem, "Tōdai no shayō ni tsukite," *Shirin*

23.2, 23.3, 23.4 (1938), both reprinted in *Tōdai shakai bunka shi kenkyū* (Tokyo: Sōbunsha, 1974).

13. See Miriam Levering, "Ta-hui and Lay Buddhists: Ch'an Sermons on Death," in David W. Chappell, ed., *Buddhist and Taoist Practice in Medieval Chinese Society: Buddhist and Taoist Studies II*, Asian Studies at Hawaii, no. 34 (Honolulu: University of Hawaii Press, 1987), pp. 181–206; and Timothy J. Brook, "Gentry Dominance in Chinese Society: Monasteries and Lineages in the Structuring of Local Society, 1500–1700" (Ph.D. dissertation, Harvard University, 1984).

14. For a listing of manuscript copies of the text, see my forthcoming study *The Scripture of the Ten Kings*. The most important studies of the text include Annemarie von Gabain, "Kṣitigarbha-Kult in Zentralasien, Buchillustrationen aus den Turfan-Funden," in Herbert Härtel and Volker Moeller, eds., *Indologentagung 1971* (Wiesbaden: Franz Steiner, 1973); Hsiao Ch'eng-fu, *Tun-huang su-wen-hsüeh lun-ts'ung* (Taipei: Commercial Press, 1988), pp. 175–292; Matsumoto Eiichi, *Tonkō ga no kenkyū* (Tokyo: Tōhō bunka gakuin, 1937), 1.402–416; Niida Noboru, "Tonkō hakken *Jūō kyō* token ni mietaru keihō shiryō," *Tōyō gakuhō* 25.3 (1938): 63–78; Sakai Tadao, "Jūō shinkō ni kansuru shomondai oyobi *Enraō juki kyō*," in *Saitō sensei koki shukuga kinen ronbun shū* (Tokyo: Katanae shoin, 1937), pp. 611–656; Sawada Mizuho, *Jigoku hen: Chūgoku no meikai setsu* (Kyoto: Hōzōkan, 1968), pp. 22–30; Tokushi Yūshō and Ogawa Kan'ichi, "*Jūō shōshichi kyō* santoken no kōzō," in *Chūō Ajia bukkyō to bijutsu,* Seiiki bunka kenkyū, vol. 5 (Tokyo: Hōzōkan, 1963), pp. 255–296; and Tsukamoto Zenryū, "Inro bosastsu shinkō ni tsuite," in *Tōhō gakuhō* 1 (1931): 130–182.

15. Tao-hsüan (596–667), *Ta T'ang nei-tien lu* 5, T 55.282a. There is every reason to trust Tao-hsüan's word in this case. Tao-hsüan himself was abbot of Hsi-ming ssu, where he claims that Fa-yün lived. Tao-hsüan lists the works of Fa-yün just before listing his own works, which would indicate that they were close contemporaries. In Tao-hsüan's brief biography of Fa-yün, Fa-yün emerges as an effective and highly motivated preacher rather than as a learned monk, and his interests tend more toward the popular than the philosophical (ibid.).

16. First translation from P no. 2003, photographically reproduced in Huang Yung-wu, ed., *Tun-huang pao-tsang* (Taipei: Hsin-wen-feng, 1981–1986), 112.28d; second translation from the same text, 112.32b.

17. My argument in the following pages concerning the function of the actual text is admittedly hypothetical, although the guesswork is based on what is known of the sociology and history of the Chinese book during the T'ang and Sung dynasties. Most of the details concerning the context and use of specific copies of the text are lost; the details that do survive are presented in my forthcoming study *The Scripture of the Ten Kings*. For an example of the first kind of manuscript, see P no. 2003. For the second kind of manuscript, see S no. 3147 (Giles no. 5448), written on a scroll, and S no. 5450 (Giles no. 1372[2]), written in a booklet. For the third kind of manuscript, see P no. 3761.

18. On the ritual functions of pictures of hell, see Stephen F. Teiser, " 'Having Once Died and Returned to Life': Representations of Hell in Medieval China," *HJAS* 48.2 (1988): 433–464.

19. See Jean-Pierre Drège, "Les cahiers des manuscrits de Touen-houang," in

Michel Soymié, ed., *Contributions aux études sur Touen-Houang,* vol. 1, Hautes études orientales, vol. 10 (Geneva: Librarie Droz, 1979), pp. 17–28.

20. See Matsumoto, *Tonkō ga no kenkyū,* 1.402–416, 2.115a–118b; and Arthur Waley, *A Catalogue of Paintings Recovered from Tun-huang by Sir Aurel Stein* (London: The British Musuem, 1931).

21. The piece is contained in Tung Kao, ed., *Ch'in-ting ch'üan T'ang-wen* (Taipei: Ching-wei shu-chü, 1965), 808.3b–4b.

22. Miao Ch'üan-sun (1844–1919), *I-feng-t'ang chin-shih wen-tzu mu,* xylograph edition, 7.9a.

23. I-ch'u (ca. 945–954), *Shih-shih liu-t'ieh,* text contained in Makita Tairyō, ed., *Giso rokujō* (Kyoto: Hōyū shoten, 1979), 16.30a–b (p. 362b).

24. The painting is reproduced in Matsumoto, *Tonkō ga no kenkyū,* 2.108.

25. See Tsukamoto, "Inro bosatsu shinkō ni tsuite," p. 173.

26. Wang Jih-hsiu (d. 1173), *Lung-shu tseng-kuang ching-t'u wen* 12, *T* 47.286c11–15. Wang was a native of Anhwei. The "Nai-ho" or "River of No Recourse" is the Buddhist River Styx, usually pictured in the second court of hell.

27. *ICC, San chih chi* 4.1331.

28. My survey of Ta pao-ting shan in these two paragraphs is based on Liu Chang-chiu et al., eds., *Ta-tsu shih-k'o yen-chiu* (Ch'eng-tu: Ssu-ch'uan sheng she-hui k'o-hsüeh-yüan ch'u-pan-she, 1985); a lecture delivered by Angela Howard to the Faculty Seminar in Buddhist Studies at Columbia University on Dec. 2, 1988; and photographic materials graciously shared with me by Angela Howard, Gary Seaman, and Anna Seidel.

29. Inscription accompanying the fourth king, reproduced in *Ta-tsu shih-k'o yen-chiu,* p. 282.

30. Tsung-chien, *Shih-men cheng-t'ung* 4, *HTC* 130.401d.

31. *Kuei-tung,* attributed to a certain Mr. Shen, Pai-pu ts'ung-shu chi-ch'eng ed. (Taipei: I-wen yin-shu-kuan, 1966), 4.7b–8a. According to Wang Yün-wu, ed., *Hsü-hsiu ssu-k'u ch'üan-shu t'i-yao* (Taipei: Commercial Press, 1972), *tzu-pu,* pp. 1758–1759, the work was compiled between 1225 and 1265 largely on the basis of other collections of ghost stories. The story in question concerns a widow Yang of Hangchow; I have not yet been able to find any reference to her in other sources.

32. See Chih-p'an, *Fo-tsu t'ung-chi* 33, *T* 49.322a–b.

33. *T'ai-shang chiu-k'u t'ien-tsun shuo hsiao-ch'ien mieh-tsui ching* (HY 378).

34. *Ti-fu shih-wang pa-tu i* (HY 215), p. 4a.

35. See, for example, the articles by Kajitani Ryōji, Kawahara Yoshio, and Nakano Teruo in *Bukkyō geijutsu* 97 (1974): 84–98, 98–123, 124–139.

36. The most important work on Sung and Yüan paintings of the ten kings is promised to be forthcoming from Minato Nobuyuki. Important published studies include Tanaka Ichimatsu, "Riku Shinchū hitsu jūō zu," *Kokka* 878 (May 1965): 27–31; Suzuki Kei, *Mindai kaiga shi kenkyū: Seppa* (Tokyo: Mokujisha, 1968), pp. 105–123. See also Lothar Ledderose, "A King of Hell," in *Suzuki Kei Sensei kanreki kinen: Chūgoku kaiga shi ronshū* (Tokyo: Yoshikawa kōbunkan, 1981), pp. 33–42.

37. See Yoshioka Yoshitoyo, "Chūgoku minkan no jigoku jūō shinkō ni tsuite," in *Bukkyō bunka ronshū* (Tokyo: Kawasaki Daishi heikanji, 1975); Geo. W. Clarke, trans., "The Yü-li or Precious Records," *Journal of the China Branch*

of the Royal Asiatic Society 28.2 (1898): 233–400; and Wolfram Eberhard, *Guilt and Sin in Traditional China* (Berkeley: University of California Press, 1967), pp. 24–59.

38. See Yoshioka, "Chūgoku minkan no jigoku jūō shinkō ni tsuite," pp. 268–270, for a representative list of titles.

39. See Julian F. Pas, "Journey to Hell: A New Report of Shamanistic Travel to the Courts of Hell," *Journal of Chinese Religions* 17 (1989): 43–60, esp. pp. 54–60.

40. I depend here on C. K. Yang's notion of "diffused" and "institutional" forms of religion; see his *Religion in Chinese Society: A Study of Contemporary Social Functions of Religion and Some of Their Historical Factors* (Berkeley: University of California Press, 1961), esp. pp. 294–340. The distinction is helpful for the discussion here, but it is also imperfect, since it lacks the conceptual clarity needed to categorize the many different kinds of religious specialists who, especially after the T'ang dynasty, fall somewhere between what Yang calls "diffused" and "institutional" forms of religion.

41. Translation from S no. 2567, printed in *T* 85.1299c. For further details see Michel Soymié's meticulous study "Les dix jours de jeûne de Kṣitigarbha," in Soymié, ed., *Contributions aux études sur Touen-Houang* 1.135–159.

42. See *T'ai-shang tung-hsüan ling-pao yeh-pao yin-yüan ching (Tao-tsang)*, 4.10a–b. For further details, see another of Soymié's meticulous studies "Les dix jours de jeûne du Taoïsme," in *Dōkyō kenkyū ronshū: Dōkyō no shisō to bunka, Yoshioka hakase kanreki kinen* (Tokyo: Kokusho kankōkai, 1977), pp. 1–21.

43. For some helpful comments, see Gary G. Hamilton, "Why No Capitalism in China? Negative Questions in Historical, Comparative Research," in Andreas E. Buss, ed., *Max Weber in Asian Studies,* International Studies in Sociology and Social Anthropology, vol. 42 (Leiden: E. J. Brill, 1985).

44. Emily Martin Ahern, *Chinese Ritual and Politics,* Cambridge Studies in Social Anthropology, no. 34 (Cambridge: Cambridge University Press, 1981), p. 109.

45. See Patricia Buckley Ebrey, "The Early Stages in the Development of Descent Group Organization," in Patricia Buckley Ebrey and James L. Watson, eds., *Kinship Organization in Late Imperial China* (Berkeley: University of California Press, 1986), pp. 16–61, esp. pp. 20–29.

46. See Janet R. Goodwin, "Shooing the Dead to Paradise," *Japanese Journal of Religious Studies* 16.1 (1989): 63–80, esp. p. 76.

47. Henry Yule, trans., *The Book of Ser Marco Polo the Venetian Concerning the Kingdoms and Marvels of the East,* 3rd ed., 2 vols. (New York: Charles Scribner's Sons, 1926), 2.132. Yule comments: "Polo here introduces a remark about the practice of burning the dead, which, with the notice of the idolatry of the people, and their use of paper-money, constitutes a formula which he repeats all through the Chinese provinces with wearisome iteration. It is, in fact, his definition of the Chinese people, for whom he seems to lack a comprehensive name" (2.133).

48. Hou Ching-lang, *Monnaies d'offrande et la notion de trésorerie dans la religion chinoise,* Mémoires de l'Institut des hautes études chinoises, vol. 1 (Paris: Collège de France, 1975), p. 130.

49. Ibid., pp. 5–6.

GLOSSARY

A-mi-t'o fo　阿彌陀佛

A-p'i-ta-mo chü-she lun　阿毘達磨俱舍論

A-p'i-ta-mo ta p'i-p'o-sha lun　阿毘達磨大毗婆沙論

Ch'a-ming ssu-lu　察命司錄

chai　齋

Ch'an　禪

Chang Yen-yüan　張彥遠

Chao Chih-feng　趙智風

chen-chün　真君

Chen-huang tung-shen t'ien-tsun　真皇洞神天尊

chi-k'u　寄庫

Chien-ssu shih-che　監司使者

Chih-p'an　志磐

Ch'ih-ch'e shih-che　赤車使者

Chin　金

Ch'in-kuang wang　秦廣王

Ch'in-ting ch'üan T'ang-wen　欽定全唐文

Ching-ai ssu　敬愛寺

Ching-lü i-hsiang　經律異相

Chu-kuan chiang-chün　諸官將軍

Ch'u-chiang wang　初江王

ch'ü　趣

Ch'uan-hsin shih-che　傳信使者

Chung t'ai-i　中太一

chung-yu　中有

Fa-yün　法雲

Fei-mo yen-ch'ing chen-chün　飛魔演慶真君

Fo-shuo yen-lo wang shou-chi ssu-chung ni-hsiu sheng-ch'i-chai wang-sheng ching-t'u ching　佛説閻羅王授記四衆逆修生七齋往生淨土經

Fo-tsu t'ung-chi　佛祖統記

Fu-chang shih-tsung　符章侍從

Hao-sheng tu-ming t'ien-tsun　好生度命天尊

Ho-chien fu　河間府

Hsi-ming ssu　西明寺

Hsia t'ai-i　下太一

Hsien-chieh ch'ien-fo　賢劫千佛

Hsü-hsiu ssu-k'u ch'üan-shu t'i-yao　續修四庫全書提要

Hsüan-chen wan-fu t'ien-tsun　玄真萬福天尊

Hsüan-shang yü-ch'en t'ien-tsun　玄上玉晨天尊

Hsüan-te miao-sheng chen-chün　玄德妙生真君

Hsüan-te wu-ling chen-chün　玄德五靈真君

Hsüan-tsang　玄奘

Hung Mai　洪邁

I-ch'u　義楚

I-feng-t'ang chin-shih wen-tzu mu　藝風堂金石文字目

Kuan-shih-yın p'u-sa　觀世音菩薩

Kuan-ting ching　灌頂經

Kuan-yin　觀音

Kuei-tung　鬼董

Li-tai ming-hua chi　歷代明畫記

Li Yen-shou　李延壽

Liu Pen-tsun　柳本尊

Lu　陸

Lu-she-na fo　盧舍那佛

Lung-shu tseng-kuang ching-t'u wen　龍舒增廣淨土文

Miao Ch'üan-sun　繆荃孫

Nai-ho　奈河

Pao-ch'ang　寶唱

pao-chüan　寶卷

Pao-su chao-ch'eng chen-chün　寶肅照成真君

Pei-ch'en　北辰

Pei-shih　北史

Pei-tou　北斗

Pei-tou ssu-sha kuei　北斗司殺鬼

P'i-lu-she-na　毘盧舍那

Pien-ch'eng wang　變成王

P'ing-teng wang　平等王

Shan-o t'ung-tzu　善惡童子

Shang t'ai-i　上太一

Shen　沈

Shih-chia-mou-ni fo　釋迦牟尼佛

shih-hsiang　食香

Shih-lun ching pien　十輪經變

Shih-lun pien　十輪變

Shih-men cheng-t'ung　釋門正統

Shih-shih liu-t'ieh　釋氏六帖

Shih-wang cheng-yeh lun　十王正業論

Shih-wang ching　十王經

Shih-wang ching pien　十王經變

Shih-wang pien　十王變

Shou-chai san-chiang-chün　守宅
　三將軍
Ssu-k'ung T'u　司空圖
Ssu-lu　司錄
Ssu-ming　司命
Ssu t'ien-wang　四天王
Sung-ti wang　宋帝王
Ta-fan t'ien-wang　大梵天王
Ta-fang-kuang shih-lun ching　大方廣
　十輪經
Ta-ling hsü-huang t'ien-tsun　大靈虛
　皇天尊
Ta pao-ting shan　大寶頂山
Ta-sheng ssu-chai jih　大乘四齋日
Ta-sheng ta-chi ti-tsang shih-lun ching
　大乘大集地藏十輪經
Ta-sheng-tz'u ssu　大聖慈寺
Ta T'ang nei-tien lu　大唐內典錄
Ta-tsu　大足
T'ai-i pa-shen shih-che　太一八神使者
T'ai-i shih-che　太一使者
T'ai-miao chih-chi t'ien-tsun　太妙至
　極天尊
T'ai-p'ing ching　太平經
T'ai Shan　泰山
T'ai-shan fu-chün　泰山府君
T'ai-shan wang　泰山王
*T'ai-shang chiu-k'u t'ien-tsun shuo
　hsiao-ch'ien mieh-tsui ching*　太上
　救苦天尊說消愆滅罪經
*T'ai-shang tung-hsüan ling-pao
　yeh-pao yin-yüan ching*　太上洞玄
　靈寶業報因緣經
*T'ai-shang tz'u-pei tao-ch'ang
　hsiao-tsai chiu-yu ch'an*　太上慈悲
　道場消災九幽懺
T'ai-su miao-kuang chen-chün　太素
　妙廣真君
T'ai-tzu　太子
tao　道
Tao-hsüan　道宣
Tao-tsang　道藏
Ti-fu shih-wang pa-tu i　地府十王拔
　度儀
Ti-tsang　地藏
Ti-tsang p'u-sa　地藏菩薩
ti-yü pien-hsiang　地獄變相
Ti-yü yu-chi　地獄遊記
Tien-ssu shih-che　典司使者
T'ien-i　天一

T'ien-kung shih-che　天公使者
T'ien ta-chiang-chün　天大將軍
T'ien-ti　天帝
T'ien-ti shih　天帝釋
T'ien-ti shih-che　天帝使者
T'ien-ti-shui san-kuan　天地水三官
t'ien-tsun　天尊
Ting-kuang ju-lai fo　定光如來佛
tsan　讚
Tsang-ch'uan　藏川
Tsei-ts'ao shih-che　賊曹使者
Tsui-sheng hui-ling chen-chün　最勝
　輝靈真君
Tsung-chien　宗鑑
Tu-hsien shang-sheng t'ien-tsun　度仙
　上聖天尊
Tu Liang　杜良
Tu-shih wang　都市王
Tung Kao　董誥
Tung-ming p'u-ching chen-chün　洞明
　普靜真君
Wang Jih-hsiu　王日休
Wei Shou　魏收
Wei shu　魏書
Wu Ching-tsang　武靜藏
Wu-hua wei-ling chen-chün　五化威
　靈真君
Wu-kuan wang　五官王
Wu-liang ta-hua t'ien-tsun　無量大華
　天尊
Wu-shang cheng-tu chen-chün　無上
　正度真君
Wu-tao chuan-lun wang　五道轉輪王
Wu-tao ta-chiang-chün　五道大將軍
Yang　楊
Yao-shih liu-li-kuang fo　藥師琉璃光
　佛
Yao-wang yao-shang p'u-sa　藥王藥
　上菩薩
Yen-lo wang　閻羅王
Yin-te ting-hsiu chen-chün　陰德定修
　真君
Yü-hsü ming-huang t'ien-tsun　玉虛明
　皇天尊
Yü I-lang　俞一郎
Yü-li　玉歷
Yü-pao huang-shang t'ien-tsun　玉寶
　皇上天尊
yung-seng　庸僧

CHAPTER 5

MYTH, RITUAL, AND MONASTIC PRACTICE IN SUNG CH'AN BUDDHISM

T. Griffith Foulk

There is no consensus among modern researchers with regard to historical periods or stages of development that the Ch'an school of Buddhism is supposed to have gone through in China, but many scholars have made use of a tripartite scheme that posits periods of incipience, flourishing, and decline. The period of incipience, usually called "early Ch'an," spans the sixth through late eighth centuries and corresponds to the age of the first six patriarchs in China (Bodhidharma, Hui-k'o, Seng-ts'an, Tao-hsin, Hung-jen, and Hui-neng) as treated in the traditional history of the Ch'an lineage. Modern historians of "early Ch'an" have concerned themselves with the teachings of the putative founder of the Ch'an lineage, Bodhidharma, and the subsequent movements (e.g., the so-called Northern, Southern, Ox-head, and Pao-t'ang schools) that claimed spiritual descent from him. The operative assumption has been that these movements, even if they were subsequently discredited or forgotten, contained the germs of distinctive ideas and practices that were fully developed by the Ch'an school during its period of greatest vitality and creativity, the so-called golden age of the late eighth through mid-tenth centuries.

The "golden age" corresponds to the period in the traditional history of the Ch'an lineage in which the Sixth Patriarch Hui-neng's Southern Lineage divided and gave rise to "five houses"—the period that saw the flourishing of such renowned patriarchs as Ma-tsu (709–788), Shih-t'ou (700–790), Nan-ch'üan (748–834), Pai-chang (749–814), Huang-po (d. 850), Chao-chou (778–897), Tung-shan (807–869), Lin-chi (d. 867), Hsüeh-feng (822–908), and Yün-men (864–949). The classical hagiographies of these monks and their contemporaries in the Ch'an lineage depict them eschewing traditional modes of Buddhist philosophical discourse and instructing their disciples in novel and striking ways—with shouts, blows, and a terse, vernacular style of rhetoric that ranged from the witty to the enigmatic, irreverent, antinomian, and iconoclastic. Modern scholars regard Ma-tsu's Hung-chou school as archetypical of "golden age" Ch'an, arguing that it was the first to employ these new methods of teaching, the first to produce the "discourse records" *(yü-lu)* literature, consisting of transcriptions of such freewheeling "encounters" *(chi-yüan)* between masters and students, and the first (led by Ma-tsu's disciple Pai-chang) to establish an independent Ch'an monastic institution.[1]

The period of ossification and decline in Chinese Ch'an, finally, is said to have begun in the Sung dynasty and to have progressed slowly all the way down to the twentieth century. Modern accounts of Ch'an intellectual history typically contrast the purported innovation and spontaneity of the "golden age" with the conservatism of Sung Ch'an, which was preoccupied with collecting, editing, and commenting on the sayings of ancient luminaries. The selection of pithy sayings from the ancient records to be used pedagogically as *kung-an*, or "test cases," was a Sung innovation, but this development too is often explained as the effort of a spiritually uncreative age to encapsulate and preserve whatever was left of the dynamic wisdom of the great T'ang masters.[2] Modern historians treating the evolution of the Ch'an monastic institution also paint a picture of decline in the Sung. In addition to absorbing elements of Buddhist ritual and devotional practice that were supposedly extraneous to the "pure" Ch'an institution founded by Pai-chang in the T'ang, Sung Ch'an monasteries are said to have suffered from increasing formalization and secularization, a growing reliance on state support and lay patronage, a corresponding increase in prayer services aimed at currying favor with patrons and the imperial court, and a heavier involvement in commercial ventures and landlordism.[3]

Although they speak in these ways of spiritual degeneration, modern historians concede that the Ch'an school enjoyed a period of unprecedented material prosperity and influence during the Sung. Officially designated Ch'an monasteries came to hold a preeminent position within the Buddhist monastic institution as a whole at this time, comprising a majority of the largest, most powerful Buddhist establishments in China —the public monasteries *(shih-fang-ch'a)*. Ch'an monastic codes known as *ch'ing-kuei* (literally, "rules of purity") were evidently so influential that the arrangements and procedures they established were followed in all public monasteries in the Sung, even ones formally dedicated to the transmission of T'ien-t'ai and Nan-shan Vinaya school teachings.[4] Many scholars regard the propagation of Ch'an monastic rules as a milestone in the sinicization of Buddhism, marking the end of the Chinese sangha's reliance on Vinaya rules that originated in India.[5] All agree, in any case, that one of the most significant changes that occurred in Chinese Buddhism in conjunction with the transition from the T'ang to the Sung was the dramatic rise in the worldly fortunes of the Ch'an school.

The tripartite scheme of incipience, flourishing, and decline is also evident in modern treatments of the history of Chinese Buddhism as a whole. Many scholars take the position that Buddhism reached its apogee as a dynamic, creative force in the social, religious, and intellectual life of China during the Sui and T'ang dynasties, after which it entered a long period of stagnation and decline that extended from the Sung down to modern times.[6] The suppression of the Hui-ch'ang era (841–846) in the late T'ang is often cited as a blow from which Buddhism never fully recovered, although it is generally accepted that under the Sung dynasty the religion continued to "flourish in countless forms of popular devotion,"[7] and "the monastic community was probably more numerous and the economic activities of the sangha were even more extensive than under the T'ang."[8] Again the degeneration of which scholars speak is not measured quantitatively; it is described, rather, as an intellectual and spiritual malaise that was associated with the "doctrinal impoverishment" and "general tendency toward syncretism" that are said to have characterized Chinese Buddhism from Sung times onward.[9] The picture that emerges of Sung Buddhism in general as well as the Ch'an school in particular is thus one of intellectual and spiritual decline in the midst of material prosperity.

This chapter subjects these theories of flourishing and decline to critical review and finds them deficient in their presentation of the historical data and flawed in their basic assumptions and methodologies. The Ch'an school gained official sanction as the leading representative of Buddhist orthodoxy and came to dominate the Buddhist monastic institution in the Sung precisely because it developed powerful new rhetorical modes and polemical strategies and produced an appealing body of quasi-historical mythological lore—the "records of the transmission of the flame" *(ch'uan-teng lu)* and "discourse records" *(yü-lu)* literature—which served to spread its message and sustain its claims to spiritual leadership. The Sung construction of the "Ch'an lineage" *(ch'an-tsung)* and its history was so ingenious and convincing that it succeeded magnificently in drawing attention away from its own creativity and directing it instead to the ostensible glories of the past. Indeed, the crux of the problem in the modern field of Ch'an studies is that the leading scholars, most of whom are affiliated with some branch of the Zen school in Japan, are still guided in their research by the normative definition of the Ch'an lineage established in the Sung and still disposed to accept Sung records as documentary evidence pertaining to the "golden age" of the T'ang rather than as works of religious literature that reflect most directly on the beliefs and concerns of the age in which they were actually compiled.

The Sung discourse records and records of the transmission of the flame, "flame histories" *(teng-shih)* for short, constituted what was essentially a body of religious mythology—a sacred history that served polemical, ritual, and didactic functions in the world of Sung Ch'an. A great deal of evidence can be adduced in support of this view, but I shall rest content with noting the following four points. First, the comparative study of Tun-huang texts and other recently discovered T'ang texts that present conflicting accounts of Bodhidharma's lineage has demonstrated conclusively that the Sung depiction of the early Ch'an lineage in compilations such as the *Ching-te ch'uan-teng lu* (Ching-te era record of the transmission of the flame; compiled by Tao-yüan in 1004) is a late fabrication.[10] Second, the hagiographies and discourse records of the T'ang Ch'an masters in the generations following Hui-neng survive only in late collections (none dating before 952) and do not appear among contemporary T'ang materials discovered in Tun-huang or preserved in Japan. Third, the literary qualities of the texts in question—especially the use of metaphor, symbolism, dramatic devices, realistic settings, and the verbatim quotation of private conversations and unspoken thoughts—are typical of fiction. Fourth, the Ch'an concept of a spiritual lineage *(tsung)* is itself essentially a religious, not a historical, category.

The account of the founding of the first independendent Ch'an monastery by Pai-chang likewise was a creation of Sung Ch'an mythology. Sources dating from the T'ang that write of Ch'an monks make no mention of independent Ch'an monasteries,[11] and most of the features attributed to Pai-chang's monastery in Sung sources were actually common in mainstream Buddhist monasteries in the T'ang.[12] Apart from the Pai-chang myth, moreover, there is no evidence to support the notion that Sung Ch'an monasteries evolved directly from a T'ang Ch'an prototype. The myth served to justify the designation of leading Buddhist establishments as Ch'an lineage monasteries—a Sung practice that had no precedent in the T'ang. It also allowed the Ch'an school to claim as its own invention certain successful features of monastic practice that were actually the common heritage of the Chinese Buddhist tradition.

The arguments that modern scholars advance about the lack of spiritual vigor and innovation in Sung Ch'an are predicated on an acceptance of the Sung flame histories and discourse records at face value as full and accurate depictions of T'ang practice in the "golden age." If, however, we see in this literature a new Buddhist ideology and mythology that was largely created in the Sung, albeit in the form of collections of ancient doctrines and records of ancestral teachers, all of those arguments are undercut. Rather than accept the texts at face value as historical documents and treat the apparent incongruity between the image of T'ang Ch'an that they project and the reality of Sung Ch'an as evidence of historical change (or degeneration), I propose to interpret the Sung records within the institutional context in which they were redacted and used in the Sung.

The charges of "doctrinal impoverishment" and "intellectual decline" in Sung Buddhism as a whole also ignore a great mass of historical evidence. Apart from the outpouring of Ch'an flame histories and discourse records, the Sung occasioned an unprecedented explosion of scholarly and literary activity in Buddhist circles. Although a thorough recounting of that activity is beyond the scope of this chapter, it included the production, beginning in 971, of numerous printed editions of a "complete" Buddhist canon,[13] the publication and study of synthetic collections of Buddhist (especially Ch'an and T'ien-t'ai) doctrinal lore,[14] and the appearance of new types of Buddhist historiography.[15]

SUNG CH'AN IDEOLOGY AND MYTHOLOGY

The ideology of Sung Ch'an was capsulized in a famous four-part slogan that was pieced together and attributed to the founding patriarch Bodhidharma: "A special transmission outside the teachings *(chiao-wai pieh-ch'uan)*; not setting up scriptures *(pu-li wen-tzu)*; pointing directly at a person's mind *(chih-chih jen-hsin)*; seeing into the nature [of the mind] and attaining Buddhahood *(chien-hsing ch'eng-fo)*."[16] This slogan was subject to a degree of conflicting interpretation within Ch'an circles in the Sung,[17] but its basic message was clear to all: the Ch'an lineage represented an elite "mind-to-mind transmission" *(i-hsin ch'uan-hsin)* of the essence of the Buddha Śākyamuni's dharma, the Buddha mind or enlightenment itself, as opposed to the transmission of dharma in the form of sūtras and philosophical treatises that characterized the so-called teachings lineages *(chiao-tsung),* such as T'ien-t'ai and Hua-yen. "Pointing directly at a person's mind" (i.e., the innate Buddha mind) was understood as a description of the unique teaching methods of Ch'an, which did not rely on philosophical discourse but used various devices such as shouts, gestures, blows, and enigmatic expressions to stimulate trainees to awaken to the Buddha nature within. It is true that more ecumenical refrains like the "unification of Ch'an and the teachings" *(ch'an-chiao i-chih)* also came into vogue in Sung Ch'an, but these were really just normative interpretations of the "special transmission" dogma. Ch'an proponents of scriptural study argued that the truth expounded by Śākyamuni in the sūtras was essentially the same as the truth vouchsafed by him in the special transmission outside the sūtras, but they did not regard doctrinal expertise as a viable substitute for "seeing into the nature and attaining Buddhahood."

The mythology of Sung Ch'an elaborated the "historical" propagation of the Ch'an lineage starting with the initial transmission of the formless dharma from the Buddha Śākyamuni to the first Indian patriarch Mahākāśyapa, who is said to have been the only person to grasp the profound meaning when Śākyamuni preached a sermon that consisted of wordlessly raising a flower.[18] The mythology was embodied in the many flame histories that were compiled during the Sung, the oldest and most influential of which is the *Ching-te ch'uan-teng lu*.[19] The notion of transmitting *(ch'uan)* a flame *(teng)* that is expressed in the titles of these works is a metaphor for the transmission of dharma, which is compared to lighting one lamp with another, passing the flame of enlightenment from one generation to the next without allowing it to be extinguished.[20] The Ch'an lineage is depicted in the *Ching-te ch'uan-teng lu* and subsequent flame histories as an extended spiritual clan consisting of all the heirs to Śākyamuni's "special transmission" of the formless dharma. The texts themselves are collections of hagiographies of individual dharma heirs in the Ch'an lineage, arranged genealogically in the manner of a family tree.

The basic outline of the lineage that became established as orthodox early in the Sung posited a single line of dharma transmission from Śākyamuni down through twenty-eight Indian patriarchs, the last of whom was Bodhidharma. Bodhidharma was believed to have come to China during the Northern Wei dynasty (424–535), thus becoming the first in a line of six Chinese patriarchs that culminated in Hui-neng. The Sung flame histories also recognized the legitimacy of a few collateral branches of the lineage that stemmed from the fourth and fifth patriarchs, notably the Northern lineage and the Ox-head lineage, but these were regarded as defunct. Following Hui-neng, the lineage was said to have split into two main branches, the lineages of Ch'ing-yüan Hsing-ssu (d. 740) and his disciple Shih-t'ou Hsi-ch'ien, and Nan-yüeh Huai-jang and his disciple Ma-tsu Tao-i . These two lines further divided into the so-called five houses in the late T'ang and Five Dynasties periods. From two of the five, namely the Lin-chi and Ts'ao-tung lines, the Sung compilers of this genealogy traced the numerous subbranches of the Ch'an lineage with which they themselves and their contemporaries claimed affiliation. Other names used more or less synonomously to refer to the lineage in its entirety were the Buddha Mind Lineage and the Lineage of Bodhidharma.[21]

Certain features of the Sung flame histories can be traced back to works such as the *Tsu-t'ang chi* (Patriarchs hall collection),[22] compiled in 952, and the *Pao-lin chuan* (Pao-lin [monastery] record),[23] written about 801. Even earlier precedents can be found in Tun-huang texts such as *Ch'uan fa-pao chi* (Annals of the transmission of the dharma treasure)[24] and *Leng-chia shih-tzu chi* (Record of masters and disciples of the Laṅkāvatāra),[25] both of which date from the first decades of the eighth century. Nevertheless, all of these prototypes of the flame history genre may be distinguished from the Sung works on one or more grounds. Most give versions of Bodhidharma's lineage that differ significantly from the early Ch'an lineage universally accepted in the Sung, and most present a lineage that is essentially unilinear, unlike the multibranched Ch'an lineage depicted in the Sung flame histories.

In addition to conventional biographical information, the Sung flame histories feature something rarely found in the earlier genre of biographies of eminent monks: ostensibly verbatim records of the Ch'an masters' dialogues with individual disciples and others who seek their instruction or challenge their understanding. This latter material often depicts the Chinese masters speaking in the vernacular and referring to matters of immediate, everyday experience to instruct their followers. The impression given is of a teaching method that does not rely much on lecturing on sūtras or systematically expounding philosophical doctrines but instead makes use of spontaneous repartee and pithy, sometimes startling or enigmatic expressions to help people gain insight into Buddhist truths. Such records of the sayings and doings of Ch'an masters take the form of brief, disconnected anecdotes and vignettes, interspersed with the standard biographical data. Each anecdote provides its own context, introduces its protagonists, and relates from beginning to end what transpired. The essentially random order of the anecdotes affords considerable insight into how these texts were probably first compiled. It also explains the ease with which certain anecdotes were taken out of the context of the Ch'an hagiographies and presented as independent "test cases" in a different genre, the *kung-an* collections.

The realism that characterizes the records of the patriarchs' words and deeds is often so finely detailed that it betrays the works as fiction. This point is particularly apt in cases where not only the exact words but also the unspoken thoughts of a master are quoted verbatim. Raconteurs, poets, and novelists are privy to the innermost thoughts and feelings of their subjects; mere reporters are not. Another factor that suggests that in many cases the use of realistic, concrete settings is a purely literary device is that the descriptions of the monastic environment of the T'ang masters often contain anachronistic details. T'ang masters are depicted in monastic settings with facilities, officers, and activities characteristic of Sung-style monasteries. The technical terms employed to refer to various features of monastic life are not found in any sources dating indisputably from the T'ang. The very realism of the settings, which would have seemed natural to readers in the Sung, gives the game away.

The Ch'an use of history (or more precisely, genealogy and hagiography) as a vehicle for religious and ideological discourse met with great success in Sung China. By taking enlightenment out of the context of abstract Indian Buddhist philosophy and mythology and depicting it in vernacular stories about the sayings and doings of "real" people, whose lives it had transformed, the flame histories struck a chord that rang true to Chinese ears. Expressions of sacred truths were skillfully harmonized with reports of mundane affairs in the hagiographies of the Ch'an masters, lending an air of down-to-earth realism to things miraculous and imbuing even ordinary events with extraordinary significance. In this way the flame histories and discourse records offered something to the world of Sung Buddhism that had scarcely been contemplated in the T'ang: native Chinese Buddhas whose modes of expression were well tuned to the sensibilities of the educated elite in China. Because the patriarchs in the Ch'an lineage were considered to be fully awakened beings comparable to the Buddha Śākyamuni, the records that contained their words and deeds were regarded as sacred literature on a par with Indian sūtras (the "discourse records" of Śākyamuni).[26]

The Sung flame histories were compiled by monk scholars who enjoyed the patronage of the imperial court and aristocracy, and the texts were published with state approval and sponsorship. The *Ching-te ch'uan-teng lu* derived its name from the fact that it was presented to Emperor Chen-tsung in the first year of the Ching-te era (1004–1007). It was published with imperial patronage shortly thereafter and was approved for inclusion in the canon. Subsequent flame histories were also known by the reign style of the era in which they were granted imperial recognition and were included in revised editions of the canon.[27]

The claim that the Ch'an lineage had continued unbroken down to the present, whereas the T'ien-t'ai lineage had ended in the twenty-fourth generation after Śākyamuni,[28] was instrumental in gaining imperial support during the Sung.[29] The inherent ambiguity and flexibility of the Ch'an conception of dharma transmission also contributed to its effectiveness as an ideological tool. The flame histories present dharma transmission in terms that mark it both as a verifiable event that takes place on the plane of human history and as an utterly transcendent religious experience. Every instance of transmission, every link in the chain of the Ch'an lineage, is set in a specific place and time and is dressed with suitable historical details as to the circumstances of the particular disciple's training under his master, the disciple's enlightenment, the master's formal approval of the disciple as a dharma heir, and so on. At the same time, the point is repeatedly made in the flame histories that the dharma transmitted from master to disciple is literally inconceivable: it has no specifiable content and no marks by which it can be recognized.[30] Indeed, it is said, dharma transmission really entails no transmission at all in the sense of something being passed from one person to another, only the awakening of the disciple to the true nature of his or her own being and a mystical realization of identity with all the Buddhas and patriarchs. Thus, on the one hand, when disputes over the true configuration of dharma lineages arose within the Sung Ch'an school or when T'ien-t'ai school opponents challenged the authenticity of Ch'an lineage records, these were regarded in principle as matters that could be resolved by the scholarly marshaling of historical evidence. On the other hand, when the textual evidence was not in their favor, proponents of the Ch'an lineage always had the option of abruptly shifting to a level of discourse where merely historical facts are inconsequential and the timeless, transcendent "fact" of enlightenment was the only thing that mattered. Whenever this sort of shift occurs, the mythical dimension of the history of the Ch'an lineage, always present beneath the surface recitation of mundane facts, comes clearly into focus. This is the dimension of sacred truth, posited by the tradition as something inviolable and utterly beyond the reach of rational criticism.

Beginning with the *T'ien-sheng kuang-teng lu* (T'ien-sheng era extensive record of the flame), each of the successive Sung flame histories drew heavily on its predecessors in recounting the history of the Ch'an lineage as it had already been established, and then extended the account by adding on new hagiographies for prominent Ch'an masters in recent generations and more detailed hagiographies for figures that had not gained much attention in previous flame histories. Such additions generally reflected the factional biases of the compilers, who tended to include more (and more detailed) biographies for masters belonging to the particular branch of the Ch'an lineage with which they themselves claimed affiliation. This activity resulted in a continual updating of the lineage records and the addition of later generations of Ch'an masters to the ranks of those who had already been canonized.

Modern scholarship on the history of Ch'an has endeavored to evaluate the ostensibly factual information presented in the hagiographies in a given Sung flame history using such categories as "patently fabricated," "dubious," "plausible but unprovable," and "factual" (well corroborated by external evidence). From the standpoint of the Sung Ch'an school itself, of course, the records of all the patriarchs in the lineage, Indian as well as Chinese, ancient as well as recent, were equally veracious. Modern scholarship takes as its task the separating out of myth from fact and tends to find proportionately less of the former commodity the farther back in time it looks. The flame histories, however, stressed the elements of continuity and sameness—continuity because the main lines of dharma transmission leading from antiquity to the present were depicted as unbroken, and sameness because the awakening of each of the Ch'an masters in the lineage was believed to have carried him beyond history and placed him on the same transcendent plane as "all the Buddhas and patriarchs." Far from distinguishing what modern scholarship is wont to call history proper from myth, the flame histories tend to weave these two elements together in one seamless fabric. Viewing the Ch'an lineage as a continuum that links the past and the present, there is a sense in which the quality of historicity (or believability) flows backwards from more recent hagiographies to older ones, while sanctity flows in the opposite direction. When each of the updated flame histories was published in the Sung, the most recently added hagiographies were of masters who would have still been remembered by the living. The aura of immediacy and reality that surrounded the hagiographies of these relatively recent ancestors lent a sense of historicity to the hagiographies of much more ancient figures in the lineage. At the same time, the hagiographies of the more recent ancestors gained sanctity and legitimacy by their association with those of the ancients.

THE PAI-CHANG MYTH AND ITS INFLUENCE ON MODERN SCHOLARSHIP

Ch'an has often been depicted as a sectarian movement that threw off all the tiresome trappings of conventional Buddhist doctrine, cult, and discipline to revel in offbeat expressions of perfect spiritual freedom. Kenneth Ch'en, summarizing the views of influential scholars such as Hu Shih, D. T. Suzuki, and Ui Hakuju, describes the rise of Ch'an as a protest against the established Chinese schools of Buddhism with their "excessive reliance on the external paraphernalia of the religion."[31] Ch'en also states that "the Ch'an masters in China broke away from the Indian dependence upon the sacred scriptures, objects of worship, rituals, and metaphysical speculation to build a school of Buddhism which favored a plain, direct, concrete, and practical approach to enlightenment."[32] The historical materials on which these theories of Ch'an iconoclasm and sectarianism are largely based are the Sung flame histories and discourse records, which depict the patriarchs of the bygone "golden age" questioning and rejecting (rhetorically, at least) various aspects of conventional Buddhist belief and practice. The Pai-chang myth, however, has also helped to sustain such theories and lend credence to the notion that Sung Ch'an was in decline.

It is assumed that because the Ch'an school arose in opposition to the mainstream Buddhist monastic establishment, it must have developed its own independent institutional base, either in the "early" or "golden age" phase of its development. Some historians argue that the formation of distinctive Ch'an monastic institutions actually took place in the so-called East Mountain communities of the fourth and fifth patriarchs of Ch'an, Tao-hsin (580–651) and Hung-jen (d. 674).[33] Others adhere to the traditional belief, widespread since the Sung, that Pai-chang Huai-hai (749–814) was the founder of the first Ch'an monastery and the author of the first Ch'an monastic rules. The locus classicus of the Pai-chang story, and the oldest historical source that deals explicitly with independent Ch'an monasteries in the T'ang, is the *Ch'an-men kuei-shih* (Regulations of the Ch'an school). This brief text was appended to Pai-chang's hagiography in the *Ching-te ch'uan-teng lu* and excerpted or paraphrased in numerous subsequent writings.[34]

According to the opening passage of the *Ch'an-men kuei-shih,* members of the Ch'an lineage from the first patriarch Bodhidharma down through the sixth patriarch Hui-neng all resided in Vinaya monasteries *(lü-ssu)*, where they had their own separate cloisters but were regulated by the ancient monastic rules handed down in the Vinaya tradition. Ch'an master Pai-chang is said to have regretted this and "conceived the idea of establishing a Ch'an monastery separately." The remainder of the *Ch'an-men kuei-shih* is given over to a sketchy description of the main organizational features of the independent Ch'an monastery that Pai-chang purportedly founded. Great importance is attached to the role played by the abbot *(chang-lao)*, who was to be a "spiritually perceptive and morally praiseworthy person." Indeed, because the abbot represented the Buddhas and patriarchs, he himself was to be regarded as the "honored one" *(tsun)*—a term usually applied to the Buddha worshiped on a monastery's central altar. Thus, no Buddha hall was needed to house an image of the "honored one," and only a dharma hall was built. There, in daily convocations, the abbot preached the dharma and engaged the assembly in debate. The abbot's quarters were also to be used for instructing disciples, not as a private bedroom. The only other facilities mentioned in the text are the quarters of ten unnamed administrative officers and the sangha hall, where all the monks who were not administrators had to reside. The sangha hall was outfitted with platforms, on which the trainees sat in meditation for long hours and reclined to sleep for brief periods. Two other routine activities mentioned are meals and communal labor, during which "seniors and juniors were required to do equal work." In addition, the text devotes considerable attention to the punishments that were meted out to troublemakers and rule breakers.

Because the *Ch'an-men kuei-shih* makes no mention of common Buddhist practices—such as scriptural study, prayers, repentances, or rituals for producing and dedicating merit for the benefit of spirits and lay patrons—it has been interpreted as corroborating the image of Ch'an iconoclasm that is projected by the hagiographies of the patriarchs of the "golden age." Modern historians have generally accepted the accuracy of the *Ch'an-men kuei-shih* account with respect to the arrangement of T'ang Ch'an monasteries and have drawn a number of inferences about the religious, social, and economic life in prototypical Ch'an monasteries as well. It has been argued, for example, that manual labor by Ch'an monks was a concrete expression of an innovative doctrine that held that Buddhist practice need not be restricted to any special religious forms or conventions but could be undertaken in the midst of all human activities.[35] By the same token, manual labor (specifically farming) is supposed to have given early Ch'an communities economic independence and obviated the necessity of performing merit-producing rituals in exchange for lay patronage and government support.[36] Buddha halls were not necessary, it is surmised, because they were centers for the type of devotional practice and services for patrons that the Ch'an school rejected.[37] Furthermore, the fact that "all were invited" *(p'u-ch'ing)* to labor, regardless of rank, is said to demonstrate the "democratic spirit" of the early Ch'an communities.[38] Most scholars agree that the "characteristic" features of T'ang Ch'an monastic life were group meditation in a sangha hall, public debate between a master and his interlocutors in a dharma hall, individual instruction in a master's room, and communal manual labor.[39] Many go a step further and take these as the "essential" features of Ch'an and Zen monasticism throughout history.

This understanding of Ch'an institutions has informed scholarly theories about the T'ang-Sung transition in Chinese Buddhism in a number of ways. It has been used, in the first place, to explain how Ch'an monasteries came to occupy such a prominent position in Sung Buddhism. Most historians agree that the stage was set for the Ch'an school's rise to preeminence in the Sung by the decimation of competing schools in the harsh suppression of the Buddhist monastic institution that was initiated by imperial decree during the Hui-ch'ang era (841–846) of the T'ang. Various reasons have been adduced for the Ch'an school's apparently singular resilience. One common theory is that Ch'an was relatively unaffected because it did not rely on the Buddhist infrastructure—the libraries, ritual sites, and other monastery facilities—that was targeted for destruction. It has been argued, for example, that because Ch'an monks "practiced Buddhism in the midst of ordinary daily life, apart from the life of textual study and observing the precepts" that went on in mainstream Buddhist monasteries, they were not affected by the suppression.[40] Another theory holds that Ch'an communities were spared because the monks engaged in manual labor and grew their own food and thus were not susceptible to the charge of economic parasitism that was leveled against the Buddhist sangha at large.[41] It has also been argued that the Ch'an school's distinctive monastic codes helped it to recover rapidly and fully when the suppression ended.[42]

The basic idea behind all these arguments is that because Ch'an-style monastic practice survived the suppression of the late T'ang, it was in a position to prosper when the Buddhist institution once again received strong support from rulers in the Five Dynasties and early Sung. That very prosperity, however, is believed to have led the Ch'an school away from the simple modes of religious practice that made it so resilient in the first place. Because scholars take the *Ch'an-men kuei-shih* account of Pai-chang's rules in the T'ang as definitive of "original" or "pure" Ch'an monasticism, they tend to view the many features of Sung Ch'an practice that find no precedent in that account as later accretions and symptoms of a degenerative syncretism that eventually (in the Yüan and Ming)

caused Chinese Ch'an to lose its iconoclastic spirit and sectarian distinct-
ness altogether.

The evidence adduced in the remaining sections of this chapter,
however, demonstrates that the very features deemed most characteristic
of Ch'an monastic practice were neither unique to nor invented by the
Ch'an school. They were, instead, common to many Buddhist monasteries (especially those that were centers of T'ien-t'ai study) during the Sui,
T'ang, Five Dynasties, and early Sung. These findings undercut the prevailing theories of the origin, flourishing, and decline of "pure" Ch'an
monasticism and demonstrate that the quasi-historical claims of the
Ch'an-men kuei-shih must be interpreted as an aspect of Sung Ch'an
polemics and mythology.

THE CH'AN LINEAGE AND THE CH'AN SCHOOL

Modern Chinese and Japanese scholars who use the Sung flame histories
to research the "history of the Ch'an lineage" often fail to distinguish
clearly the mythological and historical dimensions of their object of
study. They also tend to assume that whenever the flame histories speak
of the "Ch'an lineage" *(ch'an-tsung),* the reference necessarily implies
some sort of institutional entity or social grouping. The Ch'an lineage in
the Sung, however, was essentially a mythological entity, that is, a collection of stories about how the sacred (enlightenment) manifested itself in
the world of human beings from ancient times down to the present. Yet,
because the mythology was not only transmitted verbally and in written
form but also reenacted in concrete rituals that were recognized by the
government as well as the Buddhist community at large, the Ch'an lineage did in fact possess a certain social and institutional reality. That is to
say, there was in the Sung an elite group of Buddhist monks (and a few
nuns and laypersons) who were regarded as living members of the Ch'an
lineage by virtue of the fact that they had formally inherited the dharma
from another recognized member of the lineage in a ritual of dharma
transmission. In the accounts of the early generations of the lineage in
China, the flame histories depict the patriarchs handing over robes and
bowls to their disciples as proof of dharma transmission—visible signs
that the formless dharma had indeed been vouchsafed. In the Sung, however, it was only by the possession of an "inheritance certificate" *(ssu-
shu),* a kind of diploma received in the ritual of dharma transmission,
that a person was recognized as a member of the Ch'an lineage.

The great significance of "inheritance certificates" in the world of
Sung Buddhism was attested by the Japanese pilgrim monk Dōgen
(1200–1253) in the chapter of his *Shōbōgenzō* entitled "Shisho" (Inherit-

ance certificates).[43] These certificates were potent religious symbols, which linked the holder directly to the source of the sacred, Śākyamuni Buddha. There were some minor differences in style, but in general they were written in such a way that the names of all the persons through whom the dharma was believed to have been transmitted, beginning with the first Indian patriarch Mahākāśyapa and ending with the holder of the document, were arranged in a circle around the name of Śākyamuni and connected by a continuous line running through each name.[44] As sacred objects, inheritance certificates were kept carefully wrapped in fine cloth and rarely displayed. The opportunity to witness one and to worship it with prostrations and offerings of incense was considered (by Dōgen at least) a most auspicious occurrence. At the same time, inheritance certificates were legal documents recognized by the civil authorities as proof of succession to a dharma lineage. Such proof was necessary if a monk, having come up through the lower ranks of the monastic bureaucracy, was ever to succeed to the abbacy of an officially designated Ch'an monastery. Dōgen vividly recounts the many abuses that arose from this requirement, as ambitious monks tried to get their hands on inheritance certificates or facsimiles thereof by pestering Ch'an masters for their autographed portraits and samples of their calligraphy and bribed officials not to scrutinize their dharma transmission documents too closely.[45] He reports that inheritance certificates were routinely given to senior monastic officers, presumably so that their way to an abbacy would not be blocked.[46]

When one recalls the image of the iconoclastic Ch'an master that is projected in the hagiographical literature, the key role played in Sung Ch'an by such regalia might seem strange. It was precisely because the Ch'an lineage was defined in terms of the transmission of something utterly signless and ineffable, rather than the transmission of any particular doctrines or practices, that certification was necessary. It is easy to assume that the mark of a Ch'an master (ch'an-shih) in the Sung would have been skill in meditation (ch'an). The term ch'an-shih does in fact mean "meditation master" in texts dating from the T'ang and earlier, but many proponents of the Ch'an lineage in the Sung vigorously denied that the name Ch'an signified any particular reliance on the practice of dhyāna (ch'an-na, commonly abbreviated as ch'an). The Ch'an master Chüeh-fan Hui-hung (1071–1128), for example, stressed that Bodhidharma himself had not been a mere practitioner of dhyāna (hsi-ch'an) but was a great sage who mastered the full range of Buddhist practices.[47] What the term "Ch'an lineage" really meant in the Sung was not the lineage of meditation but the lineage of enlightenment. Masters in the Ch'an lineage could not be readily distinguished from other Buddhist monks on the basis of their ordinations, the practices they engaged in, or the arrangement of the monasteries they lived in. The elite ranks of Ch'an masters in the Sung included not only meditation specialists but also Pure Land devotees, Tantric ritualists, experts on monastic discipline, exegetes of sūtra and philosophical literature, poets, artists, and even monks with leanings toward Neo-Confucianism. Thus, apart from a familiarity with the mythology of Ch'an and an ability to mimic its rhetorical style in certain ritual settings, the only indispensable external marks of a Ch'an master in the Sung were the regalia of dharma transmission, chief among them the inheritance certificate.

The vast majority of the monks, nuns, novices, postulants, and lay patrons who lived and trained in Ch'an monasteries in the Sung were not members of the Ch'an lineage (as the term was understood at the time), because only a select few ever received dharma transmission. They did, however, have various connections with members of the Ch'an lineage, who were usually senior officers, abbots, or retired abbots.

The first step toward becoming a Buddhist monk in Sung China was to leave home *(ch'u-chia)* and become a lay postulant *(t'ung-hang or hang-che)* in a monastery. There were a number of government restrictions on this practice, including the requirement of written parental approval and the sponsorship of a high-ranking monk guarantor.[48] The guarantor might be an abbot belonging to the Ch'an lineage, but that was not a requirement imposed by the government: any abbot or senior officer would do. If the sponsoring monk moved to another monastery or died, the postulant had to go with him, find another sponsor, or return to ordinary lay life. To become a novice monk *(sha-mi),* a postulant had to pass a qualifying exam and wait for an opportunity to receive the ten novice precepts in a government-approved ordination ceremony. Again, a monk sponsor was necessary to officiate during the ceremony and to oversee the subsequent training of the novice, and that monk might or might not be a member of the Ch'an lineage. To become a fully ordained monk *(ta-seng),* a novice had to receive the full 250 precepts from a Vinaya master at a government-approved ordination platform. Full ordination was a requirement for training in the sangha halls of Ch'an monasteries and all other public monasteries in the Sung, and it is clear from the flame histories that virtually all members of the Ch'an lineage in the Sung were fully ordained. However, the ordination system was regulated by the state and the Buddhist sangha at large, and there was no such thing as a "Ch'an postulant," "Ch'an novice," or "Ch'an monk" in the sense of a monk ordained into the Ch'an lineage.

The only ritual that might be called a "Ch'an" ordination took place when members of the Ch'an lineage gave the bodhisattva precepts *(p'u-sa chieh)* to their followers, including lay patrons and monastics of all ranks. Bodhisattva ordinations did not entail any change in social status in the eyes of the government, but ceremonies for receiving them were a popular form of religious practice. The bodhisattva precepts that were used by Ch'an masters were based on the *Fan-wang ching* (Sūtra of Brahma's net)[49] and were in no way unique to the Ch'an school. Persons who received the precepts from a Ch'an master, however, were believed to have established a karmic connection with the lineage, and the ordination certificates they received resembled the certificates of dharma inheritance.[50]

The fully ordained monks who were registered for training in the sangha halls of a public monastery where the abbot was a Ch'an master included some who were personal disciples of the abbot and some who were not. Personal disciples had direct, individual access to a master in a ritual known as "entering the room" *(ju-shih)*, and it was from this group that masters usually selected their dharma heirs. Abbots also chose their personal disciples to serve them as acolytes. The various acolyte positions, which constituted a low-ranking but nevertheless prestigious branch of a monastery's bureaucracy, included the abbot's cook, valet, secretary, guest master, and attendant in rituals. To be selected as an acolyte was a boost to the career of a young monk because it meant that he had been singled out as having the potential to become a dharma heir and was being groomed for high monastic office. To be in close proximity to the abbot, even in a relatively menial position, was also regarded as an excellent opportunity for spiritual development. It is noteworthy that a monk need not have been originally sponsored by a Ch'an master in his postulancy or novitiate to become a dharma heir in the Ch'an lineage. By the same token, having a Ch'an master as a sponsor early in one's career by no means assured a monk of entry into the lineage.

The overall picture that emerges is that of individual members of an elite, highly prestigious, mythologically charged fraternity (the Ch'an lineage) holding high monastic office and having around them a wide circle of followers of varying ranks and social standings.[51] Some of those followers could aspire to attain enlightenment and be recognized by the master as a dharma heir. Clearly the realization of those aspirations would be largely contingent upon one's success in obtaining the necessary novice and full ordinations—no mean feat in an age of tight government restrictions. Many other followers of a Ch'an master, in particular those who only received the bodhisattva precepts from him or just attended his public sermons, would have been content to come into the proximity of a living Buddha and absorb some of his mana.

When Buddhists in the Sung wanted to refer to followers of Ch'an masters, they used such terms as *ch'an-ho-tzu,*[52] *ch'an-seng*[53] (both meaning "Ch'an monks"), or *ch'an-chia liu*[54] ("members of the Ch'an household"). Collectively, Ch'an masters and their followers were also referred to as the *ch'an-men* (literally, "Ch'an gate"). As explained above, a Ch'an monk in the Sung was simply a Buddhist monk who sought instruction from a Ch'an master, studied Ch'an literature, and (we may assume) aspired to succeed to the Ch'an lineage.

The distinction that I wish to draw between the Ch'an lineage and the Ch'an school should now be clear. On the one hand, most of the members of the Ch'an lineage *(ch'an-tsung)* in the Sung were ancestral figures whose sacred words and deeds were preserved in the flame histories and discourse records. Only the most recent members of the lineage were living, and even they were revered as ancestorlike personages, who in a certain sense had already departed the world of ordinary human beings and joined their predecessors.[55] The Ch'an school *(ch'an-chia, ch'an-men)*, on the other hand, consisted of everyone who believed in the Ch'an lineage, gained inspiration from its lore, worshiped its patriarchs, and followed or supported the Ch'an masters who were its living representatives.

In defining the Sung Ch'an school chiefly in terms of a shared set of beliefs rather than a set of distinctive practices, I take an approach that is different from that of modern scholarship and more in tune with the way that Sung Ch'an Buddhists themselves conceived of their tradition. The advantages of my approach will become clearer with regard to the actual organization and operation of Sung Ch'an monasteries.

THE MEANING OF THE DESIGNATION "CH'AN MONASTERY"

It was common in Sung dynasty China to distinguish various types of Buddhist monasteries, but for the sake of simplicity it may be said that there were basically two classes, which I shall call "public" and "private." The public monasteries were known as "monasteries of the ten directions" *(shih-fang-ch'a)* because they were, in theory at least, the property of the Buddhist order at large, the so-called sangha of the ten directions *(shih-fang seng)*. Strictly speaking, the public monasteries were distinguished by the fact that their abbacies were open to all eminent members of the "sangha of the ten directions" rather than restricted to disciples of previous abbots. The more technical name for them was "ten directions abbacy cloisters" *(shih-fang chu-ch'ih yüan)*. These institutions were public in the sense that they were supposed to be open to all officially ordained Buddhist clergy and were sanctioned and sometimes supported by the state. Generally speaking, the public monasteries included the larger, more famous and powerful Buddhist establishments in Sung China. They had spacious compounds encompassing over fifty major and minor structures, facilities for a rich variety of religious practices and ceremonies, and sometimes more than a thousand persons in residence, including monastic officers, ordinary monks and nuns, lay postulants and laborers. In addition, they were well endowed with estate lands and were the proprietors of other income-producing property, such as mills and oil presses. They were granted official monastery name plaques (o) to be displayed over their main gates and were often called on to dedicate merit produced in various religious rituals to the well-being of the emperor and the prosperity and defense of the state.

The private monasteries were known as "disciple-lineage cloisters" (chia-i t'u-ti-yüan) and were distinguished by the fact that the abbacy was passed down directly from master to disciple within a single teaching line. This class of monastery included some large establishments but mainly comprised numerous mid-sized and smaller ones. Private monasteries also included merit cloisters (kung-te yüan), which were sponsored by wealthy families as temples for the cult of their ancestors and (not incidentally) as tax shelters for productive lands that were donated to the temple but remained under the sponsoring family's control. Unlike their public counterparts, the communities of monks or nuns in residence in private monasteries could, in principle, be limited to the followers of a particular teacher.

Looking back at the T'ang, it is possible to find certain precedents for the Sung division between public and private monasteries. There was a basic division in the T'ang between large Buddhist monasteries that were registered with the government and smaller, privately maintained monasteries and chapels that escaped official notice. Among the former group, certain monasteries were singled out for special treatment by the court and honored with imperially bestowed name plaques (ch'ih-o). Such monasteries were given names like "Monastery for Pacifying the Nation" and "Monastery for Promoting the T'ang [Dynasty]" and were charged with producing merit to protect the emperor and the state. In return, they probably received official protection and financial support, the right to ordain a certain number of monks annually, and other perquisites such as the imperial bestowal of purple robes and "master" titles (shih-hao) upon individual monks in residence.[56] Moreover, monasteries with imperial name plaques were generally spared during crackdowns on the Buddhist institution.

By the Northern Sung, however, it seems that the practice of rulers bestowing official name plaques had become so common that the possession of such a plaque no longer entailed much special treatment for a monastery. The prestige, privileges, and duties that formerly had been the lot of the monasteries with imperial plaques shifted about this time to the newly formalized class of public monasteries.[57] It is unclear exactly when or where the first official "monasteries of the ten directions" were established, but there are indications that they began late in the T'ang and were continued on the local level during the Five Dynasties period in the would-be "empires" of Min (in what is now Fukien),⁵⁸ Ch'u, Wu, Wu-yüeh, Nan-t'ang, and Nan-han. The Southeast was an area of relative peace and prosperity in a turbulent age and provided a refuge for Buddhist monks from all over China. It was also an important place of incubation for the Ch'an and T'ien-t'ai schools, which were patronized by local rulers.⁵⁹

Sung sources also distinguish among Ch'an monasteries *(ch'an-ssu* or *ch'an-yüan),* Teachings monasteries *(chiao-ssu* or *chiao-yüan),* and Vinaya monasteries *(lü-ssu* or *lü-yüan).* All Ch'an and Teachings monasteries in the Sung belonged to the class of public monasteries, whereas Vinaya monasteries were all "disciple cloisters" until the middle of the twelfth century, when a few became public monasteries.⁶⁰ Ch'an monasteries were known technically as "ten directions Ch'an monasteries," which meant that the abbacy was restricted to monks who were dharma heirs in the Ch'an lineage but was left open and public to the extent that the abbot could come from any of the competing branches of that lineage.

The Ching-te Ch'an Monastery on Mount T'ien-t'ung, where the Japanese monk Dōgen studied under Ju-ching (1163–1228), makes a good case in point. When Dōgen first visited Mount T'ien-tung in 1223, the abbot was Wu-chi (d. 1224), a monk in the Yang-ch'i branch of the Lin-chi lineage. When he returned again in 1225, Wu-chi had died, and Ju-ching, who belonged to the Ts'ao-tung lineage, had been appointed abbot. The abbacy of the Ching-te Monastery at the time was restricted to Ch'an masters, but it was open to masters in all branches of the Ch'an lineage. When the monastery was originally rebuilt with imperial patronage in 759 at the location where Dōgen found it, it was given the name plaque "T'ien-tung Ling-lung Monastery."⁶¹ Later, during the reign of the emperor Wu-tsung (841–846), it was officially designated a "monastery of the ten directions." Its name was changed to T'ien-shou Monastery in 869. It was only in 1007 that its name was changed to Ching-te Ch'an Monastery and its abbacy was restricted to monks of the Ch'an lineage. Not only Mount T'ien-t'ung but many of the other prominent Ch'an monasteries in the Southern Sung had also become Ch'an institutions by imperial declaration rather late in their histories, after the founding of the Northern Sung in 960. The Kuang-li Ch'an Monastery on Mount A-yü-wang, for example, was given its name and declared a "ten directions Ch'an monastery" by imperial decree in 1008.⁶² Prior to that time it had had a long history of patronage by the T'ang emperors and no association with the Ch'an lineage.

It is unclear exactly when state designation of public monasteries as the domain of a particular Buddhist denomination started, but it was a common practice following the establishment of the Northern Sung dynasty and may well have taken place at the regional level during the

Five Dynasties period. It is certain, in any case, that the first public monasteries to be officially linked to a single denomination were designated as Ch'an monasteries and that the precedent set by the Ch'an school had been followed by the T'ien-t'ai school by the end of the tenth century. According to annals dating from 1011, proponents of the T'ien-t'ai teachings successfully petitioned the court in 996 for the establishment of two monasteries with "ten-directions, teachings-transmitting abbacies" (shih-fang ch'uan-chiao chu-ch'ih).[63] These were the first of the so-called Teachings monasteries.

The designation "Vinaya monastery" in the Northern Sung did not apply to public monasteries and thus does not seem to have had anything to do with membership in a Vinaya lineage as such. The term simply refers to monasteries regulated by the Vinaya, that is, ordinary Buddhist monasteries where no particular precedence was given to Ch'an or T'ien-t'ai monks. Certainly that is the meaning intended in the Ch'an-men kuei-shih, which states that before Pai-chang formulated his rules, monks belonging to the Ch'an lineage resided in "Vinaya monasteries."[64] By the thirteenth century, however, there were a handful of officially designated "ten directions Vinaya cloisters" (shih-fang lü-yüan), the abbacies of which were evidently restricted to monks in the Nan-shan Vinaya lineage. Even so, there continued to be many "disciple Vinaya cloisters" (chia-i lü-yüan), that is, private monasteries with no state-determined denominational affiliation.

There is general agreement among modern historians that the Ch'an school came to dominate the Buddhist monastic institution in the Sung. It was not the case, however, that large numbers of new Ch'an monasteries were built in the Sung in accordance with some distinctive plan handed down from Pai-chang's day. What happened, rather, was that the imperial court designated the majority of existing public monasteries as "ten directions Ch'an monasteries," thereby restricting their abbacies to monks belonging to the Ch'an lineage.[65] One of the charts in the Gozan jissatsu zu (Charts of the Five Mountains and Ten Monasteries) records what was written on the main gate name plaques, most of which were imperially bestowed, of some 88 large public monasteries. In all, 48 out of the 88 monasteries listed were designated as Ch'an monasteries or cloisters; 9 were designated as Teachings monasteries or cloisters; 4 were designated as Vinaya monasteries or cloisters; and the remaining 27 had nothing in their names to indicate any association with a particular lineage.[66] Whether those 27 monasteries were disciple cloisters, or perhaps true "ten-directions" institutions open to abbots of any lineage (Ch'an and other), is unclear. In any case, the evidence of this text lends credence to a statement made by the pilgrim monk Dōgen in the Pao-ch'ing era (1225–1228) that "what are now called Ch'an cloisters are the empire's great monasteries."[67]

Japanese scholars since the eighteenth century have believed that there was a system of "five mountains and ten monasteries" *(wu-shan shih-ch'a)* in place during the Southern Sung and that all of the monasteries in that system belonged to the Ch'an school. The *Gozan jissatsu zu,* however, contains ground plans and architectural drawings that pertain to all of the great public monasteries in the vicinity of Hangchow in the Southern Sung, not only those that were designated as Ch'an monasteries. According to the evidence in this text, there were scarcely any differences in the layouts of Ch'an, Teachings, and Vinaya monasteries. For example, the *Gozan jissatsu zu* includes complete ground plans for three major monasteries, two of them affiliated with the Ch'an school and one of them not. The ground plan of the Wan-nien Monastery on Mount T'ien-t'ai, which was not a Ch'an monastery, looks essentially the same as those of the Ching-te Ch'an Monastery on Mount T'ien-t'ung and the Ling-yin Ch'an Monastery on Mount Pei.[68] In particular, the buildings that are most often deemed characteristic of Ch'an monasteries—including a sangha hall, a dharma hall, and abbot's quarters—are found in exactly the same location in all three plans. If we consider that by the Southern Sung, at least, the public Teachings and Vinaya monasteries were regulated by monastic codes that were essentially the same as the Ch'an codes, it is even more difficult to sustain the notion of a distinctively Ch'an system of monastic organization and practice.

THE ORGANIZATION AND OPERATION OF CH'AN MONASTERIES IN THE SOUTHERN SUNG

Setting aside all preconceived notions of what facilities were essential to or characteristic of Ch'an monasteries, let us take a tour, as it were, of one representative establishment: the Ling-yin Ch'an Monastery on Mount Pei (Pei-shan ling-yin ch'an-ssu), which was located near the Southern Sung capital of Hangchow. I shall refer initially to each facility at Pei-shan (as the monastery was known colloquially) both by its name and by the number assigned it on the ground plan reproduced in figure 5.1. A list of the same facilities, categorized by function, is given in appendix 5.1. By briefly mentioning the personnel and activities associated with each of the various facilities, I hope to convey something of the complexity of the institution and the richness of the religious life that it supported. Since it is impossible to give equal treatment to every aspect of the monastery environment here, I shall focus in the greatest detail on those facilities that were used for activities involving the abbot.

According to Dōgen, who visited Pei-shan and other places like it, the major Ch'an monasteries of the Southern Sung had "more than a thousand residents and more than a hundred buildings, with storied

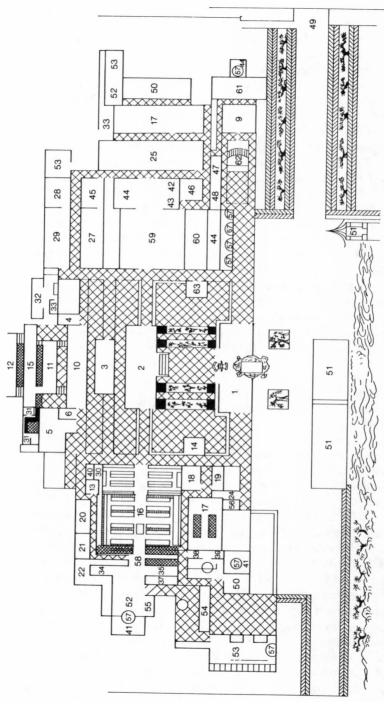

Figure 5.1. Ground plan of the Ling-yin Ch'an Monastery on Mount Pei. (Drawn by David W. Ernst based on a ground plan found in the *Gozan jissatsu zu* held at Daijōji in Kanazawa and on a reproduction of that plan in the *Daisō meiran zu* by Mujaku Dōchū. For a photographic reproduction of the *Gozan jissatsu zu* original, see *Zengaku daijiten* 3.13; for Mujaku's reproduction, see Yanagida Seisan, ed., *Zengaku sōsho* [Kyoto: Chūban shuppansha, 1977], no. 8, vol. 2, p. 1287)

pavilions arrayed from front to rear and covered corridors running from east to west, their facilities are like those of an imperial residence."[69] The figure of a hundred buildings may have been somewhat exaggerated, but in general Dōgen's description is substantiated by the Pei-shan ground plan and by a great deal of other evidence. The ground plan of Sung Ch'an monasteries (and other large public monasteries as well) was indeed modeled after that of the imperial court, with a number of imposing two- or three-storied edifices lined up along a central north-south axis, effectively dividing the many flanking buildings into east and west sectors.

At Pei-shan, the central axis was defined by a main gate [1], which had a ritual hall in the second story; a Buddha hall [2] in which an image of the "chief honored one" *(pen-tsun)* of the entire monastery, probably the Buddha Śākyamuni, was enshrined on a Sumeru altar *(hsü-mi-t'an);* a similar hall for the cult of the Buddha Vairocana [3]; a dharma hall [10]; an abbot's reception hall [11]; private abbot's quarters [15]; and a meditation room [12] for use by the abbot. On either side of the dharma hall, but still within the central courtyard, were the earth spirit hall [4], patriarchs hall [5], and donors hall [6].

With the exception of the abbot's quarters and the adjacent acolytes' quarters [31], all of the buildings on the central axis of a Ch'an monastery were in some sense public facilities. That is, the central facilities were places where all the members of a monastic community, as well as visiting monks and laymen, could gather for worship, sermons, debates, and other ceremonies. Those buildings that contained altars with images (including the main gate, the Buddha hall, the earth spirit hall, the patriarchs hall, and the donors hall) were used primarily for ritual offerings and prayers directed to the figures enshrined. The facilities on the east and west sides of a monastery housed distinct classes of persons who rarely got involved in activities on the opposite side. Most of the major buildings on the east and west sides also contained images enshrined on altars, but those were generally of deities who were conceived of as protecting or encouraging the particular activity that the building housed. Those tutelary deities were worshiped and propitiated with regular offerings and appealed to with prayers for assistance, but such worship was not the primary function of the facilities in which they were enshrined.

The main gates of Ch'an monasteries in the Sung were distinguished from those of other public monasteries chiefly by the appearance of the word "Ch'an" on the imperially bestowed monastery name plaques that hung beneath the eaves. The gates were imposing structures of two or three stories, with three portals on the ground level (hence the alternate name *san-men,* or "triple gate") and worship halls with various images installed on the upper levels. Their function was largely ceremonial and symbolic, for they were located well within a monastery's compound and the practical task of keeping out unwanted visitors was handled at the outer gate [49]. Main gates symbolized the spiritual as well as the physical boundaries of a monastery, as shown by the many prayers that asked for harmony and felicity "within the main gate" and sought to bar entry to evil spirits of discord and illness. The figures installed in the worship halls were generally associated in some way with protection of the dharma and the sangha. The four deva kings *(ssu-t'ien-wang)*, Hindu deities who were dressed as warriors and conceived as protectors of Buddhism, were sometimes enshrined in main gates. Another common arrangemment featured sets of five hundred and/or sixteen arhats arrayed behind a central figure of the bodhisattva Kuan-yin (Avalokiteśvara) or the "crowned Śākyamuni" *(pao-kuan shih-chia)*. The central figure was flanked by images of Shan-ts'ai T'ung-tzu (Sudhana) and Yüeh-kai Chang-che. We know from the verses for dedicating merit to the arhats that they were propitiated as supernatural beings who could use their magical powers to keep a monastery supplied with food and other material necessities. Yüeh-kai appeared in Buddhist mythology as a lay believer who saved his city from pestilence by calling on Kuan-yin,[70] and Shan-ts'ai was famous as the youthful pilgrim whose story was told in the "Entering the Dharmadhātu" section of the *Avataṃsaka Sūtra*.[71] The cult of all these deities and heroes belonged to the Buddhist tradition at large and was found in Ch'an and non-Ch'an monasteries alike.[72]

The ground plan of Pei-shan does not show a separate Kuan-yin pavilion [7] or an arhats hall [8], although those facilities were common at other Ch'an monasteries in the Sung. At Pei-shan, images of the bodhisattva Kuan-yin and the sixteen or five hundred arhats were probably enshrined in some other building such as the upper story of the main gate.

The Buddha halls in Sung Ch'an monasteries were first and foremost places for the worship of Buddhas. This fact needs to be stressed in order to counter the assumption that Buddha halls served mainly as places where prayer services on behalf of the emperor and monastery patrons were held.[73] Such ceremonies were by no means concentrated in the Buddha halls; they were also held in dharma halls, sangha halls, donors halls, and sūtra reading halls. There is thus no logic to the claim that the absence of a Buddha hall in the original Ch'an monastery arrangement attributed to Pai-chang signaled a lack of dependence on lay patronage. It is true that three tablets bearing the inscriptions "long life to the emperor," "prosperity to patrons," and "fire deity of the southern quarter" had a prominent place on the altar in front of the central image in Buddha halls from at least the Southern Sung. The phrasing on these tablets was derived from verses for the dedication of merit that were recited at the end of daily worship services as a device for offering the merit generated from sūtra chanting to the Buddha. The verses, however, gave voice to many different prayers, not only ones for the emperor, patrons, and protection from fire. Moreover, the primary purpose of the daily Buddha hall services was not to make prayers but to serve the Buddha whose image was enshrined (usually Śākyamuni, often flanked by Amitābha and Maitreya) with offerings of incense, food, drink, and merit accumulated by sūtra chanting. Buddha halls were also used for annual ceremonies—including ones commemorating Śākyamuni's birth, enlightenment, and entry into nirvāṇa as well as ones celebrating the emperor's birthday. During the two annual monastic retreats, each of which lasted three months, the halls were also used for Śūraṅgama assemblies *(leng-yen-hui)*, in which the monks circumambulated the altar (or walked in a "serpentine" circle in front of it) while chanting the Śūraṅgama dhāraṇī *(leng-yen-chou)*. This practice was conceived as a means of producing a great deal of merit, which was then offered to the Buddha and the earth spirit in support of special prayers for the health of the gathered monks and the success of the retreat.

Nothing about the Buddha hall and the rituals performed there was in any way unique to Ch'an monasteries,[74] except perhaps the occasional use of an image of Śākyamuni that depicted him "holding up a flower" (symbolizing the founding of the Ch'an lineage by transmitting the dharma to Mahākāśyapa).[75] Nor is there any evidence that would indicate that followers of the Ch'an school in the Sung regarded Buddha halls as somehow nonessential or extraneous to "pure" Ch'an monastic practice. Despite the isolated claim made in the *Ch'an-men kuei-shih* that Pai-chang's monastery did not have a Buddha hall, the Sung flame histories frequently depict the Ch'an masters of the "golden age" engaging in dialogues in and around Buddha halls. Whether or not the appearance of Buddha halls in the hagiographies of T'ang masters was an anachronism stemming from the Sung penchant for realistic settings, the Sung compilers of the flame histories took Buddha halls for granted.

The hall dedicated to the worship of the Buddha Vairocana at Pei-shan was probably the scene of regular devotional offerings similar to those made to Śākyamuni in the Buddha hall. Vairocana, the central deity of the *Avataṃsaka Sūtra*, was the "chief honored one" in many rituals associated with the Hua-yen school in China. The extent to which Hua-yen rituals were performed in Sung Ch'an monasteries is a matter for future research, but the size of the Vairocana hall and its placement on the central axis at Pei-shan certainly suggests that a cult of this Buddha was an important part of the religious life in at least some Ch'an establishments.

The earth spirit halls in Sung Ch'an monasteries housed images or tablets for two sorts of deities of non-Buddhist origin: the earth spirit *(t'u-ti shen)*, or god of the place where the monastery was built, and various monastery-protecting deities *(ch'ieh-lan shen)*. All were propitiated with regular offerings of food and prayed to as protectors of the dharma and guardians of the monastic community. The earth spirit at each monastery was considered to be an individual deity whose influence extended over that place alone, but none had individual names other than the generic title "this monastery's earth spirit" *(tang-shan t'u-ti)*. Monastery-protecting dieties, in contrast, were universal spirits (their power had no geographical limits), who had individual names and identities.[76] The most common set of protecting deities in Sung Ch'an monasteries were the so-called eighteen beneficent spirits *(shih-pa shan-shen)* based on the *Ch'i fo pa p'u-sa shuo ta-t'o-lo-ni shen-chou ching* (Sūtra of the Dhāraṇī taught by seven buddhas and eight bodhisattvas),[77] but other protectors, including the Hindu deities Brahma, Indra, and the four deva kings, were sometimes enshrined in earth spirit halls as well.[78] Vaiśravaṇa (P'i-sha-men), the Indian deity discussed by Valerie Hansen in this volume, was one of the four deva kings and, as such, was used as a guardian deity in Sung Ch'an monasteries,[79] but I have not found any evidence that he ever appeared alone in that capacity.[80]

The motif of suppressing and converting the gods (treated in the chapters by Hansen and Judith Boltz) does appear in the context of Ch'an monasticism, however. There were cases in which local deities (other than the nameless earth spirits) were "converted" to Buddhism and appointed as the guardians of Ch'an monasteries.[81] Moreover, Ch'an masters were sometimes caught up in contests of spiritual power with local deities and were expected by their followers to prevail. There is a significant parallel between the role played by Ch'an abbots vis-à-vis local spirits *(shen)* and that played by scholar-officials *(kuan)*. Both typically hailed from the class of the educated elite; both were often outsiders (natives of different provinces or prefectures), who were appointed by the central government to local posts for limited periods of time; and both owed their charisma to a central authority (the imperial house and the family of Śākyamuni), which claimed universal sanctity and sovereignty and thus could brook no challenge from local spirits. The Ch'an abbots' status as the final arbiters of spiritual "test cases" *(kung-an;* literally, "magistrate's table," i.e., a case in court) also paralleled the local officials' role as judges in the criminal cases and civil disputes that were brought before them. One of the Ch'an masters' favorite figurative expressions for indicating deluded thinking on the part of an interlocutor in debate was "thirty blows," a sentence that was carried out literally and immediately when pronounced by local magistrates.[82]

The patriarchs halls in Ch'an monasteries were dedicated to the veneration of key patriarchs in the Ch'an lineage and former abbots (also members of the Ch'an lineage) of the monastery. The arrangement of the halls and the services performed in them leave no doubt that they were the Ch'an school's counterpart to the Confucian-style temples that were maintained by prominent families for the worship of their ancestors. Because patriarchs halls housed funerary portraits for all of the ancestral figures commemorated, they were also called portrait halls (*chen-t'ang;* literally, "likeness halls"). The ground plan of Pei-shan shows that the patriarchs hall was a large structure containing portraits arrayed along the north wall in the following order (moving from left, west, to right, east): the first generation [abbot], the patriarch Pai-chang, the founding patriarch Bodhidharma, the second patriarch Hui-k'o, the founding abbot *(k'ai-shan),* and the second generation [abbot]. According to their places in the Ch'an lineage, however, the order is Bodhidharma, Hui-k'o, Pai-chang, the founding abbot, the first generation abbot, and the second generation abbot. Clearly the images were arranged in such a way that when one faced them, figures in all the odd-numbered generations were lined up to the left of Bodhidharma and figures in all the even-numbered generations were lined up to the right. This arrangement was inspired by the ancient Confucian model established in the "Regulations of the King" chapter of the *Li-chi* and had been followed in Ch'an portrait halls at least since Tsung-mi's (780–841) day.[83] There were, however, other possible arrangements. The Ch'an master Pai-yün Shou-tuan (1025–1071) is quoted in the *Lin-chien lu* (published 1107) as saying: "It is due to Ch'an Master Ta-chih's [Pai-chang's] power that monasteries flourish in the land. In the patriarchs hall, an image of founding patriarch Bodhidharma should be set up in the middle, an image of Ch'an Master Ta-chih [Pai-chang] should face west, and images of the founding abbot and other venerables [former abbots] should face east. Do not set up the images of the founding abbot and venerables alone, leaving out the patriarchs."[84]

Although only six figures are indicated on the Pei-shan ground plan, it is certain that the portraits of all subsequent former abbots were also enshrined there. We know from Sung Ch'an monastic codes that when an abbot died and was replaced by a new abbot, the portrait of the deceased was moved from the abbot's quarters (where it was kept after the funeral) and hung in the patriarchs hall.

The placement of spirit tablets in front of each portrait in the manner of Confucian mortuary practices does not seem to have been adopted in Ch'an patriarchs halls until late in the Southern Sung,[85] but in other respects the ritual implements used and the offerings of food and drink to the ancestral spirits were quite similar. Memorial services for each of the patriarchs and former abbots were centered on the anniversaries of their death days. On the day before the death day, the portrait was hung on the lecture platform in the dharma hall, and offering vessels were arranged on a table in front of it. That evening the great assembly of monks gathered and chanted the Śūraṅgama dhāraṇī, dedicating the merit produced to the patriarch (as an offering). On the morning of the death day, postulants lit candles and incense on the offering table and set out the offering of the morning gruel. The main service was held around the time of the forenoon meal. The abbot personally lit incense and set out the offerings of hot water, tea, and food while the monks of the great assembly chanted sūtras and dhāraṇīs to produce merit for dedication. The senior monastic officers came forward one by one and offered incense, and the ceremony closed with the entire assembly making prostrations. The portrait was returned to the patriarchs hall, and on the following day the abbot and officers congregated there after the morning meal to offer incense, tea, and snacks and to make prostrations. The entire ritual was based on the model of receiving an honored guest, feting him, and sending him off with gifts.

The explicit purpose of all the offerings, as stated in the verses for the dedication of merit, was to "raise the enlightened spirit to a more exalted status."[86] The level of exaltation attained in the human realm by the Ch'an patriarchs was a matter of real concern to living members of the Ch'an lineage, for it was the prestige of the mythological lineage that afforded them their privileged position in the Buddhist monastic institution at large. This interpretation, however, demythologizes the verses in a way that followers of the Sung Ch'an school never did. The more exalted status that the verses refer to was status in the realm of ancestral spirits, that vast celestial bureaucracy in which every family hoped to place its members to intercede on its behalf. The Chinese belief that the living must remember and nurture the ancestral spirits in order to get their help (and avoid their ire) was also clearly operative in these rites. As Pai-yün Shou-tuan stressed, for example, the prosperity of Ch'an monasteries in an empire that was not always friendly to the Buddhist institution depended on the power of the ancestral spirit Pai-chang, revered founder of Ch'an monastic practice. To lose Pai-chang's favor by leaving him out of the patriarchs hall and neglecting his memorial services would be disastrous.

It is significant that the great majority of the figures enshrined in the patriarchs halls of Ch'an monasteries were former abbots rather than the masters of the "golden age" of the lineage who were featured prominently in the flame histories and discourse records. Apart from Pai-chang, the only indispensable representative of the generations before the founding abbot was Bodhidharma.[87] This shows that the arrangement of the hall was not so much a manifestation of the mythology of Bodhidharma's lineage as a symbolic expression of how membership in the lineage qualified monks to be the abbots of public monasteries. The "successive generations" of former abbots were real persons who were remembered (at least in the more recent generations) by the living, and their portraits (often drawn from life) represented their physiognomies with considerable accuracy. Bodhidharma, Pai-chang, and other early patriarchs whom we would call semimythical were also depicted with a realism similar to that of the former abbots. The fact that these portraits were lined up together in a patriarchs hall as if there were no essential differences between them set the stage for the mutual flow of sanctity (from past to present) and historicity (from present to past) that is characteristic of Ch'an mythology. Moreover, the arrangement of Ch'an patriarchs halls conveniently obscured the identities of the true founders of the many monasteries that only became "Ch'an" institutions by imperial proclamation in the Sung. Pei-shan, for example, had been an important monastic center since the Sui and T'ang dynasties, but it was only designated a Ch'an monastery in 1007.[88] There were in its past numerous eminent monks, equivalent in stature to the Ch'an abbots of the Sung, who had no connection with the lineage of Bodhidharma. By leaving such figures out of the quasi-historical genealogical record and setting up Pai-chang in their place, the patriarchs halls also obscured the true process by which "Ch'an monasteries" in general had come into existence.

The use of the mythology of the Ch'an lineage and the symbolism of the patriarchs hall to monopolize the abbacies of leading public monasteries was a strategy that succeeded ideologically and politically, but there was a self-contradictory element in it that necessitated the performance of a mitigating ritual. The basic problem was that the Ch'an lineage was defined in terms of dharma transmission from master to disciple, whereas the lineage commemorated in the patriarchs hall was defined in terms of succession to an office (the abbacy). Thus, while a presiding abbot led the main offerings to former abbots in the patriarchs hall like the head of a clan doing his filial duty, in most cases he was not the dharma heir of any of the abbots who immediately preceded him, and he may in fact have belonged to an entirely different branch of the Ch'an lineage. The ritual impropriety of venerating someone else's spiritual ancestors while neglecting one's own would have undermined the very principles on which the mythology of Ch'an was based. So, in addition to the patriarchs hall memorial services, it was necessary to hold equally elaborate memorial services for the abbot's own dharma transmission master on the anniversary of his death. However, because the abbot's master was not enshrined in the patriarchs hall, the services for him were held entirely in the abbot's reception hall or in the dharma hall. Moreover, because the services were viewed as essentially a private affair, the abbot himself had to underwrite all the expenses incurred by the monastery. He also sponsored a feast for the senior officers and monks of the great assembly.

The arrangement of the patriarchs halls was one of the most salient features distinguishing Ch'an from non-Ch'an monasteries in the Sung, but only in the sense that the identities of the figures enshrined clearly marked the abbacy as the domain of the Ch'an lineage. Patriarchs halls themselves were not unique to Ch'an; ones very similar in layout and ritual function were also found in Teachings monasteries and Vinaya lineage monasteries. The difference was that the patriarchs and former abbots in Teachings monasteries were portrayed as members of the Chih-i's T'ien-t'ai lineage,[89] and those in Vinaya monasteries were all said to be descendants of Tao-hsüan (596–667), founder of the Nan-shan Vinaya lineage.[90]

To understand the function of patriarchs halls (portrait halls), it is important to consider the wider meaning and function of portraits *(chen)* themselves in the world of Sung Buddhism and especially Ch'an Buddhism. In the context of funeral and memorial services, portraits were considered the seat of the spirit *(ling)* of the deceased, just as the body had been earlier. The identification of a master's portrait with his body was most evident in the symbolism of the funerals that were held for abbots in Ch'an monasteries. When an abbot died, his body was seated in the abbot's quarters, and a table for offerings was placed in front of it. After three days, the body was replaced by a portrait as the focal point of offerings. When the funeral was held, the portrait was moved to the dharma hall, where it took the abbot's place on the lecture platform, as in subsequent memorial services. After the funeral the portrait was returned to the abbot's quarters, where it was served the two daily meals and even engaged in ritual debate. The portrait, or rather the spirit it harbored, was in fact still regarded as the abbot until a new abbot was formally installed, at which point it was retired and moved to the patriarchs hall. The belief that a funerary-style portrait was suffused with the charisma of the person portrayed was so strong that dozens (and in some cases hundreds) of likenesses of famous masters were commissioned by their personal disciples and lay followers, who had them inscribed with verses by the masters themselves.[91] Portraits were also used in place of living monks by persons who needed sponsors for their postulancy and novice ordinations, a practice that made sense given the religious significance attached to portraits but was condemned by the government as an abuse designed to skirt restrictions on the sangha.[92]

Dharma halls in Sung Ch'an monasteries were large structures with architectural features and appointments identical to Buddha halls, with the exception that their Sumeru altars had no Buddha images on them. Instead, dharma hall altars bore high lecture seats that were used by abbots for preaching the dharma, engaging the assembled monks and laity in debate, and other services. The association of an abbot with the Buddha in this context was unmistakable and, indeed, was voiced explicitly in the *Ch'an-men kuei-shih* passage that says that "the current abbot, representing the Buddhas and patriarchs, was to be regarded as the honored one."[93] The import of this statement was that the current abbot, ex officio, was to be worshiped as a living Buddha (or, more aptly, as a sort of flesh-and-blood Buddha image) in certain ritual settings. Thus, for example, when an abbot was on the high seat in a dharma hall, the assembly made prostrations to him that were identical in form to the prostrations made before the altar in a Buddha hall. During funerals and annual memorial services the high seat was occupied by a different but closely related sort of "Buddha image," namely the portrait of a patriarch or former abbot. Dharma halls were also the scene of novice ordinations and sūtra chanting prayer services sponsored by lay patrons.

Gatherings at which an abbot took the high seat, gave sermons, and responded to questions from the assembly were called major convocations, or "ascending the [dharma] hall" *(shang-t'ang)*. The written procedures for "ascending the hall" that survive in Sung Ch'an monastic codes make it clear that these were extremely formal ceremonies, in which the abbot's entry into the hall, preparation to speak, and departure from the hall were marked by numerous bows and prostrations on the part of the assembly. The solemnity was such that the assembly was enjoined "not to make the hall noisy by laughing aloud or even to crack a smile or sneer" if someone questioning the abbot said something laughable.[94] It was in this setting that the Sung Ch'an masters, playing the role of a living Buddha, recalled and mimicked the sparkling sayings and dramatic actions attributed to renowned T'ang patriarchs in the lineage. One of the important functions of the flame histories and discourse records was precisely to provide such models of sacred utterance and behavior for ritual reenactment. The records of Sung masters show that they used the same kinds of shouts, dramatic gestures, and enigmatic expressions that were believed to characterize the teaching styles of their predecessors. For example, on the occasion of a major convocation in his monastery's dharma hall, Yang-ch'i Fang-hui (992–1049) struck the lectern with his staff, shouted, and said: "With one shout and one blow [on the lectern] the eyes see stars, the nostrils dilate, and the eyebrows raise in surprise. If you get it, the moon sets in the western mountains; if you don't get it, wheat cakes and rice dumplings." He then got down from the lecture seat.[95] In major convocations the Sung Ch'an masters also commented frequently on the more pithy sayings of the T'ang masters. Either someone in the assembly would ask about the meaning of a particular case or the master would "raise" a case for discussion, reserving final judgment on it (and on any comments elicited from the assembly) for himself. In these verbal rejoinders and in the written commentaries that were added to each case in Sung *kung-an* collections, the Ch'an style of iconoclastic rhetoric was often turned against the revered protagonists of the ancient cases themselves. For example, Wu-men Hui-k'ai (1184–1260) treated the story of Śākyamuni holding up a flower to preach the ineffable dharma as a *kung-an* and lambasted the Buddha in his commentary as a crooked merchant who "hung up a sheep's head [as an advertisement] and sold dog meat."[96] By the Southern Sung, at least, major convocations were generally held six times a month, on the first, fifth, tenth, fifteenth, twentieth, and twenty-fifth days.[97] The ceremonies that took place on the first and fifteenth (traditionally the times of the Buddhist "sabbath," or *poṣadha*) were designated as "ascending the hall for prayers for the emperor" *(chu-sheng shang-t'ang)*. The abbot himself, from his place on the altar, held up incense and voiced prayers for the well-being of the sovereign and the stability of the state. Special prayers on the emperor's birthday were also occasions for major convocations. Other major convocations were sponsored by lay patrons, who would designate the ends to which they wished the merit formally dedicated. Major convocations were also held to celebrate the installation of a new abbot and to mark the "four great occasions" in the monastic calendar: the opening of the three-month-long retreat, the closing of the retreat, the winter solstice, and the new year. Major convocations were clearly multifaceted ritual performances, the significance of which went beyond simply providing an opportunity for teaching and public debate. It was only fitting that the Ch'an school, when it came to dominate the public monasteries in the Sung, should perform this most sacred, potent ritual in the service of the nation.

It may seem remarkable (if not positively contradictory) that a fundamentally conservative monastic institution such as that of Sung Ch'an could embrace as orthodox a body of literature that depicted ancient heroes speaking and acting in a manner that was often extremely unconventional and iconoclastic. One reason for the negative evaluation of Sung Ch'an commonly found in modern scholarship is precisely a sense that the Ch'an school in the Sung, with its great concern for monastic forms and rituals, somehow failed to live up to its own model of enlightened behavior. This area, however, is one in which scholars of Ch'an can learn from broader, comparative studies of myth and ritual in the world's religions. When we consider, for example, that one of the characteristic features of religious mythology is the tendency for gods and other sacred beings to behave outrageously and transgress the boundaries of socially accepted behavior, the Sung Ch'an use of the flame histories and discourse records no longer seems so inconsistent. In most cultures, the wild, spontaneous behavior of the mythical gods is not to be taken as a model for ordinary, everyday behavior. On special ritual occasions or during festivals and the like, however, it is common to find an acting out (either by specialists or an entire community) of the unrestrained behavior that characterizes sacred beings and forces. The Sung Ch'an ceremony of "ascending the hall" provided just such a ritual setting for the acting out, by the titular head of the community, of the spontaneous behavior of the Ch'an school's own semimythical sacred beings.

Another fruitful model for analyzing the ceremony of "ascending the hall" is Arnold van Gennep's and Victor Turner's theory of separation, liminality, and reintegration in ritual performances. When the abbot entered the hall and solemnly mounted the high seat on the altar to the accompaniment of mass prostrations, he separated from his ordinary state and became a Buddha or an ancestor. In this "liminal" state, ordinary rules of speech and behavior did not apply. Insults, blows, sacrilege, and scatalogical language all were acceptable and even expected. But then the performance was over, and the abbot descended the altar and retired to his quarters to greet and take tea with the dignitaries and government officials who attended the ceremony. Once again extreme decorum and ritual propriety were *de rigueur,* and any antisocial or insulting behavior on the part of the abbot could only jeopardize his and the monastery's standing with patrons and the state.

For the monks in training and the lesser-ranking members of a monastic community who witnessed such performances and studied the literature that inspired them, there could be no mistaking the language and behavior displayed as a model for imitation, except of course in the same sort of ritually circumscribed contexts. Severe reprimand or punishment awaited those who broke the rules of decorum or morality. Nevertheless, the message would come through that enlightenment, the goal of all their disciplined striving, was fundamentally a state of freedom and spontaneity. The injunction not to laugh that appears in the monastic rules suggests that the ceremony of "ascending the hall" provided a kind of psychological outlet, spilling over at times into comic relief, for the monks and postulants whose lives were ordinarily bound up in a very constricting set of rules and procedures. The didactic effect of the ceremony centered on its teaching an attitude of detachment from the strict monastic routine even while engaged in it.

An abbot's sermons and exchanges with interlocutors in the dharma hall were generally recorded by an acolyte. In this way, the myth of verbatim recording, which was central to the structure of the flame histories and discourse records, was itself given a concrete reenactment in a ritual setting. Again there is an artful juxtaposition of mythical and historical elements. On the one hand, the visible fact that an abbot's words were being recorded would lend credence to the claim that the records of the ancients had been compiled in a similar verbatim fashion. On the other hand, the fact of recording implied that an abbot's words on the high seat were comparable in sanctity and worth to the recorded sayings of the Buddhas and patriarchs and held out the promise that they would someday find a place alongside those older sayings in the flame histories. Indeed, if an abbot was sufficiently famous or if he had enough influential dharma heirs, eventually the more memorable of his recorded sayings, framed by a modicum of biographical information, would be included in one of the updated flame history collections that were published periodically during the Sung.

A by-product of this practice was the tremendous proliferation in the Sung of sacred literature associated with the Ch'an school. The irony of this occurrence in a tradition that claimed to eschew reliance on the written word has often been remarked on, but it is perfectly consistent with the tradition's own outlook and agenda. The polemical thrust of the claim of representing "a special transmission outside the teachings, not setting up scriptures," was to assert the precedence of the Ch'an lineage over the so-called Teachings lineages that were characterized as relying on sūtras and commentaries to transmit the Buddha-dharma. Implicit in this claim was the notion that the teachers in other traditions had only a secondhand, hearsay knowledge of awakening, whereas masters in the Ch'an lineage derived their spiritual authority from a direct experience of the Buddha-mind. In effect, the Ch'an patriarchs *were* Buddhas. That being the case, it followed that the flame history records of their words and deeds were at least equivalent to the sūtras, which recorded the words and deeds of Śākyamuni and the other Indian Buddhas, and perhaps even superior in that they were the records of native Chinese Buddhas. In short, the rhetoric of "not relying on texts" served to establish the Ch'an histories as an authoritative body of sacred literature and provided a rationale for the continual expansion of that literature as each generation of living Buddhas left its mark.

Modern scholars frequently describe dharma halls as facilities characteristic of and unique to the Ch'an school. The *Ch'an-men kuei-shih* implies that such was the case, but there is considerable historical evidence that monasteries founded by revivers of the T'ien-t'ai tradition in the Five Dynasties period had dharma halls,[98] and that dharma halls were a standard feature of Teachings monasteries throughout the Sung.[99] What distinguished the dharma halls in Sung Ch'an monasteries was neither the layout of the buildings nor the formal structure of the rituals held therein but the contents of the teachings promulgated. Abbots in Ch'an monastery dharma halls commented on and acted out the mythological lore of the Ch'an school, whereas abbots in Teachings monastery dharma halls taught the doctrines of the T'ien-t'ai school.

Somewhere near the dharma hall, Buddha hall, and other main worship halls there were quarters for monastic officers charged with maintaining the facilities and ritual implements, preparing them for ceremonies, and keeping the altars supplied with offerings. The ground plan of Pei-shan shows quarters for the hall prefect [29], who in the Southern Sung was the senior officer in charge of such affairs, and the offerings postulants [30], who served under him.

The last of the major facilities on the central axis were the two or three buildings that made up the abbot's quarters complex. The abbot's quarters proper had private rooms for the abbot's personal use. Nearby were rooms for the personnel who staffed the abbot's facilities: the monk acolytes, who assisted the abbot in all of his affairs; lay postulants [32], who worked as servants; and lay laborers [33].

The abbot's reception hall was the scene of various audiences and ceremonial events in which the abbot played a key role. Among the most important was the minor convocation *(hsiao-ts'an)*, a scaled-down version of the major convocation held in the dharma hall. Here again, the abbot played the part of a living Buddha or patriarch and was worshiped as such with prostrations and offerings of incense. The audience included the great assembly of monks in sangha hall training, the monastic officers, and on some occasions government officials and lay patrons. The latter could make special requests that the ceremony be held at the time of their visit to a monastery and presumably made a handsome donation in return. When only monks were present, the abbot would often speak on matters of monastic discipline, expounding in particular on the "house admonitions" of his particular lineage.

Either the abbot's quarters or the reception hall was also used for the ceremony of "entering the [abbot's] room" in which the abbot's personal disciples would come before him one by one to ask for instruction in a formal, semiprivate setting. Taking turns, the disciples would make prostrations and offer incense before approaching the abbot, bowing, and then standing respectfully at the southwest corner of his meditation chair. At this point, the disciple would "speak his mind" and the abbot would reply.[100] Ch'an monastic codes give no indication of the contents of the exchange, except to enjoin against talking at length or discussing mundane affairs. As soon as the exchange was over, the disciple withdrew to the center of the room, bowed, turned, and left the room. The entire procedure, I would suggest, amounted to a ritual reenactment of the encounters between Ch'an masters and disciples that were contained in the flame histories. The brevity of the flame history anecdotes and the way in which they depict the expression of sacred truths in a few short words were written into the ritual procedures. The "liminality" of the actual face-to-face confrontation with the abbot was set off by the detailed etiquette for entering into his presence and for withdrawing that the disciples had to follow. The ceremony of "entering the room" was also used to initiate new arrivals at a monastery as personal disciples of the abbot. The fact that the secret ceremony of dharma transmission also took place "in the room" supports the notion that "entering the room" was in fact a ritual reenactment of the master-disciple relationship fundamental to the definition of the Ch'an lineage established in the flame histories.

Although the oldest extant Ch'an monastic code, the *Ch'an-yüan ch'ing-kuei* (Pure rules for Ch'an monasteries; compiled in 1103), gives no hint that the verbal exchange between master and disciple in the abbot's room had any fixed content, by the Southern Sung the standard practice was for the abbot to "raise words," that is, to bring up an old anecdote from the flame histories and discourse records, and for the disciple to try to comment perceptively on them.[101] This practice was similar to the *kung-an* practice that went on in the dharma halls, but a number of questions remain unresolved. It is unclear from the surviving Sung and Yüan monastic codes, for example, whether a disciple could "raise words" for the master to respond to or whether the master always initiated the exchange. We know from the discourse records of Sung Ch'an masters that in the setting of major convocations in a dharma hall either the abbot or someone from the assembly could "raise words" for the other to comment on, but what transpired in the ritual of "entering the room" was deemed secret and thus was not included in the discourse record literature.

Other activities held in the abbot's reception hall were tea services, a ubiquitous feature of Sung Ch'an monastery life, and "ceremonies of human affairs." These ceremonies marked various transitions in personnel—such as the appointment or retirement of monastic officers and the arrival or departure of dignitaries—and major turning points in a monastery's annual schedule. Because abbots were the chief fund raisers of monastic communities as well as their administrative heads and spiritual leaders, their reception halls were also used to entertain visiting lay patrons. They had their own kitchens for preparing special feasts and were typically accoutered with fine objects of art. They also featured such refinements as moon-viewing terraces and beautiful landscape gardens. The aristocrats and high-ranking officials who came to visit Ch'an abbots would not be disappointed by the level of cultural refinement and opulence they found there.

As noted in the *Ch'an-men kuei-shih,* the name for the abbot's quarters was an allusion to the room (*fang-chang;* literally, "ten foot square [room]") of the storied Buddhist layman Vimalakīrti, which despite its size was able to hold a great host of Buddhas, bodhisattvas, and devas and had numerous miraculous qualities like those of a pure land. The *Ch'an-men kuei-shih* suggests that the concentration of spiritual authority in the person of an abbot or "elder" and the designation of abbots' quarters as sacred places to be used for preaching the dharma were Ch'an school innovations. Modern scholars frequently refer to the abbots' quarters as a characteristically Ch'an facility. However, abbot's quarters and the practice of "entering the room" existed at T'ien-t'ai monasteries in the Five Dynasties period and throughout the Sung.[102]

Generally speaking, the area to the west side of the central axis in a monastery was where fully ordained monks who were registered as permanent residents (or residents for a retreat) lived and trained. Most of the buildings on the west side of a monastery were dedicated to meeting the physical, spiritual, and ceremonial needs of this contingent, which was known as the "great assembly." At some monasteries there were also quarters for nuns [23] on the west side. The facilities on the east side of the central axis were devoted chiefly to administrative and support functions. They also housed the many residents of a monastery who were not fully ordained monks and were therefore ineligible to join the "great assembly."

The sangha hall [16] was the central facility on the west side of a monastery compound. It was a large structure (often seven bays wide and five bays deep) divided internally into an inner and an outer hall and surrounded by enclosed corridors that connected it with various nearby ancillary facilities. The inner hall was further divided into front and rear sections and featured low, wide sitting platforms arranged in several blocks in the center of the floor space and along the walls. Registered monks of the "great assembly" spent much of their time at their individual places on these platforms, sitting in meditation, taking their two daily meals, and lying down for a few hours of sleep at night. Their bowls were hung above their seats, and their few personal effects and monkish implements were stored in boxes at the rear of the platforms. Seats in the inner hall were designated for the abbot and the monastic officers and assistants who directed the training there. Monks with no special duties were seated in order of seniority, according to years elapsed since ordination. Other officers, acolytes, and unregistered monks were assigned seating places in the outer hall, where the platforms were not deep enough to recline on. They would gather in the sangha hall for meals, ceremonies, and a few periods of meditation but slept elsewhere.

Enshrined on an altar in the center of the inner hall was an image of Mañjuśrī. This bodhisattva traditionally represented wisdom (prajñā), and it may be said that he was thus a fitting figure to be placed in the sangha hall, where trainees strove to nurture that faculty. In the sangha hall setting, however, Mañjuśrī usually was not depicted in the conventional iconographical mode of a bejeweled bodhisattva holding a sword (symbolizing the wisdom that cuts through all obstructions) and seated on a lion but was portrayed instead in a monk's robes, seated in meditation. He was referred to as the Holy Monk (Sheng-seng) and was treated in every respect as the most senior monk in the hall. For example, monks and officers entering the hall on various occasions would bow first to the Holy Monk and then to the abbot. At mealtimes, a portion of the same food given the monks was placed on the Holy Monk's altar before the others were served. To the extent that he was portrayed and related to as an ordinary human being, Mañjuśrī represented an ideal of monkhood to which sangha hall trainees could aspire. At the same time, he was also an object of devotional worship before whom regular offerings of incense and prostrations were made, and he was clearly perceived as a tutelary deity who watched over the sangha hall, its occupants, and their spiritual endeavors.

The use of sangha halls for rituals other than meditation and meals is an aspect of Sung Ch'an monasticism that has been largely glossed over in modern scholarly accounts. Among the most important functions held in the sangha hall (judging from the fact that they were attended by the abbot and all of the monastic officers) were the recitation services *(nien-sung)* held six times a month. In Sung Ch'an the term *nien-sung* meant mindful recitation of the names of a Buddha or Buddhas. When performed in the sangha hall, a set verse comprising ten Buddhas' names was recited by the monks of the great assembly. This service was clearly a form of *nien-fo* practice, specifically *ch'eng-ming nien-fo,* or "focusing the mind on the Buddhas by calling their names." Prior to chanting the names, a verse was read explicitly stating the purposes, in the form of prayers, for which the recitation services were held. Three times a month the prayers were for the longevity and success of the imperial reign, the flourishing of Buddhism and the spread of the dharma, the protection of the monastery community by the tutelary deities, and the prosperity of lay patrons. On the three other occasions, prayers for the monastery and its donors were attached to a hortatory verse the gist of which was that monks should be mindful of impermanence and strive earnestly for salvation. At the end of a recitation service in the sangha hall, all of the registered monks made a circuit of the hall led by the abbot. This procession, which amounted to a circumambulation of the Holy Monk Mañjuśrī, seems to have been a merit-producing device. Similar recitation services were also held in the earth spirit hall at the opening and closing of retreats, in which case the preceding verses appealed (or gave thanks) for protection of the monastery during the retreat.

Another important ritual procedure held in the sangha hall, one that marked the formal registration of a monk in a monastery, was known as a "new arrival entering the hall." In this procedure, a newly arrived monk first entered the hall, offered incense, and made prostrations before the Holy Monk, after which he was assigned to a place on the platforms by the rector in accordance with his seniority. Even venerable elder monks who arrived at a monastery and took up residence in individual quarters had to go through this ritual in order to be regarded as full-fledged members of the community eligible to hold official positions and not simply as guests. Formal registration in the sangha hall was thus a step in the ceremony for installing a new abbot, at least in the case of eminent monks who arrived from outside to assume that position. It is clear that the sangha hall was not only a vital center of monastic life and training, but that it also had a certain symbolic value, representing the monastery proper, that is, the home base of all the ordained monks who were full members of the community.

Other ceremonies occasionally held in the sangha hall included rites marking the induction and retirement of monastic officers in the ranks of stewards and precepts, novice ordinations, sūtra chanting, prayer services sponsored by lay patrons (who would enter the hall to make cash donations and hear their prayers recited), and formal tea services. Apart from these ceremonies, however, drinking tea, sūtra reading or chanting (whether for study or devotional purposes), and writing were not allowed in the sangha hall, lest they interfere with the attitude of introspective concentration that monks were supposed to maintain there.

The institution of the sangha hall is often held up by modern scholars as the epitome of Ch'an monastic practice. The *Ch'an-men kuei-shih* implies that Pai-chang invented sangha hall training. The fact that it featured a communal form of discipline, whereas Indian Buddhist monks often had private cells where they meditated and slept, also suggests to some modern scholars that the Ch'an school was instrumental in establishing a Chinese style of group meditation practice.[103] The oldest extant set of detailed rules for monks in training on the meditation platforms in a sangha hall, however, was actually written by Tsun-shih (963–1032),[104] a T'ien-t'ai school monk who was abbot of a Teachings monastery—a fact that demonstrates that communal sangha hall training was by no means unique to Ch'an monasteries in the Sung.

Furthermore, an examination of the Vinaya literature that survives in Pāli and Chinese reveals that most of the features of the Sung sangha halls had precedents in the arrangement of facilities for meditation practice that were known in Indian and early Chinese Buddhism. Reference is found in the Vinaya, for example, to "long seats" as well as individual meditation seats, and many of the specific rules pertaining to meditation posture make it clear that the practice of meditation was often a group activity.[105] The procedure for sleeping on the platforms in the sangha hall that the *Ch'an-men kuei-shih* describes is very similar to the Vinaya rules for sleeping in a monks' quarters or a meditation hall. The *Shih-sung lü* (Ten-chapter Vinaya), for example, stipulates that a monk should place his robe beneath his head as a pillow and lie on his side on the platform.[106] The same text goes on to describe the handling of a "meditation staff" used to strike those sitting in meditation when they got drowsy; so it is clear that the monks slept and practiced meditation on the same platforms. The use of a staff for the purpose of stimulating meditators was common in Sung sangha halls. Other Vinaya texts such as the *Ssu-fen lü* (Four-part Vinaya) and the *Mo-ho-seng-ch'i lü* (Mahāsāṃghika Vinaya) also established rules for sleeping on one's right side in a meditation hall.[107] Moreover, these Vinaya texts state clearly that sleep is to be kept to a minimum so that the hours of meditation may be extended. The author of the *Ch'an-men kuei-shih* made the same comment, although he did not explain what the times for meditation were. In

Sung Ch'an monasteries there was a rule prescribing "four periods of seated meditation" every day. This rule was probably based on the Vinaya, which established similar periods of daily meditation.[108] The close connection between "Pai-chang's" rules for sangha hall training and the rules for meditation hall training found in the Vinaya comes as a surprise only because we have been so accustomed to thinking of the early Ch'an school as a radical sect that rejected mainstream Buddhist institutions and created its own new ones. The *Ch'an-men kuei-shih* speaks of Pai-chang as the architect of an independent Ch'an school, but it actually portrays him as a conservative who drew heavily on the Vinaya.

Just to the rear of the sangha hall were located quarters for the chief seat [34], a monastic officer who led the great assembly of monks in training in the hall, and the rear hall chief seat [35], a retired senior officer whose role was that of paternal advisor and assistant to the chief seat. Sometimes there were also separate quarters nearby for the Holy Monk's acolyte [36], an officer whose duty was to tend Mañjuśrī's altar. Somewhere in the vicinity of the sangha hall were quarters for the rector [37], an important officer who oversaw every aspect of the great assembly's training and discipline, including the registration of new arrivals, and acted as the leader of chanting during major ceremonies.

In order to maintain an atmosphere of sanctity and meditative concentration throughout the day and night, all sangha hall procedures were regulated by detailed rules of deportment and etiquette. Reading and writing were forbidden in the hall, as were all forms of relaxation or amusement. Generally, the place where the monks of the great assembly went to engage in such activities was the nearby common quarters [17]. The common quarters were arranged internally in much the same way as the sangha hall, with platforms on which monks were seated in order of seniority and an altar with an image of Kuan-yin, which was treated in the same manner as the Holy Monk in the sangha hall. The assignment of a place in the sangha hall to a new arrival was followed immediately by a similar assignment in the common quarters, in accordance with ritual procedures that were no less elaborate and solemn. If the sangha hall had no boxes at the rear of the platforms, new arrivals were to store all of their gear at their places in the common hall, and even if boxes were available in the sangha hall, they were to keep their personal tea cups and reading materials in the common quarters. The common quarters differed from the sangha hall in that the platforms were outfitted with desks, the ceiling had skylights to facilitate reading, and bookshelves (containing general sūtra literature as well as Ch'an records) were located between the platforms. In addition to serving as a study hall, the common quarters were equipped for serving tea. At least some of the tea services held there were highly ritualized affairs involving the monastic officers and the abbot as well as the monks of the great assembly. The location of a needle room [50] behind or sometimes in the common quarters shows that the facility was also used by the monks of the great assembly for personal tasks such as mending robes. Behind or in the rear of the building were rooms for the common quarters chief seat [38] and manager [39], the two officers in charge of the facility.

The Pei-shan ground plan shows a building called the monks' quarters [18] next to the common quarters. It is possible that this facility, not found at many other monasteries, was used by monks of the great assembly for relaxation and tending to personal affairs, thereby reserving the common quarters for more formal study and tea services. It is also conceivable that the monks' quarters were used by novices or other monks who were not registered as members of the great assembly. Such persons could have meditated and taken their meals on the narrow platforms in the outer section of the sangha hall, but they would not have had a place in the hall to sleep or store their personal belongings.

Another unusual facility that appears on the ground plan of Pei-shan is a building named after the famous statesman, literatus, and Buddhist lay practitioner Su Shih (1037–1101) [19]. My speculation, based on the location of this facility alongside the common quarters and monks' quarters, is that it was a place where laymen participating in the religious life of the sangha hall could keep their personal effects and sleep. It is also possible that Su Shih himself endowed the facility (however it was used) and gave it its name, for he did serve a stint as an official in Hangchow and, if we are to believe the Pei-shan ground plan, provided the calligraphy for the name plaque of a pavilion [51] that stood outside the monastery's main gate. The plaque read "Cold Spring Pavilion" (Leng-ch'üan t'ing), a phrase attributed to Po Chü-i (772–846), the illustrious poet who himself had served as governor of Hangchow. Whatever the historical circumstances that led to the naming of the building and the production of the pavilion plaque, it is clear that Pei-shan and other major monasteries of the Southern Sung were inclined to highlight their close associations with members of the political and cultural elite.

The common quarters were not the only facilities designed for scriptural study in Sung Ch'an monasteries. There were also sūtra-reading halls [13], equipped with desks and windows to let in light, located next to the quarters of the sūtra prefect [40], which included a library. A sacred image (not identified in the Sung Ch'an monastic codes) was enshrined in the hall, and offerings of incense and prostrations were made before it by the prefect or assistant officers at the start of a sūtra-reading session. The rules concerning behavior in and around the sūtra-reading hall—which stressed silence, proper deportment, and respectful handling of the texts—make it clear that one meaning of "sūtra reading" (k'an-ching) was quiet, individual scripture study. The term "sūtra reading," however, is also used in Sung monastic codes to refer to ceremonies in which the great assembly of monks chanted scriptures or flipped rapidly through the sūtra books in a process called "revolving reading" *(k'an-chuan)*, as a means of generating merit for dedication in support of prayers. Such ceremonies were sponsored by patrons, who would designate the aims to be prayed for and make a cash donation as part of the proceedings. The *Ch'an-yüan ch'ing-kuei* recommends staging sūtra-reading services in the dharma hall or the sūtra-reading hall and gives a detailed account of the elaborate ritual procedure. The ceremony began with the playing of cymbals, an offering of incense by the donor, the chanting of the Buddhas' names, and the recitation of a melodic Brahmanic hymn in praise of the Buddha, after which came the revolving reading and the formal donation to the monastery, itself a merit-producing act.

The revolving repositories [14] containing complete editions of the Buddhist canon were also dual-purpose facilities. On the one hand, they provided a relatively accessible storage place for the large number of scriptures that were not so frequently studied or chanted and thus were not shelved in the common quarters or sūtra prefect's collections. On the other hand, the design of the repository, which was actually a giant octagonal bookcase that could be rotated in place like a top, allowed for a "revolving reading" of the entire canon at one time, efficiently producing a great deal of merit for dedication in connection with various prayer and offering services.

In addition to the great assembly of monks in sangha hall training, the officers who led them, and any unregistered monks and laypersons who may have joined in their activities on a limited basis, there were several other classes of persons who resided on the west side of a monastery. The Pei-shan ground plan shows quarters for retired senior officers [20], retired junior officers [21], and miscellaneous persons [22], who may have been retired subordinate officers or nuns. Some other Sung monastery ground plans show nuns' quarters located in the same place as Pei-shan's "miscellaneous quarters." There were also overnight quarters [24] to provide lodging for monks who were passing through on pilgrimage and did not wish to register for training.

The remaining facilities on the west side of a monastery—including the washroom [52], toilet [53], urinal [54], laundry [55], and infirmary [56]—all served the needs of the great assembly of monks stationed in the sangha hall as well as those of the various retirees and visitors housed in the proximity. Hot water was provided for these facilities by several cauldrons [57] managed by hearth tenders [41]. Highly detailed ritual procedures for the toilet and urinal found in Sung Ch'an monastic codes,[109] based on Indian Vinaya texts,[110] are essentially the same as those found in the T'ien-t'ai rules written by Tsun-shih.[111] The so-called illuminated hall [58] was really just a passageway that linked the rear of the sangha hall with the washroom and various officers' quarters. It got its name from the windows or skylights that helped let light into the center of the sangha hall complex of buildings.

The facilities on the east side of a monastery were dedicated to administrative matters and to the housing and training of postulants. The life of a postulant combined elements of religious training and preparation for monkhood with manual labor under the supervision of monk administrators. As members of the laity, postulants wore lay clothing and let their hair grow. They took the same five precepts that were given to all Buddhist laypersons, with the exception that the precept concerning sexuality was interpreted, as for monks, to require total chastity. Facilities for the postulants on the east side mirrored those for the great assembly of monks on the west. The postulants' hall [25], sometimes called a "hall for selecting monks," functioned much like a sangha hall, with nearby common quarters [17 on east side of monastery], needle room [50 on east side], washroom [52 on east side], toilet [53 on east side], and so forth.

The central building on the east side was the priory [59], which contained the offices of the prior [42], controller [43], assistant controllers [44], and labor steward [45]. These officers were in charge of finances, supplies, and maintenance. Attached to the priory was the kitchen [60], which supplied meals for both the east and west communities, and quarters for priory postulants [46]. The latter assisted the priory officers, worked in the kitchen, and acted as waiters serving meals in the sangha hall. Near the priory was a bathhouse [61], which served the entire monastery, and the quarters of the bath prefect [47]. Also nearby were guest rooms [26] and the quarters of the guest prefect [48], who was charged with attending the many monk dignitaries, government officials, and wealthy lay patrons who would come to have audiences with the abbot, attend ceremonies, or sponsor special offerings and feasts. The east side also had quarters for eminent monks [27] and elderly monks [28]. The former were probably men of abbot rank who had held office in other monasteries but did not qualify as retired abbots of the monastery in which they were currently residing. The latter were probably elderly monks of lesser rank who likewise did not qualify for residency in the retired officers facilities on the west side.

The postulants' hall, common quarters, bathhouse, and priory hall had altars bearing images of their respective tutelary deities (the figure enshrined in the priory was Wei-t'o-t'ien), who were objects of regular offerings and prayers. The only major facilities on the east side dedicated exclusively to religious services, however, were the all beings hall [9], where esoteric rituals for feeding the hungry ghosts were held, and a pond [62], where fish were released in ritual expression of the Mahāyāna ideal of compassion.

Finally, located outside the compound and not shown on the ground plan, were facilities related to a monastery's commercial activities, such as mills [65], oil presses [66], stables [67], business cloisters [68], and offices for the management of estate lands [69]. The top administrators of these operations were fully ordained monks, who had postulants and lay servants under their command.

Modern scholars have seized on the fact that the account of Pai-chang's system of monastic practice in the *Ch'an-men kuei-shih* mentions communal labor *(p'u-ch'ing)* to paint an idealized picture of economic self-sufficiency in Ch'an monasteries during the "golden age" of the T'ang masters. A close examination of all the extant Sung and Yüan Ch'an monastic regulations shows that the term *p'u-ch'ing* (literally, "all invited") was in regular use, but that it covered a much wider range of activities than just manual labor. The term really indicated "mandatory attendance" for the abbot, officers, and monks of the great assembly at a number of functions, including feasts sponsored by lay patrons, funerals, the auctioning off of deceased monks' possessions, the appointment of new officers, the greeting of important guests, and the occasional cleaning of monastery buildings and grounds or other light work.[112] It is thus far from certain that the *Ch'an-men kuei-shih,* also a Sung text, was referring only to work when it mentioned *p'u-ch'ing* and highly unlikely that it was talking about mandatory attendance at heavy, daily manual labor of the sort necessary for agriculture. The *Ch'an-yüan ch'ing-kuei* uses the phrase "all invited to manual labor" *(p'u-ch'ing tso-wu)* in the context of outlining the duties of postulants, chiefly laboring in the kitchen and serving the monks their meals in the sangha hall.[113] There is no doubt that all of the heavy manual work done in and around Ch'an monasteries in the Sung was performed by lay postulants and laborers, overseen by monk officers.

It is true that by the Sung, partisans of the Ch'an school were stressing communal manual labor as a characteristic of Ch'an monasticism. The idea that Pai-chang, as the author of the maxim "A day without working [should be] a day without eating," was the founder of the practice of manual labor by Buddhist monks appears frequently in Sung Ch'an literature. The maxim, however, cannot be found in any source earlier than Pai-chang's hagiography in the *Tsu-t'ang chi,* compiled in 952.[114] One reason that Ch'an followers in the Sung stressed the historical importance of manual labor in their tradition was probably to define the Ch'an school as a distinctive entity and to credit it with originating what was actually an old and widespread practice in Chinese Buddhism. The Ch'an claim met with resistance from the T'ien-t'ai school, which countered that the practice of *p'u-ch'ing* began with the Buddha, as reported in the Vinaya.[115] In fact, communal manual labor appears in T'ien-t'ai monastic rules dating from the Sung and so could not have been unique to the Ch'an school at that time.[116] Moreover, there is historical evidence that suggests that farming and trade by Buddhist monks was already widespread enough in early-fifth-century China to become an object of anti-Buddhist criticism.[117] Communal labor was practiced in the seventh century at the Kuo-ch'ing Monastery on Mount T'ien-t'ai,[118] and it was noted by the Japanese pilgrim monk Ennin (792–862) in the mid-ninth century at a monastery that had no affiliation with the Ch'an school.[119] It seems clear that manual labor by monks had a long history in China and that it predated the formulation of the Pai-chang myth.

Another reason that Ch'an followers in the Sung stressed the importance of manual labor in their tradition was to deflect criticism from Confucians claiming that the Buddhist clergy was a nonproductive drain on the economic resources of the country. A good example of such criticism may be found in the *Hu-fa lun* (Discourse in defense of the dharma), written in the early twelfth century by Chang Shang-ying (1043–1121), a high government official and Buddhist layman. Chang defended the Buddhist order by stressing that monks and nuns supported themselves through agricultural production and pointed to Pai-chang and other T'ang Ch'an masters as proof that communal labor had been an important part of Buddhist monasticism since ancient times.[120] Such arguments notwithstanding, Ch'an monasteries in the Sung enjoyed imperial and aristocratic patronage and also derived income from estate lands worked by tenant farmers and commercial activities. The fully ordained monks in all public monasteries in the Sung did occasionally engage in light work such as gardening, wood cutting, building maintenance, and cleaning.[121] The practice of manual labor by monks in Sung Ch'an monasteries can be seen as a symbolic gesture, which honored the ideal embodied in Pai-chang's maxim and helped to deflect the charge of economic parasitism, even if it did not have much economic significance.

CONCLUSION

The comparative study of the organization and operation of major Buddhist monasteries in the Sung reveals that officially designated "Ch'an" establishments were distinguishable from other public monasteries chiefly by their incorporation of the mythology of the Ch'an lineage. That mythology, which was propagated in the Ch'an flame history literature and the esoteric ritual of dharma transmission, first impinged on the structure of the Buddhist institution in China during the Five Dynasties and early Sung, when rulers began to reserve the abbacies of public monasteries for monks who had dharma transmission in the Ch'an lineage. The Ch'an mythology was also reenacted and validated in rituals in which abbots played a central role, such as "ascending the [dharma] hall," "entering the [abbot's] room," and memorial services. The basic structures of those rituals were common to the Buddhist monastic tradition (all were performed in Teachings as well as Ch'an monasteries), but Ch'an abbots brought to them the special rhetorical style of the flame histories and discourse records. Other facilities and religious practices traditionally deemed characteristic or definitive of Ch'an monasticism, including communal manual labor and the routine of meditation, religious services, meals, and sleep in a sangha hall, were actually the common heritage of the Buddhist monastic tradition at large.

The suggestion that the T'ang Ch'an master Pai-chang invented the modes of training that took place in the sangha halls, dharma halls, and abbots' quarters of Ch'an and other public monasteries in the Sung is first found in a Sung text, the *Ch'an-men kuei-shih,* and is not corroborated by any evidence surviving from the T'ang. The Pai-chang myth served the interests of the Sung Ch'an school in a number of ways. It obscured the fact that many important public monasteries had been in existence long before they were arbitrarily designated as "Ch'an" establishments by the Sung court, and it provided a quasi-historical justification for the Ch'an school's domination of the Buddhist monastic institution. Since it was in actuality the propagation of a particular ideology and mythology rather than an adherence to distinctive forms of monastic discipline that gave the Ch'an school its identity, there was an element of self-contradiction in the very concept of a "Ch'an [lineage] monastery." The Pai-chang myth would have helped to mitigate that contradiction by asserting that members of the Ch'an lineage had long been concerned with monastic discipline and that certain universal features of Chinese Buddhist monasticism had in fact been "Ch'an" features from the beginning. It is no accident that the *Ch'an-men kuei-shih* account of Pai-chang's monastery focused on the selection of the abbot and on rituals in which the abbot played a central role, for these were precisely the points where the mythology of Ch'an had exerted the most influence on the organization and operation of the public monasteries that were named as "Ch'an" facilities.

To conclude that the success of the Ch'an school in the Sung was essentially the success of a newly articulated ideology and mythology and that it manifested itself only secondarily in institutional and ritual forms is to refute completely the accepted modern theories about the stages of development that the Ch'an school is supposed to have gone through. In particular, this conclusion disproves the claim that Sung Ch'an lacked intellectual creativity and spiritual vitality and exposes the notion that Sung Ch'an monasticism suffered from a process of degeneration as a historically groundless normative judgment that is based on a naive reading of the Sung mythology itself.

Modern theories of degeneration in Sung Chinese Buddhism as a whole have also gained credence from a reading of the Sung Ch'an flame histories that ignores the institutional context in which those texts were redacted and used. Kenneth Ch'en, for example, spoke for many historians in the field a generation ago when he blamed Ch'an-style practice for the purported intellectual decline of Buddhism on the grounds that "Chinese Ch'an was iconoclastic; it had no reverence for literature, images, or rituals; it discouraged the study of the texts and the exercises of the intellect."[122] This theory not only takes it for granted that the Ch'an monasteries that flourished in the Sung evolved directly from an independent Ch'an institution that is supposed to have existed in the T'ang, but it further assumes that Sung Ch'an monasteries retained the iconoclasm and simplicity that purportedly characterized Pai-chang's original system of training. This chapter has shown, however, that there is no validity whatsoever to the notion that Sung Ch'an monastic practice dispensed with literature, images, or rituals. The study of literature—including traditional sūtras, commentaries, and Vinaya texts, as well as the records of Ch'an patriarchs—was an important part of the training of lay postulants and ordained monks, and major facilities were maintained for that purpose. All Ch'an monasteries had at least one central Buddha hall and sometimes two. Images of bodhisattvas, arhats, and Ch'an patriarchs were also enshrined in their own worship halls, where they were the focal point of offering services on a daily, monthly, and annual basis. Indeed, these and many other ritual performances—including memorial services for ancestors, prayers for the emperor and patrons, and rites for the mollification of baneful spirits—filled the monastic calendar. Images of bodhisattvas and tutelary deities of Indian and Chinese origin were found in virtually every building used by the monks in their daily lives, including the sangha hall, kitchen, toilet, and bath. The idea that Buddhist practice could be carried on in the midst of everyday life was thus tied not to the abandonment of religious forms but to the sanctification of all activities—even basic bodily functions such as eating, sleeping, and washing—by turning them into precisely regulated religious rituals. The apparently radical, iconoclastic approach to spiritual training depicted in the Ch'an flame histories and discourse records was not taken literally; it was a rhetorical stance that was integrated into the fundamentally conservative Buddhist monastic institution in the Sung by being enacted in certain carefully circumscribed ritual settings.

A question that remains is why the ideology and mythology of Ch'an were so successful in gaining a following during the Sung not only among the Buddhist clergy but among the lay gentry and in governmental circles as well. I have suggested that the popularity of the Ch'an flame histories and discourse records may be attributed to a number of stylistic and substantive features that held greater appeal for educated Chinese than other, more conventional genres of Buddhist literature. Those features include the presentation of religious truths in the form of genealogical tables and historical documents, the depiction for the first time of Buddhas who were Chinese and spoke in the vernacular, and the witty, entertaining nature of the "sūtras" (recorded sayings) attributed to those native Buddhas.

Apart from the attractive literary qualities of the Ch'an flame histories and discourse records, the ideology they contained may also have been politically useful for both the Buddhist clergy and the court. Despite its polemical dimensions, the rubric "Ch'an lineage" as it came to be used in the Sung had social ramifications that were actually more unifying and conciliatory than divisive or exclusivistic. Precisely because the lineage was defined in terms of the transmission of something as utterly signless and ineffable as the Buddha-mind, not the transmission of any particular set of doctrines or religious practices, the Ch'an school was able to draw into its ranks monks and laypersons who in fact took a variety of approaches to Buddhist thought and practice. This diversity and the depiction of the Ch'an lineage as a vast extended clan that contained within itself all that was noble and successful in the Buddhist tradition provided an ideological framework in the Sung for an attempted consolidation of the Buddhist order that paralleled the political unification of the empire. That consolidation was not entirely successful, for it met with opposition from monks who promoted the T'ien-t'ai tradition, but it is easy to see why it would have appealed to and been encouraged by the court, which was ever looking for ways to control the Buddhist order.

Appendix 5.1

FACILITIES AT MAJOR BUDDHIST MONASTERIES IN THE
SOUTHERN SUNG

Facilities Used Primarily for Worship and Offerings

1. main gate *(cheng-men* 正門*)*
     a.k.a. mountain gate *(shan-men* 山門*)*
     a.k.a. triple gate *(san-men* 三門*)*
2. Buddha hall *(fo-tien* 佛殿*)*
3. Vairocana hall *(lu-she-na-tien* 盧舍那殿*)*
4. earth spirit hall *(t'u-ti-t'ang* 土地堂*)*
5. patriarchs hall *(tsu-shih-t'ang* 祖師堂*)*
     a.k.a. portrait hall *(chen-t'ang* 真堂*)*
6. donors hall *(t'an-na-t'ang* 檀那堂*)*
7. Kuan-yin pavilion *(kuan-yin-ko* 觀音閣*)*
8. arhats hall *(lo-han-t'ang* 羅漢堂*)*
9. all beings hall *(shui-lu-t'ang* 水陸堂*)*

Facilities Used Primarily for Instruction, Study, and Ceremonies

10. dharma hall *(fa-t'ang* 法堂*)*
11. abbot's reception hall *(ch'ien fang-chang* 前方丈*)*
12. abbot's meditation room *(tso-ch'an-shih* 坐禪室*)*
13. sūtra hall *(ching-t'ang* 經堂*)*
      a.k.a. sūtra-reading hall *(k'an-ching-t'ang* 看經堂*)*
14. revolving repository *(lun-tsang* 輪藏*)*
      a.k.a. sūtra repository *(tsang-tien* 藏殿*)*

Living/Training Quarters

15. abbot's quarters *(fang-chang* 方丈*)*
16. sangha hall *(seng-t'ang* 僧堂*)*
17. common quarters *(chung-liao* 衆寮*)*
      doorway plaque reads "Sandalwood Grove" *(Chan-t'an lin* 旃檀林*)*
18. monks' quarters *(seng-liao* 僧寮*)*
19. Eastern Bank [lay practitioners' quarters?] *(tung-p'o* 東坡*)*
20. retired senior officers' hall *(meng-t'ang* 蒙堂*)*
21. retired junior officers' quarters *(ch'ien-tzu-liao* 前資寮*)*
22. miscellaneous quarters *(tsa-liao* 雜寮*)*
23. nuns' quarters *(ni-liao* 尼寮*)*
24. overnight quarters *(tan-kuo* 旦過*)*
      a.k.a. transients' hall *(yün-shui-t'ang* 雲水堂*)*
25. postulants' hall *(hang-t'ang* 行堂*, hang-che-t'ang* 行者堂*)*
      doorway plaque reads "Monk-Selecting Hall" *(hsüan-seng-t'ang* 選僧堂*)*
26. guest rooms *(k'e-wei* 客位*)*
27. eminent monks' quarters *(lao-su* 老宿*, tsun-chang-liao* 尊長寮*)*
28. elderly monks *(ch'i-chiu* 耆舊*)*

Administrative Offices and Workers' Quarters

29. hall prefect *(chih-tien* 知殿 *)*
30. offerings postulants *(kung-t'ou hang-che* 供頭行者 *)*
31. acolytes *(shih-che* 侍者 *)*
32. [abbot's quarters] postulants *(hang-che* 行者 *)*
33. laborers *(jen-li* 人力 *)*
34. chief seat *(shou-tso* 首座 *)*
35. rear hall chief seat *(hou-t'ang shou-tso* 後堂首座 *)*
36. Holy Monk's acolyte *(Sheng-seng shih-che* 聖僧侍者 *)*
37. rector *(wei-na* 維那 *)*
38. common quarters chief seat *(liao shou-tso* 寮首座 *)*
    a.k.a. quarters chief *(liao-yüan* 寮元 *)*
39. common quarters manager *(liao-chu* 寮主 *)*
40. sūtra prefect *(tsang-chu* 藏主 *)*
    position divided into east collection [prefect] *(tung-tsang* 東藏 *)*
    and west collection [prefect] *(hsi-tsang* 西藏 *)*
41. hearth tender *(huo-t'ou* 火頭 *)*
42. prior *(tu-ssu* 都寺 *)*
43. controller *(chien-ssu* 監司, 監寺 *)*
44. assistant controllers *(fu-ssu* 副司 *)*
45. labor steward *(chih-sui* 直歲 *)*
46. priory underlings *(hsia k'u-ssu* 下庫司 *)*
    a.k.a. priory postulants' quarters *(k'u-hsia hang-che-liao* 庫下行者寮 *)*
47. bath prefect *(yü-chu* 浴主 *)*
48. guest prefect *(chih-k'e* 知客 *)*

Other Facilities with Practical and Ritual Functions

49. outer gate *(wai-shan-men* 外山門 *)*
50. needle room *(pa-chen-ch'u* 把針處 *)*
51. pavilion *(t'ing* 亭 *)*
52. washroom *(hsi-mien-ch'u* 洗面處, *hou-chia* 後架 *)*
53. toilet *(tung-ssu* 東司 *)*
54. urinal *(hsiao-ch'ien-so* 小遺所, *niao-liao* 尿寮 *)*
55. laundry *(hsi-i-ch'u* 洗衣處 *)*
56. infirmary *(yen-shou-t'ang* 延壽堂 *)*
    doorway plaque reads "Rest Hall" *(sheng-hsing-t'ang* 省行堂 *)*
57. cauldrons *(fu* 釜 *)*
58. illuminated hall *(chao-t'ang* 照堂 *)*
59. priory *(k'u-t'ang* 庫堂 *)*
60. kitchen *(hsiang-chi-ch'u* 香積廚 *)*
61. bathhouse *(yü-shih* 浴室 *)*
    doorway plaques read "All Cleansing" *(hsüan-ming* 宣明 *)*
62. pond *(ch'ih* 池 *)*
63. bell tower *(chung-lou* 鐘樓 *)*
64. stūpas *(t'a* 塔, *t'a-t'ou* 塔頭 *)*

Facilities for Commercial Activities

65. mill cloister *(mo-yüan* 磨院 *)*
66. oil press *(yu-fang* 油房 *)*
67. stable *(hou-ts'ao* 後槽 *)*
68. business cloister *(hsieh-yüan* 廨院 *)*
69. estate offices *(chuang-she* 莊舍 *)*

198 · T. Griffith Foulk

NOTES

1. See, for example, Yanagida Seizan, "Baso zen no sho mondai," *Indogaku bukkyōgaku kenkyū* 17.1 (1969): 33–39; idem, "The 'Recorded Sayings' Texts of Chinese Ch'an Buddhism," in Whalen Lai and Lewis Lancaster, eds., *Early Ch'an in China and Tibet* (Berkeley: Berkeley Buddhist Studies Series, 1983), pp. 186–192; Okimoto Katsumi, "Shingi kenkyū nōto," in Sasaki Kyōgo, ed., *Kairitsu shisō no kenkyū* (Kyoto: Heirakuji shoten, 1981), pp. 407–408.

2. Such theories are explained and criticized in Robert E. Buswell, Jr., "The 'Short-cut' Approach of *K'an-hua* Meditation: The Evolution of a Practical Subitism in Chinese Ch'an Buddhism," in Peter N. Gregory, ed., *Sudden and Gradual: Approaches to Enlightenment in Chinese Thought* (Honolulu: University of Hawaii Press, 1987), p. 322, n. 8.

3. Kagamishima Genryū, "Dōgen zenji to *Hyakujō shingi*," *Dōgen zenji to sono in'yō kyōten, goroku no kenkyū* (Tokyo: Kijisha, 1965), pp. 181–192; idem, "Hyakujō ko shingi henka katei no ichi kōsatsu," *Komazawa daigaku bukkyō gakubu kenkyū kiyō* 25 (1967): 1–13; idem, "Kaisetsu," Kagamishima Genryū, Satō Tatsugen, and Kosaka Kiyū, eds. and trans., *Yakuchū zennen shingi* (Tokyo: Sōtōshū shūmuchō, 1972), pp. 1–25; idem, "*Hyakujō shingi* no seiritsu to sono igi," *Aichi gakuin daigaku zen kenkyūjo kiyō* 6/7 (1967): 117–134; Kondō Ryōichi, "*Hyakujō shingi* to *Zennen shingi*," *Indogaku bukkyōgaku kenkyū* 17.2 (1969): 773–775; idem, "*Hyakujō shingi* no seiritsu to sono genkei," *Hokkaidō Komazawa daigaku kenkyū kiyō* 3 (1968): 31–39; Harada Kōdō, "*Hyakujō shingi* to *Zennen shingi*," *Sōtōshū kenkyūin kenkyūsei kenkyū kiyō* 1 (1969): 5–14; Kosaka Kiyū, "Shingi hensen no teiryū,"*Shūgaku kenkyū* 5 (1963): 126–128.

4. The *Lü-yüan shih-kuei* (HTC, vol. 106), compiled in 1325, and the *Tseng-hsiu chiao-yüan ch'ing-kuei* (HTC, vol. 101), compiled in 1347, are very similar in content to Sung and Yüan Ch'an monastic codes, especially the *Ch'ih-hsiu Pai-chang ch'ing-kuei* (T no. 2025), completed in 1343. No full-blown codes for Vinaya or Teachings monasteries survive from the Sung, but extant rules, ground plans, monastery gazetteers, and the reports of Japanese pilgrim monks leave no doubt that similar rules were already being implemented in the Sung.

5. See, for example, Tsukamoto Zenryū, "Sō jidai no zunnan shikin tokudo no seido," *Shina bukkyō shigaku* 5.1 (1941), reprinted in *Tsukamoto Zenryū chosakushū,* vol. 5 (Tokyo: Daitō, 1975), p. 52; Takao Giken, *Sōdai bukkyōshi no kenkyū* (Kyoto: Hyakkaen, 1975), p. 8; Sekiguchi Shindai, *Daruma daishi no kenkyū* (Tokyo: Shunjūsha, 1969), p. 431.

6. In a chapter entitled "Decline," Kenneth K. S. Ch'en's *Buddhism in China: A Historical Survey* (Princeton: Princeton University Press, 1964), for example, devotes a mere eighty-two pages to the entire millennium from the advent of the Northern Sung (960–1127) down to modern times.

7. Erik Zürcher, "Buddhism in China," in Mircea Eliade et al., eds., *The Encyclopedia of Religion* (New York: Macmillan, 1987), vol. 2, p. 420.

8. Ch'en, *Buddhism in China,* p. 389.

9. Zürcher, "Buddhism in China," p. 420; see also Michihata Ryōshū, *Chūgoku bukkyōshi* (Kyoto: Hōzōkan, 1957), p. 167.

10. *T* no. 2076. For a useful if somewhat dated survey of this scholarship in English, see Philip B. Yampolsky, *The Platform Sutra of the Sixth Patriarch* (New York: Columbia University Press, 1967), pp. 1–57. A thorough study of the topic may be found in Yanagida Seizan, *Shoki zenshū shisho no kenkyū* (Kyoto: Hōzōkan, 1967).

11. The terms "Ch'an monastery" *(ch'an-ssu)* and "Ch'an cloister" *(ch'an-yüan)*, understood as places where masters in the Ch'an lineage *(ch'an-tsung)* held forth or followers of the Ch'an lineage congregated, do not appear in any sources dating indisputably from the T'ang. There were monasteries in the T'ang with names that included the term *ch'an*, such as the Hsiu-ch'an Monastery and the Fo-lung Chih-che Ch'an Cloister on Mount T'ien-t'ai. In these cases, however, *ch'an* clearly indicated the practice of dhyāna and not any sort of lineage grouping or doctrinal affiliation.

12. See T. Griffith Foulk, "The 'Ch'an School' and Its Place in the Buddhist Monastic Tradition" (Ph.D. dissertation, University of Michigan, 1987), pp. 366–379.

13. For a survey in English, see Kōgen Mizuno, *Buddhist Sutras: Origin, Development, Transmission* (Tokyo: Kōsei, 1982), pp. 171–179.

14. Such as the *Tsung-ching lu* (*T* no. 2016), completed in 961 by Yung-ming Yen-shou, and the *Jen-t'ien yen-mu* (*T* no. 2006), preface dated 1188, by Hui-yen Chih-chao.

15. Such as the *Ta Sung seng-shih lüeh* (*T* no. 2126), completed in 991 by Tsan-ning; the *Lung-hsing fo-chiao pien-nien t'ung-lun* (*HTC*, vol. 130), completed in 1164 by Tsu-hsiu; and the *Fo-tsu t'ung-chi* (*T* no. 2035) completed in 1269 by Chih-p'an. For a survey in English, see Jan Yün-hua, "Buddhist Historiography in Sung China," *Deutschen Morgenländischen Gesellschaft* 114.2 (1964): 360–381.

16. Individually these phrases are found in works dating from the T'ang, but the oldest text in which they appear together is the *Tsu-t'ing shih-yüan* compiled by Mu-an in 1108 (*HTC* 113.66c). For the textual history of each of the four phrases, see Yanagida, *Shoki zenshū shisho no kenkyū*, pp. 470 ff.

17. Some Ch'an followers took the slogan literally and some favored a figurative interpretation. Mu-an, after quoting the four-part phrase in his *Tsu-t'ing shih-yüan*, makes the following remark: "Many people mistake the meaning of 'not depending on scriptures.' They speak frequently of abandoning scriptures and regard silent sitting as Ch'an. These are truly the dumb sheep of our school" (*HTC* 113.66c). Mu-an's point seems to be that it is foolish and self-contradictory to take the words literally and base an ostensibly wordless practice on them.

18. This anecdote is mentioned in the *Jen-t'ien yen-mu* (*T* 48.325b), which attributes it to an ostensibly Indian (but no doubt apochryphal) text entitled *Ta-fan t'ien-wang wen-fo chüeh-i ching* (*HTC* 87.303c, 326c). The anecdote is also found in case 6 of the *Wu-men-kuan*, a *kung-an* collection published in 1229 (*T* 48.293b). For a list of many later texts in which the anecdote appears, see Inoue Shūten, *Mumonkan no shin kenkyū*, vol. 1 (Tokyo: Hōbunkan, 1922), pp. 301–303.

19. *T* no. 2067. Some other noteworthy works belonging to the flame history genre are the *T'ien-sheng kuang-teng lu* (*HTC*, vol. 135), compiled in 1036

by Li Tsun-hsü; the *Ch'uan-fa cheng-tsung chi* (*T* no. 2078), compiled in 1061 by Ch'i-sung; the *Chien-chung ching-kuo hsü teng lu* (*HTC*, vol. 136), compiled in 1101 by Wei-po; the *Lien-teng hui-yao* (*HTC*, vol. 136), compiled in 1183 by Hui-weng Wu-ming; the *Chia-t'ai p'u-teng lu* (*HTC*, vol. 137), compiled in 1204 by Cheng-shou; and the *Wu-teng hui-yüan* (*HTC*, vol. 138), compiled in 1253 by P'u-chi.

20. The term *ch'uan-teng* is usually translated as "transmission of the lamp." *Teng* does have the meaning of "lamp" or "lantern" in Chinese, but in the Ch'an metaphor it clearly means a "flame" (the flame of awakening) that is kept alive by being passed down from teacher to disciple, just as the flame of one lamp is used to light another. For an example of the use of *teng* to mean the flame of a lamp (as opposed to the body of the lamp itself) in an early Ch'an text, see Yampolsky, *The Platform Sūtra*, §15 (p. 6 of Chinese text). Here the fundamental sameness of meditation *(ting)* and wisdom *(hui)* is compared to that of a flame *(teng)* and its light *(kuang)*. The text reads, in part, "where there is a flame, there is light." If (following Yampolsky) one reads "lamp" for "flame" here, the statement becomes patently false, and the entire metaphor loses its force, since a lamp may exist (unlit) without there being any light.

21. In the earlier Sung histories, references to specific branches of the Ch'an lineage appear much more often than references to a Ch'an lineage *(ch'an-tsung)* itself. The *Tsu-t'ang chi,* compiled in 952 a few years before the advent of the Sung, does not employ an umbrella term such as "Ch'an lineage" to refer to the lineages that were later grouped together under that rubric. The *Ching-te ch'uan-teng lu* uses the expression "Ch'an lineage" occasionally; see, for example, the occurrence in the *Ch'an-men kuei-shih,* *T* 51.250d. For an example of the expression "Buddha Mind lineage" *(fo-hsin-tsung)* in the *Ching-te ch'uan-teng lu,* see *T* 51.220a. The term "Ch'an lineage" came to be used much more frequently in sources dating from the Southern Sung and Yüan dynasties.

22. Yanagida Seizan, ed., *Sodōshū, Zengaku sōsho,* no. 4 (Kyoto: Chūbun shuppansha, 1984).

23. For a photocopy reproduction of the extant portions of the *Pao-lin chuan* (consisting of fascicles 1–5 and 8, discovered in China in 1933, and fascicle 6, discovered in Kyoto in 1932), see Yanagida Seizan, ed., *Sōzō ichin hōrinden, Dentō gyokuei shū, Zengaku sōsho,* no. 5 (Kyoto: Chūban shuppansha, 1983). For a summary of the contents, see Yampolsky, *The Platform Sutra,* pp. 47–52.

24. *T* no. 2838; P 2634; P 3858; P 3559. For a critical edition and annotated Japanese translation, see Yanagida Seizan, ed., *Shoki no zenshi,* vol. 1, *Zen no goroku,* vol. 2 (Tokyo: Chikuma shobō, 1971); for an English translation, see John R. McRae, *The Northern School and the Formation of Early Ch'an Buddhism* (Honolulu: University of Hawaii Press, 1986), pp. 255–269.

25. *T* no. 2837; P 3294; P 3436; P 3537; P 3703; P 4564; S 2054; S 4272. For a critical edition and annotated Japanese translation, see Yanagida, ed., *Shoki no zenshi,* vol 1. An English translation, entitled "Records of the Teachers and Students of the Lanka," may be found in J. C. Cleary, trans., *Zen Dawn* (Boston: Shambala, 1986).

26. The epitaphs of Sung Ch'an masters often contain elements reminiscent

of the myth of Śākyamuni's career, such as the miraculous impregnation of the mother in a dream, the discovery and division of marvelous relics after cremation, and so on.

27. The *T'ien-sheng kuang-teng lu* was presented to Emperor Jen-tsung in the seventh year of the T'ien-sheng era (1029), and the *Chien-chung ching-kuo hsü-teng lu* was presented to Emperor Hui-tsung during the Chien-chung Ching-kuo era (1101). These two flame histories were both honored with prefaces written by the reigning emperor and included in the canon by imperial order. The *Chia-t'ai p'u-teng lu,* similarly, derived its name from the fact that it was presented to Emperor Ning-tsung in the fourth year of the Chia-t'ai era (1204). It too was probably published with imperial sponsorship and included in the canon.

28. The list of twenty-four patriarchs found in Kuan-ting's introduction to the *Mo-ho chih-kuan* (*T* 46.1a–b) was based on a list of twenty-three given in the *Fu-fa-tsang chuan* (*T* no. 2058).

29. Takao Giken, *Sōdai bukkyōshi no kenkyū* (Kyoto: Hyakkaen, 1975), pp. 87–92.

30. The *Ching-te ch'uan-teng lu,* for example, calls dharma transmission "no transmission" (*T* 51.206b).

31. Kenneth K. S. Ch'en, *The Chinese Transformation of Buddhism* (Princeton: Princeton University Press, 1973), p. 11.

32. Ch'en, *Buddhism in China,* pp. 362–363.

33. This position was first taken by Ui Hakuju in his *Zenshū shi kenkyū,* vol. 1 (Tokyo: Iwanami shoten, 1935), pp. 81–90.

34. The *Ch'an-men kuei-shih* can be found in *T* 51.251c–252b. Pai-chang's role as the founder of a system of Ch'an monastic training is not mentioned in the *Ching-te ch'uan-teng lu* biography itself (*T* 51.249b–250c); nor is that role mentioned in the earlier biography of Pai-chang found in the *Tsu-t'ang chi* (see Yanagida, ed., *Sodōshū,* pp. 271a–276a). For an account of the various recensions, quotations, and pericopes of the *Ch'an-men kuei-shih,* see Foulk, "The 'Ch'an School,' " pp. 328–345.

35. Ui, *Zenshū shi kenkyū,* vol. 1, pp. 81–90.

36. Nakamura Hajime, "Zen ni okeru seisan to kinrō no mondai," *Zen bunka* 2 (1955): 32; Kondō Ryōichi, "Tōdai zenshū no keizai kiban," in Nihon bukkyō gakkai, ed., *Bukkyō to seiji, keizai* (Kyoto: Heirakuji, 1972), pp. 137–151.

37. Kagamishima Genryū, "Nansō sōrin no ichi kōsatsu," *Komazawa daigaku bukkyōgakubu kenkyū kiyō* 19 (1961): 57–59; Kondō, "*Hyakujō shingi no seiritsu to sono genkei,*" p. 41; Martin Collcutt, *Five Mountains: The Rinzai Zen Monastic Institution in Medieval Japan* (Cambridge: Harvard University Press, 1981), p. 194.

38. D. T. Suzuki, *The Training of the Zen Buddhist Monk* (1934; rpt. Berkeley: Wingbow Press, 1974), p. 34.

39. See, for example, Collcutt, *Five Mountains,* p. 134.

40. Yanagida Seizan, "Chūgoku zenshū shi," in Nishitani Keiji, ed., *Kōza zen,* vol. 3, *Zen no rekishi: Chūgoku* (Tokyo: Chikuma shobō, 1974), p. 66; Ch'en, *Buddhism in China,* p. 363.

41. Yamazaki Zen'yū, "Chūgoku zenshūshi no kenkyū: fushin samu to zun-

202 · T. Griffith Foulk

nan ni tsuite," *Sōtōshū kenkyūin kenkyūsei kenkyū kiyō* 9 (1977): 64; Heinrich Dumoulin, *Zen Buddhism: A History,* vol. 1: *India and China* (New York: Macmillan, 1988), p. 211; Ch'en, *Buddhism in China,* p. 363.

42. Suzuki Tetsuo, *Tō godai no zenshū* (Tokyo: Daitō shuppansha, 1984), p. 143.

43. Ōkubo Dōshū, ed., *Dōgen zenji zenshū,* vol. 1 (Tokyo: Chikuma shobō, 1969), pp. 337–347. My account of inheritance certificates is based largely on this source and on Dōgen's *Hōkyōki;* see Takashi James Kodera, *Dogen's Formative Years in China* (Boulder: Prajñā Press, 1980), pp. 42–46.

44. A photograph of Dōgen's inheritance certificate, now kept at Eiheiji, appears in Ōkubo, ed., *Dōgen zenji zenshū,* vol. 1, frontispiece, and vol. 2, p. 287; an illustration of the same document appears in Kodera, *Dogen's Formative Years in China,* p. 70.

45. Ōkubo, ed., *Dōgen zenji zenshū* 1.341. For an English translation, see Kōsen Nishiyama and John Stevens, trans., *Shōbōgenzō,* vol. 2 (Tokyo: Nakayama shobō, 1977), p. 181.

46. Ibid.

47. *Lin-chien lu, HTC* 148.295d.

48. Tsukamoto Zenryū, "Sō jidai no zunnan shikin tokudo no seido," pp. 54–64.

49. *T* no. 1484.

50. See Foulk, "The 'Ch'an School,' " pp. 78–87.

51. The size and composition of this following was considered a measure of a Ch'an master's success in the Sung. The epitaphs of Ch'an masters usually told how many people they gave bodhisattva precepts to, how many novices they ordained, how many personal disciples they had, and how many dharma heirs they recognized.

52. Dōgen reports on the use of this term in China in the chapter of his *Shōbōgenzō* entitled "Butsudō" (Ōkubo, ed., *Dōgen zenji zenshū* 1.376). For another example, see *Pi-yen-lu,* case 2 (*T* 48.141c).

53. For example, see *Shih-shih yao-lan,* s.v. *ch'an-seng hsing-chieh, T* 54.302a.

54. Dōgen reports on the use of this term in China in *Shōbōgenzō,* "Butsudō" (Ōkubo, ed., *Dōgen zenji zenshū* 1.376).

55. This status was symbolized in a number of ways, including the production and distribution of funerary portraits of eminent masters while they were still alive and the masters' practice of retiring to memorial cloisters in which their own stūpas were already enshrined.

56. Takao Giken, *Sōdai bukkyōshi no kenkyū,* p. 57–58.

57. Ibid., pp. 58–60.

58. For general background on the history of this period, see Edward H. Schafer, *The Empire of Min* (Tokyo: Charles E. Tuttle, 1954).

59. See Tokiwa Daijō, *Shina bukkyō no kenkyū,* vol. 2 (1943; rpt. Tokyo: Meicho fukyūkai, 1979), pp. 453–470; Michihata, *Chūgoku bukkyō shi,* pp. 163–166; Foulk, "The 'Ch'an School,' " pp. 149–152.

60. Statistics supporting this conclusion are found in the *Pao-ch'ing ssu-ming chih,* edited in 1227; cited in Takao, *Sōdai bukkyōshi no kenkyū,* pp. 66–67.

61. All of the information on Mount T'ien-t'ung given in this paragraph is

based on sources cited in Mochizuki Shinkō, ed., *Bukkyō daijiten* (Tokyo: Bukkyō daijiten hakkōjo, 1931–1936), s.v. *tendōji* (4.3812c).

62. Mochizuki, ed., *Bukkyō daijiten*, s.v. *aikuōji* (1.6a–b).

63. Takao, *Sōdai bukkyōshi no kenkyū*, pp. 61–62.

64. *T* 51.251c.

65. Evidence for the preponderance of the "Ch'an" designation in the Southern Sung is found, for example, in the *Pao-ch'ing ssu-ming chih* (cited in Takao, *Sōdai bukkyōshi no kenkyū*, p. 67) and in the *Gozan jissatsu zu*, a collection of drawings and diagrams preserved in Japan that represent the ground plans, furnishings, and other physical features of major Chinese monasteries in the early thirteenth century (*Zengaku daijiten* [Tokyo: Taishūkan, 1978], 3.10–32).

66. *Zengaku daijiten* 3.31–32; see 3.18 for a drawing of a monastery name plaque *(o)*.

67. *Hōkyōki*, in Ōkubo, ed., *Dōgen zenji zenshū* 2.382.

68. *Zengaku daijiten* 3.12–13.

69. Dōgen, *Hōkyōki*, in Ōkubo, ed., *Dōgen zenji zenshū* 2.382.

70. *T* 20.34b.

71. *T* no. 278.

72. Matsuura Hidemitsu, *Zenshū kojitsu sonzō no kenkyū* (Tokyo: Sankibō busshorin, 1971), pp. 155–164, 244–250, 261–266.

73. See, for example, Collcutt, *Five Mountains,* p. 194.

74. Śūraṅgama assemblies, for example, were also held in Teachings monasteries; see *Tseng-hsiu chiao-yüan ch'ing-kuei, HTC* 101.375d.

75. Matsuura, *Zenshū kojitsu sonzō no kenkyū*, p. 148.

76. *Shih-shih yao-lan*, s.v. *hu ch'ieh-lan shen*, *T* 54.263c.

77. *T* 21.557c.

78. *Shih-shih yao-lan*, s.v. *hu ch'ieh-lan shen, T* 54.263c; Kagamishima et al., eds., *Yakuchū Zennen shingi,* p. 76; Matsuura, *Zenshū kojitsu sonzō no kenkyū*, pp. 256–262.

79. In the Sung, statues of the four deva kings were often placed in the wings or in the second story of a monastery's main gate *(shan-men)*. By the Ming, main gates had come to be known as deva kings halls *(t'ien-wang-tien)*.

80. Tsan-ning, the author of the *Sung kao-seng chuan,* recounts the T'ang legend in which offerings and prayers to Vaiśravaṇa are said to have saved the city of An-hsi from being conquered by an enemy army and states that "this was the beginning of the practice of placing, by imperial edict, deva king images [or, the image of the deva king] *(t'ien-wang-hsiang)* in the watchtowers on city walls throughout the various circuits" (*T* 50.714a). It is not clear from the Chinese (which does not distinguish singular and plural forms of nouns) whether Tsan-ning meant that only the image of Vaiśravaṇa was placed in watchtowers or that the images of all four deva kings were placed there. Tsan-ning repeats the story in his *Ta Sung seng-shih-lüeh,* noting that not only city watchtowers but also Buddhist monasteries "were ordered to place images [or: the image] in their separate cloisters" (*T* 54.254b). Here again it is not clear whether Tsan-ning is talking about only one image or all four. Later Sung accounts, such as those of Mu-an (*HTC* 113.78a–b) and Chih-p'an (*T* 49.375b), are based on Tsan-ning and do not add any information that would help to resolve the issue. Matsuura Hidemitsu takes it for granted that Tsan-ning and Chih-p'an were explaining

how the four deva kings together came to be enshrined in the upper stories of monastery and cloister gates (*Zenshū kojitsu sonzō no kenkyū*, p. 252).

81. For example, the monastery guardian Ta-ch'üan-hsiu-li p'u-sa seems to have originated as a protector of navigation in the coastal regions around Mount A-yü-wang in Ming-chou (Chekiang province). His "conversion" to Buddhism was signaled by a legend that claimed that he was actually a son of King Aśoka (A-yü-wang), who used his magical powers to come from India to protect the great stūpa at Mount A-yü-wang, which contained the relics of Śākyamuni. The monastery on Mount A-yü-wang was declared a "ten directions Ch'an monastery" by imperial decree in 1008. Ta-ch'üan-hsiu-li p'u-sa was a protecting deity at other Ch'an monasteries in Chekiang as well and found his way to Japan in the Kamakura period as a guardian of Zen monasteries. See Matsuura, *Zenshū kojitsu sonzō no kenkyū*, pp. 420–424; Hubert Durt, "Daigenshuri Busa," in *Hōbōgirin*, vol. 6 (Tokyo: Maison Franco-Japonaise, 1983), pp. 599–609.

82. This metaphor, and indeed the use of the term *kung-an* in Ch'an literature, first appears in the discourse records of Ch'an master Yün-men (864–949): "The instant the Reverend Te-shan saw a monk enter the gate, he grabbed his staff [used by monks on pilgrimage] and drove him away. The Reverend Mu-chou, upon seeing a monk come in through the gate, said, 'It is a clear-cut case (*hsien-cheng kung-an*) [i.e., you are obviously guilty], but I absolve you of thirty blows'" (*T* 47.547a). Cf. Urs App, "Facets of the Life and Teaching of Chan Master Yunmen Wenyan (864–949)" (Ph.D. dissertation, Temple University, 1989), p. 143.

83. John Jorgensen, "The 'Imperial' Lineage of Ch'an Buddhism: The Role of Confucian Ritual and Ancestor Worship in Ch'an's Search for Legitimation in the Mid-T'ang Dynasty," *Papers on Far Eastern History*, no. 35 (Canberra: The Australian National University Department of Far Eastern History, 1987), pp. 109–111.

84. *HTC* 148.299a.

85. Matsuura, *Zenshū kojitsu sonzō no kenkyū*, p. 471.

86. *Ts'ung-lin chiao-ting ch'ing-kuei tsung-yao*, *HTC* 112.24a.

87. At Pei-shan, the second patriarch Hui-k'o was enshrined, and in other Sung Ch'an monasteries Bodhidharma may have been accompanied by the sixth patriarch Hui-neng, or the first six patriarchs may have been enshrined as a set—the historical record is vague on this point.

88. Mochizuki, *Bukkyō daijiten* 5.5025b–5026a.

89. Despite the assertion in the T'ien-t'ai school's own classical literature that the lineage had been cut off after twenty-four generations, proponents of the school in the Sung created other unbroken lineages to compete with the Ch'an lineage; see, for example, the *Ssu-ming tsun-che chiao-hsing lu*, *T* 46.915c–916a, 930c–933b; cf. the *Tseng-hsiu chiao-yüan ch'ing-kuei*, *HTC* 101.351c–352c.

90. *Lü-yüan shih-kuei*, *HTC* 106.22c–24d.

91. The discourse records of eminent Sung Ch'an masters often include a section that records the contents of these self-inscribed portrait eulogies (*chen-tsan*). See, for example, the *Hung-chih ch'an-shih kuang-lu*, *T* 48.102a–119b.

92. Tsukamoto, "Sō jidai no zunnan shikin tokudo no seido," p. 61.

93. *T* 51.252b.

94. *Ch'an-yüan ch'ing-kuei,* s.v. *shang-t'ang* (Kagamishima et al., eds., *Yakuchū zennen shingi,* p. 75).

95. *T* 47.643c.

96. *Wu-men-kuan, T* 48.293c.

97. *Ts'ung-lin chiao-ting ch'ing-kuei tsung-yao, HTC* 112.14cff.

98. *Ssu-ming tsun-che chiao-hsing lu, T* 46.925c–d.

99. *Tseng-hsiu chiao-yüan ch'ing-kuei, HTC* 101.357b–d.

100. *Ch'an-yüan ch'ing-kuei,* s.v. *ju-shih* (Kagamishima et al., eds., *Yakuchū zennen shingi,* p. 67).

101. *Ts'ung-lin chiao-ting ch'ing-kuei tsung-yao,* s.v. *ju-shih chih fa, HTC* 112.16b–c; *Ch'an-lin pei-yung ch'ing-kuei,* s.v. *ju-shih, HTC* 112.35c–d.

102. *Ssu-ming tsun-che chiao-hsing lu, T* 46.863a, 916a, 926c.

103. See, for example, Kosaka, "Shingi hensen no teiryū," p. 124.

104. *T'ien-chu pieh-chi, HTC* 101.155a–d.

105. Hirakawa Akira, "Ritsuzō ni arawareta zen no jissen," in Sekiguchi Shindai, ed., *Shikan no kenkyū* (Tokyo: Iwanami shoten, 1975), p. 54.

106. *T* 23.417b, cited in Hirakawa, "Ritsuzō ni arawareta zen no jissen," p. 61.

107. Hirakawa, "Ritsuzō ni arawareta zen no jissen," p. 62.

108. For the Vinaya rules regulating hours of meditation, see ibid., p. 61.

109. *Ju-chung jih-yung ch'ing-kuei, HTC* 111.473b–c.

110. Cf. *Mo-ho-seng-ch'i lü, T* 22.505a.

111. *T'ien-chu pieh-chi, HTC* 101.156c–d.

112. *Ch'an-yüan ch'ing-kuei* (Kagamishima et al., eds., *Yakuchū zennen shingi,* pp. 115, 215, 220, 238, 367, 385).

113. Ibid., pp. 330–331.

114. Kondō, "*Hyakujō shingi* no seiritsu to sono genkei," pp. 23–24.

115. *Tseng-hsiu chiao-yüan ch'ing-kuei, HTC* 101.388d.

116. *T'ien-chu pieh-chi, HTC* 101.155c.

117. An example of such criticism is found in the *Shih po lun* by Tao-heng (written between 405 and 417); cited by Erik Zürcher, *The Buddhist Conquest of China* (Leiden: E. J. Brill, 1959), vol. 1, p. 262.

118. Kagamishima, "*Hyakujō shingi* no seiritsu to sono igi," pp. 125, 133n.6.

119. Ennin wrote: "This cloister for the first time gathered its turnips. The Superior and all the others in the cloister went out and picked the leaves. When the monastic living quarters are out of firewood, all the monks in the cloister, regardless of whether they are old or young, go out and carry firewood" (translated in Edwin O. Reischauer, *Ennin's Diary: The Record of a Pilgrimage to China in Search of the Law* [New York: Ronald Press, 1955], p. 150).

120. Cited by Michihata Ryōshū, "Chūgoku bukkyō no keizai shisō," in Fukui hakushi juju kinen ronbunshū kankōkan, ed., *Fukui hakushi juju kinen tōyō shisō ronshū* (Tokyo, 1960), p. 658.

121. The practice of manual labor by monks in all public monasteries in Sung China was attested to by Dōgen in the chapter of his *Shōbōgenzō* entitled "Gyōji" (Ōkubo, ed., *Dōgen zenji zenshū* 1.127).

122. Ch'en, *Buddhism in China,* p. 398.

GLOSSARY

A-yü-wang　阿育王
A-yü-wang shan　阿育王山
"Butsudō"　佛道
ch'an　禪
Ch'an　禪
ch'an-chia　禪家
ch'an-chia liu　禪家流
ch'an-chiao i-chih　禪教一致
ch'an-ho-tzu　禪和子
Ch'an-lin pei-yung ch'ing-kuei　禪林備用清規
ch'an-men　禪門
Ch'an-men kuei-shih　禪門規式
ch'an-na　禪那
ch'an-seng　禪僧
ch'an-seng hsing-chieh　禪僧行解
ch'an-shih　禪師
ch'an-ssu　禪寺
ch'an-tsung　禪宗
ch'an-yüan　禪院
Ch'an-yüan ch'ing-kuei　禪苑清規
chang-lao　長老
Chang Shang-ying　張商英
Chao-chou　趙州
chen　真
chen-t'ang　真堂
chen-tsan　真讚
Chen-tsung　真宗
Cheng-shou　正受
ch'eng-ming nien-fo　稱名念佛
chi-yüan　機緣
Ch'i fo pa p'u-sa shuo ta-t'o-lo-ni shen-chou ching　七佛八菩薩説陀羅尼神呪經
Ch'i-ch'ung　契崇
chia-i lü-yüan　甲乙律院
chia-i t'u-ti-yüan　甲乙徒弟院
Chia-t'ai p'u-teng lu　嘉泰普燈錄
chiao-ssu　教寺
chiao-tsung　教宗
chiao-wai pieh-ch'uan　教外別傳
chiao-yüan　教院
ch'ieh-lan shen　伽藍神
Chien-chung ching-kuo hsü-teng lu　建中靖國續燈錄
chien-hsing ch'eng-fo　見性成佛

chih-chih jen-hsin　直指人心
Chih-i　智顗
Chih-p'an　志磐
Ch'ih-hsiu pai-chang ch'ing-kuei　勅修百丈清規
ch'ih-o　勅額
Ching-te ch'an-ssu　景德禪寺
Ching-te ch'uan-teng lu　景德傳燈錄
ch'ing-kuei　清規
Ch'ing-yüan Hsing-ssu　青原行思
chu-sheng shang-t'ang　祝聖上堂
Ch'u　楚
ch'u-chia　出家
ch'uan　傳
Ch'uan-fa cheng-tsung chi　傳法正宗記
Ch'uan fa-pao chi　傳法寶紀
ch'uan-teng　傳燈
ch'uan-teng lu　傳燈錄
Chüeh-fan Hui-hung　覺範慧洪
Dōgen　道元
Ennin　圓仁
Fan-wang ching　梵網經
fang-chang　方丈
fo-hsin-tsung　佛心宗
Fo-lung chih-che ch'an-yüan　佛瓏智者禪院
Fo-tsu t'ung-chi　佛祖統紀
Fu-fa-tsang chuan　付法藏傳
Gozan jissatsu zu　五山十刹圖
"Gyōji"　行持
hang-che　行者
Hōkyōki　寶慶記
hsi-ch'an　習禪
hsiao-ts'an　小參
hsien-ch'eng kung an　現成公案
Hsiu-ch'an-ssu　修禪寺
hsü-mi-t'an　須彌壇
Hsüeh-feng　雪峯
hu ch'ieh-lan shen　護伽藍神
Hu-fa lun　護法論
hua-yen　華嚴
Huang-po　黃檗
hui　惠
Hui-k'o　慧可
Hui-neng　慧能

Hui-tsung　徽宗
Hui-weng Wu-ming　晦翁悟明
Hui-yen Chih-chao　晦巖智昭
Hung-chih ch'an-shih kuang-lu　宏智
　禪師廣錄
Hung-chou　洪州
Hung-jen　弘忍
i-hsin ch'uan-hsin　以心傳心
Jen-t'ien yen-mu　人天眼目
Jen-tsung　仁宗
Ju-ching　如淨
Ju-chung jih-yung ch'ing-kuei　入衆日
　用清規
ju-shih　入室
ju-shih chih fa　入室之法
k'ai-shan　開山
k'an-ching　看經
k'an-chuan　看轉
kuan　官
Kuan-ting　灌頂
Kuan-yin　觀音
kuang　光
Kuang-li ch'an-ssu　廣利禪寺
kung-an　公案
kung-te yüan　功德院
Kuo-ch'ing-ssu　國清寺
Leng-chia shih-tzu chi　楞伽師資記
Leng-ch'üan t'ing　冷泉亭
leng-yen-chou　楞嚴呪
leng-yen-hui　楞嚴會
Li-chi　禮記
Li Tsun-hsü　李遵勗
Lien-teng hui-yao　聯燈會要
Lin-chi　臨濟
Lin-chien lu　林間錄
ling　靈
Ling-yin ch'an-ssu　靈隱禪寺
*Lung-hsing fo-chiao pien-nien
　t'ung-lun*　隆興佛教編年通論
lü-ssu　律寺
lü-yüan　律院
Lü-yüan shih-kuei　律苑事規
Ma-tsu　馬祖
Ma-tsu Tao-i　馬祖道一
Min　閩
Ming-chou　明州
Mo-ho chih-kuan　摩訶止觀
Mo-ho-seng-ch'i lü　摩訶僧祇律

Mu-an　睦菴
Nan-ch'üan　南泉
Nan-han　南漢
Nan-shan　南山
Nan-t'ang　南唐
Nan-yüeh Huai-jang　南嶽懷讓
nien-fo　念佛
nien-sung　念誦
Ning-tsung　寧宗
o　額
Pai-chang　百丈
Pai-chang Huai-hai　百丈懷海
Pai-yün Shou-tuan　白雲守端
Pao-ch'ing ssu-ming chih　寶慶四明志
pao-kuan shih-chia　寶冠釋迦
Pao-lin chuan　寶林傳
Pao-t'ang　保唐
Pei-shan　北山
Pei-shan ling-yin ch'an-ssu　北山靈隱
　禪寺
pen-tsun　本尊
P'i-sha-men　毘沙門
Po Chü-i　白居易
pu-li wen-tzu　不立文字
P'u-chi　普濟
p'u-ch'ing　普請
p'u-ch'ing tso-wu　普請作務
p'u-sa chieh　菩薩戒
san-men　三門
Seng-ts'an　僧璨
sha-mi　沙彌
shan-men　山門
Shan-ts'ai T'ung-tzu　善財童子
shang-t'ang　上堂
shen　神
sheng-seng　聖僧
shih-fang-ch'a　十方刹
shih-fang chu-ch'ih yüan　十方住持院
shih-fang ch'uan-chiao chu-ch'ih
　十方傳教住持
shih-fang lü-yüan　十方律院
shih-fang seng　十方僧
shih-hao　師號
shih-pa shan-shen　十八善神
Shih po lun　釋駁論
Shih-shih yao-lan　釋氏要覽
"Shisho"　嗣書
Shih-sung lü　十誦律

Shih-t'ou　石頭
Shih-t'ou Hsi-ch'ien　石頭希遷
Shōbōgenzō　正法眼藏
shou-tso　首座
Ssu-fen lü　四分律
Ssu-ming tsun-che chiao-hsing lu
　四明尊者教行錄
ssu-shu　嗣書
ssu-t'ien-wang　四天王
Su Shih　蘇軾
Su Tung-p'o　蘇東坡
Sung kao-seng chuan　宋高僧傳
Ta-chih　大智
Ta-ch'üan-hsiu-li p'u-sa　大權修利
　菩剎
*Ta-fan t'ien-wang wen-fo chüeh-i
　ching*　大梵天王問佛決疑經
ta-seng　大僧
Ta Sung seng-shih lüeh　大宋僧史略
tang-shan t'u-ti　當山土地
Tao-heng　道恆
Tao-hsin　道信
Tao-hsüan　道宣
Tao-yüan　道原
teng　燈
teng-shih　燈史
T'ien-chu pieh-chi　天竺別集
T'ien-sheng kuang-teng lu　天聖廣燈
　錄
T'ien-shou-ssu　天壽寺
T'ien-t'ai　天台
T'ien-t'ai-shan　天台山
T'ien-t'ung ling-lung-ssu　天童瓏瓏寺
T'ien-t'ung-shan　天童山
t'ien-wang-hsiang　天王像
t'ien-wang-tien　天王殿
ting　定

Tsan-ning　贊寧
Ts'ao-tung　曹洞
Tseng-hsiu chiao-yüan ch'ing-kuei
　增修教苑清規
Tsu-hsiu　祖琇
Tsu-t'ang chi　祖堂集
Tsu-t'ing shih-yüan　祖庭事苑
tsun　尊
Tsun-shih　遵式
tsung　宗
Tsung-ching lu　宗鏡錄
Tsung-mi　宗密
*Ts'ung-lin chiao-ting ch'ing-kuei
　tsung-yao*　叢林校訂清規總要
t'u-ti-shen　土地神
Tun-huang　敦煌
Tung-shan　洞山
t'ung-hang　童行
Wan-nien-ssu　萬年寺
wei-na　維那
Wei-po　惟白
Wei-t'o-t'ien　韋馱天
Wu　吳
Wu-chi　無際
Wu-men Hui-k'ai　無門慧開
Wu-men-kuan　無門關
wu-shan shih-ch'a　五山十剎
Wu-teng hui-yüan　五燈會元
Wu-tsung　武宗
Wu-yüeh　吳越
Yang-ch'i　楊岐
Yang-ch'i Fang-hui　楊岐方會
yü-lu　語錄
Yüeh-kai Chang-che　月蓋長者
Yün-men　雲門
Yung-ming Yen-shou　永明延壽

Characters for Monastic facilities can be found in appendix 5.1.

CHAPTER 6

THE RESPONSE OF THE SUNG STATE TO
POPULAR FUNERAL PRACTICES

Patricia Buckley Ebrey

In the year 1250 Chao Hsi-fen's father died. The subsequent funeral attracted attention because Chao Hsi-fen made great efforts to exclude non-Confucian funeral practices. He did not avoid the *sha* spirits; he did not employ Buddhist monks to perform services; and he gave no credence to the theories of geomancers concerning the timing of key steps in the funeral or the siting of the grave. Out of admiration for Chao's rare ability to distance himself from uncanonical practices, his contemporary Yü Wen-pao (ca. 1200–1260) wrote a brief essay on the ideas underlying these three sets of popular practices.[1] In this chapter I will use Yü's essay as a starting point for a discussion of popular funeral customs during the Sung dynasty and Confucian scholars' objections to them. I will then turn to the state's response: which practices it outlawed, which it regulated, which it ignored, and which it adopted.

The larger issues I address in this chapter concern the interconnections of power and culture. Why did those in authority—the educated elite and the state—find some practices more objectionable than others? How was the state machinery used to define correct behavior and foster conformity to it? Were other state activities, not intentionally designed to control mortuary practices, more crucial in shaping people's behavior? Or was the state largely irrelevant to the evolution of this facet of culture?

The efforts of authorities to control or suppress popular cults and to regulate, channel, and limit Buddhism and Taoism as organized religions have been profitably explored by many scholars.[2] Funerary practices differ in fundamental ways from temple-based religious worship and cults, making them an interesting topic for comparison. Social scientists have long stressed the social and psychological functions of funeral ceremonies, embedding them more fully in social context than has been done so far for Chinese popular religion.[3] Because funerals were performed within the household, they were harder for authorities to control. James Watson, nevertheless, has suggested that actions of the state had a considerable effect on the development of funeral ritual in China, particularly in fostering a high level of consistency in the basic structure of practices across place and time.[4] One goal of this chapter is to scrutinize this hypothesis by examining what, exactly, the state did.

I discuss both the state and the educated elite of men with some claim to knowledge of the Confucian classics. The state was administered by selected members of this elite, acting under the control of a relatively small number of high central government officials and ultimately the emperor. The state and the educated elite thus were not distinct entities. Historical sources, however, encourage us to stress their divergence rather than their commonalities. These sources fall into two categories: literary, historical, and philosophical writings of a tiny selection of influential members of the educated elite, many of them leaders of the Neo-Confucian movement and critical of both popular culture and state policies; and the records of government actions, such as edicts, legal decisions, and policy debates, which report the ideas of only a tiny proportion of state personnel. My reliance on these sources means that I am looking at popular practices largely from the vantage point of the educated elite and state officials, not that of ordinary unlettered people who may well have been less troubled by tensions, contradictions, or conflicting assumptions in the acts they performed.

"Popular" practice refers here not to everything commonly done at funerals but only to those practices perceived as uncanonical by the educated elite or state officials and labeled as *su* (vulgar, common, customary). Much that was commonly done by both the educated elite and ordinary peasants or townspeople was perfectly acceptable because it adhered to the outlines described in the ritual classics. Such practices as stuffing the coffin full of clothes, laying out food offerings near it, keeping it in the house for weeks, wearing coarse, undyed mourning garments, and burying containers of foodstuffs in the tomb were all common but in no way offensive, as they accorded with classical models. To keep my topic manageable, I will moreover only discuss popular practices that can be broadly categorized under Yü Wen-pao's three headings, even though there were many other customs that scholars criticized. These three areas, however, relate to three key features of current practice: the reliance on experts, the influence of religious ideas of afterlife, and the social problem of recreating family continuity and hierarchy in the face of death.

POPULAR FUNERAL PRACTICES

Much of our knowledge of uncanonical funeral practices derives from the strand of Neo-Confucian thinking, dating back to Han Yü (768–824) and especially common in the eleventh century, that called for curbing heterodox practices as an essential step toward reviving "the way of the sages." The perception that these practices were worth writing about was fairly new to the Sung, but the practices themselves had existed for centuries. Surviving sources often give the impression that these practices were becoming more prevalent in the places the authors knew, but the accuracy of this impression cannot easily be tested. Increased reference to uncanonical practices may reflect greater familiarity with common people's practices or greater interest in keeping them from contaminating the practices of the educated.

Sha Spirits

Sha were demonic spiritual forces brought into action by a death. Shortly after someone had died, *sha* came to the site of the corpse and were capable of bringing harm to anyone present. Yen Chih-t'ui (531–591+) mentioned that everyone left the house on the day the *sha* were expected to return.[5] Hung Mai (1123–1202) described avoiding *sha* as a custom of the lower Yangtze region where people believed in shamans and ghosts. When the calculated day arrived, he reported: "Everyone in the house goes outside to avoid the spirit, a practice called 'avoiding the *sha*.' They order a strong servant or a monk to guard the house."[6]

Theories of *sha* seem to have been quite varied. In some cases *sha* were conceived as giant birds. Sometimes *sha* would leave tracks on ashes from which people could infer the fate of the dead after rebirth.[7] In his essay on Chao Hsi-fen, Yü Wen-pao noted that the theory of *sha* did not go back to the classics, but he had found reference to it in the "List of One Hundred Taboos" attributed in Sung times to Lü Ts'ai of the early T'ang Dynasty.[8] According to Yü, this book recorded ways to reduce the harm caused by the *sha* of deaths:

> If the person died on a *ssu* day, there would be a male *sha* that would return on the forty-seventh day. A thirteen- or fourteen-*sui* girl would have a female *sha*, which would go to the third house to the south. *Sha* are white. In the case of men who have the surnames Cheng, P'an, Sun, or Ch'en, [the *sha*] comes back to the home of the mourners two times, on the twentieth and the twenty-ninth days. Since [Lü's] time this tradition has been handed down. When the time comes [for *sha* to return], everyone has to avoid them.[9]

Yü reported that in his time people consulted experts to discover which day they should leave the house. "For instance, if the person died on a *tzu* day, then [the *sha*] will harm people born on *tzu, wu, mao,* and *yu* days. Those who fit these categories, even the sons of the deceased, stay away when it is time for the encoffining." The experts were probably often geomancers, as two major geomancy manuals of Sung date described how to calculate when the *sha* will arrive.[10] Another Sung source reported that yin-yang experts postulated a male and a female *sha* for each person and said they could determine whether the *sha* had left by the position of the feet. If the female *sha* had not left, the right foot of the corpse would be turned to the left; if the male *sha* had not left, the left foot would be turned toward the right; and if neither had left, both feet would be turned inward.[11]

Yü Wen-pao criticized belief in *sha* spirits primarily on the grounds that the ritual classics had called for the mourners to be attentive to what was placed in the coffin and to stay near it. That is, he did not criticize belief in *sha* as ignorant but as unfilial. When they believed the *sha* would be antagonistic to them, "even the wives and daughters are not willing to look at [the body], entrusting everything to old women or household servants. Not only does this mean that the pillow and mat and other arrangements are not handled with attention to detail, but also the jewels of gold, silver, and pearl [in the coffin] may all be stolen."[12]

Criticisms of the practices of avoiding *sha* spirits are not abundant in Sung sources, which may indicate either that intellectuals were unfamiliar with the practice or that they found it unremarkable. Intellectuals could not, however, have been ignorant of the more general belief in ghosts, especially ghosts of the recent dead. Thus it is significant that Sung scholars seldom argued against the existence of ghosts or ridiculed practices or customs based on assumptions about their needs and desires.[13] Even "ghost marriages," ceremonies to join two dead souls in marriage, attracted little more than amusement.[14]

Buddhist Services

Throughout the Sung, mourners regularly engaged Buddhist monks to perform funeral services for the recent dead, generally scheduled for each seventh day until the forty-ninth day after the death. As Teiser has shown, ideas about the seven stages of judgment through which the dead must pass on their way to rebirth progressively penetrated popular culture from the late T'ang through the Sung.[15] Buddhist services were seen as a way to help the dead through these passages by transferring merit to them. The services could be held in the home of the deceased or in a temple; in either case the major activity was the chanting of sūtras. The monks who performed the services were fed vegetarian meals, and the relatives and guests who came to observe were also fed, making these services an expensive funeral activity for the bereaved family. In Kaifeng and Hangchow it was possible to hire caterers who would prepare and deliver these meals.[16] Occasionally monks might be asked to give sermons on Buddhist topics.[17] They might also be asked to perform specific ceremonies for the salvation of the soul, the most elaborate called the Great Ceremony of Land and Water.[18]

Yü Wen-pao began his discussion of the use of Buddhist clergy in funeral ceremonies by citing the famous Northern Sung scholar and statesman of two centuries earlier, Ssu-ma Kuang (1019–1086), whose testimony he apparently considered still valid:

> Wen-kung [i.e., Ssu-ma Kuang] said: "It is the current custom to believe the falsehoods of the Buddhists. At the moment of death, at each seventh day until the seventh seventh day, at the hundredth day, and at the first and second sacrifices of good fortune [on the first and second anniversaries of the death], everyone performs services to gain merit, obliterate sin, and be born in heaven. [They believe] that if they do not, [the deceased] will enter hell and be sliced, roasted, pounded, and ground. Yet with death the body decays and the spirit disperses. Even if it were sliced, roasted, pounded, and ground, how would it know of it? Li Tan said: 'If Heaven does not exist, then that is that; but if it does exist, then sages will be born there. If hell does not exist, then that is that; but if it does exist, then inferior men will enter it. Contemporaries, when a parent dies, pray to the Buddha. This is assuming one's parent is an inferior person who has sinned.' "[19]

In other words, although people perform Buddhist services according to a regular schedule, thinking that they are aiding their parents' salvation, in fact they are accomplishing nothing because the dead body cannot suffer punishment, and if perchance heaven actually exists, the good will be reborn there anyway. Yü Wen-pao thus cited Ssu-ma Kuang to attack the practice of Buddhist services on the grounds of the falsity of Buddhism. In his original essay, Ssu-ma Kuang also made fun of the idea that the Buddha could be bribed into treating sinners favorably, with its implication that the wicked will get to heaven if their children spend enough.[20] Even those more sympathetic to Buddhism were sometimes uncomfortable with the idea that Buddhist doctrine should reward the rich rather than the worthy. Lu Yu (1125–1210) insisted that the common notion that spending more for services would lead to greater blessings was a misunderstanding of the sūtras, which asserted that a single hymn could lead to immeasurable merit.[21]

Some scholars focused their criticisms of Buddhist services on the ways they conflicted with Confucian canonical rituals, especially in the use of music and other forms of entertainment. The *Li-chi* (Record of ritual) had stated that music was not to be performed at funerals,[22] a rule generally interpreted as allowing dirge singers but not instrumental music. Yü Wen-pao cited the objections of the Neo-Confucian philosopher Ch'eng I (1033–1107) to the use of cymbals and gongs in Buddhist services, as they were Indian instruments, originally used by monks out begging.[23] Lu Yu, a less doctrinaire writer, still objected to music and theatrical performances by monks at Buddhist services because they distracted the mourners from their proper task of wailing.[24] Yü Wen-pao also complained about the noise: "In ceremonies held outside [the capital], only at the beginning and end of the ceremony do they use cymbals and drums. Till the end of the evening they chant and give sermons, which serve the purpose of earnest confession of sins. In the capital today they use the Indian practice of striking the drums and cymbals throughout the service, shaking and startling people so much that they get brain-splitting headaches. How much worse it must be for the souls of the dead!"[25]

Thus not only were Buddhist services useless and foreign, but they were noisy and unfitting ways to express grief. Yü also reported that Buddhist services often were indistinguishable from entertainment, especially the evening before the funeral procession when "handsome young monks with long fingernails come out to perform on the flower gong and flower drum stick, their plan to please the women folk and plunder their wealth."[26] Confucians generally found it difficult to reconcile piety and theatrical performances. Lu Yu thought extravagant services were seldom motivated by an understanding of Buddhism, as those who "do not know who the Buddha was or what the dharma is" hold them "to make a spectacle to impress their neighbors."[27]

Taking another tack, Yü Wen-pao questioned the qualifications of the monks; some, he suggested, probably were not the scholars of the sūtras that those employing them assumed them to be: "During their recitations, they sometimes repeat a few phrases over and over, using the Sanskrit as though it was a song tune."[28] Yü was undoubtedly right in noting that some of those who performed Buddhist services were not learned monks. Sometimes laymen performed services themselves. Moreover, some of those labeled by observers as monks *(seng)* may have been self-styled monks, making a living by holding funeral services, rather than the sorts of monks at the leading monasteries, described by Foulk in this volume.[29]

Although Yü Wen-pao confined his criticism of Buddhist intrusions in funerary practices to their role in performing services, Buddhist monks and monasteries by Sung times played much broader roles in funerary activities. Buddhist clergy often led funeral processions.[30] Buddhist temples were often used as places to store coffins until burial could be arranged. Buddhist temples often aided the practice of cremation, providing crematories, storing ashes, or providing pools where ashes could be scattered. All of these practices seem to have been on the increase in Sung times, and they evoked vociferous criticism from Confucian scholars—especially cremation, which was labeled a desecration of the corpse and clear evidence that the foreign origins of Buddhism made its practices unsuitable for China.[31]

Geomancers

The third popular practice Yü Wen-pao discussed was consulting geomancers to choose the site and time for burial.[32] The underlying presuppositions of geomancy go back to the ancient idea that the living benefit when their ancestors are comfortable, but the elaboration of theories about the forces of the earth and their effect on the living seems to have begun in the Han and grown considerably in the post-Han period. These theories drew from several strains of cosmological thought, including yin-yang, five phases, and *I-ching* traditions, as well as less philosophically based divinatory traditions. Geomancy was widely used to site buildings, including temples and palaces, but the branch of geomancy of concern here is grave geomancy. The fourth-century scholar Kuo P'u (267–324) was widely credited with formulating the basic principles of grave geomancy in his influential *Book of Burials (Tsang shu,* also called *Tsang ching).* Already by the early T'ang there was a profusion of different schools of geomancy, and the emperor T'ai-tsung (r. 627–649) asked Lü Ts'ai to sift through these various theories to identify the most valid ones.[33]

The primary task of geomancers was to select grave sites and the time of interment, but they often did much more than that, determining the time the *sha* had to be avoided, how deep the grave should be, and the types and arrangement of grave goods. They sometimes performed sacrifices to the earth before excavation was begun, arranged the objects for the funerary procession, prepared the mock deeds, recited incantations at the interment, sacrificed to the gods of mountains, rivers, and soil after the tomb was finished, and so on.[34]

Yü Wen-pao began his discussion of geomancy with further quotations from Ssu-ma Kuang and Ch'eng I. From Ssu-ma Kuang he cited this passage:

> What the *Classic of Filial Piety* means by divining for the tomb site is divining whether it is auspicious or ill-omened. It is not like the yin-yang masters who inspect the configurations of wind and water to select the year, month, day, and hour, asserting that the descendants' success, wisdom, and life spans are entirely dependent on them. [Current reliance on geomancy] reaches the point where people do not bury for several years. Moreover, experts calculate people's life spans based on the five phases, which means that their fortunes are already set at birth. How can they be changed by burial sites?[35]

Yü's paraphrase touches on only a few of the many arguments Ssu-ma Kuang marshaled against the practice of geomancy, which he considered not merely illogical nonsense but immoral because it promoted delay in burial. He noted that the classics specified the length of time

between death and burial according to rank and prescribed the arrangement of graves according to birth order in the descent line.[36]

The theories of geomancy most influential in modern China were
not the dominant ones in the Northern Sung.[37] The two main schools of
modern times (the school of forms and the school of the compass)
claimed founders who predated the Sung, but their theories were not
nearly as influential as the theories of several other masters, all of whom
seem to have worked within a framework variously called the "Five Surnames," "Five Notes," or "Five Sounds." This framework was already old
in the Sung, Lü Ts'ai having criticized it at length in the early T'ang.[38] In
this theoretical framework a particular location might be auspicious for
someone in one category of surnames (based on its sound) but ill-omened
for those in others.[39] The theory of the five surname classes was repeatedly criticized by scholars in Sung times, Yü Wen-pao citing Ch'eng I's
criticism of it on the grounds that current surnames were historical products, not the original surnames of ancient times.[40]

Despite some common premises, Northern Sung geomantic theories
varied considerably not only in their vocabulary but also in their ideas
and procedures. To many Confucian scholars this diversity was grounds
enough to dismiss the theories. The philosopher Chang Tsai (1020–
1077) wrote:

> Burial methods based on wind, water, hills and ridges are completely non-
> sensical and should not be used. In the south they use *The Green Sack,*
> which can still be obtained.[41] Westerners use *I-hsing,* which is especially
> preposterous.[42] Southerners test a burial spot by taking a multicolored piece
> of silk and burying it in the ground. After a year they take it out and look at
> it. If the soil is good, the colors will not have changed, but if the *ch'i* of the
> soil is bad, they will have. People will also put a small fish in a container of
> water and bury it for a year, divining for the quality of the land according to
> whether it lives or dies or whether plants flourish or wither.[43]

One of Ssu-ma Kuang's criticisms of geomancy was that it made
people fearful. This charge was probably accurate. Sung geomantic manuals, including the government-issued *New Book of Earth Patterns* and
the privately compiled *Secret Burial Classic,* expressed geomantic principles in negative terms, specifying all the things that could go wrong if the
selection of a site were not perfect in all regards. For instance, the *Secret
Burial Classic* explained that one had to identify the dragon in a hill or
ridge and site the grave according to the parts of its body. Accuracy was
essential.

> Those who cover the dragon's head or bury in its horns will be destroyed
> within three years. Those who cover the dragon's eyes or bury in its pupils
> will have a son kill his father or a younger brother kill his older brother.

Those who cover the dragon's peak or bury in its mouth will be decapitated within three years. Those who cover the dragon's waist or bury in its cheeks will have a son or grandson pass first in the examinations. Those who cover the dragon's navel or bury in its belly will have a daughter-in-law with adulterous desires.[44]

From anecdotes we know that some people selected graves sites themselves according to geomantic principles. Nevertheless, most people must have been intimidated by the complexity of the theories and the dire consequences that awaited slight miscalculations, leading them to rely on experts.

Geomancy was also charged with provoking family quarrels. According to Lo Ta-ching (*chin-shih* 1226), when there were several surviving sons, they might fight over the selection of a site for their parents' burial, believing each brother would be affected differently by each possible site.[45] In fact, the *New Book of Earth Patterns* gives formulas for the good or bad consequences a given site would have for the parents, eldest son, middle son, and youngest son of the deceased.[46]

A particularly common complaint against geomancy was that it led to the delay of burials, sometimes for decades or even generations. Ssu-ma Kuang reported:

> When the descendants get old and decline they may forget the location of the coffin and abandon it without burying it. People want descendants in large part so someone will take care of their physical remains. When descendants act like this, wouldn't it be better to have no descendants and die by the road? Then some man of virtue might bury [the coffin]. . . . If one really supposed that burial was able to affect human fortunes, how could those who are sons and grandsons bear to cause their parents to rot and suffer exposure in order to seek profit for themselves? There are no perverse rituals that hurt moral principles more than these.[47]

When burial was delayed more than a few weeks or months, people often did not want to keep the coffin in their homes. By Sung times it had become extremely common for families to bring the encoffined body to a temple to be left there until burial could be arranged.[48] Thus geomancers and Buddhist temples complemented each other in the provision of funerary services.

Geomancy was also blamed for encouraging people to dig up bodies to bury them elsewhere. Lo Ta-ch'ing wrote that some people would decide that a site was not auspicious and would dig up the coffin, sometimes repeating this three or four times.[49] Liu K'o-chuang (1187–1269) recorded a legal case concerning a man who concluded that his grandfather's grave site was not auspicious and so dug him up for reburial.[50] Again, Sung geomantic manuals do not contradict the critics, the *New*

Book of Earth Patterns giving full instructions for a ceremony to be performed before opening a tomb to move the body for burial elsewhere, specifying the types of offerings and supplying the wording for prayers.[51] Archaeological evidence suggests that reburying bones in small boxes occurred with some frequency in North China in the Sung.[52]

Both the *New Book of Earth Patterns* and the *Secret Burial Classic* include sections on the selection of geomancers. The things to look for, they assert, are virtue, formality, intelligence, and a cultivated knowledge of the classics and apocrypha. Both say that Buddhist monks, soldiers, and the old and maimed are not satisfactory geomancers. One problem with Buddhist monks was that they had taken vows not to kill or eat meat and so could not make meat offerings to the gods of the earth, one of the responsibilities of geomancers.[53] Geomancers, it would seem, did not want competition from Buddhist monks in their particular sphere of mortuary services. Their defensive stance was apparently not totally unwarranted; not only was one of the most often cited authorities the T'ang monk I-hsing, but monks in Sung times also sometimes served as geomancers.[54] On the whole, though, in the Sung geomancers and Buddhist monks achieved a clear division of labor: Buddhists handled the ceremonies that focused on the rebirth of the soul; geomancers handled the burial of the body. Chinese graves in Sung times are full of visual and textual references to geomancy; Buddhist symbolism or language is, in contrast, striking for its rarity.

Critics of geomancy often spoke of geomancers as "rustic masters and vulgar shamans,"[55] but some geomancers were highly educated scholars, such as Ts'ai Yüan-ting (1135–1198), a friend and disciple of the great Neo-Confucian philosopher Chu Hsi (1130–1200).[56] Moreover, not all literati and philosophers condemned geomancy, and those who did criticize it did not always object to everything about it. Many later geomantic works quoted Ch'eng I's explanation that because ancestors and descendants share the same material force *(ch'i)*, when one is comfortable, the other will be also.[57] Chu Hsi, while critical of some abuses of geomancy, nevertheless accepted many of its premises. In 1194 he wrote a memorial to the throne, advising that a new imperial graveyard be started and that expert geomancers select its location. He explained the mishaps proper geomancy could avoid: "Should the selection [of the grave site] be defective, making the spot inauspicious, then there will surely be water, ants, and ground wind *(ti-feng)* that will damage the contents [of the coffin] and cause the body and spirit to be uncomfortable. As for the descendants, they may be inflicted with death and extinction [of the descent line], which are very frightening worries."[58] In other words, the fears geomancers evoked were based in fact. Chu Hsi even argued that geomancy was validated by imperial experience. By his calculations, the previous emperors had been buried in unsuitable places, and, indeed, the imperial line had suffered several tragedies.

The reasons for differences in scholars' attitudes toward geomancy range from social (some critics knew only ill-educated, lower-class geomancers, others knew highly educated experts), to situational (critics were writing from different perspectives), to philosophical (some critics were skeptical of the idea that resonances can work at a distance, others were more open to grand cosmological systems).

Let me recapitulate the main objections that Confucian scholars raised to these three sets of funerary practices: Practices associated with Buddhism were condemned most roundly, undoubtedly because of the Neo-Confucian sectarian view that the promotion of Confucianism required the suppression of Buddhism. Confucians ridiculed the doctrine of heaven and hell as inconsistent with what was known of the decay of the body and the doctrine of transferring merit as favoring the wealthy. Music, which usually accompanied services, was inappropriate when people were grieving. Cremation was desecration of the corpse. Storing coffins in temples let mourners too easily forget their heavy responsibilities and indirectly encouraged delays in final burial. The immorality of these practices was not surprising to these scholars given that Buddhism was a foreign religion.

Scholars' reactions to geomancy were more complex. Only a few scholars, such as Ssu-ma Kuang and Lo Ta-ch'ing, were sweeping in their condemnations. Others ridiculed particular theories. Geomancy could not be labeled foreign, and many of its tenets could be validated by reference to long-established cosmological ideas such as yin-yang and correlative thinking. Objections to geomantic ideas often focused on such theories as the Five Notes, rather than on underlying assumptions about the relation of the comfort of the dead to the happiness of their descendants. Most common were criticisms of people who let geomantic considerations override moral or ritual imperatives, thus delaying burials, getting into quarrels with their relatives, or digging up their ancestors for reburial. Geomancy, in other words, should be practiced in moderation.

Popular practices related to belief in ghosts or other fateful consequences of death received much less attention from Confucian scholars. Some probably shared these fears and found nothing inaccurate or immoral in them. Not only had they grown up in an environment in which such fears were commonplace, but reading would not necessarily have undermined these feelings. Recorded accounts of ghosts were plentiful, and scholars who were skeptical of popular conceptions of ghosts still might reinterpret ghostlike phenomena in terms that seemed to them more rational.[59] At any rate, since fear of ghosts led to only minor deviations from the classical ritual schedule, combatting them was not a high priority.

Attitudes toward uncanonical funerary customs were not uniform among the educated elite, even that tiny proportion of the elite whose writings survive. Not only did some defend geomancy, but many openly saved evidence of their participation in Buddhist services for friends and relatives, preserving in their collected works the prayers they wrote for these occasions.[60] Throughout the dynasty well-known literati were attracted to Buddhism or to Buddhist monks in at least some stages of their lives. Lu Yu, who criticized the vulgarity of current Buddhist funeral services, nevertheless told his sons that when he died they would not be able to avoid all popular practices; still they should keep services on a small scale, inviting one or two accomplished monks to recite the *Diamond Sūtra* or a single chapter of the *Hua-yen Sūtra*.[61] Views on these issues do not show any marked changes over time as each century of the Sung produced examples of uncompromising critics of everything uncanonical as well as other well-educated men much more tolerant of current customs.

THE RESPONSE OF THE STATE

Many modern scholars have addressed the ways Chinese have adhered to religious beliefs and practices of different origins. Finding systems that give coherence to this diversity has been a major concern.[62] Over the centuries Chinese also often tried to reconcile or synthesize key elements of these distinct traditions.[63] Here I will not try to make intellectual sense of the variety of actions commonly performed after a death in Sung China. Rather I will try to see what, if anything, the Sung state had to do with shaping the evolution of these customs.

The role of the state in the historical formation of Chinese cults has received considerable scholarly attention. In a study of the Ma-tsu cult, James L. Watson brought attention to the way local and central government authorities made use of the popularity of a local cult, transformed it through government patronage, and then reimposed it on local communities, through these actions standardizing the popular pantheon.[64] Romeyn Taylor came to a somewhat different evaluation of state effectiveness in his study of official religion of the Ming, "that comprehensive body of religious practice that was defined and prescribed in legal documents for all levels of society." Taylor argued that this official religion was inherently unstable, because, given its Confucian theoretical base, it had to lay claim to encompassing all that went on in the empire while also having to defend against corruption by nonclassical beliefs and practices. As he saw it, state efforts were also hampered by the personal idiosyncrasies of emperors and the need to resolve conflicts among Confucian ceremonialists, local elites, and Taoist priests.[65]

Funerary practices are different from worship in temples, and political and religious authorities have naturally treated them differently. Even today states regulate disposal of the dead, requiring, for instance, that bodies be promptly removed from living quarters, that they not be buried before death has been certified by an authorized person, that burial grounds be located only in certain areas, or that undertakers be licensed. These sorts of regulations are based on diverse ideas about public health, public order, and morality, as well as the interests of those who perform these services. Ecclesiastical authorities have also often taken keen interest in how people handle death, insisting that only their clergy perform rites for the dying and the dead, officiate at funeral and burial services, or supervise burial grounds or crematory.

Given Chinese ideas about the state and the moral order dating back at least to the Han, the propriety of state involvement with funerary practice was not questioned. In ancient Confucian theory, the emperor was seen as the central figure in the cosmos, the one who could, through his religious rituals, integrate the human and heavenly realms. The imperial governments from Han times on issued ritual codes that specified in considerable detail what the emperor, imperial relatives, officials, and common people could do in diverse religious and ritual situations. When their parents died, for instance, ordinary commoners could perform rites formally similar to those the emperor or nobles could perform, but at reduced levels. The size of the coffins, the quality and quantity of the objects they placed in the tomb, the length of time the body was left encoffined above ground, the steps in the funerary sacrifices, and the numbers of participants in the funeral processions all were to be similarly graded. Quantitative limits on practices were justified not only on cosmological grounds, but on political ones as well. The natural hierarchy of society is threatened when the low-ranking are allowed to put on a more splendid show than the high-ranking want to or can afford; and the national wealth is dissipated when people compete in useless ritual displays, leading to fewer resources to feed the hungry or to fill state coffers. Ethical considerations could also be introduced. In Confucian political theory, the state had an obligation to guide people in the direction of moral behavior. If leaving bodies unburied was immoral, it had to be outlawed, even if the populace at large did not perceive it as immoral and even if enforcement proved difficult.

The Sung state responded to popular funeral practices not simply by making pronouncements, but by a whole array of actions that directly or indirectly encouraged or discouraged people from performing certain practices. These state actions ranged from explicit laws imposing penalties for infractions, to administrative procedures that set up bureaucratic hurdles, to the publication and certification of books, to the example of the throne. During the Northern Sung there were strong tendencies to extend government control of the society and economy, culminating in Wang An-shih's (1021–1086) New Policies and their continuation under Ts'ai Ching (1046–1126) in the early twelfth century.[66] But state efforts to control funeral practices have no particular association with this activist phase. They seem rather to have been ad hoc responses to the complaints of officials and never to have been systematically related one to the other or consistently enforced. As will be apparent from the discussion below, the state sometimes discouraged a practice through one channel while fostering it through another.

Use of Positive Law to Outlaw Practices

When officials were firmly committed to suppressing a practice, the normal course of action was to have it declared illegal. From what survives of Sung laws, ordinances, and regulations, we know that cremation, music at funerals, and long delays in burials were declared illegal and punishable. The first to be outlawed was cremation. An edict of 962 declared: "The [ancient] kings established sizes for coffins and vaults and the system of mounds planted with trees to improve interpersonal ethics and bring unity to customs. Recently cremation has become common, which is an extreme violation of the established rituals. From now on it must be banned."[67] Thus both immorality and deviance were the grounds cited for suppressing cremation. When this edict was incorporated into the Sung code, exceptions were granted for those who died far from home, Buddhist monks and nuns, and foreigners; punishment of death was specified for all other violators.[68] In 1158 further exemptions from punishment were granted for the poor in areas where there were no free graveyards, a concession to the widespread popularity of cremation in the southeast.[69]

In 970 using Buddhists or Taoists or "people dressed up in strange colors" to lead funeral processions was banned in the capital.[70] In 982 rules for funeral processions were issued, including a ban on music. Two years after that, playing music or presenting plays in front of coffins was forbidden: violation was to be classed as unfilial conduct, a potentially very serious offense.[71] In the code "making music" was specified to refer to striking drums, or playing stringed, woodwind, or percussion instruments, whether one handled the instrument oneself or had someone else do it.[72] Since music and drama in front of coffins were often associated with Buddhist services, this edict may have been intended to set limits on such services, but Buddhist monks are not explicitly mentioned in either case.

Sometime before the end of the twelfth century the government prescribed the punishment of one hundred blows for leaving a parent's body unburied five years or longer without good reason. When the offender was an official, the case was to be reported to the censorate.[73] This law was probably intended to curb some of the excesses generally attributed to belief in geomancy. Otherwise the practice of geomancy was not limited by law. In fact, explicit exceptions were made for geomancy when in 977 local governments were ordered to investigate local yin-yang experts and diviners who were charged with deceiving the people for their own financial gain.[74]

In the Chinese context, declaring an act illegal and specifying a punishment served two distinguishable functions in controlling people's behavior: Laws were statements that labeled some behavior unacceptable, and they were part of an administrative apparatus used to punish offenders. As statements they were strongest when the fewest qualifications were added: If cremation is reprehensible, it should be reprehensible even when burial is inconvenient. Enforcing a law is an even stronger statement about the limits of acceptable behavior, but the enforcement process is complicated by the realities of political control. As guidelines for judges, qualifications to the law make it more enforceable—local officials could not cope with trying to punish everyone who played music at funerals or left a body unburied. In the case of funeral practices, the Sung state used laws both for their ritual effect and as guidelines for administrative practice. Some of the apparent vacillation on the part of the government probably reflects the tension between these two purposes and the occasional redirection of state efforts from one to the other.

Use of Administrative Apparatus to Regulate Practices

The Sung government did not confine its efforts to issuing laws; it also took administrative actions, particularly with regard to the problem of unburied coffins. In 1062 the government undertook to bury all bodies of imperial clansmen that had laid unburied for more than five years. Apparently delayed burial had reached very large proportions, for officials discovered over four hundred clansmen whose bodies had remained unburied for twelve or more years. A couple of decades later (in the Yüan-yu period, 1086–1094), any official who, without good reason, had left a parent unburied for ten or more years jeopardized his career if he did not promptly take care of the matter.[75]

In 1079 the court ordered that all local governments set up charitable graveyards. These graveyards would discourage cremation on the part of the poor by providing free grave plots and at the same time would facilitate disposing of the hundreds of coffins abandoned at temples for decades or longer. The original edict ordered the interment of any coffin unclaimed for over twenty years or for which the name of the dead person was unknown. These charitable graveyards were also to provide space to bury beggars and others who could not afford to buy grave plots. They were to be managed by Buddhist novices who would be rewarded with ordination certificates depending on the length of time they served as graveyard managers or the numbers of people they buried.[76] Archaeological evidence shows that many large graveyards were established in response to these orders.[77]

Reburials for geomantic or other reasons were made more difficult by regulations instituted before the end of the twelfth century. Anyone who wished to rebury a relative was required to notify the county government of the reason for the move and to receive approval before proceeding, with exceptions granted only for officials and their descendants.[78]

One might also note the administrative steps the government apparently did not take. The government licensed Buddhist monks and Taoist priests, establishing the requirements for ordination, the privileges of ordained clergy, and the numbers to be admitted. There is no evidence that the government made use of this power to keep clergy from performing funeral ceremonies in unacceptable ways. The state did not revoke the ordination certificates of monks or priests who performed music or plays at funerals or led funeral processions. Nor did it revoke the tax exemptions of temples or monasteries that operated crematoria or provided storage for coffins for years on end.

Use of the Power to Define and Codify

Besides defining unacceptable behavior through the legal codes, the government had the power to define correct ideas, procedures, and rituals through its publication programs. In the case of funerary practices, the Sung state, like the T'ang before it, made use of this power by issuing manuals specifying the correct versions of both geomancy and Confucian funeral rituals. To put this another way, it attempted to establish the framework within which these issues were discussed.

The first Sung emperor had commissioned a *Treasury of Heaven and Earth (Ch'ien-k'un pao-tien)*, which contained 450 sections, thirty devoted to geomancy.[79] Because scholars complained that it was full of errors, in 1034 another group of experts was assembled under Wang Ch'eng-yung to revise it, and they devoted five years to the task. In 1051, however, Tseng Kung-ting memorialized that this book was shallow and useless. This time the high official Wang Chu (997–1057) was given the task of supervising compilation of a new book. According to its preface, this book, the *New Book of Earth Patterns (Ti-li hsin-shu)*, organized existing schools according to the four directions, five phases, five surname categories, nine stars, eight trigrams, eight transformations, eight generals, three mirrors, and six roads. Pictures were added, the author said, to make the book easy for common people to use. Although the book attempted to select only the most reliable theories, the theories of shamans *(wu-shih)* were not excluded when they had solid foundations.[80]

The *New Book of Earth Patterns* survives in a Yüan edition. Its compilation could not have satisfied the critics of geomancy, as it employs the Five Notes framework, admits of the possibility that burials might best be delayed for years, calculates the auspiciousness of each grave site separately for different relatives, and even includes the specific statement that a site might be chosen because it is auspicious for the living even knowing that it is ill-omened for the dead. Compilation and circulation of this manual would have aided the professionalization of geomancers but would not have satisfied Confucian critics of geomantic theories.

Carrying on a long tradition, the Sung government also played a role in codifying Confucian funeral rituals. Early in the Sung dynasty the government issued the *K'ai-pao t'ung-li* (Comprehensive rituals of the K'ai-pao period), based closely on the *K'ai-yüan li* of the mid-T'ang.[81] In the Chia-yu period (1056–1063), Ou-yang Hsiu supervised a compendium of revisions, the *T'ai-ch'ang yin-ko li* (The revised ritual of the Court of Ritual) in one hundred *chüan*, but this book did not deal with funeral rituals for anyone outside the imperial family. A full revision, more comprehensive in scope, was done between 1107 and 1113, resulting in the 220-*chüan Cheng-ho wu-li hsin-i* (New forms for the five categories of rites of the Cheng-ho period). Compilation of this work was one of the many examples of the assertion of central government authority during the reign of Hui-tsung (r. 1101–1125). The compilers of this manual were apparently more interested than any of their predecessors in shaping rituals for commoners. An edict of 1107 stated: "The way to guard against the people's taking customary practices as their model lies in the five categories of rites."[82]

After *New Forms* was issued, serious efforts were made to get people, including commoners, to put its provisions into practice. Officials were appointed to give advice to both commoners and gentlemen on the new forms for rites, and the governor of Kaifeng was ordered to edit and print a digest of the *New Forms* suitable for common use and to distribute it widely. "This will make it possible for everyone to know the ideas of the rituals. Then those who did not carry them out can be charged with wrongdoing."[83] In 1118 the government tried positive incentives. It ordered every circuit to recommend for rewards one or two people who had properly performed the rituals prescribed in the *New Forms*. About a year and a half later negative sanctions were officially abandoned, the edict frankly discussing the problems of using the models drawn up by scholars to try to reform customs:

Recently we ordered the officials to revise the rituals and distribute them to the realm, with regulations for cappings, weddings, funerals, and sacrifices. Vulgar Confucians are stuck in the past; they can construct a text but do not know how to have it reach and affect customs. The houses lined up in the lanes, the poor people in huts do not have reception rooms or side alcoves, or steps for ascending or descending from their main rooms. The students of ritual instruct them, saying they should prepare everything [according to the *New Forms*]. If they deviate slightly, it is a violation of the law. This has reached the point where shaman diviners and wedding go-betweens do not dare do anything, so that no decisions can be made concerning cappings, weddings, funerals, or ancestral rites. We established rituals out of a desire to bring order to the people, but now we are harming the basis of the people.[84]

The Kaifeng government was ordered to stop distributing the digest of the *New Forms* and to withdraw the ritual students and other officials who had been assigned to promulgating its content.[85] The government had learned the cost of concerted efforts to change people's ritual behavior.

The government in Sung times did not try to control the writing of manuals for either geomancy or Confucian family rituals. Books on geomancy that deviated from the imperial ones were not suppressed, and even fully orthodox Confucian scholars wrote guides to family rituals that deviated from the rules in the government-sponsored manuals in significant ways.[86] All the government did was offer its own manuals to compete with other ones available.

Use of the Power of Example

In Confucian moral and political theory, the best way to govern is through example, especially the example of the Son of Heaven himself. What example did the court provide? Classical Confucian mourning practices were treated with great seriousness, and each emperor's behavior in situations of mourning was carefully scrutinized by officials and subject to debate and criticism.[87] Nevertheless, imperial actions did not undermine belief in geomancy or the utility of Buddhist services to transfer merit. While emperors were never cremated and their burials were never delayed for decades, their funeral arrangements were not purely Confucian. Taoist ceremonial had long been used to enhance the power of the throne,[88] and geomancy seems to have been used in a comparable way.

Imperial burials were regularly arranged through consultation with geomancers or at least geomantic books.[89] For instance, in 1004 officials of the Bureau of Astronomy chose geomancers (*yin-yang chia*) to select the site of the tomb for the empress dowager according to the various books on burial. The geomancers chosen decided that the burial should be delayed two years because the current year was ill-omened. Their decision evoked considerable controversy, as a long delay would interfere with the emperor's proper performance of other rites. Also for this burial, one official used the *Classic of Earth Patterns (Ti-li ching)* by the T'ang monk I-hsing to explain how the tomb should be located with respect to a prior empress' tomb.[90] In 1022 the officials in charge of Chen-tsung's tomb memorialized concerning the appropriate depth of burial, citing the conflicting figures given in Yu-wu's and I-hsing's manuals.[91] In 1067 a burial site for Ying-tsung was reported to be acceptable according to books on yin-yang and in particular the theories of surname sounds.[92] In 1142, when a site had to be selected for burial of the body of Hui-tsung, returned by the Jurchens, the surname of the imperial family was again taken into account and the site chosen was declared to be one in which "the hills and ridges are in accord with the dynasty's sound [i.e., its surname], the wind and water are appropriate with respect to earth patterns, so the site will be of advantage for a myriad generations."[93] In 1159 when a site for burying an empress was under discussion, an official analyzed three possible sites in terms of their geomantic properties: their advantage according to the imperial surname, their position with regard to roads and waterways, the likelihood of water entering the tomb, and inauspicious spirits *(hsiung-shen)*. In the end he recommended one that was not advantageous according to the imperial surname but was otherwise beneficial.[94] Similar geomantic considerations were taken into account in setting up the graveyards for imperial princes and their wives.[95]

In the case of Buddhist services, imperial example was much more limited. Buddhist services to aid the rebirth of emperors and empresses took second place to the main Confucian ceremonies (compressed into twenty-seven days when the chief mourner was the emperor) and seem most commonly to have been performed on death-date anniversaries. Evidence comes not from regulations or the *New Forms,* but from the prayers court officials had to compose for these occasions. For instance, Wang An-shih preserved the prayer for a Buddhist ceremony held on the first day of the tenth month at the tomb of Emperor Jen-tsung (d. 1063), another for a Land and Water ceremony held on the fifteenth of the seventh month for Ying-tsung (d. 1067), and another for the death-day anniversary of an imperial consort who had died in 1036.[96] Su Shih (1036–1101) preserved eighteen prayers for "transferring merit" that he wrote for imperial use on a variety of occasions. He also wrote three prayers for Land and Water ceremonies held for the recently deceased emperor Shen-tsung (d. 1085), another for a Buddhist ceremony coinciding with the Confucian rites scheduled two years after his death, and another for a ceremony to be held in a Buddhist shrine.[97] Buddhist services might also be performed near the tombs; Ssu-ma Kuang in 1064 objected to establishing a Buddhist shrine with a resident monk near the newly completed tomb of Jen-tsung.[98]

The issue of Buddhist services was raised by Emperor Hui-tsung in 1110 when scholars were debating the provisions to be included in the *New Forms*. The emperor noted that the Yü-lan-p'en festival in the seventh month was popular among both gentlemen and commoners, who thought that by making offerings to monks they were helping the dead move out of purgatory toward rebirth in Heaven.[99] Although he did not object to ordinary people performing these rites, he questioned the current practice of making this offering for the sake of imperial ancestors. Even if the Buddhist texts provided a source for this custom, he wanted to know if there was any basis for it in the Confucian classics. He also reported that on the death-day anniversaries of emperors and empresses Buddhist Land and Water ceremonies were held, with monks making the entreaty, "Do not violate the Buddha's commands." Was it right to have a foreign Buddha giving orders to a Chinese emperor? he asked. The officials who responded to his questions explained the Buddhist origins of these customs and concurred that they should not be performed in the palace.[100] Nevertheless, one continues to find in Southern Sung scholars' collected works the prayers they composed for Buddhist services for emperors and empresses.[101]

The court also tacitly accepted the role of Buddhists through its arrangements for the burial of lower-ranking imperial consorts. Empresses were given funerals much like emperors, laid out in palace buildings according to Confucian ritual classics until the coffin was taken away for burial. The deaths of lesser consorts, however, were not important enough to cause such disruption to palace routine. The mother of Jen-tsung (1023–1063), not favored by the empress dowager then powerful, had a funeral "outside," as befitted a palace lady when she died in 1032. Her body was then buried in the northwest corner of the Vast Blessing Ch'an Monastery. When Jen-tsung learned she was his true mother, he arranged to have her coffin moved.[102]

The government also provided models for emulation through the provisions it made for leading officials. The *New Forms* devoted three chapters to the funeral rites to be performed by ranked officials based on classically derived forms. Nevertheless, neither Buddhist services nor geomancy was uniformly discouraged. Higher-ranking officials were given the privilege of establishing Buddhist shrines at the sites of their ancestors' graves to perform services for their souls.[103] Among the objects the state provided when it supplied the burials of important officials were mock deeds, objects with strong ties to geomancy.[104]

Finally, the government provided an example through its charitable graveyards. By assigning the management of these graveyards and the task of making offerings to those buried there to Buddhist monasteries, the government was confirming the special connection between the Buddhist clergy and the handling of the dead.

CONCLUSION

The three practices Chao Hsi-fen renounced remained common through the rest of imperial China's history. This was true not only of practices largely ignored by the government, like avoiding the *sha*, but also of Buddhist services and geomancy.[105] Even when the state discouraged a practice, it did not do so consistently. Through its laws, its administrative apparatus, its publication programs, and the example of the throne, the Sung state unintentionally conveyed several conflicting messages, outlawing particular practices but not enforcing the laws, performing both Buddhist and Confucian ceremonies for the dead, and making full use of geomancy while outlawing the excesses geomancy often caused.

The half-heartedness of Sung official policies toward funerary practices can be explained in terms of political and cultural realities. The bureaucracy was compartmentalized, so that those writing statutes were not those writing prayers. Not all officials were singleminded Confucians. As Boltz shows in her chapter in this volume, in their personal lives and local service, officials who had passed the *chin-shih* examination might draw on diverse sets of ideas and techniques to deal with specific challenges. Even committed Confucians who saw the government's policies as contradictory might judge these contradictions to be politically necessary. To please diverse political constituencies it could make sense to incorporate something for everyone: ritual guides for Confucians, geomancy guides for geomancers, and Buddhist services for imperial mothers and other believers.

What were the effects of contradictory policies? Did state actions, no matter how contradictory they might seem to us, nevertheless contribute in a significant way to the standardization of funeral practices, as Watson argued in *Death Rituals in Late Imperial and Modern China*? Clearly state actions did not impose uniformity in anything resembling a legalistic fashion. Publishing *New Forms* did not lead officials or commoners to conform to its provisions or to refrain from practices not listed in it. Nor did laws against delaying burials do much to discourage storing coffins. The Chinese state was not nearly as intrusive as the medieval Catholic church. It did not certify the experts who officiated at funerals nor did it discipline its subjects when they failed to conform to the standards it promulgated.

Nevertheless, I would like to argue that the Sung state's response to popular funeral practices played a significant role in shaping the historical evolution of these practices. It did so not by standardizing them, nor by altering what people were in fact doing, but by influencing how they thought about their actions. State policies indirectly and unintentionally confirmed the validity and efficacy of the mixed set of practices that had become conventional. Although the state did not effectively promote a single, coherent model of what people should do, it did promote, in a fragmented, unintended way, the unorganized, unsynthesized set of practices that was coming to constitute Chinese funerary practice. In other words, imperial example showed how to cope with inconsistency. Emperors performed both Confucian and Buddhist service for the dead; they located graves by geomancy while chiding imperial kinsmen for delaying burial; they issued Confucian and geomantic manuals containing quite different versions of the ceremonies to be performed at burials. Surely if emperors could compartmentalize their activities in these ways, others with lesser claims to moral or political centrality could do so as well.

NOTES

1. *Ch'ui-chien lu* (in *Sung-jen tsa-chi pa chung* [Taipei: Shih-chieh shu-chü, 1963]), 4.124–126. Almost nothing is known of Chao Hsi-fen other than that he was a member of the imperial clan. Nor is much known of Yü Wen-pao other than what can be inferred from the essays in his book, which reveal that he shared many of the views that had been articulated by eleventh-century Neo-Confucians.

2. See, for instance, Rolf A. Stein, "Religious Taoism and Popular Religion from the Second to Seventh Centuries," in Holmes Welch and Anna Seidel, eds., *Facets of Taoism: Essays in Chinese Religion* (New Haven: Yale University Press, 1979), pp. 53–81; Stanley Weinstein, *Buddhism under the T'ang* (New York: Cambridge University Press, 1987); Valerie Hansen, *Changing Gods in Medieval China, 1127–1276* (Princeton: Princeton University Press, 1990); David Johnson, "The City-God Cults in T'ang and Sung China," *HJAS* 45.2 (1985): 365–457; Chikusa Masaaki, *Chūgoku bukkyō shakaishi kenkyū* (Tokyo: Dōhō, 1982); James L. Watson, "Standardizing the Gods: The Promotion of T'ien Hou ('Empress of Heaven') along the South China Coast, 960–1960," in David Johnson, Andrew J. Nathan, and Evelyn S. Rawski, eds., *Popular Culture in Late Imperial China* (Berkeley: University of California Press, 1985), pp. 292–324; C. K. Yang, *Religion in Chinese Society: A Study of Contemporary Social Functions of Religions and Some of Their Historical Factors* (Berkeley: University of California Press, 1961), esp. 180–217; Emily Martin Ahern, *Chinese Ritual and Politics* (Cambridge: Cambridge University Press, 1981). See also the chapters in this volume by Hansen and Boltz. There are also many studies of the state cults loosely associated with Confucianism. See Lester James Bilsky, *The State Religion of Ancient China* (Taipei: Orient Cultural Service, 1975); Howard J. Wechsler, *Offerings of Jade and Silk: Ritual and Symbol in the Legitimation of the*

T'ang Dynasty (New Haven: Yale University Press, 1985); Romeyn Taylor, "Official and Popular Religion and the Political Organization of Chinese Society," in Kwang-Ching Liu, ed., *Orthodoxy in Late Imperial China* (Berkeley: University of California Press, 1990), pp. 126–157; Stephan Feuchtwang, "School-Temple and City God," in G. William Skinner, ed., *The City in Late Imperial China* (Stanford: Stanford University Press, 1977), pp. 581–608; and A. R. Zito, "City Gods, Filiality, and Hegemony in Late Imperial China," *Modern China* 13 (1987): 333–371.

3. On the ritual handling of death, see Bronislaw Malinowski, *Magic, Science and Religion* (Garden City, NY: Doubleday, 1954), esp. pp. 47–53; Arnold van Gennep, *The Rites of Passage* (Chicago: The University of Chicago Press, 1960), esp. pp. 146–165; Robert Hertz, "A Contribution to the Study of the Collective Representation of Death," in Rodney and Claudia Needham, trans., *Death and the Right Hand* (Glencoe: The Free Press, 1960); Richard Huntington and Peter Metcalf, *Celebrations of Death: The Anthropology of Mortuary Ritual* (Cambridge: Cambridge University Press, 1979); and Maurice Bloch and Jonathan Parry, eds., *Death and the Regeneration of Life* (Cambridge: Cambridge University Press, 1982). For Chinese funerals, see J. J. M. de Groot, *The Religious System of China* (Leiden: E. J. Brill, 1892–1910); and James L. Watson and Evelyn S. Rawski, eds., *Death Ritual in Late Imperial and Modern China* (Berkeley: University of California Press, 1988).

4. "The Structure of Chinese Funerary Rites: Elementary Forms, Ritual Sequence, and the Primacy of Performance," in Watson and Rawski, *Death Ritual in Late Imperial and Modern China*, pp. 10–11, 17–18.

5. Wang Li-ch'i, ed., *Yen-shih chia-hsün chi-chieh* (Hong Kong: Ming-wen, 1982), 2.103. Cf. Teng Ssu-yü, trans., *Family Instructions for the Yen Clan* (Leiden: E. J. Brill, 1968), p. 36.

6. *ICC, I-chih,* 19.352. This text gives *fang* instead of *sha* but notes that another edition gives *sha,* which is probably correct.

7. See, for example, *TPKC* 366.2905; Lien Hsüan, *Ch'ing-tsun lu* (Pi-chi hsiao-shuo ta-kuan 5 edition), pp. 1612–1613; *ICC, I-chih,* 19.352. See also Sawada Mizuho, *Chūgoku no minkan shinkō* (Tokyo: Kōsekusha, 1982), pp. 406–450.

8. This book is reported in a Sung bibliography, Ch'en Chen-sun's *Chih-chai shu-lu chieh-t'i* (*TSCC* edition), 12.357, to be full of popular superstitions and most likely not actually by Lü Ts'ai, though he had in fact written a book of that title with a section on burials. On Lü Ts'ai, see Carol Morgan, "T'ang Geomancy: The Wu-hsing ('Five Names') Theory and Its Legacy," *T'ang Studies* 8–9 (1990–1991): 45–76.

9. *Ch'ui-chien lu* 4.124.

10. *Ti-li hsin-shu* (Yüan fifteen-*chüan* edition), *chüan* 15; *Ta Han yüan-ling mi-tsang ching* (Yung-lo ta-tien edition), *chüan* 8199.31b.

11. Ch'u Yung, *Ch'ü-i shuo* (Pai-pu ts'ung-shu chi-ch'eng edition), 19b–20a. *Sha* did not derive from Buddhist cosmology, but sometimes Buddhist monks seem to have participated in this tradition. In one anecdote a monk was described as an expert in the theory of the eight *sha* (Chou Mi, *Ch'i-tung yeh-yü* [Chung-hua shu-chü], 16.300–301).

12. *Ch'ui-chien lu* 4.124.

13. Hung Mai, in the anecdote cited above, provided an alternative explanation for what was taken as the action of *sha* but in general was quite willing to accept the possibility that ghosts could affect human affairs.

14. K'ang Yü-chih, *Tso-meng lu* (Pi-chi hsiao-shuo ta-kuan 6 edition), 8b–9a, for example, discusses as a curiosity the custom in the north of having go-betweens who specialized in handling the marriages of those who had reached marriageable age but had died before marriage, the ceremonies combining elements of standard weddings, funerals, and ancestral rites.

15. See Stephen F. Teiser, " 'Having Once Died and Returned to Life': Representations of Hell in Medieval China," *HJAS* 48.2 (1988): 433–644, and his chapter in this volume.

16. Meng Yüan-lao, *Tung-ching meng-hua lu wai ssu-chung* (Shanghai: Chung-hua shu-chü, 1962), 4.26; Wu Tzu-mu, *Meng-liang lu* (in *Tung-ching meng-hua lu wai ssu-chung*), 19.302.

17. Miriam Levering, "Ta-hui and Lay Buddhists: Ch'an Sermons on Death," in David W. Chappell, ed., *Buddhist and Taoist Practice in Medieval Chinese Society: Buddhist and Taoist Studies II,* Asian Studies at Hawaii, no. 34 (Honolulu: University of Hawaii Press, 1987), pp. 181–206.

18. The Land and Water ceremony was commonly performed in the Sung either for the recently deceased or for ghosts that had not settled satisfactorily. It frequently figures in *I-chien chih;* see, for instance, *ICC, Ping-chih,* 7.422–423, 11.457, 11.461, 12.465, 15.497. Taoist clergy also could perform funeral services, instead of or in addition to Buddhist services, though in Sung times such services do not seem to have been as common as Buddhist ones. In the *I-chien chih,* for instance, when an official's wife died, his son-in-law invited a Tung-chen Taoist master to perform a Nine Shades ceremony on the fourth seven. Because the service was so impressive, the official asked the same master to return on the fifth seven to perform a Yellow Registers ceremony (*ICC, Ping-chih,* 10.448). As this account indicates, Taoist services were also performed on the seven sevens. Lu Yu speculated that Taoists had invented these rites to compete with the Buddhists in earning money by offering funeral services (*Fang-weng chia-hsün* [*TSCC* edition], p. 2). He also reported that the "Yellow hats" (Taoist priests) said they could send souls to Heaven, could issue amnesties in the place of Heaven, and could perform purification rites referred to as "salvation through refinement." On Taoist rites in the Sung, see Judith Boltz, "Opening the Gates of Purgatory: A Twelfth-Century Taoist Meditation Technique for the Salvation of Lost Souls," in Michel Strickmann, ed., *Tantric and Taoist Studies in Honour of R. A. Stein,* vol. 2: *Mélanges chinois et bouddhiques* 21 (1983): 487–511. For Buddhist and Taoist funeral practices in general, see Matsumoto Koichi, "Sorei, sairei ni miru Sōdai shūkyōshi no ichi keikō," in *Sōdai no shakai to bunka* (Tokyo: Kyūko, 1983), pp. 169–194.

19. *Ch'ui-chien lu* 4.124. Ssu-ma Kuang's original text is in *Ssu-ma shih shu-i* (*TSCC* edition), 5.54–55. Yü Wen-pao miscopied the "Tan" in Li Tan as "Chou." Li Tan was an official in the T'ang. Ssu-ma Kuang indicated that this passage was from a letter Li Tan wrote to his younger sister. For Ssu-ma Kuang's views on contemporary customs, see Patricia Buckley Ebrey, *Confucianism and Family Rituals in Imperial China: A Social History of Writing about Rites* (Princeton: Princeton University Press, 1991), pp. 49–50, 55–56, 60–62, 75–76, and 89–97.

20. Ssu-ma Kuang was ignorant of or did not choose to discuss the Buddhist explanation for these practices in terms of transferring merit and increasing the value of offerings made to the dead by giving them to the sangha rather than directly to the dead person. On these ideas, see Stephen F. Teiser, *The Ghost Festival in Medieval China* (Princeton: Princeton University Press, 1988), pp. 196–213.

21. *Fang-weng chia-hsün*, p. 2.

22. See James Legge, trans., *Li Chi, Book of Rites* (New Hyde Park: University Books 1967, reprint of 1885 edition), 1:103.

23. From *Erh-Ch'eng chi* (Peking: Chung-hua shu-chü edition, 1981), *i-shu* 10.114.

24. Lu Yu, *Fang-weng chia-hsün*, p. 2.

25. *Ch'ui-chien lu* 4.125.

26. Ibid.

27. *Fang-weng chia-hsün*, p. 2.

28. *Ch'ui-chien lu* 4.125

29. *ICC, San-chih-jen,* 6.1512–1513, includes the following example of laymen organizing to perform less expensive services:

> Young men who are a little clever in Po-yang like to form associations to chant sūtras and make confessions. To perform Buddhist services they organize ten men into a unit. If any of them has a wedding, funeral, or special need, they go together to perform the ceremony. They fast, chant Sanskrit, strike the bell, and hit the drum, from the beginning of the night until the fourth drum, exactly like a Buddhist ritual. They all endeavor to be accurate and sincere, and there are no expenses for contributions or gifts [as there are to monks]. They will also go to those who are not members of their unit if the latter send a letter of invitation. In this region followers are very numerous and, as they often wear white robes, they are called the "white clothes associations." The city resident Chiang Erh, a commoner, is their leader. He normally makes his living by manufacturing and selling incense.

30. Wang Yung, *Yen-i i-mou lu* (Peking: Chung-hua shu-chü, 1981), 3.24; Lu Yu, *Fang-weng chia-hsün*, p. 3.

31. See Patricia Ebrey, "Cremation in Sung China," *American Historical Review* 95.2 (1990): 406–428.

32. In Sung sources, geomancers were called "burial masters" *(tsang-shih),* "yin-yang masters" *(yin-yang chia),* "experts" *(shu-chia),* and related terms, and their science "wind and water" *(feng-shui),* "earth patterns" *(ti-li),* or "carriage and cover" *(k'an-yü).*

33. *CTS* 79.2719–2727; see also Morgan, "T'ang Geomancy."

34. These activities are all discussed in two geomantic manuals of Sung or slightly later date, the imperially sponsored *New Book of Earth Patterns (Ti-li hsin-shu)* and the *Secret Burial Classic (Mi-tsang ching),* both of which are discussed below.

35. *Ch'ui-chien lu* 4.125–126, paraphrased from *Ssu-ma shih shu-i* 7.75.

36. *Ssu-ma shih shu-i* 7.75; cf. *Ssu-ma Wen-cheng kung ch'uan-chia chi* (Kuo-hsüeh chi-pen ts'ung-shu edition), 27.381.

37. On modern theories, see Stephan D. R. Feuchtwang, *An Anthropological Analysis of Chinese Geomancy* (Vientiane: Vithagna, 1974); Andrew L.

March, "An Appreciation of Chinese Geomancy," *JAS* 27.2 (1968): 253–267; Steven J. Bennett, "Patterns of the Sky and Earth: A Chinese Science of Applied Cosmology," *Chinese Science* 3 (1978): 1–26; de Groot, *The Religious System of China* 3.936–975; and Robert P. Weller, *Unities and Diversities in Chinese Religion* (Seattle: University of Washington Press, 1987), pp. 173–184.

38. *CTS* 79.2720–2721. Fragments of geomantic texts using this framework that have survived at Tun-huang are analyzed in Morgan, "T'ang Geomancy."

39. These sounds have connections to rhymes and tones, but their correspondences are not exact. The *Secret Burial Classic* claimed that they were based on the position of the tongue. In pronouncing the *shang* note the tongue was extended, in the *chih* it was against the teeth, in the *chüeh* it was contracted, and so on, so that some sounds were throat sounds, others teeth or lip sounds, and so on (*Mi-tsang ching,* pp. 3b–4a). Geomantic manuals that have survived from Tun-huang, the Northern Sung *New Book of Earth Patterns,* and the slightly later *Secret Burial Classic* all give formulas for this theory, such as "surnames that correspond to *chüeh* ought to use a *ping* site in a *ken* grave."

40. Another component of Northern Sung geomantic theories that is repeatedly referred to in the *New Book of Earth Patterns* is a tie between burial location and the way the dead person is treated by the gods of the underworld. It was important for there to be a suitable spirit (god) path for the *kung-ts'ao* to communicate between Hao-li and the Yellow Springs (*Ti-li hsin-shu, chüan* 12). Hao-li was a place on Mt. T'ai where the dead were judged; the Yellow Springs was a general term of ancient origin for the destination of the dead. This theory of paths seems to have been especially associated with Sun Chi-yung, who lived in the T'ang or earlier and whose book linked burials to long lists of gods, with burial in certain sites by people of certain surnames disturbing specific gods (*Ti-li hsin-shu, chüan* 15). I have not found any criticisms of this strand of geomantic thought.

41. Books with this title were often attributed to Yang Yün-sung, of the tenth century, recognized in later periods as one of the founders of a major school of geomancy.

42. I-hsing (683–727) was an eminent monk of the T'ang, noted especially for his studies of the calendar. See *CTS* 191.5111–5113. Several geomantic manuals were attributed to him, such as the *Classic of Earth Patterns (Ti-li ching)* in twelve *chüan* mentioned in *SS* 206.5253. His mathematical contributions are discussed by Christopher Cullen, "An Eighth-Century Chinese Table of Tangents," *Chinese Science* 5 (1982): 1–34. A Buddhist astrological work often attributed to I-hsing is discussed in Raoul Birnbaum, "Seeking Longevity in Chinese Buddhism: Long Life Deities and Their Symbolism," *Journal of Chinese Religion* 13–14 (1985–1986): 143–176, esp. pp. 158–160.

43. *Chang Tsai chi* (Peking: Chung-hua shu-chü edition), p. 299.

44. *Mi-tsang ching* 1b–2a.

45. *Ho-lin yü-lu, Ping* 6.344–345. See also Chen Te-hsiu, *Hsi-shan tu-shu chi (SKCS* edition) 11.58a–b. Competition among brothers seems often to have occurred in modern times.

46. *Ti-li hsin-shu* 12.

47. *Ssu-ma shih shu-i* 7.75.

48. *ICC* records many cases of people of middling means storing coffins in

temples, but even high officials made use of temples in this way. For instance, Sung Ch'i, in *Ching-wen chi* (*TSCC* edition), 60.815, reports that, after his mother died in 1032, the high official Chang Te-hsiang (978–1048), hoping to get the chance to bring her coffin back to be buried along side his father's coffin in Fukien, had it placed in a temple in the capital. After five years he decided instead to bury her near the capital.

49. *Ho-lin yü-lu*, *Ping* 6.344.

50. *Hou-ts'un hsien-sheng ta-ch'üan chi* (*SPTK* edition), 192.9b.

51. *Ti-li hsin-shu* 15. The *Secret Burial Classic* provided brief instructions on how to open a grave and remove the bones for burial elsewhere. The bones should be wiped clean, starting with the head, then placed in a wooden box, the kind of wood depending on the five sound categories, and the box was then to be packed with cotton padding (*Mi-tsang ching* 13a).

52. Hsü P'ing-fang, "T'ang-Sung mu-tsang-chung ti 'Ming-ch'i shen-sha,' yü 'mu-i' chih-tu—tu 'Ta-Han yüan-ling mi-tsang ching' cha-chi," *K'ao-ku* 1963.2: 100. Archaeological evidence does not indicate whether reburial was for geomantic or other, more widely accepted reasons such as the desire to return remains to an ancestral graveyard.

53. *Erh-Ch'eng chi*, *Wen-chi* 10.623.

54. *Chu Wen-kung wen-chi* (*SPTK* edition), 15.34a–b. For more details on Chu Hsi's attitudes and this incident, see my "Neo-Confucian Attitudes Toward Geomancy," draft chapter for a festschrift for Wing-tsit Chan and Wm. Theodore de Bary.

55. For example, Chen Te-hsiu, *Hsi-shan tu-shu chi* 11.58a.

56. Yeh Shao-weng (ca. 1175–1230) reported that Chu Hsi had come to "clearly understand the numbers of heaven and earth, master musical theory, and incorporate knowledge from books on yin-yang and geomancy *(feng-shui)*" from his friend Ts'ai Yüan-ting (*Ssu-ch'ao wen-chien-lu* [*TSCC* edition], *I-chi*, p. 38). See also Ts'ai's biography in *SS* 434.12875–12876.

57. For some examples, see Wang Ming-ch'ing, *Hui-chu lu* (*TSCC* edition), *Hou-lu* 11.667–668; Yu Chi, *Wan-liu ch'i-pien chiu-hua* (*TSCC* edition), p. 6. Some Buddhists, however, also drew a line between themselves and geomancy. A Chinese sūtra found at Tun-huang argued that monks should be without fears or taboos and applied this principle to grave geomancy. The Buddha was asked why people do not bury until they have checked to find an auspicious day and an auspicious site, and why, having taken such precautions, they still sometimes ended up poor, their descent lines broken. He replied that in reality all years were good years, and there was no need to "inquire about east, west, south, or north." To obtain blessings, one should instead recite this sūtra during the burial ceremonies. See Daniel L. Overmyer, "Buddhism in the Trenches: Attitudes Toward Popular Religion in Indigenous Scriptures from Tun-huang," *HJAS* 50 (1990): 197–222.

58. *Ti-li hsin-shu* 15; *Mi-tsang ching* 31b.

59. Chapter 3 of Chu Hsi's collected conversations (*Chu-tzu yü-lei* [Chung-hua shu-chü, 1986]) is devoted to analyzing ghosts and spirits in terms of positive and negative cosmological forces.

60. See, for example, Su Shih, *Su Shih wen-chi* (Peking; Chung-hua shu-chü, 1986), 62.1909–1935; *Hou-ts'un hsien-sheng ta-ch'üan chi*, *chüan* 171; Ch'en

Chu, *Pen-t'ang chi* (*SKCS* edition), 93.10b–11b; Hung Kua, *P'an-chou wen-chi* (*SKCS* edition), 70.11b–16b; Chou Pi-ta, *Wen-chung chi* (*SKCS* edition), *chüan* 37. In most of these cases, the authors also preserved prayers or other documents for Taoist and more strictly Confucian ancestral rites as well.

61. *Fang-weng chia-hsün*, p. 2.

62. See, for instance, Maurice Freedman, "On the Sociological Study of Chinese Religion," in Arthur P. Wolf, ed., *Religion and Ritual in Chinese Society* (Stanford: Stanford University Press, 1974), pp. 19–42; Weller, *Unities and Diversities;* Teiser, *Ghost Festival in Medieval China.*

63. On this process, see Judith A. Berling, *The Syncretic Religion of Lin Chao-an* (New York: Columbia University Press, 1980), especially pp. 1–61.

64. "Standardizing the Gods: The Promotion of T'ien Hou ('Empress of Heaven') Along the South China Coast, 960–1960," in David Johnson, Andrew J. Nathan, and Evelyn S. Rawski, eds., *Popular Culture in Late Imperial China* (Berkeley: University of California Press, 1985), pp. 292–324.

65. Taylor, "Official and Popular Religion," quote on p. 128.

66. On these policies, see Paul J. Smith, "State Power and Economic Activism During the New Policies," in Robert P. Hymes and Conrad Schirokauer, eds., *Ordering the World: Approaches to State and Society in Sung Dynasty China* (Berkeley: University of California Press, forthcoming).

67. Li T'ao, *Hsü tzu-chih t'ung-chien ch'ang-pien* (Chung-hua shu-chü edition), 3.65.

68. Tou I et al., *Sung-hsing t'ung* (Taipei: Wen-hai, 1964; rpt. of 1918 edition), 18.8a–9a.

69. *SS* 125.2919.

70. *SS* 125.2917; Wang Yung, *Yen-i i-mou lu* 3.24.

71. *SS* 125.2917–2918.

72. *Sung hsing-t'ung* 1.11a.

73. *Ch'ing-yüan t'iao-fa shih-lei* (Taipei: Hsin-wen-feng reprint of Seikadō manuscript copy, 1976), 77.24a (p. 557). What constituted "good reason" is not specified. It was common when one's mother died before one's father to wait until after he died to arrange a major funeral, burying both together. Possibly such cases could also be excused on the grounds that the woman was still someone's wife, and the law said nothing about neglecting the burial of wives or children.

74. *Sung ta-chao-ling chi* (Peking: Chung-hua shu-chü, 1962), 198.731.

75. *SS* 124.2912.

76. See my "Cremation in Sung China."

77. See "Ssu-ch'uan kuan-ch'ü-nien T'ang-Sung-Ming mu ch'ing-li chien-pao," *K'ao-ku t'ung-hsün* 1956.5: 31–38; Ho Cheng-huang, "Sung wu-ming shih mu-chuan," *Wen-wu* 1966.1: 53–54; "Ho-nan Nan-yang fa-hsien Sung-mu," *K'ao-ku* 1966.1: 54; and Sung Ts'ai-i and Yü Sung, "T'an Ho-nan Nan-hua hsien fa-hsien Pei-Sung ti lou-tse yüan," *Ho-nan ta-hsüeh hsüeh-pao* 1986.4: 53–58.

78. *Ch'ing-yüan t'iao-fa shih-lei* 7.28a (p. 559).

79. *Ti-li hsin-shu*, preface. *SS* 206.5250 lists this book as being by Shih Hsü (935–1010), in 455 *chüan.*

80. *Ti-li hsin-shu*, preface.

81. On the *K'ai-yüan li*, see David McMullen, "Bureaucrats and Cosmology:

The Ritual Code of T'ang China," in David Cannadine and Simon Price, eds., *Rituals of Royalty: Power and Ceremonial in Traditional Societies* (Cambridge: Cambridge University Press, 1987), pp. 181–236.

82. *Cheng-ho wu-li hsin-i (SKCS* edition), *Chüan-shou* 6a.

83. *SS* 98.2423.

84. *Sung ta-chao-ling chi* 148.548.

85. The government did not abandon all interest in bringing people to perform funerals and other family rituals according to these forms. Not only did local officials take initiative in these regards, but the government also sponsored further efforts. During the Shao-hsi period (1190–1194) a ritual official recommended that the sections of the *New Forms* that concerned life-cycle rites of officials and commoners be reissued, with modification based on the privately written ritual manuals by Ssu-ma Kuang and Kao K'ang, and distributed to prefectures and counties throughout the country. This book, in fifteen chapters, was extant in the early thirteenth century (*SS* 430.12791; *Chih-chai shu-lu chieh-t'i* 6.179). See also Chu Hsi's efforts to get a revised version of the *New Forms* issued for use by local magistrates, discussed in Ebrey, *Confucianism and Family Rituals,* p. 117.

86. See my "Education Through Ritual: Efforts to Formulate Family Rituals During the Sung Period," in John W. Chaffee and Wm. Theodore de Bary, eds., *Neo-Confucian Education: The Formative Stage* (Berkeley: University of California Press, 1989), pp. 277–306.

87. See, for instance, Carney T. Fisher, "The Ritual Dispute of Sung Ying-tsung," *Papers on Far Eastern History* 36 (1987): 109–138. For imperial funeral practices in later periods, see Evelyn S. Rawski, "The Imperial Way of Death: Ming and Ch'ing Emperors and Death Ritual," in Watson and Rawski, eds., *Death Ritual in Late Imperial and Modern China,* pp. 228–253.

88. See John Lagerwey, *Taoist Ritual in Chinese Society and History* (New York: Macmillan, 1987), pp. 253–264.

89. For a T'ang precedent, see Wang P'u, *T'ang hui-yao* (Taipei: Shih-chieh shu-chü, 1968), 20.396–397.

90. *SHY, Li,* 31.30a–35a; 37.50a–55a.

91. *SHY, Li,* 29.23a –24b.

92. *SHY, Li,* 37.12b.

93. *SHY, Li,* 37.18b–19a.

94. *SHY, Li,* 37.70b–71a. See also discussions in 1194, 1200, and 1224, in *SHY, Li,* 37.25a–27a.

95. *SHY, Li,* 39.1a–12a.

96. *Wang Lin-ch'uan chi* (Taipei: Shih-chieh shu-chü, 1966), 47.270.

97. *Su Shih wen-chi* 44.1275–1284.

98. *Ssu-ma Wen-cheng kung ch'uan-chia chi* 30.412–413.

99. On these ceremonies, see Teiser, *The Ghost Festival in Medieval China,* chapter 3.

100. *Cheng-ho wu-li hsin-i, Chüan-shou,* 31b–34a. Hui-tsung generally favored Taoism over Buddhism, which may have contributed to his efforts to remove Buddhist ceremonies from palace routine. On sponsorship of Taoism in this period, see Michel Strickmann, "The Longest Taoist Scripture," *History of Religions* 17 (1978): 331–354.

101. See, for example, Liu K'o-chuang, *Hou-ts'un hsien-sheng ta-ch'üan chi* 171.9b–13a.

102. *SS* 242.8616–8617; *SHY, Li,* 32.15a–21a. See also *Shao-shih wen-chien lu* (Peking: Chung-hua shu-chü edition), 8.76–77.

103. On this practice , see Chikusa Masaaki, "Sōdai funji kō," *Tōyō gakuhō* 61.1, 2 (1978): 35–66.

104. *SS* 124.2910; Ch'en Po-ch'üan, "Chiang-hsi ch'u-t'u ti-ch'üan tsung-shu," *K'ao-ku* 1987.3: 223–231, gives several examples of mock deeds from official graves.

105. The custom of avoiding *sha* is much more fully documented for modern times than for the Sung. See de Groot, *Religious System* 5.469–477; Hsü Ch'ien-hsüeh, *Tu-li t'ung-k'ao* (*SKCS* edition), 116.37a–39a; and especially Sawada, *Chūgoku no minkan shinkō*, pp. 406–450. On other funerary practices, see de Groot, *Religious System*, passim, and Watson and Rawski, eds., *Death Rituals in Late Imperial and Modern China*.

GLOSSARY

Chang Te-hsiang　章得象
Chang Tsai　張載
Chang Tsai chi　張載集
Chao Hsi-fen　趙希弁
Chen Te-hsiu　真德秀
Ch'en　陳
Ch'en Chen-sun　陳振孫
Ch'en Chu　陳著
Cheng　鄭
Cheng-ho wu-li hsin-i　政和五禮新儀
Ch'eng I　程頤
Ch'i　氣
Ch'i-tung yeh-yü　齊東野語
Ch'ien-k'un pao-tien　乾坤寶典
chih　徵
chih-chai shu-lu chieh-t'i　直齋書錄解題
chin-shih　進士
Ching-wen chi　景文集
Ch'ing-tsun lu　清尊錄
Ch'ing-yüan t'iao-fa shih-lei　慶元條法事類
chou　舟
Chou Mi　周密
Chou Pi-ta　周必大
Chu Hsi　朱熹
Chu Tzu yü-lei　朱子語類
Chu Wen-kung wen-chi　朱文公文集
Ch'u Yung　儲泳

Ch'ü-i shuo　祛疑説
chüeh　角
Ch'ui-chien lu　吹劍錄
Erh-Ch'eng chi　二程集
fang　放
Fang-weng chia-hsün　放翁家訓
feng-shui　風水
Han Yü　韓愈
Hao-li　蒿里
Ho-lin yü-lu　鶴林玉露
Hou-ts'un hsien-sheng ta-ch'üan-chi　後村先生大全集
Hsi-shan tu-shu chih　西山讀書志
hsiung-shen　凶神
Hsü Ch'ien-hsüeh　徐乾學
Hsü Sung　徐松
Hsü tzu-chih t'ung-chien　續資治通鑑
Hsü tzu-chih t'ung-chien ch'ang-pien　續資治通鑑長編
Hui-chu lu　揮塵錄
Hung Kua　洪适
Hung Mai　洪邁
I-ching　易經
I-hsing　一行
K'ai-pao t'ung-li　開寶通禮
K'ai-yüan li　開元禮
k'an-yü　堪輿
K'ang Yü-chih　康與之
Kao K'ang　高閌

ken　庚
kung-ts'ao　功曹
Kuo P'u　郭璞
Li-chi　禮記
Li Tan　李丹
Li T'ao　李燾
Lien Hsüan　廉宣
Liu Hsü　劉昫
Liu K'o-chuang　劉克莊
Lo Ta-ching　羅大經
Lu Yu　陸游
Lü Ts'ai　呂才
mao　卯
Meng-liang lu　夢粱錄
Meng Yüan-lao　孟元老
Mi-tsang ching　秘藏經
Ou-yang Hsiu　歐陽修
P'an　潘
P'an-chou wen-chi　盤洲文集
Pen-t'ang chi　本堂集
Pi Yüan　畢沅
ping　丙
seng　僧
sha　煞
shang　商
Shao-shih wen-chien lu　邵氏聞見錄
Shih Hsü　史序
shih-ta-fu　士大夫
shu-chia　術家
ssu　巳
Ssu-ch'ao wan-chien lu　四朝聞見錄
Ssu-ma Kuang　司馬光
Ssu-ma shih shu-i　司馬氏書儀
Ssu-ma Wen-cheng kung ch'uan-chia
　chi　司馬文正公傳家集
su　俗
Su Shih　蘇軾
Su Shih wen-chi　蘇軾文集
Sun Chi-yung　孫季邕
Sung Ch'i　宋祁
Sung hsing-t'ung　宋刑統
Sung hui-yao chi-pen　宋會要輯本
Sung ta-chao-ling chi　宋大詔令集
Ta Han yüan-ling mi-tsang ching
　大漢原陵秘葬經
T'ai-ch'ang yin-ko li　太常因革禮

tan　丹
T'ang hui-yao　唐會要
ti-feng　地風
ti-li　地理
Ti-li ching　地理經
Ti-li hsin-shu　地理新書
T'o T'o　脫脫
Tou I　竇儀
Ts'ai Ching　蔡京
Ts'ai Yüan-ting　蔡元定
Tsang ching　葬經
tsang-shih　葬師
Tsang shu　葬書
Tseng Kung-ting　曾公定
Tso-meng lu　昨夢錄
Tu-li t'ung-k'ao　讀禮通考
Tung-chen　洞真
*Tung-ching meng-hua lu wai
　ssu-chung*　東京夢華錄外四種
tzu　子
Wan-liu ch'i-pien chiu-hua　萬柳溪邊
　舊話
Wang An-shih　王安石
Wang Ch'eng-yung　王承用
Wang Chu　王洙
Wang Lin-ch'uan chi　王臨川集
Wang Ming-ch'ing　王明清
Wang P'u　王溥
Wang Yung　王栐
Wen-chung chi　文忠集
Wen-kung　溫公
wu　午
wu-shih　巫史
Wu Tzu-mu　吳自牧
Yang Yün-sung　楊筠松
Yeh Shao-weng　葉紹翁
Yen Chih-t'ui　顏之推
Yen-i i-mou lu　燕翼詒謀錄
Yen-shih chia-hsün chi-chieh　顏氏家
　訓集解
yin-yang chia　陰陽家
yu　酉
Yu chi　尤玘
Yu-wu　由吾
Yü-lan-p'en　盂蘭盆
Yü Wen-pao　俞文豹

CHAPTER 7

NOT BY THE SEAL OF OFFICE ALONE:
NEW WEAPONS IN BATTLES WITH THE
SUPERNATURAL

Judith Magee Boltz

Three days after the Honorable Ou-yang had taken up his post as prefect of Ying-t'ien [Honan], he received a local shrine keeper and was told that the Shrine of the Five Gentlemen (Wu-lang miao) was exceedingly numinous. The shrine keeper advised the prefect to pay his respects. Failure to do so, he was reminded, would most certainly provoke disaster. His Honor declined.

One day, as the prefect was taking his meal, a pair of chopsticks suddenly vanished. The next day they were found resting in the hand of a clay image at the shrine. The prefect immediately ordered the shrine barred shut. As he imprinted the seal of his regency, Ou-yang declared by way of warning: "Not to be reopened until after I leave [office]." He was thereby freed from any further disturbances.

The episode above appears in the ten-chapter version of the *Po-chai pien,* an anthology of anecdotes collected by Fang Shao (1066–1141+) from both hearsay and eye-witness accounts.[1] The absence of the protagonist's full name is unlikely to have puzzled the compiler's intended audience. Even if they might have been hard-pressed to supply any evidence, Fang's contemporaries surely realized that the prefect in question was none other than the renowned literatus Ou-yang Hsiu (1007–1072). A chronicle of his life indicates that Ou-yang Hsiu did in fact serve simultaneously as prefect of Ying-t'ien and regent of the southern capital, from the seventh month of 1050 to the third month of 1052.[2] No confirmation of this incident emerges from either biographical data or any of Ou-yang's collected writings. Regardless of its questionable validity, this anecdote and others like it have much to tell us about popular perceptions of Chinese officeholders and their relation to the supernatural. Such accounts offer an invaluable complement to historiographic sources on the subject of the eternal struggle between the realms of *kuan* (officials) and *shen* (spirits).

An astounding range of variations on this theme are to be found in centuries of Chinese narrative literature. It is an anecdotal type that invites formulaic analysis in terms of a challenge and a response. In the challenge, a *kuan* is confronted by the presence of a *shen* as manifested, for example, by a tutelary deity, a medium, a ghost, or a possessing spirit. Intermediaries such as shrine keepers and devotees often alert an official to local guardians. Dreams, visions, and victims of spirit possession serve as additional channels. The response and results are as follows: (a) Appeasement of demands voiced in the name of *shen* is likely to be rewarded. (b) Resistance may incite disturbances, including injuries and fatalities, ascribed to the offended spirit, thereby provoking either delayed compliance or intensified defiance. (c) Continued resistance ultimately leads to the suppression of the *shen* or defeat of the *kuan*.

A comprehensive exposition of this type of narrative is beyond the scope of this study. The content, rather than structural features, of such stories are of interest here. The overriding value of such narratives is the window they provide on the power struggles faced by those in positions of authority. Above all, I would suggest, these stories demonstrate how personal dilemmas are played out in the supernatural arena.[3] To understand the language of that choreography is to gain a clearer perspective on the nature of conflict and its resolution in Chinese society.

How, then, are we to interpret the story of the struggle in which Prefect Ou-yang was putatively forced to engage? He had occupied his new post for but three days when the keeper of a local shrine called on him. The prefect's guest presumed to speak on behalf of the spiritual presence enshrined in the house of worship he maintained. He boasted of its unequivocal powers. Had that been the extent of the keeper's claims, the Honorable Ou-yang might well have agreed to visit the shrine. Prefects and magistrates alike traditionally found it to their advantage to support temples of proven merit within their jurisdiction. It was to these very shrines that local administrators could appeal for divine assistance in times of need.

Ou-yang's collected writings reveal that he was not in the least adverse to the idea of calling on the sacred. In one prayer beseeching an end to rain, Ou-yang declared the spirit realm responsible for overcoming natural disasters such as floods and drought—in short, anything beyond human capacity to resolve.[4] On another occasion he even evoked the aid of another tutelary spirit of Ying-t'ien to alleviate inclement weather that caused him great personal distress. As Tseng Min-hsing (1118–1175) explains, incessant rain prevented Ou-yang from transporting his mother's coffin back home to Chi-chou (Kiangsi) for burial. A village elder reportedly volunteered that the enshrinement of a former prefect was known to grant relief from problematic weather. Ou-yang thus submitted an invocation at the shrine, seeking a three-day curtailment of rain. His prayers were answered, and Ou-yang is said to have commended the spirit to the throne.[5]

To Ou-yang's way of thinking, responsible spirits were those with a record of serving the people. Why, then, would he have denied homage to the Shrine of the Five Gentlemen? In Fang Shao's version of events, Ou-yang was given sufficient reason to question the merit of this particular enshrinement. The only form of power to which the keeper alluded was the inevitability of disaster should the prefect fail to pay obeisance. Just what sort of deity did the Shrine of the Five Gentlemen represent? A substantial body of lore regarding spirits called *wu-lang* or *wu-t'ung* indicates a distinctly notorious reputation during Ou-yang's time. Accounts vary, but they are generally portrayed as grotesque incubi with the habit of preying on young women.[6] Since Fang Shao provides no clues as to the history or nature of the shrine in Ying-t'ien, it is difficult to know whether the name alone would have condemned it for his readers. There is no question that Ou-yang, in daring to rebuff the spirit, invited a testing of his will. Although a minor incident, the disappearance of the chopsticks was meant as a direct challenge to the new prefect's authority. The battle lines came into even sharper relief when the missing utensils were found in the hand of the image at the shrine. It was a feat that invited confirmation of the popular adage that angry spirits took revenge. Ou-yang, on the contrary, did not accuse the deity of being light-fingered. He seems to have been acutely aware that devotees rather than the spirits they patronized were likely to be behind such trickery.[7] His response was both decisive and flexible. Many in his position might have peremptorily closed the shrine without any allowance for its reopening. The calm that greeted the new prefect's compromise could only have served to underscore his victory. Ou-yang had prevailed by his seal of office alone.

I have chosen the story of Ou-yang Hsiu as an introduction to a body of literature devoted to the theme of *kuan* versus *shen* set in the period of transition from Northern to Southern Sung. The first half of this study focuses on the diverse range of such accounts in the *I-chien chih* of Hung Mai (1123–1202). But before turning to a survey of pertinent anecdotes in this anthology, I want first to speculate a bit further on the overall significance of narrative accounts formulated on the theme of rivalry between officials and the spirit realm. Episodes conventionally framed according to this scheme appear to have more than a grain of truth in them. The power struggles they portray almost invariably mask conflicts of a much more mundane sort. What is staged as a drama featuring supernatural elements is often a recasting of the endless tug of war between the governed and the government. And who but the newly posted agent of the throne is likely to suffer the brunt of such challenges? As an outsider in alien territory, prefects like Ou-yang Hsiu were behooved to assert their authority in order that the potential for disruption could be curbed. How they managed to link up with existing channels of influence in their adopted homes had much to do with the success or failure of their tenures. Community support was essential to the undertakings of all temporarily stationed heads of local bureaucracy. Thus it was of utmost importance that Ou-yang establish his alignments in Ying-t'ien with caution. His decision not to patronize the Shrine of the Five Gentlemen reflected more than simply his disapproval of a deity portrayed as an extortionist.

Representatives of the state traditionally issued declarations in condemnation or praise of shrines within their jurisdiction. The language used is formulaic in part, conditioned by centuries of imperial efforts to establish limits on what the throne was willing to sanction as acceptable religious practice. Places of worship perceived as intolerable were invariably branded *yin-tz'u,* or "excessive shrines."[8] Human sacrifice was the most egregious form of excess to be outlawed, but conspicuous displays of sacrificial offerings were also commonly deemed offensive if they were thought to cause economic strain on a community. Any institution that boded ill rather than good for the people was subject to restraint. Although the definition of what constituted injury may have varied somewhat from one regime to the next, the underlying concept behind government regulation of religious practice remained unchanged. Anything connected with shrines that was regarded as excessive served as just cause for censorship. Officially, shrines were shut down and their keepers dismissed on charges of deception and fraudulent practice. Such charges were no doubt justly applied in many cases. But in other instances it was as much the welfare of the state as the good of the people that weighed on the mind of the official in charge.

Government servants in positions such as Ou-yang held generally perceived the spirit realm as a party to their own efforts in maintaining an orderly society. Difficulties arose when they discovered that their constituents entrusted their welfare to spirits that were presented as challenges to, rather than subsidiaries of, the imperial bureaucracy. Behind such spirits were embodied the most serious threats to an official's capacity to rule, for shrines that harbored extortionist spirits were without exception founded out of fear.[9] Such was apparently the nature of the Shrine of the Five Gentlemen in Ying-t'ien during Ou-yang's term of office. It was his task to transfer the sense of awe generated therein to his own seat of authority. For him to have bowed down in fear would simply have placed the new prefect in a position subordinate to the shrine and all it represented.

And just what might the Shrine of the Five Gentlemen have represented in Ying-t'ien? If patronized by a majority of citizens, it could easily have served as a symbol of solidarity against outsiders in the community. Allegiance to popularly supported shrines had the potential for encouraging local autonomy in the face of unwanted government presence. That Ou-yang reputedly suffered no further consequences following his closure of the Shrine of the Five Gentlemen suggests, however, that he had determined that it held no substantial threat to his governance. A shrine with a large following presumably would not have met its silencing so meekly. We can only conclude that neither the keeper nor the patrons of the shrine wielded any significant influence in Ying-t'ien.

Anecdotes in the *I-chien chih* suggest that many administrators encountered far more powerful opposition from channels of the spirit realm. Such narratives seem to attest to both a sharpening of attacks on and increasing resourcefulness by officials serving at the crossroads of Northern and Southern Sung. It would appear that many of Ou-yang's successors in office overcame perceived threats to their sense of both public and personal welfare by availing themselves of something markedly more potent than their seal of office. The new arms to which they gained access were drawn from contemporary Taoist exorcistic practice. Just how, why, and what made this ritual rearmament so appealing and effective are questions taken up in the second half of this study. The phenomenon of reinforcement through Taoist exorcistic rites is, I suggest, but a product of its time, a reflection of both the changing demands on and resources of the governing class.

HUNG MAI AND THE *I-CHIEN CHIH*

Hung Mai's literary output reveals a man with a profound curiosity about the society in which he lived. The *I-chien chih* in particular is a product of his interest in human nature. The entire work, issued sporadically over a span of nearly forty years, once totaled 420 *chüan*. Only about half of the original is extant. The first fascicle was completed around 1161, and the latest surviving preface dates to 1198. Hung put together the bulk of the collection while in retirement back home at P'o-yang (Kiangsi). He came to collect much of his material, however, as he moved from one official post to the next. As the former prefect of various locales, Hung Mai learned firsthand about the joys and travails of serving in government. His success in curtailing extortionary practices of the local militia in Kan-chou (Kiangsi) and in ameliorating factional feuds in Chien-ning (Fukien) suggests that Hung was notably effective at recognizing and resolving conflicts.[10] And it is the nature of conflict that dominates countless episodes recorded in the *I-chien chih*.

The fact that many stories of this anthology owe their heritage to a rich *chih-kuai* (curiosa) tradition tends to obscure the value of the *I-chien chih* as a document on the social history of the Sung in its own right. While unabashedly fond of curiosities, Hung Mai was nonetheless concerned with distinguishing fact from fantasy. He took much on faith and only later realized that some of his informants had supplied him with derivative, if not entirely fabricated, anecdotes. The discovery made him all the more vigilant about checking the authenticity of his accounts. He also took great pains to identify the sources of the stories he recorded in the *I-chien chih*.

Initially Hung Mai drew his material from the sort of stories heard at local taverns or told by strangers passing through. Eventually everyone he met, from domestic servant to reclusive monk, was a potential source for the *I-chien chih*. Later fascicles were occasionally drawn in part from written accounts. And sometimes Hung Mai relied exclusively on one of his colleagues for the contents of an entire segment. Members of his own family, agnatic and affinal relatives alike, also prove to have been a major resource for the *I-chien chih*. Numerous anecdotes are retellings of events either personally experienced or witnessed by informants.

A high concentration of stories center on the dilemmas encountered by officials posted to unfamiliar terrain. Several address the special problems inherent in the reestablishment of the Sung court in the south. Although he was but an infant at the time of this major dislocation of imperial authority, Hung Mai manifests an uncommon interest in the resulting hardships suffered by migrant families as well as those with roots in the south. Lessons thus learned about the give-and-take of society find their expression time and again in the *I-chien chih*.

As the selections below demonstrate, Hung Mai was remarkably attuned to the various means by which officials of the state sought to save face amidst a growing complexity of assaults on the well-being of one's person, family, and society. He and his informants exhibit an acute awareness of what appears to be the new-found resourcefulness of officeholders in his age. The conflicts staged as power struggles between *kuan* and *shen* were often perceived as irrevocable tragedies. The question of how one prevailed over mounting adversity dominates all such dramas. The answers offered rest on whether one attempted to make peace or war with the powers present. The following summary is organized in illustration of the full range of strategies adopted, from compliance to defiance, as outlined in the formulaic pattern above.

Recognition and the Potential for Reward

Newly commissioned officials, once they had taken up residence at their assigned posts, customarily made a circuit of all the shrines within their jurisdictions. The prefect of Ts'ai-chou (Honan), on just such a tour of inspection, went so far as to authorize the recarving of a stele honoring the enshrinement of a T'ang guardian.[11] Government functionaries were equally likely to pay their respects at various sanctuaries encountered en route to office or in the course of duty. A native of Le-p'ing (Kiangsi), for example, was on his way to the capital to take up his post as gate guardian of the Court of Judicial Review when he stopped with his maidservant to pray for good fortune at an unidentified shrine of Shang-jao (Kiangsi).[12] The defender of Chiang county (Shansi) was similarly moved to pay his respects at the Shrine of the Perfected (Chen-jen tz'u) as he passed by Mount Ku-she. His voluntary act of devotion was rewarded shortly thereafter by an encounter with the deity enshrined, the renowned transcendent Lü Tung-pin.[13]

The terms *miao* and *tz'u* traditionally denoted ancestral shrines but in time came to be applied to sanctuaries dedicated to a wide range of spirits. The two designations are by and large used interchangeably in the *I-chien chih*. Both "Lei miao" and "Lei tz'u," for example, appear in reference to a single Thunder Shrine.[14] *Wu,* or sorcerers, are commonly named as the caretakers of *tz'u*. Either *wu*—or more typically *chu (miao-chu),* that is, supplicants—are identified as the overseers of *miao*.[15] Shrines commanding homage are ordinarily characterized in the *I-chien chih* as *ling* (numinous), *ling-hsien* (numinously manifest), or *ling-hsiang* (numinously responsive). The only shrines that generally survived widespread purges were precisely those that had a reputation of omnipotence. But, as the episode regarding Ou-yang Hsiu illustrates, even putatively powerful seats of divine authority were subject to closure if that authority were abused. The salvation of shrines whose influence was uncertain rested largely on an official's receptivity to persuasion.

Chiang Ching (*chin-shih* 1079) of I-hsing (Kiangsu) apparently faced just such a quandary.[16] Upon assuming his post as magistrate of An-jen (Kiangsi), Chiang is said to have ordered the destruction of three hundred "excessive shrines," the remains of which were then cast into the river. He also forbade the residents of An-jen to continue their practice of submitting sacrificial offerings. Only one shrine was spared, according to Sun Chiu-ting (fl. 1113–1123), source of this anecdote and a former vice-director of the Imperial Library. The temple that Magistrate Chiang hesitated to demolish honored a certain General Liu. Of all sanctuaries in the county it was considered to command the most power.

Although Chiang allowed the shrine to stand, he decided at one point that a large juniper standing within its courtyard had to be cut down. Before he had a chance to put his plan into action, Chiang had an ominous dream. There appeared before him an armored figure on horseback. The apparition identified himself as a long-term resident and thanked the "rector" for extending his protection. In fifteen years time, he promised, they would meet again. Chiang awoke from the dream and concluded that it must have been the spirit of General Liu who had inexplicably addressed him as "rector." The vision left such an impression on him that he changed his mind about having the juniper tree removed and instead authorized repair of the shrine.

The shrine to General Liu apparently flourished throughout Chiang's tenure as magistrate. When his term of office expired, Chiang reportedly paid his respects at the shrine and inscribed a verse on one of its walls. The opening line of his farewell address dismissed the notion of dreams as a reflection of reality. Chiang admitted, nonetheless, that the general had discreetly made known his divine powers. The splendor of the shrine from that time forth he also willingly acknowledged. Chiang closed his tribute, as if to mock his initial declaration of skepticism in oneiromancy, by stating he anticipated bowing down before the spirit once again in fifteen years time.

The transcription of the verse alone was clearly intended to dispel any doubt as to the veracity of the story. As if offering further testimony to its authenticity, Hung Mai reveals that a stone incised with Chiang's verse could be found at the site in his time. A summary of the magistrate's subsequent posts points out, moreover, that the prophecies of his dream were fulfilled. Exactly fifteen years later he did indeed find himself back in An-jen county, as the military administrator of the Chiang-tung circuit. And the last office Chiang Ching held was as rector of a preparatory branch of the National University.

The concise biography of Chiang Ching in the *Sung shih* offers only limited evidence in support of this anecdote.[17] Chiang's career as magistrate of An-jen, according to this account, was marked by a vigorous campaign against the sorcerers in whom residents of the county placed their trust. An-jen is further characterized as a place where many fatalities resulted from widespread refusal of medical treatment for epidemic diseases.[18] The description of Chiang's strategy recalls the language of the *I-chien chih* episode. Here the magistrate is reported to have confiscated three hundred offensive images, which were then destroyed and cast into the river. Unlike Hung Mai's version of events, no allowance is made for any flexibility on the part of Chiang Ching. This is but one example of how anecdotal material offers a necessary corrective to the biographies generated by imperial committees.

The official persona conveyed, that of the austere and unforgiving magistrate, yields in this case to that of a sensitive and thoughtful negotiator. Chiang Ching's decision to cut down the juniper tree suggests he sought ways to curb the appeal of General Liu's shrine. It is not clear whether anyone became aware of his decision, but the fact that it seems to have provoked his dream implies that Chiang at least expected to face considerable opposition. The dream allowed him to resolve subconsciously what must have been a conspicuous difference of opinion festering between himself and those he governed. It gave him just cause not only to sanction the presence of the shrine but also to authorize its renovation. The gratitude voiced by the spirit for continued protection, while it committed Chiang to changing his course of action, also gave him a sense of empowerment. The dream, in other words, served to reassure the magistrate that he remained in charge even as he joined the residents of An-jen in honoring their most potent guardian deity. Although Chiang may not have responded with reverence equal to that of the community, he was at least persuaded that it was his responsibility to enhance rather than diminish the sacred space devoted to General Liu. The anecdote, on the one hand, provides an explanation of how a single shrine managed to thrive at a time when all others had been eliminated. The faithful, we can imagine, would have been inclined to believe that the force of the spirit himself saved their shrine. The fulfillment of General Liu's prophecy, on the other hand, suggests a magistrate blessed not only with the wisdom of reconciliation but also with the power of prescience.

The spirit of accommodation in the face of budding conflict also lies at the heart of anecdotes in which devotees themselves figure as the successful agents of persuasion. For example, apparent thefts were linked to offended spirits, the appeasement of which was all that was necessary to ensure the recovery of the missing items. One episode of this sort concerns the mysterious loss of wine from the storehouse of Kuang-te prefecture (Anhwei) in the year 1155. The incident was brought to Hung Mai's attention by an eyewitness named Ch'en Tai.[19] While serving as administrator for public order in Kuang-te, Ch'en was informed that several hundred kegs of wine were missing. Ch'en at first attributed the loss to petty thieves. Several days later it was discovered that the lower level of the storehouse had been completely emptied of its contents. A thorough search of the premises left Ch'en absolutely baffled. There was not the least bit of evidence, he claimed, that anyone had even tampered with the locks on the storehouse. Ch'en reportedly was not at that time prepared to associate the loss with some sort of ghostly phenomena.

Several more days passed before he returned to the storehouse. This time Ch'en went in the company of Revenue Manager Shen Wen.[20] The quantity of wine that had vanished by then was evidently beyond calculation. Shen initially suggested that perhaps the floor had caved in. When that proved not to be the case, he proposed taking up the matter with Prefect Shen Chieh.[21] At that point civil and military staff members alike made it known that Shen Wen's predecessor in office had abruptly removed a shrine that had long stood at the storehouse. The current crisis, they advised, might very well be attributable to this action. The revenue manager took their counsel to heart. He discreetly arranged for the purchase of sacrificial animals and fermented beverages. And with these offerings displayed before him, Shen Wen bowed down to pray for assistance and pledged that he would have the shrine restored. The next day the kegs of wine miraculously reappeared in the storehouse. True to Shen's vow, a shrine was once more put in place at the site.

Restoration of the shrine was a pragmatic move, to be sure. But here

Hung Mai introduces one official who found the accommodation of local sentiment an expedient way to avert an obvious pilfering of state property. By acceding to the prevailing desire for the reestablishment of a guardian shrine, Shen spared himself the onerous task of informing the prefect of a theft of goods for which he would be held responsible. It was a clever move to raise the possibility of approaching higher authority within earshot of local staff members. Shen Wen thus not only allowed himself to save face but also provided the necessary cover for the restitution of the wine. Such graceful acknowledgment of local channels to the spirit realm, as exemplified by both Shen and Chiang, was not always within the capacity of their peers.[22] Many in a position of authority obviously had just cause to resist. Some were thought to have suffered for it. Others in the end proclaimed victory.

Defiance and the Question of Retribution

Adjustment to their home away from home proved difficult for many commissioned officials. Some assignments during times of political uncertainty forced the officeholder to leave his family behind as he took up residence in a sensitive area.[23] Those posted in the more remote regions of the continent often found themselves confronting lawless tribes.[24] Others found living standards falling short of the level to which they were accustomed and sometimes even attempted to raise the cultural awareness of their adoptive communities. Misunderstandings arose when northerners simply failed to understand the customs of the south.[25] Perhaps most crucial to the successful relocation of high-ranking officials such as magistrates and prefects was the sort of relations they were able to cultivate with their subordinates. Clerks and other menials drawn from the local population and earning little or no salary could make or break a career. As in Shen Wen's case cited above, staff members served as invaluable informants on local traditions of importance to the community. Officeholders who crossed their subordinates were popularly perceived as having put themselves at great risk.[26]

Yang Kuang is one prefect presented in the *I-chien chih* as a tempter of fate.[27] A grandnephew by the name of Hung Fu provided Hung Mai with an account of Yang's unfortunate experience. Yang Kuang was posted in 1195 to Yung-k'ang (Szechwan), where a grandly enfeoffed shrine to the spirit of Kuan-k'ou stood as the pride of the locale. This temple compound, established in honor of Li Ping, is the ancestor of the Erh-wang miao located near the popular tourist site at Tu-chiang-yen.[28] In Sung times, it was the custom for all who worshiped at the shrine, rich or poor, to submit an offering of lamb. Each lamb brought inside the city walls was subject to a substantial tax. The collection of this tax is said to have kept the coffers of the local gentry full to overflowing.

On the day marking Li Ping's birthday, every resident within the prefecture, from ranking officials to clerks and commoners, paid obeisance at the shrine. One person in 1195 remained conspicuous in his resolve not to join in the celebration. That person was Yang Kuang himself. Described as an obstinate man with absolutely no belief in the possibility of extraordinary phenomena, the new prefect refused to yield to the pleas of his subordinates to pay his respects at the shrine. Yang chose instead to hold his own private party. That night a fire broke out, leaving the prefectural headquarters in shambles. Several days later Yang learned that his family home to the southwest in Han-chia had also burned to the ground on that very same night. The shock is said to have made him realize, all too late, that he had aroused the anger of the spirit. It seems more likely, however, that Yang suffered the vengeance of those who stood to lose face, not to mention income, should his disrespectful behavior go unpunished. No one with his hand in the incense pot, so to speak, was about to allow seeds of disaffection to be sown. Thus it was inevitable that an act of divine retribution be witnessed, even if that meant wanton sabotage. Yang paid dearly for his arrogance, but he was the victim of human, not holy, wrath.

A spirit sufficiently outraged was often popularly perceived as capable of rendering punishment far more grievous than the theft or destruction of property. Two instances where fatalities are linked to denying or hindering homage to a local shrine are recorded in a single entry of the *I-chien chih*.[29] Hung Mai is reluctant to endorse the concept of retribution in the first incident, but he remains silent regarding the significance of the second. Central to the opening episode is the welfare of a Shrine to Three Worthies (San-sheng miao) located adjacent to the headquarters of the vice-magistrate of Chü-jung (Kiangsu). Such shrines are reputed to have been common throughout Chien-k'ang prefecture. They typically featured a single image, but no one seemed to be able to identify the deity represented. Each spring the submission of pigs and lambs to the shrine reportedly created a great commotion throughout the compound, from morning to night. In 1191 the new vice-magistrate Yen Shu-p'ing sought to reduce this disturbance by proposing to shut off the courtyard so as to divert patrons of the shrine away from his office.[30] Civil and military functionaries alike insisted that such action would invite certain disaster, so Yen in the end backed down. But the following year he managed to have a low retaining wall built. It forced devotees to circle around the back of his headquarters to reach the shrine. The number paying homage is reported thereby to have dropped off considerably in comparison with years past. By the summer of 1194, Yen had fulfilled his term of office. He requested and received authorization to return home. On his departure, the residents of Chü-jung made a special procession to the shrine. They pleaded with their tutelary deity not to blame them for the past reduction in sacrifices. The responsibility for diminished patronage, they asserted, rested squarely with the former vice-magistrate. Yen made it home only to fall ill very suddenly. One night later he was dead. Hung Mai, like Yen's friends and colleagues, admitted that he found it difficult to accept the loss of such a privileged and promising young official. He cautioned that it would be inadvisable simply to conclude a spirit had snatched Yen away before his time.[31]

The second half of this entry concerns Liu Tsai (1166–1239) of Tan-yang (Kiangsu), defender of Chiang-ning county (Kiangsu). A shrine of comparable eminence to that in Chü-jung is said to have commanded the devotion of all officeholders in Chiang-ning save Liu. Such was his disdain that Liu reportedly raised his sleeve every time he passed by so as to avoid having even to look at the shrine. Disaster soon struck. First, Liu's younger brother, a member of his staff, suddenly passed away after a minor illness. Liu's wife Ms. T'ao (1170–1193) had an ominous dream shortly thereafter. The spirit of the shrine, she claimed, told her that he had taken Liu's brother because of her husband's impudence. She said he also threatened to seize her if Liu did not repent. The defender would not believe that his wife's dream was of any significance. Then she, too, passed away, heavy with child. Only then is Liu said to have gone in remorse to the shrine to beg forgiveness.[32]

Liu Tsai's putative conversion is remarkable in view of the historical and literary writings that survive in documentation of his career. As it turns out, Liu could not have been much over twenty-five years of age at the time he took up the post of defender of Chiang-ning. It was his first commission following attainment of the chin-shih degree in 1190. According to both the Sung shih and the Ching-k'ou ch'i-chiu chuan, a biographical work compiled apparently by a Tan-yang contemporary, Liu Tsai found his jurisdiction overrun with sorcerers.[33] He engaged the local militia in an effort to keep their activities in check. Eventually Liu even succeeded in transforming these channels of the spirit realm into tillers of the soil. He is additionally credited with destroying eighty-four "excessive shrines" during the course of his official career.

Given these data, the narrative in the I-chien chih might be somewhat exaggerated if not apocryphal.[34] Unlike his account on the plight of Yen Shu-p'ing, Hung Mai refrained from commenting on the devastating blows suffered by Liu Tsai during his first term of office. Devotees to the shrine in Chiang-ning, however, would most certainly have viewed Liu's losses as verification of the power of their deity, the font of their local identity. Such is the force of faith conditioned by the fear of retribution. Trust in the omnipotence of guardian spirits allowed no expression of doubt as to the controlling force within a community. Such faith lost its grip only when alternative sources of authority were seen to dominate.

Many episodes in the I-chien chih center on officials who overrode popular anticipation of divine vengeance. One outstanding selection of this sort features Chang Kuei-mo (*chin-shih* 1169) of Sui-ch'ang (Chekiang). As prefect of Ch'ang-chou (Chekiang), Chang faced much the same predicament noted in Chiang Ching's official biography.[35] During the spring and summer of 1195 nine out of ten households under his jurisdiction fell victim to an epidemic disease. Even though Chang arranged for the distribution of effective medication throughout the prefecture, he found that very few took advantage of it. The local gentry he questioned all told him that they worshiped the spirits of pestilence *(wen-shen)* at a shrine maintained by four sorcerers. Anyone who fell ill was obliged to go to the shrine to pray, Chang learned. Medicine was forbidden, moreover, and for that reason no one dared avail himself of any supplied by the prefect's office.[36] Utterly dismayed, Chang set out for the shrine the very next day. He had been told that it stood behind the Circuit Palace of the Sacred Mountain of the East (Tung-yüeh hsing-kung). The temple compound appeared to him to be completely desolate. So Chang turned to his subordinates and asked them to direct him to the temple of the spirits of pestilence. They assumed the prefect intended to pay homage. Incense was lit and a prayer mat spread out for his use. Chang pushed everything aside.

The appearance of the prefect is said to have caused quite a stir at the shrine. Old and infirm women who had previously been engaged in submitting offerings and prayers struggled to crowd around him. Chang pointed to the central, most imposingly adorned image and asked its name. The sorcerers informed him that it was the Numinous Lord of Jupiter (T'ai-sui ling-chün). Chang then inquired about several figures standing to the left and right, posed as if ready for combat. He was told that these were the spirits of the Bureau of Pestilence (Wen-ssu).

The prefect thereupon launched into an impromptu lecture on how the hierarchies of the mundane and spirit realms were governed alike by rules of propriety. How, he demanded to know, could the subordinates of the Lord of Jupiter display such a loss of propriety? Where was their sense of responsibility to the public? Lest the significance of his accusations be lost, Chang immediately had the four sorcerers arrested and sent to his headquarters. Twenty militiamen were gathered together, plied with liquor, and sent out to smash all images in the shrine. The remaining sacrificial vessels were distributed to various Buddhist monasteries. Chang also arranged for the shrine itself to be dismantled so that the materials could be used to rebuild the central hall of the Monastery of Commended Blessings (Chien-fu ssu), which had recently burnt down. Once the site of their activity had been swept clean, the sorcerers were punished with a lashing and sent into exile. Hung Mai, presumably echoing the voice of his informant Ch'ien Shen-chih, added in closing that the people in their ignorance were sure the prefect had invited the wrath of the spirits.[37] Contrary to public expectation, however, the epidemic abated, the vulgarity of local customs was somewhat amended, and Chang was summoned to serve as director of the Ministry of Personnel. He even received the honor of this post before he had completed his term of office in Ch'ang-chou.

When Efforts Toward Appeasement Failed

Hung Mai also includes many accounts about officeholders who sought the help of local exorcists in dislodging ill-boding forces. Appeals to indigenous exorcists, however, did not always yield positive results. The experience of Hao Kuang-ssu, newly commissioned administrative supervisor of Kuang-chou, is a case in point.[38] In the year 1150, the supervisor's household reportedly suffered repeated intrusions of a demonic phantom. No quarters were left unviolated, from bedrooms to the kitchen and bathhouse. In one instance a fire broke out within a clothing hamper. Hao tried to salvage what he could from the blaze and ended up with severely burned hands. He found his official gowns ruined beyond repair. Luckily, his certificate of appointment and seal of office escaped undamaged.

Then one day Hao discovered the seal itself was missing, although the case in which it had been locked showed no signs of tampering. Hao summoned a local sorcerer to investigate. When his efforts proved of no avail, Hao attempted to resolve the matter himself. He swept out a room and gravely lit incense on behalf of what he apparently took to be a troubled spirit in residence. Approximately twenty days elapsed without any sign of the seal. Since none of the officers and clerks serving under Hao could be paid without its authorization, the effect of the seal's loss was felt bitterly throughout the ranks. Finally it reappeared. It seemed to drop down out of nowhere, bouncing like a large stone on a table in the room set aside for the offering of incense. Seven days later Hao passed away. Even after his family moved out of the supervisor's quarters, the same demonic force is said to have pursued them relentlessly until they left the region and went back north.

Like many anecdotes in the *I-chien chih,* this episode serves foremost to emphasize just how difficult it was for officeholders of northern origin to gain acceptance in the south. That the Kuang-chou sorcerer did not prevail speaks not of his failure to command divine forces but rather of his complicity with the putative demon behind the siege of the supervisor's household. Conjuring spirits and the ability to make objects disappear through magic were long recognized to be among the skills of sorcerers. It was just such trickery that lay behind the missing chopsticks at Ou-yang Hsiu's table. The challenge Supervisor Hao faced was clearly more serious. The successful abduction of his seal of office was truly a most flagrant offense. Without it Hao could no longer conduct business as usual, and, worse yet, everyone on his staff had to go without pay. The seal's sudden reappearance was presumably timed to allow mounting unrest to reach its peak. Its return by no means signaled the submission of the resident phantom. For even with the seal back in hand, Hao was not to last much longer in office. Although his death one week later is not explicitly linked with the haunting of his house, Hao was perceived to have been a victim of circumstances beyond his control. The opposition to him in Kuang-chou simply proved too great to overcome. What better endorsement of local autonomy than the apparent ability to hound an alien functionary to death and to chase his family away besides.

Hao Kuang-ssu, in seeking some way to surmount resistance to his presence, did what any official in his position might have done. The odds, however, were so stacked against him that even his own effort to appease the offending spirit proved futile. Were there no other avenues of communication with the spirit realm that he might have pursued so as to reestablish equilibrium within his quarters? What if he had been able to call on an exorcist who bore no allegiance to the community in Kuang-chou? Was there no network of ritual experts with whom he might have made profitable contact? Perhaps Hao himself could have acquired training in more effective ritual techniques.

Taoist Exorcistic Practice to the Rescue

Numerous episodes in the *I-chien chih* reveal that it was not uncommon for officials to call on the assistance of specialists in Taoist exorcistic traditions. Other episodes indicate that men of official rank were among those who came to acquire and apply expertise in Taoist rites of exorcism. Chinese officeholders can be said traditionally to have served in an exorcistic capacity.[39] Many cults were, in fact, founded on the popular perception of an official's command of supernatural powers.[40] Hung Mai's anthology indicates that by the twelfth century it was not unusual for someone to serve both in an official post and in the role of exorcist. Officeholders who had no training in Taoist exorcistic practice called time and again on those who did.

The descriptions of exorcistic practice in the *I-chien chih* suggest more than a passing acquaintance with variant traditions of Taoist ritual. Hung Mai spoke of specialists in the Cheng-i (i.e., Celestial Master), T'ien-hsin (Celestial Heart), and Wu-lei (Five Thunder) rituals—in short, the entire range of Taoist traditions prevalent in his time. The Correct Rites of the Celestial Heart (T'ien-hsin cheng-fa) is by far the Taoist legacy most often mentioned. Its prominence within the pages of the *I-chien chih* is doubtless related to the fact that the origins of T'ien-hsin are traced to Mount Hua-kai, just south of Hung's home in P'o-yang.[41] The south-central river basins were also host to a wide range of Thunder Ritual *(lei-fa)* traditions.[42]

The feature fundamental to all varieties of Taoist exorcistic practice is a technique known as *k'ao-chao fa,* or the "rites of evocation by interrogation." As the term *k'ao-chao* implies, it was by various means of ritual interrogation that specialists in this technique sought to resolve conflicts manifested in the spirit realm. These specialists are commonly referred to as *fa-shih,* or ritual masters.[43] Their task was to learn the identity and nature of spirits troubling their clients. Both written and oral communications figured in the rites of *k'ao-chao.* Written notifications and inquiries were submitted to members of the local spirit hierarchy within whose domain offenses were thought to have been committed. Responses from both these guardian figures as well as possessing spirits were often voiced by mediums *(t'ung-tzu)* in service to the ritual master. Resolutions varied, but appeasement of troubled spirits by the sponsorship of a Fête of the Yellow Register (Huang-lu chiao) was frequently prescribed. Such was the language of Taoist exorcistic practice with which Hung Mai and his informants were familiar. As the anecdotes summarized below indicate, they bore witness to the rise of a new breed of officeholder cum exorcist.

Two episodes reveal that a descendant of the imperial line named Chao Tzu-chü served in both an official and a ritual capacity.[44] One account, apparently supplied by Chao's nephew, describes how he came to be trained.[45] Like many who become healers, Chao took up a career in exorcism following his remarkable recovery from a severe affliction.[46] His health began to fail after the death of his wife. Her loss is said to have left Chao so obsessed with longing that he began deluding himself into thinking that she had returned. By the time a *Tao-jen,* or "man of the Tao," appeared begging at his doorstep, Chao was close to a stupor and extremely debilitated for lack of food or drink. The adept immediately perceived that Chao was keeping company with a ghost.[47] He warned him that an early death was inevitable should the situation continue. If Chao but allowed himself to be taught the Correct Rites of T'ien-hsin, the adept told him, the ghost could be provoked to leave. Chao, shocked to his senses, immediately accepted instruction. After six months of rigorously observing the code of practice and devotion prescribed, Chao finally gained release from the phantom of his wife. He had in essence been taught to cure himself.

Following his recovery, Chao Tzu-chü dedicated himself all the more intently to his ritual training. He soon gained the reputation of being able to heal others. Among his clients was Hung Mai's father-in-law, Chang Yüan-tao. In 1128, shortly after the fall of Northern Sung, Chang had taken refuge with his family in the Lung-hsing Monastery of Yang-chou (Kiangsu). He called on Chao, who also happened to be at the monastery, to attend to the grandmother of his wife. She was found to be suffering disturbing visits from the ghosts of two relatives lost in the recent chaos. Chao correctly identified her tormentors and assured Chang that the two ghosts would depart once appropriate offerings were made.

Chao's ability to appease ghosts is also highlighted in another anecdote set approximately a decade later. By then, he had been posted to Yen-chou (Chekiang) as supervisor of the militia. His client is identified as the son of an eminent prefect who had lost his life in the north around 1126. Hung Mai inserts a note stating that he was unwilling to record the man's name. He describes how the prefect's son suffered a vivid nightmare some ten years after his father's death. He is said to have dreamed that several hundred ghosts approached supporting a millstone bearing his father's head, dripping with blood. Chao Tzu-chü was engaged to preside over a Fête of the Yellow Register, which the son sponsored on behalf of his parents at considerable expense.[48]

Other members of Hung Mai's extended family are also reported to have had occasion to call on the assistance of fellow men of rank with training in Taoist rites of exorcism. In 1183, during the New Year's celebrations, a "Court Gentleman for Ceremonial Service" named Yao answered the summons of cousin Hung Ching-kao, magistrate of Chin-ling (Kiangsu).[49] It was Yao's ability to apply the Rites of Five-Thunder Celestial Heart that recommended him to treat the magistrate's ten-year-old son. The young boy had suddenly collapsed in a state of dementia following a visit to the home of a local official named Fan An. He and his friends had stopped there for refreshments after viewing the lanterns on display at the Circuit Shrine of the Sacred Mountain of the East (Tung-yüeh hsing-miao).

To diagnose this case of apparent spirit possession, Yao summoned the God of the Earth (T'u-ti) for cross-examination. Speaking through a young medium, the tutelary deity insisted that the magistrate's compound was impenetrable to aberrant forces and, furthermore, that no ghosts were about that he could be expected to apprehend. Yao went into retreat at his home and, after ten days of submitting talismanic communications, he was able to evoke a young woman. The ghost, channeled apparently by Yao's young accomplice, identified herself as the mother of Hung Hsün, an adolescent stepbrother of the magistrate. A subsequent dispatch to the City God (Ch'eng-huang) forced her to admit that she had taken possession of the magistrate's son when he appeared at Fan An's home. It was there, in fact, that she had passed away. The magistrate, Hung Mai notes, had placed the woman and her son in Fan's care because he feared she had contracted a contagious disease and did not want to risk the infection of his own household.[50] Arrangements were then made to transfer her coffin to a local monastery.[51] The succession of visits to the temple and her place of death were apparently sufficient to evoke severe anxiety in the magistrate's son, presumably a close confidant of the orphaned boy.[52] Proper mortuary observances were determined to be the obvious solution. Yao prescribed offerings of fermented beverages, food, incense, and paper money. He also dispatched a notification to the Bureau of Mount T'ai to assure reincarnation of the deceased. Once these measures had been taken and the coffin burned, the magistrate's son immediately recovered.[53]

According to another account in the *I-chien chih,* one high-ranking military official found his efforts to apply teachings in Taoist ritual to be less than successful.[54] That man was Fu Hsüan, vice commander-in-chief of military affairs in Kiangsi. While stationed at Yü-chang, Fu invited Wang Wen-ch'ing (1093–1153) of Lin-ch'uan to come and instruct him in Thunder Rites. Wang was popularly regarded as heir to the legacy of Lin Ling-su (1076–1120), codifier of the Shen-hsiao theocracy embraced by Sung Hui-tsung (r. 1101–1125).[55] Wang's obstinacy in dealing with the vice commander-in-chief apparently very nearly cost him his life. He is said to have found Fu Hsüan to be exceedingly repugnant. Even so, the reputedly outspoken Wang was sufficiently in awe of Fu's innate cruelty that he dared not deny him instruction. His solution was to provide him with but the basic rudiments so that Fu could at least impress his friends. Problems arose, however, when Fu felt he was ready to test the new skills he had acquired. His goal was to bring down a stūpa towering in the distance. This feat Fu attempted to achieve by lighting a talisman. A fire soon broke out inside the stūpa but burned out, leaving only a trail of smoke. The structure itself was left standing, completely unmarred.[56] Outraged that Wang had conveyed less than a full course of study, Fu called for his execution. Wang knew well in advance what Fu's intentions were and loudly condemned his disciple as unworthy. He then applied the rituals essential to dispatching a reprimand on high so that Fu would be deprived of the divine forces required for the practice of Thunder Rites. Thereafter, Fu's efforts to make use of his instruction were reportedly ineffective.

Another high-ranking military officer's reputation as an accomplished exorcist appears to have overshadowed his career in the armed forces. Altogether four anecdotes in the *I-chien chih* center on the exploits of the omnipotent Sung An-kuo. His application of the Rites of T'ien-hsin, according to one account, were known to be unfailing at the time Sung was stationed at Hu-chou (Chekiang) as military director-in-chief of the Che-hsi circuit.[57] Such was his fame that a family in Te-ch'ing county invited Sung to rescue them from the annoyance of a malign force. His initial attempt to overcome this provocation proved to be uncharacteristically fruitless. Indeed, Sung is said to have been infuriated at being made the object of ridicule. He withdrew and took refuge at a

Taoist abbey in a nearby village. There he undertook a seven-day fast and devoted himself to inscribing talismans and reciting incantations. Upon completion of this intensive regimen, he unbound his hair, took up his sword, and marched back to the residence under attack. Sung headed directly toward a giant tree standing behind the family's living quarters and circled around it in the pace of Yü.[58] His efforts were rewarded when a loud crash of thunder split the tree in half. Subsequent tremors reduced the entire grove in the end to tinder no larger than bamboo tallies. All traces of the resident phantom are said to have been thereby eliminated.

Three additional episodes in the *I-chien chih* featuring Sung's exorcistic achievements make no mention of either an official career or expertise in the Rites of T'ien-hsin. He is identified in one case as a *fang-shih,* or technocrat, and in another as a *shan-shu-che* (lit., one skilled in magical arts), a term applicable to exorcists, fortune-tellers, physiognomists, and geomancers. The absence of any label whatsoever regarding Sung An-kuo's profession suggests that the narrator of the anecdote preserved in the supplement to the *I-chien chih* felt his protagonist needed no introduction.[59] In this episode, Sung's application of the rites of interrogation is reputed to have disclosed that Grand Guardian Hsing Hsiao-yang's new home in Lin-an was overrun with countless ghosts of those previously slaughtered in combat. He recommended that the family sponsor a grand Fête of the Yellow Register by way of relief and offered to preside over it. On the eve of *lien-tu,* or salvation by refinement, Sung supervised the entrapment of all lost souls lingering at the site.[60] The residence is said to have thenceforth been restored to a state of peace and quiet.

Another episode recounts how the "technocrat" Sung An-kuo overcame vengeful ghosts roaming the estate of General Han Shih-chung (1089–1151) in Lin-an. The general's son Han Yen-chih (1131–1200) provided Hung Mai with this story.[61] It concludes with lavish praise for Sung's abilities. His power over malign forces is reputed to have been achieved without the aid of either talismanic registers or *k'ao-chao* procedures. No one, it is said, could match his incisiveness and subtlety. Ultimately, Sung's success in resolving both this case and that of Grand Guardian Hsing's haunted house appears to have rested in large part on his awareness of Lin-an atrocities.[62]

The episode featuring the "magician" Sung An-kuo is also set in Lin-an.[63] It centers on the difficulties of a soldier named Li Li serving in the palace command. Li was known to have been of little means. His sudden accumulation of valuables thus aroused considerable suspicion. When his peers accused him of thievery, the general in charge proceeded to conduct his own private investigation. He is said to have sensed that something extraordinary was at hand. Sung took over at that point and reportedly evoked, presumably through Li himself, a young woman claiming to be the offspring of the Hsiao family dating to the T'ang.[64]

She asserted, moreover, that she had been betrothed to Li when, in his prior incarnation, he had been a gentleman of rank. Her discovery of Li's current state of impoverishment, she continued, led her to shower him with presents. Sung countered by asking if those presents were not in fact stolen goods. Ms. Hsiao denied the charge and insisted that she had merely relieved the wealthy of their overabundance.

Following his ritual interrogation, Sung dismissed the possessing spirit and warned her not to come back lest real trouble erupt. He promised, in addition, to send off a declaration to the Sacred Mountain of the East so that her reincarnation would be assured. Soldier Li, the episode concludes, found himself no better off than before the incident. Here, in other words, was a man who had helped himself to what he considered to be the excess bounty of the rich. His commander wisely found the means for Li to be exonerated of his crimes. In taking on the role as mediator, Sung An-kuo essentially allowed the soldier to save face. The success of his intervention as an exorcist rested on his ability not only to draw forth a scapegoat but also to persuade his client to agree to a truce. The embarrassment of internal conflict among the ranks was thus relieved. Whether or not Sung himself maintained a post in the armed services, his prestige as an exorcist was clearly not lost on his compatriots. He seems to have served foremost, in other words, as the therapist on call to career officers in the military command. Sung An-kuo was apparently among those who could be trusted to negotiate resolutions to battles that fell beyond the periphery of conventional martial training.

If anyone can be said to have been Sung's counterpart among members of the civil service, it would be Lu Shih-chung (fl. 1107–1134). More than half a dozen episodes in the *I-chien chih* attest to the exploits of Lu, "Officer of Perfection" (Chen-kuan). As one account sums it up, Lu's ability to suppress ghosts by the application of talismanic registers was well known to *shih-ta-fu* (literati and officials).[65] Although evidence of an official career is scant, Lu presumably thought of himself as belonging to the *shih-ta-fu*. In an episode highlighting his demonstration of the Correct Rites of T'ien-hsin, Fang Shao indicates that Lu had been awarded the rank of "Gentleman for Closing Court."[66] Lu himself speaks of serving as vice-prefect of Chin-ling (Kiangsu). Taking up this post reportedly gave him the opportunity to follow up on a vision experienced several years earlier. The circumstances behind his vision in 1120 and how it led to the recovery of secret writings concealed at Mao shan are summarized in the opening chapter of Lu Shih-chung's *Great Rituals of the Jade Hall*. This synthesis of T'ien-hsin and Shen-hsiao ritual practice also includes an account of how Lu received divine communications through spirit writing. Lu claims that he and his disciple Chai Ju-wen (1076–1141) recorded the voice of revelation as late as 1134.[67] This discipleship, however, remains to be confirmed. The single entry in the

I-chien chih to mention Chai places him in Ch'ang-chou (Kiangsu), just outside of Mao shan.[68] Another episode suggests that Chai's association with Lu Shih-chung may be traced not to Mao shan but to Ch'en-chou (Honan).[69] It tells the story of how the prefect of Ch'en-chou overcame his reservations about a vice-prefect named Lu and allowed him to perform a ritual that, as local elders had promised, brought relief from a drought. Indexes to the *I-chien chih* identify Vice-Prefect Lu as Lu Shih-chung.[70] The fact that Chai is known to have served as prefect of Ch'en-chou invites speculation as to whether this account provides the background to his recognition of Lu Shih-chung as his master.[71]

There was apparently some confusion in Hung Mai's time not only about Lu Shih-chung's rank and positions held but also about his ancestry. He is identified in one anecdote as the son of Lu Kuan, magistrate of Shang-shui (Honan). Hung Mai later reported that T'eng Yen-chih informed him that Lu Kuan was actually an uncle of Lu Shih-chung.[72] T'eng himself claimed to be Lu Shih-chung's nephew and described how he together with his brothers and cousins once begged their uncle Lu Shih-chung to teach them a simple technique for their own protection. Instead of complying with their request, Lu told them stories about his own narrow escapes from tragedy. On one occasion, Lu reported, he had been passing through Yen-chou (Chekiang) when he was called to treat a young, unmarried woman who had apparently been overtaken by a demonic force. He found his initial efforts to be singularly ineffective. Humiliated by the defeat, Lu took refuge in a Taoist abbey at some distance from the home of the afflicted. Two nights later he sent a novice back to investigate. The power of his intensive devotions was realized when the novice returned to report that the shrine of the God of the Earth had burned to the ground. When Lu went back to check on his client, the entire family came out to congratulate him. The young woman, who had by then recovered, described how she had been seized and held hostage by a matchmaker. Everyone fled, she said, upon the arrival of the "Officer of Perfection," and when he led her away, the young woman added, she looked back to see the residence of her abductor go up in flames.

This story is reportedly one of three that Lu recounted in order to impress upon his nephews the gravity of ritual pursuits. He claimed to have very nearly lost his life in this one encounter alone. Hung Mai states that Lu's nephew T'eng passed away before he was able to repeat the other two stories to him. Additional accounts in the *I-chien chih* reveal that many besides T'eng supplied Hung Mai with testimony to Lu's successes. Among his putative clients were the prefect of Ch'ing-chou (Shantung), the vice-prefect of Ying-t'ien (Honan), and the magistrate of Ling-pi county (Anhwei).[73] Lu is also reported to have applied his ritual skills on behalf of a government clerk in Ch'ing-t'ien (Chekiang) and a ferry captain stationed at I-ch'un (Kiangsi).[74] An episode in Tseng Min-hsing's *Tu-hsing tsa-chih,* moreover, finds Lu Shih-chung summoned to the imperial compound to treat a maidservant suffering from spirit possession.[75]

As mentioned above, a significant number of anecdotes came to Hung Mai by way of his own family. Of particular interest are two episodes contributed by his brothers, which describe how their own relatives prevailed over false commanders of mass allegiance by calling on personal reserves of divine authority. The protagonist in Hung Ching-p'ei's account is his wife's maternal grandfather, Ch'ien Tang of Lin-an.[76] Ch'ien's confrontation with a putative channel of supernatural power came at the beginning of the Shao-hsing period (ca. 1131), just after he took office as magistrate of Nan-ling (Anhwei). Residents of the county are reported to have been utterly devoted to a shrine honoring a Bee King (Feng-wang). It was apparently established solely on the basis of a sorcerer's claims that the Bee King represented the ultimate embodiment of "numina" *(ling).* Beyond those claims, no one seemed able to say much about the spirit they claimed as guardian. In addition to a house of worship, a portable shrine was also built to house the Bee King for transport during ceremonial processions.

The Bee King was brought to Magistrate Ch'ien's attention when, shortly after his arrival in Nan-ling, it became necessary to offer prayers in supplication of rain. Clerks on his staff and local residents alike assured Ch'ien that it was a spirit on which he could rely. And so it happened that the portable shrine was solemnly conveyed to the magistrate's headquarters. At first, Ch'ien submitted offerings of incense before the shrine in honest sincerity. But then he discovered that it was not an image before which he bowed but rather a bee flying about in a cage. Ch'ien's assiduous practice of the Correct Rites of T'ien-hsin is credited with providing him with the wherewithal to realize that he faced a bogus spirit. Hurling denunciations at the cage, he loudly proclaimed the Bee King to be nothing but an insentient little creature on whose behalf the people had been swindled out of offerings of flesh. Ch'ien declared, moreover, that he was not afraid to die and challenged the Bee King to come out and bite him. Failure to respond, he promised, meant that he would reduce it to ashes and thereby cleanse Nan-ling of its foolish practices. Ch'ien was greeted with silence. Both the portable shrine and the temple to the Bee King were summarily set afire. The residents of Nan-ling, the episode concludes, never again spoke of it. Hung Mai does not divulge the fate of the sorcerer who had promoted the shrine. Given Ch'ien's decisive action, however, it is unlikely that he would have had any further influence in the community.

The final episode under consideration concerns a distant uncle of Hung Mai by the name of Hung Pang-chih *(chin-shih* 1148).[77] Since his collected writings are lost and biographical data are minimal, it has much to contribute to our understanding of his reputation as a servant of the people. The first post Hung Pang-chih is known to have held is that of defender of Wu-yüan (Anhwei).[78] He was subsequently promoted to serve as magistrate. Hung's success in implementing a policy of famine relief reportedly endeared him to the inhabitants of Wu-yüan and won him commendation from the throne as well.[79] It is his tenure as magistrate that serves as the setting for a story told by Hung Mai's brother Hung Yüan-chung.

The anecdote opens with a description of the figure who came to be regarded as the curse of Wu-yüan. He is identified as a village sorcerer by the name of Chang. His powers were such, it is said, that Chang had the capacity to bring down great misfortune on others. He set himself up in the canton of Huai-chin, where he extorted cash and rice from all households of wealth. Anyone who happened to offend Chang reportedly suffered ulcerous sores that in some cases even proved fatal. Not a single person is said to have felt anything less than terror in his presence. Assemblies were held every day in his home. On these occasions Chang adorned himself in crimson robes and a towering cap and then seated himself on a high throne. Approximately thirty devoted followers gathered regularly to hear his impromptu sermons. One of his patrons, a scholar named Wang T'ing-jui, came to serve as his assistant, motivated in part, it seems, by the desire to share in Chang's ill-begotten wealth. Among Wang's contributions was a signboard inscribed "Gateway for Paying Homage to Heaven" (Ch'ao-t'ien men), which he hung in front of Chang's residence.

Magistrate Hung apparently first learned of Chang after a retainer on his staff by the name of Wang Tsao happened to invite his wrath. Chang had rebuked him for passing by without coming in to pay his respects by presenting offerings of incense. When Wang found himself forced inside, he went through the motions in an effort to comply. Even so, Chang commanded his attendants to seize and bind the retainer. Rather than submit, Wang challenged the sorcerer to have the soldiers of the netherworld grab him and flog him in midair. Otherwise, he said he would report him to the magistrate. Chang let him go.

Wang followed up on his threat and described in great detail the treatment he had suffered at Chang's hands. Magistrate Hung had Chang arrested and brought to his headquarters. When Hung questioned his devious ways, Chang haughtily denied that he had ever engaged in sorcery. He proudly declared himself to be a practitioner of the Correct Rites of T'ien-hsin, graced with the special capacity to cure others of their afflictions. Hung countered his false claims by issuing an ultimatum. He promised to release Chang if he could leap over the drum tower in the somersaulting technique by which he was reputed to achieve great heights. It was a demand that Chang could not possibly accommodate. He had no choice but to prostrate himself before the magistrate and beg for mercy. Hung had him thrown in prison.

The very next day Hung Pang-chih went in person to conduct an exhaustive interrogation. Armed with the Seal for Vanquishing Demons (Hsiang-mo yin) of the Cheng-i Register, the magistrate defied Chang to tell him what he held in his hand. It was his intention, as he informed Chang, to test the powers of precognition and communication with the divine about which Chang had so boldly bragged. Stunned by the challenge, Chang found himself at a complete loss for words. He was subsequently sentenced to twenty lashes and banished from the region. The large sum of cash found in his coffers was confiscated and consigned to the local treasury. Everyone is said to have rejoiced, save Chang's scholar-accomplice, who chose to flee rather than face inevitable punishment. Thus, the story concludes, did Magistrate Hung win the hearts of the people. His victory over villain Chang, it should be added, was achieved not by his investiture with the seal of the magistracy but with the seal he held embodying the authority of the Celestial Master patriarchy.[80]

BEYOND HUNG MAI

The full significance of the *I-chien chih* passages noted above can only be appreciated within a larger context than I have outlined thus far. In the remaining discussion, I would like to sketch out the framework against which this line of inquiry might be further pursued. The questions raised by this preliminary study on the narrative theme of *kuan* versus *shen* can be reduced to questions of supply and demand. The summary below points out various aspects of the demand for as well as the availability and nature of instruction in Taoist ritual practice. Of concern above all is how and why members of the government bureaucracy were drawn to acquire and apply such training. As I stated at the outset, it is my opinion that Hung Mai attests to the rise of a network of gentry invested with the tokens and weapons of divine as well as imperial authority. To what degree are we to understand the ritual rearmament of officeholders during the Sung as a manifestation of changing times? Does it speak, in other words, not only of an era of new resources but also of a new-found sense of resourcefulness?

The questions of how and why ultimately lead to the question of what made Taoist ritual practice so inviting to members of the Sung civil and military service. In what way can new ritual codifications be said to be a reflection of their time? Although the tradition of oral transmission cannot be denied, we must ask whether the apparent proliferation of written manuals during the Sung answered an enhanced need for exorcistic measures. How precisely did the instructions themselves come to define the targets and means by which divine wrath was to be unleashed? To what features in particular might we attribute the extraordinary appeal of Taoist ritual innovations introduced in the Sung?

On the Demands for and of Discipleship

It would be facetious to suggest that men in positions of authority prior to the Sung were not known to gain and apply instructions in exorcistic techniques. A distinction, however, must be made between those who bore official and ritual entitlements simultaneously and those who were in service to the throne as religious professionals. I am not concerned here, in other words, with the history of imperial employment of channels of the spirit realm such as occupied posts in the ministries of Rites and War during the Chou and in the Imperial Medical Office of the Sui and T'ang.[81] My focus rests rather on the phenomenon whereby members of the gentry class came to be identified by both official title or post and their expertise in Taoist ritual practice.

Early cults evolving around such officials can be traced to their legendary victories over indigenous supernatural forces. But, as mentioned above, such folk heroes typically devoted themselves entirely to contemplative pursuits following a public demonstration of superior divine power. The decision to resign office in favor of the life of a religious is noted, moreover, in centuries of hagiographic lore.[82] The phrase *ch'i-kuan ju-tao* (lit., to abandon office and enter into [a study of] the Tao) and variations on this formula dominate to the point of suggesting that administrative and spiritual pursuits were ultimately considered incompatible. There is, to be sure, a long historical precedent in China for committing oneself solely to either a worldly post or a life of meditation.[83] Outside of the many who found themselves naturally inclined toward the latter, there is also a considerable legacy of the disenchanted scholar forsaking office to follow an eremetic path. Certainly the history of disillusionment with public office could not but have reinforced the ideal of the detached contemplative.

The question that remains is whether, in fact, there is any evidence beyond the lore of folk heroes to suggest something on the order of the official-cum-exorcist immortalized by Hung Mai. I have found in a survey of pre-Sung narrative literature two accounts that attest to but a single facet of what I designate as the ritual rearmament of officials. Both feature officeholders resolving cases of spirit possession by talismanic applications.[84] Such accounts are doubtless but a sample of what must have been a very substantial body of early oral, if not written, literature on the subject. They do not in any way reflect the range of exorcistic practice undertaken by men of office whose careers are publicized in the *I-chien chih*. Remedies for spirit possession can be said to have constituted what might be called the therapeutic role of specialists in exorcistic rites during the Sung. As demonstrated above, Hung Mai's informants witnessed the application of such training toward the restoration of order not only in the family but also within work units and the community at large. Aside from a wider applicability, moreover, schooling in Taoist rites during the Sung clearly entailed the mastery of techniques above and beyond the rudimentary prescription of talismans. Talismanic applications, as demonstrated in the *I-chien chih* episodes above, were typically preliminary to rites of interrogation. And it was not uncommon for such procedures to find their resolution in fêtes on behalf of the dead or in the destruction of an offending spirit's enshrinement. The picture Hung Mai paints of officials armed with Taoist ritual techniques is far more complex than that conveyed by his predecessors.

Indeed, if the *I-chien chih* is any measure, individual talismans or incantations of reputed omnipotence were considered an easily obtainable commodity in the Sung. Such embodiments of divine power were largely sought for demonifuge purposes. Hung Mai himself wrote of learning how to inscribe a talisman recognized as effective in warding off manifold threats. His teacher Li Hao (1116–1176), a recorder in the Court of Imperial Sacrifices, even claimed that he had used it to relieve his cousin's wife of a possessing spirit.[85] Although Hung admits that he had never made use of this particular talisman, he does highly recommend, apparently on the basis of personal experience, an incantation for dispelling nightmares.[86] By the mere fact of recording such incantations, he has himself contributed to their dispersal. The fact that many such apotropaic measures became part of the public domain speaks both of a marked demand for and willingness to believe in divine guardianship. Faith would appear to have been the only price exacted for the transmission of popularly circulating wisdom of this sort.

Those who applied themselves to a rigorous program of ritual training were often found to be less readily inclined to pass on their knowledge. Lu Shih-chung, for example, sought to discourage his nephews from seeking protective techniques by telling them stories of his harrowing experiences. He obviously meant thereby to impress upon the youngsters the solemnity of and the risks innate to gaining such instruction. Additional anecdotes in the *I-chien chih* reveal, moreover, that training in exorcistic rites was not to be undertaken lightheartedly. To identify oneself as a disciple under the authority of a higher cosmic force was understood to entail nothing less than a lifelong commitment to a restrictive code of behavior. Those who fell short were thought to have suffered for it. A disciple of the Correct Rites of T'ien-hsin named Ch'en Chüeh, for instance, reputedly met a violent end as punishment for neglecting his training after assuming a new post late in life.[87] Another devotee of T'ien-hsin, Jen Tao-yüan of Fu-chou, was reportedly made to endure terrifying visions that led ultimately to his demise. The grievous manner of his death was perceived as retribution for engaging in exceedingly shameful conduct while administering a Fête of the Yellow Register.[88]

Thus it was with good reason that demands for discipleship did not always meet with compliance. Even Wang Wen-ch'ing's refusal of full instruction to Vice Commander-in-Chief Fu Hsüan, explained as a personality conflict, is revealed in the end to be well grounded on principle. Fu's impetuous attempt to flaunt his training in Thunder Rites condemned him as an unworthy disciple. He was by no means uniquely deprived. Many are those who have requested instruction and been found wanting. A concrete grasp of Taoist exorcistic practice was simply not something that could be conveyed on whim alone. The lesson that only those deemed both capable and responsible might hope to be rewarded with discipleship is expressed time and again in hagiographic literature.[89]

With the burden of ritual training so great and its acquisition restricted, we are left to wonder how anyone might have been motivated to seek it out. Accounts in the *I-chien chih* suggest that sons of office-holders were especially drawn to such schooling. It may be that they devoted themselves to Taoist ritual training at times when the direction of their careers remained uncertain. Commitment to a program of ritual study also seems to have been the preferred path of many who found their careers in office derailed, whether by slander or by political upheaval. What ultimately appears to be at issue here is the increasing tendency for members of the gentry to explore new options when facing instability. Schooling in Taoist rituals might also have been regarded as a means by which to maintain, if not bolster, one's potential as a public servant. In Hung Mai's time, certainly, a command of Taoist exorcistic practice would have been regarded as one sure measure of success among gentry.

However vaguely motivations have been defined, the *I-chien chih* leaves no doubt as to the sociopolitical needs that were met by office-holders with expertise in Taoist rituals. The era about which Hung Mai wrote was above all a time of transition. The forced relocation of the imperial house can be said to have left its mark on every aspect of life across the central and southern reaches of the empire. As the episodes summarized above demonstrate, Hung appears to have been instinctively alert to the difficulties inherent to an age characterized by major realignments of power. He and his informants documented everything from haunted houses and the ghosts of the dead to obstreperous clerks and coercive sorcerers. Nothing that fell within the range of potential perils awaiting the newly placed official seems to have escaped their attention.

Emigrants from the north were found to be especially vulnerable to the intrusions of the ghosts of family members left behind. Their well-being was also threatened by terrifying visions of indigenous yet, to them, alien forces. Possessing spirits were simply not known to discriminate between oldtimers and newcomers.

Locals and transplanted officials alike were compelled to redefine their supporting networks as vast numbers sought refuge in the south. As disturbances arose at home or office, the dilemma faced overall was to find someone on whom to rely, someone who knew how to explain, if not resolve, the mysteries staged as supernatural dramas. Many episodes in the *I-chien chih* indicate that local sorcerers, physicians, and Taoist masters all found their clientele. But there is evidence to suggest a growing preference for calling on someone with whom one could identify, someone of comparable breeding and entitlement who came recommended as a master of exorcistic rites. Practitioners of T'ien-hsin and cognate Thunder Rites born of genteel families are on record for having proved themselves, often to the point of fame. Few types of psychic conflict, from mysterious thefts and vandalism to delirium and other behavorial aberrations, fell beyond their capacity to diagnose. Their services came to be indispensable, for they possessed the acumen essential to gaining consensus in identifying scapegoats of the spirit realm on whom any untoward affront might be pegged.

Face-to-face combat with channels of the spirit realm of a more pernicious nature also fell within the capacity of this new breed of official. Empowered by the seal of divine as well as state authority, they became agents of reform, whose very presence could not have been anything less than formidable. Just as they found their calling as family and company therapists, so too did Hung Mai's generation struggle to maintain equilibrium in the community at large. Recent research points to a growing sense of local solidarity as a manifestation of the elite's changing perceptions of its role in society.[90] It appears to have been precisely the entrenchment of local authority figures that came to pose the most implacable challenges to newly installed officials. Episodes featuring communities that openly defied representatives of imperial authority offer a glimpse of the institutional centers around which disputes over territorial dominion evolved. Some officials saved face by yielding to overwhelming support of enshrinements where pride of locale was inextricably bound. Many who sought to diminish such foci of local identity were seen to have done so at great risk of life and limb. Central to stories in which presiding officials overcame threats to their autonomy was a show of force. But, as Hung Mai discloses, that show of force was often backed up with the armature of Taoist rites. The demands for weapons of ritual authority can thus be explained in part as a manifestation of an era in which public servants had no choice but to look beyond imperial investiture in asserting their presence. The erosion of what in the past were assumed to be invincible tokens of power was clearly among the factors contributing to a rising demand for ritual reinforcement. Threats to both personal and public welfare, increasing during the Southern Sung, found their remedy in the adoption of more menacing weapons in return. Taoist ritual practice in truth offered new means with which to fight fire with fire.

Instruction in Taoist Rites of Exorcism

The accounts in the *I-chien chih* provide few clues as to the accessibility of teachings in Taoist rites. Opportunities for taking up such studies often appear to have arisen from mere happenstance. Names of masters willing to take on disciples are seldom supplied. A chance encounter with a stranger of unusual mien is the most common explanation offered. The haphazard way in which such alliances were formed suggests an itinerant body of ritual practitioners who roamed as free agents, unattached to temple compounds.[91] The manner in which they conveyed their secrets is as mysterious as their backgrounds. As is still largely the case, relations between master and disciple were doubtless defined in accordance with a legacy of oral transmissions. Texts of sacred writ are also likely to have changed hands, as one generation passed down teachings to the next. Traditional pedagogy would also find the novice copying out manuals of instruction in his master's possession.

The increasing production of printed texts during the Sung cannot be ignored. Ritual Master Yüan Miao-tsung, in preparing a corpus of T'ien-hsin and related teachings, stated that it was his intention to supply instruction that he found otherwise unavailable. His anthology is among the few in the present Taoist canon that can be traced to the canonic compilation authorized by Sung Hui-tsung. The emperor himself is reported to have sought in vain a complete work on "thunder writings" to include in the new canon.[92] But there is apparently no way to know just how many manuals of this sort came to be incorporated into the Taoist canon printed at the end of the Northern Sung. Nor do we know how many copies of the canon or portions of it may have been issued and distributed, much less the extent to which private printings of such literature were undertaken at the time.

By the Southern Sung, however, at least one Thunder Ritual master is known to have recommended dissemination of his teachings through publication. A letter preserved in an anthology of writings ascribed to Pai Yü-ch'an (fl. 1209–1224) expressly advises that ten copies of an existing woodcut printing of the *Jade Scripture of Thunderclap (Lei-t'ing yü-ching)* be distributed among the gentry of Kiangsi.[93] There is considerable evidence to suggest that many others preferred to guard the secrecy of

Thunder Ritual writings.[94] Pai's move to disperse *lei-fa* teachings was presumably tied to his warnings against falling under the sway of masters promoting false teachings. Particularly treacherous, to his mind, were sorcerers who claimed the authority of ritual codes but who in fact fabricated what they called the secret transmissions of spirit writing. Pai even joked about a sorcerer who spouted nonsense because he misunderstood the inscription on a talisman that had itself, characteristically, been appropriated from venerable teachings in the name of Lord Lao.[95]

Pai's astute comments point out the features of Taoist formulations that set them apart from the legacy of sorcerers. First and foremost, Taoist ritual traditions are based on the written word. It is this aspect, more than any other, that historically distinguishes the Taoist exorcist from the common sorcerer. He is, in truth, its literate counterpart. Although both concentrate on the exposure of perverse forces, the Taoist exorcist finds his closest correspondence in what might best be termed an expert in martial and legal affairs. He marches into battle like a commander-in-chief and issues orders like a judge. He perceives himself as a master of cosmic power whose calling is to resolve upheavals in the spirit realm as mirrored in the mundane. Thus, like a clever civil or military official, the Taoist exorcist must remain ever vigilant to the events and circumstances shaping the conflicts he may be expected to remedy. Essential to every step of the entire ritual procedure of exorcism, from the embodiment of divine authority to the dispatch of cosmic warriors, is the inscription and conveyance by fire of communications on high.

In addition to the written foundation of Taoist ritual, Pai Yü-ch'an's remarks recall that Taoist exorcistic codifications and government directives have long found an enemy in common. The nemesis they shared comprised the *yin-ssu* and *yin-tz'u,* or "excessive cults and shrines," and the *wu,* that is, sorcerers, presiding over them. Such enemies are specified in centuries of writings preserved in the Taoist canon, from the early Shang-ch'ing revelations, Ling-pao scriptures, and Cheng-i formulations to the immense codifications of Lu Hsiu-ching (406–477) and T'ao Hung-ching (456–536). Many texts simply advocate a policy of *p'o-miao,* or the smashing of shrines. As T'ao Hung-ching explains in his commentary to a synthesis of Shang-ch'ing writings, shrines were to be destroyed if they harbored any intent to render harm, whether it be the provocation of illness or more lethal attacks. The intent to do injury, T'ao continues, characterized the altars of sorcerers sustained throughout the countryside by offerings of food. The remedy cited for overcoming these shrines and their perverse inhabitants merely consists of an invocation of the lord of heaven together with 120 commanders.[96]

T'ao Hung-ching's successors down through the T'ang appear to offer nothing more specific regarding either target or method of control. Among ritual codifiers to take up the subject in the Northern Sung was

Ritual Master Yüan Miao-tsung. But even his corpus on T'ien-hsin practice fails to supply more than broad guidelines. In one passage he defines objectionable shrines as those honoring inauthentic spirits, such as were identified with trees and streams, which had not been entered into the imperial Canon of Sacrifices. Yüan's definition also evokes T'ao's commentary, for he adds that the shrines to be suppressed were precisely those that extorted offerings of flesh while threatening reprisals. Unlike the verbal invocation recorded by T'ao, Yüan prescribes a remedy based on the written word. He calls for the inscription and dispatch of a petitionary report to the Sacred Mountain of the East and a memorial to the uppermost celestial realm. The force of these communications, according to Yüan, was to "send down celestial troops to seize the perverse spirits who bring injury through fraud and to burn down their shrines."[97] Subsequent passages in Yüan's anthology are no more specific regarding how the actual destruction of the shrines might be carried out.[98]

Discourse on the subject of who should be suppressed and how becomes considerably more animated by the Southern Sung. Tropes such as *yin-ssu* and *p'o-miao* finally begin to be defined with somewhat more clarity. To Thunder Ritual Master Pai Yü-ch'an himself is ascribed a remarkably enlightening introduction to variant traditions of *wu-fa,* or the rites of sorcerers.[99] In answer to a question posed by one of his disciples, Pai is reported to have traced the history of *wu-fa* from its transmission to P'an-ku. The fact that the Yao minority claims the legendary P'an-ku as its ancestor suggests that the rites of P'an-ku to which Pai refers were those practiced by Yao sorcerers.[100] Here, I would suggest, is a clue to a major motivating force behind ritual rearmament during the Sung.

The magical feats of ethnic minorities in south China caught the attention of many literati over the centuries. One fifth-century account reports on how a sorcerer of the Man minority taught someone the means by which to transform himself into a tiger.[101] Anecdotes inspiring awe soon gave way to horror stories. Meng Kuan, writing of bizarre phenomena in Ling-nan during the ninth century, traces the history of a false shrine established by Annamese to a dragon spirit.[102] To Chou Ch'ü-fei (*chin-shih* 1163), who compiled a comparable account of Ling-nan, the terms *wu* and *yin-tz'u* appear to have been considered synonymous with the mediumistic practices of minorities in the south.[103] Memorials issued periodically toward the suppression of "sorcerers" and "excessive cults," in fact, frequently targeted the regions south of the Yangtze.[104] Thus it would seem that *wu* and *yin-ssu* also came to serve as official euphemisms for aggregations of minorities. The unarticulated yet implicit agenda of such declarations would appear to have been the assertion of state rule over local autonomy. Many, if not all, of the enshrinements featured in the *I-chien chih* episodes fell under the aegis of sorcerers whom the state perceived as potential leaders of opposition to the throne.

Although Hung Mai remains vague as to the ethnic identity of the sorcerers confronting agents of the central government, some may very well have been the designated heads of minority followings. It is the sorcerer, after all, who has traditionally served as the village chieftain of the Yao minority. Old folksongs of the Yao, moreover, attest to a long history of animosity toward Han officials.[105]

The significance of Pai Yü-ch'an's mention of sorcery in the name of P'an-ku is further elucidated by the writings of Lu Shih-chung. Lu states unequivocally in his *Great Rituals of the Jade Hall* that "the emanations of ghosts prevail most abundantly among the hundred tribes south of the Yangtze."[106] With this declaration, Lu reveals himself to be at the forefront of efforts to sinicize minorities. He condemns false gods of all kinds. Those venerating ghosts and perverse spirits are but victims of their own blind faith, he adds, and are unaware of how they thereby provoke injury to themselves. Once armed with *cheng-fa*, or "correct rites," Lu's argument proceeds, the patrons of such counterfeit, ill-boding forces would be able to eradicate the source of misery in their lives.

Lu distinguishes two types of perversity, the great and the small. The small he identifies as the *hun*-souls who await release from the netherworld. Great perversities are defined as the false enshrinements within Buddhist and Taoist abbeys, spirits attached to mountains and forests, and the affiliates of *shen-miao*, or spirit shrines. The "correct rites," Lu emphasizes, offer refuge against the harm perpetrated by all of these aberrations. Lu Shih-chung, in other words, urged nothing less than the reform of all those who fell under the grip of the sorcerers of the south. Hung Mai recorded a similar message of reform in the voice of the T'ien-hsin practitioner Magistrate Ch'ien Tang, as he destroyed the shrine of a Bee King under the charge of an anonymous sorcerer.[107] It was a message that at least by the mid-thirteenth century the Yao are known to have taken to heart. Their assimilation of the Correct Rites of T'ien-hsin appears to have been directly related to Sung imperial efforts to sinicize minority tribes.[108] Such efforts also seem to have been the unspoken agenda of magistrates such as Ch'ien Tang.

On the Power of Thunder Rites

It is to the cognate formulations of Thunder Rites that I turn in closing for a clearer picture of the new weaponry available to officeholders by the Sung. Variant codes of *lei-fa* arose throughout the south, across the very terrain where thunderbolts struck with the greatest intensity.[109] All manuals of Thunder Rites, whatever the regional variety, find a common heritage in the ever burgeoning body of thunder lore that one generation passed down to the next. As the harbinger of rain, the crash of thunder and flash of lightning inspired numerous cults. Communities whose welfare depended on the yield of the land typically looked to guardian spirits, often serpentine in origin, for timely rainfall.[110] Among the most widely acclaimed was the thunder spirit enshrined in the prefecture named for its frequent thunderstorms, Lei-chou (Kwangtung).[111] Lei-kung, or Sire Thunder, as this spirit came to be known, was the name coined in antiquity for a deity popularly envisioned beating on drums to evoke thunder and wielding a dagger to punish wrongdoers.[112] The latter aspect owes much to the firmly held belief that fatal strikes of lightning bore proof positive of the power of divine retribution.[113]

Masters of Thunder Rites may be considered in essence the worldly counterparts to Lei-kung. Just as the primordial thunder deity was thought to embody complementary aspects, thunder ritual specialists perceived themselves both as rainmakers and as the combatants of all sinister forces preying on the masses.[114] Although necessarily opaque in language, the remedies prescribed in *lei-fa* manuals for overcoming so-called perverse sorcerers and enshrinements prove to be somewhat more explicit than the writings on the subject surveyed heretofore. The sheer variety of Thunder Rites practiced in the Sung can be considered remarkable in itself. Pai Yü-ch'an lists altogether thirty-six different traditions of *lei-fa* in a petition dating to 1216.[115] Texts of instruction for many in his count are found in the 268-*chüan Tao-fa hui-yüan,* the most voluminous anthology of Thunder Rites to survive. The provenance of this monumental work is uncertain, but internal evidence reveals it to date no earlier than the late fourteenth century. That the opening fifty-five chapters, which are entirely devoted to the Ch'ing-wei ritual tradition, evoke the memory of the Ch'ing-wei patriarch Chao I-chen (d. 1382) suggests that one of Chao's disciples may have been responsible for its compilation.[116] All manuals in the *Tao-fa hui-yüan* name worthies of ages past by way of establishing a venerable line of transmission. Many are anonymous compilations, but a notable few bear prefaces or colophons identifying them as products of the Sung. Several, furthermore, designate Thunder Ritual masters prominent during the twelfth and thirteenth centuries as the prevailing practitioners.

Like T'ien-hsin codifications, several *lei-fa* manuals in the *Tao-fa hui-yüan* are promoted as the single, true *cheng-fa* (correct rites). Inherent in these competing claims is a barely concealed undercurrent of rivalry. The innate theatricality of the rites themselves seems to offer additional evidence for what must have been a highly competitive field of specialty. Even so, all of these exorcistic ritual codes agree that the common enemy was any manifestation of malevolence, be it vengeful ghost or village sorcerer. A remarkable expression of this consensus is recorded in one of the concluding chapters of the *Tao-fa hui-yüan*. To an analyst who remains anonymous, there are but two forms of *lei-fa:* correct *(cheng)* and perverse *(hsieh)*. One must discriminate, he counsels, between correct rites and the perverse rites of sorcerers *(shih-wu hsieh-fa)*.[117] Thus, however correct rites may be defined, there is no mistaking their most highly visible competitor. We can conclude that a primary goal of those seeking training in Thunder Rites was to master techniques that would prove superior to the forms of "thunder magic" practiced by southern sorcerers.[118] The preeminence of black magic was, in short, to be challenged by a more potent range of ritual artillery than had previously been known to exist.

The nature of battles fought between sorcerers and Thunder Ritual masters is initially suggested by the language of instruction itself. The inscription of the word *sha,* or "kill," is a well-recognized feature of Taoist talismans. Early incantations, moreover, evoke visions of the beheading, dismemberment, and disembowelment of demonic forces.[119] There is no question that Taoist exorcistic rites are fundamentally framed as acts of violence.[120] Much less clear is the extent to which they can be said actually to have sanctioned the rampages evoked both by the choice of words and by the graphic aids specified. This issue raises a question of significance to all ritual traditions. Is there any justification for seeking meaning beyond the metaphorical language of ritual instruction? Manuals of Thunder Rites surely invite a second reading. Chief among the lessons these complex writings teach is that what is not said may be as important or more important than what is. We are left to consider whether the corrective rites of *lei-fa* entail measures equal to the violence inherent in the black magic of sorcerers. Are we to understand that those who took up Thunder Rites thereby appropriated the license to kill as well as to search and destroy? To answer this question, I turn to an examination of the means by which the threats of annihilation issued under the aegis of "correct rites" were to have been carried out.

Fighting Sorcery. Manuals on Thunder Rites printed in the Taoist canon, although highly suggestive, rarely offer very much in the way of concrete instruction on how to combat sorcery. There is, however, no lack of reference to the undesirability of the presence of *wu.* One notable example is found in a manual that is ascribed to the Ling-pao patriarch Ko Hsüan (164–244) but appears to have been compiled sometime between 1104 and 1246.[121] Central to this veritable compendium of Lei-chou lore is an outline of everything considered to be subject to the wrath of thunder. Worldly criminals singled out include "perverse sorcerers," who deceive and harm the masses by their "perverse magic."[122] The authority to punish such wrongdoers is said to be preordained, but just how executions were to be carried out by the authority of thunder is left to the reader's imagination.

The license to kill is more explicitly divulged in a text drawn from the Lei-kung legacy that survives only in fragmentary form outside the Taoist canon. Portions of two works centering on the cosmic board and seals of Sire Thunder are recorded in sequence within a fascicle of the Ming encyclopedia *Yung-le ta-tien*.[123] An attribution to the renowned general Li Ching (571–649) embedded within this composite transcription is presumably fictive.[124] The text on seals bears the title *Lei-kung yin-wen ching* (Scripture on the seal inscriptions of Sire Thunder). A similar title in three *chüan* is registered in the bibliographic monograph of the *Sung shih*.[125] The fourth in the first series of twelve seals illustrated is expressly designated as a seal with the capacity for *yen-sha* (lit., to stifle to death), that is, to induce fatal nightmares. "If you intend to kill someone," the instructions continue, "inscribe the person's full name in vermilion on the doorway of earth (*ti-hu*, i.e., the southeast corner) of the cosmic board. [With the seal in hand,] pace the seven stars [i.e., of the Northern Dipper] and press the seal on it [i.e., the cosmic board]. That very night twelve generals, thirty-six spirit lords, and eighty-four thousand spectral troops will stifle that person to death."[126] The fact that this passage is followed by directions on how to revive the dead would seem to suggest that the instructions for terrorizing someone to death by inducing nightmares were to be understood figuratively, not literally.[127] The intent to kill is nonetheless implicit.[128]

The *Scripture on the Seal Inscriptions of Sire Thunder* offers no clarification regarding to whom the ritual of *yen-sha* might be directed. The Lei-kung procedures are dedicated overall to the protection of one's person and to the assistance of the state, aims that find their match in T'ien-hsin and related codifications.[129] Did its provocative instructions recommend against the text's inclusion in the Taoist canon? Can it be considered an example of the sort of black magic that Taoist traditions of exorcism came to apply but ordinarily guarded with the utmost secrecy?

Narrative accounts of the tenth century register conflicting perceptions of the Lei-kung legacy. Tu Kuang-t'ing (850–933), for example, tells the story of how Yeh Ch'ien-shao of Hsin-chou (Kiangsi) effectively applied the talismanic teachings conveyed to him by Sire Thunder.[130] Echoes of his training in calling on the five thunder lords are found in a manual on Thunder Rites, the inspiration for which is traced, in a preface ascribed to Ch'en Nan (d. 1213), to the descent of Hsü Sun (239–292/374?).[131] Most remarkable among other manuals traced to this patriarch of Ching-ming enshrined in central Kiangsi is a codification presented as the Great Rites of the Thunder of the [Southern] Man.[132] This formulation and others similarly titled are among the most likely to be adaptations of the "thunder magic" associated with the Man of south China.

Is there any evidence that links the rites of Sire Thunder with minority ritual practice? An anecdote ascribed to the *Pei-meng so-yen* seems to imply just such a connection.[133] A Register of Sire Thunder is reported to have been in circulation among villagers of the Pa-Shu (Szechwan) region sometime after the K'ai-yüan era (713–714). It is also said to have been in the possession of a Taoist master in the village of Chiang-ling (Hupeh). Some were of the opinion, the anecdote concludes, that this register was forbidden by patriarchs of the Celestial Master lineage. It was rejected apparently on two grounds. First, the Register of Sire Thunder reportedly was not to be found within the Taoist canon. Second, it appears to have been condemned for its potential destructiveness. Perverse applications, the closing declaration reads, would most certainly invite divine retribution.

A late manual on Thunder Rites in the *Tao-fa hui-yüan* appears to have been aimed precisely at those who practiced the sort of *yen-sha* prescribed in the *Scripture on the Seal Inscriptions of Sire Thunder*. The "Rites for Seizing Perverse Sorcerers" *(Shou-she hsieh-wu fa)*, compiled by Lu Yeh and annotated by his disciple Hsü Pi-ta (fl. 1258), provide some of the most specific instructions within the Taoist canon on the curtailment of sorcery.[134] Several restrictions governed their application. First, the "Rites of Seizure" were to be authorized only in cases where it had been determined that a "perverse sorcerer" had committed egregious crimes. Second, it is stated that prior to initiating the ritual procedure, one must inform the censor-in-chief as well as the astral deity T'ien-p'eng.[135] The level of offense justifying the ritual procedure is spelled out in the sample of the notification form to be submitted to the censor-in-chief. Sorcerers who led the masses astray by their perverse ways and then induced fatal nightmares when they did not get what they wanted are deemed subject to the "Rites of Seizure."[136]

The procedure is alternatively dubbed "Rites for Decapitating *Hun*-Souls" *(Chan-hun fa)*. As this designation implies, the rites are presented fundamentally as a form of sympathetic magic whereby one envisions the capture and confinement of the villain's *hun*-souls and other vital forces within talismans resembling human figures (figure 7.1).[137] An incantation to be recited upon visualizing the seizure itself, however, seems to suggest that this ritual of substitution may have been conducted in direct correspondence to the censor-in-chief's actual pursuit of the sorcerer at large.[138] Decapitation by hachet is the punishment specified for any who dared resist the forces under the command of T'ien-p'eng. A rigorous interrogation awaited captives. Although the ultimate measures to be taken remain indistinct, the underlying force of the "Rites of Seizure" is perhaps best conveyed by two strongly worded admonitions incorporated within the text. The procedure itself was considered to be so potentially treacherous that the utmost discretion is advised for anyone attempting to apply it. Those who take it upon themselves to engage in

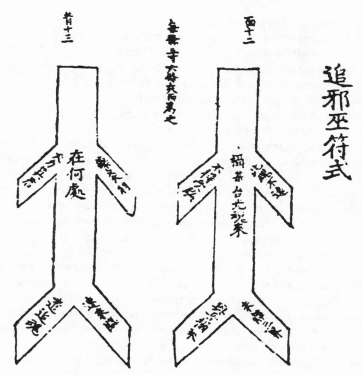

Figure 7.1. The "Rites for Seizing Perverse Sorcerers" require that multiple copies of the "Talisman for Pursuing Perverse Sorcerers" be rendered as illustrated. Inscriptions on front and back include the name of the sorcerer sought as well as the sorcerer's domicile. (*Tao-fa hui-yüan* [HY 1210], 264.6b)

the seizure and interrogation of sorcerers for personal reasons, moreover, are warned to expect the death penalty for their violation of the ritual code. Above all else, these advisories seem to reaffirm the inherent severity of the "Rites of Seizure." The instructions are a reminder, moreover, that exorcistic procedures both reinforced and were reinforced by all who served to maintain law and order in society. Black magic, as practiced by sorcerers such as Chang who confronted Magistrate Hung Pang-chih, had obviously met its match in more ways than one.

Demolishing Shrines. Guidelines on the destruction of shrines recorded in manuals on Thunder Rites prove to be slightly more far-ranging than those on eradicating sorcery itself. The two aims are not mutually exclusive. The abolition of practitioners of sorcery housed in shrines may be considered implicit, if not explicit, in the phrase *fa-miao ch'u-hsieh* (destroy shrines and eradicate perversity). Wang Wen-ch'ing and Pai Yü-ch'an are among renowned experts in Thunder Rites to have used precisely these words in listing threats to be overcome.[139] A wide array of weapons became available for the accomplishment of this goal. Both the variety and creativeness exhibited by this new arsenal bespeak a markedly competitive era of Taoist exorcistic practice.

Among the most eye-catching instructions are those found in the manuals of Thunder Rites formulated in the name of the astral deity Ma Sheng. One text incorporated within the Ch'ing-wei corpus of the *Tao-fa hui-yüan* features an incantation describing his attributes and the force of his weapons. A three-headed, nine-eyed manifestation of Ma Sheng is to be envisioned mounted on a scarlet rhinoceros. "Fire-crows released in wrath set aberrant shrines ablaze; iron ropes brandished in glee entwine 'round mountain goblins," reads one couplet.[140] Variant formulations of the rites of Ma Sheng supplement this incantation with talismanic renditions of the weapons enumerated. A version of the "Fire-Crow Talisman" appears, for instance, in a *k'ao-chao* ritual code putatively transmitted by the Shen-hsiao codifier Lin Ling-su (1076–1120).[141] Each component is separately illustrated, together with the line of incantation to be recited upon inscription (figure 7.2). The recitation prescribed for producing the bird's head includes the lines "Flames of fire spewn from the mouth, scorching to death perverse forces."[142] But, rather than the fire-crow, it is Ma Sheng's steed, the fire-rhinoceros, that, according to this code, is the

Figure 7.2. The flame-splitting fire-crow is among the weapons borne by the astral deity Ma Sheng. The instructions call for inscribing the "Fire-Crow Talisman" in black on yellow paper. (*Tao-fa hui-yüan* [HY 1210], 222.15b–16a)

weapon of choice against undesirable shrines. Lighting the abstract talismanic configuration representing this beast is said to provoke a clap of
thunder that will immediately result in the conflagration of all shrines
harboring injurious forces. A more complex vision of destruction is
introduced in an alternative manual on the rites of Ma Sheng, the provenance of which is uncertain. The repression of shrines is among fourteen different applications specified for an inscription recorded in this
manual under the title "Talisman for Remote Seizure" *(Yüan-cho fu)*.
Following its rendition on stone or on an iron tablet, one is to visualize
Commander Ma standing inside the shrine targeted for destruction. It
will burst into flames, according to these instructions, as one envisions
the emergence of Ma Sheng's fire-wheel and fire-gourd, together with his
fire-spitting snake.[143]

Strikingly similar images dominate a selection of Thunder Rites centering on the spirit of lightning, Teng Po-wen. Shrines and sorcerers
alike, according to one manual, are deemed subject to the flames surging
from the beak of the bird-headed Teng himself.[144] A single talismanic
charge in the same text, moreover, evokes a stampede of fire-breathing
animals, including everything from crows and hawks to camels, elephants, dragons, horses, lions, dogs, and even unicorns.[145] Another
manual dedicated to Teng Po-wen features instructions specifically
devised for overcoming "perverse shrines." A "Talisman for Sealing
Shrines" *(Feng-miao fu)*, imprinted with the Seal of Sire Thunder, is to be
used in securing the gateways of offensive structures. The incantation to
be recited as the gates are sealed implies that the shrine will thereby
instantaneously collapse. But the actual demolition is understood to be
accomplished with the aid of a complementary inscription, the "Talisman
of the Fire-Wheel" (figure 7.3). The incantation recited for empowering
this talisman evokes not only the spit-fire snake depicted but also a herd
of celestial beasts spewing flames over great distances.[146] The guidelines
governing its application, on the one hand, are pointedly ambiguous. Initially, one is instructed to envision someone else carrying forth the talisman. As the fire-wheel burns, the shrine itself, which is to be visualized
as a grass hut, is described as succumbing to flaming chariots and con-
veyors of foul-smelling smoke. The closing comments, on the other
hand, imply that a more active role than mere visualization is required. A
memorial expression of gratitude is to be released, the text advises, prior
to taking one's leave. "Do not look back once you come out of the
shrine," reads the concluding admonition.[147]

Equally enigmatic instructions are recorded for applying a "Talisman
of the Great Spirit of Crackling Fire." This talisman features a depiction
of the bird-beaked Teng Po-wen soaring above a fire-breathing dragon
(figure 7.4). It is recorded in a manual on Thunder Rites, which opens
with a preface ascribed to Wang Wen-ch'ing.[148] Shrines housing spectral
forces who delude the masses and steal their goods, among other crimes,

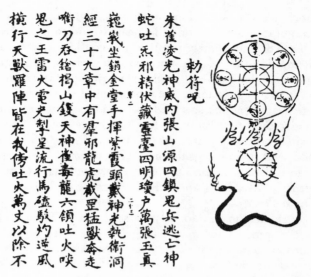

朱雀凌光神威內張山源四鎮鬼兵逃亡神
蛇吐炁邪精伏藏靈臺四明瓊戶萬張玉真
巃巍坐鎮金堂手揮紫霞頭戴翠神光執衛洞
經三十九章中有犖邪龍虎藏罡猛獸奔走
嚼刀吞鎗捫山鎈天神雀毒龍六領吐火唉
鬼之王雷火電光制星流行馬磕灼遊風
橫行天獸羅陣皆在我傍吐火萬丈以除不

勅符呪

Figure 7.3. The "Fire-Wheel Talisman" is to be inscribed in vermilion on magenta paper. Recitations identifying the symbolic force embodied within each stroke are recorded in the lengthy analysis preceding the illustration. The accompanying incantation (*left*) also enumerates the various thunder spirits and fire-breathing animals evoked upon the application of this talisman. (*Tao-fa hui-yüan* [HY 1210], 115.27a–29a)

are reported to be liable to the fury of Teng Po-wen. The dispatch of communications to the requisite office on high is listed as the first order of business. The spirits thereby notified are expected to assemble on the day set aside for the demolition of the shrine. One then proceeds to the site at the appointed time, armed with the seals of the "Purple Radiance of the Cinnabar Heavens" and the "Inscription of the Fire-radiating Thunder." Once the "Talisman of the Great Spirit of Crackling Fire" has been attached to the gateway of the shrine, preparations are to be made for submitting offerings to the spirits of thunder. A mound in the wilderness a short distance away is designated as the appropriate setting for presenting oblations. If one then calls out loudly: "Go immediately to that site, burn down the shrine, and seize all spectral bandits!" a thunderstorm will reportedly erupt in swift response. "Be not afraid," the text advises. Readers are further reminded that a reckless application of these rites not only risks injury to others but also invites punishment in return.[149]

A corresponding set of instructions for "Destroying Perversity and

Figure 7.4. The bird-beaked Teng Po-wen, embodiment of lightning, is featured surmounting a fire-dragon in the "Talisman of the Great Spirit of Crackling Fire." As the analysis indicates, bolts of lightning are thought to emerge from the crack of his rope, signaling a thunderous holocaust. (*Tao-fa hui-yüan* [HY 1210], 56.22a–23a)

Smashing Shrines" *(fa-hsieh p'o-miao)* is found in a late Shen-hsiao codification that also appears to reflect the legacy of Wang Wen-ch'ing.[150] The procedures outlined here are to be followed upon receiving notification of the presence of any enshrinements unauthorized by the Canon of Sacrifices or of any aberrant forces occupying the mountains or forests. Plaints submitted in writing must specify in detail how such perversities wrongfully extract offerings by violating homes and fields alike. A sequence of communiqués may then be issued to alert a deputation of guardian spirits to make its presence known in advance. The practitioner applying these rites must then take on himself the role of spirit commander, after achieving divine transformation. Not unlike the rites of Teng Po-wen, the instructions subsequently call for a contingent of cosmic troops to escort someone bearing a talisman into the shrine under siege. The master of ceremonies cum spirit commander is to call down an entourage of thunder spirits to accompany him to the front of the shrine. Spectral forces are reportedly seized at his command. The demolition of the shrine itself is to be accomplished with the release of a "Thunder-Fire Talisman" *(Lei-huo fu)*. As the talisman is consumed in flames, the instructions continue, "the master visualizes flashes of lightning, claps of thunder rumble forth, and a fire rages throughout the void." Finally, to prevent the return of spectral inhabitants, four iron tablets engraved with talismans are to be nailed inside the shrine, one to each wall. This closing directive seems to suggest that although a shell may remain, the force of the talisman can be assumed to have reduced everything within to ashes. The procedure at any rate is considered to be so miraculous that, as the instructions conclude, one is forbidden to apply them except on rare occasions.

I would suggest that both the visual and auditory features of these instructions offer substantial clues regarding the weaponry behind Thunder Rites. The procedures in which fire-breathing animals are evoked appear fundamentally to culminate in a burst of flames. The talismans central to these rites, moreover, recall the fire-birds and fire-beasts that are known to have been employed in Chinese warfare since very early times. Illustrations of this primitive form of arms in the *Wu-ching tsung-yao,* dating to 1044, seem to attest to something more than a glancing similarity. Two types of fire-birds featured in this extraordinary handbook on martial arts, for example, are pictured banded with small receptacles of burning moxa tinder (figure 7.5).[151] These avian destroyers were sent by the dozens to fly over enemy encampments and granaries, setting them afire. So-called fire-beasts were similarly prepared for battle. Particularly evocative is an illustration in the *Wu-ching tsung-yao* depicting wild beasts bearing gourds of burning moxa tinder on top of their heads.[152] These illustrations bring to mind most immediately the fire-crows and fire-gourds depicted within Ma Sheng's arsenal. Fire-breathing snakes and dragons, not to mention exotic species such as rhinoceroses, camels, elephants, and unicorns, might best be regarded as the inspirations of minds well acquainted with the tradition of employing

Figure 7.5. The pheasant and sparrows banded with nutfuls of burning moxa tinder, as depicted in the *Wu-ching tsung-yao,* find their correspondence in the fire-spitting crows and hawks featured in various manuals on Thunder Rites. (*Wu-ching tsung-yao* 11.21a–22b)

beasts of burden as weapons of war.[153] And like their counterparts on the battlefield, practitioners who called on flocks and herds of fire fighters by talisman and incantation may have been employing much the same weaponry. Talismanic renditions of fire-spitting birds and beasts, in short, would seem to be but shadows of the worldly species dispatched to set enemy shrines afire.

New Weaponry. On closer examination the manuals on Thunder Rites yield hints of weapons of far greater potency than incendiary devices had to offer. The evidence rests in not what the talismans depict but in what they were heard to deliver. Talismans of the fire-rhinoceros, crackling fire, and thunder-fire all gave way to claps of thunder. And within those rumblings is the key to a new form of weaponry behind Thunder Rites. Thunder Rites, in effect, gave new definition to the long-held perception that the greatest weapon of exorcism was command of the loudest noise.[154]

The narrative legacy of Thunder Rites is exemplified in Hung Mai's story of Sung An-kuo's defeat of an arboreal spirit. His rites of exorcism, it will be recalled, culminated in a clap of thunder that reduced the offending tree to cinders. Such anecdotes are found in a wide range of texts. Hagiographic accounts that feature the outbreak of thunderstorms on the release of a talisman may be considered a prototype of this genre.[155] But just as the legacy of rainmaking magic underlies this type, so too may its counterparts be considered the offspring of Thunder Ritual lore.

Stories centering on the destruction of perverse enshrinements are particularly common in hagiographies of figures who came to be adopted as patriarchs of various traditions of Thunder Rites. A late biography of the Ching-ming patriarch Hsü Sun, for example, finds him, much like Sung An-kuo, prevailing over a pernicious tree spirit.[156] Hsü reportedly witnessed villagers making offerings of flesh to a spirit who threatened dire consequences upon denial. He subsequently evoked wind and thunder to uproot its forest domain and declared the blackmailing perversity gone.

A significant variation on this theme is recorded in a story about another figure central to the Ching-ming heritage. Here the sound of thunder evoked by Hu Hui-ch'ao (d. 703) reduced a shrine to ashes.[157] Hu reportedly appeared in the Hsi shan region sometime around 674 or 675 and later oversaw the restoration of a temple there marking Hsü Sun's ascent. His victory over a nefarious spirit is reminiscent of the legend of Hsi-men Pao's confrontation with the god of the Yellow River. Hu Hui-ch'ao is portrayed as the salvation of a family whom he happened to encounter on a stroll through the marketplace of Hung-chou (Kiangsi). Their apparent bereavement caught his attention. He learned that they were grieving over their daughter's selection as the next bride of a local spirit.[158] His shrine is said to have been consumed in flames the instant Hu roared out a command giving charge to wind and thunder.

A similar account may be found in the hagiography of the martial lord known as Wen Ch'iung (b. 702).[159] The thirtieth-generation Celestial Master Chang Chi-hsien (1092–1126) is credited with promoting rites in his name. A disciple named Wu Tao-hsien, according to hagiographic legend, was sent as Lord Wen's agent to destroy an unsavory shrine in Min-hsien (Fukien). A storm reportedly broke out as the vision of Lord Wen appeared. As if in response to a single clap of thunder, the shrine targeted for destruction burst into flames.

Are such stories to be regarded simply as a continuation of the lore evolving around retributive lightning strikes? I think not. They seem rather to signify an advanced form of exorcistic practice. An apt expression of this higher level of training is found in a concise biography of Hsieh T'ien-yü, a practitioner active in the Hsien-tu mountains (Chekiang) during the thirteenth century. Listed among Hsieh's attributes is the capacity to "demolish shrines by the evocation of thunder" *(hsing-lei fa-miao)*.[160] To explain the skills implied in the coining of this phrase, I turn in closing to the life of an expert in Thunder Rites by the name of Sa Shou-chien (fl. 1141–1178).

The legends evolving around Sa Shou-chien center largely on the origins of the cult of Wang Ling-kuan, the fearsome red-haired martial lord who typically stands as the guardian deity of Taoist abbeys. According to the version of the story recorded in a supplement to Chao Tao-i's (fl. 1294–1307) hagiographic corpus, Sa initially took up the study of medicine but was led to abandon his practice after a faulty prescription resulted in the death of one of his patients.[161] Sa reportedly undertook a journey in search of the ritual teachings of the renowned Celestial Master Chang Chi-hsien, Lin Ling-su, and Wang Wen-ch'ing. At one point in his travels three men appeared, and, when they learned of his mission, each conveyed one item of instruction. One of the three is said to have introduced Sa to *lei-fa*. It was only after a subsequent visit to Lung-hu shan (Kiangsi), seat of the Celestial Master patriarchy, that Sa learned the identity of his roadside teachers. A letter he had carried at their behest revealed them to be none other than the transcendents Chang, Lin, and Wang themselves.

After completing his studies at Lung-hu shan, Sa began to apply his ritual training with great success. He had occasion to test his skills on a visit to the temple of a city god named Wang Shan.[162] Some days after his arrival the prefect chased him out, according to orders the deity had conveyed to him in a dream. At a distance outside the city, Sa happened to encounter someone carrying a pig to the temple as an offering. He prevailed upon this patron of the city god to take some incense and light it on his behalf. The man did as he was told, whereupon a single clap of thunder was heard. The temple was immediately consumed in flames, yet all other buildings in the area were said to have remained unscathed. Three years later, as Sa's life story concludes, Wang Shan reappeared and begged to be taken on as the master's assistant. Thus ends the saga of how a wayward spirit was subdued and later accepted as a guardian.[163]

The point of interest here is the devastating clap of thunder that followed the offering of incense at the temple. How might burning incense result in a thunderous burst of flames? This is a question that the Jesuit priest Pierre Huang came to ask in the late nineteenth century. It is raised in his discussion of a late version of the story of Sa Shou-chien copied from a gazetteer of Hunan province.[164] The sound of thunder and the source of the fire, Huang concludes, must have come from the application of gunpowder. In this suggestion, I am convinced, rests the secret of Thunder Rites.

As Joseph Needham has pointed out, the compounding of explosive mixtures arose as a by-product of systematic efforts to produce the elixir of life.[165] An alchemical handbook in the Taoist canon entitled *Chen-yüan miao-tao yao-lüeh* includes a passage pertinent to this subject. It appears in a catalogue of thirty-five errors known to have been committed by those lacking a discerning master. To heat sulphur, realgar, and saltpeter together with honey is said to have resulted not only in burned hands and faces but also in the destruction of buildings by fire.[166] The first three items are precisely the ingredients essential to the making of gunpowder, the earliest formulae for which are recorded in the *Wu-ching tsung-yao* of 1044.[167] The history of the composite work received in the canon under the title *Chen-yüan miao-tao yao-lüeh* is problematic. It is ascribed to Cheng Ssu-yüan, that is, Cheng Yin, whose expertise in alchemy was well publicized by his disciple Ko Hung (283–343). There is little doubt, however, that this attribution reflects but an effort to identify the text with one of the earliest acclaimed masters of alchemy. Internal evidence argues for a compilation date no earlier than the mid-tenth century.[168] It thus seems to attest to an awareness of the essentials behind the preparation of gunpowder approximately one century prior to the appearance of the *Wu-ching tsung-yao*.

However early the origins of gunpowder in China may prove to be, I think we might entertain the possibility that Thunder Rites may be traced to its invention. What I am suggesting is that *lei-fa* may owe its inspiration to the very discovery of the explosive properties of the combination of sulphur, realgar, and saltpeter. This is perhaps the secret that remains concealed within both the manuals and narrative accounts of Thunder Rites. The incense offering of Sa Shou-chien finds its counterpart in the talismans lit within shrines doomed to destruction. In addition to evoking the sound of exploding gunpowder, manuals on Thunder Rites also appear to evoke its smell, as in the "stinking smoke" denoted in talismans and incantations alike. The sheer hazards of such rites, which are repeatedly voiced in the manuals, offer resounding reminders of the caution put forth in the *Chen-yüan miao-tao yao-lüeh*. The risk of engaging in Thunder Rites, we are led to believe, was real indeed.

Its very capacity to masquerade as a thunderbolt appears, in fact, to explain the immediate appeal of gunpowder as a weapon. Is it possible that stories told by Tu Kuang-t'ing and Hung Mai about thunderbolts quelling the menace of Southern Man also have the smell of explosive compounds behind them?[169] To read such accounts as mere sermons on the recompense of lightning is perhaps to miss their true significance. Like stories on the demolition of shrines, they too seem to speak to the legacy of gunpowder.

The difficulty of distinguishing between a genuine thunderbolt and its artificial cousin is raised in an interesting legal case of 1732. Villagers in Hopei reportedly understood the death of one of their residents to be due to a strike of lightning.[170] A local magistrate investigating this fatality determined, however, that the deceased had been the victim of a crime of passion. The culprit, who had taken the widow as his wife, was condemned on the one hand by his inability to explain large purchases of combustible agents. The magistrate also observed that the deceased's home would have caved in had it been struck by lightning. Only a deadly explosion set off within the house, he concluded, could have caused it seemingly to erupt.

The wisdom demonstrated by the Hopei magistrate in 1732 was wisdom his predecessors in office had gained centuries earlier. The invention of gunpowder appears to have altered not only the way in which war came to be conducted but also the way in which peace was to be sustained throughout the countryside. The evolution of Thunder Rites would seem to have provided a protective shield for the application of explosives in securing the state against indigenous challenges to its authority. The ability to set off explosive compounds by divine authority could not but have contributed to a redefinition of the battle lines between *kuan* and *shen*. It was presumably the most important weapon in the expanding arsenal of exorcistic rites with which officeholders of the Sung became increasingly familiar. As the stability of the imperial house was shaken, new generations of elite must have taken heart in visions of divine guardians bearing arms representing the highest technology available.[171] The percussive roll of thunderclaps that came to rumble with greater frequency throughout the countryside was surely music to their ears. It was a roar that found its echo in the firecrackers exploding on the operatic stage as Wang Ling-kuan banished all demons from his presence.[172] All demons in the end, of course, rest in the eye of the beholder.

NOTES

1. Fang Shao, *Po-chai pien* (Peking: Chung-hua shu-chü, 1983), 6.34.
2. See *Ou-yang Wen-chung ch'üan-chi* (*SPPY* edition), *Lu-ling Ou-yang Wen-chung kung nien-p'u* 5b–6a.
3. My analysis is shaped by readings in anthropological literature centered on interpretations of phenomena such as possessing spirits, sorcery, and witchcraft as clarifications of social relations, as exemplified in E. E. Evans-Pritchard, *Witchcraft, Oracles, and Magic among the Azande* (Oxford: Clarendon Press, 1937); John Middleton and E. H. Winter, eds., *Witchcraft and Sorcery in East Africa* (New York: Frederick A. Praeger, 1963); and Mary Douglas, ed., *Witchcraft: Confessions & Accusations* (London and New York: Tavistock Publications, 1970).
4. *Ou-yang Wen-chung ch'üan-chi* 70.3a. See also the discussions in Liu Tzu-chien, *Ou-yang Hsiu ti chih-hsüeh yü ts'ung-cheng* (Hong Kong: Hsin-ya yen-chiu-so, 1963), pp. 108–128, and James T. C. Liu, *Ou-yang Hsiu, An Eleventh-Century Neo-Confucianist* (Stanford: Stanford University Press, 1967), pp. 155–172.
5. Tseng Min-hsing, *Tu-hsing tsa-chih* (Shanghai: Ku-chi ch'u-pan-she, 1986), 5.41–42, includes a portion of the prayer recorded in *Ou-yang Wen-chung ch'üan-chi*.
6. See Ursula-Angelika Cedzich, "Wu-t'ung: Zur bewegten Geschichte eines Kultes," in Gert Naundorf et al., eds., *Religion und Philosophie in Ostasien* (Würtzburg: Königshausen & Neumann, 1985), pp. 33–60.
7. The first episode in *TPKC* 73, ascribed to the *Chi-wen*, observes that sorcerers were adept at filching goods by masquerading as ghosts and spirits.
8. The classic study on state and church response to *yin-tz'u* remains Rolf A. Stein, "Religious Taoism and Popular Religion from the Second to Seventh Centuries," in Holmes Welch and Anna Seidel, eds., *Facets of Taoism: Essays in Chinese Religion* (New Haven: Yale University Press, 1979), pp. 53–81.
9. Anecdotal literature appears to verify this observation, tentatively formulated in Judith M. Boltz, *A Survey of Taoist Literature, Tenth to Seventeenth Centuries*, China Research Monograph no. 32 (Berkeley: Institute of East Asian Studies, 1987), p. 293, n. 254.
10. Biographical accounts of Hung Mai include *SS* 373 and the *Hung Wen-min kung nien-p'u*, compiled by Ch'ien Ta-hsin (1728–1804), in *Ch'ien-yen t'ang ch'üan-shu*, vol. 5 (Changsha, 1884). A reedition of Ch'ien's chronicle is found in Wang Te-i, "Hung Jung-chai hsien-sheng nien-p'u," Sung shih tso-t'an-hui, ed., *Sung shih yen-chiu chi* (Taipei: Chung-hua ts'ung-shu pien-shen wei-yüan-hui, 1964), vol. 2, pp. 405–474. Chang Fu-jui, "Le *Yi kien tche* et la société des Song," *Journal Asiatique* 256 (1968): 55–91, concludes that the initial fascicle of the ICC was completed in 1161, but Ōtsuka Hidetaka, "Kō Mai to Iken-shi—rekishi to genjitsu no hazama nite," *Tōdai Chūtetsubun gakkai-hō* 5 (1980): 75–96, dates it to early 1159.
11. *ICC, Chia* 2.13–14. Note also *ICC, Chih-i* 7.844–845, concerning a vision associated with the authorization of the prefect of Yüeh-yang (Hunan) of the restoration of an image of Lü Tung-pin and the prefect's subsequent sponsorship of the printing of a *chin-tan* manual ascribed to the transcendent, a version

of which can be found in Tseng Ts'ao's (fl. 1131–1155) *Tao shu* (HY 1011), 25.1a–11b.

12. *ICC, Chia* 15.132–133. The terminology given in Charles O. Hucker, *A Dictionary of Official Titles in Imperial China* (Stanford: Stanford University Press, 1985), is adopted here, with the exception of "clerk," rather than Hucker's "subofficial functionary," for *li,* and "county," rather than Hucker's "district," for *hsien.*

13. *ICC, Chia* 6.49–50. Note also *ICC, Ping* 3.385, concerning a Ch'iung-chou (Szechwan) prefect's frequent visits to the Chang Ssu-lang shrine at Mount Pai-ho.

14. *ICC, Chih-ching* 9.954–955.

15. *ICC, Chia* 5.43, 13.111–112.

16. *ICC, Chia* 1.2. Resources on Chiang Ching are cited in *SJSY,* pp. 3771–3772. Background on Sun Chiu-ting is found in the preceding and initial episode of *ICC, Chia* 1.1–2. According to *ICC, Chia* 1.3 and *Pu* 11.1649, Sun himself wrote down a number of such episodes, all of which were recent events.

17. *SS* 356.11211.

18. The link implied here between faith in sorcerers and denial of medical treatment has a long history in China. Although this issue is not raised in the *I-chien chih* episode concerning Chiang Ching, it figures in other anecdotes, one of which is discussed below (see n. 36).

19. *ICC, Ping* 5.408–409. This is the last episode in a chapter entirely credited to Ch'en Tai of Chin-yün (Chekiang). An entry in *SJSY,* p. 2488, identifies Ch'en Tai as the son of Ch'en Ju-hsi (*chin-shih* 1097), a native of Ch'ing-t'ien (Chekiang).

20. An entry for a Shen Wen (*chin-shih* 1148) of K'ai-feng is given in *SJSY,* p. 670, without reference to this post.

21. The sources cited in an entry for Shen Chieh (*chin-shih* 1138) of Wu-hsing (Chekiang) in *SJSY,* p. 670, do not mention the post of prefect of Kuang-te.

22. Of note among additional episodes on the theme of accommodation is *ICC, Chih-chia* 6.761, regarding an administrator of the foundry of Kan-chou (Kiangsi) by the name of Wang. A doorkeeper guided Wang to a local shrine to resolve the mystery of the apparent theft of soybean extract sold outside his residence. Like Ou-yang's chopsticks, the soybean extract was found inside the shrine. Rather than take offense, Wang chose to warm up the liquid so that it might properly serve as an offering. He also paid for it out of his own pocket. The account is all the more remarkable for its characterization of the shrine as one capable of provoking misfortune. Although Wang was certainly not coerced into honoring a site that many in his place would have found reason to condemn, he is portrayed as the willing pawn in a devotee's subterfuge.

23. See, for example, *ICC, I* 1.190–191, 5.223, 18.337.

24. See, for example, *ICC, Chia* 15.127.

25. Among the more memorable episodes concerning the difficulties of northerners relocating in the south is one recorded in *ICC, Ping* 10.452. It concerns a retired prefect whose death was erroneously perceived to have been the direct result of the sorcery of hired laborers.

26. According to *ICC, I* 3.210, a clerk actually managed to have a fatal dose of poison administered to a magistrate who had vowed to see him punished for

criminal activities. On the responsibilities of the clerical subbureaucracy and the opportunities for corruption, see Brian E. McKnight, *Village and Bureaucracy in Southern Sung China* (Chicago and London: University of Chicago Press, 1971), pp. 5, 20–22, 26, 48, 59, 61–62, 65–66, 70, 74, 124, 146, 176–177. The dependency of magistrates on clerks and the potential for corruption is also discussed in Denis C. Twitchett, "Patterns of Provincial Autonomy in the T'ang Dynasty," in John Curtis Perry and Bardwell L. Smith, eds., *Essays on T'ang Society: The Interplay of Social, Political and Economic Forces* (Leiden: E. J. Brill, 1976), pp. 90–109. The issue of corruption is further explored in Twitchett, "The Seamy Side of Late T'ang Political Life: Yü Ti and his Family," *Asia Major*, 3d series, 1.2 (1988): 29–63.

27. *ICC, Chih-ting* 6.1017–1018. It is not clear whether the Yang Kuang of Han-chia featured in this episode is to be identified with the Yang Kuang of Tzu-chou (Szechwan), whose candidacy for the provincial examination of 1178 Hung Mai is unable to verify, according to *ICC, Chih-kuei* 2.1236–1237.

28. The entry on the Erh-wang miao in Chuang Ssu-heng and Cheng Ti-shan, eds., [*Tseng-hsiu*] *Kuan-hsien chih* (1886), 3.20a, alludes to this episode in the *ICC*; additional lore regarding Li Ping is recorded in 9.40a–42a, 13.39b–45b. See also *ICC, Ping* 9.439.

29. *ICC, Chih-ching* 9.948–949. Yü Chi-ssu is identified as the source of this double entry, as well as the two succeeding episodes, one of which documents Ch'en Chüeh's career, as mentioned below. Hung Mai's preface to the *Chih-ching* segment is dated the tenth month of 1195. Other episodes also date to that year, some as late as the seventh month. Four episodes in *ICC, Chih-ting* 6.1011–1014, are credited to a Yü Wei-ssu, perhaps a scribal or printer's error for Yü Chi-ssu.

30. Yen Shu-p'ing's father is identified as Yen Lu-tzu, that is, Yen Tu, a native of K'un-shan (Kiangsu), according to *SJSY*, p. 4209.

31. See also the anecdote of *ICC, Ping* 12.468–469, in which Hung Mai voices consternation regarding the destiny of two brothers highly regarded for their literary studies, who seemingly fell victim to an "excessive shrine" that one had sought to eliminate.

32. Entries for both Liu Tsai and his wife Ms. T'ao (T'ao-shih) are found in *SJSY*, pp. 3863–3864.

33. *SS* 401.12167–12169. According to the *Ching-k'ou ch'i-chiu chuan* (Taipei: Kuang-wen shu-chü, 1969), 9.7b, Liu Tsai was still in office as defender of Chiang-ning during the drought of 1194.

34. A preliminary survey of what survives of Liu Tsai's writings reveals no corroboration of the *I-chien chih* episode. Commemorative prayers honoring his deceased brother and wife are recorded in *chüan* 26 of Liu's collected works, the 36-*chüan Man-t'ang* [*wen-*]*chi* (SKCS edition). This anthology represents less than half of his total output, according to *Ssu-k'u ch'üan-shu tsung-mu t'i-yao* 3386. Additional biographical materials are found in the prefaces and supplementary chapter of the *Chia-yeh t'ang ts'ung-shu* printing of the *Man-t'ang wen-chi* (Wu-hsing, 1918–1930), vols. 177–188.

35. *ICC, Chih-wu* 3.1074–1075. Biographical records on the life of Chang Kuei-mo, cited in *SJSY*, pp. 2413–2414, offer no confirmation of this account.

36. Early testimony to popular refusal of medical treatment due to faith in

sorcerers may be found in Ssu-ma Ch'ien's biography of the eminent physician Pien Ch'üeh in the *Shih chi* (Peking: Chung-hua shu-chü, 1959; rpt. 1964), 105.2794, and Ko Hung's essays in Wang Ming, ed., *Pao p'u-tzu nei-p'ien chiao-shih* (Peking: Chung-hua shu-chü, 1985), 5.113 and 9.173. The seriousness of the problem during the Sung is noted in Chang Pang-chi (d. 1150+), *Mo-chuang man-lu* (*TSCC* edition), 8.90–91. Two of three episodes noted in Tseng Min-hsing, *Tu-hsing tsa-chih,* 2.13 and 3.27–28, are corroborated in *SS* 283.9571 and 334.10729.

37. The episode recorded in *ICC, Chih-wu* 3.1076, gives Ch'ien Shen-chih's age in the year 1160 as thirty-plus.

38. *ICC, Chia* 19.174. The account is credited to Hsieh Chih (*chin-shih* 1148), on whom see the entry in *SJSY*, p. 4102. The phenomenon of haunted quarters, as exemplified in this episode, merits a study in its own right. Such accounts typically center on the temporary residence of a newly arrived official. The haunted house motif, I would suggest, is but one variation on the theme of the conflict between outsider and insider, as manifested through the rubric of *kuan* versus *shen.*

39. Recent contributions on the subject include Jean Lévi, "Les fonctions religieuses de la bureaucratie céleste," *L'homme* 101 (1987): 35–57; "Les fonctionnaires et le divin," *Cahiers d'Extrême-Asie* 2 (1986): 81–100; and *Les fonctionnaires divins: Politique, despotisme et mystique en Chine ancienne* (Paris: Éditions du Seuil, 1989), esp. pp. 234–269.

40. Examples of such cults that come to mind are those dedicated to the memory of Hsü Sun (see Boltz, *Survey of Taoist Literature,* pp. 70–78, 197–199) and the spirit of Kuan-k'ou (see above, n. 28). Hagiographic lore in both cases, according to *Sou-shen chi* (HY 1466), 2.10a, 3.13a–13b, (see Boltz, *Survey of Taoist Literature,* pp. 61–62), indicates that, following miraculous deeds, each abandoned office and moved on to higher pursuits.

41. Codifications of T'ien-hsin ritual include the ten-*chüan T'ai-shang chu-kuo chiu-min tsung-chen pi-yao* (HY 1217), compiled in 1116 by Ritual Master Yüan Miao-tsung, and the seven-*chüan Shang-ch'ing t'ien-hsin cheng-fa* (HY 566), compiled by Teng Yu-kung (1210–1279). A code of governance for both practitioners and the spirit realm compiled by Teng Yu-kung, the three-*chüan Shang-ch'ing ku-sui ling-wen kuei-lü* (HY 461), corresponds to *chüan* 6 in Yüan Miao-tsung's work (Boltz, *Survey of Taoist Literature,* pp. 33–35).

42. A major resource on variant schools of Thunder Ritual, the 268-*chüan Tao-fa hui-yüan* (HY 1210), is discussed in Piet van der Loon, "A Taoist Collection of the Fourteenth Century," in Wolfgang Bauer, ed., *Studia Sino-Mongolica: Festschrift für Herbert Franke* (Wiesbaden: Franz Steiner, 1979), pp. 401–405, and Boltz, *Survey of Taoist Literature,* pp. 47–49.

43. Kristofer Schipper makes a distinction between the classical legacy of ritual as practiced by *Tao-shih* (Taoist masters) and the vernacular, originally illiterate, tradition of *fa-shih* (ritual masters), but, as he points out, the term *fa-shih* has historically been applied to a diverse range of practitioners, including mediums ("Vernacular and Classical Rituals in Taoism," *JAS* 45 [1985]: 21–57). The history of the term demands further study. In the episodes below, *fa-shih* denotes literate practitioners who are exorcists foremost.

44. *ICC, I* 6.235–236, *Ping* 16.504–505. Note also *ICC, Chih-ting* 1.971,

regarding a Ritual Master Chao of the imperial line, who confronted the tutelary deity of Wu-hsing (Chekiang); *Chih-keng* 7.1191, concerning another descendant of the imperial family practicing the Rites of T'ien-hsin in Ming-chou (Chekiang); *Pu* 23.1759–1761, centering on the exorcistic rites of a Chao Shan-tao; and *Ping* 8.429–430, featuring a Chao Shih-e, who, in 1152, was able to cure a colleague of consumption according to his command of the "Ritual Registers of the Most High."

45. Although no informant's name appears immediately after the entry in *ICC, I* 6.235–236, Chao's nephew Chao Po-t'i would be the likely source, since he is credited with the succeeding entry regarding a cousin who unsuccessfully imitated his father in attempting exorcisms according to the Rites of T'ien-hsin.

46. See, for example, Boltz, *Survey of Taoist Literature,* pp. 38–39, 41, regarding two codifiers of the Ch'ing-wei ritual legacy, Huang Shun-shen (1224– ca. 1286) and Chao I-chen (d. 1382), who took up their professions after experiencing seemingly miraculous recoveries from illness.

47. The ability to identify on sight victims of possessing spirits is commonly ascribed to T'ien-hsin practitioners as, for example, in the case of Yang Chung-kung, administrative supervisor of Tao-chou (Hunan), according to *ICC, Chih-chia* 5.745.

48. *ICC, Ping* 16.504–505. Hung Mai names Wang Chü (d. 1173) as the source of this episode, based on the eyewitness account of Chang Ch'i, a younger brother of Chang Shao (1096–1156). Wang Chü also provided the story in *ICC, I* 7.244, on how the eldest son of Minister Li Pang-yen (d. 1130) came to give up practice of T'ien-hsin ritual. Also of note is the episode in *ICC, Chih-i* 9.866– 867, regarding the son of a "Gentleman for Court Service" named Hsü, of Hu-chou (Chekiang). The son, identified as "official no. 13," is said to have achieved great success as an expert in the *k'ao-chao* rites of T'ien-hsin, the practice of which he undertook after witnessing instances of spirit possession in his family.

49. *ICC, Chih-i* 7.846. Yao is said to have purchased his office by submitting payment in millet. See also *ICC, Chih-ching* 2.890, featuring a District Defender Yao, known to be skilled in exorcistic ritual, who helped overcome the haunted house of the supervisor of the granary in Kuei-chi (Chekiang). A more humorous account in *ICC, I* 19.347, tells how an uncle of Hung Mai's wife, who found himself troubled by a ghost, eventually gained relief by applying his training in T'ien-hsin ritual.

50. The woman and her son are said to have earlier resided with Hung Mai's older brother Hung Kua (1117–1184) at the time he served as overseer-general of the Huai-tung circuit. Ch'ien Ta-hsin (1728–1804) notes that Hung Kua took up the post of overseer-general of military stipends of the Huai-tung circuit in 1162, a year earlier than the date given this anecdote in the *ICC* (*Hung Wen-hui kung nien-p'u,* in *Ch'ien-yen t'ang ch'üan-shu* [Changsha, 1884], 5.7a). The lack of medical care in the Huai-tung circuit is said to have led to Hung Kua's transfer of mother and child to the home of Hung Ching-kao. The comments ascribed to the God of the Earth suggest that the deceased had been a concubine of Hung Hao. On the status and treatment of women in this position, see Patricia Ebrey, "Concubines in Sung China," *Journal of Family History* 11.1 (1986): 1–24.

51. The coffins of those without means or for whom immediate burial was unfeasible were often entrusted to Buddhist monasteries. *ICC, Ping* 6.410–411,

notes the pitifully shallow grave of an impoverished clerk buried in front of the Shrine of the City God of Ch'ing-t'ien (Chekiang).

52. As issue of Hung Hao (1088–1155), the son of the deceased would have been approximately eight years old or two years younger than the afflicted at the time of this incident. Although lantern festivals were traditionally joyous celebrations, we can imagine that the boy may have been attracted to the scenes of torture in purgatory that typically graced temples dedicated to T'ai shan.

53. The burning of the coffin would seem to have been the preferred method of corpse disposal when death occurred away from home. This practice was customarily recommended as a means to overcome the malevolent emanations of the dead, as noted in *ICC, Chih-ching* 9.948. See Patricia Ebrey's chapter on funeral practices in this volume for further comments on this subject.

54. *ICC, Chih-i* 5.832–833. According to *ICC, Chia* 2.16, Fu Hsüan served in 1134 as commander of a vanguard force in Kiangsi, the presence of which led to the surrender of rebel forces.

55. Accounts of the Shen-hsiao codification are found in Michel Strickmann, "The Longest Taoist Scripture," *History of Religions* 17.3–4 (1978): 331–354, and Boltz, *Survey of Taoist Literature,* pp. 26–30.

56. A similar failure by an attendant censor of Ch'ien-t'ang (Chekiang) applying T'ien-hsin ritual is described in *ICC, Ting* 14.653–654.

57. *ICC, Ting* 4.568. Hung Mai credits this and two succeeding episodes to an Ou-yang Chün of Chen-chiang (Kiangsu).

58. Variant choreographic guides recorded under the rubric of *Yü-pu* are included in *Tai-shang chu-kuo chiu-min tsung-chen pi-yao* (HY 1217), 8.1a–12b, and *Tao-fa hui-yüan* (HY 1210), 160.1a–16a. A description is given in Kristofer Schipper and Wang Hsiu-huei, "Progressive and Regressive Time Cycles in Taoist Ritual," in J. T. Fraser, N. Lawrence, and F. C. Haber, eds., *Time, Science, and Society in China and the West* (Amherst: University of Massachusetts Press, 1986), pp. 185–205, esp. 199–201.

59. *ICC, Pu* 17.1710–1711. Hung Mai ascribes this account to a Chao Yen-tse, apparently the ancestor of a Chao Shih-chin (fl. 1187) featured in *ICC, Chih-ting* 5.1005.

60. A manual of instruction on the contemplative procedures for achieving *lien-tu* is translated and analyzed in Judith M. Boltz, "Opening the Gates of Purgatory: A Twelfth-Century Taoist Meditation Technique for the Salvation of Lost Souls," in Michel Strickmann, ed., *Tantric and Taoist Studies in Honour of R. A. Stein,* vol. 2: *Mélanges chinois et bouddhiques* 21 (1983): 488–510.

61. *ICC, I* 16.320–321, gives Sung An-kuo's cognomen as T'ung-fu, the second component of which figures in the cognomens of four of the six sons of Sung Sheng (1152–1196), whose names are known and recorded in Wang Tzu-ts'ai (1792–1851), *Sung Yüan hsüeh-an pu-i* (Ssu-ming ts'ung-shu edition), 71.55a. Sung An-kuo's association with Hsing Hsiao-yang and Han Shih-chung, however, dates him at least a generation earlier than even Sung Sheng himself. Whether or not Sung An-kuo was born of another branch of this Sung lineage from Chin-hua (Chekiang) cannot be determined until further background on his life is discovered. Accounts of Han Shih-chung's family are given in *SS* 364 and Teng Kung-san, *Han Shih-chung nien-p'u* (Chungking: Tu-li ch'u-pan-she, 1944).

62. An episode in *ICC, I* 20.360–361, also demonstrates that alertness to local scandal resulted in the successful exorcism of ghosts.

63. *ICC, Ting* 18.691. This episode, which Hung Mai credits to a T'ung Min-te, opens with a description of how Li Li putatively happened to encounter the ghost who came to speak through him as a possessing spirit.

64. The surname Hsiao presumably evokes memory of the imperial family of the Southern Ch'i, who, as Patricia Buckley Ebrey observes in *The Aristocratic Family of Early Imperial China: A Case Study of the Po-ling Ts'ui Family* (Cambridge: Cambridge University Press, 1978), successfully transformed itself into an aristocratic family of eminence during the T'ang (pp. 11, 23, 29–30).

65. *ICC, I* 7.237–239, concerns the affairs of a magistrate.

66. The episode in *Po-chai pien* 7.42 appears to be derivative of an earlier account in *Sou-shen hou-chi* (Peking: Chung-hua shu-chü, 1981, rpt. 1983), 7.106–107.

67. *Wu-shang hsüan-yüan san-t'ien yü-t'ang ta-fa* (HY 220), 1.7a–7b; 28.1b–8b. The date given for the revelations received jointly with Chai Ju-wen, the year *wu-yin* of the Shao-hsing period (1158), should presumably be corrected to the year *chia-yin* (1134) or *wu-wu* (1138). Variant accounts of Lu's enlightenment are recorded in *ICC, Ping* 13.479, and *Tu-hsing tsa-chih* 10.93.

68. *ICC, Pu* 18.1714, describes how a physician denied Chai medical treatment on the grounds that he accepted only highly prestigious clients.

69. *ICC, San-chi* 8.1362–1363. All episodes in this chapter, according to *ICC, San-chi* 8.1368, are Hung Mai's embellishments of accounts in Li Yung's (d. 1188) *Lan-tse yeh-yü.*

70. See Chang Fu-jui, *I-chien chih t'ung-chien* (Taipei: Hsüeh-sheng shu-chü, 1966, rpt. 1967), and Ho Cho's index to the Chung-hua shu-chü edition of the *ICC.*

71. It is significant that Kuo T'uan (*chin-shih* 1165), *K'uei-ch'e chih* (*TSCC* edition), 3.24–25, tells the story of how Chai Ju-wen, while serving as military commissioner of Kuei-chi (Chekiang), recommended a successful remedy for overcoming spirit possession and relates that a preface to a ritual corpus entitled *Huang-lu meng-chen yü-chien* is preserved in Chai's collected writings, *Chung-hui chi* (*SKCS* edition), 8.8b–9a. See also his biography in *SS* 372.11543–11545.

72. *ICC, Ping* 13.479, *Ting* 18.684–685. In his 1198 preface to *ICC, San-chi,* p. 1303, Hung Mai identifies T'eng Yen-chih as prefect of Jao-chou (Kiangsi) and alludes to his account of Lu Shih-chung's command of ritual and near defeat by a Ms. Fang.

73. *ICC, I* 6.232, 237–239, *San-chi* 8.1362.

74. *ICC, Ping* 5.403–404, *Pu* 5.1594.

75. *Tu-hsing tsa-chih* 10.93.

76. *ICC, Chih-i* 5.830. Ch'ien Tang's daughter is identified as the wife of Fang Tzu-chang, father-in-law of Hung Ching-p'ei. Hung Mai also credits Hung Ching-p'ei with a story concerning Fang's haunted house (*ICC, Chih-ching* 2.892).

77. *ICC, Chih-ting* 4.995.

78. Hung Pang-chih held the post of defender of Wu-yüan in the year 1153, according to *ICC, Chia* 13.112.

79. *SJSY,* p. 1516.

80. This anecdote merits comparison with an episode credited to Huang Chün in *ICC, Ping* 20.532, which recounts how a magistrate of Chiang-ling (Hupeh) risked censure as well as his life in combating a sorcerer reputed to be directing the destiny of the masses by his magical manipulations. The prefect of the region is said to have endorsed the magistrate's forceful measures and to have ordered the sorcerer executed.

81. See, for example, the entries in Hucker, *Dictionary of Official Titles,* nos. 1902 and 7807, for the Ministry of War; nos. 5814 and 5913, for the Ministry of Rites; and nos. 1337–1339 for specialists in exorcism in the Imperial Medical Office during the Sui and the T'ang. Similarly, the history of official posts for Taoist clergy, as noted in nos. 1654–1656, lie beyond the scope of this study.

82. The pattern of taking up a study of the Tao upon resigning from office is common to the hagiographies for a number of prominent patriarchs. See, for example, Sung Lien's (1310–1381) preface and the biography of Chang Tao-ling (fl. 142), initial patriarch of the Celestial Master lineage, in *Han T'ien-shih shih-chia* (HY 1451), 2.2a–2b; and the biographies of the third and tenth Celestial Masters, Chang Lu (fl. 190–220) and Chang Tzu-hsiang (fl. 590), in Chao Tao-i (fl. 1294–1307), *Li-shih chen-hsien t'i-tao t'ung-chien* (HY 296), 19.2b–3a, 5b; and for biographies of Shang-ch'ing patriarchs Hsü Mi (303–373) and T'ao Hung-ching (456–536), see ibid., 21.14b–15a, 24.12b–23b. Representative biographies in *Wu-tang fu-ti tsung-chen chi* (HY 960), 3.21a–23a, completed in 1291 by Liu Tao-ming, and in *San-tung ch'ün-hsien lu* (HY 1238), 4.5a; 9.6a; 10.6b; 12.10a; 13.1b–2a; 14.6b, 7b–8a, 9a; 16.9a, completed ca. 1154 by Ch'en Pao-kuang, are drawn from a range of earlier writings spanning the Han to the T'ang. Brief introductions to the four anthologies noted above may be found in Boltz, *Survey of Taoist Literature,* pp. 56–65, 119–121.

83. The sentiment that the study of the Tao is incompatible with holding office is expressed in an episode of Sun Kuang-hsien (d. 968), *Pei-meng so-yen* (*TSCC* edition), 12.99. Scholars who chose in the end to devote themselves to a study of the Tao are enumerated in Wang Ting-pao (*chin-shih* 900), *T'ang chih-yen* (Shanghai: Ku-chi ch'u-pan-she, 1978), 8.92.

84. The two episodes, recorded as the ninth and first entries of *TPKC* 298 and 447, respectively, are both ascribed to the *Kuang-i chi,* an anthology compiled by Tai Fu (*chin-shih* 757), which does not survive intact. As Glen Dudbridge points out in "*Kuang-i chi* ch'u-t'an," *Hsin-ya hsüeh-pao* 15 (1986): 395–414, many entries in the *TPKC* are falsely attributed to the *Kuang-i chi.* The victim's visionary confirmation of her rescue recounted in the first episode finds its echo in the story by Lu Shih-chung cited above.

85. According to *ICC, Ping* 14.486–487, Li Hao prevailed upon the magistrate of Hsiang-yang (Hupeh) to teach him the talisman after seeing him successfully apply it in 1151 to quell a flood. The talisman reportedly had the capacity for warding off not only floods, but also drought, epidemics, armed attacks, ghosts, and spirits, as well as phantoms inhabiting mountains and forests. Hung Mai came into its possession at the time he served as vice-director of the Ministry of Rites, a post gained in 1160. The fascicle in which this episode appears was completed in 1171.

86. *ICC, Pu* 14.1680–1681. See also *ICC, Pu* 14.1681–1682, for a mantra reputed to be effective in evading armed forces, and *ICC, Pu* 23.1764–1765, for

an incantation prescribed for overcoming poisonous bites. Hung Mai's brother Hung Yüan-chung, moreover, is identified as the source in *ICC, Chih-ting* 4.996, for an incantation popular among P'o-yang sorcerers for treating burns. A study of incantations recorded in the *ICC* has been taken up in Sawada Mizuho, "Sōdai no shinju shinkō: *Iken-shi* no setsuwa o chūshin toshite," *Tōhō shūkyō* 57 (1980): 71–77. Also of note is the incantation associated with the Correct Rites of T'ien-hsin recorded in Su Shih (1036–1101), *Ch'ou-ch'ih pi-chi* (*TSCC* edition), pp. 1–2.

87. *ICC, Chih-ching* 9.949–950. Additional biographical notes are found in *Mao shan chih* (HY 304), 16.8a–8b (Boltz, *Survey of Taoist Literature,* pp. 103–105), and *Ching-k'ou ch'i-chiu chuan* 1.6b–7a.

88. *ICC, Chih-wu* 5.1089–1091. Jen Tao-yüan was the son of Jen Wen-chien (*chin-shih* 1135), vice-minister of the Court of Imperial Sacrifices. Hung drew this episode from the *Nan-pu yen-hua lu* of his eldest son Hung Hsin. As Chang Fu-jui points out in "L'influence du *Yi-kien tche* sur les oeuvres littéraires," *Études d'histoire et de littérature chinoises offertes au Professeur Jaroslav Průšek, Bibliothèque de l'Institut des hautes études chinoises,* vol. 24 (Paris: Presses universitaires de France, 1976), p. 53, this account served as the foundation for the narrative in Ling Meng-ch'u (1580–1644), *Ch'u-k'o p'ai-an ching-ch'i* 17.

89. See, for example, accounts from various sources on instruction denied cited in *San-tung ch'ün-hsien lu* (HY 1238), 13.3b–4a; 15.4a–4b; and 20.4b, 10a.

90. See, for example, Robert P. Hymes, *Statesmen and Gentlemen: The Elite of Fu-chou, Chiang-hsi, in Northern and Southern Sung* (Cambridge: Cambridge University Press, 1986).

91. Although beyond the scope of this study, the history of monastic institutions serving as schools merits a full investigation. Su Ch'e (1039–1112), *Lung-ch'uan pieh-chih* (*TSCC* edition), 2.23, remarks on Ch'ien Jo-shui's (960–1003) experience in just such a school. His brother Su Shih names the Taoist master who served as his teacher when he attended primary school at the age of eight (*Ch'ou-ch'ih pi-chi,* p. 4). The availability of ordination certificates during the Sung also pertains to the question of discipleship. Officials who are said to have received registers (*shou-lu*), implying a level of ordination, are noted in *Li-shih chen-hsien t'i-tao t'ung-chien* (HY 296), 22.9a–9b, 41.17a–20a.

92. Piet van der Loon, *Taoist Books in the Libraries of the Sung Period: A Critical Study and Index,* Oxford Oriental Institute Monographs, no. 7 (London: Ithaca Press, 1984), p. 44.

93. The letter is found in *Hai-ch'iung Pai chen-jen yü-lu* (HY 1296), 4.16b–21a, a composite work based on the transcriptions of Pai Yü-ch'an's disciples and put into final form by P'eng Ssu (fl. 1229–1251); see Boltz, *Survey of Taoist Literature,* pp. 177–178.

94. Secrecy is counseled in many manuals of the *Tao-fa hui-yüan.* See also observations regarding contemporary practice in Michael Saso, "The Liturgical Heritage of the Hsinchu Taoist," *Cahiers d'Extrême-Asie* 4 (1980): 175–180.

95. *Hai-ch'iung Pai chen-jen yü-lu* (HY 1296), 2.15a–15b, 1.9a.

96. *Teng-chen yin-chüeh* (HY 421), 3.21b, corresponds to *Ch'ih-sung-tzu chang-li* (HY 615), 2.21b.

97. *T'ai-shang chu-kuo chiu-min tsung-chen pi-yao* (HY 1217), 1.6a–6b;

Stein, "Religious Taoism and Popular Religion," pp. 67–68. Edouard Chavannes, "Le jet des dragons," *Mémoires concernant l'Asie orientale* 3 (1919):
214, n. 167, links these instructions to vague remarks on the destruction of
shrines found in T'ang formularies.

98. *T'ai-shang chu-kuo chiu-min tsung-chen pi-yao* (HY 1217), 8.16a
records instructions for manipulations labeled "ju-miao" (entering a shrine) and
"p'o-miao" (smashing a shrine) and *chüan* 6, which is entirely devoted to a code
of regulations governing practitioners and the spirit realm (see n. 41 above), specifies punishments for offensive spirits.

99. *Hai-ch'iung Pai chen-jen yü-lu* (HY 1296), 1.8b–9a.

100. Michel Strickmann, "The Tao among the Yao: Taoism and the Sinification of South China," in *Rekishi ni okeru minshū to bunka* [Festschrift in Honor
of Sakai Tadao] (Tokyo: Kokusho kankōkai, 1982), pp. 23–30.

101. A tiger drawing and a talisman figure in this magical transformation,
according to the first entry of *TPKC* 284, ascribed to Wang Yen's (fl. 470) *Ming-
hsiang chi*.

102. A prefect found it to his advantage to exploit the faith of the ignorant
masses in this shrine, according to the third entry of *TPKC* 458, ascribed to
Meng Kuan's (fl. 835) *Ling-nan i-wu chih*.

103. Chou Ch'ü-fei, *Ling-wai tai-ta* (*TSCC* edition), 10.120–126.

104. See, for example, *SS* 9.178, regarding the prohibition announced by
Sung Jen-tsung in 1023 against sorcerers, extortionists, and anyone who brought
harm by trickery throughout Liang-Che, Chiang-nan, Ching-hu, Fu-chien, and
Kuang-nan lu.

105. *Yao-tsu chien-shih* (Nan-ning: Kuang-hsi min-tsu ch'u-pan-she, 1983),
p. 126; Ch'en Mo-jen and Hsiao T'ing, *Yao-tsu ke-t'ang ch'ü* (n.p.: Hua-ch'eng
ch'u-pan-she, 1981, rpt. 1984), pp. 24–26.

106. *Wu-shang hsüan-yüan san-t'ien yü-t'ang ta-fa* (HY 220), 27.5a–5b.

107. An investigation into the history of enshrinements honoring a Bee King
is likely to clarify the significance of this episode. The story of a Bee King cavern
in Yunnan, said to have been popular among the Chuang minority since the
Sung, for example, is noted in Yüan K'o, ed., *Chung-kuo min-tsu shen-hua tz'u-
tien* (Chengtu: Ssu-ch'uan sheng she-hui k'o-hsüeh yüan, 1989), p. 116.

108. Strickmann, "Tao among the Yao," pp. 26–27. Manuscripts of Yao
priests, together with a charter issued to the Yao in 1260 by Sung Li-tsung, are
reproduced in Shiratori Yoshirō, *Yōjin bunsho* (Tokyo: Kōdansha, 1975), color
plates.

109. Liu Chih-wan, "Raijin shinkō to raihō no tenkai," *Tōhō shūkyō* 67
(June 1986): 1–21, esp. pp. 2, l7, points out that it was the region south of the
Yangtze, noted for its thunderstorms, where thunder deities were venerated and
where Thunder Rites arose.

110. The origins of the Wen-ch'ang cult, for example, may be traced to
thunder lore evolving around snake cults, as Terry Kleeman points out in this
volume.

111. Texts giving considerable account to the thunder lore of Lei-chou
include Chou Ch'ü-fei, *Ling-wai tai-ta* 10.120, and *Sou-shen chi* (HY 1466),
1.23b–24a. See also the episode in *ICC, Chih-ching* 9.954–955, cited in n. 14
above and in Hymes, *Statesmen and Gentlemen*, p. 191.

112. Henri Maspero, *Taoism and Chinese Religion,* trans. Frank A. Kierman, Jr. (Amherst: University of Massachusetts Press, 1981), pp. 97–98, considers the beak-faced Sire Thunder to be "one of the ancient divinities whom modern religion has retained almost unmodified." Additional summaries on the lore of Lei-kung include Henry Doré, *Researches into Chinese Superstitions,* part 2: *The Chinese Pantheon,* vol. 10: *Boards of Heavenly Administration,* trans. D. J. Finn (Shanghai: T'usewei Printing Press, 1933; rpt. Taipei: Ch'eng-wen Publishing Co., 1967), pp. 4–14, and Wolfram Eberhard, *The Local Cultures of South and East China,* trans. Alide Eberhard (Leiden: E. J. Brill, 1968), pp. 253–261.

113. Animals as well as humans were deemed subject to the retribution of lightning strikes, according to anecdotes in Chang Tu (fl. 853), *Hsüan-shih chih* (Pi-chi hsiao-shuo ta-kuan edition), 5.5a–5b, 7.2a–3a, and in *ICC, Ting* 8.601, *Chih-wu* 8.1116. A critical account of belief in lightning as punishment is given in *Lun Heng,* part 1: *Philosophical Essays of Wang Ch'ung,* trans. Alfred Forke (Leipzig: Otto Harrassowitz et al., 1907), pp. 285–297. Also of note is the discussion in Chou Mi (1232–1308), *Ch'i-tung yeh-yü* (Peking: Chung-hua shu-chü, 1983), 12.218–219.

114. Prayers for rain are the first cited in the lists of responsibilities falling to practitioners of Five-Thunder Rites in the *Wu-i chi* anthology of Pai Yü-ch'an's writings, printed in *Hsiu-chen shih-shu* (HY 263), 47.9a, 16b–17a; see Boltz, *Survey of Taoist Literature,* pp. 178–179, 234–237. Also of special interest is an account on the shrine to Thunder Ritual Master Wang Wen-ch'ing in Ch'eng Chü-fu (1249–1318), *Ch'eng Hsüeh-lou wen-chi* (Taipei: National Central Library, 1970), 11.3a–3b. Ch'eng, much like Ou-yang Hsiu, found himself pleading for divine assistance in the alleviation of torrential rains preventing the timely burial of his mother. On the recommendation of a family member, he sought intervention through Assistant Magistrate Teng Kuei-sun, recognized heir to Wang's ritual legacy. Many other literary anthologies as well as miscellanea are likely to yield additional evidence attesting to a tradition of officeholders with training in Taoist exorcistic rites continuing far beyond Hung Mai's time.

115. *Hsiu-chen shih-shu* (HY 263), 47.10a–17b.

116. Kristofer M. Schipper, "Master Chao I-chen (?–1382) and the Ch'ing-wei School of Taoism," in Akizuki Kan'ei, ed., *Dōkyō to shūkyō bunka* (Tokyo: Hirakawa shuppansha, 1987), pp. 715–734. See also the studies cited in n. 42 above.

117. *Tao-fa hui-yüan* (HY 1210), 250.15a.

118. For this suggestion I am indebted to Professor Timothy H. Barrett, who served as a discussant at Hacienda Heights. See his "Taoist Ritual and Development of Chinese Magic," *Modern Asian Studies* 14.1 (1980): 164–169, and "Towards a Date for the *Chin-so liu-chu yin,*" *Bulletin of the School of Oriental and African Studies* 53.2 (1990): 292–294, esp. n. 5.

119. See Michel Strickmann, "History, Anthropology, and Chinese Religion," *HJAS* 40.1 (June 1980): 201–248, esp. p. 228, for a partial translation of the T'ien-p'eng spell, an incantation featuring genocidal language that entered the fourth-century Shang-ch'ing corpus and remains central to many traditions of Thunder Rites.

120. The theme of religion as a shelter from and unto violence, as articulated in René Girard, *Violence and the Sacred,* trans. Patrick Gregory (Baltimore and

London: The Johns Hopkins University Press, 1977, rpt. 1984), is pivotal to the analysis of *k'ao-chao* procedures in Judith Magee Boltz, "Taoist Rites of Exorcism" (University of California, Berkeley, Ph.D. dissertation, 1985).

121. An honorific title authorized in 1104 precedes Ko Hsüan's name as it is recorded in *Tao-fa hui-yüan* (HY 1210), 73.1a, whereas an additional epithet granted in 1246 is conspicuously absent.

122. *Tao-fa hui-yüan* (HY 1210), 73.6a.

123. *Yung-le ta-tien* (Peking: Chung-hua shu-chü, 1959–1960), vol. 178, *chüan* 19782, pp. 7a–22b.

124. A prefatory discussion on the construction of a cosmic board is ascribed to Li Ching in *Yung-le ta-tien* 19782.12b–13a. Writings in the name of such culture heroes typically owe their inspiration to later generations of followers.

125. The title *Lei-kung yin-wen ching* appears in *Yung-le ta-tien* 19782.20a. The bibliographic monograph in SS 206.5248, 5262 lists a *Lei-kung shih-chü* in one *chüan* and a *Lei-kung yin-fa* in three *chüan*, respectively. A variation on the former title, *Lei-kung shih-ching*, in one *chüan*, is entered in the bibliographic monograph of HTS 59.1555.

126. *Yung-le ta-tien* 19782.18a. The readings suggested in brackets are based on comparable, generally more explicit, instructions recorded for the application of all twelve seals on pp. 17b–20a. The celestial entourage invoked here are precisely the troops understood to be embodied within the seals.

127. The inducement of fatal nightmares does not figure in the summary on sorcery in J. J. M. de Groot, *The Religious System of China* (Leiden: E. J. Brill, 1892–1910; rpt. Taipei: Ch'eng-wen Publishing Co., 1972), 5.813–923, but see pp. 699–701 for a description of the "demoniacal nightmare" as "a sleeper labouring under this sensation seems crushed down under the weight of a demon riding on his chest" and for the techniques Ko Hung recommended for reviving such victims by calling back their souls. Accounts concerning revival of the dead are also found in vol. 4, pp. 123–142.

128. Of note among the applications prescribed for the first in this set of twelve seals in *Yung-le ta-tien* 19782.17a, is the evocation of cosmic troops to beat to death wild animals such as the lions, tigers, and wolves one might encounter on excursions into the mountains.

129. Variants on the expression *hu-shen tso-kuo* recorded in *Yung-le ta-tien* 19782.14a, may be found, for example, in *T'ai-shang chu-kuo chiu-min tsung-chen pi-yao* (HY 1217).

130. The anecdote in *Shen-hsien kan-yü chuan* (HY 592), 1.3b–4b, may be compared with the versions recorded as the eleventh episode of *TPKC* 394 and in *Yün-chi ch'i-ch'ien* (HY 1026), 112.1b–2b; see Boltz, *Survey of Taoist Literature*, pp. 229–231.

131. *Tao-fa hui-yüan* (HY 1210), 122–123; note esp. 123.13a for an enumeration of five thunder guardians, which corresponds remarkably to Tu Kuang-t'ing's account of Yeh Ch'ien-shao's experience. An alternative biography of Yeh in *Hsü-hsien chuan* (HY 295), 2.16b–18b, by Tu's contemporary Shen Fen, makes no mention of Sire Thunder but observes that Yeh took up the study of the practices of Hsü Sun and Wu Meng under a Taoist master at Hsi shan, the site of Hsü's enshrinement. Also of note is a story ascribed to the *Kuang-i chi* in the ninth episode of *TPKC* 231 and in *San-tung ch'ün-hsien lu* (HY 1238), 10.7a,

which speaks of the appearance of a sword inscribed with Hsü Sun's name that came to be recovered following an appearance of Sire Thunder in Ching-chiang (Kwangsi).

132. *Tao-fa hui-yüan* (HY 1210), 125. Writings pertinent to Hsü Sun and the Ching-ming legacy are introduced in Boltz, *Survey of Taoist Literature,* pp. 70–78, 197–199.

133. The third episode of *TPKC* 395, ascribed to the *Pei-meng so-yen,* is not included in the received text (*TSCC*) but is recorded in the supplementary selection of accounts in *Pei-meng so-yen* (Shanghai: Ku-chi ch'u-pan-she, 1981), p. 165.

134. *Tao-fa hui-yüan* (HY 1210), 264. See also a preface by Liu Yü (fl. 1258) in 198.25b–27a, which traces the transmission of Shen-hsiao rites as promoted by Lin Ling-su to his master Lu Yeh; 134.2a and 198.12b for passing references to overcoming transient sorcerers encountered by chance; and the manuals in *chüan* 215, 227, and 258, which advocate rituals by which sorcerers could be induced to suffer the injuries perpetrated. A story concerning this latter technique is recounted in Michael R. Saso, *The Teachings of Taoist Master Chuang* (New Haven: Yale University Press, 1978), pp. 117–118. The technique is used in overcoming the black magic of a "Mao Shan Taoist," which, like "new Shen-hsiao Taoism," purportedly "makes use of evil talismans to kill, injure, or harm people in the community" (p. 239).

135. *Tao-fa hui-yüan* (HY 1210), 264.1a–1b. See Strickmann, "History, Anthropology, and Chinese Religion (cited in n. 119)," for the T'ien-p'eng spell.

136. *Tao-fa hui-yüan* (HY 1210), 264.3a–3b.

137. Surrogate figures were commonly used to induce misfortune, as noted in discussions of black magic in de Groot, *Religious System* 5.888–896, 905, 908–913, 920–926. Their use to avert demonic forces in exorcistic rites is noted in de Groot, *Religious System* 6.1098–1106 and Kristofer Schipper, "La représentation du substitut dans le ritual taoïste," in "Psychanalyse et approche familiale systémique," transcripts of presentations at the Centre d'étude de la famille, Paris, 16 December 1984, pp. 35–54. Instructions in *Tao-fa hui-yüan* (HY 1210), 215, directed toward overcoming sorcerers who apply "demonic needles," apparently refer to the practice of sticking needles into puppets to reinforce curses, as described in de Groot, *Religious System* 5.921.

138. *Tao-fa hui-yüan* (HY 1210), 264.10a. Interpretation of this incantation rests on whether the designation for "censor-in-chief" is to be understood to refer to a worldly or a celestial office. The former seems to be implied by the fact that the name Wei Po-hsien appears with this title in 265.15b.

139. *Tao-fa hui-yüan* (HY 1210), 56.1a–3b; *Hsiu-chen shih-shu* (HY 263), 47.9a.

140. *Tao-fa hui-yüan* (HY 1210), 36.2b.

141. *Tao-fa hui-yüan* (HY 1210), 221.1b–2a; see pp. 23a–23b for a variant version of the invocation cited above.

142. *Tao-fa hui-yüan* (HY 1210), 222.15b.

143. *Tao-fa hui-yüan* (HY 1210), 224.10a. The vision of Ma Sheng introduced in 225.1a–1b features the fire-crow emerging from a fire-gourd resting on his back. The fire-wheel, fire-gourd, and fire-spitting snake appear separately and in combination in talismans featured in *chüan* 222–223 and 225.

144. *Tao-fa hui-yüan* (HY 1210), 80.24b–25a, 43a–44a, 45a–45b.

145. *Tao-fa hui-yüan* (HY 1210), 80.21a.

146. *Tao-fa hui-yüan* (HY 1210), 115.29a–29b.

147. *Tao-fa hui-yüan* (HY 1210), 115.30b–31a; see also 122.17b–18a for a "Talisman of the Stinking Smoke of the Fire-Hawk." A subsequent chapter of these Thunder Rites, ascribed to Ch'en Nan, includes concise instructions on demolishing shrines according to three talismanic applications: (1) attachment to the gateway, (2) burial inside the shrine, and (3) as a summons to spirit generals (123.10a).

148. *Tao-fa hui-yüan* (HY 1210), 56.1a–3b. The rites of Teng Po-wen featured in *chüan* 114–120 include an anonymous disciple's account of how his master, "Attendant to the Throne," advised him on applying the rites for destroying shrines (116.26a–26b). A variant version recorded in 129.3a–3b identifies the "Attendant to the Throne" as Wang, i.e., Wang Wen-ch'ing. The destructive power of the thunder-fire talisman is reported to be entirely dependent upon its timely application on those days when baleful stars were known to be in evidence.

149. *Tao-fa hui-yüan* (HY 1210), 56.33a–33b, 57.1a–4a.

150. *Kao-shang shen-hsiao yü-ch'ing chen-wang tzu-shu ta-fa* (HY 1209), 12.6b–7b.

151. Pheasants and sparrows are suggested in Tseng Kung-liang (998–1078) et al., *Wu-ching tsung-yao* (*SKCS* edition), 11.21a–22b. The technique of tying nutfuls of burning moxa tinder to birds is mentioned as early as 759, according to Joseph Needham, with Ho Ping-yü, Lu Gwei-Djen, and Wang Ling, *Science and Civilisation in China*, vol. 5: *Chemistry and Chemical Technology: Spagyrical Discovery and Invention*, part 7: *Military Technology: The Gunpowder Epic* (Cambridge: Cambridge University Press, 1986), pp. 210–211.

152. Wild boars and roebucks are suggested in *Wu-ching tsung-yao* 11.24b. See Needham, *Science and Civilisation*, vol. 5, part 7, pp. 65, 70, 211–218, for the history of using "expendable animals" in this manner since pre-Han times.

153. The image of Ma Sheng's fire-crow also finds its correspondence in the so-called soaring crow of divine fire *(shen-huo fei-ya)* depicted in a military manual dating to 1412, which is thought to be derived from a text compiled ca. 1330. On such winged rocket-bombs and dragon-shaped automata for carrying bombs or land mines, see Needham, *Science and Civilisation*, vol. 5, part 7, pp. 213, 218, and 498–505. See also Jixing Pan, "On the Origin of Rockets," *T'oung Pao* 73 (1987): 2–15, for evidence suggesting the use of rockets as early as 1161.

154. On the legacy of the exorcistic power of noise, see de Groot, *Religious System* 6.941–946.

155. See, for example, accounts concerning the Celestial Master lineage in *Han T'ien-shih shih-chia* (HY 1451), 3.2a–2b, 14a, 18b–19a.

156. The locale of this enshrinement is not identified in the versions of this anecdote in *Hsiu-chen shih-shu* (HY 263), 33.5a; *Li-shih chen-hsien t'i-tao t'ung-chien* (HY 296), 26.5a; *Hsü T'ai-shih chen-chün t'u-chuan* (HY 440), 1.17a–17b; *Hsü chen-chün hsien-chuan* (HY 447), p. 4b; and *Hsi shan Hsü chen-chün pa-shih-wu hua lu* (HY 448), 1.10a. Context places the event in Hung-chou (Kiangsi) in the versions recorded in *Ching-ming chung-hsiao ch'üan-shu* (HY 1102), 1.3a, dating to 1327, and *Hsiao-yao hsü-ching* (HY 1453), 2.9a of Hung Ying-ming (fl. 1596).

157. Significant variants on the version of the story in *Ching-ming chung-hsiao ch'üan-shu* (HY 1102), 1.15b, are found in the thirteenth-century anthologies *Hsiu-chen shih-shu* (HY 263), 36.8b; *Li-shih chen-hsien t'i-tao t'ung-chien* (HY 296), 27.14a; and *Hsi shan Hsü chen-chün pa-shih-wu hua lu* (HY 448), 3.20a–20b.

158. As revealed by episodes recorded in *ICC, San-jen* 4.1497–1498 and *Pu* 14.1683–1684, and studies such as Sawada Mizuho, "Satsujin saiki," *Tenri daigaku gakuhō* 43 (1964): 1–22; rpt. with supplement in *Chūgoku no minkan shinkō* (Tokyo: Dai-ichi insatsu kabushiki kaisha, 1982), pp. 332–373, the practice of human sacrifice was commonly associated with sorcerers in south China.

159. *Ti-ch'i shang-chiang Wen T'ai-pao chuan* (HY 779), pp. 7b–8a, compiled in 1274 by Huang Kung-chin; see Boltz, *Survey of Taoist Literature,* pp. 97–99. See also the analysis in John Lagerwey, *Taoist Ritual in Chinese Society and History* (New York: Macmillan, 1987), pp. 241–252.

160. *Hsien-tu chih* (HY 602), 2.2a, dating to 1348; see Boltz, *Survey of Taoist Literature,* pp. 113–115.

161. *Li-shih chen-hsien t'i-tao t'ung-chien hsü-pien* (HY 297), 4.1a–3a.

162. The locale of the temple to Ch'eng-huang is not indicated in this version of Sa Shou-chien's biography. Later renditions place it in Hsiang-yin (Hunan); see n. 164 below.

163. The portrayal of a city god in need of censure contrasts sharply with the general perception that such deities were the masterful spokesmen of the elite and thus above reproach, as observed in David Johnson, "The City-God Cults of T'ang and Sung China," *HJAS* 45.2 (1985): 363–457. The reform of demonic forces and taming of indigenous gods to serve as guardian figures is a common feature of many religious traditions, as noted, for example, in contributions to Alf Hiltebeitel, ed., *Criminal Gods and Demon Devotees: Essays on the Guardians of Popular Hinduism* (Albany: State University of New York Press, 1987).

164. Huang Po-lu, *Chi-shuo ch'üan-chen* (revised edition, Shanghai 1906), p. 305a. The Hunan gazetteer cited locates the temple of the city god in Hsiang-yin.

165. See Needham, *Science and Civilisation,* vol. 5, part 7; and idem, *Gunpowder as the Fourth Power, East and West,* Hong Kong University Press Occasional Papers' Series, no. 3 (Hong Kong: Hong Kong University Press, 1985).

166. *Chen-yüan miao-tao yao-lüeh* (HY 923), p. 3a; Needham, *Science and Civilisation,* vol. 5, part 7, pp. 111–112.

167. *Wu-ching tsung-yao* 12.65a–65b.

168. *Chen-yüan miao-tao yao-lüeh* (HY 923), p. 19a, refers to Yen-lo-tzu, whom hagiographies identify as a comrade of Cheng Ao (866–939). Weng T'ung-wen, "*Chen-yüan miao-tao yao-lüeh* ti ch'eng-shu shih-tai chi hsiang-kuan ti huo-yao shih wen-t'i," *Nan-yang ta-hsüeh hsüeh-pao* 5 (1971): 73–80, suggests that the attribution may refer to a Cheng Ssu-yüan of the tenth century, but this seems unlikely, given the name recognition of Ko Hung's master. On the other hand, Ssu-ma Kuang (1019–1086), *Su-shui chi-wen* (Peking: Chung-hua shu-chü, 1989), 6.125, includes an intriguing entry regarding Sung Chen-tsung's (r. 998–1022) summons and entitlement of a Cheng Yin of Hua shan.

169. *Tao-chiao ling-yen chi* (HY 590), 9.7a–8b, 15.1a–1b; *ICC, Chia* 15.127. Equally suggestive is the story of sorcerers struck down in a thunder-

storm, recorded in *Hua-kai shan Fou-ch'iu Wang Kuo san chen-chün shih-shih* (HY 777), 4.22b; see Boltz, *Survey of Taoist Literature,* pp. 78–81.

170. Chi Yün (1724–1805), *Yüeh-wei ts'ao-t'ang pi-chi* (Shanghai: Ku-chi ch'u-pan-she, 1980), 4.65.

171. The adaptability of guardian figures such as the sword-bearing Hsü Sun to new formulations of *lei-fa* may be compared with the decline in the popularity of St. George (d. ca. 303), which, according to David Hugh Farmer, *The Oxford Dictionary of Saints* (Oxford: Oxford University Press, 1982), p. 166, may be attributed to "the invention of gunpowder and the consequent diminution of the importance of sword and lance."

172. The theatrical tradition of impersonating Wang Ling-kuan in rites of purification is discussed in Piet van der Loon, "Les origines rituelles du théâtre chinois," *Journal asiatique* 265 (1977): 141–168; esp. 162–163.

GLOSSARY

Chai Ju-wen　翟汝文
Chan-hun fa　斬魂法
Chang Chi-hsien　張繼先
Chang Ch'i　張祁
Chang Kuei-mo　張貴謨
Chang Lu　張魯
Chang Pang-chi　張邦基
Chang Shao　張邵
Chang Ssu-lang　張四郎
Chang Tao-ling　張道陵
Chang Tu　張讀
Chang Tzu-hsiang　張子祥
Chang Yüan-tao　張淵道
Chao I-chen　趙宜真
Chao Po-t'i　趙伯禔
Chao Shan-tao　趙善蹈
Chao Shih-chin　趙師縉
Chao Shih-e　趙士遏
Chao Tao-i　趙道一
Chao Tzu-chü　趙子舉
Chao Yen-tse　趙彥澤
Ch'ao-t'ien men　朝天門
Chen-jen tz'u　真人祠
Chen-kuan　真官
Chen-yüan miao-tao yao-lüeh　真元妙
　道要略
Ch'en Chüeh　陳栝
Ch'en Ju-hsi　陳汝錫
Ch'en Nan　陳楠
Ch'en Pao-kuang　陳葆光
Ch'en Tai　陳棣

Cheng Ao　鄭遨
cheng-fa　正法
Cheng-i　正一
Cheng Ssu-yüan　鄭思遠
Cheng Ti-shan　鄭瑞山
Cheng Yin　鄭隱
Ch'eng Chü-fu　程巨夫
Ch'eng Hsüeh-lou wen-chi　程雪樓
　文集
Ch'eng-huang　城隍
Chi-shuo ch'üan-chen　集說詮真
Chi-wen　記聞
Chi Yün　紀昀
ch'i-kuan ju-Tao　棄官入道
Ch'i-tung yeh-yü　齊東野語
Chia-yeh t'ang ts'ung-shu　嘉業堂
　叢書
Chiang Ching　蔣靜
Chien-fu ssu　薦福寺
Ch'ien Jo-shui　錢若水
Ch'ien Shen-chih　錢伸之
Ch'ien Ta-hsin　錢大昕
Ch'ien Tang　錢譓
Ch'ien-yen t'ang ch'üan-shu　潛研堂
　全書
Ch'ih-sung-tzu chang-li　赤松子章曆
chin-tan　金丹
Ching-k'ou ch'i-chiu chuan　京口耆
　舊傳
Ching-ming chung-hsiao ch'üan-shu
　淨明忠孝全書

Ch'ing-wei　清微

Chou Ch'ü-fei　周去非

Chou Mi　周密

Ch'ou-ch'ih pi-chi　仇池筆記

chu　祝

Ch'u-k'o p'ai-an ching-ch'i　初刻拍案
　驚奇

Chuang　狀

Chuang Ssu-heng　莊思恆

Chung-hui chi　忠惠集

Erh-wang miao　二王廟

fa-hsieh p'o-miao　伐邪破廟

fa-miao ch'u-hsieh　伐廟除邪

fa-shih　法師

Fan An　范安

Fang Shao　方勺

fang-shih　方士

Fang Tzu-chang　方子張

Feng-miao fu　封廟符

Feng-wang　蜂王

Fu Hsüan　傅選

Hai-ch'iung Pai chen-jen yü-lu　海瓊
　白真人語錄

Han Shih-chung　韓世忠

Han T'ien-shih shih-chia　漢天師世家

Han Yen-chih　韓彥直

Hao Kuang-ssu　郝光嗣

Hsi-men Pao　西門豹

Hsi shan Hsü chen-chün pa-shih-wu
　hua lu　西山許真君八十五化錄

Hsiang-mo yin　降魔印

Hsiaò　蕭

Hsiao-yao hsü-ching　消搖墟經

hsieh　邪

Hsieh Chih　謝芷

Hsieh T'ien-yü　謝天與

Hsien-tu chih　仙都志

Hsing Hsiao-yang　邢孝陽

hsing-lei fa-miao　興雷伐廟

Hsiu-chen shih-shu　修真十書

Hsü chen-chün hsien-chuan　許真君
　仙傳

Hsü-hsien chuan　續仙傳

Hsü Mi　許謐

Hsü Pi-ta　徐必大

Hsü Sun　許遜

Hsü T'ai-shih chen-chün t'u-chuan
　許太史真君圖傳

Hsüan-shih chih　宣室志

Hu Hui-ch'ao　胡惠超

hu-shen tso-kuo　護身佐國

Hua-kai shan Fou-ch'iu Wang Kuo
　san chen-chün shih-shih　華蓋山浮
　丘王郭三真君事實

Huang Chün　黃鈞

Huang Kung-chin　黃公瑾

Huang-lu chiao　黃籙醮

Huang-lu meng-chen yü-chien　黃籙
　盟真玉檢

Huang Po-lu　黃伯祿

Huang Shun-shen　黃舜申

hun　魂

Hung Ching-kao　洪景高

Hung Ching-p'ei　洪景裴

Hung Fu　洪倗

Hung Hao　洪皓

Hung Hsin　洪梓

Hung Hsün　洪迅

Hung Kua　洪适

Hung Mai　洪邁

Hung Pang-chih　洪邦直

Hung Wen-hui kung nien-p'u　洪文惠
　公年譜

Hung Wen-min kung nien-p'u　洪文
　敏公年譜

Hung Ying-ming　洪應明

Hung Yüan-chung　洪元仲

Jen Tao-yüan　任道元

Jen Wen-chien　任文薦

ju-miao　入廟

Kao-shang shen-hsiao yü-ch'ing
　chen-wang tzu-shu ta-fa　高上神霄
　玉清真王紫書大法

k'ao-chao fa　考召法

Ko Hsüan　葛玄

Ko Hung　葛洪

kuan　官

[Tseng-hsiu] Kuan-hsien chih　[增修]
　灌縣志

Kuan-k'ou　灌口

Kuang-i chi　廣異記

K'uei-ch'e chih　睽車志

Kuo T'uan　郭彖

Lan-tse yeh-yü　蘭澤野語

Lei-fa　雷法

Lei-huo fu　雷火符

Lei-kung　雷公
Lei-kung shih　雷公式
Lei-kung shih-ching　雷公式經
Lei-kung shih-chü　雷公式局
Lei kung yin-fa　雷公印法
Lei-kung yin-wen ching　雷公印文經
Lei-miao　雷廟
Lei-t'ing yü-ching　雷霆玉經
Lei-tz'u　雷祠
li　吏
Li Ching　李靖
Li Hao　李浩
Li Li　李立
Li Pang-yen　李邦彥
Li Ping　李冰
Li-shih chen-hsien t'i-tao t'ung-chien　歷世真仙體道通鑑
Li-shih chen-hsien t'i-tao t'ung-chien hsü-pien　歷世真仙體道通鑑續編
Li Yung　李泳
Liang Chung-li　梁仲禮
lien-tu　鍊度
Lin Ling-su　林靈素
ling　靈
ling-hsiang　靈響
ling-hsien　靈顯
Ling Meng-ch'u　凌濛初
Ling-nan i-wu chih　嶺南異物志
Ling-pao　靈寶
Ling-wai tai-ta　嶺外代答
Liu Tao-ming　劉道明
Liu Tsai　劉宰
Liu Yü　劉玉
Lu Hsiu-ching　陸脩靜
Lu Kuan　路瓘
Lu-ling Ou-yang Wen-chung kung nien-p'u　廬陵歐陽文忠公年譜
Lu Shih-chung　路時中
Lu Yeh　盧埜
Lü Tung-pin　呂洞賓
Lung-ch'uan pieh-chih　龍川別志
Lung-hsing ssu　龍興寺
Lung-hu shan　龍虎山
Ma Sheng　馬勝
Man　蠻
Man-t'ang [wen-]chi　漫堂[文]集
Mao shan chih　茅山志
Meng Kuan　孟琯

miao　廟
miao-chu　廟祝
Ming-hsiang chi　冥祥記
Mo-chuang man-lu　墨莊漫錄
Nan-pu yen-hua lu　南部煙花錄
Ou-yang Chün　歐陽雋
Ou-yang Hsiu　歐陽修
Ou-yang Wen-chung ch'üan-chi　歐陽文忠全集
Pai Yü-ch'an　白玉蟾
P'an-ku　盤古
Pei-meng so-yen　北夢瑣言
P'eng Ssu　彭耜
Pien Ch'üeh　扁鵲
Po-chai pien　泊宅編
p'o-miao　破廟
Sa Shou-chien　薩守堅
San-sheng miao　三聖廟
San-tung ch'ün-hsien lu　三洞群仙錄
sha　煞
shan-shu-che　善術者
Shang-ch'ing　上清
Shang-ch'ing ku-sui ling-wen kuei-lü　上清骨髓靈文鬼律
Shang-ch'ing t'ien-hsin cheng-fa　上清天心正法
shen　神
Shen Chieh　沈介
Shen Fen　沈汾
Shen-hsiao　神霄
Shen-hsien kan-yü chuan　神仙感遇傳
shen-huo fei-ya　神火飛鴉
shen-miao　神廟
Shen Wen　沈文
shih-ta-fu　士大夫
shih-wu　師巫
shih-wu hsieh-fa　師巫邪法
shou-lu　受籙
Shou-she hsieh-wu fa　收攝邪巫法
shu　術
shu-shih　術士
Sou-shen chi　搜神記
Sou-shen hou-chi　搜神後記
Ssu-ma Kuang　司馬光
ssu-tien　祀典
Su Ch'e　蘇轍
Su Shih　蘇軾
Su-shui chi-wen　涑水記聞

Sun Chiu-ting　孫九鼎
Sun Kuang-hsien　孫光憲
Sung An-kuo　宋安國
Sung Lien　宋濂
Sung Sheng　宋甡
Sung Yüan hsüeh-an pu-i　宋元學案
　補遺
Tai Fu　戴孚
T'ai-shang chu-kuo chiu-min
　tsung-chen pi-yao　太上助國救民總
　真秘要
T'ai-sui ling-chün　太歲靈君
T'ang chih-yen　唐摭言
Tao-chiao ling-yen chi　道教靈驗記
Tao-fa hui-yüan　道法會元
Tao-jen　道人
Tao-shih　道士
Tao-shu　道樞
T'ao Hung-ching　陶弘景
T'ao[-shih]　陶[氏]
Teng-chen yin-chüeh　登真隱訣
Teng Kuei-sun　鄧桂孫
Teng Po-wen　鄧伯溫
Teng Yu-kung　鄧有功
T'eng Yen-chih　滕彥智
Ti-ch'i shang-chiang Wen T'ai-pao
　chuan　地祇上將溫太保傳
ti-hu　地戶
T'ien-hsin cheng-fa　天心正法
T'ien-p'eng　天蓬
T'ien-shih　天師
[Tseng-hsiu] Kuan-hsien chih　[增修]
　灌縣志
Tseng Kung-liang　曾公亮
Tseng Min-hsing　曾敏行
Tseng Ts'ao　曾慥
Tu-hsing tsa-chih　獨醒雜志
Tu Kuang-t'ing　杜光庭
T'u-ti　土地
Tung-yüeh hsing-kung/miao　東岳行
　宮/廟
T'ung Min-te　童敏德
t'ung-tzu　童子
tz'u　祠
Wang Chü　王柜
Wang Ling-kuan　王靈官
Wang Shan　王善

Wang Ting-pao　王定保
Wang T'ing-jui　王廷瑞
Wang Tsao　汪早
Wang Tzu-ts'ai　王梓材
Wang Wen-ch'ing　王文卿
Wang Yen　王琰
Wei Po-hsien　魏伯賢
Wen Ch'iung　溫瓊
wen-shen　瘟神
Wen-ssu　瘟司
wu　巫
Wu-ching tsung-yao　武經總要
wu-chu　巫祝
wu-fa　巫法
Wu-i chi　武夷集
Wu-lang miao　五郎廟
Wu-lei　五雷
Wu Meng　吳猛
Wu-shang hsüan-yüan san-t'ien yü-
　t'ang ta-fa　無上玄元三天玉堂大法
Wu-tang fu-ti tsung-chen chi　武當福
　地總真集
Wu Tao-hsien　吳道顯
wu-t'ung　五通
Yang Chung-kung　楊仲弓
Yang Kuang　楊光
Yao　瑤
Yao [Chiang-shih]　姚[將仕]
Yeh Ch'ien-shao　葉遷紹
Yen-lo-tzu　煙蘿子
yen-sha　厭煞
Yen Shu-p'ing　顏叔平
Yen Tu　顏度
yin-hsiang　淫像
yin-ssu　淫祀
yin-tz'u　淫祠
Yü Chi-ssu　余稷思
Yü[-pu]　禹[步]
Yü-t'ang ta-fa　玉堂大法
Yü Wei-ssu　余魏思
Yüan-cho fu　遠捉符
Yüan Miao-tsung　元妙宗
Yüeh-wei ts'ao-t'ang pi-chi　閱微草堂
　筆記
Yün-chi ch'i-ch'ien　雲笈七籤
Yung-le ta-tien　永樂大典

CHAPTER 8

CHANNELS OF CONNECTION IN SUNG
RELIGION: THE CASE OF PAI YÜ-CH'AN

Judith A. Berling

Scholars today have been able to gain a good grasp of some of the customs, ideas, traditions, and institutions that, taken as a whole, constituted Chinese religion. Scriptures are good sources for ideas; hagiographies allow analysis of the self-definition of religious communities; government records reveal the role of the state in overseeing and patronizing religious establishments; inscriptions and other local records show the evolution of cults and sacred places. To avoid seeing Chinese religion as simply a conglomeration of diverse, unconnected ideas, practices, and local traditions, however, we need to develop models of the larger "economy" of Chinese religion. We need to ask how devotion and scholarship, local and imperial traditions, laypersons and clergy impinged on each other. What was the relationship between local centers? How were new ideas and practices diffused and spread? Who were the carriers? What cultural mechanisms were available for the spread of religious ideas? How did developments in one religious transmission affect other religious groups around it? How did religious pluralism work? How were masters and students of these traditions exposed to other traditions, elite or local?

To uncover the channels of connection in the Sung Chinese religious economy, we must perforce turn to textual evidence. This evidence, however, tends to "fix" events, practices, institutions, and personalities. Many of the texts used for the study of Sung religion clearly were intended to "order" lineages, institutions, or rituals in ways that do not reflect their actual complexity. Yet the growth of printing in the Sung dynasty led to the publication of a wide variety of records, allowing us to "recomplexify" our picture of Sung religion.

This chapter will explore religious connections in the Sung period through the examination of texts attached in one way or another to the figure of Pai Yü-ch'an, best known in Taoist circles as a specialist in Thunder Rites,[1] as "the effective founder of Taoism's Southern School."[2]

and as a supporter of the cult of Hsü Sun of the Ching-ming Tao.[3] Pai Yü-ch'an thus was connected to a variety of the streams of religious development in southeast China.[4] Rather than undertaking an intellectual biography of Pai, in this chapter I use sources and traditions that coalesce around him to glimpse some of the dynamics of religious interaction in the Sung.

PORTRAITS OF PAI YÜ-CH'AN

Sources for the study of Pai Yü-ch'an's life are not rich; most are short hagiographies, found in local gazetteers, particularly temple gazetteers.[5] Pai Yü-ch'an was born Ko Ch'ang-keng to Ko Yu-hsing of Min-ch'ing, Fukien.[6] Traditional biographies have established his dates as 1134–1229, noting his long life as a practitioner of the Tao. Miyakawa Hisayuki, after close textual analysis, believes that his actual birthdate was 1194 and that his biographers reinterpreted the dates (reading the cyclical dates a full sixty-year cycle earlier), thus casting Pai in their image of a successful Taoist.[7] Pai is said to have been adept at poetry by the age of seven *sui* and to have memorized the nine classics. His father died in his youth, and his mother remarried into the Pai clan of Lei-chou in Canton. Pai did not follow his mother, nor does he seem to have been adopted by another member of his father's clan. Instead he left home to follow the Taoist master Ch'en Nan (Ni-wan; 1171?–1213) and to learn from him the arts of physiological alchemy and Taoist Thunder Rites. He studied and traveled with Ch'en for some nine years, on land and on sea. At one point their travels took them to Lei-chou. Pai used the occasion to visit his mother and was brought into the Pai clan, thus adopting the name Pai Yü-ch'an.

The records are silent on why Pai's father's death led to his severing ties with his father's patrilineal relatives, assuming some lived nearby. Whatever the cause, at the age of twelve *sui* this bright young man was patrilineally rootless. It is not surprising that he left home to follow a Taoist master. It is perhaps more surprising that he joined his mother's new husband's clan, taking an entirely new name. His actions suggest not only a strong attachment to his mother but also his radical sense of disconnectedness from his natal patrilineage. Ko's (or Pai's) unusual early life history suggests that the Taoistic notion of living *fang-wai* (outside the bounds of normal society), sometimes—perhaps often—had real social roots; some Taoists left home, but some, like Ko Ch'ang-keng, were left rootless by circumstances beyond their control. The cultural trope of the Taoist wandering "beyond the bounds" thus offered a means for coming to terms with their anomalous status.

The second major phase of Pai Yü-ch'an's life covers the nine years from 1205 to 1214, when he studied and wandered with Ch'en Nan. Ch'en, later recognized as the Fifth Patriarch of the so-called Southern Lineage, is renowned as a specialist in physiological alchemy and Thunder Rites. The sources suggest that Pai became Ch'en's formal disciple in 1205, kneeling to receive an oral transmission.[8] After nine years Pai realized the Way for himself *(te-Tao)* and was formally initiated by Ch'en, at which time students and scholars of the four directions gathered around him "like the hairs on a bull."[9] Pai was then only twenty years old.

Ch'en Nan was honored by Pai Yü-ch'an as his master and was later incorporated into the Southern Lineage.[10] He was, however, not a figure through whom Pai Yü-ch'an would gain respectability within the lineages of Taoism. Ch'en's biographies in the standard Taoist sources, such as the *Li-shih chen-hsien t'i-tao t'ung-chien,* depict Ch'en as one of the freefloating, disheveled, nonconformist Taoists following the general cultural trope of the Seven Sages of the Bamboo Grove of the Six Dynasties.[11] He was a commoner with dirty hair and ragged clothes who made wood and bamboo eating utensils, was always drunk, and frequently ate dog meat. In 1213, on his way to meet some other Taoists, he was apprehended by authorities, who were suspicious of his appearance. He may even have died under less than auspicious circumstances.[12] The evidence suggests that in the early thirteenth century Ch'en was not yet connected with an established lineage.[13] Nonetheless Pai evidently found him an excellent teacher and continued to honor him throughout his life.

Pai Yü-ch'an drew deeply from the common well of Chinese religious practices, teachings, and symbols, reappropriating ideas from it along with those he had acquired from Ch'en Nan. Pai did not restrict himself to the oral teachings of Ch'en Nan. His writings indicate that he read widely, either during the time he studied with Ch'en or thereafter. One biographical source cites him as a disciple of Chang Po-tuan (d. 1082), alleged author of the *Wu-chen p'ien* (Folios on the apprehension of perfection). Chang Po-tuan was a major intellectual figure in Sung Taoism, but he died more than a century before Pai Yü-ch'an was born. Nonetheless the corpus of writings attributed to Pai Yü-ch'an contains a "Reply to Chang Tzu-yang [Po-tuan]."[14] Whether or not Pai authored this text, the religious traditions and practices suggested in it are consistent with the other writings and activities attributed to Pai in his published corpus.

Pai Yü-ch'an in time became renowned for his ritual expertise. Nevertheless, perhaps because of his connections with a then nonestablishment Taoist master, he seems to have never received formal ordination. There is no record of ordination in any of his biographies, nor in the genealogies of the schools. He was once ejected from Lung-hu shan, the center of the Cheng-i lineage of the Celestial Masters.[15] The record does not say that he had gone there seeking ordination, but that is at least a reasonable supposition. He is never, to my knowledge, referred to as a ritual master (fa-shih) or a Taoist master (Tao-shih)[16]—terms most frequently applied to ordained masters—but rather as a transcendent (chen-jen), teacher (hsien-sheng), or (in ritual contexts) transcendent official (hsien-kuan).

During the next stage of his life (1214–1222), Pai reached the apex of his career as an expert in ritual arts and a scholar-participant in the religious interchanges and developments in southeast China. After he realized the Tao, he established a hermitage on Mount Wu-i, on the border of Kiangsi and Fukien. During this period he also made a number of trips to visit other religious centers and sites, often having been invited there to share his ritual expertise or officiate at rites. In his hermitage he gathered some disciples and was visited by many more scholars and religious personalities, and on his travels he met many priests and scholars. He was thus active in the religious discourse of his day, exchanging letters, poems, inscriptions, and other occasional writings with a wide range of colleagues and acquaintances, although not persons of particularly great renown.[17] According to his biographies, he was widely respected for his ritual expertise and knowledge; he trained Taoists in the use of the Thunder Rites and was invited to erect chiao altars and to officiate in these rites at a number of temples.

About 1222, the picture changes again slightly. Reports indicate that around this date Pai attracted a reputation as a tipster and a public rowdy; there is even a report of his arrest by authorities and his involvement in heterodox arts (tso-tao).[18] It is difficult to know how to interpret such reports. There are indications that Pai associated with persons who had fallen out of favor, and thus he may have been the victim of slander by association. However, there are other reports that during this period his fame as a poet and calligrapher was growing and that he frequently shared wine and companionship with other wen-jen (in this context, perhaps artistic free spirits), ignoring or stretching social proprieties. It is likely that his changed reputation is a combination of the above factors.

The dual portraits of Pai as a highly skilled ritual expert and a free-spirited, iconoclastic poet wandering "outside the bounds" are captured in the two existing portraits of him (see figures 8.1 and 8.2). One, labeled "The Great Philosophical Master of the Southern Lineage, Pai Yü-ch'an, Fifth Patriarch," depicts him with his hair in a Taoist bun and sporting a trimmed beard, holding animals and ritual implements.[19] He stands next to a cauldron, evoking the alchemical process. His stance conveys knowledge and ritual prowess. The second, labeled "Portrait of the Perfected One Pai Yü-ch'an," depicts a younger, beardless man, barefoot, with loose hair, holding a fly whisk. His stance is relaxed, and the flow of his robes is graceful and almost feminine, as in portraits of the

Figure 8.1. The Great
Philosophical Master of the
Southern Lineage, Pai Yü-
ch'an, Fifth Patriarch.
(*Sung Pai chen-jen Yü-ch'an
ch'üan'chi*, p. 11)

Seven Sages. The second portrait suggests a combination of graceful
refinement and iconoclastic looseness (the bare feet and hair); it exudes
calm and beauty rather than power and authority. One admirer of his
poetry and calligraphy called him a youth with a "jade face."[20] Both sides
of the portrait and memory of Pai had connections to the label "Taoist" in
Chinese history, albeit with constrasting connotations of the ritual expert
versus the cultivated artist-eccentric. Not tied to a particular place or an
established transmission, Pai was able to roam freely along the byways
culturally labeled "Taoist" as well as in the broader common arena of
Chinese religious life.

As an author, Pai was renowned for his expertise in the Thunder
Rites. His writings in this field occur throughout the corpus attributed to
him, and Judith Boltz claims that the detailed exposition in the ritual
communications he issued in 1215 and 1216 "clarifies many of the codi-

Figure 8.2. Portrait of the Perfected One Pai Yü-ch'an. (*Sung Pai chen-jen Yü-ch'an ch'üan-chi*, p. 18)

fications" in the *Tao-fa hui-yüan* (Corpus of Taoist ritual).[21] Pai also wrote knowledgeably about physiological alchemy and contemplation, and, in the period from 1215 to 1218, he wrote several pieces on this topic.[22]

Technical writings aside, four major themes pervade Pai Yü-ch'an's thought: (1) the higher truth of the transcendent, formless Tao; (2) the linked manifestations of Tao in many levels of reality, conveyed through his use of symbolism in poetry and discourse; (3) a sustained interest in local religious traditions; and (4) a deep sense of the wholeness and unity of apparently diverse religious traditions.

Pai's intellectual contributions were summed up by the Ming syncretist Lin Chao-en (1517–1598) in his *Joint Chronicle of the Three Teachings (San-chiao hui-pien yao-lüeh)* in this way:

1232. Pai Yü-ch'an, broadly knowledgeable in Confucian writings and having fully plumbed Ch'an principles, produced sayings and writings that added no unnecessary flourishes. He once said: "People of the world who hold theories of alchemical drugs and the timing of alchemical fires and who see these as physical things and forms cannot attain sudden enlightenment. How can they understand the state before original chaos? . . . We describe the original Tao of no shape and form with the parable of the dragon and the tiger. We take the original named Tao to be the lead and the mercury."[23] . . . He also said: "Before Heaven and Earth are yet *ch'ien* and *k'un* [two of the eight trigrams of the *I-ching*, the primal symbols of Heaven and Earth], the ten thousand things in themselves are *ch'ien* and *k'un*. Before the sun and moon are yet *li* and *k'an* [trigrams that function in the *I-ching* as primal symbols of Fire and Water], the ten thousand things in themselves are *li* and *k'an*."[24]

Lin saw Pai's discussions of the symbols and processes of physiological alchemy (alchemical drugs; the timing of the fires; the symbolic struggle and interplay of dragon and tiger, representing the elements fire and water; and lead and mercury, the main ingredients of the elixir) as grounded not only in Taoism but also in a broader and more synthetic knowledge of the Three Teachings, including Buddhism and Confucianism. The passages he cited show Pai's ability to employ technical symbols of Taoism while insisting on their transcendent "formless" connections. The cosmological processes of Taoist physiological alchemy take place in the realm of the "ten thousand things," but they are grounded in the cosmological patterns of the formless Tao or the metaphysical principles *(hsing-erh-shang)* of the Neo-Confucians. The means and channels by which Pai Yü-ch'an was connected to these various traditions of Sung religious and intellectual life may be examined from four perspectives: (1) ritual expertise, (2) sacred places, (3) Sung religious discourse, and (4) poetry.

RITUAL EXPERTISE

During his lifetime Pai Yü-ch'an was not part of an established Taoist lineage or associated with a major Taoist center, yet his expertise in Thunder Rites and the *chiao* seems to have provided him multiple entrées into the fluid religious world of the Southern Sung. In 1215, just a year after he had established his hermitage on Mount Wu-i as an independent master, he revisited Lung-hu shan, the renowned center of the Cheng-i lineage from which he had been earlier expelled. This visit went rather differently. It is recorded that at this time he was welcomed by the abbot *(kung-chu)* Wang Nan-chi. He read and recited the *Shang-ch'ing lu* (Record of Shang-ch'ing) and became so thoroughly versed in the arts of the Taoist masters *(Tao-shih)* that it was rumored that he was a reincarnation of one of the Celestial Masters.[25] This report bears all the earmarks of hagiographical justification of his subsequent renown as a ritual expert. Yet, since there is no record of anyone ever challenging his credentials to build *chiao* altars or to officiate at *chiao* rituals, he must have had some familiarity with the rituals practiced by the Cheng-i Taoist masters, and he seems to have exchanged ritual information with them. His friendly relations with the Cheng-i lineage are reflected in the eulogistic poems he wrote for thirty-two generations of Celestial Masters.[26]

In his period on Mount Wu-i, he built his hermitage near the Taoist monastery Ch'ung-yu kuan. There he instructed the Taoist masters in Thunder Rites and officiated in *chiao* rituals, using the title *hsien-kuan*. Scattered throughout his writings—in poems, inscriptions, and correspondence—are references to his being invited to participate in *chiao* rituals in a number of temples and communities. He established a *chiao* altar southeast of Ch'ung-yu kuan on Wu-i shan in 1215, and in 1218 he presided over a state *chiao* at Jui-ch'ing kung in southern T'ung-shan hsien of Hupei.[27] In 1224 he performed a *chiao* in a small village near Yü-chang in honor of a local notable, while one of his disciples performed rites to banish dragons and thunder and attract rain.[28] Ritual expertise was one of his links to officialdom, since *chiao* ceremonies were understood as support for the state and community. As Judith Boltz documents in this volume, local officials in the Sung used Taoist rituals as part of their governing repertoire, and experts like Pai Yü-ch'an, who had some classical education as well as ritual expertise, could help officials expand their arsenal of weapons in the fight against the forces of disorder. Pai was also invited in 1218 to officiate at a *chiao* to be offered at the Yü-lung kung on Hsi shan, in Nan-ch'ang fu, Kiangsi, the center of the newly revived Ching-ming Tao. He at first refused the invitation, but the messengers stayed at the gate of his hermitage and repeatedly pleaded until he relented.

Ching-ming Tao began as a local popular religion based on wonder-working spiritual arts, particularly exorcistic demonifuge rites, and some rudimentary forms of ritual and self-cultivation from the common store of Chinese religious cosmology and practices. The Hsiao-tao rituals associated with the early cult appear to have been "an early regional variation on the deeply rooted Ling-pao ritual heritage."[29] The cult of Hsü Sun, by Pai's time firmly associated with the Ching-ming Tao, also had a long history. In the late T'ang and Sung, Hsü's original career as an outstanding local magistrate—whose religious arts helped the people to battle threatening demons and plagues and whose later powers as a deity helped besieged communities defend themselves against bandits—gave the cult some fame as a "defender of the state," thus attracting elite patronage.[30] Several influential persons helped to revive the cult, which had died out after several generations of leadership (despite cult legends of a continuous transmission), and by the Southern Sung it had attracted imperial patronage. Because of such patronage, Yü-lung kung became a Taoist temple in which *chiao* rites for the benefit of the state had to be performed regularly.

After arriving at Hsi shan, Pai became close friends with the head of Yü-lung kung, and he stayed there for most of the year studying the cult and its history. He left a record of the flourishing of this local religion and its incorporation into "Taoism" by means of imperial patronage. His writings about this local religion suggest that he was deeply impressed by the revival and religious vitality of Ching-ming Tao in his day. In this instance, at least, he did not simply hire himself out as a ritual expert; his visit to Hsi shan involved him in the life and history of that religious community beyond the limits of his original assignment.

SACRED PLACES AS SITES FOR RELIGIOUS INTERACTION

Much of Pai's contact with lay believers, religious adepts, and mildly curious Confucian scholars took place at sacred sites. The Chinese are famous for their pragmatic approach to religion, their interest in this-worldly boons and benefits. They also, like many peoples, grounded religion, associating religious figures, persons, events, and practices with particular places. Temples, shrines, hermitages, steles, pagodas, and stone piles in the shape of pagodas dotted the traditional Chinese landscape, reminding locals and travelers alike of the sacred history and the sacred inhabitants of the terrain. These visible markers were the foci for worship and reverence, and means of popular education that made the transcendent realities of religion highly visible. Each site was also in competition with other sacred sites for patronage and position in the hierarchy of religious places.

For the majority of his life as a religious master, Pai Yü-ch'an was associated with Mount Wu-i on the border of Fukien and Kiangsi. A sacred mountain of long and eminent history, Mount Wu-i contained traces of several dozen deities dating back hundreds of years.[31] In his inscription commemorating the building of his hut, Pai briefly sketched some of the high points of the sacred history of the mountain and its thirty-six peaks. He noted numerous temples and shrines of Buddhist, Taoist, and local provenance. But the location of his hermitage was unequaled in spirituality; it was perched above a steep embankment at a point where the river burbled its way over rocks; below it was a pond known as Heaven's mirror, above it the Grotto for Ascent to the Absolute (Sheng-chen tung). Pai also noted his proximity to the Jen-chih t'ang

(Hall of Humane Wisdom), established by the great Neo-Confucian master Chu Hsi (1130–1200).[32] Nevertheless, the mountain was dominated by the Taoist monastery Ch'ung-yu kuan, and Pai Yü-ch'an built his hermitage almost literally in its shadow (see map of Mount Wu-i, figure 8.3). His hermitage was thus on the path to a major pilgrimage site.

Taoist pilgrims were not the only ones to visit this mountain. Not far from Pai Yü-ch'an's hermitage was a private academy *(ching-she* or *shu-yüan)* founded by Chu Hsi at a place where he felt the mysterious confluence of the nine turns of the Wu-i River and the mountain created a hamlet for ghosts and spirits.[33] Because later official *shu-yüan* were often located among the official government halls in the prefectural city, there is a tendency to envision them in the ordered urban world of the Confucians. In fact, as Linda Walton shows in this volume, Confucian academies were often housed in former Taoist or Buddhist temples or shrines and thus were often located amid the spiritual rocks and cliffs of a sacred mountain.

Living and teaching in close proximity to Chu Hsi's academy, Pai Yü-ch'an found inspiration in the teachings of the great master. There is no evidence of formal face-to-face exchanges between Pai and students or teachers at Chu's academy, but Pai's writings include direct and indirect evidence of how deeply he was "perfumed" (as the Buddhists say) by the presence of Chu Hsi's academy and his students. The academy contained various shrines and commemorations of Chu Hsi's presence, including a portrait for which Pai wrote an inscription. Characteristically, it was in this poetic form that Pai expressed most directly his reverence for Chu Hsi. The inscription praised Chu as a truly great master, whose numinous presence filled the entire cosmos but noted that his spiritual presence was especially keen in the mountains, cliffs, trees, and monkey cries of Mount Wu-i, although Chu could no longer be seen or heard there. Chu's portrait, however, provided a focal point for his presence so that his civilizing effects *(wen)* were not dissipated. Pai concluded his inscription: "Only those with a rectified mind and sincere will *(cheng-hsin ch'eng-i)* can understand this; those who aspire thoroughly to realize the preservation of the spirit can speak about it."[34]

Sacred mountains such as Mount Wu-i were not solely religious centers; they were also renowned as scenic spots visited for their natural beauty. Scholars on an outing or local officials getting to know their territory would visit such sites, have a cup of tea at a temple, and pay a courtesy call. The steles and memorial plaques dotting the mountain would guide visitors on their way, sometimes inspiring them to visit a local hermit or compose a poem or an inscription to mark the site. It can be assumed that many Confucian scholars visited Pai in his hermitage on Mount Wu-i.

During this period, however, he did not always stay in his hermit-

Figure 8.3. Comprehensive map of Wu-i shan. Indicated are (1) Pai's Chih-chih an, (2) Taoist monastery Ch'ung-yu kuan, and (3) approximate location of Chu Hsi's *shu-yüan*. (*Wu-i shan-chih, chüan* 4)

age. Religious figures such as Pai were not located in fixed spots at which seekers and disciples found them. They also wandered about visiting other temples, eager to participate in a ritual or festival, curious to meet a famous master or to read a text, or intent on expanding their own religious experiences through formal or informal pilgrimage. The improvements in transportation along commercial routes in the Sung dynasty made such travel easier and encouraged interaction across distances.

Pai Yü-ch'an's writings on Ching-ming Tao, in the ostensible form of a biography of its "founder" Hsü Sun, provide a delightful record of Sung pilgrimage connected with a local religion.[35] The first *chüan* of the biography recorded in detail events and miracles connected with Hsü's life, with each event carefully located. In the second *chüan* Pai provided an account of the pilgrimage held each year to commemorate the ascension of the founder and the events at each of the significant sites connected with his life. The pilgrimage path was believed to retrace the routes that Hsü had traveled as a local magistrate; the old road was windy, but when the pilgrims had tried to take a newer road instead, the omens grew inauspicious and they went back to the old path.[36] Each twist and turn of the path, each ford of a river had a story or tradition connected with Hsü's life.[37]

The revival of the Ching-ming Tao at Hsi shan illustrates the relation of sacred place and respect for the written record in the history of Chinese religion. The men who revived Ching-ming Tao went back to all of the textual evidence they could find, concluding that the religious events of Hsü Sun's life centered on Hsi shan. Unfortunately, the devotees of the original community had moved, and there was no reliable record of the exact location of the original Hsi shan, and there were a number of mountains of the same name in southeast China. Judging by the textual evidence, the revivers decided on the present site in Nanch'ang fu, Kiangsi; when they went there, they found all of the physical traces of Hsü Sun's career referred to in the biographical sources.[38] According to Akizuki, however, they had almost certainly misidentified the site; nonetheless the "traces" were identified and the location was perceived to be invested with the numinous presence of Master Hsü.

This incident exemplifies the dynamics of Chinese religion. The revival of Hsü Sun's teachings was religiously motivated; later figures found in this figure and what he stood for some basis for a teaching and practice relevant for their times. They saw in Hsü Sun a model magistrate, a learned scholar-official, a skilled practitioner of spiritual arts, and an effective representative of broad social and religious values.[39] They turned to him to legitimize, spiritually and historically, their ethical and religious visions. Legitimation was sought through historical and religious texts, drawing on an age-old Chinese respect for the written word. With texts providing the guidelines, the community found the physical traces or relics of the religion that were necessary to reestablish the spiritual presence or numinosity *(ling)* of the deity. The community was able to use the textual evidence as its warrant even though they were in fact mistaken about its reading.

RELIGIOUS DISCOURSE AND BOUNDARIES IN SUNG RELIGION

As all of the chapters in this volume confirm, the Sung religious arena was characterized by remarkable fluidity across lines of textual and ritual transmissions, by the movement of famous masters and teachers visiting each other and a variety of sacred places, by the lively exchange of poetry and correspondence, and by the publication of a broad range of texts facilitated by the advances in printing. As a result of all of these factors, there was a common font of religious texts, practices, symbols, and ideas from which religious thinkers could draw to reappropriate "authentic" religious practice in their own terms. Despite the open and fluid religious boundaries, however, virtually all teachers and writers of the Sung also drew boundaries between themselves and others, locating themselves in terms of their understanding of the "true Way." Precisely because of the fluidity of boundaries in the Sung religious arena, it was important to define a discourse that related to past and present religious traditions and ideas in a way that delimited a coherent and distinctive approach to religious life; religious thinkers had to position themselves among the range of possibilities and practices.

Yü-lu, or discourse records, provided a means for religious traditions to define their boundaries. This genre seems to have begun among Ch'an Buddhists with an interest in transmitting the teachings of famous T'ang masters.[40] During the Southern Sung, however, Buddhists, Neo-Confucians, and Taoists were all publishing *yü-lu* of eminent masters. Although there are some differences in the genre in different traditions, there are also common features.

Yü-lu often present discourses as though they were records of actual conversations; in fact, these collections were edited—sometimes years after the fact—by disciples of the master based on notes taken and kept by disciples, lay students, and/or visiting officials. In some cases, such as the *yü-lei* (classified recorded sayings) of Chu Hsi, the intent was a thoroughgoing record of every surviving scrap of the master's exchanges with students. Chu Hsi's sayings were arranged by topic, thus abstracting them from their actual context of interchanges among living personalities. Other collections were arranged by context; that is, they recorded the master's discourse at a specified time and place, sometimes naming the recorder. Many of these collections, particularly in the later Sung and beyond, were highly edited and perhaps fictionalized in order to create a brief interchange with symbolically representative interlocutors. This literary device located the master's position pithily but effectively among the religious options of the day.[41]

Pai Yü-ch'an's disciples edited his *yü-lu* to record his exchanges with religious leaders, disciples, and other interlocutors. Pai's *yü-lu* extends beyond the normal limits of "recorded sayings." It includes a broad range of texts that amount to "a collage of firsthand accounts attesting to Pai's mission, compiled at different times by a number ·of disciples."[42] Although the anthology includes verses, sermons, and other materials, the bulk of it is the recorded discourses, usually in question-and-answer format, between Pai and a range of interlocutors. In his exchanges with Taoists in the first *chüan* of his record, Pai consistently pointed beyond literal meanings of symbols to higher, symbolic meanings. For instance:

> The *Classic of the Big Dipper (Pei-tou ching)* was not written by T'ai-shang [Lao-chün] but rather comprises Chang Cheng-i's record of the essence of T'ai-shang's teaching during the Han dynasty. But today people do not understand its meaning. They only worship the stars and sacrifice to the dipper. Now the single ether of the human self rises in the east and settles in the west; it moves up and down like [the ether of] heaven and earth. The ether of heaven and earth is called yin and yang; what humans are endowed with is similar to it. Now the Big Dipper in heaven constantly revolves day and night in order to differentiate yin and yang and thus establish the divisions of the hours. Heaven and earth are thereby constantly preserved. Why consider that it is the single ether of the human body controlling it? One who can understand what controls it can thereby understand the Big Dipper in the human self.[43]

The classic, he argued, is not about astral worship but rather provides the cosmological grounding for the contemplative practices of physiological alchemy.

The corpus of texts in the *Tao-tsang* gives witness to a broad range of religious practices, ritual arts, and beliefs, including traditions of astral worship and rituals. Sung Taoists like Pai Yü-ch'an who developed and transmitted the teachings on physiological alchemy according to the Ch'üan-chen or Southern Lineage, had a strong hermeneutical tendency to read all Taoist practices as pointing beyond their literal or surface meanings to the functioning of general cosmological principles that were also the foundation of physiological alchemy. All ritual and all practices were in their view grounded in the general rhythms and patterns of the cosmos, of the formless Tao beyond its myriad manifestations. Thus this view provided a cosmological unity and coherence to the immensely fragmented Taoist heritage. Moreover, in their view, to accept the surface meaning was to miss the foundation and its connection to the proper integration of the microcosm within the self. This view, then, not only refined and sustained an intellectual foundation for Taoism but also created the principles for discriminating between higher and lesser understandings of the Way. For instance, Li Tao-ch'un (fl. 1288–1290), a disciple of Pai, published a description of thirteen vehicles of physiological alchemy, which laid out higher and higher understandings of the symbols and practices of Taoism.[44] Thus Pai argued that the *Classic of the Big Dipper* was properly understood as a description of the cosmological principles and rhythms that underlie the reintegration of the various aspects of the self in the practice of physiological alchemy.

As one active in officiating in rituals, Pai Yü-ch'an had strong feelings about the integrity of rituals and was critical of priests and believers who allowed the incorporation of inauthentic popular practices in order to increase their wealth: "Those who say one must offer paper money to the supreme absolute during the *chiao* ceremony are profaning the rite. The ancients had ritual implements but no paper money. This practice appeared only in the late Han dynasty. One can use it for sacrifices to ghosts and spirits of hell, but how is it appropriate for the rites of the heavenly absolute?"[45]

This comment is an excellent example of boundary drawing. Pai did not repudiate the use of paper money in offerings to ghosts and spirits of the underworld, nor was he critical of the existence of such religious practices. His point was that this practice was inappropriate in the conduct of the *chiao* ceremony, which belongs to a different aspect of the Sung religious world. It encouraged a materialistic and excessively pragmatic attitude in a ceremony dedicated to the renewal of the human world through petitions to the highest deities of Heaven.

Modern anthropological studies of Chinese religion have noted that different forms of worship and offerings are appropriate to different levels of deities. One does not give a hungry ghost the same offering or liturgical piety one offers a spirit. Spirits are fed and fêted ceremoniously, whereas hungry ghosts are given scraps in the back alley like beggars bribed not to cause trouble.[46] Michael Saso's study of contemporary *chiao* in Taiwan demonstrated that during a high *chiao* the spirits who normally occupy the place of honor in the temple are moved to become spectators (and worshipers) like the humans, giving honor to the Three Pure Ones who are installed for the ceremony.[47] We cannot with confidence project the levels and codes documented by contemporary fieldwork into the practices of the Sung dynasty, but Pai's argument about the inappropriateness of paper money offerings during the *chiao* documents that levels of liturgical practice were being defined and defended during the Sung. As new practices and religious communities emerged, religious thinkers were busy both drawing from the common pool of Chinese religious practice and drawing boundaries to maintain their sense of appropriateness, of true and authentic practice.

In his sayings, Pai both interpreted the elaborate symbolism of

Taoist ritual and meditation and also constantly reminded his conversation partners that these were "mere" symbols; the Great Way was beyond both the symbolism and any language he could use to describe it: "Another interlocutor asked: 'Why do the transmissions of the great schools lose the Way and get caught in the details of the written word? Over eight hundred thousand kalpas they gradually sink into oblivion.' Pai replied: 'All that does (yu-wei) is an allusion. The formless (wu-hsiang) is the absolute.' "[48]

The third chüan of the yü-lu contained a set piece in which Pai engaged in turn representatives of the Ch'an school, a Taoist master, and a Confucian scholar and earned their respect for his insightful discourse.[49] Although somewhat tamer in rhetorical style, these exchanges resemble the "dharma battles" through which Ch'an adepts demonstrated their embodiment of the Way in Ch'an collections. The episode, clearly highly edited, sought both to locate Pai's teachings within the common arena of discourse and to assert his eminence among the many teachers of the day vying for respect and recognition. Collections of yü-lu by disciples asserted the importance and distinctiveness of their master's teachings.

POETRY AS A MEDIUM OF RELIGIOUS EXCHANGE AND RECOGNITION

When one looks beyond the Taoist canon, the temple gazetteers, and the major Taoist compendia in researching Pai Yü-ch'an, one immediately finds another sort of record of this man. He was noted in Sung dynasty travel books and in collections of poetry as an outstanding poet and calligrapher.[50] These sources mentioned his Taoist connections and the Taoist themes of his poetry, then cited one or two of his poems.

Pai Yü-ch'an's poetic corpus is substantial. A modern anthology has included 1079 poems in various genres.[51] Yet even a cursory comparison of the table of contents of that anthology with other collections of Pai's poetry in Japanese libraries shows that it is incomplete. Pai's style ranges across a broad continuum, from standard commemorative and occasional poems, through "Taoistic" nature poetry in the tradition of poets such as Su Shih (1037–1101), all the way to verses in which the technical imagery and recondite symbolism of Taoism is used to create dense layers of public and esoteric meaning.

Pai's poetry served several purposes. First, as Judith Boltz has noted in her study of Ch'üan-chen literature, poetry was an important means of communication among the early masters of this lineage.[52] Wang Che (1112–1170) and Ma Yü (1123–1183) even practiced an elaborately stylized form of poetry exchange in which the poet "not only had to accommodate the prescribed metrical pattern and rhyme scheme, but also had to evoke the opening word from a component of the last word in the verse."[53] These poetic exchanges, like the discourse records, were stylized forms of Taoist discourse meant to convey and refine the understanding of the Tao. Like the Ch'an masters who often certified their disciples' enlightenment with verses, these Ch'üan-chen masters sharpened their discourse by means of poetry. It was for Taoists a remarkably apt medium, for the multivalent symbols and language of poetry could express layers of simultaneous meaning.

Even if the use of poetry by Ch'üan-chen and Southern Lineage Taoists was in part influenced by Ch'an uses of poetry, there was another side to the role of poetry in the Sung religious and literary world. Every educated man needed at least a rudimentary skill in poetry to commemorate visits, outings, and other special occasions. Precisely because there had been from the time of the Six Dynasties a long tradition of nature poetry in which Taoist tropes, motifs, and symbols played a significant role, poetry was one of the most broadly accepted means of communicating Taoist points of view. There was an enduring interest in "literary" or "poetic" Taoism among educated admirers of nature poetry, even ones uninterested in Taoist rituals or physiological alchemy.[54]

Pai Yü-ch'an left hundreds of poems at places he visited around south China. A great many were occasional pieces, commemorating his visit to a particular place or a meeting with a friend or acquaintance. He sometimes penned his poems on the walls of the inns and teahouses where he stayed on his travels, and later travelers, inspired by the beauty of the poetry and his calligraphy, would collect them as souvenirs.[55] The temples he visited often kept his poems and seem to have shown them to other visitors. Thus Pai Yü-ch'an left his mark across the religious landscape of southeast China. Scholars, teachers, poets, monks, and travelers who had never met Pai Yü-ch'an encountered his poetry and thus knew his name and something of the flavor of his teaching.

His skill at poetry, calligraphy, and other forms of formal writing also drew Pai Yü-ch'an into a network of written formal exchanges. Like many men of letters, Pai wrote prefaces, inscriptions, postfaces, couplets, and commemorative essays for his acquaintances. Toward the end of his life, he seems to have become actively engaged with a group of literati, with whom he drank and exchanged poems and pleasantries. He was commended to the court by Wang Chü-an for his poetry, calligraphy, and general refinement as a man of letters sometime between 1213 and 1220.[56] Thus, even though he led his life "beyond the bounds" in the world of temples and religious hermitages, his writings connected him with the literary world and its networks of exchange of ideas and sentiments.

Pai's poetry was typically "Taoist" in its literary tropes. He evoked the pleasures of retreating into the deep stillness of nature, away from the human world of dust. One example is his "Constructing my Hermitage."

> Constructing the hermitage, I live in deep mountains.
> And within stillness regard the ten thousand things.
> Green moss seals in the morning clouds;
> Greener vines bind the evening moon.
> Crying birds hang atop boulders
> While dark waters wash the bones of rock.
> Wind rises, the mountains seem to thunder;
> The ocean tosses, waves like snow.
> Days of youth will never return
> While in this world of mortals, in vain white hair.[57]

Pai often enfolded into his poems symbols of physiological alchemy. An example of a poem with symbolism evoking Sung dynasty Taoist practices is "Preface to a Friend's *Evening Light* Poetry Collection":

> At the sea's bottom is a bright moon
> Rounder than our bright moon's wheel.
> Catch but an inch of its light and
> You can buy ten thousand ancient springs.
> On the rocks plant the fragrance of flowers.
> From fire's center fish up a snow man.
> Walking, ride a water buffalo.
> Then you'll know a priceless treasure.[58]

In this poem, the moon also stands for *k'an* (water), a pair to fire in the sixth line. Fire and water (*li* and *k'an*) represent the two inner lights cultivated in Taoist alchemical meditation. In fact, it is full of images from Taoism and Buddhism. In addition to describing a moonlit scene, for the informed reader it depicts the achievement of a priceless treasure through physiological alchemy. The allusion to the bright moon in the first line, for instance, refers to the moment in physiological alchemy when sun and moon (*li* and *k'an*, fire and water) directly face or balance each other. At that moment yin ether reaches its nadir, and it is then that the True Lead, the light representing the refinement and sublimation of vital forces, appears.[59] "Catching an inch of its light" refers to the practice of learning to circulate this light through the inner passages of physiological alchemy, so that eventually it will combine with the light of spirit (True Mercury) to conceive the new self; hence the promise of an immortal existence, buying ten thousand springs. Planting the fragrance of flowers on the rocks (in the fifth line) refers to the planting of the congealed spirit in the cave of ether,[60] the cavity within the inner cavity, where the spirit of the new self can be refined and nurtured in the alchemical process. When the spirit or embryo is ready to emerge, the adept sees snow and flowers blowing in the wind of the inner microcosm; at that moment the adept must concentrate attention on leading the new self out of the fire of the alchemical furnace, up the spine, and through the opening at the top of the head.[61] Thus the poem's reference to fishing a snow man from the fire's center refers to this delicate and fragile process. The reference to riding a water buffalo while walking is presumably a reference to the famous "Ten Ox-herding Pictures" of Ch'an Buddhism, which were seen as a metaphor for the gradual mastery of enlightenment.[62] In Taoist terms, the image of buffalo herding presumably refers to the need to learn to control and master the new self after it has appeared, lest it become capricious and misuse its powers or fall prey to the temptations of demons.[63] Thus, the deeper the reader's knowledge of the esoteric practices is, the more layers of meaning appear.

Poetry, then, was not only a medium of exchange and a channel for interconnections; in addition, each poet sought to convey his (rarely her) vision of the world and to invoke images he or she felt to be powerful. Thus the exchange of poetry was a means of exchanging, sustaining, and refining the images, symbols, and motifs that expressed the aesthetic and religious ethos of the Sung.

CONCLUSION

The career and activities of Pai Yü-ch'an—both religious and literary— help to illustrate the many ways in which persons, texts, symbols, histories, and practices flowed across time, space, and "tradition" in Sung times. As the two portraits of Pai indicate, he had two sides: the ritual expert who entered into Sung exchanges about the place of Taoist practices and symbols in the Sung religious world and the poet and man of letters who became renowned for his calligraphy and elegant writings on religious themes. The first portrait is of a "Taoist," but one who crossed boundaries and communities within the lineages and traditions of Taoism; the second is less narrowly "Taoist," representing a broader cultural trope of Taoism. To these two portraits one might add a third: the historian of Ching-ming Tao. Although Pai was not incorporated into the lineage of that community, his lengthy biography of Hsü Sun is one of the community's most important documents. In writing this carefully documented biography, Pai took on the role of a scholar in order to preserve a local religious tradition.

Although Pai Yü-ch'an was ultimately identified as heir to the Southern Lineage, his openness toward other communities is characteristic of him and perhaps of the Sung religious ethos as a whole. In his supervision of ceremonies, his visits to sacred sites and temples, his documentation of religious revivals and imperial patronage, his face-to-face interaction with representatives of many religious practices, and his poetry and writings, one can see the many ways in which he crossed social and intellectual boundaries. In his discourse records we also see Pai and the disciples who edited those records establishing his distinctive boundaries and locus as a teacher. Pai Yü-ch'an may be taken as a symbol of the permeability of boundaries between religious groups and traditions during the Sung period and the process by which one could establish a place in the Sung religious world.

NOTES

I am grateful to the American Council of Learned Societies for a grant that made the initial research on this topic possible and to the National Endowment for the Humanities for a Summer Stipend, which funded research in Japanese libraries. I would also like to thank the colleagues who attended the conference on which this volume was based for their helpful criticisms and Margaret McLean of the Graduate Theological Union for her careful reading and incisive suggestions.

1. This aspect of Pai's career is treated in more detail in the chapter by Judith Boltz. See also Judith M. Boltz, *A Survey of Taoist Literature, Tenth to Seventeenth Centuries,* China Research Monograph Series, no. 32 (Berkeley: Institute of East Asian Studies, 1987), pp. 176–179.

2. Michel Strickmann, Review Article, *HJAS* 40.1 (1980): 245. On the ex post facto reconstruction of the Southern School or Southern Lineage, see Boltz, *Survey,* pp. 173–175.

3. See Akizuki Kan'ei, *Chūgoku kinsei dōkyō no keisei* (Tokyo: Sōbunsha, 1978).

4. Miyakawa Hisayuki, "Nansō no Dōshi Haku Gyozen no jiseki," in *Uchida Gimpū hakushi shōju kinen tōyōshi ronshū* (Kyoto: Dōhōsha, 1978), pp. 499–517. In addition to having connections with physiological alchemy (Chin-tan Tao), he is claimed in the lineage of I-kuan Tao, a later syncretic movement; he is heir to the so-called Southern Lineage in the line of Ma Tan-yang; he is considered by some a follower of the Sixth Patriarch of Ch'an Buddhism; and he is known in Japan in connection with the Ōbaku sect of Zen (p. 499). Lin Chao-en (1517–1598) considered him an important link in the true transmission of the Three Teachings. See Judith A. Berling, *The Syncretic Religion of Lin Chao-en* (New York: Columbia University Press, 1980), esp. pp. 38–40 and 202–203.

5. The fullest accounts appear in *Li-shih chen-hsien t'i-tao t'ung-chien* (HY 296), 49.16b–18a. See Boltz, *Survey,* pp. 56–59; *Hai-ch'iung Yü-ch'an hsien-sheng shih-shih,* in *Sung Pai chen-jen Yü-ch'an ch'üan-chi* preface by Hsiao T'ien-shih (Taiwan: Committee to Publish Pai Yü-ch'an's Works, 1976); *Pai chen-jen shih-chi san-t'iao* from *Tao-tsang chi-yao;* and *Jih-yung chi Pai-chi* 4, as cited in Miyakawa, "Dōshi Haku Gyozen," p. 502. Even with these accounts, however, the facts are somewhat sketchy.

6. Boltz notes that a biography compiled by Pai's disciple Hsüeh Shih-ch'un in *Tao-fa hui-yüan* (HY 1210), 147.1a–4a, claims that Pai was a native of Hainan and gives his original name as Chu-ko Meng; see her *Survey*, p. 318, n. 456. However, the vast majority of sources cite the Ko tradition, and thus Miyakawa has followed it ("Dōshi Haku Gyozen," p. 502).

7. Miyakawa, "Dōshi Haku Gyozen," p. 501.

8. *Jih-yung chi*, cited in Miyakawa, "Dōshi Haku Gyozen," p. 502. Pai has left a record of his studies and interactions with Ch'en in "Hsiu-hsien pien-huo lun," in *Hsiu-chen shih-shu*, anonymous, late thirteenth century (HY 263), 4.1a–10a. On the dating of *Hsiu-chen shih-shu*, I follow Boltz, *Survey*, pp. 234–237.

9. *Li-shih chen-hsien t'i-tao t'ung-chien*, cited in Miyakawa, "Dōshi Haku Gyozen," p. 502.

10. According to that tradition, Ch'en received instruction from Hsüeh Tzu-hsien (d. 1191) at Li-mu shan on the island of Hainan. The fourteenth-century preface to the one text attributed to Ch'en Nan claims, as Boltz has noted, "that Ch'en's text represents the culmination of all there was to learn about *chin-tan* procedures" (Boltz, *Survey*, p. 175).

11. On the Seven Sages, see Richard B. Mather, "The Controversy over Conformity and Naturalness During the Six Dynasties," *History of Religions* 9.2/3 (1969–1970): 160–180; see also Ellen Johnston Laing, "Neo-Taoism and the 'Seven Sages of the Bamboo Grove' in Chinese Painting," *Artibus Asiae* 36.1/2 (1974): 5–54.

12. *Li-shih chen-hsien t'i-tao t'ung-chien*; see Miyakawa, "Dōshi Haku Gyozen," pp. 503–504.

13. Boltz's research suggests that the Southern Lineage was a later reconstruction (*Survey*, pp. 173–175), and my analysis of Pai's "encounter" with Chang Po-tuan (immediately following) supports that conclusion, especially since that text may suggest an alternate or variant "lineage." There was, it seems, considerable fluidity or ambiguity about the status of the major figures during the Sung. Pai's turn to Chang Po-tuan may have been an attempt to ground his understanding of the Way in a lineage broader and deeper than the teachings of Ch'en Nan.

14. *Hsiu-chen shih-shu* 6.1a–5a. Because it lacks a date and place and is somewhat too "neat," there is reason to doubt Pai's authorship of the "reply"; it has the earmarks of a genealogical document fashioned later by adherents of the Southern Lineage and attributed to the pen of an important figure. The author "Pai" traced the genealogy back through his master Ch'en Nan to former Ch'an master Hsüeh Tzu-hsien, to Shih T'ai (Chün; d. 1158), and then back to Chang Po-tuan himself. Note that the man later identified as the founder of the Southern Lineage, Liu Ts'ao (fl. 1031) plays virtually no role in this text (see Boltz, *Survey*, pp. 173–179). Moreover, Pai entered into a dialogue with Chang in which he as a disciple clarified his understanding of the correct transmission; he reverently presented his "reply" with an offering of incense to Chang. It is not entirely clear whether this document is presented in a form of veneration of a religious forefather or whether the author is portrayed as having a vision or dream in which he is in direct contact with the late master. The latter seems likely, since such dreams and visions were not uncommon within Chinese Taoism. However, it is clear that this document is an attempt to establish in a religiously appropriate way a geneal-

ogy of the true transmission of the Tao (*Hsiu-chen shih-shu* 6.4a–4b). There are interesting parallels and contrasts in attempts to establish genealogies in Confucianism and Buddhism; see Thomas A. Wilson, "Genealogies of the Way: Representing the Confucian Tradition in Neo-Confucian Philosophical Anthologies" (Ph.D. dissertation, University of Chicago, 1988).

15. Miyakawa, "Dōshi Haku Gyozen," p. 510.

16. Following the usage by Judith Boltz in this volume.

17. Miyakawa has documented examples of correspondence with members of middle-level officialdom, notably Li Ch'en (1144–1218) and Ch'iao Ling-hsien (1155–1222) ("Dōshi Haku Gyozen," p. 512), and there are a few disciples who have left some writings. My attempts to identify eighty or more persons named in poems and occasional writings proved fruitless. Pai's activities were primarily local and mostly among the subelite, although his contacts with abbots on Lung-hu shan and at Hsi shan are reasonably well documented. They will be discussed elsewhere in the chapter. One splendid example of the literary output of his interactions with other places and religious leaders is that an entire *chüan* of the *Shang-ch'ing chi* (An anthology of Shang-ch'ing) comprises poems and inscriptions commemorating visits to temples and other religious figures. See *Hsiu-chen shih-shu, chüan* 40.

18. Miyakawa, "Dōshi Haku Gyozen," p. 512.

19. According to the tradition of the Southern Lineage, Ch'en Nan, not Pai Yü-ch'an, was the Fifth Patriarch (see Boltz, *Survey,* p. 173). Why, then, is the title given to Pai in this portrait? If it is not simply an error, it may be evidence of a rival lineage, as suggested in Pai's "Reply to Chang Tzu-yang," consisting of (1) Chang Po-tuan, (2) Shih T'ai, (3) Hsüeh Tzu-hsien, (4) Ch'en Nan, and (5) Pai Yü-ch'an. This issue merits further research. *Hsiu-chen shih-shu* 6.1a–5a.

20. Miyakawa, "Dōshi Haku Gyozen," p. 510.

21. Boltz, *Survey,* p. 179; see also *Tao-fa hui-yüan* (HY 1210).

22. Preserved in *Hsiu-chen shih-shu* (scattered throughout) and particularly in the *Shang-ch'ing chi, chüan* 37–44. See Boltz, *Survey,* p. 178.

23. Quotation from "Hsiu-hsien pien-huo lun," in *Hsiu-chen shih-shu* 4.3a–3b.

24. *Lin-tzu chüan-chi* (compiled in 1567 and preserved in the Sonkeikaku Bunko, vol. 12), 9.11b–12a. This *chüan* was reviewed and ordered for publication by disciples Wang Hsing and Ch'en Piao. The Joint Chronicle is dated 1562 in the *Lin-tzu nien-p'u,* ed. Lin Chao-k'o, 1610. Lin's Joint Chronicle presents his version of an orthodox genealogy of the Three Teachings heritage. Although deeply intertextual in providing citations for most thinkers cited, Lin does not provide references and he sometimes paraphrases slightly. Our first passage, as noted in the last note, was an exact quote from an essay by Pai. I have been unable as yet to locate the second quote in Pai's collected writings. Lin Chao-en's remarks on Pai are cited as a rare pre-modern assessment of Pai's role in Chinese intellectual and religious history.

25. Miyakawa, "Dōshi Haku Gyozen," p. 510. The *Shang-ch'ing lu* was given to Taoist ordinands as part of their ordination ceremony; however, Miyakawa does not say that Pai "received" the text, only that he read and recited it. For whatever reasons, the historical record does not provide clear evidence of ordination, although these sources may be suggesting indirectly that Pai may have been ordained.

26. *Sung Pai chen-jen Yü-ch'an ch'üan-chi,* pp. 364–369.

27. Miyakawa, "Dōshi Haku Gyozen," p. 510.

28. Ibid., p. 513.

29. Boltz, *Survey,* p. 71. Akizuki Kan'ei has written a history of Ching-ming Tao from its inception through the Yüan dynasty entitled *Chūgoku kinsei dōkyō no keisei,* cited above. According to Akizuki's research, the founder of the cult was Wu Meng, but sometime in the T'ang, between 644 and 670, Hsü Sun (third–fourth century), who was originally Wu Meng's disciple, began to move to the center of the legend as the founder of the cult. By the late T'ang he was firmly established as one of the cult's twelve perfected gentlemen *(chen-chün).* Devotion to Hsü Sun was well established on Hsi shan, and shrines to him appeared all over southeast China from the Sung dynasty onward (see Akizuki, *Chūgoku kinsei dōkyō no keisei,* pp. 6–10, 27–31).

30. The first *chüan* of Pai Yü-ch'an's detailed biography of Hsü Sun provides a detailed record of Hsü's spiritual prowess as a local magistrate. "Ching-yang Hsü chen-chün chuan," in *Yü-lung chi, chüan* 33–34, preserved in *Hsiu-chen shih-shu.*

31. That history is recorded in a number of works written about the mountain, most notably *Wu-i shan-chih,* 24 *chüan,* Tung T'ien-kung ed. (1846), reprinted in *Chung-kuo ming-shan sheng-chi ts'ung-k'an.* The gazetteer includes maps and charts; myths and traditions about temples, shrines, and sacred places; documents about establishing or reviving temples; and numerous poems written by resident monks and priests and visiting worthies. There are also a number of "travel records" *(yu-chi)* of visits to the mountains by Taoists, Buddhists, and laypersons. Most extant versions are from the Ming and Ch'ing.

32. *Wu-i chi,* preserved in *Hsiu-chen shih-shu* 45.1a–4a.

33. Chu Hsi, *Chu Wen-kung wen-chi* (*SPTK* condensed version), 9.146–147. I am indebted to Lionel Jensen for calling my attention to this passage.

34. "Chu Wen-kung hsiang shu," in *Shang-ch'ing chi* (HY 263), 43.3b.

35. Pai's biography drew on an extensive corpus of earlier works. See Boltz, *Survey,* pp. 71–73, and Akizuki, *Kinsei dōkyō,* pp. 3–37, on the history of sources for the biography of Hsü Sun.

36. *Yü-lung chi* 34.10a.

37. Ibid. 34.8b. The return to the old route should not be seen as a rejection of the new commercialism of the Sung; Pai explicitly reports that at major shrines and temples on the pilgrimage route shops and stalls lined the way to serve the crowds of pilgrims, creating a lively bustle.

38. Akizuki, *Kinsei dōkyō,* pp. 42–59.

39. Boltz, *Survey,* pp. 72–73, comments on the striking way in which the Sung lore on Hsü Sun's life came to reflect Hui-tsung's interests and preoccupations, revealing "how easily such literature adapts to the realities of its time."

40. Judith A. Berling, "Bringing the Buddha Down to Earth: Notes on the Emergence of *Yü-lu* as a Buddhist Genre," *History of Religions* 27.1 (1987): 56–88; see also Yanagida Seizan, "Goroku no rekishi," *Tōhō gakuhō* 57 (1985): 211–663.

41. Judith Boltz has written of Taoist *yü-lu* (which she translates "dialogic treatise") as "characteristic of what was apparently a new age of religious creativity." She notes that there are abundant examples of this genre in the *Tao-tsang,* suggesting that "Taoist Masters seem to have favored this genre as an instrument

of didactic persuasion nearly as keenly as did their Ch'an counterparts" (*Survey*, p. 138). As in the case of Ch'an and Neo-Confucian *yü-lu*, these collections were edited and published by disciples, sometimes from notes and sometimes from memory. They are not a literal record, but a re-presentation, and the genre, as Boltz notes, "occasionally exhibits a level of narrative inventiveness that would make any professional storyteller proud" (p. 138). Boltz's survey of Taoist *yü-lu* led her to conclude that these works are both instruments of persuasion and records of pedagogical styles. She also notes that the Ch'üan-chen lineage's historical connection with Ch'an Buddhism may well have contributed to the importance of this genre in their literary corpus (pp. 138–139). My study of the evolution of *yü-lu* as a Ch'an genre would both confirm Boltz's judgment and suggest some further interpretations. In addition to being persuasive and recording the pedagogical styles of great masters, the *yü-lu* served two purposes in Ch'an history: (1) they made a theological statement by having living masters in particular and unidealized settings "stand in" for the role the Buddha would have played in sūtra literature as the conveyer of the dharma; in other words, they reinforced the Mahāyāna notion that "this very body is the Buddha"; (2) they portrayed the paradoxical and startling dynamics of the nondiscursive, nondualistic discourse of the Ch'an Buddhist lineage. Thus, the masters and monks were not only engaged in persuading each other about the excellence of a particular master's teachings and insights; the "dharma battles" were also enactments of a distinctively Ch'an approach to discourse. It is not unreasonable to assume that Taoist *yü-lu* served similar purposes, mutatis mutandis.

42. Boltz, *Survey*, pp. 177–178; *Hai-ch'iung Pai chen-jen yü-lu*, 4 *chüan* (HY 1296). It was put into its final form by Pai's most eminent disciple, P'eng Ssu (fl. 1229–1251).

43. Pai, quoted in *Hai-ch'iung Pai chen-jen yü-lu* 1.2b–3a.

44. See Berling, *Lin Chao-en*, pp. 101–103, for a discussion and partial translation of this text.

45. Pai, quoted in *Hai-ch'iung Pai chen-jen yü-lu* 2.10b.

46. See Arthur P. Wolf's classic "Gods, Ghosts, and Ancestors," in idem, ed., *Religion and Ritual in Chinese Society* (Stanford: Stanford University Press, 1974), pp. 131–182.

47. Michael R. Saso, *Taoism and the Rite of Cosmic Renewal* (Pullman: Washington State University Press, 1972), pp. 38–41.

48. *Hai-ch'iung Pai chen-jen yü-lu* 3.5b.

49. Ibid., 3.6b–8b.

50. His poems are included in various anthologies and in travel literature. For instance, the *Sung-Yüan ming-jen kung shih-chi*, ed. P'an Shih-jen (1615), contains forty-five of Pai's poems in several sections of the anthology. In addition, there are numerous extracanonical collections of his poetry, including (1) *Hai-ch'iung Pai hsien-sheng shih-chi*, 29 *chüan* (hand-copied manuscript in the Naikaku Bunko, Tokyo, Japan); (2) *Ch'iung-kuan Pai hsien-sheng wen-chi*, 14 *chüan*, ed. Liu Shih-an (Ming edition); (3) *Ch'iung-kuan Pai chen-jen wen-chi*, 12 *chüan*, ed. Ho Chi-kao (preface 1594); and (4) *Yü-ch'an hsien-sheng wen-chi*, 6 *chüan*, ed. Chu Ch'üan (Ming).

51. *Sung Pai chen-jen Yü-ch'an ch'üan-chi*.

52. Boltz, *Survey*, pp. 139–173.

53. Ibid., p. 146.

54. See, for instance, Yoshikawa Kojiro, *An Introduction to Sung Poetry,* trans. Burton Watson, Harvard-Yenching Institute Monograph Series, vol. 17 (Cambridge: Harvard University Press, 1967).

55. See, for instance, two poems dedicated to hostels and inns, in *Wu-i chi,* preserved in *Hsiu-chen shih-shu* 49.5b and 49.6a.

56. Miyakawa, "Dōshi Haku Gyozen," p. 510, citing *SS* 405.12255.

57. *Sung Pai chen-jen Yü-ch'an ch'üan-chi,* p. 126, translation adapted from a draft by Neil Bolick titled "An Examination of Patterns of Imagery, Metaphor, and Allusion in Pai Yü-ch'an's Poetry," (Indiana University seminar paper), 1985. Neither this poem nor the next appears in the *Tao-tsang* collections; modern anthologies include a great many poems from extracanonical collections.

58. Ibid., p. 127; again adapted from Neil Bolick's translation.

59. Tai Yüan-chang, ed., *Tao-hsüeh tz'u-tien* (Taipei: Chen-shan-mei ch'u-pan-she, 1971), p. 94.

60. Tai Yüan-chang, ed., *Hsien-hsüeh tz'u-tien* (Taipei: Chen-shan-mei ch'u-pan-she, 1970), p. 127.

61. Tai, ed., *Hsien-hsüeh tz'u-tien,* p. 129.

62. See Philip Kapleau, *The Three Pillars of Zen: Teaching, Practice, and Enlightenment* (Boston: Beacon Press, 1967), pp. 301–314, for illustrations and explanations of these famous pictures.

63. See Lu K'uan-yü, *Taoist Yoga: Alchemy and Immortality* (New York: Samuel Weiser Inc., 1970), pp. 160–173.

GLOSSARY

Chang Cheng-i　張正一
Chang Chih-liang　張志諒
Chang Po-tuan (Tzu-yang)　張伯端（紫陽）
chen-chün　真君
chen-jen　真人
Chen-tsung　真宗
Ch'en Nan (Ni-wan)　陳楠（泥丸）
Ch'en Piao　陳標
cheng-hsin ch'eng-i　正心誠意
Cheng-i　正一
chiao　醮
Ch'iao Ling-hsien　譙令憲
ch'ien　乾
Chih-chih an　止止庵
Chin-tan Tao　金丹道
Ching-ming Tao　淨明道
ching-she　精舍

Ching-yang Hsü chen-chün chuan　旌陽許真君傳
Ch'iung-kuan Pai chen-jen wen-chi　瓊琯白真人文集
Ch'iung-kuan Pai hsien-sheng wen-chi　瓊琯白先生文集
Chu Hsi　朱熹
Chu-ko Meng　諸葛猛
Chu-tzu wen-chi　朱子文集
Chu Wen-kung hsiang shu　朱文公像疏
Ch'üan-chen　全真
Chung-kuo fang-chih ts'ung-shu　中國方志叢書
Ch'ung-tsuan Fu-chien t'ung-chih　重纂福建通志
Ch'ung-yu kuan　沖佑觀
fa-shih　法師

fang-wai　方外
Fu-chou fu-chih　福州府志
Fu-ning fu-chih　福寧府志
Hai-ch'iung Pai chen-jen yü-lu　海瓊
　白真人語錄
Hai-ch'iung Pai hsien-sheng shih-chi
　海瓊白先生詩集
Hai-ch'iung Yü-ch'an hsien-sheng
　shih-shih　海瓊玉蟾先生事實
Ho Chi-kao　何繼高
Hsi shan　西山
Hsiao-tao　孝道
Hsiao T'ien-shih　蕭天石
hsien-kuan　仙官
hsien-sheng　先生
hsing-erh-shang　形而上
Hsiu-chen shih-shu　修真十書
"Hsiu-hsien pien-huo lun"　修仙
　辨惑論
Hsü Sun (Ching-yang)　許遜(旌陽)
Hsüeh Shih-ch'un　薛師淳
Hsüeh Tzu-hsien (Tao-kuang)　薛紫
　賢(道光)
Hui-tsung　徽宗
I-ching　易經
I-kuan Tao　一貫道
Jen-chih t'ang　仁智堂
Jih-yung chi　日用記
Jui-ch'ing kung　瑞慶宮
k'an　坎
Ko Ch'ang-keng　葛長庚
Ko Yu-hsing　葛有興
kuan　觀
k'un　坤
kung　宮
kung-chu　宮主
Lei-chou　雷州
li　離
Li Ch'en　李訦
Li-mu shan　黎姆山
Li Pa　李拔
Li-shih chen-hsien t'i-tao t'ung-chien
　歷世真仙體道通鑑
Li Tao-ch'un　李道純
Lin Chao-en　林兆恩
Lin Chao-k'o　林兆克
Lin-tzu nien-p'u　林子年譜
ling　靈

Ling-pao　靈寶
Liu Shih-an　劉氏安
Liu Ts'ao　劉操
Lung-hu shan　龍虎山
Ma Yü (Tan-yang-tzu)　馬鈺(丹陽子)
Min-ch'ing　閩清
Min-ch'ing hsien-chih　閩清縣志
Nan-ch'ang fu　南昌府
Ōbaku　黃檗
Ou-yang Yung-min　歐陽傭民
Pai chen-jen shih-chi san-t'iao　白真
　人事蹟三條
Pai Yü-ch'an　白玉蟾
P'an Shih-jen　潘是仁
Pei-tou ching　北斗經
P'eng Ssu　彭耜
piao-wen　表文
San-chiao hui-pien yao-lüeh　三教會
　編要略
Shang-ch'ing chi　上清集
Shang-ch'ing lu　上清錄
Shang-ti　上帝
Sheng-chen tung　昇真洞
Shih T'ai (Chün)　石泰(君)
shu-yüan　書院
ssu　寺
Su Shih　蘇軾
Sui Yang-ti　隋煬帝
Sun Erh-chun　孫爾準
Sung Pai chen-jen Yü-ch'an ch'üan-chi
　宋白真人玉蟾全集
Sung-shih　宋史
Sung-Yüan ming-jen kung shih-chi
　宋元名人公詩集
T'ai-shang (Lao-chün)　太上(老君)
Tao-shih　道士
Tao-tsang　道藏
Tao-tsang chi-yao　道藏輯要
te-Tao　得道
tso-tao　左道
Tung-shan kung　東山宮
Tung T'ien-kung　董天工
T'ung-shan hsien　通山縣
Wang Che　王嚞
Wang Chü-an　王居安
Wang Hsing　王興
Wang Nan-chi　王南玘
wen　文

wen-jen　文人
Wu-chen p'ien　悟真篇
wu-hsiang　無相
Wu-i chi　武夷集
Wu-i shan　武夷山
Wu-i shan-chih　武夷山志
Wu Meng　吳猛
Yang Tsung-ts'ai　楊宗彩
yao-ch'i　妖氣
Ying-hsien tao-yüan　迎仙道院
yu-chi　遊記

yu-wei　有偽
Yü-ch'an hsien-sheng wen-chi　玉蟾
　先生文集
Yü-chang　予章
Yü Cheng　喻政
yü-lei　語類
yü-lu　語錄
Yü-lung chi　玉隆集
Yü-lung kuan　玉隆觀
Yü-lung kung　玉隆宮

CHAPTER 9

SOUTHERN SUNG ACADEMIES
AS SACRED PLACES

Linda Walton

Illumined Way Academy in Chiang-ning (modern Nanking) began around 1175 as a shrine *(tz'u)* to the great Neo-Confucian philosopher Ch'eng Hao (1032–1085).[1] In its origin as a shrine and in the vicissitudes of its recorded history, it was typical of many Southern Sung academies.[2] Illumined Way was formally established as an academy in 1215 during the tenure of Commissioner Chen Te-hsiu (1178–1235), who wrote an inscription for it. The academy fell into disrepair shortly thereafter, eventually becoming a hostel for soldiers.[3] When it was restored in the mid-thirteenth century, the emperor bestowed a name plaque on it, much as he might have on a Buddhist monastery. A "famous classicist" was invited to become the head of the academy, recalling the system of abbot selection employed by the Southern Sung state.[4] Descendants of Ch'eng Hao were appointed to administer the academy, while the post of headmaster was filled by officials from the local prefectural office appointed by the Ministry of Personnel.[5] Rules for administering the academy were adapted from Chu Hsi's (1130–1200) famous White Deer Hollow Academy. These rules reveal that academy life had some parallels with life in a Buddhist monastery—such as formal lectures, rituals, and regulation for relations with the outside world. "Every ten days the headmaster entered the hall and gathered the staff and students to hear a lecture. . . . There were thirty-eight lectures on the Classics and sixteen on the Histories." Topics followed a schedule: "During the first ten days were 'Questions on the Classics.' During the middle ten days were 'Questions on History.' The last ten days were left for instruction." A rector *(chih-hsüeh)* kept records of the progress of each student, while a dean *(chih-shih)* had charge of such disciplinary matters as requests for leave. "If without reason [students] did not visit the shrine, attend lectures, or prepare their lessons, up to three demerits were recorded in the register."[6]

In addition to the similarities between academies and Buddhist monasteries suggested here, there were significant parallels in the regulation of communal life and in the attendant physical structure, which included dormitories, kitchen, bath, granary, and so on (see figure 9.1). Like the shrine to Ch'eng Hao that was the foundation of Illumined Way, nearly every academy had shrines to Confucius, his disciples, Neo-Confucian philosophers, or "local worthies." These shrines were similar to the Buddha and patriarch halls in a monastic complex (as described by Foulk in this volume). Academies also normally included a central lecture hall, often simply referred to as the *chiang-t'ang,* which was comparable to the dharma hall in a Buddhist monastery. As the abbot of a monastery would ascend to the high lecture seat in the dharma hall to preach the dharma, so the headmaster of the academy would ascend the platform at the center of the lecture hall, surrounded by students who were gathered to hear his lecture on *The Great Learning* or *The Doctrine of the Mean.* Just as Buddhist monasteries had libraries and sponsored the printing of the Buddhist canon, so too, as the term *shu-yüan* (book hall) implies, large academies had substantial libraries and sponsored the printing of books. Illumined Way, for example, edited and printed the writings of Ch'eng Hao.[7]

Southern Sung academies like Illumined Way have hitherto been viewed primarily as semiprivate educational institutions that played a major role in the propagation of Neo-Confucian ideas.[8] During the early Northern Sung, academies evolved from private scholarly retreats to semiofficial schools, established by private scholars but often sponsored by local officials and supported by public land endowments. The decline of the great academies of the Northern Sung in the mid-eleventh century was a result of the expansion of state schools as training institutions for examination candidates and the employment of scholars as officials in the central government's Directorate of Education (Kuo-tzu chien), the Imperial University (T'ai-hsüeh), or local schools. In the Southern Sung, criticism of the examination system contributed to a revival of academies. By the late Southern Sung, official support for Chu Hsi's thought transformed White Deer Hollow Academy into the centerpiece of the Southern Sung academy movement and linked these institutions directly to the rise of Neo-Confucianism.[9]

Focus on the Neo-Confucian identity of Southern Sung academies has obscured other important dimensions, particularly those related to the intense religious activity of an era characterized by profound social and economic change. Just as Buddhist and Taoist temples housed images of Buddhas, bodhisattvas, patriarchs, immortals, and sundry deities, so shrines at academies contained images of scholars and officials. Scholars included Confucius, his disciples, and scholars primarily (although not exclusively) associated with the School of the Way (Tao-hsüeh). Officials venerated were often ones who had suffered disgrace and dismissal in the course of factional intrigues.[10]

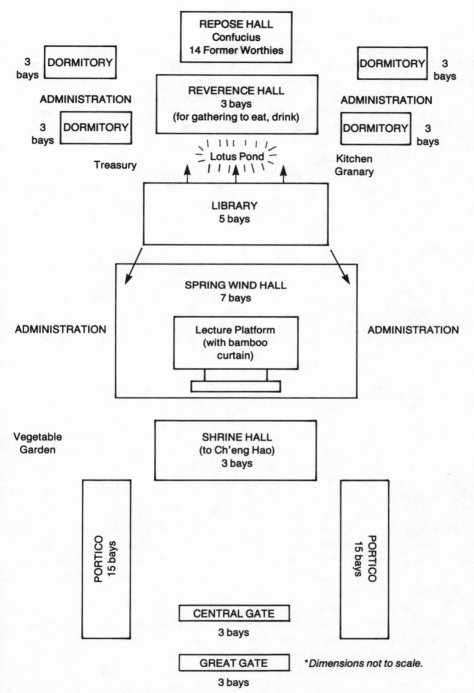

Figure 9.1. Illuminated Way Academy, early thirteenth century (ca. 1215). (*Chien-k'ang chih* 29.2b–4b)

The regular performance of rituals was probably the most important element in bonding the academy members together as a community. Illumined Way Academy explicitly followed the model of White Deer Hollow in carrying out the "vegetarian offering" *(shih-ts'ai)* rites as stipulated in the *Li chi*.[11] These rites involved the presentation of offerings to Confucius and other teachers at the opening of each academic session. Chu Hsi's brief description of these rites, as appended to his *White Deer Hollow Teaching Regulations,* can be cited as an illustration of the religious dimension of an outwardly secular ceremony. After quoting various authorities, including Lü Ta-lin (1044–1093), who stated that "the vegetarian offerings are the utmost in simplicity, and they do not lie in having many things but in ennobling one's sincerity," Chu Hsi continued:

> The White Deer rites are carried out every year in the first month of spring. The prefect sends the various students into the academy, then carries out [the rites]. In the first ten-day period [of the month], the Hollow students and teaching officials select an auspicious day. They request sacrificial implements to carry out the rites. They fast [by abstaining from meat and certain other things] for three days. On the last day the prefect makes the offerings. After the rites are completed, he ascends the hall and instructs all the students.[12]

Similar rites were practiced regularly at other academies. For instance, at Elephant Mountain Academy, the seat of Lu Chiu-yüan's (1139–1193) learning, in the spring of 1232 the "vegetarian offering" rites were held to honor the former sages, whereupon the participants "withdrew to visit the shrine to the Three Gentlemen [Lu Chiu-yüan, Yang Chien (1141–1226), and Yüan Hsieh (1144–1224)]." The solemn students, in formal dress, acted as though they were in the presence of their deceased teachers.[13]

Adherents of the "School of the Way," broadly defined, formed a major part of the community active in the academy movement, but they were by no means the entire community. The individuals for whom academy shrines were dedicated were not all patriarchs of Neo-Confucianism or their disciples. Even when individual scholars were linked with major Neo-Confucian figures, such as the Ch'eng brothers or Chu Hsi, as much if not more emphasis might be given in commemorative inscriptions to other aspects of their lives. An ambivalent attitude toward official service was evoked by the political and cultural heroes honored at academies: scholars whose reputations as teachers or thinkers drew attention to them, men whose political skills and fortune brought them high office, and loyal officials victimized by imperial whims or political struggles at court were all honored.

SHRINES TO NEO-CONFUCIAN PATRIARCHS

Academies were frequently built around shrines to one or more of the great Sung philosophers.[14] These include not only Chu Hsi,[15] but also his lesser known disciples, such as Wei Liao-weng (1178–1237), whose sobriquet, Ho-shan, was used to name several academies concentrated in, but not limited to, his native Szechwan.[16] There were also numerous academies named to commemorate Northern Sung forerunners of Chu, like Chou Tun-i (1017–1073), usually called Lien-ch'i after his sobriquet.[17] The Lien-ch'i Academy at Mount Lu in northern Kiangsi, for example, represents a common pattern in the construction of academies. It began with the identification of a sacred site where Chou had built a study in 1070. More than a century later (1176) the local prefect renovated the study "in order to make sacrifices to Chou."[18] Chu Hsi's inscription on Lien-ch'i Academy places Chou in the historical context of the transmission of the Tao from Mencius and is infused with the metaphysics of "Heavenly Principle," inspired by the beauty of the landscape that attracted Chou to build his study there.[19]

Not infrequently academies contained shrines dedicated to a group of major thinkers: Chou, the Ch'eng brothers, Chang Tsai (1020–1077), and Chu himself. Heaven Gate Academy at T'ai-p'ing (Chekiang) was typical. Established by the prefect early in the thirteenth century, it included the "Seven Worthies Hall," venerating Chou Tun-i, the Ch'eng brothers, Chang Tsai, Chu Hsi, Chang Shih (1133–1180), and Lü Tsu-ch'ien (1137–1181).[20] There were several academies dedicated specifically to Yang Shih (1053–1135), who was credited with transmission of the Ch'eng brothers' ideas to the south.[21] A shrine established in the early Southern Sung at Yang Shih's residence in Nan-chien prefecture (Fukien) was made into Turtle Mountain Academy by Ch'en Mi (1171–1230) around 1225.[22]

Spring Mountain Academy in Ch'üan-chou along the Fukien coast was founded around 1268 to venerate Chu Hsi. An inscription by Liu K'o-chuang (1187–1269) refers to other famous Southern Sung academies that used White Deer as a model.[23] Liu also provides detailed information on the individuals venerated at Spring Mountain (see figure 9.2). They include the usual members of the Confucian and Neo-Confucian pantheon, such as Confucius and his disciples, Mencius, Chou Tun-i, Shao Yung, Chang Tsai, and the Ch'eng brothers of the Northern Sung. But those venerated also include Ssu-ma Kuang, a historian and statesman rather than a philosopher, as well as Lü Ta-lin (1046–1092) a student of the Ch'eng brothers and younger brother of Lü Ta-chün, the author of the famous Lan-t'ien Lü-shih *hsiang-yüeh* (community compact), which was adapted by Chu Hsi in the hope of promoting community harmony and solidarity. Lü Ta-lin, along with Hsieh Liang-tso

(1050–1135), Yu Tso (1053–1123), and Yang Shih were known as the Four Masters of the Ch'eng School. Hu Yin (1048–1156), Hu An-kuo (1074–1138), Hu Hsien (1086–1162), Liu Tzu-hui (1101–1147), and Liu Mien-chih (1091–1149) were all natives of Ch'ung-an, where Chu Hsi settled after his father died, and were all students of the major Northern Sung thinkers, Yang Shih and the Ch'eng brothers. All the Hus were related, and, after the death of Chu Hsi's father, both Liu Tzu-hui and Liu Mien-chih treated Chu Hsi as their own son.[24] Lo Ts'ung-yen (1072–1135), a native of Nan-chien, was also a student of Yang Shih and the Ch'eng brothers and was praised by Chu Hsi. Yin Ch'un (1071–1142), a native of Honan, was a student of Ch'eng I summoned by Emperor Kao-tsung to lecture in the Imperial Seminar at the Southern Sung capital.[25] A shrine to him was the foundation of Tiger Hill Academy at Soochow (discussed below). Chang Shih and Lü Tsu-ch'ien were, of course, two prominent friends of Chu Hsi.[26] Those venerated in the inner sanctum, Chu Hsi's sacrificial temple, included Huang Kan, his major disciple, Chao Shih-hsia (1190 *chin-shih*), a former prefect of Nan-k'ang and disciple of Chu Hsi, Chen Te-hsiu, and Ch'en Mi, the prefect of Nan-chien responsible for establishing three academies there.

The emphasis on natives of Fukien, even of the same county (in this case Ch'ung-an), suggests that it was considered important to establish a link between the region and the transmission of learning from the Northern Sung. The most obvious link was provided by Yang Shih, but it is significant that lesser figures in the Neo-Confucian pantheon, such as Hu Yin, were also included, presumably because of their identity with the area. A second noteworthy aspect of many of these late Northern Sung and early Southern Sung figures is their opposition in office to compromise with the Jurchen Chin. Nearly all were known as confirmed opponents of peace with the Chin, and Chang Shih was the son of the general Chang Chün (1096–1164). The combination of Neo-Confucian scholarship and irridentist loyalty was particularly significant in the transmission of the Tao-hsüeh tradition through Yang Shih, a Fukienese student of the Ch'eng brothers and a staunch opponent of concessions to the Jurchen.

Academies were, of course, not confined to the orthodox Ch'eng-Chu line. They apparently served much the same functions for followers of Lu Chiu-yüan as they served for those of Chu Hsi and others. In addition to Elephant Mountain Academy, which was established at Lu Chiu-yüan's lecturing place in his native area of Kuei-ch'i county (Hsin prefecture, Kiangsi),[27] Locust Tree Hall Academy was founded in 1233 by the magistrate of Ch'in-ch'i county (Fu, Kiangsi) to venerate Lu Chiu-yüan and his brother Lu Chiu-ling (1132–1180).[28] There was also an academy that commemorated Yang Chien (1141–1226), Lu's principal disciple, in his native county of Tz'u-ch'i in Ming (Chekiang). The shrine was set up

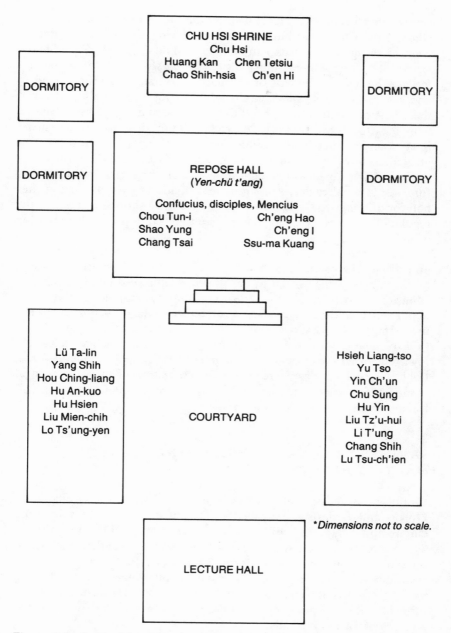

Figure 9.2. Spring Mountain Academy (latter thirteenth century). (Liu K'o-chuang, *Hou-ts'un hsien-sheng ta ch'üan-chi* 93.15b–16a)

shortly after his death by local men on the shores of Compassion Lake, where Yang Chien had built a residence during his lifetime. A decade later the shrine was moved to an islet in the middle of the lake, and in the last years of the Southern Sung a retreat *(ching-she)* was built by the prefect on the lake to the east of a T'ien-t'ai temple, and official land in another county was allocated for the support of rituals performed there.[29] A few years after the fall of the Southern Sung, priests from the temple, with official support, "usurped its land, destroyed its sacrificial images, and slandered all its students to the officials."[30] Almost immediately after, however, Yüan government officials restored the former residence of Yang Chien and made it into an academy.[31] This academy was foremost a ritual center. Among its first buildings were a revering rites hall for offerings to the former sage and a stately shrine pavilion for the regulation of sacrifices. Only later were the lecture hall and four study chambers built.[32]

Like other patriarchs of Neo-Confucianism, Yang Chien served as an official. Neo-Confucian idealism did not help to advance his career; on the contrary, his earnest moral stance, exemplified by his defense of Minister Chao Ju-yü (1140–1196), got him into trouble. Ambivalence about office holding characterized the career of the most prominent figure in the Tao-hsüeh movement, Chu Hsi, and this attitude could also be said to have typified the official lives of many other scholars. Deeply loyal but often victimized by the bureaucratic system or political factionalism, such scholars were seen as representatives of a Confucian ideal of ministerial service and frequently were revered as models for their colleagues and heirs in academy shrines.

SHRINES TO LOYAL OFFICIALS AND MARTIAL HEROES

Confucian ideals associated with official service were complicated ones. Loyalty and patriotism that called men to put service to the emperor and empire above self and family were encouraged and validated by history. At the same time, there was a romantic idealization of individuals, beginning with Ch'ü Yüan, whose firm, almost obsessive, loyalty brought them disaster. The demotion, dismissal, or punishment of worthy and well-intentioned officials is a common theme in Chinese historical literature that often inspired the establishment of academies to honor the memory of such individuals.

Recognition of the insecurity of official life is reflected in the shrine to three generations of loyal officials of the Liu family that served as the foundation for West Brook Academy at Kao-an county in Jui (Kiangsi).

The shrine was erected during the Shao-hsing period (1131–1165). After its destruction in the early thirteenth century, the prefect established an academy in 1236 to the east of the prefectural seat.[33] West Brook Academy was designed to function as a ritual center, venerating not only Confucius and his disciples but also local men who exemplified certain values in their professional careers.[34] All three Lius are cited as being principled officials who were demoted as a result of offending those in power during the Northern Sung.[35] The inscription for West Brook Academy cites the precedent of White Egret Islet in the Kan river basin prefecture of Chi, where former prime minister Chiang Wan-li (1198–1275) established an academy to venerate the Ch'eng brothers and their father.[36] During the Yüan, both Chiang Wan-li, who served in Lu-ling county (Chi, Kiangsi), and Ou-yang Shou-tao (1209–?), who was from there, were honored in a shrine at White Egret Islet Academy.

Shrines were sometimes dedicated to high officials idealized as upright models of virtue undone by arbitrary decisions and political circumstances beyond their control. Li Kang (1083–1140), prime minister under Kao-tsung, whose strong opposition to the Chin got him into political trouble, was venerated at Ch'iao Creek Academy in Fukien as well as at Nine Peaks Academy in Sung-chiang (Soochow), where he was born.[37] The T'ang chief minister, Lu Chih (754–805), exiled to the south in 795 by Emperor Te-tsung (r. 780–805), was commemorated at a shrine in an academy in Hsiu prefecture (Chekiang), established at the end of the Sung. Other academies commemorated the residence in exile or office holding of Northern Sung figures such as Fan Chung-yen (989–1052), Su Ch'e (1039–1112), or Su Shih (1036–1101).[38]

Some academies celebrated military accomplishments. Ch'en Wei (ca. 1180–1261), the elder brother of the prefect who established West Brook Academy, built Former Worthies Academy in Kan at the southern end of the Kan river basin at the site of a scholar's study.[39] He was also associated with the founding of an unconventional academy in Fukien. As specially appointed pacification commissioner, Ch'en Wei had led a campaign to suppress bandits in the Fukien hinterland in 1229–1230.[40] His success was attributed to his skillful military strategy, and his abilities were commemorated in the establishment of Sleeping Dragon Academy, named for Chu-ko Liang (181–234), the famous strategist of the Three Kingdoms period. An image of Chu-ko Liang was placed in the academy, and phrases from his writings were inscribed on the wall. This academy commemorated Chu-ko Liang and Ch'en Wei and taught the strategic skills associated with Chu-ko Liang.

Another layer is added to this story by Chen Te-hsiu's fortuitous recording in 1231 of an account of a "shrine for the living" *(sheng-tz'u)*[41] erected to Ch'en Wei.[42] After repeating the story of Ch'en Wei's strategic success in eradicating the bandits in Fukien, Chen described the steps taken by the people of Yen-p'ing to honor Ch'en Wei and noted the historical precedents drawn upon by them:

> The scholars and people of Yen-p'ing gathered to plan and said: "The merit (kung-te)[43] of Ch'en was received by seven [prefectures of] Min, but ours received the most. How could we ignore such extreme benevolence?" Therefore, they divined the old site of the Dragon Ford postal station to the east of the prefectural city to make a "shrine for the living" for sacrificing to his image. They took the T'ang precedent of Ti Liang-kung [Ti Jen-chieh, 630–700] to name its hall, called "Love Looking Up," for the people of Chien loved Ch'en Wei as the people of Wei loved Ti Liang-kung. They further used the precedent of remonstrator Hsien-yü to name the pavilion, called "Prosperity Star," to tell of Ch'en Wei's enriching the people of Chien as Hsien-yü enriched Ch'ing-she.[44]

When Ch'en Wei heard of the plans, he modestly argued that he had only been doing his duty and did not merit such attention, but the people persisted. Not only did they paint an image of Ch'en to be venerated at the shrine, but they also painted images of the fiscal intendant for Fukien, Shih Mi-chung (d. 1244), a cousin of chief councillor Shih Mi-yüan, and the military commissioner for western Huai, Tseng Shih-chung. The historical precedents noted by Chen Te-hsiu linked Ch'en Wei with past heroes, thereby suggesting his influence on Yen-p'ing paralleled that of the two earlier figures. Ti Jen-chieh was the model of the upright and talented minister who faithfully served his sovereign, Empress Wu, even when her policies were questionable, trying to moderate her mistakes and encourage wiser courses of action.[45] Chen Te-hsiu presented Ch'en Wei as equally beloved by the local population and in that way conferred on him some of the aura of greatness surrounding Ti Jen-chieh.

What did it mean for an official to be venerated at such a shrine? How did this shrine differ from shrines to local deities? That so orthodox a Neo-Confucian as Chen Te-hsiu would write so positive an account of the erection of Ch'en's shrine suggests that this practice elicited no censure from Neo-Confucian ideologues. The latter part of this inscription reveals the Neo-Confucian interpretation of Ch'en's success and thus sheds some light on the religious and intellectual justification for shrine building:

> Ch'en clearly obtained the great merit of the empire from Heaven. From his youth he was extraordinary. . . . His talents and simplicity went beyond others. . . . [When he responded to the crisis] . . . it was the determination (ming) of myriad vital spirits (sheng-ling). Thus his sincerity and talent con-

verged. It is appropriate that he was able to manage great affairs. The former classicists said: "What will be wrought by Heaven in the transformation of our world will be produced by people." The bandits rose in Min, and Ch'en was born in Min. Heaven truly engaged Ch'en in order to carry out its transformation. His pure loyalty was Heaven's heart manifested in him. . . . Such is Heaven's and man's mutual convergence. It was fitting that he was able to accomplish the great merit. Alas! How can we attribute this simply to chance?[46]

The point is clear: Heaven only operates through human beings, and they can thus be worshiped as manifestations and agents of Heaven's will. This passage does not, however, say what meaning to ascribe to the erection of a "shrine for the living"; nor does it tell how this kind of shrine differed from shrines to local deities. This example does suggest, however, that a shrine to a living official in recognition of meritorious acts of service may have been a response to the proliferation of shrines to local deities and the cults surrounding them. Southern Sung records abound with accounts of officials attempting to stamp out such cults. The erection of a shrine to venerate an official might well have been intended as a means to redirect popular energies away from such cults. Although the sources make it sound as though there was a popular clamor for the shrine to Ch'en Wei, it is not at all clear what community the shrine served. The erection of the shrine could well have been a self-justifying and self-gratifying orchestration on the part of members of the local elite, led by the prefect. In that case, the common people would have been kept at a distance, although perhaps subject to the "civilizing" influence represented by the shrine's subject.

In addition to Sleeping Dragon Academy, named for him, Chu-ko Liang was also venerated,[47] along with a Northern Sung military hero, K'ou Chun (961–1023), at Nan-yang Academy in Ching prefecture (Hupei). K'ou Chun was instrumental in the outcome of the battle of Shan-yüan (1004) against the Khitan. When others advised the emperor to flee, he urged the emperor to lead the troops himself. The emperor followed his advice, the enemy retreated, and a peace treaty was signed. Nan-yang Academy was one of two academies Meng Kung (1195–1246) built to provide refuge for scholars fleeing Mongol invasions of the middle and upper Yangtze valley in the mid-1230s. Meng Kung was a scion of a military family that had moved south after the fall of the Northern Sung and was "by repute the last great Sung military figure."[48] Inscriptions on both of these academies emphasize the importance of supporting scholars in distress by providing them a modest means to live and study. They quote extensively from Mencius on the ability of the true scholar to suffer physical hardship in the interest of learning.[49] The other academy,

Bamboo Grove, was established in 1243 at the site of K'ou Chun's grave in Kung-an county, where a bamboo grove was said to have sprung up magically.

A spirit of martial loyalty and patriotic fervor pervaded the atmosphere surrounding the establishment of these two academies. The connection with the spirits of departed loyalist heroes was physically embodied in the bamboo grove at K'ou Chun's grave, and Nan-yang Academy was built at the place where Chu-ko Liang had taken up farming to support himself. Shrines to these figures were a central part of each academy, reinforcing the idea that scholars were to value military skills and soldiers were to protect scholars.[50]

SHRINES TO EREMITES

The early origins of academies in the T'ang were deeply rooted in an eremitic tradition; similarly, many Sung academies were founded at the sites of retreats associated with this tradition. Some academies were founded to honor posthumously an eremite scholar who did not hold office but whose life represented certain principles of official service. One such academy was established at Yen-ling (Yen prefecture, Chekiang) during the first half of the thirteenth century at the site of a shrine to an eremite of the Han period, Yen Kuang (37 B.C.–A.D. 43).[51] An intimate associate of Emperor Kuang-wu (r. 25–57), Yen had rejected office and retired there. During the Northern Sung, a shrine was erected at the site of Yen's fishing place in the Fu-ch'un Mountains while Fan Chung-yen was prefect. Angling Terrace Academy was later established at the shrine in 1226 by the son of Southern Sung poet Lu Yu while he was prefect of Yen.[52] By then, Chu Hsi's disciple Ch'en Ch'un had given a famous series of lectures there on Neo-Confucianism, and followers of Lu Chiu-yüan were active in the area as well.[53]

Each step of the development of the shrine to Yen Kuang into an academy, beginning with the shrine itself, was initiated by prefects, but the descendants of Yen Kuang contributed to its support as well.[54] By the time of its completion in 1251, the academy was clearly well supplied and functioning as a school; in the following year, the prefectural school professor began to serve concurrently as the academy headmaster.[55] Within ten years, however, the academy was in decline. At least part of its grounds had been absorbed by Buddhist priests, who built a dharma hall on the former site of one of its pavilions.[56] Despite orders from the prefect and several years of litigation, only half of the original land absorbed by the Buddhists was returned to the academy, and the academy's support consequently was substantially reduced.[57] The account in the local history, however, suggests that spiritual power returned when the prefect ordered the Buddhists to return the land where they had built a dharma hall.[58]

In an inscription for "Pristine Wind Hall," the lecture hall of Angling Terrace Academy, Fang Hui (1227–1306), a former prefect of Yen, related the name of the hall to Yen Kuang, and through him to the legendary Po-i, who starved in the wilderness rather than submit to an illegitimate sovereign: "Po-i preferred to die in order to complete his humanity. He was one who desired to clarify for myriad generations the proper relationship between ruler and minister. Tzu-ling [Yen Kuang] did not bend the Way in order to extend his life. He desired to clarify for myriad generations the proper relationship between friends."[59] The shrine and later the academy, especially the "Pristine Wind Hall," linked contemporaries to past heroes such as Yen Kuang.

The Southern Sung loyalist Hsieh Ao (1249–1295), who was buried at Angling Terrace, had deeply mourned Wen T'ien-hsiang's (1236–1283) death at the hands of the Mongol conquerors, and he invoked Ch'ü Yüan, Yen Kuang, and Wen T'ien-hsiang in a continuum of heroes in history.[60] These three figures represent somewhat different ideals: Ch'ü Yüan, the loyal minister undeservedly dismissed by his ruler; Yen Kuang, upholding ideals of merit rather than personal ties as the criterion for office; and Wen T'ien-hsiang, a loyal martyr to the legitimate rule of his Chinese sovereign. But all of these ideals were related in a spectrum of values that define the principles of official service and justify the alternative of eremitism.

Eremitism was often either an individual response to official censure or a group reaction to illegitimate political authority, such as the Jurchen conquest of the north or Mongol rule. Mount T'ao Tall Bamboo Academy at Jui-an county in Wen prefecture (Chekiang) was established at the grave of Lu Tien (1042–1102), the poet Lu Yu's grandfather.[61] During the Northern Sung, Lu Tien earned Wang An-shih's disfavor and retired to Mount T'ao to collect books and study.[62] Wang Ying-sun, who founded this academy, belonged to a circle of eremite literati who retired after the fall of the Southern Sung and lived near the former capital.[63] Wang had offended the prime minister when first appointed to office, leading to his life as an eremite scholar.[64] His eremitism can be seen as both a personal response to political difficulty and part of a wider reaction among literati to the Mongol conquest. Similarly, Lu Yu (1125–1210) bitterly resented the loss of the north, where his ancestors were buried, and was specially protective of his grandfather's grave as the sole family grave not under Chin control. The personal experiences of Lu Tien and Wang Ying-sun as recluses at Mount T'ao also echoed the early association of the place with the Taoist master T'ao Hung-ching (452–536) and thus Taoist eremitism.

The eremitic tradition in Confucianism had many links to Taoism.

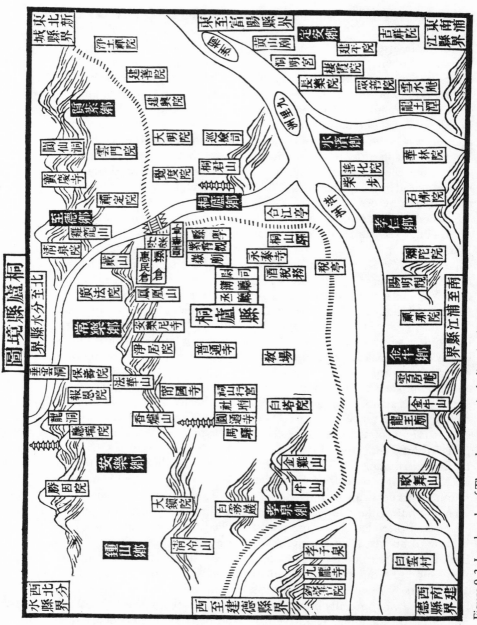

Figure 9.3. Landmarks of T'ung-lu county, including Angling Terrace Academy. (*Yen-chou, t'u-ching*, p. 6)

Individuals became eremites because they were excluded from office for one reason or another; they could also reject service to an unjust ruler and wait to attend a new, legitimate sovereign. But eremitism was not simply a passive response to unfavorable political conditions. The Confucian eremitic tradition clearly suggests rejection of the official world frequently associated with Taoism as well as elements of a monastic tradition identified primarily with Buddhism.

ACADEMIES AND MONASTERIES

Both academies and monasteries were sacred places. There were many similarities in the ways they were organized, and they were often located near each other or at similar sites. Figure 9.3 shows the location of Angling Terrace Academy in hills which also were dotted with many temples and monasteries. References to academies located at former Buddhist or Taoist temple sites, at places where numinous essences were thought to collect and emerge from the earth, suggest that there were areas commonly regarded as "sacred." Conflicts over land between academies and Buddhist or Taoist institutions suggest that they were engaged in ongoing competition for both sacred sites and economic resources. Neo-Confucians, Buddhists, and Taoists also competed for support from and influence over the local populace.

The concept of *chiao-hua,* "cultural transformation," may be understood as a form of Confucian proselytization. The term is frequently used in accounts praising the building of schools or the pacification of an unruly population by an official. It is also used in connection with academies.[65] Han-shan Academy in Ch'ao (Kwangtung) was dedicated to the central figure in the late T'ang Confucian revival, Han Yü (768–824).[66] The academy was built on the site of the temple to Han Yü commemorating his encouragement of schools in the area when he held office there. In Lin Hsi-i's (1210–1273) inscription on the academy's restoration in 1269, he compared Han Yü's influence on education there to Han period figures noted for their support of schools in Szechwan and Fukien.[67] A particularly straightforward account of *chiao-hua* comes from Wen T'ien-hsiang, in his inscription for Peace Lake Academy in Hsing-kuo county of Kan prefecture at the southern end of the Kan river basin (Kiangsi). The county magistrate built the academy to encourage the "Confucianization" of the area, reputed to be disorderly and uncivilized. When the building was completed and Confucian rites were held there, "all those who watched held their breaths in wonder," even the women and children.[68] As a sign of its cultural transformation, this place was renamed "Ju-hsüeh" (Confucian learning).[69] "The distant and uncultivated are 'cleansed' and instructed," through such missionary efforts, and "The ruler's will spreads and daily grows more profound."[70]

Passages in many academy inscriptions allude to the vitality of "other" traditions, in terms of numbers of temples as well as their influence over people's thought and behavior. In his inscription on Tiger Hill Academy in Soochow, Liu Tsai (1166–1239) praised the official who restored Yin Ch'un's residence and founded the academy, noting that the region of Wu (the Soochow area) had been "seduced by Buddhism" until this official turned back the tide by supporting the academy and thus purifying the region's customs (chiao-hua).[71] Chou Pi-ta's (1126–1204) inscription on Dragon Islet Academy (Chi, Kiangsi), in justifying the need for the academy, first described the hierarchy of schools in antiquity and then contrasted the relative paucity of schools in his own time with the flourishing of Buddhist and Taoist temples.[72]

Peripheral areas were particularly susceptible to seduction by "other" religions. Mount Tai Academy in Ch'ang-kuo county (Ming prefecture, Chekiang), located on an island in the sea, was seen as a mission outpost in an uncultivated area.[73] Similarly, Weng Islet Academy, also in the same area, was seen as a mission establishment, bringing civilization to the coastal inhabitants.[74] A late Yüan inscription for it described the numerical strength of Taoist and Buddhist institutions: "They are spread out here and there, like figures on a chessboard, lined up like the innumerable stars."[75] Such claims were frequently used to justify the need for academies in order to transform and Confucianize (chiao-hua) people who were susceptible to the influences of Buddhism and Taoism.

In most cases where a common site was used, it appears that academies were built on the foundations of defunct Buddhist or Taoist temples, such as Goose Lake Academy at the site of Goose Lake Temple where the famous debate between Chu Hsi and Lu Chiu-yüan had been held. The best location for Spring Mountain Academy in Chüan-chou was "divined" to be at the abandoned site of T'ien-ning Temple.[76]

Occasional references to land disputes between academies and temples indicate that conflict sometimes occurred as both attempted to occupy the same sacred space. For example, Compassion Lake Academy in Ming (Chekiang) was established on the edge of temple grounds and may actually have usurped some temple property, leading to the effort by priests from that temple to restore their control. Eastern Yung Academy, also in Ming, was built in the mid-thirteenth century by chief councillor Cheng Ch'ing-chih (1176–1251) to honor his teacher, Lou Fang, on the site of a Buddhist temple, presumably an active one, since it is recorded that Buddhist priests were "removed" in 1281.[77] Tung-lin Academy, famous after its restoration in the Ming, began as a shrine to Yang Shih at Wu-hsi near Soochow and became an academy in the late Southern Sung.[78] The name was adopted from the Buddhist patriarch Hui-yüan's temple in the foothills of Mount Lu, and, before it was restored in the Ming, this academy was converted to a Buddhist temple.[79] Following the Yüan restoration of Angling Terrace Academy, "neighboring Buddhist priests exploited and took its property for their own."[80] There is no consistent pattern evident in the relationships between academies and temples. In some instances, the state intervened to restore land or to take land from a Buddhist institution to provide support. But there were also cases in which the state was apparently either unwilling or unable to aid academies in such conflicts.

Taoist temple sites were attractive too, as were places with long Taoist associations. Stone Drum was said to be at the foundation of an old Taoist temple.[81] Both Stone Drum and Yüeh-lu, two of the four stellar academies of the Southern Sung movement, were located in the shadow of Mount Heng, one of the five sacred mountains. The prototypical White Deer Hollow Academy was in the foothills of Mount Lu, a place replete with both Buddhist and Taoist sites.

Some scholars seem to have felt a need to deny association between Taoism and the location of academies in scenic mountain settings. The author of an inscription for an academy Chu Hsi established in Fukien wrote:

> When I held office in Chien-an, my friend Chu Hsi lived there on Wu-fu of the Wu-i Mountains. . . . He and his students used to tuck their books under their arms and go out to chant old poems and drink wine. . . . Thus the enjoyment of these places was Chu Hsi's private pleasure. . . . [He] later built a retreat (ching-she) here, using a Taoist hut. . . . [But] Chu Hsi was a classicist (ju). He used his learning to conduct himself in his locality and to improve his disciples. He was not like the improper men who sequester themselves in the mountains and valleys, clothing themselves in air and eating fungus in order to imitate the prevalent customs of the Taoists.[82]

Given the pleasures enjoyed by Chu Hsi and his friends in the Wu-i Mountains, the author of the inscription apparently felt obliged to make explicit the distinction between Chu Hsi and Taoist eremites.[83]

Such Neo-Confucian disclaimers suggest that Taoist influence was perhaps not entirely insignificant. Wang Ying-ch'en (1119–1176), an associate of Chu Hsi, wrote an inscription for T'ung-yüan Academy in Hsin (Chiang-tung), his native area.[84] This academy was the family school of the Kao, an eminent lineage from Kuei-ch'i county that traced its descent from a T'ang officeholder. The school was open to the community as well, and Wang's inscription makes reference to the classical model of community schools in describing T'ung-yüan Academy.[85] He concluded by suggesting that the purpose of this and other academies was to educate students to progress to the prefectural school and then to the Imperial University.[86] Sandwiched between prosaic comments about the importance of Confucian virtues and the final passage is a startling digression filled with Taoist imagery and vocabulary on the meaning of a "place" for study:

> That people study in an academy, this is something everyone knows. [But] the place for study, [this is something] they perhaps don't completely know. How can it be only a beautiful residence with broad pavilions and clear windows, that kind of ephemeral meaning? The heart is simply the study. In this way I am able to purify the dwelling of spiritual clarity by reading "my book." Thus, discourse on the *Mencius,* the *Mean,* and [the rest of] the *Four Books* does not take place on the bookshelf but in the midst of the "cinnabar chamber" *(tan-fu).* The teachings of the Six Classics, the Philosophers, and the Histories are found not in the documents, but within my "spirit tower" *(ling-t'ai).* Ingesting its beauty and imbibing its rich incense, how can there be limits?[87]

This passage can be interpreted in terms of *hsin-hsüeh* (learning of the heart and mind). Nonetheless, the use of terminology such as *tan-fu* or *ling-t'ai,* although not exclusively Taoist, at least imparts a Taoist flavor, and Wang Ying-ch'en's own background also suggests a Taoist interpretation.[88]

The role of the state in mediating among competing religious universes and their institutions is unclear, but it appears that the state (particularly the Mongol state) may have coopted shrines and formalized them as academies. Allocating "officially confiscated land" to academies newly founded or restored with official sanction was a means for the state to wrest land from Buddhist or Taoist temples and bring it into the state's domain as an academy. Formal recognition of academies as state institutions with imperially bestowed name plaques dates back to the Northern Sung but peaked in the Southern Sung during the reign of Li-tsung in the mid-thirteenth century.[89]

CONCLUSION

Rituals commemorating individual philosophers, officials, local scholars, and teachers were central to the function of academies, just as shrines dedicated to these individuals were central to the physical structure of the academy. In inscriptions written for the founding or restoration of academies, much attention was paid to ceremonial rites recognizing the cultural bequest of "former worthies." The lives and deeds of culture heroes—virtuous scholars, loyal officials, skillful administrators, adept strategists, and noted poets were commemorated in shrines. Often these culture heroes stood out because they had been undeservedly demoted or dismissed, a telling detail about the motivation for erecting shrines and the roles these shrines played both in academy life and in the larger context of Southern Sung cultural and political life.

Academies in the Ming have generally been associated with political activism. The case has yet to be made for the Sung, except insofar as the initial repression of Tao-hsüeh thinkers motivated the revival of academies in the Southern Sung. It is also possible to see political meaning in the erection of shrines at academies. The veneration of people whose careers suffered because of some upright moral stance or who rejected office entirely could be seen as a critique of the official system as well as of specific policies, such as compromise with the Jurchen. Many Southern Sung writers associated with the Tao-hsüeh school, most notably Chu Hsi, criticized the examinations, for example, as symptomatic of the ills of the bureaucratic system. Shrines at academies formed in connection with the Tao-hsüeh movement often venerated individuals whose very careers implied criticism of the system. Political reform, dating to Northern Sung statesmen like Fan Chung-yen and Ou-yang Hsiu (1007–1072), was closely tied to the moral reformation of society, a primary concern of Tao-hsüeh schoolmembers.

Chang Tsai, the Northern Sung thinker and precursor of Tao-hsüeh, linked the moral reformation of society to ritual. Ritual veneration of culture heroes at shrines was an important part of academy life, commemorating lives as well as ideas. Ritual recalled the antiquity of the sages; it was also a process that historicized individuals and ideas. Preserving the memory of individual lives and the ideals they represented was an important function of commemorating people through rituals at shrines. Bitter factionalism in political life contributed to the establishment of shrines as a means to remember the victims of political controversy, as the shrines could be seen as a kind of unofficial historical record.

Religion, no less than politics, is concerned with power. Who benefited from the erection of shrines? Why did people commit resources to these shrines and, by extension, to academies? Often shrines and academies were set up by officials at the urging of local people. In analyzing the role played by government officials in ostensibly private academies, we might make use of ideas put forward by James Watson in a discussion of the Ma-tsu cult.[90] He suggests that there was an interplay between state authority and popular pressure in standardizing the Ma-tsu cult. He also argues that the cult's structure, but not its content, was imposed by the state and that the ambiguity of the symbols used allowed a wide array of beliefs to be encompassed. Considering Neo-Confucian academy shrines from this perspective, we might speculate that, although state officials played a large role in founding and funding both shrines and academies, they did not necessarily determine the meaning of the symbols invoked by the shrines. Officials, as representatives of the state, would probably not be inclined to give public support to shrines for people harmed by the official system. At the same time, making these shrines (and academies themselves) into officially sanctioned sacred places brought potentially disruptive forces into a structure that was state ordained. It is significant that the state intervened in academy life in much the same way it did in Buddhist and Taoist institutional life. From the naming of abbots and the bestowal of name plaques at Buddhist monasteries to the appointment of officials to sinecures at Taoist temples, the Southern Sung state exercised some authority over these religious institutions. Similarly, the state appointed academy headmasters, allocated lands and other support, and bestowed name plaques signifying imperial sanction.

Academies, like Buddhist or Taoist temples, reinforced the ideas they stood for through ritual practice. The cohesion of the community of scholars and officeholders was enhanced by performing these ritual acts, much as the religious rites at Buddhist or Taoist institutions consolidated those communities. The identity of the Neo-Confucian community at academies was defined by the ritual commemoration of the sages and their Tao-hsüeh heirs in later times, including those known for their administrative or martial leadership rather than scholarship. Among the figures venerated were eremites who rejected office and officeholders who were forced into retirement by political circumstances. All exhibited in their lives and careers essential Confucian ideals. These ideals, however, were ambiguous: not holding office—either actively refusing it or being forced out—was validated at the same time that loyal service to the state was praised. It is not surprising that figures venerated at academy shrines could have different meanings for those representing state interests and those—temporarily or permanently—on the outside.

NOTES

1. See Chou Ying-ho, comp., *Ching-ting Chien-k'ang chih* (SYTFC), 29.1a–42a.

2. The major sources for information on Sung academies are inscriptions written to commemorate their founding or restoration. Commemorative inscriptions typically discuss people who founded or restored the academy and individuals for whom shrines were established. They describe the founding or restoration, when it was carried out, and how it was funded. Accounts of academies in local histories, such as that on Illumined Way in the gazetteer for Chien-k'ang, provide basic information about the date of establishment, funding, and so on, and often include inscriptions with more detail and literary elaboration. Only occasionally and peripherally is there information about what actually went on at academies. There are some exceptions, and those will be discussed here.

3. The use of temples as hostels for travelers is well documented, and it is

clear that academies in many cases had a similar function. The rules at West Brook Academy, for example, stated that scholars who came to stay temporarily would be allowed three days of rice; if they wanted to stay on as resident scholars, they would be supplied with rice on that basis (Wang I-shan, *Chia-ts'un lei-kao* [*SKCS*], 8.3b).

4. See, for example, Kanai Noriyuki, "Sōdai no Bukkyō ni tsuite—Sōdai shakai ni okeru ji'in to jujisei no mondai," *Rekishi kyōiku* 10.8 (August 1962): 52–58. Headmasters were often named concurrently with appointment to a professorship *(chiao-shou)* at a prefectural school, after recognition of the academy by the state through the bestowal of a name plaque. Terms used to refer to headmasters, particularly *shan-chang* (mountain master), also evoke strong Buddhist or Taoist connotations.

5. Chou Ying-ho, *Chien-k'ang chih* 29.15a, 29.20b.

6. Ibid., 29.5b–6a.

7. Ibid., 29.13b–14a.

8. For background on Sung academies, see inter alia Sun Yen-min, *Sung-tai shu-yüan chih-tu chih yen-chiu* (Taipei: Cheng-chih ta-hsüeh, 1963).

9. For a critical perspective on the role of White Deer Hollow in the academy movement, see John W. Chaffee, "Chu Hsi and the Revival of the White Deer Grotto Academy, 1179–1181 A.D.," *T'oung Pao* 17 (1985): 40–62.

10. One might link the proliferation of academies not only with the prohibition against *wei-hsüeh* in 1195 but also more generally with political factionalism in the Sung.

11. Chou Ying-ho, *Chien-k'ang chih* 29.5b. For classical references to these rites, see Morohashi Tetsuji, *Dai Kanwa jiten* (Tokyo: Taishūkan shoten, 1955–1960), 11.410a

12. Chu Hsi, *Pai-lu shu-yüan chiao-kuei (TSCC)*, p. 5. Chu Hsi gives a detailed description of these rites as they were carried out at the Ts'ang-chou Retreat (see *Chu-tzu wen-chi* [*TSCC*], 13.479–480). Since many academies were built around shrines of some kind, and all had at least a place for veneration of Confucius, it would be valuable to know more about how the ceremonies were conducted, their canonical bases, and their significance for the participants.

13. Yüan Fu, *Meng-chai chi (TSCC)*, 13.187.

14. See Ellen Neskar, "The Cult of Worthies: Shrines Honoring Former Confucian Worthies in the Sung Dynasty, 960–1279" (Ph.D. dissertation, Columbia University, 1992), which provides a detailed study of Neo-Confucian shrines in the Sung.

15. In the lower Yangtze valley, Chi-shan Academy in Yüeh (Chekiang) began with a shrine in the mid-thirteenth century to Chu Hsi because he had held office there (*Ta Ming i-t'ung chih* [1461 edition], 45.10a); Ch'uan-i Academy in Hsiu (Chekiang) was built by Fu Kuang, a student of both Lü Tsu-ch'ien and Chu Hsi, at his study place in 1269, and there were sacrifices to Chu Hsi in it (Hsü Shih, *Chih-yüan Chia-ho chih* [*SYTFC*], 7.6a, 25.9b–12a). In the eastern periphery of the middle Yangtze region there was Lin-ju Academy in Fu (Kiangsi), built to venerate Chu Hsi by a local official who had been his student (Wu Ch'eng, *Wu Wen-cheng kung chi* [*SKCS*], 37.14a–14b; Chuang Cheng-fan, comp., *Nan-Sung wen-fan* [1888 edition], 46.12a–12b). Many further examples could be cited in every region of the Southern Sung empire.

16. Ho-shan Academy, established by Wei Liao-weng in Ching (Hunan) (*Ta

Ming 66.16a); Wei Liao-weng and Ho-shan academies in Ch'eng-tu (*Ta Ming* 72.7a); Ho-shan Academy in Chia-ting, established by Wei Liao-weng (*Ta Ming* 72.18b); Ho-shan Academy in Soochow (*Ta Ming* 8.9a).

17. In the lower Yangtze valley there was Lien-ch'i Academy in Jun (Chekiang), founded at the former residence of Chou Tun-i (*Ta Ming* 11.6a). In the middle Yangtze valley there was Dragon Stream Academy in Chi (Kiangsi), founded for both Chou Tun-i and a local scholar (*Ta Ming* 56.11a); Tsung-lien Academy in Lung-hsing (Hung, Kiangsi), where Chou Tun-i had held office (*Ta Ming* 57.19b); Lien-ch'i Academy in Chiang and Kan (Kiangsi), and Yung (Hunan) (*Ta Ming* 52.21a, 58.7a, 65.17b). In the upper Yangtze valley there was Lien-ch'i Academy in Tz'u-chou (Szechwan) (*Ta Ming* 69.22a). In Kwangtung there was Lien-ch'i Academy in Nan-en (Liu Po-chi, *Kuang-tung shu-yüan chih-tu* [Canton: Commercial Press, 1938; Taipei rpt., 1978], p.15); Lien-ch'üan and San-chou (1261) academies in Chao-ch'ing (Kwantung) (*Ta Ming* 79.11a, 81.10a); Hsiang-chiang (ca. 1250) and Lien-ch'i (1246) academies in Shao (Kwangtung) (*Ta Ming* 79.26b; Liu Po-chi, *Kuang-tung*, p. 15). Tao-chou Lien-hsi Academy (Hunan) was established to commemorate Chou, whose native place was Tao county (Honan) (Ou-yang Shou-tao, *Hsün-chai wen-chi* [SKCS], 14.3a]; Liu Po-chi, *Kuang-tung*, p. 15, refers to this as Lien-ch'i Academy.

18. Chu Hsi, *Chu-tzu ta-ch'üan (SPPY)*, 78.13a–13b.

19. Shrines to other scholars were also numerous. Li-tse Academy was founded at the site of Lü Tsu-ch'ien's lecturing place in Wu (Chekiang) during the late 1230s (*Ta Ming* 42.7b); Tung-lai Academy was established where Lü Tsu-ch'ien had studied in T'an (Hunan) (*Ta Ming* 63.13b). Nan-hsüan at Yüan (Kiangsi) in the middle Yangtze valley centered on a shrine to Chang Shih (*Ta Ming* 57.19b); Hsüan-ch'eng Academy was established ca. 1260 at Kuei-lin (Kwangsi) to commemorate travel there by Chang Shih and Lü Tsu-ch'ien (*Ta Ming* 83.10a). Pi-ch'üan Academy was founded in T'an (Hunan) at the site of the Neo-Confucian scholar Hu An-kuo's (1074–1138) dwelling, where his son Hu Hung (1105–1155) and Chang Shih lectured (*Ta Ming* 63.13b); Yü-chang Academy at Nan-hsiung in the Kwangtung hinterland was founded at Lo Yü-chang's (Ts'ung-yen) study place (Liu Po-chi, *Kuang-tung*, p. 14). Shang-ts'ai Academy was founded in 1260–1264 to revere Hsieh Liang-tso in T'ai (Chekiang) (*Ta Ming* 47.10b).

20. *Ta Ming* 15.6a. Other examples include Ch'ien-kang Academy, established ca. 1245 in Lin-chiang (Kiangsi) with a sacrificial hall for Chou Tun-i, Chang Tsai, the Ch'eng brothers, and Chu Hsi (*Ta Ming* 57.19b). Tao-yüan Academy at Nan-an in Kan (Kiangsi) was founded to revere Chou Tun-i and the Ch'eng brothers (*Ta Ming* 58.17b).

21. In the lower Yangtze region Kuei-shan Academy in Ch'ang (Chekiang) was built ca. 1230 by the prefect because Yang Shih had lectured there (*Ta Ming* 10.9a). Kuei-shan Academy in Hangchow was established to commemorate Yang Shih's having been prefect there and the people's admiration for him (*Ta Ming* 38.13b). In the middle Yangtze region Wen-ching Academy at Ch'ang-sha (Hunan) was named for Yang Shih's posthumous honorific because he had once held office there (*Ta Ming* 63.14a).

22. An inscription by Liu Ch'en-weng (1231–1294) on this Turtle Mountain Academy contains an interesting, probably apocryphal, account of the origin of the shrine: "During 1127 to 1131 bandits destroyed Chiang-lo. Only when they

got to the gate of Yang Shih did they stop and say that this was his home and could not be burned. From this, his residence became a shrine" (*Hsü-ch'i chi* [Yü-chang ts'ung-shu edition], 1.5b–6a). This account attributes to the unnamed bandits a remarkable reverence for learning and for the scholarly achievements of Yang Shih. The author of the inscription may be reflecting here an assumption that even the unlettered respected the sanctity of this scholar's home, or he may be cynically attempting to suggest a common cross-class bond between the bandits and Yang Shih.

Ch'en himself, a native of P'u-t'ien along Fukien's southern coast, was a follower of Chu Hsi's learning through his disciple Huang Kan (1152–1221). See *SJSY* 3.2441; Huang Tsung-hsi et al., *Sung-Yüan hsüeh-an (SPPY)*, 69.12b–13a; *SS* 408.12312. He had been prefect of Nan-k'ang, where he rebuilt Chu Hsi's White Deer Hollow Academy; later, as prefect of Nan-chien, he built two other academies in addition to Turtle Mountain: Southern Way, originally a shrine to Yang Shih and later transformed into an academy, and Yen-p'ing, modeled on White Deer Hollow and named to honor Li T'ung, Chu Hsi's teacher and a native of Yen-p'ing. Wang Tz'u-ts'ai and Feng Yün-hao, comps., *Sung-Yüan hsüeh-an pu-i* (Shih-chieh shu-chü edition), 70.33a9; Liu Ch'en-weng, *Hsü-ch'i chi* 1.5b–6a; *Ta Ming* 77.6b.

23. Liu K'o-chuang, *Hou-ts'un hsien-sheng ta ch'üan-chi (SPTK)*, 93.15a–16b.

24. *SJSY* 5.3919, 3970.

25. *SJSY* 1.94.

26. See the inscription of Tiger Hill Academy by Liu Tsai, *Man-t'ang chi (SKCS)*, 23.29a–31a.

27. Yüan Fu, *Meng-chai chi (TSCC)*, 13.186–188; *Ta Ming* 54.8a–b; Sun, *Sung-tai shu-yüan*, p. 27.

28. Yüan Chüeh, *Yen-yu* [1314–1321] *Ssu-ming chih (SYTFC)*, 14.30a, 36a.

29. Ibid., 14.30a.

30. This chronology of the establishment of Compassion Lake Academy follows the record in the local history for the early fourteenth century. *Sung-Yüan hsüeh-an pu-i*, 74.67a3, simply records that the circuit military commissioner established Compassion Lake Academy around 1275. The term "academy" (*shu-yüan*) is one applied loosely in later eras to a wide range of institutions that were not initially founded as academies but rather as shrines or retreats. They were later formalized, notably under the Yüan, as academies. Precise dating and terminology remain problematic.

31. Wang Yüan-kung, ed., *Chih-cheng (1341–1367) Ssu-ming hsü-chih (SYTFC)*, 8.8b.

32. Wang I-shan, *Chia-ts'un lei-kao* 8.1b.

33. Ibid.

34. Ibid.

35. The first Liu in the early Northern Sung is said just to have "opposed higher officials." But his son, who worked on Ssu-ma Kuang's history, eventually lost his post in the Imperial Library because he criticized Wang An-shih; similarly his grandson offended against Ts'ai Ching and lost his post. *SJSY* 5.3875 (Liu Huan); see also pp. 3869 (Liu Ju), 3995 (Liu Hsi-chung).

36. Wang I-shan, *Chia-ts'un lei-kao* 8.3a.

37. *Ta Ming* 9.5a.

38. Hsi-tung Academy at Yüeh (Hunan) was established to commemorate Fan Chung-yen's once traveling there (*Ta ming* 62.39b); P'ing-hu and Wen-ming academies in Lei-chou (Kwangtung) and Tung-p'o Academy in Ch'iung (Kwangtung) were all established to commemorate the exile of Su Ch'e and Su Shih to the Kwangtung coastal periphery (*Ta Ming* 82.11b–12a, 22b).

39. See *Sung-jen chuan-chi* 3.2529.

40. For the inscription providing information on this academy, see Ch'en Yüan-chin, *Yü-shu lei-kao (SKCS),* 5.4b–7a.

41. For historical references to the practice of erecting "living shrines," see Morohashi Tetsuji, *Dai Kanwa jiten* (Tokyo: Taishūkan shoten, 1955–1960; 2d printing, 1966–1968), 7.7940b–7940c. Further references (provided to me by Judith Boltz) include Chu I, *I-chüeh liao tsa-chi* (Pi-chi hsiao-shuo ta-kuan edition), 2.20b–21a; Chu Pien, *Ch'ü-wei chiu-wen (TSCC),* 3.20; Kung Ming-chih, *Chung Wu chi-wen* (Pi-chi hsiao-shuo ta-kuan ed.), 2.5a–b, 4.9b–10a.

42. Chen Te-hsiu, *Hsi-shan hsien-sheng Chen Wen-chung kung wen-chi (SPTK),* 25.15a–17b.

43. This term is commonly used by Buddhists. Although it probably does not have a Buddhist meaning here, its ambivalent connotation is still significant.

44. According to Morohashi, *Dai Kanwa jiten,* the double surname Hsien-yü derives from King Wu of the Chou enfeoffing a son in Korea. The reference in Morohashi to the place name Ch'ing-she (*Dai Kanwa jiten* 12.12704) states that this was the shrine of Ch'i in the east, identified by the green colored earth used for its altar.

45. Ti Jen-chieh was also venerated at Southern Lake Academy in Fu-chou, Hupei (see *Ta Ming* 66.3b). His biography in CTS 89.2895 records a *sheng-tz'u* established in honor of him (I am indebted to Judith Boltz for this reference).

46. Chen Te-hsiu, *Hsi-shan hsien-sheng* 25.17a.

47. Ch'en Mi, prefect of Nan-k'ang who restored White Deer Hollow, and also of Yen-p'ing (where Sleeping Dragon was), where he established Southern Way and Yen-p'ing academies, was said to have "loved Chu-ko Liang deeply." See *Sung-Yüan hsüeh-an* 69.13a.

48. For information on Meng Kung, see the entry by Charles Peterson in Herbert Franke, ed., *Sung Biographies* (Wiesbaden: Franz Steiner Verlag, 1976), pp. 779–786. See also *SJSY* 2.1300–1301.

49. See Li Tseng-po, *K'o-chai tsa-kao (SKCS),* 5.1a–2b; Ch'eng Chü-fu, *Hsüeh-lou chi* (Yüan-tai chen-pen wen-chi edition), 11.16b–17b; and Kao Ssu-te, *Ch'ih-t'ang ts'un-kao* (Wu-ying-tien edition), 4.5a–7a.

50. In addition to the cases cited above, there are other examples with less detailed information that appear to share common attributes, such as the academy founded at the site of the military leader Chang Chün's study in his native Szechwan or Ming-cheng Academy in Ch'ü (Chekiang), founded to commemorate six upright officials. See *Ta Ming* 67.16a; Huang Chin, *Huang Wen-hsien kung chi* (Chin-hua ts'ung-shu edition), 8.12a–13a.

51. Huang Chin, *Huang Wen-hsien kung chi (TSCC),* 7 shang, 265–266.

52. For Lu Tzu-i, see *SJSY* 3.2665. Prior to his appointment as prefect of Yen, Lu had acquired a reputation for demon quelling and the suppression of local religious beliefs and practices associated with shamanism. During his tenure

as magistrate of Li-yang county in Chiang-ning (Kiangsi), he "exorcised demons" and set up a school where rites were taught in order to transform local customs.

53. For a discussion of this philosophical background, see the introduction to Wing-tsit Chan, trans. and ed., *Neo-Confucian Terms Explained (Pei-hsi tzu-i by Ch'en Ch'un)* (New York: Columbia University Press, 1986), pp. 22–32.

54. Cheng Yao and Fang Jen-jung, comps., *Ching-ting Yen-chou hsü-chih (SYTFC)*, 3.2b.

55. Cheng Yao and Fang Jen-jung, *Yen-chou* 3.3a–3b.

56. Ibid., 3.3b; Huang Chin, *Huang Wen-hsien kung-chi*, 7 shang, 265.

57. Huang Chin, *Huang Wen-hsien kung chi*, 7 shang, 265.

58. Cheng Yao and Fang Jen-jung, *Yen-chou* 3.3b.

59. Fang Hui, *T'ung-chiang hsü-chi (SKCS)*, 35.5a.

60. For an interesting discussion of the poetic and artistic tradition surrounding Angling Terrace and Yen Kuang, including this reference to Hsieh Ao, see Alan John Hay, "Huang Kung-wang's Dwelling in the Fu-ch'un Mountains: The Dimensions of a Landscape" (Ph.D. dissertation, Princeton University, 1978), pp. 311 ff.

61. See the inscription by Lin Ching-hsi, *Chi-shan hsien-sheng chi* (Chih-pu-tsu chai ts'ung-shu edition), 4.6a–8a.

62. Ibid., 4.7b; *SJSY* 3.2649.

63. See *SJSY* 1.323. See also Etienne Balazs and Yves Hervouet, eds., *A Sung Bibliography* (Hong Kong: Chinese University Press, 1978), p. 475; Franke, *Sung Biographies*, pp. 261–268, for the biography of Chou Mi, one of Wang Ying-sun's associates.

64. Lin Ching-hsi, *Chi-shan hsien-sheng chi* 4.7b.

65. When used in reference to the establishment of a school or academy in a previously unruly area, *chiao-hua* seems to be understood as an almost magical process whereby the very presence of the school would somehow pacify the local population, even though only the elite would presumably have access to it.

66. There was another academy, Tsun-Han, in Kuang-chou, established to commemorate the fact that Han Yü studied there (*Ta Ming* 79.11a).

67. Lin Hsi-i, *Chu-ch'i hsien-chai shih-i kao hsü-chi (SKCS)*, 11.9b–11a.

68. Wen T'ien-hsiang, *Wen-shan hsien-sheng ch'üan-chi (SPTK)*, 9.19a.

69. Ibid., 9.19b.

70. Ibid.

71. Liu Tsai, *Man-t'ang chi* 23.29a–29b.

72. Chou Pi-ta, *Chou I-kuo wen-chung kung chi* (1848 edition), 19.8a.

73. See especially the inscription by Huang Chen in *Yen-yu Ssu-ming chih* 14.27b–29b.

74. See, for example, an inscription on this academy by Ying K'uei-weng in *Chih-cheng Ssu-ming* 8.5b–6b.

75. Ibid., 8.6a.

76. *Sung-Yüan hsüeh-an pu-i* 70.29b2; Liu K'o-chuang, *Hou-ts'un hsien-sheng* 93.15a–15b.

77. Huang Chen, *Yen-yu Ssu-ming chih* 14.38a–38b.

78. For background on Tung-lin Academy in the Ming, see Heinrich Busch, "The Tung-lin Academy and Its Political and Philosophical Significance," *Monumenta Serica* 14 (1949–1955): 1–163.

79. For background on Hui-yüan and the original Tung-lin Temple, see, for example, Erik Zürcher, *The Buddhist Conquest of China: The Spread and Adoption of Buddhism in Early Medieval China,* (Leiden: E. J. Brill, 1972 [1959]), 1.208.

80. Huang Chin, *Huang Wen-hsien kung chi, 7 shang,* 265.

81. See Sheng Lang-hsi, *Chung-kuo shu-yüan chih-tu* (Shanghai: Commercial Press, 1935; Taipei rpt., 1978), p. 11.

82. Tai Hsien, comp., *Chu-tzu shih-chi* (Kinsei kanseki sōkan edition), 24b–26a/696–699.

83. A remarkably similar statement is made in the course of an inscription on Mt. Tai Academy in Ch'ang-kuo county in the Chou-shan archipelago off the coast of Ming: "Yüan-hui [Chu Hsi] was a classicist *(ju).* When he used learning to manage his locality and to perfect his disciples, it was not like the solitary men and eremites who seclude themselves in the mountains and valleys, clothing themselves in air and [living on] fungus in order to imitate the prevalent customs of the Taoists" (Huang Chen, *Yen-yu Ssu-ming chih* 14.25b–26a).

84. Wang Ying-ch'en, *Wen-ting chi* (Wu-ying-tien edition), 9.17a–18b.

85. Ibid., 9.17b.

86. Ibid., 9.18a–b.

87. Ibid., 9.18a.

88. See Morohashi, *Dai Kanwa jiten* 1.555a, for *tan-fu,* which is rendered, with examples, as a very Confucian-sounding "sincerity." The term still suggests a Taoist connotation because of the many Taoist phrases that include *tan.* See ibid., 12.92d–93a, where *ling-t'ai* is glossed first with a quote from Chuang-tzu and then with one from the *Shih-ching,* where the term is associated with King Wen.

89. In her chapter in this volume, Valerie Hansen notes a similar phenomenon with regard to popular deities.

90. James Watson, "Standardizing the Gods: The Promotion of T'ien Hou ('Empress of Heaven') along the South China Coast, 960–1960," in David Johnson, Andrew Nathan, and Evelyn Rawski, eds., *Popular Culture in Late Imperial China* (Berkeley: University of California Press, 1985), pp. 292–324.

GLOSSARY

chai 齋
Chang Chün 張浚
Chang Shih 張栻
Chang Tsai 張載
Chao Ju-yü 趙汝愚
Chao Shih-hsia 趙師夏
Chen Te-hsiu 真德秀
Ch'en Ch'un 陳淳
Ch'en Mi 陳宓
Ch'en Wei 陳韡
Ch'en Yüan-chin 陳元晉
Cheng Ch'ing-chih 鄭清之
Cheng Yao 鄭瑤

Ch'eng Chü-fu 程鉅夫
Ch'eng Hao 程顥
Chi-shan 稽山
Chi-shan hsien-sheng chi 霽山先生集
ch'i 氣
Chia-ts'un lei-kao 稼村類藁
Chiang-ning 江寧
chiang-t'ang 講堂
Chiang Wan-li 江萬里
chiao-hua 教化
chiao-shou 教授
Ch'iao 樵
Chien 劍

Ch'ien-kang　鈐岡

*Chih-cheng (1341–1367) Ssu-ming
　hsü-chih*　至正四明續志

chih-hsüeh　直學

chih-shih　職事

Chih-yüan (1271–1294) Chia-ho chih
　至元嘉禾志

Ch'ih-t'ang ts'un-kao　恥堂存稿

Chin　金

chin-shih　進士

Ch'in Kuei　秦檜

ching-she　精舍

ching-shen　精神

Ching-ting Chien-k'ang chih　景定建
　康志

Ching-ting Yen-chou hsü-chih　景定
　嚴州續志

ch'ing　頃

ch'ing-she　青社

Chou I-kuo wen-chung kung chi
　周益國文忠公集

Chou Pi-ta　周必大

Chou Tun-i (Lien-ch'i)　周敦頤（濂溪）

Chou Ying-ho　周應合

Chu-ch'i hsien-chai shih-i kao hsü-chi
　竹溪鬳齋十一藁續集

Chu Hsi (Yüan-hui)　朱熹（元晦）

Chu I　朱翌

Chu-ko Liang　諸葛亮

Chu Pien　朱弁

Chu Sung　朱松

Chu-tzu nien-p'u　朱子年譜

Chu-tzu shih-chi　朱子實記

Chu-tzu ta-ch'üan　朱子大全

Ch'ü-wei chiu-wen　曲洧舊聞

Ch'ü Yüan　屈原

Chuan-i　傳貽

Chuang Chung-fang　莊仲方

Chuang-tzu　莊子

Chung-wu chi-wen　中吳紀聞

ch'ung-li tien　崇禮殿

fa-t'ang　法堂

Fan Chung-yen　范仲淹

Fang Hui　方回

Fang Jen-jung　方仁榮

feng　奉

feng hsien-sheng　奉先聖

feng-ssu　奉祀

Fu-ch'un　福春

Fu Kuang　輔廣

Han Yü　韓愈

Ho-shan　鶴山

Hou Chung-liang　侯仲良

Hou-ts'un hsien-sheng ta-ch'üan-chi
　後村先生大全集

Hsi-chien chü-shih　西澗居士

Hsi-chung　義仲

*Hsi-shan hsien-sheng Chen
　　Wen-chung kung wen-chi*　西山先
　生真文忠公文集

Hsi-tung　溪東

hsiang (image)　像

hsiang (locality)　鄉

Hsiang-chiang　相江

Hsieh Ao　謝翱

Hsieh Liang-tso　謝良佐

hsien-hsien　先賢

Hsien-yü　鮮于

hsin-hsüeh　心學

Hsü-hsi chi　須溪集

Hsü Shih　徐碩

hsüan　軒

Hsüan-ch'eng　宣成

Hsüeh-lou chi　雪樓集

Hsün-chai wen-chi　巽齋文集

Hu An-kuo　胡安國

Hu Hsien　胡憲

Hu Hung　胡宏

Hu Yin　胡寅

Huang Chen　黃震

Huang Chin　黃溍

Huang Kan　黃榦

Huang Tsung-hsi　黃宗羲

Huang Wen-hsien chi　黃文獻集

Huang Wen-hsien kung chi　黃文獻
　公集

Hui-yüan　慧遠

I-chüeh liao tsa-chi　猗覺寮雜記

ju　儒

Ju-hsüeh　儒學

Kao Chieh-shih　高節始

kao-fu　膏馥

Kao Ssu-te　高斯得

Kao-tsung　高宗

K'o-chai tsa-kao　可齋雜藁

K'ou Chun　寇準

Kuang-wu 光武
Kuei-shan 龜山
Kung Ming-chih 龔明之
kung-te 功德
Kuo-tzu chien 國子監
Lan-t'ien Lü-shih hsiang-yüeh 藍田呂氏鄉約
Lao-tzu 老子
Li chi 禮記
Li Kang 李綱
Li-tse 麗澤
Li Tseng-po 李曾伯
Li-tsung 理宗
Li T'ung 李侗
Lien-ch'i 濂溪
Lien-ch'üan 濂泉
Lin Ching-hsi 林景熙
Lin Hsi-i 林希逸
Lin-ju 臨汝
ling-t'ai 靈臺
Liu Chao 劉肇
Liu Ch'en-weng 劉辰翁
Liu Hsi-chung 劉羲仲
Liu Huan 劉渙
Liu K'o-chuang 劉克莊
Liu Mien-chih 劉勉之
Liu Po-chi 劉伯驥
Liu Shu 劉恕
Liu Tsai 劉宰
Liu Tzu-hui 劉子翬
Lo Ts'ung-yen 羅從彥
Lo Yü-chang (Ts'ung-yen) 羅豫章（從彥）
Lou Fang 樓昉
Lu 廬
Lu Chih 陸贄
Lu Chiu-ling 陸九齡
Lu Chiu-yüan 陸九淵
Lu Tien 陸佃
Lu Tzu-i 陸子遹
Lu Yu 陸游
Lü Ta-chün 呂大鈞
Lü Ta-lin 呂大臨
Lü Tsu-ch'ien 呂祖謙
Ma-tsu 媽祖
Man-t'ang chi 漫塘集
Meng-chai chi 蒙齋集
Meng Kung 孟珙

miao 廟
ming 命
Ming-cheng 明正
mo-kuan chih t'ien 沒官之田
Nan-hsüan 南軒
Nan-Sung wen-fan 南宋文範
Nan-yang 南陽
Ou-yang Hsiu 歐陽修
Ou-yang Shou-tao 歐陽守道
Pai-lu shu-yüan chiao-kuei 白鹿書院教規
Pao-shan 包山
Pi-ch'üan 碧泉
P'ing-hu 平湖
Po-i 伯夷
San-chou 三洲
shan-chang 山長
Shan-yüan 澶淵
Shang-ts'ai 上蔡
Shao-hsing 紹興
Shao Yung 邵雍
sheng-ling 生靈
sheng-tz'u 生祠
Shih-ching 詩經
Shih Mi-chung 史彌忠
Shih Mi-yüan 史彌遠
shih-ts'ai 釋菜
shu-yüan 書院
ssu 祀
Ssu-ma Kuang 司馬光
Su Ch'e 蘇轍
Su Shih 蘇軾
Sung-Yüan hsüeh-an 宋元學案
Sung-Yüan hsüeh-an pu-i 宋元學案補遺
Ta Ming i-t'ung chih 大明一統志
Tai 岱
Tai Hsien 戴銑
T'ai-hsüeh 太學
tan-fu 丹府
Tan-yang 丹陽
Tao-chou 道州
Tao-hsüeh 道學
Tao-yüan 道源
T'ao 陶
T'ao Ch'ien 陶潛
T'ao Hung-ching 陶弘景
Te-tsung 德宗

Ti Liang-kung (Ti Jen-chieh)　狄梁公
　（狄仁傑）
tien-yeh　奠謁
T'ien-ning　天寧
T'ien-t'ai　天台
T'o T'o　脱脱
Ts'ai Ching　蔡京
Tseng Shih-chung　曾式中
Tseng-tzu　曾子
Tsun-Han　尊韓
Tsung-lien　宗濂
Tung-lai　東萊
Tung-lin　東林
Tung-p'o　東波
T'ung-chiang hsü-chi　桐江續集
T'ung-yüan　桐源
Tzu-ling　子陵
tz'u　祠
Wang An-shih　王安石
Wang I-shan　王義山
Wang Mao-hung　王懋竑
Wang Te-i　王德毅
Wang Tz'u-ts'ai　王梓材
Wang Ying-ch'en　汪應辰
Wang Ying-sun　王英孫
Wang Yüan-kung　王元恭
Wei　魏
wei-hsüeh　偽學
Wei Liao-weng　魏了翁
Wen-ching　文靖

Wen-chung chi　文忠集
Wen-ming　文明
Wen-shan hsien-sheng ch'üan-chi
　文山先生全集
Wen T'ien-hsiang　文天祥
Wen-ting chi　文定集
wu　廡
Wu (empress)　武
Wu (king)　武
Wu Ch'eng　吳澄
Wu-i　武夷
Wu Wen-cheng chi　吳文正集
Yang Chien　楊簡
Yang Shih　楊時
Yen Hui　顏回
Yen Kuang　嚴光
Yen-p'ing　延平
yen-tz'u t'ing　嚴祠庭
Yen-yu Ssu-ming chih　延祐四明志
Yin Ch'un　尹焞
Ying K'uei-weng　應奎翁
Yu Tso　游酢
Yü-chang　豫章
Yü-shu lei-kao　漁墅類稿
Yüan Chüeh　袁桷
Yüan Fu　袁甫
Yüan Hsieh　袁燮
Yüeh-lu　嶽麓
Yung　甬

Contributors

JUDITH A. BERLING, now dean of the Graduate Theological Union, Berkeley, previously taught Chinese religion at Indiana University. A specialist on Taoism, she has published *The Syncretic Religion of Lin Chao-en* (1980) and is currently working on a study of Taoism in the Sung period.

JUDITH MAGEE BOLTZ completed her Ph.D. in the Department of Oriental Languages of the University of California, Berkeley. Her publications include *A Survey of Taoist Literature, Tenth to Seventeenth Centuries* (1987).

PATRICIA BUCKLEY EBREY, professor of East Asian Languages and Cultures at the University of Illinois, is a specialist in Sung social history. Her most recent books are *Confucianism and Family Rituals in Imperial China: A Social History of Writing about Rites* (1991) and *The Inner Quarters: Marriage and the Lives of Chinese Women in the Sung Period* (1993).

T. GRIFFITH FOULK currently teaches as an assistant professor in the Buddhist Studies program at the University of Michigan. His dissertation (1987) focused on the idea of the Ch'an school and its place in the Buddhist monastic tradition. He is currently completing a manuscript on the Ch'an monastic institution in the Sung dynasty.

PETER N. GREGORY is an associate professor in the Program for the Study of Religion and Department of East Asian Languages and Cultures at the University of Illinois and the executive director of the Kuroda Institute for the Study of Buddhism and Human Values. His research has focused on medieval Chinese Buddhism. In addition to three edited volumes, he has also published *Tsung-mi and the Sinification of Buddhism* (1991).

VALERIE HANSEN received her Ph.D. from the University of Pennsylvania and is now an associate professor in the Department of History at Yale University. Her first book, *Changing Gods in Medieval China, 1127–1276* (1990), dealt with popular religion in the Southern Sung. She continues to work in Sung social history.

TERRY F. KLEEMAN, an assistant professor in the Department of Oriental Studies at the University of Pennsylvania, received his Ph.D. from the University of California, Berkeley. A specialist in Taoism and Chinese religion, he is currently completing a manuscript on Wen-ch'ang.

STEPHEN F. TEISER, an assistant professor in the Department of Religion at Princeton University, has focused his research on Chinese religion and Buddhism. In addition to his *The Ghost Festival in Medieval China* (1988) his recently completed study of *The Scripture of the Ten Kings* is slated for publication in 1994.

LINDA WALTON, associate professor of history at Portland State University, received her Ph.D. from the University of Pennsylvania. Her interests in the conjunction of intellectual and social history have led to several articles and book chapters on academies and other social institutions of the educated class in Southern Sung times.

Index

Page numbers in italics refer to figures.